NEW YORK CITY
FROM $80 A DAY

Here's what the critics say about Frommer's:

"Amazingly easy to use. Very portable, very complete."
—*Booklist*

♦

"The only mainstream guide to list specific prices. The Walter Cronkite of guidebooks—with all that implies."
—*Travel & Leisure*

♦

"Complete, concise, and filled with useful information."
—*New York Daily News*

♦

"Hotel information is close to encyclopedic."
—*Des Moines Sunday Register*

♦

"The best series for travelers who want one easy-to-use guidebook."
—*U.S. Air Magazine*

Other Great Guides for Your Trip:

Frommer's New York City

Frommer's Portable New York City

Frommer's New York City with Kids

Frommer's Irreverent Guide to Manhattan

The Mad Monks' Guide to New York City

The Unofficial Guide to New York City

Frommer's Memorable Walks in New York

Frommer's Manhattan by Night

Frommer's Born to Shop New York

Frommer's Wonderful Weekends from New York City

The New York Times Weekends

Frommer's 2000®

NEW YORK CITY
FROM $80 A DAY

The Ultimate Guide to
Comfortable Low-Cost Travel

by Cheryl Farr Leas

with research assistance from Nathaniel R. Leas

Walking tours by Reid Bramblett

with Frommer's Online Directory by Michael Shapiro

MACMILLAN • USA

ABOUT THE AUTHOR

Cheryl Farr Leas was senior editor at Macmillan Travel before embarking on a freelance writing career. She also authors *Frommer's New York City* and *The Complete Idiot's Travel Guide to Hawaii,* and contributes to *Frommer's USA.* When she's not traveling, she's at home in Park Slope, Brooklyn with her groovy husband, Rob, and their happy dog, Monty. Feel free to write her directly at rncleas@yahoo.com.

MACMILLAN TRAVEL

Macmillan General Reference USA, Inc.
1633 Broadway
New York, NY 10019

Find us online at **www.frommers.com**.

ISBN 0-02-863036-X
ISSN 8755-5433

Editor: Justin Lapatine
Production Editor: Jenaffer Brandt
Photo Editor: Richard Fox
Design by Michele Laseau
Staff Cartographers: John Decamillis, Roberta Stockwell
Page Creation by Sean Monkhouse and Ellen Considine
Front cover photo: The Lower Manhattan skyline as seen from the Brooklyn Promenade

SPECIAL SALES

Bulk purchases (10+ copies) of Frommer's and selected Macmillan travel guides are available to corporations, organizations, mail-order catalogs, institutions, and charities at special discounts, and can be customized to suit individual needs. For more information write to Special Sales, Macmillan General Reference, 1633 Broadway, New York, NY 10019.

Manufactured in the United States of America

5 4 3 2 1

Contents

List of Maps　viii

1　The Best of the Big Apple　1

1　How This Guide Can Save You Money　2

2　Frommer's Favorite Affordable Experiences　3

3　Best Affordable Hotel Bets　6

4　Best Affordable Dining Bets　7

2　Planning an Affordable Trip to New York City　10

1　60 Money-Saving Tips　10

2　Visitor Information　21

3　Money　22

4　When to Go　24

New York City Calendar of Events 25

5　Health & Insurance　32

6　Tips for Travelers with Special Needs　34

7　Getting There　37

Money-Saving Package Deals 38

3　For Foreign Visitors　46

1　Preparing for Your Trip　46

2　Getting to the United States　51

3　Getting Around the United States　52

How to Save on International Airfares 53

Fast Facts: For the Foreign Traveler 54

4　Getting to Know New York City　59

1　Orientation　59

The New York Tabloids Revealed! 61

Manhattan's Neighborhoods in Brief 63

2　Getting Around　74

Deals for Visitors with Wheels: Cheap Parking Tips 80

3　Playing It Safe　81

Fast Facts: New York City 82

5　Accommodations You Can Afford　86

1　TriBeCa　87

2　The Lower East Side　88

3　The East Village　88

Getting the Most for Your Money, Part I: Weekend Packages 90

4　Greenwich Village　92

5　The Flatiron District & Gramercy Park　93

6　Chelsea　94

7　Times Square & Midtown West　98

8 Midtown East & Murray Hill 104
   Getting the Most for Your Money, Part II: Dealmaking with the Chains 106
9 The Upper West Side 108

Affordable Family-Friendly Hotels 112
10 The Upper East Side 116
11 Harlem 117

6 Great Deals on Dining 118

1 Restaurants by Cuisine 119
2 South Street Seaport & the Financial District 122
3 TriBeCa 125
4 Chinatown & Little Italy 127
   Bargain Alert—Great Prix-Fixe Lunch Deals 128
5 The Lower East Side 130
6 SoHo & NoLiTa 132
7 The East Village & NoHo 135
   The New York Deli News 140
8 Greenwich Village 142
9 The Flatiron District, Union Square & Gramercy Park 148

10 Chelsea 152
11 Times Square & Midtown West 154
   Theme Restaurant Thrills! 162
12 Midtown East & Murray Hill 165
   Affordable Family-Friendly Restaurants 167
13 The Upper West Side 168
14 The Upper East Side 174
15 Harlem 176
16 Waterfront Dining in Brooklyn 176

7 Exploring New York City 178

1 Sights & Attractions by Neighborhood 179
2 In New York Harbor: Lady Liberty, Ellis Island & the Staten Island Ferry 181
   Cheap Thrills: What to See & Do for Free 182
3 Historic Lower Manhattan's Top Attractions 185
   A Walking Tour of Wall Street & the Financial District 194
4 The Top Museums 202
   Free Culture at Big Apple Museums 206
   In Search of Historic Homes 208
5 More Manhattan Museums 209
   Art for Art's Sake: The Gallery Scene 216

6 Skyscrapers & Other Architectural Marvels 218
7 Affordable Sightseeing Tours 225
   Show Me, Show Me, Show Me: Free Walking Tours 229
   A Self-Guided Walk Through Greenwich Village's Literary Past 231
8 Urban Oases: Central Park & Other Places to Play 243
9 Talk of the Town: Free TV Tapings 251
10 Especially for Kids 253
11 Highlights of the Outer Boroughs 255
12 Spectator Sports 262

8 Shopping for Big Apple Bargains 264

1 The Top Shopping Streets &
  Neighborhoods 265
  *The Lowdown on Sidewalk
  Vendors 267*

2 The Department Stores 272

3 Shopping A to Z 274
  Where the Fleas Are 275
  Scouring the Sample Sales 281

9 New York City After Dark 296

1 All the City's a Stage: The
  Theater Scene 297
  *Bargain Alert—How to Save on
  Theater Tickets 301*

2 Opera, Classical Music &
  Dance 302
  *Bargain Alert—The Classical
  Learning Curve 304*

3 Major Concert Halls &
  Landmark Venues 307
  *Park It! Shakespeare & Other
  Free Fun 308*

4 Live Rock, Jazz, Blues &
  More 311
  Free Music 315

5 Comedy & Cabaret 319

6 Bars & Cocktail Lounges 321

7 Dance Clubs & Party Scenes 331
  It Might As Well Be Swing 334

8 The Lesbian & Gay Scene 336

Frommer's Online Directory 339

Index 350

General Index 350
Accommodations Index 356

Restaurant Index 356

Index 350

List of Maps

New York Metropolitan Area 41
Manhattan Neighborhoods 65
Downtown Accommodations 89
Midtown Accommodations 96
Uptown Accommodations 110
Lower Manhattan, TriBeCa &
  Chinatown Dining 123
East Village & SoHo Area
  Dining 131

Greenwich Village Dining 143
Midtown Dining 156
Uptown Dining 170
Downtown Attractions 186
Midtown Attractions 188
Uptown Attractions 190
Upper Manhattan Attractions 192
Walking Tour: Wall Street & the
  Financial District 195
Walking Tour: Greenwich Village's
  Literary Past 232
Central Park 245

Brooklyn Heights Attractions   259
The Theater District   299

AN INVITATION TO THE READER

In researching this book, we discovered many wonderful places—hotels, restaurants, shops, and more. We're sure you'll find others. Please tell us about them, so we can share the information with your fellow travelers in upcoming editions. If you were disappointed with a recommendation, we'd love to know that, too. Please write to

Frommer's New York City from $80 a Day 2000
Macmillan Travel
1633 Broadway
New York, NY 10019

AN ADDITIONAL NOTE

Please be advised that travel information is subject to change at any time—and this is especially true of prices. We therefore suggest that you write or call ahead for confirmation when making your travel plans. The authors, editors, and publisher cannot be held responsible for the experiences of readers while traveling. Your safety is important to us, however, so we encourage you to stay alert and be aware of your surroundings. Keep a close eye on cameras, purses, and wallets, all favorite targets of thieves and pickpockets.

WHAT THE SYMBOLS MEAN

✪ Frommer's Favorites

Our favorite places and experiences—outstanding for quality, value, or both.

The following abbreviations are used for credit cards:

AE	American Express	EC	Eurocard
CB	Carte Blanche	JCB	Japan Credit Bank
DC	Diners Club	MC	MasterCard
DISC	Discover	V	Visa
ER	enRoute		

FIND FROMMER'S ONLINE

Arthur Frommer's Budget Travel Online (**www.frommers.com**) offers more than 6,000 pages of up-to-the-minute travel information—including the latest bargains and candid, personal articles updated daily by Arthur Frommer himself. No other Web site offers such comprehensive and timely coverage of the world of travel.

The Best of the Big Apple

1

Welcome to New York City—the only city on the planet brazen enough to call itself "The Capital of the World." New York has never been subtle, self-effacing, or coy. This is the Muhammad Ali of cities: We Are the Greatest!

It's precisely this kind of urban machismo that makes people either love New York or hate it—or both. Either you'll be enthralled by the tempo, glamour, and sheer excitement of it all, or you'll be stunned by the noise, the intimate mingling of inhuman poverty and unimaginable wealth, the smog, and the callousness that's an everyday occurrence on these city streets. If your emotional metronome swings back and forth from one moment to the next, take heart: We New Yorkers have a never-ending love-hate relationship with this awful, wonderful town. We talk endlessly about escaping for the weekend, commiserate about subways that arrive late, bemoan the noise, the rents, the crowds, the cab drivers who don't seem to know Lincoln Center from the Lower East Side. Yet still we stay.

The questions beg to be asked: Why do we stay? And what is it about New York City that makes you, dear reader, want to join us?

Any attempt to define New York today recalls the Zen wisdom that you can't step in the same stream twice. The city is so mutable, so constantly changing, that it's almost impossible to get a fix on. Restaurants and nightclubs become trendy overnight, then die under the weight of their own popularity. Fashions, almost by definition, change in the time it takes to try on a pair of vinyl pants. Broadway shows, exercise fads, even neighborhoods are all subject to the same Big Apple fickleness. But within this ebb and flow lies the answer: No other place keeps any of us on our toes quite like New York City. Nowhere else is the challenge so tough, the pace so relentless, the stimuli so ever-changing and insistent—and the payoff so rewarding. Simply put, New York never gets boring. Anything can happen here.

The city has a special magnetism—a charisma, if you will—that pulls in the intelligent, the creative, the determined, the overbearing, and the overblown from all over the world. Just about any language and any dialect is spoken here, from Mandarin to Brooklynese; no other dot on the map is quite so ethnically, culturally, and socially diverse. This is the nerve center of world finance and trade. The international hub of advertising, publishing, entertainment, and fashion. The creative core for the arts. The top showcase for pure celebrity. And, now as never before, a huge magnet for travelers from all over the country and around the globe.

The only credential the city asked was the boldness to dream. For those who did, it unlocked its gates and its treasures, not caring who they were and where they came from.

—Moss Hart

The end [of the world] wouldn't come as a surprise here. Many people already bank on it.

—Saul Bellow

You've probably heard the good news: The city is in top form, its finest in more than 50 years. The economy is up, and crime is down. Everywhere you look, things are being refurbished and the city is steadily improving. It has even become, why, *family friendly*—just look at the new peep-show-and-porn-free Times Square. New Yorkers love to complain about Hizzoner, Mayor Rudy Giuliani, because he likes to take the lion's share of credit—more than he deserves, methinks. But few alive today have ever seen the city so radiant, so manageable; and he's had the good fortune to usher in the Renaissance. New Yorkers love to wax nostalgic about the good-old, bad-old days, but the fact is that we're reveling in our own good fortune. Now is a great time to be in New York.

Visitors, pumped with curiosity about this "new" New York, are arriving by the millions, swarming the city's streets, sights, hotels, museums, restaurants, nightclubs, and theaters. And the city, aglow in its newfound optimism, is welcoming them, and you, with open arms. So come—and be prepared to be overwhelmed, exasperated, delighted, and utterly charmed. That, after all, is what the Big Apple is all about.

1 How This Guide Can Save You Money

New York, as everyone knows, is perpetually short on space and overflowing with people. And the city's huge popularity these days means that more people are coming to visit—or to stay—than ever. It's a situation that turns the economy of supply and demand in the seller's favor, with vendors charging whatever the market will bear for goods and services. The result has been stratospheric prices, generally the highest you'll find in the country. Average hotel rates are now hovering around $195, and New Yorkers don't bat an eye at dropping a hundred bucks on a modest dinner for two. If you're used to getting a simple motel room for $35 to $50, the kind of basic accommodations available all over the United States, get set for a shock. With hotel occupancy rates hovering perilously close to 90%, most hoteliers laugh at the notion of giving away any hotel room for $100 or less.

That's the bad news—but there's plenty of good news to tell, too. Simply put, you *can* stay in New York City comfortably, eat well, and see and do everything you want without blowing your budget. There are plenty of great deals in every category for the intrepid traveler who knows where to look for good value and mine for discounts. And you've taken the right first step—buying this book. I've done the initial legwork for you, scouring the city from top to bottom and loading the pages that follow with the best money-saving advice, leads on the top values and bargains, and the kind of New York travel know-how that only comes with years of research and experience.

Accommodations will be your biggest hurdle. Most other aspects of New York are budgetable if you look before you leap, which is precisely how we regular New Yorkers manage to live here on regular salaries. The city tends to snag people who, exhausted, sit down at the first meal they see and end up with a huge bill—or those who stumble into a chic boutique to buy a standard replacement item or a souvenir that can be had for a fraction of the price with just a little effort. Keep an eye on the goal and you'll soon see that New York has more affordable culinary and bargain-hunters' delights than you'll have time to enjoy.

With average museum admissions hovering around 10 bucks a pop and guided bus tours starting out near $25 for the basic look-see, you could spend a fortune on sightseeing and activities—but you don't have to. Start perusing these pages and you'll soon find more to see and do for free and on the cheap than you could possibly squeeze into one vacation (or two or three or four). I'm not suggesting that you skip anything that has a price tag; certain New York experiences shouldn't be missed, money be damned. But read the pages that follow and you'll know what's worth your dough—and what's not.

THE NEW YORK–FROM-$80-A-DAY PREMISE
This premise may seem like a pipe dream, but it's not. The idea is this: With good planning and a watchful eye, you can keep your basic daily living costs—accommodations and three meals a day—down to as little as $80. This budget model works best for two adults traveling together who have at least $160 a day to work with and can share a standard room for two (as you're probably well aware, single rooms are much less cost-efficient). This way, if you aim for accommodations costing around $100 double, you'll be left with about $30 per person per day for food (less drinks and tips).

If you want to do it even cheaper by spending even less on accommodations, I'll show you how to do that, too. But in defining this basic premise we at Frommer's have assumed that you want to travel comfortably, with your own room rather than a hostel bunk, dining on good food rather than fast food at every meal. This book will also serve you well even if you don't need to keep your two-person budget to a strict $160 a day, but you want to keep the tabs down and get the most for your money at every turn.

Of course, the cost of sightseeing, transportation, and entertainment are all extras. But don't worry—I'll offer plenty of suggestions on how to keep those bills down, too. What you choose for entertainment will have a huge effect on your overall budget. If you frequent nightclubs every night, you'll come home with a lighter wallet than if you spend time taking in free concerts or browsing galleries. If you seek top-name entertainment on Broadway or the cabaret circuit, you'll pay more than if you take a risk on tomorrow's stars at an off-Broadway show or a no-cover bar. Only you know how much money you have to spend—but follow my advice, and you'll be able to make informed decisions on what to see and do so that it's money well spent. Even if you stick with freebies, the Big Apple guarantees a memorable time. After all, to paraphrase Quentin Crisp, every flat surface in New York is a stage—and you're guaranteed a nonstop show.

2 Frommer's Favorite Affordable Experiences

- **Sailing to the Statue of Liberty.** If you have time to do only one thing in New York, this is what it should be. No monument so embodies the nation's, and the world's, notion of political freedom and economic potential more than Lady Liberty. As silly as this may sound, the view never loses its power—and neither does the Manhattan skyline, which is breathtaking from this perspective. The ferry that takes you out to Liberty Island also stops at the historic federal immigration station on Ellis Island, gateway to America for nearly half of our forefathers and foremothers. The museum's exhibits illustrate, with moving simplicity, what coming to the "promised land" was all about. If you want the view but prefer to skip the tourist crowds—and the fare—consider catching the free Staten Island Ferry, a city icon unto itself, instead. See chapter 7.

- **Visiting the Museums.** The Metropolitan Museum of Art, the American Museum of Natural History, the Museum of Modern Art, the Whitney Museum of American Art, the Guggenheim—museum hopping just doesn't get any better than this. The number of masterworks housed in this city is mind-boggling. But don't just stick to the biggies; New York boasts a wealth of smaller, lower-profile museums that speak to specific interests—from folk art to photography to financial history—and house some phenomenal treasures. For a complete rundown, see chapter 7—and don't miss the box "Free Culture at Big Apple Museums," which will fill you in on which ones offer free or discounted admission on select days.

- **Strolling the Neighborhoods.** One of the greatest things about New York is the distinct character of each of its neighborhoods. Rather than trying to quick-scan them all, I highly recommend picking one and really getting to know it. Wend your way through the historic streets of Greenwich Village, saunter the cast-iron canyons of SoHo, or explore the lovely, trendy Flatiron District. All you really need is a map and a sense of adventure. If you prefer a little structure, consider taking one of the many excellent walking tours that are available; there's no better way to get to know a 'hood than with an expert at the helm. Some of the city's best guided tours are even free. See chapters 4 and 7.

- **Walking the Brooklyn Bridge.** A marvel of civic engineering when it first connected Brooklyn to Manhattan in 1883, the Brooklyn Bridge still awes even the most jaded New Yorkers. I, for one, never tire of admiring its Gothic-inspired stone pylons and intricate steel-cable webs. Get an up-close look, and some marvelous views of Manhattan, by taking the easy stroll from end to end. Start on the Brooklyn side for best effect, and consider pairing your walk with a stroll through historic Brooklyn Heights for a lovely afternoon. See chapter 7.

- **Being on Top of the World.** Go to the top. Straight to the top—higher than you've ever been before. New York is made to be seen from above, in the full light of day or in the full glitter of night—it's your choice. Better yet, get both perspectives. Head up to the Top of the World observation deck at the World Trade Center where, if you're lucky, you'll be able to go out on the rooftop promenade, the world's highest open-air observation deck. If you'd rather avoid the tourist crowds, head to the Greatest Bar on Earth, on the top floor of the second tower, which boasts the same incredible views for the price of a cocktail. And don't forget about the Empire State Building—not quite as high up, but doubly romantic. Well worth the price of admission. **Money-saving tip:** Consider buying a **CityPass,** which gives you 50% off admission to the World Trade Center and Empire State observation decks as well as four other top attractions. See "60 Money-Saving Tips" in chapter 2 as well as chapters 7 and 9.

- **Star Gazing at Grand Central Terminal.** Always a beaux arts gem, this majestic 1913 railroad station received a remarkable facelift, unveiled in late 1998, that has made it a must-see. Every surface glitters with renewed optimism—but none more than the masterful ceiling, once again brilliant with 24-karat gold zodiac constellations against a gorgeous blue-green sky. Walk in, throw your head back, and watch the stars gleam. See chapter 7.

- **Ogling the City's Art-Deco Marvels.** Nothing embodies the city's historic sense of optimism more so than its streamline masterpieces. And nowhere is the art-deco style more passionately realized than at Rockefeller Center, the business-and-entertainment center at the heart of midtown. The most romantic of the city's skyscrapers, the chrome-topped Chrysler Building, is another art-deco gem; look for the gargoyles jutting out from the upper floors. And when you visit the marvelous Empire State Building, don't miss the mural in the lobby in your rush to get to the top. See chapter 7.

- **Wandering Central Park.** This beautiful accident of civic planning makes the otherwise uninterrupted urban jungle tolerable for workaday New Yorkers. Don't skip the chance to enjoy its wonders. Be sure to seek out Strawberry Fields, the living memorial to John Lennon. Without this great green park, I couldn't imagine life in the city. See chapter 7.

- **Watching Your Favorite Talk Show Being Taped.** If you have the forethought (to send away months in advance) or the patience (to wait in the standby line), you can watch Dave, Conan, Rosie, Sally, or the ladies of *The View* work their TV magic. If sketch comedy or sitcoms are more your speed, think *Spin City, Cosby,* or—the holy grail of TV audience wannabes—*Saturday Night Live.* To start planning—or tips on how to score tickets at the last minute—see chapter 7.

- **Dining Out.** New York is the world capital of great eating—and the true beauty of New York's restaurant scene is that you don't have to spend a fortune to eat well. You'll find cheap but dazzling Chinese in Chinatown, pastrami to die for at any number of Jewish delis, pasta and pizza that your Italian grandmother could love . . . the list goes on and on. See chapter 6.

- **Watching the Curtain Rise on a Play.** There's nothing like the immediacy and excitement of a stage production in action. Movie and TV stars know it, which is why more and more are showing their stuff on the New York stage. Make it a priority to catch a live theater production while you're in town. Sure, tickets are expensive—but creative minds almost never have to pay top dollar. First of all, consider the city's wealth of affordable off-Broadway productions. Who knows? You could be the first on your block (or in your state) to catch the next *Rent.* If your heart's set on a big Broadway musical (or any theater production, for that matter), buy your tickets through the TKTS booth, where you can save 25% to 50% off face value. See chapter 9 for details.

- **Catching a Baseball Game.** There's no better place to experience the trademark "Noo Yawk" attitude than at a ball game. New York fans have a love/hate relationship with their Boys of Summer—they're saints when they win, bums when they lose. There's never a dull moment: Everybody has an opinion, and it's all part of the show. Check out the Yankees at Yankee Stadium, or the Mets at Shea. You can decide to catch a game a couple of hours before the first pitch, hop on the subway, and buy your tickets at the stadium (thereby saving on advance-purchase service charges). At the House that Ruth Built, unreserved bleacher seats go for just $8. For better sightlines and a more refined crowd, go for the $14 upper-tier reserves. At Shea, the upper-tier reserves are just $10—not bad for an only-in–New York experience. See chapter 7.

- **Celebrating the Holidays in the City.** Sure, Christmas and New Year's can be nightmarish times in New York, with crowds choking the entire city and every merchant in town charging top dollar. But the city can be a dream on other, less attention-grabbing holidays, and a veritable bargain to boot. On Chinese New Year, a bright dragon promises great fortune ahead—and bargain-basement winter getaway rates. With the promise of summer heat keeping both visitors and city dwellers out of town, a peaceful hush comes over the city on July 4th—until the fireworks explode overhead, lighting up the night sky with patriotic flair. The huge hot-air balloons of the Macy's Thanksgiving Day Parade bring out the kid in all of us—and it's a little-known fact that some of the best hotel bargains in the city can be had over the holiday weekend away from the parade route. See "When to Go" and the "Calendar of Events" in chapter 2.

- **Taking Advantage of Freebies.** Always financially pressed in this perpetually too-expensive city, New Yorkers and visitors alike love nothing better than a bargain. But even longtime locals often don't realize just how much wonderful stuff there is to see and do in the Big Apple that's absolutely free. Be sure to check out "Cheap Thrills: What to See & Do for Free" in chapter 7.

3 Best Affordable Hotel Bets

There's no way around it—you're going to spend more than you like on a hotel room. But lest you worry that your credit card can't handle the stress, never fear: New York has plenty of good wallet-friendly choices, and even some downright bargains, for those who know where to look. For the details on these and other affordable city hotels, see chapter 5.

- **Best Overall Value—Downtown:** It's hard to beat the **Cosmopolitan Hotel–Tribeca,** 95 W. Broadway (☎ 888/895-9400), for value. Each of the small but comfy, modern rooms comes with its own petite but immaculate private bath for as little as $99 a night. The high-rent neighborhood is hip as can be, and subway-convenient to the rest of the city.
- **Best Overall Value—Midtown:** No midtown choice is better located or more consistently value-priced than the **Hotel Edison,** 228 W. 47th St. (☎ 800/637-7070), a mammoth hotel with freshly renovated, perfectly comfortable rooms for just $140 (double) right in the heart of the Theater District. As Gershwin himself said, who could ask for anything more?
- **Best Overall Value—Uptown:** I was thrilled to find the **Hotel Newton,** 2528 Broadway (☎ 888/HOTEL58), the one budget hotel in the city that doesn't expect you to put up with a miniscule room or myriad inconveniences just because you don't have a king's ransom to spend. The rooms are spacious and well outfitted, and the staff couldn't be more professional. With rates running just $99 to $135 for a double with private bath, you'll more than get your money's worth here—and you'll save an additional 10% if you're a AAA member.
- **Best Value for Bargain-Hunters Who Don't Mind Sharing:** If you're willing to share a hall bath with your fellow travelers, you'll be pleased as punch with the charming **Larchmont Hotel,** in the leafiest, loveliest part of Greenwich Village at 27 W. 11th St. (☎ 212/989-9333). If you want to spend less than $100 a night, you won't do better for the money.
- **Best Classic New York Appeal:** I just love the **Wyndham,** 42 W. 58th St. (☎ 800/257-1111). This family-owned charmer boasts simply enormous rooms and the same old-time staff that was here when Jimmy Carter was in the White House. The eclectic (some might say wacky) decor isn't for everybody, but it's gives the old girl character. And the location is terrific, on a great block just steps from Fifth Avenue shopping and Central Park.
- **Best Service for the Budget-Minded:** The professional staff at the **Broadway Inn,** 264 W. 46th St. (☎ 800/826-6300), just may be the most helpful in the city. They're so committed to making their guests feel welcome and at home in New York that they give you a hotline number to call when you're out and about if you need directions, advice on where to eat, or any other assistance. When you come home from your long day of sightseeing, they'll be happy to order in delivery from any of the nearby restaurants for you. And you thought New York wasn't friendly!

- **Best for Families:** Located on the Upper West Side, one of the city's most desirable and kid-friendly residential neighborhoods, is the **Milburn,** 242 W. 76th St. (☎ **800/833-9622**), whose one-bedroom suites are the most affordable in town. A queen-size sleeper sofa in the living room makes the suites large enough to comfortably accommodate four, and a kitchenette with microwave, minifridge, and coffeemaker means mom and dad can save on breakfast bills. And the kids-under-12-stay-free policy makes the Milburn an even better value for budget-minded families.
- **Best for a Romantic Getaway:** Even if money were no object, I'd send you to **Country Inn the City,** on the Upper West Side on W. 77th St. (☎ **212/580-4183**), one of the most impeccable guest houses I've ever seen. Couples will have everything they need at hand—including plenty of privacy.
- **Best Accommodations for Arty Types:** If you're a youth-minded traveler looking for an artsy environment, you have two choices: The super-cool, Factory-esque **Gershwin Hotel,** 7 E. 27th St. (☎ **212/545-8000**), where Billy Name is the house photog—what more do I need to say? There's also the even wilder and cheaper **Carlton Arms,** 160 E. 25th St. (☎ **212/679-0680**), where freedom reigns but creature comforts fall short; for shoestring-budget travelers only.
- **Best for Style Hounds on a Shoestring:** The brand-new **Habitat Hotel,** 130 E. 57th St. (☎ **800/255-0482**), is carving out quite a niche for itself as the "upscale budget" choice among style-conscious consumers. The narrow rooms are fresh and outfitted with flair, and the neighborhood is about as high fashion as it gets.
- **Best Freebie: Travel Inn,** 515 W. 42nd St. (☎ **800/869-4630**), wins on not just one, but *two* counts. First is the free garage parking—otherwise completely unheard of in Manhattan, and a $25-a-day value at minimum for visitors driving to the city. Freebie number two is for summer visitors, who can take advantage of Travel Inn's excellent rooftop swimming pool and huge sundeck.
- **Best Weekend Packages:** Weekend and holiday visitors should definitely check with the **Millenium Hilton,** 55 Church St. (☎ **800/835-2220**), whose luxury rooms tend to go for a relative song once business travelers flee Wall Street for home.
- **Best for Disabled Travelers:** Disabled travelers no longer have to spend a fortune to stay in a hotel that can accommodate them. At press time, the **Milburn,** 242 W. 76th St. (☎ **800/833-9622**), was adding five new lobby-level wheelchair-accessible rooms to their selection of comfortable, budget-minded accommodations.
- **Best Splurge:** On the Upper West Side is the **Lucerne,** 201 W. 79th St. (☎ **800/492-8122**), a sophisticated hotel that's big on comforts and service but not on price. If you'd rather be in Midtown, opt instead for the Lucerne's sister hotel, the **Belvedere,** 319 W. 48th St. (☎ **888/HOTEL58**), or the art-deco-style **Hotel Metro,** 45 W. 35th St. (☎ **800/356-3870**), both excellent midpriced hotels that feel more expensive than they actually are.

4 Best Affordable Dining Bets

One of the great joys of being in New York is that there's fabulous food at nearly every turn—and you don't have to be toting a gold card to pay for it. Go ethnic—Chinese, Jewish, Italian, and much, much more—to indulge in the best cheap eats you'll find anywhere. For the details on these and other terrific affordable city restaurants, see chapter 6.

- **Best for a Special Occasion:** TV chef Mario Batali's charming **Pó,** 31 Cornelia St. (☎ 212/645-2189), manages to feel special while still remaining affordable, and his inspired pastas are more impressive than those served in much pricier restaurants around town. If you can't get into Pó (which has been known to book up a full month in advance), try Cornelia Street neighbor **Home,** at no. 20 (☎ 212/243-9579), which oozes Village charm and boasts an intimate outdoor garden.
- **Best Spot for a Business Lunch:** If you want to impress with your New York acumen, head to the **Oyster Bar,** on the lower level of Grand Central Terminal (☎ 212/490-6650), a New York classic that's a perfect spot to seal the deal.
- **Best Chinese:** With all the culinary wonders that Chinatown has to offer, this is a tough choice. But whenever I think about the steamy soup dumplings at **Joe's Shanghai,** 9 Pell St. (☎ 212/233-8888), I can't help but swoon.
- **Best Affordable French:** It's expensive enough to warrant a splurge, but your best bet is **Le Gigot,** 18 Cornelia St. (☎ 212/627-3737), for a true slice of St-Germain. If Le Gigot is too rich for your wallet, grab a bottle of wine and head to **Tartine,** 253 W. 11th St. (☎ 212/229-2611), where the well-priced bistro fare is more than worth the wait.
- **Best Affordable Italian:** For bang-for-your-buck Italian, the award goes to **Bar Pitti,** 268 Sixth Ave. (☎ 212/982-3300), a wonderfully authentic Tuscan-style trattoria. And, of course, there's super-popular **Pó,** 31 Cornelia St. (☎ 212/645-2189)—pasta simply doesn't get any better than this.
- **Best Affordable Seafood:** You can't do better for your money than at **Pisces,** 95 Ave. A (☎ 212/260-6660), where the top-quality fish is always fresh and creatively prepared. The early-bird prix-fixe dinner makes an already terrific value even more wallet-friendly.
- **Best Home-Style Cooking:** No other restaurant warms my heart more than the aptly named **Home,** 20 Cornelia St. (☎ 212/243-9579); don't skip the silky-smooth chocolate pudding that even Mom would admit is better than hers.
- **Best Newcomer:** NoLiTa's **Cafe Habana,** 17 Prince St. (☎ 212/625-2001), has wooed and won the downtown crowd with its nuevo-luncheonette look and pretension-free Cubano fare.
- **Best Jewish Deli:** Kosher **Second Avenue Deli,** 156 Second Ave. (☎ 212/677-0606), is New York's deli of choice among those who know their kreplach, matzo, and pastrami. No cutesy sandwiches named for celebrities here—just top-notch Jewish classics, all at wallet-friendly prices.
- **Best Gourmet Sandwiches:** Nobody does BLTs better than NoLiTa newcomer, **Bread & Butter,** 229 Elizabeth St. (☎ 212/925-7600). In Midtown, there's retro-hip **Island Burgers & Shakes,** 766 Ninth Ave. (☎ 212/307-7934), for excellent grilled-chicken sandwiches (churascos).
- **Best Burger and Beer:** Ask a hundred New Yorkers, and you'll get a hundred opinions. But for my money, there's no better choice than **Old Town Bar & Restaurant,** 45 E. 18th St. (☎ 212/529-6732). Whether you go low-fat turkey or bacon-chili-cheddar, the burgers at this venerable 19th-century pub are perfect every time. The fries are addictively crisp, and there's a whole selection of great beers are on tap.
- **Best Pizza:** Pizza doesn't get any better than the coal oven-baked, fresh-mozzarella-topped pie at **Patsy Grimaldi's Pizzeria,** 19 Old Fulton St., Brooklyn Heights (☎ 718/858-4300). If you're unwilling to travel across the river, head to **Lombardi's,** 32 Spring St. (☎ 212/941-7994), which has been baking up its own coal-oven pies since 1905.

- **Best Diner:** As any aficionado knows, the true mark of a good diner is the quality of their chicken noodle soup, the ultimate comfort food. **Bendix Diner,** 219 Eighth Ave. (☎ 212/366-0560), takes the soul-warming prize.
- **Best Fine-Dining Bargain:** Dining values don't get any better than the **Tavern Room at Gramercy Tavern,** 42 E. 20th St. (☎ 212/477-0777), which allows you to experience one of the city's finest restaurants for a fraction of what expense-account diners pay in the main dining room. I actually prefer this friendly bistro-style alternative, which offers excellent New American food without the pretension.
- **Best Year-Round Prix-Fixe Lunch Deal:** Lots of fine-dining restaurants offer specially discounted fixed-price lunches during Restaurant Week, or even for the entire summer (see "Bargain Alert—Great Prix-Fixe Lunch Deals" in chapter 6). But for a midday bargain at any time of year, your best bet is **Molyvos,** 871 Seventh Ave. (☎ 212/582-7500). This warm and inviting upscale taverna offers a generous three-course fixed-price lunch for just $20. You'll have a short but excellent list to choose from at every course; on my last visit, the prix-fixe menu even included the stellar lemon and garlic–seasoned roasted free-range chicken, one of the best birds I've ever had the pleasure to enjoy. The baklava is a must-have for fans.
- **Best Prix-Fixe Dinner Deal:** If you don't mind dining early and you have the willpower to stick to the prix-fixe menu, the two-course $20 dinner at **Alison on Dominick Street,** 38 Dominick St. in SoHo (☎ 212/727-1188), is a smokin' deal. Since seatings are between 5 and 6:30pm, you can even take advantage of Alison on Dominick as a pre-Broadway choice, as long as you allow yourself time to get Uptown (the nearby 1 or 9 train will get you to the Theater District in 15 minutes).
- **Best Spot for Weekend Brunch:** Uptown, head to **Sarabeth's Kitchen,** 423 Amsterdam Ave. (☎ 212/496-6280), whose omelettes, pancakes, and pastries are unrivaled—go early or expect a wait. Downtown, **Le Gigot,** 18 Cornelia St. (☎ 212/627-3737) is the Village's best-kept brunch secret—until now, that is. The crispy potatoes are downright addictive.
- **Best People-Watching Spot:** With its model-caliber waitstaff and hipper-than-thou clientele, the **Coffee Shop,** 29 Union Sq. W. (☎ 212/243-7969), may be the best place to spy on the beautiful people; in warm weather, come early to snag one of the coveted alfresco tables overlooking Union Square.
- **Best for Aspiring Cooks:** Shabu Tatsu, 216 E. 10th St. (☎ 212/477-2972), is loads of interactive fun. Come in a group to enjoy the Japanese specialty shabu-shabu, a dish you cook yourself in the hotpot of boiling water built into the center of your table. The waiters bring the plateful of raw meat and veggies, and you'll have a blast doing the rest.
- **Best Late-Night Hangout:** Half authentic French bistro, half all-American diner, **Florent,** 69 Gansevoort St. (☎ 212/989-5779), is the hipster crowd's favorite after-hours hangout. Thanks to its good food, great people watching, and wonderful sense of humor, it's mine, too.
- **Best Wine Deal:** Tuesday isn't just Tuesday anymore—at least not at the **Bridge Cafe,** 279 Water St. (☎ 212/227-3344), where it's Wine Discovery Tuesday. Every bottle on the restaurant's already–well-priced all-American wine list is 30% off. This deal should still be on while you're in town, but call ahead to be sure.
- **Best Dessert:** There are a lot of stellar pastry chefs in town, but you'd be hard-pressed to do better than the remarkable confections at **Payard Pâtisserie and Bistro,** 1032 Lexington Ave. (☎ 212/717-5252), which is well located for a pastry break during a day of Upper East Side museum hopping.

2 Planning an Affordable Trip to New York City

In the pages that follow, you'll find everything you need to know to handle the practical details of planning your trip in advance—airlines and area airports, a calendar of events, resources for those with special needs, and much more—with time-tested advice on how to save money at every turn.

1 60 Money-Saving Tips

Be prepared—hotels are likely to take a far larger chunk out of your travel budget than you'd like. And then there's airfare to pay for, which is always pricey. But don't be discouraged if you feel like you've spent most of your vacation money even before you've packed your bags. New York is so exciting on its own that there's no need to spend a fortune on expensive activities and sightseeing tours. And this city is the capital of cheap ethnic eats, so it's easy to eat well without overspending.

Here are some tips to help you keep your travel costs down:

1. **Buy a money-saving package deal.** A travel package that includes your plane tickets and hotel stay for one price may just be the best bargain of all. In some cases, you'll get airfare, accommodations, transportation to and from the airport, plus extras—maybe an afternoon sightseeing tour, or restaurant and shopping discount coupons—for less than the hotel alone would have cost had you booked it yourself. For the lowdown on where and how to get the best package, see the box "Money-Saving Package Deals" later in this chapter.

2. **Buy a *New York for Less* guidebook.** The primary value in buying this guide ($19.95) is the discount card within, which offers hundreds of discounts of 20% or more at restaurants, attractions (including the Empire State Building, the Museum of Modern Art, and the World Trade Center observation deck), guided tour operators, shops, theaters, and nightlife spots around Manhattan. The card is good for up to four people for up to 8 days and comes with a handbook detailing all the places that honor New York for Less. You can order *New York for Less* by calling ☎ 888/463-6753 or online at **www.for-less.com**.

3. **If you're an American Express cardholder, check for AmEx-only special offers.** American Express offers its cardholders a surprisingly good array of discounts at local and national merchants via its Web site at **www.americanexpress.com**. At the

---

Planning Tip

Check out Frommer's Online Directory, in the back of this book, for further information on Web sites covering airfares, lodgings, restaurants, and attractions that will help you plan an exciting and affordable trip to New York.

---

home page, click on See SPECIAL OFFERS under PERSONAL, then click on CARDMEMBER SPECIAL OFFERS, which in New York can range from a free sandwich at the Official All-Star Cafe to 15% off tickets for *Ragtime*. The restaurant discounts are often particularly good (I once got 20% off my entire dinner bill at the Bridge Cafe, a wonderful restaurant in South Street Seaport). Be sure to scroll down to the national offers, where you might find such bargains as fifth-night free hotel stays at reliable chains, 20% discounts on rental cars, and $3 off shipping from Mail Boxes, Etc. The discount certificates are right online; all you have to do is print them out and bring them with you. American Express is terrific about keeping these offers current, but be sure to check the expiration dates as well as the terms and conditions carefully.

WHEN TO GO

4. **Choose your season carefully.** The biggest factor that will affect how much you pay for your hotel room and airfare is the season in which you travel. Prices on hotel rooms, in particular, can vary dramatically—by hundreds of dollars in some cases—depending on what time of year you visit. Winter from January to mid-April is the best season for bargains, with summer from June to mid-August being second-best. Spring and fall are the busiest and most expensive seasons after Christmas, but negotiating a decent rate is doable, especially in spring. Budget-minded travelers should skip Christmas and New Year's altogether, when visitors pay top dollar for everything. Thanksgiving, however, is a little-known bargain-hunter's delight. For more on this subject, see "Money Matters" under "When to Go" later in this chapter.

GETTING TO NEW YORK CITY
AIR TRAVEL

5. **Plan ahead, and be flexible.** On most flights, even the shortest hops, the full fare is close to $1,000 or more, but you'll most likely pay a lot less if you buy a 7-, 14-, or 21-day advance purchase ticket. If you don't mind staying over Saturday night or are willing to travel on a Tuesday, Wednesday, or Thursday, you'll likely save even more. Many airlines won't volunteer this information, so be sure to ask.

6. **Always ask for the lowest fare.** Yes, reservations and travel agents should take for granted that you want the lowest possible fare—but they don't always do so. Be sure to ask specifically for the lowest fare, not just a discount fare. And, as with every aspect of your trip, ask about discounts for groups, seniors, children, and students.

7. **Consider all three airports when you're shopping around.** Fares can be markedly different depending on which airport you fly into—LaGuardia, JFK, or Newark, NJ—and none of them are that far from Manhattan. Continental, for instance, almost always has cheaper flights into Newark, since it's one of their main hubs. In fact, even though it's in the next state over, Newark may often be more convenient to your Manhattan destination than the other two airports, and the public buses that run between the airport and the city are cheap and easy to use.

8. **Keep an eye out for promotional rates or special sales.** Periodically, airlines lower prices on their most popular routes, which often include New York. Check your newspaper for advertised discounts or call the airlines directly and ask if any special deals are available. You'll almost never see a sale during the peak summer vacation months of July and August, or during the Thanksgiving or Christmas seasons; but in periods of low-volume travel, you should pay no more than $400 for a cross-country flight.

   Note, however, that the lowest-priced fares are often nonrefundable, require advance purchase of 1 to 3 weeks, a certain length of stay, and carry penalties for changing dates of travel. So, when you're quoted a fare, make sure you know exactly what the restrictions are before you commit.

9. **Try the discount carriers, too.** When shopping the airlines, don't forget to check with the smaller, no-frills airlines that fly to New York, including Tower Air, ATA, and Spirit Airlines. You may not get the same kind of service or frequent-flyer bonuses that you will get from the majors, but you may save a lot of dough. See "Getting There," below, for a rundown of discount carriers that fly into area airports.

10. **Check for discounted fares with consolidators.** Also known as bucket shops, consolidators are a good place to find low fares, often below even the airlines' discounted rates. There's nothing shady about the reliable ones—basically, they're just big travel agents that get discounts for buying in bulk and pass some of the savings on to you. Before you pay, however, ask for a confirmation number from the consolidator and then call the airline itself to confirm your seat. Be aware that consolidator tickets are usually non-refundable or come with stiff cancellation penalties.

    Small ads for consolidators usually run in the Sunday travel section at the bottom of the page, but I recommend going with one of these reliable companies: I've gotten great deals on a number of occasions from **Cheap Tickets** (☎ 800/377-1000 or 212/570-1179; www.cheaptickets.com). **Council Travel** (☎ 800/226-8624; www.counciltravel.com) and **STA Travel** (☎ 800/781-4040; www.sta.travel.com) cater especially to young travelers, but their bargain-basement prices are available to travelers of all ages. **Travel Bargains** (☎ 800/AIR-FARE; www.1800airfare.com) was formerly owned by TWA but now offers the deepest discounts on many other airlines, with a 4-day advance purchase. Other reliable consolidators include **1-800-FLY-4-LESS; Cheap Seats** (☎ 800/ 451-7200; www.cheapseatstravel.com); **1-800-FLY-CHEAP** (www. 1800flycheap.com); or "rebators" such as **Travel Avenue** (☎ 800/333-3335 or 312/876-1116) and **Smart Traveller** (☎ 800/448-3338 or 305/448-3338), which rebate part of their commissions to you. **TFI Tours International** (☎ 800/745-8000 or 212/736-1140), which serves as a clearinghouse for unused seats, also has good fares, but I've found their operators to be less than polite on more than one occasion.

11. **Search the Internet for cheap advance-purchase fares.** Online booking services can be especially useful because they show you all the options, and some even make lower-priced suggestions on alternatives to your requested itinerary. Keep in mind, though, that it's a good idea to compare your findings with the research of a dedicated travel agent, if you're lucky enough to have one, before you buy, especially when you're booking more than just a flight.

    A few of the better-respected virtual travel agents are **Travelocity** (www. travelocity.com) and **Microsoft Expedia** (www.expedia.com). Each has its own little quirks—Travelocity and Expedia both require you to register with them—but they all provide variations of the same service. Just enter the dates you want to fly and the cities you want to visit, and the computer roots out the lowest fares. Expedia's site will e-mail you the best airfare deal once a week if you so choose. Travelocity uses the SABRE computer reservations system that most travel agents use, and has a "Last Minute Deals" database that advertises really cheap fares for those who can get away at a moment's notice. I've also had good luck with the **Internet Travel Network** (www.itn.net). No other fare-finding site is as thorough as this one: When it pulls up flights that meet your itinerary, it includes each flight's on-time record, plus its exact distance so you know how many frequent-flyer miles you'll earn. You can even call them (☎ **800/253-9822** or 650/494-1557) before or after you make your reservation if you have any questions or concerns about what you see onscreen.

Another good bet is **Arthur Frommer's Budget Travel** (www.frommers.com), which offers detailed information on 200 destinations around the world, plus ways to save on flights, hotels, car reservations, and cruises. Book an entire vacation online, or direct travel questions to Arthur himself. The newsletter is updated daily to keep you abreast of the latest ways to save.

12. **Sign up for e-mail notification of last-minute fare deals.** Great last-minute deals are available through E-savers, free e-mail services provided directly by the airlines. Each week, the airline sends you a list of discounted flights, usually leaving the upcoming Friday or Saturday and returning the following Monday or Tuesday. You can sign up at each airline's Web site (see "Getting There: By Plane" later in this chapter for Web addresses).

    Better yet, save yourself the headache and register with **Smarter Living** (www.smarterliving.com). Every week you'll get a customized e-mail summarizing the discount fares available from your departure city. Smarter Living tracks more than 15 different airlines, so it's a worthwhile time-saver. The site also features concise lists of links to hotel, car rental, and other hot travel deals.

13. **If you purchase refundable tickets, keep checking fares even after you've received them.** The availability of bargains changes daily; as your departure date draws nearer, more seats may become available at lower prices. Even with the change penalty factored in, it may be cheaper to make the switch.

14. **Book a seat on a charter flight.** Most charter operators advertise and sell their seats through travel agents, thus making these local professionals your best source of information for available flights. Before deciding to take a charter flight, however, check the restrictions on the ticket: You may be asked to purchase a package tour, pay in advance, be amenable to a change in departure date, pay a service charge, fly on an airline you're not familiar with (although this is not usually the case), and/or pay harsh penalties if you cancel—as well as be understanding if the charter doesn't fill up and is canceled up to 10 days before departure. Summer charters fill up more quickly than others and are almost sure to fly, but if you decide on a charter flight, seriously consider cancellation and baggage insurance.

15. **Look into courier flights.** They're usually unavailable on domestic flights, but it's worth checking into if you're committed to flying for as little as humanly possible. Companies that hire couriers use your luggage allowance for their business baggage; in return, you get a deeply discounted ticket. Flights are often offered at the last minute, and you may have to arrange a pretrip interview to make sure you're right for the job. **Now Voyager** (☎ **212/431-1616;** www.nowvoyager-travel.com) has cross-country flights for as little as $199 round-trip and also offers non-courier discounted fares, so call the company even if you don't want to fly as a courier.

OTHER TRANSPORTATION OPTIONS

16. **Consider taking a train or bus instead of flying.** Traveling by train or bus is usually considerably cheaper than flying. More importantly, it saves you money upon arrival and departure, since you'll come right into and leave right out of Manhattan (where you want to be). If you're as close to New York as Washington D.C., these alternate methods can also save time, once you factor in the time spent going to and from the airport. Keep in mind, though, that the cheapest transportation method, the bus, can eat up a lot of time and be pretty uncomfortable.

17. **Have a flexible schedule when booking train travel, and always ask for the lowest fare.** When you're offered a fare, always ask if you can do better by traveling at different times or days. You can often save money by traveling at off-peak hours and on weekends. And don't forget to ask for discounts for kids, seniors, passengers with disabilities, military personnel, or anything else that you think may qualify you for a lower fare.

18. **Keep an eye out for fare sales.** Go to the "Schedules & Fares" page at **www.amtrak.com** and click on RAIL SALE, where you'll find segments discounted up to 90% on select routes. Keep in mind, though, that if you buy a rail sale ticket, it is not refundable and cannot be exchanged. If you register your e-mail address you'll be notified of rail sale fares as they happen.

    Greyhound advertises fare sales right on their home page at **www.greyhound.com**. This national bus line usually has a number of money-saving deals, ranging from "Friends and Family Ride Free" companion deals to 21-day "Go Anywhere" fares for as little as $99.

19. **Make reservations as soon as possible.** As with the airlines, discounts on buses and trains are often based on advanced purchase.

GETTING AROUND NEW YORK CITY

20. **Don't rent a car.** Save your money—you don't need one. Driving is a nightmare and parking is ridiculously expensive (or near-to-impossible in some neighborhoods). It's much easier to get around using public transportation.

21. **Take a bus or the subway from the airport.** A shuttle bus connects JFK Airport to the A train, which whisks you right into the city, and the M60 bus comes into Manhattan from LaGuardia for $1.50. From Newark, convenient and affordable buses can drop you off at various points around the city. You may have to allot a bit more time, but public transportation offers great savings over taxis and car services.

22. **Use the subway and bus systems as you travel around the city.** The transit system is probably the city's best bargain. It's safe, relatively clean (the bus, anyway), quick, efficient, and very, very cheap. Use taxis only late at night, when trains and buses can be few and far between, or when traveling a short distance in a group of three or four, when the fare may be less than a bunch of subway tokens.

23. **Buy a MetroCard.** With the MetroCard, you can enjoy free transfers between bus and subway for 2 hours. And you can save even more money if you evaluate how you're going to use your MetroCard: If you're going to be in the city for a few days, or you're traveling in a group (up to four people can use a MetroCard at any given time), buy a $15 pay-per-ride MetroCard, which will get you 11 rides for the price of 10. If you're going to do a lot of running around the city, consider a $4 **daily Fun Pass** or a $17 **7-Day MetroCard,** each of which allows unlimited rides for the life of the card. There's one strong caveat, however: Every

person has to have his or her own unlimited-use MetroCard; you can't double-up like you can with pay-per-ride MetroCards.

24. **In the daytime, walk.** No other American city is more welcoming or so rewarding to explore on foot. Walking will save you a bunch of money—and work off all the fab meals you'll no doubt buy with the savings.

ACCOMMODATIONS

25. **Visit over a weekend.** If you trip includes a weekend, you might be able to save big. Business hotels tend to empty out, and rooms that go for $300 or more Monday through Thursday can drop dramatically once the midlevel execs have headed home. At the Millenium Hilton, for instance, a $300–$350 room goes for as little as $120 on the weekend. These deals are especially prevalent in the Financial District, but they're often available even in tourist-friendly midtown. They're frequently advertised on the hotel's Web site, or just ask when you call. See the box "Getting the Most for Your Money, Part I: Weekend Packages" in chapter 5 for tips on where to check.

26. **Watch for advertised discounts.** Scan ads in the Travel section of your local Sunday paper, which can be an excellent source for up-to-the-minute hotel deals. Also check the back of the Travel section of the Sunday *New York Times*, where the best weekend deals and other hotel bargains are usually on offer.

27. **Don't be afraid to bargain.** Always ask for a lower price than the first one quoted. Most rack rates include commissions of 10% to 25% or more for travel agents, which many hotels will cut if you make your own reservations and haggle a bit. Always ask politely whether a less-expensive room is available than the first one mentioned, or whether any special rates apply to you. You may qualify for corporate, student, military, senior citizen, or other discounts. Be sure to mention membership in AAA, AARP, frequent-flyer programs, corporate or military organizations, or trade unions, which may entitle you to special deals as well. The big chains, such as Sheraton, tend to be good about trying to save you money, but reservation agents often won't volunteer the information—you have to pull it out of them.

28. **Dial direct.** When booking a room in a chain hotel, call the hotel's local line, as well as the toll-free number, and see where you get the best deal. The clerk who runs the place is more likely to know about booking patterns and will often grant deep discounts in order to fill up.

29. **Call a travel agent.** Certain hotels give travel agents discounts in exchange for steering business their way, so if you're shy about bargaining, an agent may be better equipped to negotiate discounts for you.

30. **Shop online.** New York hotels often offer "Internet-only" deals that can save you 10% to 20% over what you'd pay if you booked by telephone. Also, hotels often advertise all of their available weekend and other package deals on their Web site. In addition, some of the discount reservations agencies (see below) have sights that allow you to book online.

31. **Investigate reservation services.** These outfits usually work as consolidators, buying up or reserving rooms in bulk, and then dealing them out to customers at a profit. They do garner special deals that range from 10% to 50% off; but remember, these discounts apply to rack rates, inflated prices that people rarely end up paying. You're probably better off dealing directly with a hotel, but if you don't like bargaining, this is certainly a viable option. Most of them offer online reservation services as well. Here are a few of the more reputable providers:

Accommodations Express (☎ 800/950-4685; www.accommodationsxpress. com); **Quikbook** (☎ 800/789-9887, includes fax-on-demand service; www. quikbook.com); and **Room Exchange** (☎ 800/846-7000 in the United States, 800/486-7000 in Canada). The New York Convention and Visitors Bureau offers a direct link to the **Hotel Reservations Network** (☎ 800/846-7666; www.newyork-hotel.com), which charges no fee for booking your hotel, and can save you up to 65% on the cost of your room at 140 city hotels ranging from budget to deluxe. **Microsoft Expedia** (www.expedia.com) features an online "Travel Agent" that will also direct you to affordable lodgings.

Another good bet is **Hotel ConXions** (☎ 800/522-9991 or 212/840-8686; www.hotelconxions.com), a consolidator that handles hotels in only a few select destinations, including New York. Not only can they check pricing and availability on a number of hotels with just one phone call, but they can sometimes save you up to 40% off rack rates. Also, because Hotel ConXions has guaranteed room blocks in select properties, they can often get you into a hotel that's otherwise sold out.

Important tips: Never just rely on a reservations service. Do a little homework; compare the rack rates that we've published to the discounted rates being offered by the service to see what kind of deal they're offering. And always check the rate a reservations service offers you with the rate you can get directly from the hotel, which can actually be better on occasion. If you're being offered a stay in a hotel I haven't recommended, do more research to learn about it, especially if it isn't a reliable brand name like Holiday Inn or Best Western. It's not a deal if you end up at a dump.

32. **If you find a rate that seems a particularly good value, book it early.** If somebody quotes you an attractive rate, don't assume it'll be there waiting for you in a month, a week, or even a day from now. Occupancy rates are through the roof in New York these days, and everyone, like you, is on the lookout for a decent rate. As hotels fill up and the number of empty rooms go down, rates go up. You can even get burned at those hotels that don't jack up their rates according to demand, since hotels often have only a limited number of rooms in a particular price category, and the most affordable ones usually go first.

33. **If you find yourself without a room at the last minute, work it to your advantage.** I never recommend coming to town without reservations; you never know when a convention or some other event can hit town and fill up the city's hotels in a snap. But if you find yourself in the city without a room, you may be able to strike quite a bargain. As the hours progress, the hotel becomes more anxious to fill empty rooms, and will lower the rate to get your business. I've seen desk clerks sell $179 rooms for $79 more than once. But remember—this is a risky way to go, because if the hotel is full, you're out of luck.

34. **Be willing to share a bathroom.** For the best bargains in town, do as the Europeans do: Share a hall bath with your fellow travelers. Usually there's two or three baths to a floor, often with separate rooms for the toilet and the shower and/or tub, so all the facilities aren't tied up at once. If you can wrap your mind around this idea—it's not much different than sharing with your siblings when you were a kid—you can get a lot of bang for your buck. If you're on a tight budget, you'll be able to stay at a much nicer hotel than if you insist on a private bath. Many rooms even have private sinks, which means you can brush your teeth or wash your face without leaving the room. And, chances are, you'll never even have to wait for the shower anyway.

35. **Consider a suite.** It sounds like the ultimate splurge, but if you're traveling with another couple or your family, a suite can be a terrific bargain. They're always cheaper than two hotel rooms. The living room almost always features a sofa bed, and there's often a kitchenette where you can save money by preparing coffee and light meals for yourself. Remember that some places charge for extra guests beyond two, some don't.

36. **Look into group or long-stay discounts.** If you come as part of a large group, you should be able to negotiate a bargain, since the hotel can then guarantee occupancy in a number of rooms. Even if you're just an average-size family, ask if there's a discount for booking two adjacent rooms. If you're planning a long stay in town (usually 5 to 7 days or more), you may qualify for a discount, so be sure to ask.

37. **Consider a bed-and-breakfast or homestay.** There are thousands of B&Bs in New York, ranging from Spartan to splendid, and they usually fall on the lower end of the price continuum. A few words of warning, however: Credit cards are often accepted only for the deposit; you may have to pay the balance with a traveler's check, certified check, or cash. We've received complaints about B&Bs and homestays that offer one thing and deliver another, so be sure to get all promises in writing and an exact total up front. And try to pay entirely by credit card if possible, so you can dispute payment if the B&B fails to live up to its promises.

    ✪ **Homestay New York** (☎/fax **718/434-2071;** www.homestayny.com) can book you into a private room with a New York City family that regularly welcomes travelers into their well-kept home. Many homes are in very nice residential neighborhoods in the outer boroughs, but all are within a half hour of Manhattan via subway or bus. Not only can this option save you a lot of money, but it can be fun, too: Visitors are matched to hosts by age and interests, and the carefully chosen hosts are more than happy to provide advice and assistance. Rates start at $80 single, $90 double with shared bath in a Brooklyn or Queens home, $120 in a Manhattan home. A daily breakfast buffet and dinner every other night at the host's home is included in the rate. Also included is an unlimited-ride MetroCard and a phone card (values depend on the length of your stay), making Homestay New York an excellent value. A 2-night minimum is required, and no credit cards are accepted.

    Manhattan Getaways (☎ **212/956-2010;** fax 212/265-3561; www.manhattangetaways.com) can book you into a selection of B&B rooms and private apartments that they have personally inspected, starting at $95 a night. There's a three-night minimum, monthly rates are available, and credit cards are accepted.

    Manhattan Lodgings (☎ **212/677-7616;** fax 212/253-9295; www.manhattanlodgings.com), also provides B&B stays and private apartments for stays lasting 3 days to 3 months. Rates start at $85 per night. Credit cards are accepted for deposits, but you'll have to pay the balance with cash, money order, or traveler's checks. **New York Bed and Breakfast Reservation Center** (☎ **800/747-0868** or 212/977-3512) provides a similar service, but they do not accept credit cards.

    New York Habitat (☎ **212/255-8018;** fax 212/627-1416; www.nyhabitat.com), is a real-estate brokerage that offers all kinds of services, including short-term (from 1 month to 1 year) and very short-term (4 nights to 1 month) apartment rentals, as well as B&B stays, for as low as $67 a night, or $600 per month. Accommodations are mostly in Manhattan, but some outer borough apartments are available, too.

38. **If you're on a shoestring budget, book a hostel bed.** You'll have no privacy whatsoever—you'll share a room with fellow travelers from all over the world and all facilities are common—but there's no arguing with the rate. The largest hostel

in the **Hostelling International–American Youth Hostels** system (☎ **800/ 444-6111** or 202/783-6161; www.hiayh.org) houses travelers in bunk-bedded rooms for $22 to $27 per person, per night. You'll save about $3 a night if you become an AYH member, which is worth looking into if you're coming to the city for an extended stay or if you plan on doing other hostel-based traveling around the world. Also consider the dorms at the better-located **Gershwin Hotel,** costing just $22 per person, per night.

39. **Try the Y.** The Y isn't as cheap as hostel living, but the facilities are much better. The **YMCA of Greater New York,** 333 Seventh Ave., New York, NY 10001 (☎ **212/630-9600;** www.ymcanyc.org), has eight residences for travelers throughout the city's five boroughs. You'll have a private room (some have private bathrooms) and access to the on-site fitness center—many feature extensive state-of-the-art equipment, pools, and a full slate of exercise classes—for absolutely free. The atmosphere is usually on the quiet side, since the Y is popular with families, older travelers, and singles. A number of Ys also feature a calendar of cultural and other events, which fosters a warm community spirit. The main Manhattan branches, all of which are extremely well located, are reviewed in chapter 5; always book as far in advance as possible, as these Ys are extremely popular. For complete information on other New York–area locations, visit the Y's Web site and click on RESIDENCES & RESERVATIONS.

40. **Do as little business as possible through the hotel.** Any service the hotel offers will come with a stiff premium. You can easily find dry cleaners or other services in most areas of Manhattan. Find out before you dial whether your hotel imposes a surcharge on local or long-distance calls; it may be cheaper to use the pay phone in the lobby instead.

41. **If you're driving into the city and will need to garage your car, check parking rates with the hotel before you book.** Many hotels negotiate discounted parking rates at nearby garages. Choose a hotel that has negotiated a good rate, or you may end up paying a fortune for parking (thereby negating any savings you've earned by booking a cheap hotel). For more on this subject, see the box "Deals for Visitors with Wheels: Cheap Parking Tips" in chapter 4.

DINING

42. **Book a hotel room with an efficiency.** Booking a standard room (or a suite, if you're traveling with family or in a group) with a kitchenette allows you to grocery shop and eat some meals in. Even if you only use it to prepare breakfast, you're bound to save money on food this way.

43. **Stay at a hotel, guest house, or bed-and-breakfast that includes breakfast in the rate.** However, be sure to confirm what's included before you book, because some city guest houses keep rates down by not offering breakfast. If breakfast is offered, ask what's included, especially if you're used to starting the day with a hearty meal; the offerings will most likely be a limited continental breakfast.

44. **Use any coupons you can get your hands on.** In addition to the sources listed in tips 2 and 3, (above), the New York Convention & Visitors Bureau offers a free visitor's guide that includes discount coupons in the back. Even if you order one in advance (see "Visitor Information," below), stop into the local visitor centers while you're in town, where the wall racks sometimes have coupons and advertisements for freebies, two-for-ones, and other dining discounts. If you do use a dining discount coupon, remember to tip your waiter based on the full value of the meal; he's on a budget, too.

45. **Eat ethnic.** New York has what's probably the best collection of ethnic restaurants in the country, and the best of them offer first-class eats for low, low prices. Chinatown is always a good bet for top-quality meals, as are the restaurants lining East Sixth Street east of Second Avenue, known as Little India. Jewish delis are first-rate in Manhattan—and the pile of pastrami can keep you well-fueled for days. New York's excellent selection of pizza parlors serve up dining bargains by the slice all over town. For tips on where to go, see chapter 6.

46. **During warm weather, picnic.** New York is full of marvelous delicatessens, greenmarkets, and gourmet groceries where you can assemble a delicious, affordable meal—almost always one much finer than you'd get for the same price at a restaurant. The city is full of small parks that serve as great picnic spots, such as Battery Park, Bryant Park, and Union Square—and don't forget Central Park, where a picnic just doesn't get any better on a nice day. If you don't feel like going through the hassle of assembling a picnic at a grocery, try take-out, which will save you the cost of the tip if you ate in.

47. **Eat street food.** While dirty-water hot dogs and soft pretzels still have their appeal, New York's street-food offerings have expanded considerably in recent years. You'll find vendors on street corners all over the city hawking gourmet soups, gyros, falafels, freshly baked potatoes with a variety of toppings, fresh fruit, and much more. The best vendors congregate in high-end business districts, such as around Rockefeller Center in Midtown (vendors often line up just off Sixth Ave.; 50th St. is a hot corner) and in the Financial District (the 1-block park bordered by Broadway, Church, Liberty, and Cedar streets is a hub of good, cheap eats). Sixth Avenue is lined with open plazas where you can enjoy your alfresco lunch, and Downtown offers a wealth of even more pleasant open spaces.

48. **Fill up at lunch, when prices are generally lower.** Eating your main meal at midday and following up with a lighter dinner can save you money. Lunch prices are usually lower, and at many restaurants you'll get the same size portions you'd get at dinner anyway. This is especially good advice if you plan on splurging on a pricey meal, since fancier restaurants are almost always a much better bargain at lunch.

49. **Order the prix-fixe special.** Fixed-price specials that include appetizers, side dishes, and dessert (as well as beverages in some cases), will almost always get you more bang for your dining buck.

50. **Bring your own wine.** This is a great way to save on huge wine markups. Some restaurants, even those with their own wine lists, will let you bring your own bottle if you just call and ask. At press time, places that are BYOB as policy include **Kitchenette,** the **Zen Palate** in Union Square, **Tartine,** and just about any restaurant in Little India; all of these places are happy to open your bottle and provide glasses. However, *always* call and ask permission in advance—never just show up with your own bottle. (The only exception to this rule is Little India, where you can just arrive with a bottle or a six-pack and ask at the door.) If the answer is "no," be gracious and accept it without argument. If the answer is "yes," be sure to ask if a corkage fee is charged, so there's no unpleasant surprise at bill time. See chapter 8 for tips on shops with good values on wine.

51. **Go to food courts.** The one at the **Mid-Manhattan Mall,** on 33rd and Broadway, claims to be one of the largest in the world. Prices are reasonable, there are many choices (so everyone in your group is satisfied), and there's no tipping. The street level of the **World Trade Center** mall offers a wealth of cheap-eating options at lunch. Another good bet is **Eatzi's,** in the cellar at Macy's, where you can graze on pre-prepared foods.

SIGHTSEEING

52. **Buy a CityPass.** Pay one price ($27.50) for admission to six top attractions—the Top of the World observation deck at the World Trade Center, the Metropolitan Museum of Art, the Museum of Modern Art, the Empire State Building, the American Museum of Natural History, and the *Intrepid* Sea-Air-Space Museum—which would cost you fully twice as much to visit if you paid for each one separately. This just may be New York's best sightseeing deal, especially for newcomers intent on hitting all the big sights. More importantly, CityPass is not a coupon book; it contains actual admission tickets, so you can bypass lengthy ticket lines. CityPass is good for 9 days from the first time you use it. It's sold at all participating attractions, and discounted rates are available for kids and seniors. If you want to avoid that first line, order your CityPass online at **www.citypass.net** or www.ticketweb.com. For phone orders, call **Ticketweb** at ☎ 212/269-4TIX. Call **CityPass** at ☎ 707/256-0490 for further details.

53. **Take advantage of freebies.** You'll be surprised to discover how many there are to be had. Many of the best things to do and see in Manhattan are absolutely free, from walking the Brooklyn Bridge to riding the Staten Island Ferry to exploring Central Park to attending TV show tapings. Additionally, a number of organizations now offer neighborhood walking tours at absolutely no charge. And many museums and attractions that charge admission have free or pay-as-you-wish programs one day or evening a week. For details, see the boxes in chapter 7: "Cheap Thrills: What to See & Do for Free"; "Show Me, Show Me, Show Me: Free Walking Tours"; and "Free Culture at Big Apple Museums."

SHOPPING

54. **Ship major purchases home.** If you're buying high-ticket items, you can often save on the exorbitant New York sales tax by having items shipped home. Depending on the laws of your state, you can pay a lesser tax or skip the duty completely.

55. **Seek out sample sales.** Garment designers and manufacturers often sell off their newest items (sometimes not even available in the store yet) for a song to raise quick cash; see "Scouring the Sample Sales" in chapter 8.

56. **Do your homework and bargain on electronic equipment.** New York may not exactly be a Casablanca bazaar, but you'll find that prices are a lot more flexible than what you're used to in retail outlets at home. Play hard to get and you may get lucky. I've seen prices tumble precipitously the closer I got to the door. But trust me on this: The only way you'll do well is if you know your stuff. If you have your eye out for a digital camera, say, or a new CD player, do some research before you leave home and know what the going prices are. These dealers know how to make a huge markup sound like the bargain of the century, and they won't hesitate to rip you off.

57. **Always ask for a better price on anything used or vintage.** It won't always work, but lots of vintage, antique, and collectibles dealers—even those with nice shops in high-rent districts like SoHo and the Village—will drop their price if you're just savvy enough to ask. Always be polite, however, and don't push if you're told "no."

PERFORMING ARTS & NIGHTLIFE

58. **Buy discounted same-day theater tickets at the TKTS booth.** If your heart is set on seeing a particular show, you should buy full-price advance tickets before

you come to the city. But if you're flexible about what you see, check out TKTS, which sells day-of-show tickets to popular plays both on Broadway and off at 25% to 50% off. Many theater box offices also sell discounted day-of-show tickets directly. For details, see "Top Ticket-Buying Tips" in chapter 9.

59. **Take advantage of freebies.** Summertime is a great time to be in the city if you're a culture buff. Some of the city's top cultural organizations offer free outdoor events, from Shakespeare in the Park to the Metropolitan Opera. For details, see "Park It! Shakespeare & Other Free Fun" in chapter 9. But you don't have to wait until summer to enjoy yourself for free: Comb the listings in *Time Out New York, New York* magazine, the *New Yorker,* and the *New York Times* for listings of free performances throughout the city, which may range from free dance performances to book talks at Barnes & Noble. If you want to do some research before you arrive, hop online; see "Site Seeing: The Big Apple on the Web" under "Visitor Information," below.

60. **Eschew high-priced, high-profile performances for lesser-known, lower-priced surprises.** Sure, attending a performance at the New York Philharmonic or a big-name Broadway extravaganza is a must if you can afford it. But you'll save money—and maybe even enjoy yourself more—by looking beyond the obvious to lower-profile options. For instance, the nation's top music education institution, the **Julliard School,** offers a full slate of free and cheap events, from first-rate student concerts to lectures by visiting celebrities of the performing-arts world. Smaller venues like **Bargemusic,** the **92nd Street Y,** and the **Amato Opera Theatre** offer more intimate, only-in–New York performances, sometimes by nationally known artists, at rock-bottom prices.

Off- and off-off Broadway theater is usually significantly less expensive than the shows offered on the Great White Way, and the quality doesn't have to suffer one bit—witness this year's Pulitzer Prize winner, *Wit,* which just moved to an off-Broadway theater after a long and successful off-off Broadway run (I saw it for about $35, versus the going rate of around $75 for Broadway tix). If you're visiting between early February and late April, be sure to look into the **Passport to Off Broadway,** which can save you even more money—between 10% and 50%—on more than 200 off- and off-off-Broadway shows. Go online at **www.newyork.sidewalk.com/passport** or call the Visitors Bureau for further information.

2 Visitor Information

For information before you leave home, your best source (besides this book, of course) is the **New York Convention & Visitors Bureau** (NYCVB). You can call the bureau's 24-hour hotline at ☎ **800/NYC-VISIT** or 212/397-8222 to order a **Big Apple Visitors Kit,** detailing hotels, restaurants, theaters, attractions, events, and more. It costs $5.95 (payable by credit card) and will arrive at most U.S. addresses within a week or two. If you don't want to pay the six bucks, they'll send you the guide that's the heart of the kit for free, but expect it to take 4 to 6 weeks to reach you. The bureau also has a terrific Web site at **www.nycvisit.com**. To speak to a travel counselor who can answer specific questions, call ☎ **212/484-1222** Monday through Friday from 9am to 5pm EST (multilingual counselors are available). Or write for information to the NYCVB at 810 Seventh Ave., New York, NY 10019.

For visitor center and information-desk locations once you arrive, see "Visitor Information" in chapter 4.

FOR U.K.-BASED VISITORS In late 1998, an **NYCVB Visitor Information Center** opened in London at 33–34 Carnaby St. (☎ **020/7-437-8300**). The new center offers a wealth of information and free one-on-one travel-planning assistance to New York–bound travelers. It's open Monday through Friday from 10am to 4pm.

SITE SEEING: THE BIG APPLE ON THE WEB

The NYCVB's **www.nycvisit.com** is a terrific online resource offering tons of information on the city, from trip-planning basics to tips on where to take the kids. But there's much more to be learned from the Web than the official line. Sure, there's a lot of junk out there in cyberspace—but the net boasts some terrific sites on the city, the best of which can supply up-to-the-minute news, current events calendars, information for those of you with special interests, or just another point of view. Here are our favorite general-information sites (we'll also recommend subject-specific sites in the chapters that follow):

- **www.newyork.sidewalk.com** The Microsoft-backed Sidewalk is an excellent source for up-to-the-minute information on what's happening in the city. It's a particularly good for the latest nightlife information—you'll find reviews of current theater, music, and other performing-arts events, and most club listings even feature day-to-day schedules. I also like Sidewalk for the latest restaurant dish and sample sales, but at press time competitor Citysearch's (see below) shopping listings were more comprehensive.

- **www.newyork.citysearch.com** Done in cooperation with the *Daily News* and *Time Out* magazine—hands down the best weekly source for what's going on in the city—Citysearch is much more organized than Sidewalk and much quicker to load. They're also all over current happenings, with direct links to recommended events. The listings are as comprehensive as Sidewalk's, sometimes more so, but new stuff almost always hits Sidewalk first. I suggest checking them both out—that's what I do!

- **www.nytoday.com** Set up in an easy-access daily calendar format, the site is an expanded version of the *New York Times* cultural coverage. You'll find even more events listings and critics' reviews in this electronic version, including museum schedules and sports events, plus the *Times'* definitive restaurant reviews.

- **www.papermag.com** The online version of the glossy alterna-monthly *Paper* serves as good prep for those of you who want to experience the hipper side of the city. There's opinionated coverage of clubs and bars (including extensive gay scene coverage)—virtually all downtown, of course.

- **www.panix.com/clay/nyc** Commonly referred to as New York City Reference, this handy site is a virtual hyperlink index of New York–related sites. It's regularly updated, and at press time there were about 2,000 links covering every subject area from "The Best Public Toilets in New York City" (**www.angelfire. com/ny/NYCtoilets** if you want to bypass the middleman) to "Webcams: Live Pictures of New York City."

3 Money

You never have to carry too much cash in New York, and while the city's pretty safe these days, it's best not to overstuff your wallet (although always make sure you have at least $20 in taxi fare on hand). Credit cards and traveler's checks are accepted almost everywhere—plastic is even accepted in the subway system now—and ATMs are almost always on hand in case you need the green stuff.

Avoid poorly lit or out-of-the-way ATMs, especially at night. New York is pretty safe these days, but it's not a good idea to put yourself in a compromising position. Use an indoor machine, or one at a well-trafficked, well-lit location. Put your money away discreetly; don't flash it around or count it in a way that could attract the attention.

ATMS

Almost all New York City ATMs are linked to a national network that most likely includes your bank at home. **Cirrus** (☎ 800/424-7787; www.mastercard.com/atm) and **Plus** (☎ 800/843-7587; www.visa.com/atms) are the two most popular networks; check the back of your ATM card to see which network your bank belongs to. The city's biggest ATM networks belong to Citibank, Chase, and Fleet banks, which belong to both networks.

In the most popular Manhattan neighborhoods, there's a bank with ATM machines on every other corner or so. The only places you may have some difficulty in are more far-flung neighborhoods, like the far East Village or far uptown in Harlem. If you don't easily spot an ATM, use the 800 numbers to locate one near you.

New York's Consumer Affairs chief has tried to ward off additional ATM charges for consumers, but it seems to be a losing battle. The last holdout from additional charges, Chase, had just given in to $1-per-transaction charges at press time. In general, expect to pay $1 each time you withdraw money from an ATM, in addition to what your home bank charges. Try to stay away from commercial machines, like those in hotel lobbies and corner delis, which often charge $2 or more per transaction. If you find an ATM with no additional charge, consider yourself lucky.

TRAVELER'S CHECKS

Traveler's checks are something of an anachronism these days. They seem less necessary now that 24-hour ATMs allow you to withdraw small amounts of cash as needed—and thus avoid the risk of carrying a fortune around. But New York is an expensive city, capable of sucking money right out of your pocket. And if you're withdrawing money every day, you might be better off with traveler's checks—provided that you don't mind showing identification every time you want to cash one.

You can get traveler's checks at almost any bank. **American Express** offers denominations of $10, $20, $50, $100, $500, and $1,000. You'll pay a service charge ranging from 1% to 4%. You can also get American Express traveler's checks over the phone by calling ☎ 800/221-7282; by using this number, Amex gold and platinum cardholders are exempt from the 1% fee. AAA members can obtain checks without a fee at most AAA offices.

Visa offers traveler's checks at Citibanks nationwide, as well as several other banks. The service charge ranges between 1½% and 2%; checks come in denominations of $20, $50, $100, $500, and $1,000. **MasterCard** also offers traveler's checks. Call ☎ 800/ 223-9920 for a location near you.

CREDIT CARDS

Credit cards are invaluable when traveling. They're a safe way to carry money and provide a convenient record of all your expenses. American Express, MasterCard, and Visa are accepted virtually everywhere in New York. Discover is also popular, and Carte Blanche and Diner's Club are making a comeback, especially in hotel circles. Since New York has such a heavy influx of international visitors, cards like enRoute and JCB are also widely accepted, particularly at hotels.

Still, it can be smart to keep some cash on hand for small expenses, like cab rides, or for that rare occasion when a restaurant or small shop doesn't take plastic, which can happen in New York if you're dining at a neighborhood joint or buying from a small vendor.

THEFT Almost every credit-card company has an emergency 800 number that you can call if your wallet or purse is stolen. They may be able to wire you a cash advance off your credit card immediately, and in many places, they can deliver an emergency credit card in a day or two. The issuing bank's 800 number is usually on the back of the credit card—though that doesn't help you much if the card was stolen. The toll-free information directory will provide the number if you dial ☎ **800/555-1212.** Citicorp **Visa's** U.S. emergency number is ☎ **800/336-8472. American Express** cardholders and traveler's check holders should call ☎ **800/221-7282** for all money emergencies. **MasterCard** holders should call ☎ **800/307-7309.**

If you opt to carry traveler's checks, be sure to keep a record of their serial numbers, separately from the checks of course, so you're ensured a refund in just such an emergency.

Odds are that if your wallet is gone, the police won't be able to recover it for you. However, after you realize that it's gone and you cancel your credit cards, it's still worth informing them. Your credit-card company or insurer may require a police report number.

4 When to Go

Summer or winter, rain or shine, New York City always has great things going on, so there's no real "best" time to go.

MONEY MATTERS If money is your biggest concern, you might want to visit in winter, between the first of the year and early April. Sure, the weather can suck, but hotels are suffering the post-holiday blues, and rooms often go for a relative song. In the winter of 1999, the truly comfortable Comfort Inn Midtown had rooms for as low as $79.

Spring and fall are the busiest, and most expensive, seasons after holiday time. Don't expect hotels to be handing you deals, but you still may be able to negotiate a good rate.

New York's spit-shined image means that the city is drawing more families these days, and they usually visit in the summer. Still, the prospect of heat and humidity keeps some people away, making June, July, and the first half of August a generally cheaper time to visit than later in the year. Surprisingly good hotel deals are often available.

At Christmas, all bets are off—expect to pay top dollar for everything. There's no denying that it's a terrific time to be here—celebrations of the season abound, and seasonal sales take over the city's stores—but hotel prices go sky high and the crowds are almost intolerable. If you'd rather have more of the city to yourself, with better chances at discount Broadway show tickets and easier access to museums and other attractions, you'll be happier visiting at another time of year, anyway.

But Thanksgiving can be a great time to come, believe it or not: Business travelers have gone home for the holiday, and the holiday shoppers haven't yet arrived. It's a little-known secret that most hotels away from the Thanksgiving Day parade route have empty rooms sitting, and they're usually willing to make great deals to fill them.

WEATHER The worst weather in New York is during that long week or 10 days that seems to arrive each summer between mid-July and mid-August, when temperatures go up to around 100°F with 100% humidity. You feel sticky all day, the streets smell horrible, everyone's cranky, and the concrete canyons become furnaces. It can be no fun walking around in this weather. Don't get put off by this—summer has its compensations, such as wonderful free open-air concerts and events, as I've already mentioned—but bear it in mind. And you may luck out—the last few summers have been downright lovely. But if you're planning on visiting in the summer and are at all temperature sensitive, your odds of getting comfortable weather are better in early June or September.

Another period when you might not like to stroll around the city is during January or February, when temperatures are commonly in the 20s (-6C) and those concrete canyons turn into wind tunnels. The city looks gorgeous just after a snowfall, but the streets soon become an ugly, slushy mess. Again, you never know—temperatures have regularly been in the mild 40s during the past few winters. If you hit the weather jackpot, you could have a bargain bonanza (see "Money Matters," above).

Fall and spring are the best times in New York. From April to June and September to November, temperatures are mild and pleasant, and the light is beautiful. With the leaves changing in Central Park and just the hint of crispness in the air, October is a fabulous time to be here—but expect to pay for the privilege (see "Money Matters," above).

If you want to know how to pack just before you go, check the Weather Channel's online 5-day forecasts at **www.weather.com** or **www.ny1.com**.

New York's Average Temperature & Rainfall

	Jan	Feb	Mar	Apr	May	June	July	Aug	Sept	Oct	Nov	Dec
Daily Temp. (°F)	38	40	48	61	71	80	85	84	77	67	54	42
Days of Rain	11	10	11	11	11	10	11	10	8	8	9	10

New York City Calendar of Events

As with any schedule of events, the following information is always subject to change. Always confirm information before you make plans around an event. Call the venue or the city's Visitors Bureau at ☎ **212/484-1222** (Mon–Fri 9am–5pm EST), or go to **www.nycvisit.com/cgi/calendar.html** for the latest details on these or other events taking place during your trip.

January

- **New York National Boat Show.** Slip on your docksiders and head to the Jacob K. Javits Convention Center, which promises a leviathan fleet of boats and marine products from the world's leading manufacturers. Call ☎ **212/922-1212.** January 8–16.
- **Winter Antiques Show at the Seventh Regiment Armory.** This is New York's most important, prestigious, and expensive antiques show. You may not be able to buy anything, but it's well worth browsing if you're a fan. Call ☎ **718/292-7392.** January 14–25 (preview January 13).
- **Antiques at the Other Armory.** Younger, trendier dealers with more affordable collectibles show at the 26th Street Armory (at Lexington Avenue) during the first weekend of the Winter Antiques Show. A free shuttle runs between the two locations. Call ☎ **212/255-0020.** January 14–16.

February

- **Chinese New Year.** Every year Chinatown rings in its own New Year (based on a lunar calendar) with 2 weeks of celebrations, including parades with dragon and lion dancers, vivid costumes of all kinds, and fireworks (though the city has been cracking down on their use in recent years). In 2000 (4698 in the Chinese designation), the Year of the Dragon, the Chinese New Year falls on February 5. Call ☎ **212/484-1222** or the Chinese Center at 212/373-1800.

- **Valentine's Day Marriage Marathon at the World Trade Center.** Once again, 110 people will be married at the top of the city's tallest skyscraper during the annual Valentine's Day Marriage Marathon. Applicants for "marrying slots" will be accepted from January 1, 2000; a maximum of 55 couples will be selected by February 1. To be considered, contestants are usually required to write a one-page typewritten essay entitled "Why We Want to Get Married at the Highest Place in New York"; call ☎ **212/580-9548.** A similar event is held on the observation deck at the **Empire State Building;** call ☎ **212/736-3100** or visit **www. esbnyc.org.** February 14.

- ✪ **Westminster Kennel Club Dog Show.** Some 30,000 dog fanciers from the world over congregate at Madison Square Garden for the "World Series of Dogdom." All 2,500 dogs are American Kennel Club Champions of Record, competing for the Best of Show trophy. The ultimate purebred pooch fest. Call ☎ **800/455-3647** for information. Tickets become available after January 1 through **Ticketmaster** (☎ **212/307-7171** or 212/307-1212; www.ticketmaster. com). February 14–15.

- **International Cat Show.** More than 800 fabulous felines, from rare and exotic purebreds to household pets, also compete for Best of Show honors at the Garden. Lectures by vets, special competitions (including cat photo contests), and the largest "feline shopping mall" anywhere are all part of the fun. Call ☎ **212/465-6741.** Tickets usually become available after February 1 through **Ticketmaster** (☎ **212/307-7171** or 212/307-1212; www.ticketmaster.com). Late February or early March.

March

- ✪ **Manhattan Antiques and Collectibles Triple Pier Expo.** The city's largest and most comprehensive antiques show takes place over two consecutive weekends, as more than 600 dealers exhibit their treasures, ranging from ephemera to jewelry to home furnishings, on three piers along the Hudson River between 48th and 51st streets. Pier 88 features 20th-century collectibles; pier 90 all manner of Americana, including country rustic, folk art, and arts and crafts; and pier 92 for 18th- and 19th-century formal European antiques. Call ☎ **212/255-0020** or surf to **www.antiqnet.com/Stella** for this year's dates. Usually mid-March, and again in mid-November.

- **St. Patrick's Day Parade.** More than 150,000 marchers join in the world's largest civilian parade, as Fifth Avenue from 44th to 86th streets rings with the sounds of bands and bagpipes, and an inordinate amount of beer is consumed (much of it green). The parade usually starts at 11am, but go extra early if you want a good spot. Wear green and insist you're Irish if anyone asks—you are, at least for today. Call ☎ **212/484-1222.** March 17.

- **Ringling Bros. and Barnum & Bailey Circus.** The circus comes to town in grand style as elephants and bears and other performing animals parade down the city streets from the railroad at Twelfth Avenue and 34th Street to Madison Square Garden early on the morning before the first performance (usually well before daybreak). Call ☎ **212/465-6741** for this year's dates, or **Ticketmaster** (☎ **212/307-7171** or 212/307-1212; www.ticketmaster.com) for tickets. Usually late March to early April.

- ✪ **New Directors/New Films.** The kleig lights are turned on up-and-coming directors at this film series co-sponsored by the Museum of Modern Art (MoMA) and the Film Society of Lincoln Center and screened at MoMA. Notable debuts in recent years have included *Smoke Signals, Buffalo '66,* and π. Call ☎ 212/875-5610 or visit **www.filmlinc.com** for this year's calendar.

April

⊗ **The Easter Parade.** This isn't a traditional parade, per se: There are no marching bands, no baton twirlers, no protesters. Once upon a time, New York's gentry came out to show off their tasteful but discreet toppings. Today, it's more about flamboyant exhibitionism, with hats and costumes that get more outrageous every year—and anybody can join right in for free. The parade generally runs Easter Sunday from about 10:30am to 3pm along Fifth Avenue from 48th to 57th streets. Call ☎ **212/484-1222.** April 23.

• **Greater New York International Auto Show.** Hot wheels from all over the world whirl into the Jacob K. Javits Convention Center for the largest auto show in the United States. Many concept cars show up that will never roll off the assembly line, but they're fun to dream about nonetheless. Call ☎ **800/282-3336** or 212/216-2000. One week in early or mid-April.

May

⊗ **Bike New York: The Great Five Boro Bike Tour.** The largest mass-participation cycling event in the United States attracts about 30,000 cyclists from all over the world. After a 42-mile ride through the five boroughs, finalists are greeted with a traditional New York–style celebration of food and music. Starting line is at Battery Park in Manhattan; the finish line is at Fort Wadsworth Naval Station on Staten Island. If you plan on entering, expect a stop-and-start ride. (Ever been caught in bike gridlock? Another New York first.) Call ☎ **212/932-0778** or visit **www.bikenewyork.org** to register. May 7.

• **Ninth Avenue International Food Festival.** Cancel dinner reservations and spend the day sampling sizzling Italian sausages, homemade pierogi, spicy curries, and an assortment of other ethnic dishes. Street musicians, bands, and vendors add to the festive atmosphere at one of the city's best street fairs, stretching along Ninth Avenue from 37th to 57th streets. Call ☎ **212/581-7217.** One weekend in mid-May.

⊗ **Fleet Week.** About 10,000 Navy and Coast Guard personnel are "at liberty" in New York for the annual Fleet Week at the end of May. Usually from 1 to 4pm daily, you can visit the ships and aircraft carriers that dock at the piers on the west side of Manhattan, and watch some dramatic exhibitions by the U.S. Marines. Kids love this event hosted by the *Intrepid* Sea-Air-Space Museum. But even if you don't take in any of the events, you'll know it's Fleet Week, since those 10,000 sailors invade Midtown in their starched white uniforms. It's simply wonderful— *On the Town* come to life. Call ☎ **212/245-2533,** or visit **www.uss-intrepid. com**. Late May.

• **Washington Square Outdoor Art Exhibition.** This Greenwich Village tradition, in its 69th year, features the works of 250 artists displayed on 20 blocks in and around Washington Square Park. Call ☎ **212/982-6255.** May 27–29 and June 3–5, and again in September.

June

• **The Belmont Stakes.** The third jewel in the Triple Crown is held at the Belmont Park Race Track in Elmont, Long Island. If a triple-crown winner is to be named, it will happen here. For information, call ☎ **516/667-5055** or 718/641-4700. Early June.

⊗ **Lesbian and Gay Pride Week and March.** A week of cheerful happenings, from simple parties to major political fund-raisers, precedes a zany parade commemorating the Stonewall Riot of June 27, 1969, which for many marks the beginning of the gay liberation movement. Fifth Avenue goes wild as the gay/lesbian community celebrates with bands, marching groups, floats, and plenty of panache. The parade starts on upper Fifth around 52nd Street and continues into the Village, where a street festival and a waterfront dance party with fireworks cap the day. Call ☎ **212/807-7433**. Mid- to late June.

✪ **SummerStage.** A summer-long festival of free or low-cost outdoor concerts in Central Park, featuring world music, pop, folk, and jazz artists ranging from Ziggy Marley to Yoko Ono to Morrissey. Call ☎ **212/360-2777**. June through August.

• **Metropolitan Opera in the Parks.** Free evening performances are given in the city parks. Past performers have included the likes of Luciano Pavarotti and Kathleen Battle. Call ☎ **212/362-6000** or visit **www.metopera.org**. June through July.

✪ **Shakespeare in the Park.** The Delacorte Theater in Central Park is the setting for first-rate free performances under the stars, often with stars on the stage. Recent performers have included Patrick Stewart (*The Tempest*) and Andre Braugher (*Henry V*). Be prepared to line up hours in advance for tickets; you're allowed to collect two. For more details, see "Park It! Shakespeare & Other Free Fun" in chapter 9. Call ☎ **212/539-8750** or 212/539-8500, or point your web browser to **www.publictheater.org**. June through August.

✪ **Restaurant Week.** Dine for only $20 at some of New York's finest restaurants. Participating places vary each year, so watch for the full-page ads in the *New York Times* and other publications, or call ahead to the visitors bureau, since they usually have a list of restaurants by mid- or late May. Reserve instantly. One week in late June; some restaurants extend their offers through summer to Labor Day.

• **JVC Jazz Festival.** The biggest names in jazz play sites like Avery Fisher Hall, Carnegie Hall, the Beacon Theater, and Town Hall; free concerts at Bryant Park may also be in this year's mix. Call ☎ **212/501-1390**, or go online at **www.jvc-america.com/jazz**. Late June to early July.

July

✪ **Independence Day Harbor Festival and Fourth of July Fireworks Spectacular.** Start the day amid the patriotic crowds at the Great July Fourth Festival in Lower Manhattan, watch the tall ships sail up the Hudson River in the afternoon, and then catch Macy's great fireworks extravaganza (one of the country's most fantastic) over the East River (the best vantage point is from the FDR Drive, which closes to traffic several hours before sunset). Call ☎ **212/484-1222**, or Macy's Special Events at 212/494-2922. July 4.

✪ **Lincoln Center Festival 2000.** This festival celebrates the best of the performing arts from all over the world—theater, ballet, contemporary dance, opera, even puppet and media-based art. Schedules are usually available in mid-March, and tickets go on sale in late May or early June. Call ☎ **212/546-2656**, or visit **www.lincolncenter.org**. July.

✪ **Midsummer Night's Swing.** Dancing duos head to the Lincoln Center Fountain Plaza for romantic evenings of big band swing, salsa, and tango under the stars. Dance lessons are offered with the purchase of a ticket. Call ☎ **212/875-5766**, or visit **www.lincolncenter.org**. July and August.

• **Mostly Mozart.** World-renowned soloists and ensembles—Alicia de Larrocha and André Watts have performed in the past—are featured at this month-long series at Avery Fisher Hall. Schedules are usually available in mid-April. Call ☎ **212/875-5103** or 212/546-2656, or visit **www.lincolncenter.org**. July and August.

August

- **Lincoln Center Out-of-Doors.** This series of free music and dance performances is held outdoors at Lincoln Center. Schedules are available in July. Call ☎ 212/875-5108, or visit **www.lincolncenter.org**. August to September.
- **New York Fringe Festival.** Held in a variety of tiny Lower East Side venues for a mainly hipster crowd, this arts festival presents alternative as well as traditional theater, musicals, dance, comedy, and all manner of performance art, including new media. Literally hundreds of events are held at all hours over about ten days in late August. The quality can vary wildly (lots of performers use Fringe as a workshop to develop their acts and shows) and some performances really push the envelope, but you'd be surprised at how many shows are actually *good.* Call ☎ 888/FRINGENYC or 212/307-0229, or visit **www.fringenyc.org**. Mid- to late August.
- ✪ **U.S. Open Tennis Championships.** The final grand slam of the tennis season is held at the slick new facilities at Flushing Meadows Park in Queens. Tickets go on sale in May. The event sell out far in advance, since many of the tickets are held by corporate sponsors who hand them out to customers. (It's worth it to check the list of sponsors to determine if anyone you know has a connection for getting tickets.) You can usually buy tickets from a scalper outside the complex (an illegal practice, of course), which is right next to Shea Stadium. Of course, the last few matches of the tournament are most expensive, but you'll see a lot more tennis early on, when your ticket allows you to wander the outside courts, viewing several different matches. Call ☎ 718/760-6200 or Telecharge at ☎ 800/524-8440 for tickets as far in advance as possible; visit **www.usopen.org** for additional information. Two weeks surrounding Labor Day.
- **Harlem Week.** The world's largest African-American and Hispanic cultural festival, lasting about 2 weeks, includes the Black Film Festival and the Taste of Harlem Food Festival. Expect a whole slate of music, from gospel to hip-hop, and lots of other festivities. Call ☎ 212/862-7200 or 212/484-1222 for this year's schedule of events and locations. Mid-August.

September

- **West Indian–American Day Parade.** This annual Brooklyn event is New York's largest street celebration. Come for the extravagant costumes, pulsating rhythms (soca, calypso, reggae), bright colors, folklore, food (jerk chicken, oxtail soup, Caribbean soul food), and 2 million hip-shaking revelers. The parade runs down Eastern Parkway in Brooklyn. Call ☎ 212/484-1222 or 718/774-8807 Labor Day. September 4 in 2000.
- ✪ **Wigstock.** Come see the Lady Bunny, Hedda Lettuce, Lypsinka, and even RuPaul—plus hundreds of other fabulous drag queens—strut their stuff. The crowd is usually wilder than the stage acts. A true East Village event, Wigstock outgrew its original location, Tompkins Square Park, and has been held on the pier at 11th Street in recent years, but another move could be in the offing. For a preview, see Goldwyn's *Wigstock: The Movie.* For information, visit **www.wigstock.nu** or call ☎ 800/494-TIXS or the Lesbian and Gay Community Services Center at ☎ 212/620-7310. Labor Day weekend.
- **Washington Square Outdoor Art Exhibition.** The May event returns for Labor Day, when the works of 250 artists are displayed in and around Washington Square Park. Call ☎ 212/982-6255. September 2–4 and 9–10.
- **Broadway on Broadway.** This free afternoon show features the songs and casts from virtually every Broadway production performing on a stage erected in the middle of Times Square. Call ☎ 212/768-1560. Early or mid-September.

- **Feast of San Gennaro.** An atmospheric and festive Little Italy street fair honoring the patron saint of Naples, with great food, traditional music, carnival rides, games, and vendors set up along Mulberry Street north of Canal Street. Usually mid-September.

✪ **New York Film Festival.** Legendary hits *Pulp Fiction* and *Mean Streets* both had their U.S. premieres at the Film Society of Lincoln Center's 2-week festival, a major stop on the film-fest circuit. Schedules in recent years have included advance looks at *The Sweet Hereafter, Gods and Monsters,* and *Rushmore.* Screenings are held in various Lincoln Center venues; advance tickets are a good bet always, and a necessity for certain events (especially evening and weekend screenings). Call ☎ **212/875-5610,** or visit **www.filmlinc.com.** Two weeks from late September to early October (Sept 22–Oct 9 in 2000).

✪ **BAM Next Wave Festival.** One of the city's most important cultural events takes place at the Brooklyn Academy of Music. The months-long festival showcases experimental new dance, theater, and music works by both renowned and lesser-known international artists. Recent celebrated performances have included Astor Piazzolla's *Maria de Buenos Aires,* featuring Piazzolla disciple Gidon Kremer; the 25th anniversary of the Kronos Quartet; and choreographer Bill T. Jones's *We Set Out Early . . . Visibility Was Poor,* set to the music of Stravinsky, John Cage, and Peteris Vask. Call ☎ **718/636-4100** or visit **www.bam.org**. September through December.

October

- **Ice-Skating.** Show off your skating style in the limelight at the diminutive **Rockefeller Center** rink (☎ 212/332-7654), open from mid-October to mid-March (you'll skate under the magnificent Christmas tree for the month of December) or at the larger **Wollman Rink** in Central Park, at 59th Street and Sixth Avenue (☎ **212/396-1010**), which usually closes in early April, depending on the weather.

✪ **Feast of St. Francis.** Animals from goldfish to elephants are blessed as thousands of Homo sapiens look on at the Cathedral of St. John the Divine. This is a magical experience; pets, of course, are welcome. A festive fair follows the blessing and music events. Buy tickets in advance; they can be hard to come by. Call ☎ **212/316-7540** or visit **www.stjohndivine.org**. Early October.

- **International Fine Arts and Antiques Dealers Show.** Considered by many as the opening of the fall arts season, this show attracts dealers and collectors from all over the world to the Seventh Regiment Armory. Call ☎ **212/642-8572** or 212/877-0202. Mid-October.

✪ **Greenwich Village Halloween Parade.** This is Halloween at its most outrageous. You may have heard Lou Reed singing about it on his classic album *New York*—he wasn't exaggerating. Drag queens and assorted other flamboyant types parade through the village in wildly creative costumes. The parade route has changed over the years, but most recently it has started after sunset at Spring Street and marched up Sixth Avenue to 23rd Street or Union Square. Check the papers for the exact route so you can watch—or participate, if you have the threads and the imagination. October 31.

November

✪ **New York City Marathon.** Some 25,000 hopefuls from around the world participate in the largest U.S. marathon, and at least a million fans will cheer them on as they follow a route that touches on all five New York boroughs and finishes in Central Park. Call ☎ **212/860-4455,** or visit **www.nyrrc.org**. Call for the date (most likely to be November 4 or 11 in 2000).

- **Ice Skating at the South Street Seaport.** The rink is petite, but the waterfront setting is grand. Call ☎ **212/SEA-PORT** or 212/809-6080. November through March.
- **Radio City Music Hall Christmas Spectacular.** A rather gaudy extravaganza, but lots of fun nonetheless. Starring the Radio City Rockettes and a cast that includes live animals (just try to picture the camels sauntering in the Sixth Avenue entrance!). For information, call ☎ **212/247-4777** or visit **www. radiocity.com**; buy tickets at the box office or via Ticketmaster's **Radio City Hotline** (☎ **212/307-1000**). Mid-November to early January.
- ✪ **Manhattan Antiques and Collectibles Triple Pier Expo.** The city's largest antiques show takes place over two consecutive weekends, usually just before Thanksgiving; for details, see March, above. Call ☎ **212/255-0020** or visit **www.antiqnet.com/Stella** for this year's dates.
- ✪ **Macy's Thanksgiving Day Parade.** The procession from Central Park West and 77th Street down Broadway to Herald Square at 34th Street continues to be a national tradition. Huge hot-air balloons of Rocky and Bullwinkle, Snoopy, Underdog, the Pink Panther, Bart Simpson, and other cartoon favorites are the best part of the fun. The night before, you can usually see the big blow-up on Central Park West at 79th Street; call in advance (☎ **212/494-5432** or 212/ 494-2922) to see if it will be open to the public again this year. November 23 in 2000.
- ✪ **Big Apple Circus.** New York City's homegrown, not-for-profit circus is a favorite with children and the young at heart. A tent is pitched in Damrosch Park at Lincoln Center. Call ☎ **212/268-2500**. November to January.
- *The Nutcracker.* Tchaikovsky's holiday favorite is performed by the New York City Ballet at Lincoln Center. Tickets are usually available starting in early October. Call ☎ **212/ 870-5570**, or visit **www.nycballet.org**. Late November through early January.

December

- ✪ **Lighting of the Rockefeller Center Christmas Tree.** The annual lighting ceremony is accompanied by an ice-skating show, singing, entertainment, and a huge crowd. The tree stays lit around the clock until after the new year. Call ☎ **212/ 632-3975**. Early December.
- ✪ **Holiday Trimmings.** Stroll down festive Fifth Avenue, and you'll see doormen dressed as wooden soldiers at FAO Schwarz, a 27 foot sparkling snowflake floating over the intersection outside Tiffany's, the Cartier Building ribboned and bowed in red, wreaths warming the necks of the New York Public Library's lions, and fanciful figurines in the windows of Saks Fifth Avenue and Lord & Taylor. Throughout December.
- **Christmas Traditions.** In addition to the **Radio City Music Hall Christmas Spectacular** and the New York City Ballet's staging of *The Nutcracker* (see November, above), traditional holiday events include *A Christmas Carol* at the Theater at Madison Square Garden (☎ **212/465-6741** or www.thegarden.com; ☎ **212/307-7171** or www.ticketmaster.com for tickets), usually featuring a big name or two to draw in the crowds (Roger Daltrey in 1998). At Avery Fisher Hall is the National Chorale's sing-along performance of Handel's *Messiah* (☎ **212/ 875-5030**; www.lincolncenter.org). Don't worry if the only words you know are "Alleluia, Alleluia!"—a lyrics sheet is provided.
- **Lighting of the Hanukkah Menorah.** Everything is done on a grand scale in New York, so it's no surprise that the world's largest menorah (32 feet high) is at Manhattan's Grand Army Plaza, Fifth Avenue and 59th Street. Hanukkah

celebrations begin December 22 in 2000 with the lighting of the first of the giant electronic candles.

○ **New Year's Eve.** The biggest party of them all happens in Times Square, where hundreds of thousands of raucous revelers count down in unison the year's final seconds until the new lighted ball drops at midnight at 1 Times Square. I personally don't understand it, since its always a crowded, cold, boozy madhouse, but hey! Call ☎ **212/354-0003** or 212/484-1222. December 31.

There's also **First Night,** a liquor-free gala celebration held at venues all around town. Just purchase a button for admission to any of these; they're available throughout December at various locations around the city. Events include swing dancing in the magnificent concourse of Grand Central Terminal, taking in the view at the Empire State Building observation deck, world music concerts, children's events, and more. Call the **First Night Hotline** at ☎ 212/922-9393.

Other unique events include **fireworks** followed by a **5-mile midnight run** sponsored by the New York Road Runners Club (☎ 212/860-4455; www.nyrrc.org) in Central Park. The **Cathedral of St. John the Divine** (☎ 212/316-7540; www.stjohndivine.org) is known for its New Year's Eve concert.

5 Health & Insurance

It can be hard to find a doctor you can trust when you're in an unfamiliar place. Try to take proper precautions the week before you depart to avoid falling ill while you're away from home. Amid the last minute frenzy that often precede a vacation break, make an extra effort to eat and sleep well—especially if you feel an illness coming on. It's a drag to be sick on vacation, and a head cold can make a plane flight intolerable.

WHAT TO DO IF YOU GET SICK AWAY FROM HOME

If you worry about getting sick away from home, you may want to consider **medical travel insurance** (see the section on travel insurance below). In most cases, however, your existing health plan will provide all the coverage you need. Be sure to carry your identification card in your wallet.

If you suffer from a chronic illness, consult your doctor before your departure. For conditions like epilepsy, diabetes, or heart problems, wear a **Medic Alert Identification Tag** (☎ 800/825-3785; www.medicalert.org), which will immediately alert doctors to your condition and give them access to your records through Medic Alert's 24-hour hotline. Membership is $35, plus a $15 annual fee.

Pack prescription medications in your carry-on. Carry written prescriptions in generic, not brand-name form, and dispense all medications from their original labeled vials. If you wear contacts, pack an extra pair in case you lose one.

FINDING A DOCTOR If you do get sick, ask the concierge at your hotel to recommend a local doctor, even his or her own. This will probably yield a better recommendation than any 800 number would. There are also several walk-in medical

Travel Tip

If you're buying a package vacation or tour, don't buy your trip-cancellation insurance from your tour operator—talk about putting all of your eggs in one basket! Buy it from an outside vendor instead.

centers, like the **New York Healthcare Immediate Care,** 55 E. 34th St., between Park and Madison avenues (☎ **212/252-6001**), for non-emergency illnesses. The clinic, affiliated with Beth Israel Medical Center, is open Monday to Thursday 8am to 8pm, Fri 8am to 7pm, Saturday 9am to 3pm, and Sunday 9am to 2pm. A 24-hour referral service for doctors who make house calls can be reached by calling ☎ **212/737-2333.**

If you have dental problems, a nationwide referral service, **1-800-DENTIST** (☎ 800/336-8478), will provide the name of a nearby dentist or clinic. **Preventive Dental Associates** at (☎ **212/683-2530**) accepts same-day appointments and has a 24-hour answering service.

If you can't find a doctor who can help you right away, try the emergency room at the local hospital. Many emergency rooms have walk-in-clinics for emergency cases that are not life threatening. You may not get immediate attention, but you won't pay the high price of an emergency-room visit (usually a minimum of $300 just for signing your name, plus the price of whatever treatment you receive). For a list of local hospitals, see "Fast Facts: New York City," in chapter 4.

TRAVEL INSURANCE

There are three kinds of travel insurance: trip cancellation, medical, and lost-luggage coverage. **Trip-cancellation insurance** is a good idea if you have paid a large portion of your vacation expenses up front. The other two types of insurance, however, don't make sense for most travelers. Rule number one: Check your existing policies before you buy any additional coverage.

Your existing health insurance should cover you if you get sick while on vacation (though if you belong to an HMO, you should check to see whether you are fully covered when away from home). For independent travel health-insurance providers, see below.

Your homeowner's or renter's insurance should cover stolen luggage. The airlines are responsible for $1,250 on domestic flights if they lose your luggage; if you plan to carry anything more valuable than that, keep it in your carry-on bag.

The differences between **travel assistance** and insurance are often blurred, but in general the former offers on-the-spot assistance and 24-hour hotlines (mostly oriented toward medical problems), while the latter reimburses you for travel problems (medical, travel, or otherwise) after you have filed the paperwork. The coverage you should consider will depend on how much protection is already contained in your existing health insurance or other policies. Some credit- and charge-card companies may insure you against travel accidents if you buy plane, train, or bus tickets with their cards. Before purchasing additional insurance, read your policies and agreements carefully. Call your insurers or credit/charge-card companies if you have any questions.

If you do require additional insurance, try one of the companies listed below. But don't pay for more than you need. If you need only trip-cancellation insurance, don't purchase coverage for lost or stolen property, which should be covered by your homeowner's or renter's policy. Trip cancellation insurance costs approximately 6% to 8% of the total value of your vacation.

Among the reputable issuers of travel insurance are:

Access America, 6600 W. Broad St., Richmond, VA 23230 (☎ 800/284-8300; www.accessamerica.com); **Travel Guard International,** 1145 Clark St., Stevens Point, WI 54481 (☎ 800/826-1300; www.travel-guard.com); **Travel Insured International,** Inc., P.O. Box 280568, East Hartford, CT 06128 (☎ 800/243-3174); **Travelex Insurance Services,** P.O. Box 9408, Garden City, NY 11530-9408 (☎ 800/228-9792).

6 Tips for Travelers with Special Needs

FOR FAMILIES

You don't have to leave the kids home, Mom and Dad. These days, New York City is just as big a playground for the younger set as it is for you. For the best places to stay and eat, see "Affordable Family-Friendly Hotels" in chapter 5 and "Affordable Family-Friendly Restaurants" in chapter 6. For details on sightseeing specifics, check out the section "Especially for Kids" in chapter 7. If you want a guide devoted exclusively to travel with children, pick up a copy of *Frommer's New York City with Kids.*

Good bets for the most timely information include the "Weekend" section of Friday's the *New York Times,* which has a whole section dedicated to the week's best kid-friendly activities; weekly *New York* magazine, which has a full calendar of children's events in its "Cue" section; and *Time Out New York,* which also has a great weekly kid's section with a bit of an alternative bent.

Good Web sources for up-to-date information and advice include **New York Family** (☎ 914/381-7474) which features an online calendar and other family-friendly Big Apple advice at **www.family.go.com/Local/nyfm**; and **Big Apple Parent** (☎ 212/533-2277) offering similar information and links at **www.family.go.com/Local/bapp**. Both *New York Family* and the *Big Apple Parents' Paper* are usually available for free at children's stores and other locations in Manhattan. Call to find out how to order advance copies.

FINDING A BABY-SITTER   The first place to look for baby-sitting is in your hotel (better yet, ask about baby-sitting when you reserve). Most budget hotels don't provide baby-sitting services, but can they can often provide you with lists of reliable sitters. If this doesn't pan out, there's the **Baby Sitters' Guild** (☎ 212/682-0227) or the **Frances Stewart Agency** (☎ 212/439-9222). The sitters are licensed, insured, and bonded, and can even take your child on outings.

FOR TRAVELERS WITH DISABILITIES

A disability shouldn't stop anyone from traveling. The Americans with Disabilities Act and state and local laws require an increasing number of buildings and other public spaces to accommodate people with disabilities, making New York more accessible to travelers with disabilities than ever before. The city's bus system is wheelchair-friendly, and most of the major sightseeing attractions are easily accessible. Even so, always call first to be sure that the places you want to go to are fully accessible.

Most city hotels are ADA compliant, with suitable rooms for wheelchair-bound travelers as well as those with other disabilities. But before you book, **ask lots of questions** based on your needs. Many budget hotels are housed in older buildings that have had to be modified to meet requirements; still, elevators and bathrooms can both be on the small side, and other impediments may exist. If you have mobility issues, you'll probably do best to book into one of the city's newer hotels, which tend to be more spacious and accommodating.

Some Broadway theaters and other performance venues provide total wheelchair accessibility; others provide partial accessibility. Many also offer lower-priced tickets for disabled theatergoers and their companions, though you'll need to check individual policies and reserve in advance.

GENERAL TRAVEL INFORMATION   The **Moss Rehab Hospital** (☎ 215/456-9600; www.mossresourcenet.org) has been providing friendly and helpful phone advice and travel-agent referrals to disabled travelers for years through its **Travel Information Service** (☎ 215/456-9603). Another great source is **www.access-able.com**.

You'll find relay and voice numbers for hotels, airlines, and car-rental companies on this user-friendly site, as well as links to accessible accommodations, attractions, transportation, and tours; local medical resources and equipment repairers; and much more.

Reliable operators of guided tours for travelers with disabilities include **Flying Wheels Travel** (☎ **800/535-6790;** www.flyingwheels.com) and **Accessible Journeys** (☎ **800/TINGLES** or 610/521-0339; www.disabilitytravel.com), whose tours for slow walkers and wheelchair travelers tend toward outdoor and adventure destinations. They can arrange for a healthcare professional to serve as a traveling companion to you.

You can join **The Society for the Advancement of Travel for the Handicapped** (SATH), 347 Fifth Ave. Suite 610, New York, NY 10016 (☎ **212/447-7284;** www.sath.org), for $45 annually ($30 for seniors and students), to gain access to their vast network of connections in the travel industry.

CITY-SPECIFIC INFORMATION   **Hospital Audiences, Inc.,** has an information hotline (☎ **888/424-4685,** Mon–Fri 9am–5pm) providing details about accessibility at cultural institutions, hotels, restaurants, and transportation, as well as cultural events adapted for people with disabilities. Trained staff members answer specific questions based on your particular physical needs and the dates of your trip. The nonprofit organization also publishes *Access for All,* a guidebook on accessibility at many of the city's cultural institutions, available by sending a $5 check to **Hospital Audiences, Inc.,** 220 W. 42nd St., 13th floor, New York, NY 10036 (☎ **212/575-7676;** TTY 212/575-7673; www.hospitalaudiences.org). They also have a range of other services, including "Describe!" which allows visually impaired theatergoers to enjoy theater events; and an omnibus program that transports the disabled to cultural events.

Another terrific source for travelers with disabilities is **Big Apple Greeter** (☎ **212/669-8159;** TTY: 212/669-8273; www.bigapplegreeter.org). Their Greeter Access Project is geared to travelers with disabilities interested in getting to know the Big Apple. All of their employees are extremely well versed on access issues. They can provide a list of agencies that serve the city's disabled community, and sometimes have special discounts for theater and music performances. Big Apple Greeter even offers one-to-one tours that pair volunteers with disabled visitors; they can even introduce you to the public transportation system if you like. Reserve at least 1 week ahead.

Other helpful organizations are the **American Foundation for the Blind,** 11 Penn Plaza, Suite 300, New York, NY 10001 (☎ **800/232-5463** or 212/502-7600); **The Lighthouse, Inc.,** 111 E. 59th St., New York, NY 10022 (☎ **800/829-0500** or 212/821-9200; www.lighthouse.org), which arranges activities for people with impaired vision and sells Braille subway maps; and the **New York Society for the Deaf,** 817 Broadway, 7th floor, New York, NY 10003 (☎ **212/777-3900**).

GETTING AROUND   **Gray Line Air Shuttle** (☎ **800/451-0455** or 212/315-3006) operates minibuses with lifts from JFK, La Guardia, and Newark airports to Midtown hotels by reservation; be sure to arrange pick-up 3 or 4 days in advance.

A licensed ambulette company, **Upward Mobility Limousine Service** (☎ **718/645-7774;** www.brainlink.com/~phil) is a wheelchair-accessible car service that can provide door-to-door airport shuttle service as well as taxi service anywhere in the metropolitan area. Arrange airport pickups with as much advance notice as possible.

Taxis are required to carry people with folding wheelchairs and Seeing Eye or hearing dogs. However, don't be surprised if they don't run each other down trying to get to you; even though you shouldn't have to, you may have to wait a bit for a friendly (or fare-desperate) driver to come along.

Public buses are an inexpensive and easy way to get around New York. All buses' back doors are supposed to be equipped with wheelchair lifts (though the city has had complaints that not all are in working order). Buses also "kneel," lowering their front steps for people who have difficulty boarding. Passengers with disabilities pay half-price fares (75¢). Call the **Accessible Line** at ☎ 718/596-8585 (daily 6am–9pm) for bus and subway transit info, or visit **www.mta.nyc.ny.us/nyct.** The subway isn't yet fully wheelchair accessible, but a free brochure about subway accessibility, *Accessible Transfer Points,* is available by contacting MTA Customer Assistance, 370 J St., Room 702, Brooklyn, NY 11201 (☎ **718/330-3322;** TTY: 718/596-8273). A list of accessible subway stations is also on the MTA Web site.

You're better off not trying to rent your own car to get around the city. But if you consider it the best mode of transportation for you, **Wheelchair Getaways** (☎ **800/ 379-3750** or 516/939-0372; www.wheelchair-getaways.com) rents specialized vans with wheelchair lifts and other features for those with disabilities throughout the New York metropolitan area.

FOR SENIOR TRAVELERS

One of the benefits of age is that travel often costs less. New York subway and bus fares are half price (75¢) for people 65 and older. Many museums and sites (and some theaters and performance halls) offer discounted entrance and tickets to seniors, so don't be shy about asking. Always bring an ID card, especially if you've kept your youthful glow.

Always mention the fact that you're a senior citizen when you first make your travel reservations. Both **Amtrak** (☎ **800/USA-RAIL;** www.amtrak.com) and **Greyhound** (☎ **800/752-4841;** www.greyhound.com) offer discounts to persons over 62, and most of the major domestic airlines offer discount programs for senior travelers. Many hotels also offer senior discounts; **Choice Hotels** (which include Comfort Inns, some of my favorite affordable midtown hotels; see chapter 5), for example, give 30% off their published rates to anyone over 50, provided you book your room through their nationwide toll-free reservations number (that is, not directly with the hotels or through a travel agent). For a complete list of Choice Hotels, visit **www. hotelchoice.com.**

Members of the **American Association of Retired Persons (AARP),** 601 E St. NW, Washington, DC 20049 (☎ **800/424-3410** or 202/434-2277; www.aarp.org), get discounts not only on hotels but on airfares and car rentals, too. The AARP offers members a wide range of special benefits; if you're not already a member, do yourself a favor and join.

Some thugs and unscrupulous tricksters try to take advantage of seniors. Be as skeptical as a New Yorker whenever you're approached, especially by someone who has a long story that promises to give you something for nothing. For safety tips, see "Playing It Safe" in chapter 4. Your experience and common sense equips you with more savvy than most con artists will ever have.

FOR GAY & LESBIAN TRAVELERS

Gay and lesbian culture is as much a part of New York's basic identity as yellow cabs, high-rises, and Broadway theater. Indeed, in a city with one of the world's largest, loudest, and most powerful gay and lesbian populations, homosexuality is hardly seen as an "alternative" these days—it's squarely in the urban mainstream. So city hotels tend to be neutral on the issue, and gay couples shouldn't have a problem. Still, if you'd like to stay in a particularly gay-friendly inn, see "Staying Out" in the introduction to chapter 5. You'll also want to see "The Lesbian & Gay Scene" in chapter 9 for nightlife suggestions.

If you want help planning your trip to New York, **The International Gay & Lesbian Travel Association** (IGLTA) (☎ **800/448-8550** or 954/776-2626; fax 954/776-3303; www.iglta.org) can link you up with the appropriate gay-friendly service organization or tour specialist. With around 1,200 members, it offers quarterly newsletters, marketing mailings, and a membership directory that's updated quarterly. Members are kept informed of gay and gay-friendly hoteliers, tour operators, and airline and cruise-line representatives.

All over Manhattan, but especially in neighborhoods like the **West Village** (particularly Christopher Street, famous the world over as the main drag of New York gay-male life) and **Chelsea** (especially Eighth Avenue from 16th to 23rd streets and West 17th to 19th streets from Fifth to Eighth avenues), shops, services, and restaurants have a lesbian and gay flavor. **A Different Light Bookstore,** 151 W. 19th St. (☎ **800/343-4002** or 212/989-4850; www.adlbooks.com), and the **Oscar Wilde Bookshop,** 15 Christopher St. (☎ **212/255-8097;** www.oscarwildebooks.com), are the city's best gay and lesbian bookstores; both are good sources for information on the city's gay community.

The **Lesbian and Gay Community Services Center,** 1 Little W. 12th St., between Ninth Avenue and Hudson Street, one block south of West 13th Street (☎ **212/620-7310;** www.gaycenter.org), is open daily 9am to 10:30pm. (This is its temporary home for about 2 years while its headquarters at 208 W. 13th St. is being renovated.) The center is the meeting place for more than 400 lesbian, gay, and bisexual organizations. The center also runs 26 programs of its own, including one for gays and lesbians newly relocated to New York. Their Community Calendar of Events lists happenings like lectures, dances, concerts, readings, and films.

The **Gay and Lesbian Switchboard of New York** (☎ **212/989-0999;** www.glnh.org) offers peer counseling and information on upcoming events.

Another good source for lesbian and gay events during your visit is *Homo Xtra* (*HX*)*,* a weekly magazine you can pick up in appropriate bars, clubs, and stores throughout town. Lesbians now have their own version, *HX for Her.* Both mags have information online at **www.hx.com.** In addition, the weekly *Time Out New York* boasts a terrific gay and lesbian section. For other online information sources, see "Site Seeing: The Big Apple on the Web" under "Visitor Information" earlier in this chapter.

FOR STUDENTS

Many attractions and theaters offer reduced admission to students, so don't forget to bring your valid student ID and proof of age.

Your best resource is the **Council on International Educational Exchange** (CIEE). They can set you up with an International Student ID card, and their travel branch, **Council Travel** (☎ **800/226-8624;** www.counciltravel.com) can get you discounts on plane tickets and the like. City locations include 254 Greene St., between Waverly and 8th Street in the Village (☎ **212/254-2525**).

The biggest hostel in the **Hostelling International–American Youth Hostels,** 733 15th St. NW, Suite 840, Washington, DC 20005 (☎ **800/444-6111** or 202/783-6161; www.hiayh.org), system is in New York City; see chapter 5 for a complete review.

7 Getting There

BY PLANE

Three major airports serve New York City: **John F. Kennedy International Airport (JFK;** ☎ 718/244-4444) in Queens, about 15 miles (or 1 hour's driving time) from Midtown Manhattan; **LaGuardia Airport** (☎ 718/533-3400) also in Queens, about

Money-Saving Package Deals

Before you start your search for the lowest airfare, you may want to consider booking your flight as part of a travel package.

Package tours are not the same as escorted tours. They are simply a way to buy airfare and accommodations (and sometimes extras like sightseeing tours and hard-to-get theater tickets) at the same time. For New York, a package can be a smart way to go. In many cases, one that includes airfare, hotel, and transportation to and from the airport will cost you less than the hotel alone would have had you booked it yourself. That's because packages are sold in bulk to tour operators, who resell them to the public at a cost that drastically undercuts standard rates.

Packages, however, vary widely. Some offer a better class of hotels than others. Some offer the same hotels for lower prices. With some packagers, your choice of accommodations and travel days may be limited. Which package is right for you depends entirely on what you want. Here are a few tips to help you tell one from the other, and figure out which one is right for you:

- **Read this guide.** Do a little homework; read up on New York. Compare the rack rates that we've published to the discounted rates being offered by the packagers to see what kinds of deals they're offering. If you're being offered a stay in a hotel I haven't recommended, do more research to learn about it, especially if it isn't a reliable brand name like Holiday Inn or Best Western. It's not a deal if you end up at a dump.
- **Read the fine print.** Make sure you know *exactly* what's included in the price you're being quoted, and what's not. Are hotel taxes and airport transfers included, or will you have to pay extra? Conversely, don't pay for a rental car you don't need—and you won't need one in New York. Before you commit to a package, make sure you know how much flexibility you have, say, if your kid gets sick or your boss suddenly asks you to adjust your vacation schedule. Some packagers require iron-clad commitments, while others will go with the flow, charging minimal fees for changes or cancellations.
- **Use your best judgement.** Stay away from fly-by-nights and shady packagers. If a deal sounds too good to be true, it probably is. Go with a reputable firm with a proven track record. This is where your travel agent can come in handy; he or she should be knowledgeable about different packagers, the deals they offer, and the general rate of satisfaction among their customers.

Finding a Package Deal   The best place to start your search is the travel section of your local Sunday newspaper. Also check the ads in the back of national travel

8 miles (or 30 minutes) from Midtown; and **Newark International Airport** (☎ 201/961-6000) in nearby New Jersey, about 16 miles (or 45 minutes) from Midtown. Online information on all three airports is available at **www.panynj.gov**.

Almost every major domestic carrier serves at least one of these airports; most serve two or all three. **America West** (☎ 800/235-9292; www.americawest.com), **American** (☎ 800/433-7300; www.americanair.com), **Continental** (☎ 800/525-0280 or 800/523-3273; www.flycontinental.com), **Delta** (☎ 800/221-1212; www.deltaair.com), **Northwest** (☎ 800/225-2525; www.nwa.com), **TWA** (☎ 800/221-2000; www.twa.com), **US Airways** (☎ 800/428-4322; www.usairways.com), and **United** (☎ 800/241-6522; www.ual.com).

magazines like *Travel & Leisure, National Geographic Traveler,* and *Conde Nast Traveler.*

One of the biggest packagers in the Northeast, **Liberty Travel** (☎ **888/271-1584** to be connected to with the travel agent closest to you; www.libertytravel.com) boasts a full-page ad in many Sunday papers. You won't get much in the way of service, but you will get a good deal. They offer great-value 2–7-night New York packages that usually include such freebies as a Circle Line cruise and discounts at Planet Hollywood, plus lots of good hotels to choose from.

Major airlines also offer good-value packages to New York: **Continental Airlines Vacations** (☎ 800/634-5555; www.coolvacations.com) featured a limited selection of hotels at press time, but among the choices was the Hotel Metro, one of my mid-priced favorites. **Delta Vacations** (☎ 800/872-7786; www.deltavacations.com) boasts a very good selection of hotels, including the Hotel Metro, Loews New York, and the Doubletree Guest Suites (a great family choice if you can land an afford-able deal). **United Vacations** (☎ 800/328-6877; www.unitedvacations.com) and **US Airways Vacations** (☎ 800/455-0123; www.usairwaysvacations.com) each offers a pleasing range of hotels, plus Broadway tickets as part of their add-on options. **American Airlines Vacations** (☎ 800/321-2121; aav3.aavacations.com) has an extensive but mixed selection of hotels, so be careful where you book (skip the Ameritania and the Park Central altogether). **Northwest WorldVacations** (☎ 800/800-1504; www.nwa.com/vacpkg) is another option, but their prices weren't that attractive last time I checked. You may want to choose the airline that has frequent service to your hometown or the one on which you accumulate frequent-flyer miles (you may even be able to pay with your trip using miles).

For one-stop shopping on the Web, go to **www.vacationpackager.com**, a search engine that will link you to many different package-tour operators offering New York City vacations, often with a profile summarizing the company's basic booking and cancellation terms.

In New York, many **hotels** also offer package deals, especially for weekend stays. Some of the best deals in town are those that include theater tickets, some-times for otherwise sold-out shows like *The Lion King.* (Most aren't air/land combos, however; you'll have to book your airfare separately.) I've included tips on hotels that regularly offer them in chapter 5, but always ask about available packages when you call any hotel.

In recent years there has been a rapid growth in the number of start-up, no-frills air-lines serving New York. These smaller, sometimes struggling airlines usually offer lower fares, but don't expect the same kind of service you get from the majors. Still, if you're looking to save, check out **AirTran** (☎ 800/AIRTRAN; www.airtran.com), **ATA** (☎ 800/I-FLY-ATA; www.ata.com), **Frontier** (☎ 800/432-1359; www.frontier air. com), **Midway** (☎ 800/446-4392; www.midwayair.com), **Midwest Express** (☎ 800/ 452-2022; www.midwestexpress.com), **Spirit Airlines** (☎ 800/772-7117; www.spiritair. com), **SunJet International** (☎ 800/4-SUNJET; www.sunjet.com), **Sun Country** (☎ 800/752-1218; www.suncountry.com), and **Tower Air** (☎ 800/34-TOWER or 718/553-8500; www.towerair.com). In addition, a new airline, **New**

Air, is scheduled to begin serving New York at great discounts in fall 1999, but no other details were available at press time. And the nation's leading discount airline, **Southwest** (☎ 800/435-9792; www.iflyswa.com), announced flights to Long Island's Islip Airport, 40 miles east of Manhattan, but there are no current plans to fly into the city's airports.

Most major international carriers also serve New York; see chapter 3 for details.

Keep in mind that it's more convenient to fly into Newark than Kennedy if your destination is Manhattan, and consider that fares to Newark are often cheaper than the other airports. Newark can also be the most convenient if you hotel is in Midtown West or Downtown near the World Trade Center.

For advice on how to get the best airfare, see "60 Money-Saving Tips" earlier in this chapter.

TRANSPORTATION TO & FROM THE NEW YORK AREA AIRPORTS

Since there's no need to rent a car for a visit to New York, you're going to have to figure out how you want to get from the airport to your hotel and back.

For complete transportation information for all three airports (JFK, La Guardia, and Newark), call **Air-Ride** (☎ 800/247-7433); it gives recorded details on bus and shuttle companies and private-car services registered with the New York and New Jersey Port Authority.

On the arrivals level at each airport, the Port Authority also has Ground Transportation Information counters where you can get information and book transport. Most transportation companies also have courtesy phones near the baggage-claim area.

Generally, travel time between the airports and Midtown Manhattan by taxi or car is 1 hour for JFK, 45 minutes for La Guardia, and 50 minutes for Newark. Always allow extra time, though, especially during rush hour, peak holiday travel times, and if you're taking a bus.

SUBWAYS & PUBLIC BUSES Taking the MTA to and from the airport can be a hassle, but it's the cheapest way to go—just $1.50 each way. However, keep in mind that the subways and buses that currently serve the airports involve multiple transfers and staircases; count on more hauling to your hotel (or a taxi fare) once you arrive in Manhattan. This won't work for travelers with too much luggage, because you won't have anywhere to store it on the bus or subway train. You might not want to take the bus or the subway if you're traveling too early in the morning or late at night; you'll be passing through some less-than-desirable neighborhoods.

For additional subway and bus information, see "Getting Around" in chapter 4.

From/to Kennedy Airport You can take the **A train** to Kennedy airport, which connects to one of two free **shuttle buses** that serve all the JFK terminals. Plan on 2 hours in each direction, maybe more if you're traveling at rush hour: The subway ride from midtown takes about 75 minutes, and you'll need another 20 to 30 minutes for the shuttle ride to your terminal; also be sure to factor in waiting time at both ends.

Upon exiting the terminal, pick up the shuttle bus (marked LONG TERM PARKING LOT) out front; it takes you to the Howard Beach station, where you pick up the A train to the west side of Manhattan. Service is every 10 to 15 minutes during rush hour and every 20 minutes at midday. If you're traveling to JFK from Manhattan, be sure to take the A train that says FAR ROCKAWAY or ROCKAWAY PARK—*not* LEFFERTS BOULEVARD. Get off at the Howard Beach/JFK Airport station and connect to the shuttle bus, A or B, that goes to your terminal (they're clearly marked, and there's usually a guide to point you to the right one). The subway can actually be more reliable than taking a car or taxi at the height of rush hour.

New York Metropolitan Area

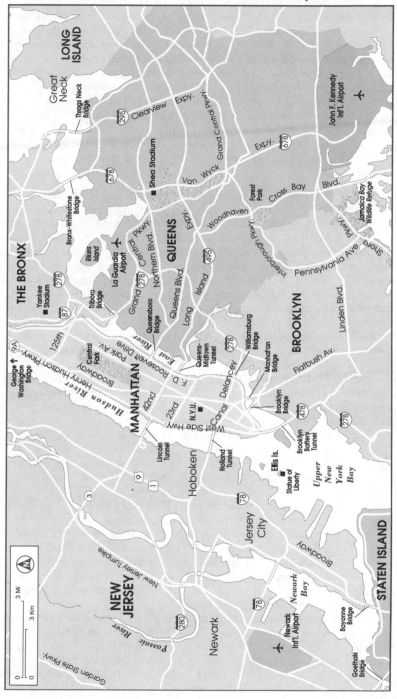

From/to LaGuardia   The **M60 bus** serves all LaGuardia terminals. When leaving LaGuardia, follow the GROUND TRANSPORTATION signs and look for the M60 stop sign at the curb. The bus will take you to Broadway and 116th Street on Manhattan's west side, where you can transfer to a downtown bus or the 1 or 9 subway; you can also pick up the N subway into Manhattan by disembarking at the Astoria Boulevard station in Queens. The bus runs daily between 6am and 1am, leaving at roughly half-hour intervals and taking about 50 minutes. (From Manhattan, you can pick up the bus as early as 4:30am from Broadway and 106th St.) Be sure to allow at least 1¼ hour, however—you never know about traffic. *Money-saving tip:* Use a MetroCard to pay your fare and you'll save the extra $1.50 it usually costs for the transfer. For the complete schedule and other pickup and drop-off points, visit **www.mta.nyc.ny.us/nyct/ service/m60.htm**.

From/to Newark   Sorry, there's no public transportation; use one of the private bus services listed below.

PRIVATE BUSES & SHUTTLES   Buses and shuttle services are more expensive than using the MTA for airport transfers, but they're more comfortable and less expensive than taxis (but usually more time-consuming). Gray Line Air Shuttle and Super Shuttle serve all three airports; New York Airport Service serves JFK and La Guardia; Olympia Trails serves Newark. This is my favorite option for getting to and from Newark during peak travel times, because the drivers usually take lesser-known surface streets that make the ride much quicker than if you go with a taxi or car, which will virtually always stick to the traffic-clogged main route.

   Gray Line Air Shuttle (☎ 800/451-0455 or 212/315-3006; www.graylinenewyork. com) vans depart JFK, La Guardia, and Newark every 20 minutes 7am to 11:30pm and will drop you off at most hotels between 23rd and 63rd streets in Manhattan, or Port Authority (34th Street and Seventh Avenue) or Grand Central (42nd Street and Park Avenue) terminals if you need to catch a subway to another part of town or a train to the 'burbs. No reservation is required; just go to the ground-transportation desk or use the courtesy phone in the baggage-claim area and ask for Gray Line. Service from most major mid-Manhattan hotels to all three airports operates 5am to 7pm; you must call a day in advance to arrange a hotel pickup. The one-way fare for JFK is $19, for La Guardia $16, and for Newark $19, but you can save a few bucks by prepaying your round-trip at the airport ($28 for JFK and Newark, $26 for LaGuardia).

   The familiar blue vans of **Super Shuttle** (☎ 800/258-3826 or 718/482-9703; www.supershuttle.com/nyc.htm) serve all three airports, providing door-to-door service to Manhattan and points on Long Island every 15 to 30 minutes around the clock. As with Gray Line, you don't need to reserve your airport-to-Manhattan ride; just go to the ground-transportation desk or use the courtesy phone in the baggage-claim area. Hotel pickups for your return trip require 24 to 48 hours' advance booking. Fares are $15 one-way to and from JFK, $14 one-way to and from LaGuardia, $17 one-way to and from Newark.

   New York Airport Service (☎ 718/706-9658) buses travel from JFK and La Guardia to the Port Authority Bus Terminal (42nd St. and Eighth Ave.), Penn Station (34th St. and Seventh Ave.), Grand Central Terminal (Park Ave. between 41st and 42nd sts.), or your midtown hotel, plus the Jamaica LIRR Station in Queens, where you can pick up a train for Long Island. Follow the GROUND TRANSPORTATION signs to the curbside pickup or look for the uniformed agent. Buses depart the airport every 20 to 70 minutes (depending on your departure point and destination) between 6:30am and midnight. Buses to JFK and La Guardia depart the Port Authority and

Grand Central Terminal on the Park Avenue side every 15 to 30 minutes, depending on the time of day and day of the week. To request direct shuttle service from your hotel, call the above number at least 24 hours in advance. One-way fare for JFK is $13, $10 for La Guardia; children under 12 ride free with a parent.

Olympia Trails (☎ **888/662-7700** or 212/964-6233; www.olympiabus.com) provides service every 5 to 15 minutes (less frequently during off hours) from Newark Airport to four Manhattan locations: the World Trade Center (on West St., next to the Marriott World Trade Center Hotel), Penn Station (the pickup point is the northwest corner of 34th St. and Eighth Ave. and the drop-off point the southwest corner), the Port Authority Bus Terminal (on 42nd St. between Eighth and Ninth aves.), and Grand Central Terminal (41st St. between Park and Lexington). Passengers to and from the Grand Central Terminal location can connect to Olympia's Midtown shuttle vans, which service most hotels between 30th and 65th streets. From the above departure points in Manhattan, service runs every 15 to 30 minutes depending on your pickup point; call for exact schedule. The one-way fare is $10, $15 if you connect to the hotel shuttle.

If you're traveling to a borough other than Manhattan, call **ETS Air Service** (☎ 888/467-4996 or 718/221-5341) for shared door-to-door service.

TAXIS   Taxis are a quick and easy way to travel to and from the airports, but you'll pay for the convenience of door-to-door service. They're available at designated taxi stands outside the terminals, with uniformed dispatchers on hand during peak hours (follow the GROUND TRANSPORTATION or TAXI signs). There may be a long line, but it generally moves pretty quickly. Fares, whether fixed or metered, don't include bridge and tunnel tolls ($3.50 to $4) or tip (15% to 20% is customary). They do include all passengers in the cab and luggage—never pay more than the metered or flat rate, except for tolls and a tip (from 8pm to 6am a 50¢ surcharge also applies on New York yellow cabs). Taxis have a limit of four passengers. For more on taxis, see "Getting Around" in chapter 4.

- **From JFK:** At press time, the flat rate of $30 to and from Manhattan (plus any tolls and tip) was still in effect. The meter will not be turned on and the surcharge will not be added. If the flat rate has been overturned by the time you arrive (the cabbies really hate it), expect the fare to be metered and run $30 to $40.
- **From La Guardia:** $20 to $25, metered.
- **From Newark:** The dispatcher for New Jersey taxis gives you a slip of paper with a flat rate ranging from $30 to $45 (toll and tip extra), depending on where you're going in Manhattan, so you'll have to be precise about your destination. New York yellow cabs aren't permitted to pick up passengers at Newark. The yellow-cab fare from Manhattan to Newark is the meter amount plus $10 and tolls (about $40 to $50, perhaps a few dollars more with tip). New Jersey taxis aren't permitted to take passengers from Manhattan to Newark.

An Airport Warning

Never accept a car ride from the hustlers who hang out in the terminal halls. They're illegal, don't have proper insurance, and aren't safe. You can tell who they are because they'll approach you with a suspicious, conspiratorial air, and ask if you need a ride. Not from them, you don't! Sanctioned city cabs and car services wait outside the terminals

PRIVATE-CAR & LIMOUSINE SERVICES   Private-car and limousine companies provide convenient 24-hour door-to-door airport transfers. The advantage over taking a taxi is that you can arrange your pickup in advance and avoid the hassles of the taxi line. Call at least 24 hours in advance (even earlier on holidays), and a driver will meet you near baggage claim or at your hotel for a return trip. You'll probably be asked to leave a credit-card number to guarantee your ride; you'll likely be offered the choice of indoor or curbside pickup. Vehicles range from sedans to vans to limousines and tend to be relatively clean and comfortable. Prices vary slightly by company and the size of car reserved, but expect to pay around the same as you would for a taxi for a basic sedan with one stop; toll and tip policies are the same. (Note that car services are not subject to the flat-rate rule that taxis are for rides to and from JFK.) Ask when booking what the fare will be and whether you can use your credit card to pay for the ride. There may be waiting charges tacked on if the driver has to wait an excessive amount of time for your plane to land when picking you up, but the car companies will usually check on your flight beforehand to get an accurate landing time.

I've had the best luck with **Carmel** (☎ 800/922-7635 or 212/666-6666); **Executive Town Car & Limousines** (☎ 800/716-2799 or 516/538-8551), which also serves New Jersey and Connecticut; **Allstate** (☎ 800/453-4099 or 212/741-7440); and **Tel-Aviv** (☎ 800/222-9888 or 212/777-7777). All have good cars, responsive dispatchers, and polite drivers.

BY TRAIN

Amtrak (☎ **800/USA-RAIL;** www.amtrak.com) runs frequent service to New York City's Pennsylvania Station (Seventh Ave. between 31st and 33rd streets), where you can easily pick up a taxi, subway, or bus to your hotel. Trains are a great bet for short routes—especially if you live on the Boston–Washington, D.C. corridor—since they're usually cheaper than airfares and can often get you into the city quicker, if you factor in the time it takes getting to and from the airport. Trains can also be less of a hassle for any traveler, since they take you right into Manhattan (thereby avoiding complicated and expensive airport transfers). To get the best rates, book early (as much as 6 months in advance) and travel on weekends. See "60 Money-Saving Tips," above, for more wallet-friendly advice, and check Amtrak's Web site for special discounted fares.

BY BUS

Buses arrive at the Port Authority Terminal (Eighth Ave. between 40th and 42nd sts.), where you can easily transfer to your hotel by taxi, subway, or bus. Buses are slow and uncomfortable, but fares are usually much lower than train and airline fares: For example, you'd pay between $90 and $100 for a round-trip ticket between Boston and New York on Amtrak, while the same route on Greyhound is just $60. The trips are pretty comparable in length (between 4½ and 6 hours each way), but the train may be quicker depending on your departure point, and it will always be more comfortable. Buses are also subject to traffic, which can slow them down.

For complete schedule and fare information, contact **Greyhound Bus Lines** (☎ **800/231-2222;** www.greyhound.com). You'll find a complete list of their special fares and discounts on their Web page; be sure to ask for complete details if you call instead.

While the bus is likely to be the cheapest option, don't just assume. Always compare fares; sometimes, a full-fare bus ticket is no cheaper than the train. If you get lucky, you might even catch an airline fare sale that will make flying the most prudent option.

BY CAR

From the **New Jersey Turnpike** (I-95) and points west, there are three Hudson River crossings into the city's west side: the Holland Tunnel (Lower Manhattan), the Lincoln Tunnel (Midtown), and the George Washington Bridge (Upper Manhattan).

From **upstate New York,** take the New York State Thruway (I-87), which crosses the Hudson on the Tappan Zee Bridge and becomes the Major Deegan Expressway (I-87) through the Bronx. For the east side, continue to the Triborough Bridge and then down the FDR Drive. For the west side, take the Cross Bronx Expressway (I-95) to the Henry Hudson Parkway or the Taconic State Parkway to the Saw Mill River Parkway to the Henry Hudson Parkway south.

From **New England,** the New England Thruway (I-95) connects with the Bruckner Expressway (I-278), which leads to the Triborough Bridge and the FDR on the east side. For the west side, take the Bruckner to the Cross Bronx Expressway (I-95) to the Henry Hudson Parkway south.

Note that you'll have to pay tolls along some of these roads and at most crossings.

Once you arrive in Manhattan, park your car in a garage (expect to pay at least $20 to $35 per day) and leave it there. Don't use your car for traveling within the city. Public transportation, taxis, and walking will easily get you where you want to go without the headache of parking, gridlock, and dodging crazy cabbies. For tips on parking, see "Deals for Visitors with Wheels: Cheap Parking Tips" in chapter 4.

3 For Foreign Visitors

You've seen it all already—the high-rises, the bustling crowds, the glittering nightlife, and the shopping. New York's global media profile might make it appear familiar, but movies and TV, music videos, and news images all distort as much as they reflect. The gap between image and reality can make certain situations puzzling for the foreign—or even domestic—visitor. This chapter will help prepare you for the more common problems that you may encounter.

1 Preparing for Your Trip

ENTRY REQUIREMENTS

Immigration laws are a hot political issue in the United States these days, and the following requirements may have changed somewhat by the time you plan your trip. Check at any U.S. embassy or consulate for current information and requirements, or plug into the U.S. State Department's Web site at **http://travel.state.gov**. Go to **http://travel. state.gov/visa_services.html** for the latest entry requirements.

VISAS The U.S. State Department has a **Visa Waiver Pilot Program** allowing citizens of certain countries to enter the United States without a visa for stays of up to 90 days. At press time these included Andorra, Argentina, Australia, Austria, Belgium, Brunei, Denmark, Finland, France, Germany, Iceland, Ireland, Italy, Japan, Liechtenstein, Luxembourg, Monaco, the Netherlands, New Zealand, Norway, San Marino, Slovenia, Spain, Sweden, Switzerland, and the United Kingdom. Citizens of these countries need only a valid passport and a round-trip air or cruise ticket in their possession upon arrival. If they first enter the United States, they may also visit Mexico, Canada, Bermuda, and/or the Caribbean islands and return to the United States without a visa. Further information is available from any U.S. embassy or consulate. Canadian citizens may enter the United States without visas; they need only proof of residence.

Citizens of all other countries must have (1) a valid passport that expires at least 6 months later than the scheduled end of their visit to the United States, and (2) a tourist visa, which may be obtained without charge from any U.S. consulate.

Obtaining a Visa To obtain a visa, the traveler must submit a completed application form (either in person or by mail) with a 1½-inch-square photo, and must demonstrate binding ties to a residence abroad. Usually you can obtain a visa at once or within 24 hours, but it may take longer during the summer rush from June through August. If you cannot go in person, contact the nearest U.S. embassy or consulate for directions on applying by mail. Your travel agent or airline office may also be able to provide you with visa applications and instructions. The U.S. consulate or embassy that issues your visa will determine whether you will be issued a multiple- or single-entry visa and any restrictions regarding the length of your stay.

British subjects can obtain up-to-date passport and visa information by calling the **U.S. Embassy Visa Information Line** (☎ **0891/200-290**) or the **London Passport Office** (☎ **0990/210-410** for recorded information).

IMMIGRATION QUESTIONS   Telephone operators will answer your inquiries regarding U.S. immigration policies or laws at the **Immigration and Naturalization Service's Customer Information Center** (☎ **800/375-5283**). Representatives are available Monday through Friday from 9am to 3pm. The INS also runs a 24-hour automated information service, for commonly asked questions, at ☎ **800/755-0777**. You'll find them online at **www.ins.usdoj.gov.**

MEDICAL REQUIREMENTS   Unless you're arriving from an area known to be suffering from an epidemic (particularly cholera or yellow fever), inoculations or vaccinations are not required for entry into the United States. If you have a disease that requires treatment with narcotics or syringe-administered medications, carry a valid signed prescription from your physician to allay any suspicions that you may be smuggling narcotics (a serious offense that carries severe penalties in the United States).

For HIV-positive visitors, requirements for entering the United States are somewhat vague and change frequently. According to the latest publication of *HIV and Immigrants: A Manual for AIDS Service Providers,* although INS doesn't require a medical exam for every one trying to come into the United States, INS officials may keep out people who they suspect are HIV positive. INS may stop people because they look sick or because they are carrying AIDS/HIV medicine.

If an HIV-positive non-citizen applying for a non-immigrant visa knows that HIV is a communicable disease of public health significance but checks "no" on the question about communicable diseases, INS may deny the visa because it thinks the applicant committed fraud. If a non-immigrant visa applicant checks "yes," or if INS suspects the person is HIV positive, it will deny the visa unless the applicant asks for a special waiver for visitors. This waiver is for people visiting the United States for a short time, to attend a conference, for instance, to visit close relatives, or to receive medical treatment. It can be a confusing situation, so for up-to-the-minute information concerning HIV-positive travelers, contact the Centers for Disease Control's **National Center for HIV** (☎ **404/332-4559;** www.hivatis.org) or the **Gay Men's Health Crisis** (☎ **212/367-1000;** www.gmhc.org).

DRIVER'S LICENSES   Foreign driver's licenses are mostly recognized in the United States, although you may want to get an international driver's license if your home license is not written in English.

PASSPORT INFORMATION

Safeguard your passport in an inconspicuous, inaccessible place like a money belt. If you lose it, visit the nearest consulate of your native country as soon as possible for a replacement (a list of major consulates can be found in "Fast Facts" at the end of this chapter). Passport applications are downloadable from the Internet sites listed below.

For Residents of Canada   You can pick up a passport application at one of 28 regional passport offices or most travel agencies. The passport is valid for 5 years and costs $60. Children under 16 may be included on a parent's passport but need their own to travel unaccompanied by the parent. Applications, which must be accompanied by two identical passport-sized photographs and proof of Canadian citizenship, are available at travel agencies throughout Canada or from the central **Passport Office, Department of Foreign Affairs and International Trade**, Ottawa K1A 0G3 (☎ **800/567-6868;** www.dfait-maeci.gc.ca/passport). Processing takes 5 to 10 days if you apply in person, or about 3 weeks by mail.

For Residents of the United Kingdom   To pick up an application for a regular 10-year passport (the Visitor's Passport has been abolished), visit your nearest passport office, major post office, or travel agency. You can also contact the London Passport Office at ☎ **0171/271-3000** or search its Web site at www.open.gov.uk/ukpass/ukpass.htm. Passports are £21 for adults and £11 for children under 16.

For Residents of Ireland   You can apply for a 10-year passport, costing IR£45, at the Passport Office, Setanta Centre, Molesworth Street, Dublin 2 (☎ **01/671-1633;** www.irlgov.ie/iveagh/foreignaffairs/services). Those under age 18 and over 65 must apply for a IR£10 3-year passport. You can also apply at 1A South Mall, Cork (☎ **021/272-525**) or over the counter at most main post offices.

For Residents of Australia   Apply at your local post office or passport office or search the government Web site at www.dfat.gov.au/passports. Passports for adults are A$126 and for those under 18 A$63.

For Residents of New Zealand   You can pick up a passport application at any travel agency or Link Centre. For more info, contact the Passport Office, P.O. Box 805, Wellington (☎ **0800/225-050**). Passports for adults are NZ$80 and for those under 16 NZ$40.

CUSTOMS
What You Can Bring In

Every visitor over 21 years of age may bring in, free of duty, the following: (1) 1 liter of wine or hard liquor; (2) 200 cigarettes, 50 cigars (but not from Cuba), or 2 kilograms (4.4 pounds) of smoking tobacco; and (3) $100 worth of gifts. These exemptions are offered to travelers who spend at least 72 hours in the United States and who have not claimed them within the preceding 6 months. It is altogether forbidden to bring into the country foodstuffs (particularly fruit, cooked meats, and canned goods) and plants (vegetables, seeds, tropical plants, and the like). Foreign tourists may bring in or take out up to $10,000 in U.S. or foreign currency with no formalities; larger sums must be declared to U.S. Customs on entering or leaving, which includes filing form CM 4790. For more specific information regarding U.S. Customs, contact your nearest U.S. embassy or consulate, or the **U.S. Customs** office at ☎ **202/927-1770** or www.customs.ustreas.gov.

What You Can Bring Home

U.K. citizens returning from a non-EC country have a customs allowance of: 200 cigarettes; 50 cigars; 250g of smoking tobacco; 2 liters of still table wine; 1 liter of spirits or strong liqueurs (over 22% volume); 2 liters of fortified wine, sparkling wine or other liqueurs; 60cc (ml) perfume; 250cc (ml) of toilet water; and £145 worth of all other goods, including gifts and souvenirs. People under 17 cannot have the tobacco or alcohol allowance. For more information, contact HM Customs & Excise, Passenger Enquiry Point, 2nd Floor Wayfarer House, Great South West Road, Feltham, Middlesex TW14 8NP (☎ **020/8-910-3744;** from outside the United Kingdom 44/20-8-910-3744), or consult their Web site at www.open.gov.uk.

   For a clear summary of **Canadian** rules, write for the booklet *I Declare,* issued by **Revenue Canada,** 2265 St. Laurent Blvd., Ottawa K1G 4KE (☎**613/993-0534**).

Canada allows its citizens a $500 exemption, and you're allowed to bring back duty-free 200 cigarettes, 2.2 pounds of tobacco, 40 imperial ounces of liquor, and 50 cigars. In addition, you're allowed to mail gifts to Canada from abroad at the rate of Can$60 a day, provided they're unsolicited and don't contain alcohol or tobacco (write on the package "Unsolicited gift, under $60 value"). All valuables should be declared on the Y-38 form before departure from Canada, including serial numbers of valuables you already own, such as expensive foreign cameras. Note: The $500 exemption can only be used once a year and only after an absence of 7 days.

The duty-free allowance in **Australia** is A$400 or, for those under 18, A$200. Personal property mailed back should be marked "Australian goods returned" to avoid payment of duty. Upon returning to Australia, citizens can bring in 250 cigarettes or 250 grams of loose tobacco, and 1,125ml of alcohol. If you're returning with valuable goods you already own, such as foreign-made cameras, you should file form B263. A helpful brochure, available from Australian consulates or Customs offices, is *Know Before You Go.* For more information, contact **Australian Customs Services,** GPO Box 8, Sydney, NSW 2001 (☎ **02/9213-2000**).

The duty-free allowance for **New Zealand** is NZ$700. Citizens over 17 can bring in 200 cigarettes, or 50 cigars, or 250 grams of tobacco (or a mixture of all three if their combined weight doesn't exceed 250 grams); plus 4.5 liters of wine and beer, or 1.125 liters of liquor. New Zealand currency does not carry import or export restrictions. Fill out a certificate of export, listing the valuables you are taking out of the country; that way, you can bring them back without paying duty. Most questions are answered in a free pamphlet available at New Zealand consulates and Customs offices: *New Zealand Customs Guide for Travellers, Notice no. 4.* For more information, contact New Zealand Customs, 50 Anzac Ave., P.O. Box 29, Auckland (☎ **09/359-6655**).

INSURANCE

Although it's not required of travelers, health insurance is highly recommended. Unlike many European countries, the United States does not usually offer free or low-cost medical care to its citizens or visitors. Doctors and hospitals are expensive, and in most cases will require advance payment or proof of coverage before they render their services. Policies can cover everything from the loss or theft of your baggage and trip cancellation to the guarantee of bail in case you're arrested. Good policies will also cover the costs of an accident, repatriation, or death. See "Health & Insurance" in chapter 2 for more information. Packages such as **Europ Assistance** in Europe are sold by automobile clubs and travel agencies at attractive rates. **Worldwide Assistance Services, Inc.** (☎ **800/821-2828**) is the agent for Europ Assistance in the United States.

Though lack of health insurance may prevent you from being admitted to a hospital in non-emergencies, don't worry about being left on a street corner to die: The American way is to fix you now and bill the living daylights out of you later.

For British Travelers   Most big travel agents offer their own insurance and will probably try to sell you their package when you book a holiday. Think before you sign. Insist on seeing the policy and reading the fine print before buying travel insurance. **The Association of British Insurers** (☎ **020/7-600-3333**) gives advice by phone and publishes the free *Holiday Insurance,* a guide to policy provisions and prices. You might also shop around for better deals: Try **Columbus Travel Insurance Ltd.** (☎ **020/7-375-0011**) or, for students, **Campus Travel** (☎ **020/7-730-2101**).

For Canadian Travelers   Canadians should check with their provincial health plan offices or call **HealthCanada** (☎ **613/957-2991**) to find out the extent of their coverage and what documentation and receipts they must take home in case they are treated in the United States.

MONEY

CURRENCY   The U.S. monetary system is painfully simple: The most common bills (all ugly, all green) are the $1 (colloquially, a "buck"), $5, $10, and $20 denominations. There are also $2 bills (seldom encountered), $50 bills, and $100 bills (the last two are usually not welcome as payment for small purchases). Note that a newly redesigned $100 and $50 bill were introduced in 1996, and a redesigned $20 bill in 1998. Expect to see redesigned $10 and $5 notes in the year 2000. Despite rumors to the contrary, the old-style bills are still legal tender.

There are six denominations of coins: 1¢ (1 cent, or a penny); 5¢ (5 cents, or a nickel); 10¢ (10 cents, or a dime); 25¢ (25 cents, or a quarter); 50¢ (50 cents, or a half dollar); and, the rare $1 piece. A new gold $1 piece will be introduced by the year 2000.

The "foreign-exchange bureaus" so common in Europe are rare even at airports in the United States, and nonexistent outside major cities. You'll find them in New York's prime tourist areas like Times Square, but expect to get extorted on the exchange rate. **American Express** (☎ **800/AXP-TRIP;** www.americanexpress.com) has many offices throughout the city, including at the New York Hilton, 1335 Sixth Ave., at 53rd Street (☎ 212/664-7798); the New York Marriott Marquis, 1535 Broadway, in the 8th floor lobby (☎ 212/575-6580); on the mezzanine level at Macy's Herald Square, 34th Street and Broadway (☎ 212/695-8075); and 65 Broadway, between Exchange Place and Rector Street (☎ 212/493-6500). **Thomas Cook Currency Services** (☎ **212/753-0132;** www.thomascook.com) has locations at JFK Airport; 1590 Broadway, at 48th Street (☎ 212/265-6049); 317 Madison Ave., at 42nd Street (☎ 212/883-0040); and 511 Madison Ave., at 53rd St. (☎ 212/753-2398).

It's best not to change foreign money (or traveler's checks denominated in a currency other than U.S. dollars) at a small-town bank, or even a branch in New York or any other American city. In fact, it's best to just leave any currency other than U.S. dollars at home—it may prove a greater nuisance to you than it's worth.

TRAVELER'S CHECKS   Though traveler's checks are widely accepted, make sure that they're denominated in U.S. dollars, as foreign-currency checks are often difficult to exchange. The three traveler's checks that are most widely recognized—and least likely to be denied—are **Visa**, **American Express**, and **Thomas Cook.** Be sure to record the numbers of the checks, and keep that information separately in case they get lost or stolen. Most businesses are pretty good about taking traveler's checks, but you're better off cashing them in at a bank (in small amounts, of course) and paying in cash. Remember: You'll need identification, such as a driver's license or passport, to change a traveler's check.

CREDIT CARDS & ATMs   Credit cards are the most widely used form of payment in the United States: **Visa** (BarclayCard in Britain), **MasterCard** (EuroCard in Europe, Access in Britain, Chargex in Canada), **American Express, Diners Club, Discover,** and **Carte Blanche;** New York vendors may also accept international cards such as **enRoute, EuroCard,** and **JCB,** but not as universally as AmEx, MasterCard, or Visa. There are, however, a handful of stores and restaurants that do not take credit cards, so be sure to ask in advance. Most businesses display a sticker near their entrance to let you know which cards they accept. And be aware that often businesses require a minimum purchase price, usually around $10 or $15, to use a credit card.

It is strongly recommended that you bring at least one major credit card. Hotels, car-rental companies, and airlines usually require a credit-card imprint as a deposit against expenses, and in an emergency a credit card can be priceless.

You'll find **automated teller machines (ATMs)** on just about every block in Manhattan. Some ATMs will allow you to draw U.S. currency against your bank and credit

---
Travel Tip

Be sure to keep a copy of all your travel papers separate from your wallet or purse, and leave a copy with someone at home should you need it faxed in an emergency.

---

cards. Check with your bank before leaving home, and remember that you will need your personal identification number (PIN) to do so. Most accept Visa, MasterCard, and American Express, as well as ATM cards from other U.S. banks. Expect to be charged up to $3 per transaction, however, if you're not using your own bank's ATM.

SAFETY

Tourist areas in Manhattan are generally safe, and the city has experienced a dramatic drop in its crime rate in recent years. Still, crime is a national problem, and U.S. urban areas tend to be less safe than those in Europe or Japan. You should always stay alert, use common sense, and trust your instincts. If you feel you're in an unsafe area or situation, you probably are and should leave as quickly as possible.

GENERAL SAFETY SUGGESTIONS   Leave your valuables at home if you can live without them. Don't display expensive cameras, flashy jewelry, or electronic equipment as you walk around the city. If you are using a map, consult it as discreetly as possible, with one eye on what's going on around you at all times. Hold your pocketbook across your shoulder and in front of you at all times, and place your billfold in an inside pocket. In theaters, restaurants, subways, and other public places, keep a hand on your possessions at all times. Put your purse at your feet rather than slinging it over the back of a chair, where it can be lifted without you knowing it.

Remember also that hotels are open to the public, and in a large hotel, security may not be able to screen everyone entering. Always lock your room door—don't assume that once inside your hotel you are automatically safe and no longer need to be aware.

Avoid deserted areas, especially at night, and don't go into public parks at night unless there's a concert or similar occasion that will attract a crowd.

For more about personal security in Manhattan, see "Playing It Safe" in chapter 4.

DRIVING   An inviolable rule of thumb for New York: Don't even think of driving within the city (especially not in neighborhoods you don't know). Like many cities, New York has its own arcane rules of the road, confusing one-way streets, incomprehensible street-parking signs, and outrageously expensive parking garages. Public transport—whether buses, subways, or taxis—will get you anywhere you want to go quickly and easily, and that's where you'll be most comfortable.

If you do drive to New York in a rental car, return it as soon as you arrive and rent another when you're ready to leave the city. If you dare to arrive in your own car, park it in a garage and don't take it out again until you leave the city. Always keep your car doors locked. Never leave any packages or valuables in sight, because thieves will break car windows. If someone attempts to rob you or steal your car, don't resist. Report the incident to the police department immediately.

2 Getting to the United States

In addition to the domestic airlines listed in chapter 2, many international carriers serve John F. Kennedy International and Newark airports. **British Airways** (☎ 0345/222-111 in the United Kingdom; www.british-airways.com) has daily service from London as well as direct flights from Manchester and Glasgow. **Virgin Atlantic** (☎ 01293/747-747 in the United Kingdom; www.fly.virgin.com) flies from London's Heathrow to New York.

Canadian readers might book flights on **Air Canada** (☎ 800/776-3000; www. aircanada.ca), which offers direct service from Toronto, Montreal, Ottawa, and other cities, or on **Canadian Airlines** (☎800/426-7000; www.cdair.ca).

Continental (☎ 01293/776-464 in the United Kingdom; www.flycontinental. com) flies to Newark from London, Manchester, Madrid, Paris, and Frankfurt. **Aer Lingus** flies from Dublin and Shannon to New York (☎ 01/844-4747 in Dublin or 061/415-556 in Shannon; www.aerlingus.ie). **TWA** (☎ 800/892-4141 in the United Kingdom; www.twa.com) has nonstop service to New York from Barcelona, Madrid, Milan, Paris, and Rome. **United** (☎ 020/8-990-9900 in the United Kingdom; www.ual.com) serves those cities and London, Amsterdam, Brussels, and Zurich. **American** (☎ 020/8-572-5555 in the United Kingdom; www.americanair.com) flies nonstop from London, Manchester, Paris, Brussels, and Zurich. **Delta** (☎ 0800/ 414-764 in the United Kingdom; www.delta-air.com) flies to New York from most major European cities.

Qantas (☎ 13-12-11 in Australia; www.qantas.com.au) and **Air New Zealand** (☎13-2476 in New Zealand; www.airnewzealand.co.nz) fly to the West Coast and will book you straight through to New York City on a partner airline.

Canadians visiting from Toronto and Montreal can also travel to New York via **Amtrak** (☎ 800/USA-RAIL; www.amtrak.com). For more details on arriving by train, see "Getting There" in chapter 2.

IMMIGRATION AND CUSTOMS CLEARANCE   Visitors arriving by air, no matter what the port of entry, should cultivate patience and resignation before setting foot on U.S. soil. Getting through immigration control may take as long as 2 hours on some days, especially on summer weekends, so be sure to have this guidebook or something else to read. Add the time it takes to clear Customs, and you'll see that you should make a 2- to 3-hour allowance for delays when you plan your connections between international and domestic flights.

In contrast, for the traveler arriving by car or rail from Canada, the border-crossing formalities have been streamlined to the vanishing point. People traveling by air from Canada, Bermuda, and some places in the Caribbean can sometimes clear Customs and Immigration at the point of departure, which is much quicker.

3 Getting Around the United States

If you'll be traveling beyond New York, you'll have to think about how you'd like to get around.

BY PLANE   The United States is a massive country, so the fastest way to cover large distances is by airplane. Some large airlines (for example, Northwest and Delta) offer travelers on their transatlantic or transpacific flights special discount tickets under the name **Visit USA,** allowing mostly one-way travel from one U.S. destination to another at very low prices. These discount tickets must be purchased abroad in conjunction with your international ticket. This system is the best and easiest way to see the United States at low cost. You should obtain information well in advance from your travel agent or the office of the airline concerned, since the conditions attached to these discount tickets can be changed without advance notice.

BY CAR   After airplanes, the most cost-effective, convenient, and comfortable way to travel around the United States is by car. The interstate highway system connects cities and towns all over the country; in addition to these high-speed, limited-access roadways, there's an extensive network of federal, state, and local highways and roads. Some of the national car-rental companies include **Avis** (☎ 800/331-1212), **Budget**

How to Save on International Airfares

The idea of traveling abroad on a budget is something of an oxymoron, especially when pricey New York City is your destination. However, you can reduce the price of a plane ticket by several hundred dollars if you take the time to shop around.

If you're on a tight budget and you're coming from Europe, you might want to consider traveling to New York between January and March. That's when airlines like British Airways and Virgin Atlantic pull out all the stops to fill their post-holiday flights, and fares plummet. Hotels are also suffering the after-Christmas blues, and rooms often go for a relative song.

If you're coming from anywhere overseas, take advantage of APEX (Advance Purchase Excursion) reductions offered by all major U.S. and European carriers year-round. These usually require 7 to 21 days advance booking, cannot be canceled, and may come with significant change fees, but they'll save you hundreds of dollars over full-fare rates. For the best deals, compare fares by calling a number of airlines that serve your departure city and be flexible with your dates and times of travel.

Operated by the ETN (European Travel Network), **Discount Tickets** (www.discount-tickets.com) is a great online source for both regular and discounted airfares to New York and other destinations around the world. You can also use this site to compare rates and book accommodations, car rentals, and tours. Click on SPECIAL OFFERS for the latest package deals.

For more money-saving airline advice, see "Getting There" in chapter 2.

(☎ 800/527-0700), **Dollar** (☎ 800/800-4000), **Hertz** (☎ 800/654-3131), and **National** (☎ 800/227-7368).

To rent a car in the United States you need a valid driver's license, a passport, and a major credit card. The minimum age is usually 25, but some companies will rent to younger people and add a surcharge. It's a good idea to buy maximum insurance coverage unless you're positive your own auto or credit-card insurance is sufficient. All major car-rental agencies have branches in Manhattan; check the Yellow Pages directory under "Automobile Renting" for locations. Rates vary, so it pays to call around. Stick to the major companies (Avis, Budget, Dollar, Enterprise, Hertz, National) because what you might save with smaller companies might not be worth the headache if you have mechanical troubles on the road.

In New York it's sometimes much less expensive to rent a car from a nearby smaller town or from an airport rather than from the city center. You might consider taking the train to a destination outside the city and then renting and returning your car there. Compare the rates—and figure in the transportation costs and inconveniences—before you decide on this option.

If you're planning to buy or borrow a car, automobile-association membership is recommended; see "Fast Facts," below, for details.

BY TRAIN   If you're making a short hop to another East Coast city, such as Boston, Philadelphia, or Washington, D.C., rail is the best way to go. **Amtrak** (☎ **800/ USA-RAIL;** www.amtrak.com) trains leave from New York's Pennsylvania Station, at Seventh Avenue and 34th Street. Although bus travel is available for short hops, it can also be slow and uncomfortable, and no less expensive than the far more luxurious trains.

If you're visiting more than one city, you may want to consider purchasing a **USA Railpass,** available to international visitors only and good for 15 or 30 days of unlimited travel on Amtrak. The pass is available through many foreign travel agents. Prices in 1999 for a 15-day pass are $285 off-peak, $425 peak; a 30-day pass costs $375 off-peak, $535 peak. (With a foreign passport, you can also buy passes at some Amtrak offices in the United States, including New York.) Reservations are generally required and should be made as early as possible.

Fast Facts: For the Foreign Traveler

Also see "Fast Facts: New York City" in chapter 4 for more city-specific information.

Automobile Organizations Auto clubs will supply maps, suggested routes, guidebooks, accident and bail-bond insurance, and emergency road service. The **American Automobile Association (AAA)** (☎ 800/222-4357) is the major auto club in the United States. If you belong to an auto club in your home country, inquire about AAA reciprocity before you leave. AAA is actually an organization of regional auto clubs; so look under "AAA Automobile Club" in the White Pages of the telephone directory. AAA has a nationwide emergency road service telephone number (☎ 800/AAA-HELP).

Business Hours See "Fast Facts: New York City" in chapter 4.

Currency & Currency Exchange See "Money" under "Preparing for Your Trip," above. For the latest market conversion rates, visit **www.cnn.com/travel/currency**.

Drinking Laws The legal age for purchase and consumption of alcoholic beverages is 21; proof of age is required and often requested at bars, nightclubs, and restaurants, so it's always a good idea to bring ID when you go out. Liquor stores, the only retail outlets for wine as well as hard liquor in New York, are closed on Sundays, holidays, and election days while the polls are open. Beer can be purchased in grocery stores and delis all day Monday to Saturday and Sunday after noon.

Do not carry open containers of alcohol in your car or any public area that isn't zoned for alcohol consumption. The police can, and probably will, fine you on the spot. And nothing will ruin your trip faster than getting a citation for DUI ("driving under the influence"), so don't even think about driving while intoxicated.

Electricity Like Canada, the United States uses 110 to 120 volts AC (60 cycles), compared to 220 to 240 volts AC (50 cycles) in most of Europe, Australia, and New Zealand. If your small appliances use 220 to 240 volts, you'll need a 110-volt transformer and a plug adapter with two flat parallel pins to operate them here. Downward converters that change 220–240 volts to 110–120 volts are difficult to find in the United States, so bring one with you.

Embassies/Consulates All embassies are in Washington, D.C. Some countries have consulates in major U.S. cities, and most have a mission to the United Nations in New York City. If your country isn't listed below, call for directory information in Washington, D.C. (☎ 202/555-1212) or visit **www.embassy.org/embassies** for the number of your national embassy.

Australia: Consulate General, 630 Fifth Ave., New York, NY 10111 (☎ 212/351-6500; www.austemb.org). **Canada:** Consulate General, 1251 Ave. of the Americas, New York, NY 10020 (☎ 212/596-1600; www.cdnemb-washdc.org).

Ireland: Consulate General, 345 Park Ave., New York, NY 10154-0037 (☎ 212/319-2555; www.irelandemb.org). **Japan:** Embassy, 2520 Massachusetts Ave. NW, Washington, DC 20008 (☎ 202/238-6700; www.embjapan.org). **New Zealand:** Consulate General, 780 Third Ave., New York, NY 10017 (☎ 212/832-4938; www.emb.com/nzemb). **United Kingdom:** Consulate General, 845 Third Ave., New York, NY 10022 (☎ 212/745-0202).

Emergencies   Call ☎ **911** to report a fire, call the police, or get an ambulance anywhere in the United States. This is a toll-free call (no coins are required at public telephones).

If you have a medical emergency that doesn't require an ambulance, you can walk into a hospital's 24-hour emergency room (usually a separate entrance). For a list of hospitals, see "Fast Facts: New York City" in chapter 4. Because emergency rooms are often crowded and the waits are long, one of the walk-in medical centers listed under "Finding a Doctor" under "Health & Insurance" in chapter 2 might be a better option. Otherwise, call ☎ **212/737-2333,** a referral service available 8am to midnight, for doctors who make house calls. Don't be surprised if the first question you are asked is, "Do you have medical insurance?"

Gasoline (Petrol)   Petrol is known as gasoline (or simply "gas") in the United States, and petrol stations are known as both gas stations and service stations. Gasoline costs about half as much here as it does in Europe (about $1.05 per gallon at press time), and taxes are already included in the printed price. One U.S. gallon equals 3.8 liters or .85 Imperial gallons.

Holidays   Banks, government offices, post offices, and many stores, restaurants, and museums are closed on the following legal national holidays: January 1 (New Year's Day), the third Monday in January (Martin Luther King Day), the third Monday in February (Presidents' Day, Washington's Birthday), the last Monday in May (Memorial Day), July 4 (Independence Day), the first Monday in September (Labor Day), the second Monday in October (Columbus Day), November 11 (Veterans Day/Armistice Day), the fourth Thursday in November (Thanksgiving Day), and December 25 (Christmas). Also, the Tuesday following the first Monday in November is Election Day and is a federal government holiday in presidential-election years (held every four years, and next in 2000).

Legal Aid   The foreign tourist will probably never become involved with the American legal system. If you are stopped for a minor infraction (for example, speeding), never attempt to pay the fine directly to a police officer; this could be construed as attempted bribery, a much more serious crime. If it's a traffic infraction, do not get out of the car; stay seated, with your hands on the steering wheel until the officer approaches you. Pay fines by mail, or in person to the clerk of the court. If accused of a more serious offense, say and do nothing before consulting a lawyer. Here the burden is on the state to prove a person's guilt beyond a reasonable doubt, and everyone has the right to remain silent, whether he or she is suspected of a crime or actually arrested. Once arrested, a person can make one telephone call to a party of his or her choice. Call your embassy or consulate.

Mail   If you aren't sure what your address will be in the United States, mail can be sent to you, in your name, c/o General Delivery at the main post office in New York City, at Eighth Avenue between 31st and 33rd streets, which is open 24 hours. To receive general-delivery mail in New York City, call ☎ **212/330-3099.** The addressee must pick up mail in person and must produce proof of identity (driver's license, passport, and so on). Most post offices will hold your mail for up to 1 month.

Generally found at intersections, mailboxes are blue with a red-and-white stripe and carry the inscription U.S. MAIL. If your mail is addressed to a U.S. destination, don't forget to add the five-digit postal code (or Zip code), after the two-letter abbreviation of the state to which the mail is addressed.

At press time domestic postage rates were 20¢ for a postcard and 33¢ for a letter. For international mail, a first-class letter of up to one-half ounce costs 60¢ (46¢ to Canada and 40¢ to Mexico); a first-class postcard costs 50¢ (40¢ to Canada and 35¢ Mexico); and a preprinted postal aerogramme costs 50¢. **www.usps.gov** has complete U.S. postal information, or call ☎ **800/275-8777** for information on the nearest post office. Most branches are open Monday to Friday from 8am to 5 or 6pm, and Saturday from 9am to 3pm.

Newspapers/Magazines In addition to the *New York Times* and other city papers, many newsstands in New York City carry a selection of international newspapers and magazines. For nearly all major newspapers and magazines from around the world, head to **Universal News & Magazines,** 977 Eighth Ave., at 57th Street (☎ **212/459-0932**), or **Hotalings News Agency,** 142 W. 42nd St., between Broadway and Sixth Avenue (☎ **212/840-1868**).

Taxes In the United States there is no value-added tax (VAT) or other indirect tax at the national level. Every state, county, and city has the right to levy its own local tax on all purchases, including hotel and restaurant checks, airline tickets, and so on. Sales tax is usually not included in the price tags on merchandise but is added at the cash register. These taxes aren't refundable. In New York City, the **sales tax** is 8.25%, but there has been talk of reducing or eliminating it. The **hotel tax** is 13.25% plus $2 per room per night (including sales tax). The **parking garage tax,** added to already high basic fees, is 18.25%.

Telephone, Telegraph, Telex & Fax The telephone system in the United States is run by private corporations, so rates, especially for long-distance service and operator-assisted calls, can vary widely. Generally, hotel surcharges on long-distance and local calls are astronomical, so you're usually better off using a **public pay telephone,** which you'll find in most public buildings and private establishments as well as on the street. Convenience grocery stores and gas stations always have them. Many convenience groceries and packaging services sell **prepaid calling cards** in denominations up to $50; these can be the least expensive way to call home. Many public phones at airports now accept American Express, MasterCard, and Visa credit cards. **Local calls** made from public pay phones usually cost 25¢ for the first five minutes, but sometimes it's 35¢. Pay phones do not accept pennies, and few will take anything larger than a quarter.

In New York, I advise caution when using pay phones. In fact, I use only pay phones bearing the distinctive green-and-blue **Bell Atlantic** logo, or the sleek new multimedia phone booths from **AT&T,** another reliable company. Many other phones belong to unscrupulous companies that provide bad service and charge unconscionably high rates.

Most long-distance and international calls can be dialed directly from any phone. **For calls within the United States and to Canada,** dial 1 followed by the area code and the seven-digit number. **For other international calls,** dial 011 followed by the country code, city code, and the telephone number of the person you are calling. Often the city code is preceded by a "zero." This should be dropped when calling from another country. Some country and city codes are as follows: **Australia** 61, Melbourne 3, Sydney 2; **Ireland** 353, Dublin 1; **New**

Zealand 64, Auckland 9, Wellington 4; **United Kingdom** 44, Belfast 232, Birmingham 21, Glasgow 41, London 20. If you're calling the **United States** from another country, the country code is 1.

For **reversed-charge, collect, operator-assisted, and person-to-person calls,** dial 0 (zero, not the letter O) followed by the area code and number you want; an operator will then come on the line, and you should specify that you are calling collect, or person-to-person, or both. If your operator-assisted call is international, ask for the overseas operator.

For **local directory assistance** ("Information"), dial 411; for long-distance information, dial 1, then the appropriate area code and 555-1212.

Most hotels have **fax machines** available for guest use (be sure to ask about the charge to use it), and many hotel rooms are even wired for guests' fax machines. A less expensive way to send and receive faxes may be at stores such as Mail Boxes Etc., a national chain of packing service shops (look in the Yellow Pages directory under "Packing Services").

Telegraph and telex services are provided primarily by Western Union. You can bring your telegram into the nearest Western Union office (there are hundreds across the country) or dictate it over the phone (☎ **800/325-6000**). You can also telegraph money or have it telegraphed to you very quickly over the Western Union system, but this service can cost as much as 15% to 20% of the amount sent.

There are two kinds of telephone directories in the United States. The so-called **White Pages** list private households and business subscribers in alphabetic order. The inside front cover lists emergency numbers for police, fire, ambulance, the Coast Guard, poison-control center, crime-victims hotline, and so on. The first few pages will tell you how to make long-distance and international calls, complete with country codes and area codes. Government numbers are usually printed on blue paper within the White Pages. Printed on yellow paper, the so-called **Yellow Pages** list all local services, businesses, industries, and houses of worship according to activity with an index at the front or back. (Drugstores/pharmacies and restaurants are also listed by geographic location.) The Yellow Pages also include city plans or detailed area maps, postal Zip codes, and public transportation routes. A useful online Yellow Pages for finding phone numbers and addresses in New York and other U.S. cities is **www.yp.ameritech.net**.

Time The continental United States is divided into **four time zones:** eastern standard time (EST), the zone New York is in, which is five hours behind Greenwich Mean Time (GMT); central standard time (CST); mountain standard time (MST); and Pacific standard time (PST). Alaska and Hawaii have their own zones. For example, noon in New York City (EST) is 11am in Chicago (CST), 10am in Denver (MST), 9am in Los Angeles (PST), 8am in Anchorage (AST), and 7am in Honolulu (HST).

Money-Saving Travel Tip

Calls to area codes **800, 888,** and **877** are toll-free. However, calls to numbers in area codes **700** and **900** (chat lines, bulletin boards, "dating" services, and so on) can be very expensive—usually a charge of 95¢ to $3 or more per minute, and they sometimes have minimum charges that can run as high as $15 or more. Your best bet is to avoid them altogether.

Daylight saving time is in effect from 1am on the first Sunday in April through 1am the last Sunday in October, except in Arizona, Hawaii, part of Indiana, and Puerto Rico. Daylight saving time moves the clock 1 hour ahead of standard time. When daylight saving time is in effect, New York is only 4 hours behind Greenwich Mean Time.

For the correct local time in New York, dial ☎ 212/976-1616.

Tipping   Tips are a very important part of certain workers' salaries, so it's necessary to leave appropriate gratuities. Unlike in most of Europe, tips aren't automatically added to restaurant and hotel bills. **In restaurants,** tipping the waitperson 15% to 20% of the total check is customary (in New York City, just double the 8.25% tax to figure the appropriate tip).

Other tipping guidelines: 15% to 20% of the fare to taxi drivers, 10% to 15% of the tab to bartenders, $1 to $2 per bag to bellhops, $1 to $2 per day to hotel maids (more if you've made a big mess), $1 per item to checkroom attendants, $1 to valet parking attendants, and 15% to 20% to hairdressers. Tipping theater ushers, gas-station attendants, and cafeteria and fast-food restaurant employees isn't expected.

Toilets   In general, you won't find public toilets or "rest rooms" on the streets in New York, but they can be found in hotel lobbies, bars, restaurants, museums, department stores, or railway and bus stations. See "Rest Rooms" under "Fast Facts: New York City" in chapter 4.

Traveler's Assistance   See "Fast Facts: New York City" in chapter 4.

Getting to Know New York City

This chapter gives you an insider's take on Manhattan's most distinctive neighborhoods and streets, tells you how to get around town, and serves as a handy reference to everything from personal safety to libraries and liquor laws.

1 Orientation

VISITOR INFORMATION

INFORMATION OFFICES Here are convenient addresses where you can collect free details about the city:

✪ The **Times Square Visitors Center,** 1560 Broadway, between 46th and 47th streets (where Broadway meets Seventh Ave.), across from the TKTS booth (☎ **212/768-1560;** www.timessquarebid.org), is the city's top info stop. Run by the Times Square Business Improvement District and occupying the renovated 1925 Embassy Theatre, this center features a helpful information desk offering loads of citywide information. There's also a tour desk selling tickets for Gray Line bus tours and Circle Line boat tours; a Metropolitan Transportation Authority (MTA) desk staffed to sell MetroCards, provide free public transit maps, and answer all of your questions on the transit system; a Broadway Ticket Center providing show information and selling full-price show tickets (although we suggest you get your tickets across the street from the discount TKTS booth or directly at the box office); ATMs and currency exchange machines; computer terminals with free Internet access, courtesy of Yahoo; an international newsstand; and more. It's open daily from 8am to 8pm.

• At press time, the New York Convention and Visitors Bureau had just opened the **NYCVB Visitor Information Center** at 810 Seventh Ave., between 52nd and 53rd streets. In addition to loads of information on citywide attractions and a multilingual information counselor on hand to answer questions, the center also has interactive terminals that provide free touch-screen access to visitor information via Citysearch and sell advance tickets to major attractions (which can save you from standing in long ticket lines once you arrive). There's also an ATM, a gift shop, and a bank of phones that connect you directly with American Express cardmember services. The center is open Monday through Friday from 8:30am to 5:30pm, Saturday and Sunday from 9am to

5pm. For over-the-phone assistance, call ☎ **212/484-1222** weekdays from 9am to 5pm EST.

- **Grand Central Partnership,** at Grand Central Terminal, East 42nd Street at the corner of Vanderbilt Avenue (☎ **212/818-1777**). There's an information window inside the newly restored Grand Central Terminal and a cart out front, open Monday to Friday 8:30am to 6:30pm and Saturday and Sunday 9am to 6pm.
- **34th Street Partnership,** in Penn Station, Seventh Avenue between 31st and 33rd streets (☎ **212/868-0521**). This window is open Monday to Friday 8:30am to 5:30pm and Saturday and Sunday 9am to 6pm. The group also maintains carts at the Empire State Building (year-round), Fifth Avenue and 34th Street; outside Madison Square Garden, Seventh Avenue at 32nd Street (except when it's colder than 30°F outside); and in Greeley Square, 32nd Street where Broadway and Sixth Avenue cross (summer only). The carts are open from 9:15am to 4:45pm.
- **Lower East Side Business Improvement District,** 261 Broome St., between Orchard and Allen streets (☎ **888/VALUES-4-U** or 212/226-9010). The Lower East Side's Visitor Center is open Sunday through Friday from 10am to 4pm. Stop in for a free Orchard Street Bargain District shopping guide (which they can also send you in advance), plus other neighborhood information. They also have public rest rooms.

PUBLICATIONS   For comprehensive listings of films, concerts, performances, theaters, operas, ballets, sporting events, museum and gallery exhibits, street fairs, and special events, there are many local publications to choose from. The following are your best bets:

The *New York Times* (www.nytimes.com) features terrific arts and entertainment coverage, particularly in the two-part Friday "Weekend" section and the Sunday "Arts & Leisure" section. Both days boast full guides to the latest happenings in Broadway and off-Broadway theater, classical music, dance, pop and jazz, film, and the art world. Friday is particularly good for cabaret, family fun, and general-interest recreational and sightseeing events.

Time Out New York (www.timeoutny.citysearch.com) is my favorite weekly magazine. Dedicated to weekly goings-on, it's attractive, well organized, and easy to use. *TONY* features excellent coverage in all categories, from live music, theater, and clubs (gay and straight) to museum shows, dance events, book and poetry readings, and kids' stuff. The regular "Check Out" section, unequaled in any other listings magazine, will fill you in on upcoming sample and closeout sales, crafts and antiques shows, and other shopping-related scoop. A new issue hits newsstands every Thursday.

The free weekly *Village Voice* (www.villagevoice.com), the city's legendary alterna-paper, is available late Tuesday downtown and early Wednesday in the rest of the city. From classical music to clubs, the arts and entertainment coverage couldn't be more extensive, and just about every live music venue advertises its shows here. But I find the paper a bit unwieldy to navigate, and the tone of its features can be tiresome.

Other useful weekly rags with city information and events listings include the glossy *New York* magazine (www.newyorkmag.com), whose "Cue" section is a selective guide to city arts and entertainment; the *New Yorker,* which features an artsy "Goings On About Town" section at the front of the magazine; and the alternative *New York Press* newspaper, available free around Manhattan. Monthly *Paper* (www.papermag.com) is a glossy alterna-mag that's serves as good prep for those of you who want to experience the hipper side of the city.

The New York Tabloids Revealed!

Welcome to a world where New Yorkers live in "nabes" (neighborhoods), and express outrage over "slays" (murders). Mayor Rudolph Giuliani is "Rudy," or "Hizzoner" (New York-ese for "His Honor"); President Clinton becomes "Prez" or "Bill"; and Michael Jackson is *only ever* "Jacko," "Jax," or often, "Wacko Jacko."

This is the world according to our tabloids. Presently, the nearly 200-year-old *New York Post* dukes it out with the *Daily News* for the city's readership. It's a long-standing battle, and they pull no punches.

Take for example, the headlines. Everyone has his favorite. Who can forget, during the 1976 budget crisis, FORD TO CITY: DROP DEAD? And the *New York Post* headline that is now so famous you can buy it on a t-shirt: HEADLESS BODY IN TOPLESS BAR. No subject is too prurient (WHAM! BAM! GEORGE SAYS HE'S *TRES* GAY, after George Michael's bathroom escapade), no crime too heinous (DAD'S DEATH NOTE TO KIDS: MOM'S IN THE FREEZER"), no tale too tragic (when preparations for Diana's funeral hit a snag, the *Post* trumpeted, CHUCK TO QUEEN'S STAFFER: STUFF IT!). Sometimes the patently irreverent results elicit a giggle (ICY HILL GIVES BILL A CHILL, regarding the mood of the First Marriage), sometimes a groan (CLOSE BUT NO CIGAR, after Clinton's acquittal), sometimes a puzzled frown (The Michael Jackson–Lisa Marie Presley divorce became, inexplicably, LISA NIXED MA ROLE, SO JAX SPLIT).

The papers' strength lies in their zeal to uncover what it is that makes this city great/terrifying/hilarious—a populist local focus the cerebral *New York Times* sacrifices in order to be the "paper of record." Nothing makes a tabloid editor salivate like the chance to champion The Little Guy, right The Egregious Wrong, or cackle over The Blatant Stupidity.

Case in point: the city, inexplicably, places a fire hydrant 5 feet into a Bronx street months before widening the sidewalk. The offending item is splashed across the front page of the *Daily News,* along with a pithy, one-word headline (DUH!). Next day, the hydrant's back on the curb where it belongs. They're loud. They're obnoxious. But they get results.

Critics bemoan today's in-your-face sensationalism, but those who cringe at "trial of the century" coverage like, COPS PUT THE SQUEEZE ON O.J. forget that 50 years earlier, during the Lindbergh Baby Trial, accused kidnapper Bruno Richard Hauptmann routinely faced headlines that screamed his guilt, despite convincing evidence to the contrary. And at the turn of the century, the "yellow journalism" wars between Joseph Pulitzer's *World* and William Randolph Hearst's *Journal* whipped public frenzy over Cuba to such a fever pitch that President William McKinley felt compelled to instigate the Spanish-American War. How's that for the power of the press?

So while I may wince at their tactics, I realize the tabloids are simply a mirror of the city itself. For every stuffy, tea-sipping society dame with her nose buried in the arts pages, you're sure to find a scrappy, beer-drinking, lay-it-on-the-line mensch who "sez" what's on his mind and sticks to his guns.

—*Kelly Regan*

Orientation Tips

I've indicated the cross streets for all destinations in this book, but be sure to ask for the cross street (or avenue) if you're ever calling for an address.

When you're give a taxi driver an address, always specify the cross streets. New Yorkers, even most cab drivers, probably wouldn't know where to find 994 Second Ave., but they do know where to find 51st and Second. If you're heading to the restaurant Le Bernadin, for example, tell them that it's on 51st Street between Sixth and Seventh avenues. The exact number (in this case, no. 155) is given only as a further precision.

If you have only the numbered address on an avenue and need to figure out the cross street, refer to the address locator at the front of the Yellow Pages.

CITY LAYOUT

Open the sheet map that comes free with this book and you'll see the city is comprised of five boroughs: **Manhattan,** where most of the visitor action is; the **Bronx,** the only borough connected to the mainland United States; **Queens,** where Kennedy and La Guardia airports are located and which borders the Atlantic Ocean and occupies part of Long Island; **Brooklyn,** south of Queens, which is also on Long Island and is famed for its attitude, accent, and Atlantic-front Coney Island; and **Staten Island,** the least populous borough, bordering Upper New York Bay on one side and the Atlantic Ocean on the other.

But it is Manhattan, the long finger-shaped island pointing southwest off the mainland—surrounded by the Harlem River to the north, the Hudson River to the west, the East River (really an estuary) to the east, and the fabulous expanse of Upper New York Bay to the south—that most visitors think of when they envision New York. Despite the fact that it's the city's smallest borough (13½ miles long, 2¼ miles wide, 22 square miles in all), Manhattan contains the city's most famous attractions, buildings, and cultural institutions. For that reason, all of the accommodations and most of the restaurants suggested in this book are in Manhattan.

In most of Manhattan, finding your way around is a snap because of the logical, well-executed grid system by which the streets are numbered. If you can discern Uptown and Downtown, and East Side and West Side, you can find your way around pretty easily. In real terms, **Uptown** means north of where you happen to be and **Downtown** means south, although sometimes these labels have vague psychographical meanings (generally speaking, "Uptown" chic versus "Downtown" bohemianism).

Avenues run north–south (Uptown–Downtown). Most are numbered. **Fifth Avenue** divides the East Side from the West Side of town, and serves as the eastern border of Central Park north of 59th Street. **First Avenue** is all the way east and **Twelfth Avenue** is all the way west. The three most important unnumbered avenues on the East Side are between Third and Fifth avenues: **Madison** (east of Fifth), **Park** (east of Madison), and **Lexington** (east of Park, just west of Third). Important unnumbered avenues on the West Side are **Avenue of the Americas,** which all New Yorkers call Sixth Avenue; **Central Park West,** which is Eighth Avenue north of 59th Street as it borders Central Park on the west (hence the name); **Columbus Avenue,** which Ninth Avenue north of 59th Street; and **Amsterdam Avenue,** or Tenth Avenue north of 59th.

Broadway is the exception to the rule—the only major avenue that doesn't run Uptown–Downtown. It cuts a diagonal path across the island, from the northwest tip down to the southeast corner. As it crosses most major avenues, it creates squares (Times Square, Herald Square, Madison Square, and Union Square, for example).

Streets run east–west (crosstown) and are numbered consecutively as they proceed Uptown from Houston Street. So to go Uptown, simply walk north of, or to a higher-numbered street than, where you are. Downtown is south of (or a lower-numbered street than) your current location. If you can see a major landmark like the Empire State Building or the World Trade Center, it's easy to determine Uptown from Downtown if you know what street you are on and remember that the former is on 34th Street and the latter is almost on the southern tip of the island.

As I've already mentioned, Fifth Avenue is the dividing line between the **East Side** and **West Side** of town (except below Washington Square, where Broadway serves that function). On the east side of Fifth Avenue, streets are numbered with the distinction East, on the west side of that avenue they are numbered West. East 51st Street, for example, begins at Fifth Avenue and runs to the East River, and West 51st Street begins at Fifth Avenue and runs to the Hudson River.

If you're looking for a particular address, remember that even-numbered street addresses are on the south side of streets and odd-numbered addresses are on the north. Street addresses increase by about 50 per block starting at Fifth Avenue. For example, nos. 1 to 50 East are just about between Fifth and Madison avenues, while nos. 1 to 50 West are just about between Fifth and Sixth avenues. Traffic generally runs east on even-numbered streets and west on odd-numbered streets, with a few exceptions, like the major east–west thoroughfares—**14th, 23rd, 34th, 42nd, 57th, 72nd, 79th, 86th,** and so on—which have two-way traffic. Therefore 28 W. 23rd St., is a short walk west of Fifth Avenue; 325 E. 35th Street would be a few blocks east of that road.

Avenue addresses are irregular. For example, 994 Second Ave. is at East 51st Street but so is 320 Park Ave. Therefore, it's important to know a building's cross street to find it easily.

Unfortunately, these rules don't apply to neighborhoods in Lower Manhattan, south of 14th Street—the Financial District, Chinatown, SoHo, TriBeCa, the Village—since they sprang up before engineers devised this brilliant grid scheme. A good map is essential when exploring these areas.

STREET MAPS   You'll find a useful pull-out street-by-street map of Manhattan at the back of this book. There's also a decent one available for free as part of the Big Apple Visitors Kit if you write ahead for information (see "Visitor Information" in chapter 2); you can also pick it up for free at most of the visitor centers listed above.

Even with all these freebies at hand, I suggest investing in a map with more features if you really want to zip around the city like a pro. **Hagstrom** maps are terrific because they feature block-by-block street numbering—so instead of trying to guess what the cross street for 125 Prince St. is, you can see right on your map that it's Greene Street. Another great bet is H.M. Gousha's **Fastmap,** which folds in only three places and is laminated. Easy to handle and pack away, it can also be read discreetly, which is a major deterrent to crime. Van Dam's **New York Unfolds,** a pop-up map that unfolds and refolds like an origami flower, serves the same function. Spiral- or staple-bound notebook-size maps are another good idea, but many of these cover all five boroughs, which is probably more information than you need. These and other visitor-friendly maps are available at just about any good bookstore, including the Barnes & Noble and Borders Books & Music branches around town; see "Shopping A to Z" in chapter 8 for locations.

Manhattan's Neighborhoods in Brief

Since they grew up over the course of hundreds of years, all Manhattan neighborhoods have multiple, splintered personalities and fluid boundaries. Still, it's relatively easy to agree upon what they stand for in general terms—so if you stop a New Yorker on the street and ask him to point you to, say, the Upper West Side or the Flatiron District, he'll know where you want to go. From south to north, here is how I've defined Manhattan's neighborhoods for use throughout this book. It's a good idea to refer to the fold-out map in the back of this book as you review this section in order to get your bearings.

DOWNTOWN

Lower Manhattan: South Street Seaport & the Financial District   For hundreds of years, this was New York. Originally established by the Dutch in 1625 (hence the city's original name, Nieuw Amsterdam), the first settlements sprung up here, on the southern tip of Manhattan Island, while everything uptown was farm country and wilderness. All that's changed, but this is still the best place to search for the past. George Washington was first inaugurated president here. **Fraunces Tavern,** on Pearl Street, was the site of countless great moments in city history. (The Wall Street and Financial District walking tour in chapter 7 can guide you through Lower Manhattan's past.) The now-touristy South Street Seaport area is surrounded by reminders of when shipping was the raison d'etre of the city. The **Brooklyn Bridge** stands proudly as the symbol of a new world of engineering marvels that came to the city in the 19th century. Wall Street—now a state of mind much grander than the actual narrow street— dominates the global mindset with the **New York Stock Exchange** and the towering **World Trade Center** (also known as the Twin Towers). Battery Park City is where downtown residents are found, while **Battery Park** itself is your point of departure for the Statue of Liberty, Ellis Island, and Staten Island.

Lower Manhattan constitutes everything south of Chambers Street. Battery Park is on the very south tip, while South Street Seaport a bit north on the east coast (just south of the Brooklyn Bridge). The rest of the area is considered the Financial District, which is anchored by the World Financial Center, the World Trade Center, and Battery Park City to the west, with Wall Street running crosstown to the south. City Hall is at the northern border of the district, abutting Chambers Street (look for City Hall Park on the map). Most of these streets are narrow concrete canyons, with Broadway serving as the main Uptown–Downtown artery. Just about all of the major subway lines congregate here before they either end or head to Brooklyn (the Sixth Ave. B, D, F, Q line being the chief exception—it crosses into Brooklyn from the Lower East Side, over the Manhattan Bridge).

During the week, this neighborhood is the heart of capitalism and city politics, and the sidewalks are crowded with the business-suit set. But despite the fact that some office buildings have been redeveloped into high-end apartments, the neighborhood still feels rather desolate after work and on the weekends. Still, you might consider staying down here on the weekend or during the holidays, when you can find an accommodations bargain in the luxury hotels that business travelers have abandoned for home; for details, see the box called "Getting the Most for Your Money, Part I: Weekend Packages" in chapter 5.

TriBeCa   Bordered by the Hudson River to the west, the area north of Chambers Street, west of Broadway, and south of Canal Street is the *Tri*angle *Be*low *Ca*nal Street, or TriBeCa. Since the 1980s, when SoHo became saturated with chic, the spillover has been quietly transforming TriBeCa into one of the city's hippest residential neighborhoods, where celebrities and families quietly coexist in cast-iron warehouses converted into spacious, expensive loft apartments. Artists' lofts and galleries as well as hip antique and design shops pepper the area, as do some of the city's best (and most expensive) restaurants. Robert DeNiro gave the neighborhood a tremendous boost

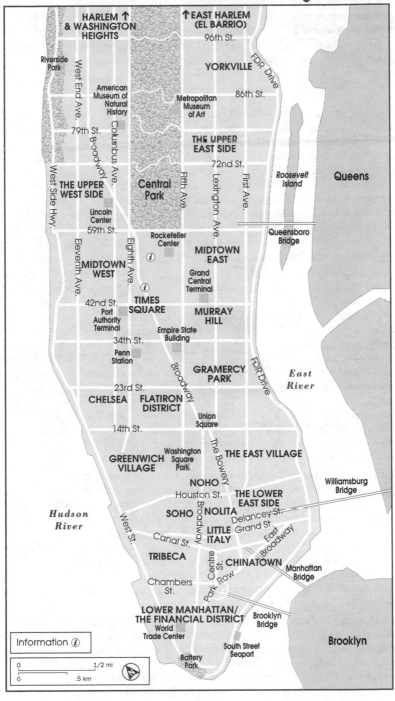

Manhattan Neighborhoods

HARLEM ↑
& WASHINGTON
HEIGHTS

↑EAST HARLEM
(EL BARRIO)

96th St.

Riverside
Park

YORKVILLE

FDR Drive

West End Ave.

86th St.

American
Museum of
Natural
History

Metropolitan
Museum
of Art

79th St.

THE UPPER
EAST SIDE

72nd St.

Broadway

Columbus Ave.

Central
Park

Fifth Ave.

Lexington Ave.

First Ave.

Roosevelt
Island

Queens

West Side Hwy.

THE UPPER
WEST SIDE

Lincoln
Center

59th St.

Queensboro
Bridge

Eighth Ave.

Rockefeller
Center

MIDTOWN
EAST

Eleventh Ave.

MIDTOWN
WEST

Grand
Central
Terminal

42nd St.

Port
Authority
Terminal

TIMES
SQUARE

MURRAY
HILL

34th St.

Empire State
Building

Penn
Station

Broadway

GRAMERCY
PARK

FDR Drive

East
River

23rd St.

CHELSEA

FLATIRON
DISTRICT

Union
Square

14th St.

GREENWICH
VILLAGE

Washington
Square
Park

THE EAST VILLAGE

The Bowery

NOHO

Houston St.

THE LOWER
EAST SIDE

Williamsburg
Bridge

Hudson
River

SOHO

Broadway

NOLITA

Delancey St.

LITTLE
ITALY

Grand St.

West St.

Canal St.

East Broadway

TRIBECA

Park Centre St.

CHINATOWN

Manhattan
Bridge

Chambers
St.

Park Row

LOWER MANHATTAN/
THE FINANCIAL DISTRICT

World
Trade Center

Brooklyn
Bridge

Brooklyn

South Street
Seaport

Information ⓘ

Battery
Park

0   1/2 mi
0   .5 km

Impressions

Can we actually "know" the universe? It's hard enough finding your way around Chinatown.

—Woody Allen

when he established the **Tribeca Film Center,** and Miramax headquarters gave the area further capitalist-chic cachet. Still, historic streets like White (especially the Federal-style building at no. 2) and Harrison (the complete stretch west from Greenwich Street) evoke a bygone, more human-scaled New York, as do a few hold-out businesses and unpretentious, Old World pubs. I love this neighborhood, because it seems to have brought together the old city and the new without bastardizing either. It also happens to be home to one of my favorite budget hotels in the city (see chapter 5). The main Uptown–Downtown drag is West Broadway (2 blocks to the west of Broadway), and the main subway line is the 1/9, which stops at Franklin in the heart of TriBeCa. Take your map; the streets are a maze.

Chinatown　New York City's most famous ethnic enclave is bursting past its traditional boundaries and encroaching on Little Italy, much to the chagrin of civic fathers there. The former marshlands northeast of City Hall and below Canal Street, from Broadway to the Bowery, are where Chinese immigrants arriving from San Francisco were forced in the 1870s. This booming neighborhood is now a conglomeration of Asian populations. As such, it offers tasty cheap eats from Szechuan to Hunan, Cantonese to Fujian, Vietnamese to Thai. Exotic shops offer strange foods, herbs, and souvenirs. Bargains on clothing and leather are plenty. The area is also home to sweatshops, however, and doesn't have quite the quaint character you'd find in San Francisco. Still, walking down Canal Street, peering into the myriad electronics and luggage stores and watching crabs cut loose from their handlers at the exotic fish markets, is some of the city's best free entertainment. The Grand Street (B, D, Q) and Canal Street (J, M, Z, N, R, 6) stations will get you to the heart of the action. The streets are crowded during the day and empty out after around 9pm; they remain quite safe, but the neighborhood is more enjoyable during the bustle.

Little Italy　Little Italy is just as ethnic and culinarily compelling as Chinatown to the south, but it's not quite as vibrant. Traditionally the area east of Broadway between Houston and Canal streets, these days the shrinking community is limited mainly to **Mulberry Street,** where you'll find the majority of restaurants, and a just few offshoots thanks to the encroachment of thriving Chinatown. With rents going up in the increasingly trendy Lower East Side, a few chic spots are moving in as well, further intruding upon the Old World landscape. To reach Little Italy, your best bet is to walk up Mulberry Street from the Grand Street Station, or east from the Spring Street Station on the no. 6 line. September is a great time to visit, when Mulberry Street comes alive during the **Feast of San Gennaro.**

The Lower East Side　In 1894, the 4 square miles that made up the Lower East Side were the most densely populated on earth. Of all the successive waves of immigrants and refugees who passed through here from the mid-19th century to the 1920s, it was the Eastern European Jews who left the most lasting impression on the neighborhood, which runs between Houston and Canal streets, east of the Bowery.

Drugs and crime ultimately supplanted the Jewish communities that first popped up here, dragging the Lower East Side into the gutter until recently. While the Lower East Side has been gentrifying over the last few years—lots of hip bars and clubs have sprung up, prompting complaints from long-standing residents who seem to have preferred the desolation and crime of the old days—the area can still be very dicey in spots. Stick with the crowd and avoid desolate streets late at night. There are some remnants of what was once the largest Jewish population in America along Orchard Street, where you'll find great bargain hunting in its many fabric and clothing stores. There's a good visitor center, where you can get your bearings and pick up a shopping guide, just around the corner from **Orchard Street** at 261 Broome St. Keep in mind that as an Orthodox Jewish community, many places (including the visitor center) close early on Friday afternoon and all day on Saturday (the Sabbath). The trendy set can be found mostly along **Ludlow Street** north of Delancey, especially just south of Houston. This area is not well served by the subway system (one cause for its years of decline), so your best bet is to take the F train to Second Avenue and walk east on Houston; when you see Katz's Deli, you'll know you've arrived.

SoHo & NoLiTa   No relation to the London neighborhood of the same name, SoHo is an abbreviation of "South of Houston Street" (pronounced *house*-ton). This super-fashionable neighborhood extends down to Canal Street, between Sixth Avenue to the west and Lafayette Street (one block east of Broadway) to the east.

An industrial zone during the 19th century, SoHo retains the impressive cast-iron architecture of the era, and in many places, cobblestone peeks out from beneath the street's asphalt. In the early 1960s, cutting-edge artists began occupying the drab and deteriorating buildings, soon turning it into the trendiest neighborhood in the city. SoHo is now a prime example of urban gentrification and a major New York attraction thanks to its impeccably restored buildings, influential arts scene, fashionable restaurants, and stylish boutiques. On weekends, the cobbled streets and narrow sidewalks are crowded with gallery goers and shoppers; the prime action is between Broadway and Sullivan Street north of Grand Street.

Some critics claim that SoHo is becoming a victim of its own popularity—witness the recent departure of several imaginative galleries and independent boutiques to TriBeCa and Chelsea as well as the influx of suburban mall–style stores like J. Crew, Victoria's Secret, and Smith & Hawken. However, SoHo is still one of the best shopping neighborhoods in the city, with everything from pricey boutiques to high-end street peddlers. At night, the neighborhood is transformed into a terrific, albeit pricey, dining and bar-hopping neighborhood (although I recommend some appealing and affordable options, too; see chapter 6). The neighborhood is easily accessible by subway: take the B, D, F, or Q train to the Broadway–Lafayette stop; the N, R to the Prince Street Station; or the C, E to Spring Street.

In recent years SoHo has been crawling its way east, taking over Mott and Mulberry streets—and white-hot Elizabeth Street in particular—north of Kenmare Street, an area now known as **NoLiTa** for its *No*rth of *Li*ttle *Ita*ly location. NoLiTa is becoming increasingly well known for its hot shopping prospects. Some of the city's most promising young clothing designers have taken up residence here, but don't expect bargains. Good, affordable restaurants abound, though, making the neighborhood well worth a browse. Taking the 6 to Spring Street will get you closest by subway, but it's just a short walk east from SoHo proper.

Impressions

Nobody's going to come from the boondocks anymore and live in SoHo and be an artist. You can't afford to park there, let alone live there.

—Pete Hamill

| **Free Touring Tip** |

If you're looking to tour a specific neighborhood with an expert guide, call **Big Apple Greeter** (☎ **212/669-8159;** www.bigapplegreeter.org), preferably at least 1 week ahead of your arrival. It's a non-profit organization of specially trained New Yorkers who volunteer to take visitors around town for a free 2 to 4–hour tour of a particular neighborhood. And they say New York isn't friendly! The office is open Monday to Friday 10am to 5:30pm.

The East Village & NoHo   The **East Village,** which extends between 14th Street and Houston Street, from Broadway east to First Avenue and beyond to avenues A, B, C, and D, is where the city's real Bohemia has gone. Once, flower children tripped along **St. Mark's Place** and listened to music at the Fillmore East; now the East Village is a fascinating mix of some of the city's best wallet-friendly restaurants; upstart clothing designers and kitschy boutiques offering affordable, one-of-a-kind fashions and souvenirs; punk-rock clubs (yep, still) and folk cafes; plus a half-dozen or so off-Broadway theaters—all of which give the neighborhood a youthful vibe and a low-budget appeal for both visitors and locals with limited resources.

The gentrification that has swept the city has made a huge impact on the East Village, but there's still a seedy element that some of you won't like. Now yuppies and other ladder-climbing types make their homes alongside Old World Russian immigrants who have lived in the neighborhood forever, and the cross-dressers, squatters, and artists who settled here in between. The neighborhood still embraces great ethnic diversity, with strong elements of its Ukrainian and Irish heritage, while more recent immigrants have taken over Sixth Street between First and Second avenues, turning it into a haven of cheap eats known as Little India.

The East Village isn't very accessible by subway; unless you're traveling along 14th Street (the L line will drop you off at Third and First avenues), your best bet is to take the N, R to 8th Street or the 6 to Astor Place and walk east. Always stay alert in the East Village. The landscape changes from one block to the next, especially the farther east you go. Venture only with care into Alphabet City (avenues A, B, C, and D)—while the neighborhood has improved dramatically in recent years, drug dealers still peddle openly and some streets can be dangerous.

The southwestern section, around Broadway and Lafayette between Bleecker and 4th streets, is called **NoHo** (for *No*rth of *Ho*uston), and has a completely different character. As you might have guessed from its name, this area is more in tune to its neighbor to the south, SoHo. Here you'll find a growing crop of trendy lounges, stylish restaurants, cutting-edge designers, and upscale antiques shops. NoHo is pricey but wonderful fun to browse; the Bleecker Street stop on the no. 6 line will land you right in the heart of it, and the Broadway-Lafayette stop on B, D, F, Q lines will drop you right at its edge.

Greenwich Village   Tree-lined streets crisscross and wind, following ancient streams and cow paths. Each block reveals yet another row of Greek-Revival town houses, a well-preserved Federal-style house, or a peaceful courtyard or square. This is "the Village," from Broadway west to the Hudson River, bordered by Houston Street to the south and 14th Street to the north. It defies Manhattan's orderly grid system and unless you live here it may be impossible to master the lay of the land—so be sure to have a map on hand as you explore. The Seventh Avenue line (1, 2, 3, 9) is the area's main subway artery, while the West 4th Street stop (where the A, C, E lines meet the B, D, F, Q lines), serves as its central hub.

It was 19th-century artists like Mark Twain, Edgar Allan Poe, Henry James, and Winslow Homer who first gave the Village its reputation for embracing the unconventional. This reputation flourished as later generations of groundbreaking artists, literary giants, and radical thinkers claimed the Village as their own. (To learn more about the Village's literary and counterculture past, take the walking tour in chapter 7.)

Gentrification and escalating land values have conspired to push out the artistic element, but culture and counterculture still rub shoulders in cafes, internationally renowned jazz clubs, neighborhood bars, off-Broadway theaters, and an endless variety of tiny shops and restaurants. The Village is probably the most chameleon-like of Manhattan's neighborhoods; indeed, it changes faces depending on what block you're on. Some of the highest-priced real estate in the city runs along lower Fifth Avenue, which dead-ends at **Washington Square Park.** Serpentine **Bleecker Street** stretches through most of the neighborhood, and is emblematic of the area's historical bent. A tolerant, anything-goes attitude has fostered a large gay community, which is still largely in evidence around **Christopher Street** and Sheridan Square. The streets west of Seventh Avenue, an area known as the **West Village,** boast a more relaxed vibe and some of the city's most charming and historic brownstones. Three colleges—New York University, Parsons School of Design, and the New School for Social Research—keep the area thinking young—hence the popularity of Eighth Street, lined with shops selling cheap, hip clothes to bridge-and-tunnel kids and the college crowd.

With a few charming and affordable hotels on hand, the Village makes a great base for independent-minded visitors who prefer to avoid more touristy areas in favor of a quirkier, more residential view of the city.

Village streets are often crowded with weekend warriors and teenagers, especially on Bleecker, West 4th, 8th, and surrounding streets, so keep an eye on your wallet when navigating the weekend throngs. Washington Square Park was cleaned up a couple of years back, but there's never any telling when the dealers will be back, so stay away after dark.

MIDTOWN

Chelsea   This neighborhood is coming on strong of late as a hip address, especially for the gay community. A low-rise composite of town houses, tenements, lofts, and factories, Chelsea roughly comprises the area west of Sixth Avenue from 14th to 30th streets. (Sixth Ave. itself below 23rd St. is actually considered part of the Flatiron District; see below). Its main arteries are Seventh and Eighth avenues, and it's primarily served by the C, E and 1, 9 subway lines. The Chelsea Piers sports complex to the far west and a host of shops (both unique boutiques and big names like Williams-Sonoma), well-priced bistros, a handful of new and renovated hotels and inns, and thriving bars along the main drags have contributed to the area's rebirth. Even the Hotel Chelsea—the neighborhood's most famous architectural and literary landmark, where Thomas Wolfe and Arthur Miller wrote, Bob Dylan composed, and Sid Vicious killed girlfriend Nancy Spungeon—has undergone a renovation. You'll find a number of very popular flea markets set up in parking lots along Sixth Avenue, between 24th and 27th streets, on the weekends.

One of the most influential trends in Chelsea has been the establishment of a **"gallery row"** on far West 22nd Street and its vicinity; this is where you'll find the cutting edge of today's New York art scene. The neighborhood is also home to the Joyce Theater, New York's principal modern-dance venue.

The Flatiron District, Union Square & Gramercy Park   These adjoining and at places overlapping neighborhoods are some of the city's most appealing. Dotted with four small historic parks (Union Square, Gramercy, Madison Square, and Stuyvesant), their streets have been rediscovered by New Yorkers and visitors alike thanks to great shopping and dining opportunities. The commercial spaces are often large loft-like expanses with witty designs and graceful columns.

The **Flatiron District** lies south of 23rd Street to 14th Street, between Broadway and Sixth Avenue, and centers around the historic Flatiron Building on 23rd (so named for its triangular shape) and Park Avenue South, which has become a sophisticated new Restaurant Row. Below 23rd Street along Sixth Avenue mass-market discounters like Filene's Basement, Bed Bath & Beyond, Old Navy, and others have moved in. The shopping gets classier on Fifth Avenue, where you'll find a mix of national names (including Emporio Armani, Kenneth Cole, Banana Republic, and the super-trendy Restoration Hardware) and hip boutiques. Lined with Oriental carpet dealers and high-end fixture stores, Broadway is becoming the city's home-furnishings alley; its crowning jewel is the justifiably famous, and humongous ABC Carpet & Home.

Union Square is the hub of the entire area; the N, R, 4, 5, 6, and L trains stop here, making it easy to reach from most other city neighborhoods. Long in the shadows of the more bustling (Times and Herald) and high-toned (Washington) city squares, Union Square has experienced a major renaissance in the last decade. Local businesses joined forces with the city to rid the park of drug dealers, and now it's a delightful place to spend an afternoon. Union Square is perhaps best known as the setting for New York's premier greenmarket every Monday, Wednesday, Friday, and Saturday, where it's easy to assemble a cheap and healthy picnic. Musical acts often play the small pavilion at the north end of the park, and in-line skaters take over the market space in the after-work hours. A number of hip, mostly affordable restaurants rim the square, as do superstores like Toys 'Я' Us, the city's best Barnes & Noble superstore, a brand-new Virgin Megastore, and an equally infant 14-screen movieplex. The shopping gets dubious along 14th Street, which also becomes rather unsightly as you move away from the square.

From about 16th to 23rd streets, east from Park Avenue South to about Second Avenue, is the leafy, largely residential district known as **Gramercy Park.** The pity of the Gramercy Park district is that so few can enjoy the park of the same name: Built by Samuel Ruggles in the 1830s to attract buyers to his other property in the area, it is the only private park in the city and is locked to all but those who live on its perimeter (the rule is that your windows have to look over the park for you to have a key). Located at the southern endpoint of Lexington Avenue (at 21st St.), it is one of the most peaceful spots in the city. If you know someone who has in, go there. Or better yet, book a room at the splurge-worthy Gramercy Park Hotel, whose guests have park privileges.

At the northern edge of the area, fronting the Flatiron Building on 23rd Street and Fifth Avenue, is another of Manhattan's lovely little parks, **Madison Square.** Across from its northeastern corner once stood Stanford White's original Madison Square Garden (in whose roof garden White was murdered in 1906 by possibly deranged, but definitely jealous, millionaire Harry K. Thaw). It's now majestically presided over by the massive New York Life Insurance Building, the masterful New York State Supreme Court, and the Metropolitan Life Insurance Company.

Times Square & Midtown West   Midtown West, the vast area from 34th to 59th streets west of Fifth Avenue to the Hudson River, encompasses several famous names: Madison Square Garden, the Garment District, Rockefeller Center, the Theater District, and Times Square. This is New York's tourism central, where you'll find the bright lights and bustle that draws people from all over the world. As such, this is also the city's biggest hotel neighborhood, with lots of budget and midpriced choices

I'm opposed to the redevelopment. I think there should be one neighborhood in New York where tourists are afraid to walk.

—Fran Lebowitz on the "new" Times Square

amidst the famous-name luxury hotels. The 1, 2, 3, 9 subway line serves the massive neon station at the heart of Times Square, at 42nd Street between Broadway and Seventh Avenue, while the B, D, F, Q lines run up Sixth Avenue to Rockefeller Center. The N, R lines cuts diagonally across the neighborhood, following the path of Broadway before heading up Seventh Avenue at 42nd Street. The A, C, E line serves the West Side, running along Eighth Avenue.

If you know New York but haven't been here in a few years, you'll be quite surprised by the "new" **Times Square.** Longtime New Yorkers like to kvetch nostalgic about the glory days of the old peep-show-and-porn-shop Times Square that this cleaned-up, Disneyfied one supplanted, but the truth is that it's a hugely successful regentrification. Grand old theaters have come back to life as Broadway and children's playhouses, scores of new family-friendly restaurants and shops have opened (including the terrific Virgin Megastore on Broadway as well as Disney and Warner Bros. studio stores), and plenty of businesses have moved in—MTV studios overlook Times Square at 1515 Broadway, and, taking a key note from the far more successful *Today* show, *Good Morning America* is in the process of launching its own street-facing studio at Broadway and 44th Street, which should be up and running by the time you arrive. The neon lights have never been brighter, and middle America has never been more welcome.

Most of the great Broadway theaters light up the streets just off Times Square, in the West 40s just east and west of Broadway. At the heart of the **Theater District,** where Broadway meets Seventh Avenue, is the TKTS booth, where crowds line up daily to buy discount tickets for tonight's shows.

Unlike neighboring Times Square, gorgeous **Rockefeller Center** needs no renovation. Situated between 46th and 50th streets from Sixth Avenue east to Fifth, this art-deco complex contains some of the city's great architectural gems that house hundreds of offices, a number of NBC studios (including *Saturday Night Live, Late Night with Conan O'Brien,* and the famous glass-walled *Today* show studio at 48th St.), and some pleasing upscale boutiques (attention, shoppers: Saks Fifth Avenue is just on the other side of Fifth). Holiday time is a great time to be here, as ice skaters take over the central plaza and the huge Christmas tree twinkles against the night sky.

Along Seventh Avenue south of 42nd Street is the **Garment District,** of little interest to most visitors except for its sample sales, where some great new fashions are sold cheap to serious bargain hunters willing to scour the racks (see chapter 8 for details). Other than that, it's a pretty grim commercial area. Between Seventh and Eighth avenues and 31st and 33rd streets, Penn Station sits beneath **Madison Square Garden,** where the Rangers and the Knicks play. Taking up all of 34th Street between Sixth and Seventh avenues is Macy's, the world's largest department store; exit Macy's at the southeast corner and you'll find more famous-label shopping around **Herald Square.**

Farther north, despite the presence of grand dame Carnegie Hall, West 57th Street has become a theme restaurant bonanza, with Planet Hollywood (for now, anyway, until it moves to the in-the-works Planet Hollywood Hotel in Times Square), the Harley-Davidson Cafe, the Motown Cafe, Brooklyn Diner USA, and the venerable Hard Rock in residence. There are a good number of hotels in all price categories in this area, and their convenience to Central Park (which starts at 59th St.) is an extra plus.

If you're looking for something a little more culture-rich than an over-priced burger and a logo T-shirt, Midtown West is also home to the Museum of Modern Art, Radio City Music Hall, and the *Intrepid* Sea-Air-Space Museum.

Midtown East & Murray Hill   Midtown East, the area including Fifth Avenue and everything east from 34th to 59th streets, is the more upscale side of the Midtown map. This side of town is short of subway trains, served primarily by the Lexington Avenue 4, 5, 6 line.

Midtown East is where you'll find the city's finest collection of grand hotels, mostly along Lexington Avenue and near the park at the top of Fifth, with a handful of affordable choices dotting the luxury landscape (although far fewer than you'll find in Midtown West). The stretch of Fifth Avenue from Saks at 49th Street extending to FAO Schwarz at 59th is home to the city's most high-profile haute shopping, including Tiffany & Co., Cartier, and Bergdorf Goodman, but more midpriced names like Banana Republic, Ann Taylor, and Liz Claiborne have moved their superstores in of late. The stretch of 57th Street between Fifth and Lexington avenues is also known for high-fashion boutiques (Chanel, Hermès) and high-ticket galleries, but change is underway since Warner Brothers (at the intersection with Fifth), Levi's, and Niketown squeezed in. You'll find plenty of spillover along Madison Avenue, a great strip for shoe shopping in particular, some of it priced for real people.

Magnificent architectural highlights include the recently repolished **Chrysler Building,** with its stylized gargoyles glaring down on passersby; the beaux arts tour de force that is the newly renovated **Grand Central Terminal;** magnificent **St. Patrick's Cathedral;** and the glorious **Empire State Building,** offering oh-so-romantic views from its observation deck.

Far east, swank Sutton and Beekman places are enclaves of beautiful town houses, luxury living, and tiny pocket parks that look out over the East River. The **United Nations,** which isn't officially in New York City, or even the United States, but is on a parcel of international land belonging to member nations, sits along the river.

Claiming the territory east from Madison Avenue, **Murray Hill** begins somewhere north of 23rd Street (the line between it and Gramercy Park is fuzzy), and is most clearly recognizable north of 34th Street to 42nd Street. This residential quarter, lined with lovely brownstones, is largely a quiet residential neighborhood, notable for its handful of good budget and midpriced hotels.

UPTOWN

The Upper West Side   North of 59th Street and encompassing everything west of Central Park, the Upper West Side contains Lincoln Center, arguably the world's premier performing-arts center; the American Museum of Natural History, whose renovated Dinosaur Halls garner justifiably rave reviews; and a number of midpriced hotels whose larger-than-midtown rooms and nice residential location make them particularly good bets for families, or anybody looking for affordable sleeps in an extra-nice neighborhood. Unlike the more stratified Upper East Side, the Upper West Side is home to an egalitarian mix of middle-class yuppiedom, laid-back wealth (lots of celebs and monied media types call the grand apartments along Central Park West home), and ethnic families who have survived gentrification.

The neighborhood runs all the way up to Harlem, around 125th Street, and encompasses Morningside Heights, where you'll find Columbia University and the perennial construction project known as the Cathedral of St. John the Divine. But prime Upper West Side—and the part you're most likely to explore—is the area running from Columbus Circle at 59th Street into the 80s, between the park and

Broadway. North of 59th Street is where Eighth Avenue becomes Central Park West, the eastern border of the neighborhood (and the western border of Central Park); Ninth Avenue becomes Columbus Avenue, lined with attractive boutiques and cafes; and Tenth Avenue becomes Amsterdam Avenue, less appealing than Columbus to the east and less trafficked than bustling Broadway to the west, whose highlights are the gourmet mega-marts Zabar's and Fairway (both great places to assemble a gourmet picnic to enjoy in Central Park). You'll find Lincoln Center at the lower end of the neighborhood, in the mid-60s, where Broadway crosscuts Amsterdam. Two major subway lines service the area: the 1, 2, 3, 9 line runs up Broadway, while the B and C trains run up glamorous Central Park West, stopping right at the historic Dakota apartment building (where John Lennon was shot and Yoko still lives) at 72nd Street, and at the Museum of Natural History at 81st Street.

The Upper East Side North of 59th Street and east of Central Park is some of the most expensive residential real estate in the city—and probably the world. This is New York at its most gentrified: Walk along Fifth and Park avenues, especially between 60th and 80th streets, and you're sure to encounter some of the wizened WASPs and Chanel-suited socialites who make up the most rarefied of the city's population. Madison Avenue to 79th Street is the monied crowd's main shopping strip, recently vaunting ahead of Hong Kong's Causeway Bay to become to most expensive retail real estate *in the world.* This is an area for browsing only, unless you book a room or attend a program at the 92nd Street Y, one of the city's best arts and cultural institutions, particularly for culture vultures with limited budgets (see chapters 5 and 9 for details).

The main attraction of this neighborhood is **Museum Mile,** the stretch of Fifth Avenue fronting Central Park that's home to no fewer than 10 terrific cultural institutions, including Frank Lloyd Wright's Guggenheim, and anchored by the mind-boggling Metropolitan Museum of Art. But the elegant rows of landmark town houses are worth a look alone: East 70th Street, from Madison east to Lexington, is one of the world's most charming residential streets. If you want to see where real people live, move east to Third Avenue and beyond; that's where affordable restaurants and active street life start popping up.

A second subway line is in the works, but it's still no more than an architect's blueprint. For now, the Upper East Side is served solely by the Lexington Avenue line (4, 5, 6 trains), so wear your walking shoes (or bring taxi fare).

Harlem Harlem is really two areas. Harlem proper stretches from river to river, beginning at 125th Street on the West Side and 96th Street on the East Side. **Spanish Harlem** (El Barrio), an enclave east of Fifth Avenue, runs between East 100th and East 125th streets.

Parts of Harlem are benefiting from the same kinds of revitalization that have swept over so much of the city, with national-brand retailers moving in and visitors arriving to tour historical sites related to the Golden Age of African-American culture. In the 1920s and 1930s, great bands like the Count Basie and Duke Ellington orchestras played at the Cotton Club and Sugar Cane Club, and literary giants like Langston Hughes and James Baldwin soaked up the scene. Some of the best brownstone mansions in the city are here, dating back to a time when the area was something of a country retreat. On Sugar Hill (from 143rd St. to 155th St., between St. Nicholas and Edgecombe aves.) and Striver's Row (West 139th St. between Adam Clayton Powell Jr. and Frederick Douglass blvds.) are a significant number of fine town houses. For cultural visits, there's the Morris-Jumel Mansion, the Schomburg Center, the Studio Museum, and the Apollo Theater.

By all means, come see Harlem—it's one of the city's most vital and historic neighborhoods. Intrepid travelers now even have a place to stay in the neighborhood (see chapter 5). But for most visitors, the best bet is to take a guided tour (see chapter 7). Sights tend to be far apart, and neighborhoods change quickly. Don't wander thoughtlessly through Harlem, especially at night.

Washington Heights & Inwood Located at the northern tip of Manhattan, Washington Heights (the area from 155th St. to Dyckman St., with adjacent Inwood running to the tip) is home to a large segment of Manhattan's Latino community. **Fort Tryon Park** and the **Cloisters** are the two big reasons to come up this way. The Cloisters houses the Metropolitan Museum of Art's stunning medieval collection; in a building perched atop a hill, with excellent views across the Hudson to the Palisades. Committed off-the-beaten-path sightseers might also want to visit the Dyckman Farmhouse, a historic jewel built in 1783 and the only remaining Dutch-Colonial structure in Manhattan.

2 Getting Around

Frankly, Manhattan's transportation systems are a marvel. It's simply miraculous that so many people can gather on this little island and move around it. For the most part, you can get where you're going pretty quickly and easily using some combination of subways and buses, with maybe a pricier cab ride here and there if you're traveling in a group or late at night. This section will tell you how to use the city's public systems with the confidence and skill of a native New Yorker.

But between traffic gridlock and subway delays, sometimes you just can't get there from here—unless you walk. Walking can be the fastest way to navigate the island. During rush hours, you'll easily beat car traffic while on foot, as taxis and buses stop and groan at gridlocked corners (don't even *try* going crosstown in a cab or bus in Midtown at midday). You'll also see a whole lot more by walking than you will if you ride beneath the street in the subway or fly by in a cab. So pack your most comfortable shoes and hit the pavement—it's the best, cheapest, and most appealing way to experience the city.

On the Sidewalks

What's the primary means New Yorkers use for getting around town? The subway? Buses? Taxis? Nope. Walking. They stride across wide, crowded pavements without any regard for the light, weaving through crowds at high speeds, dodging taxis and buses whose drivers are forced to interrupt the normal flow of traffic to avoid flattening them. **Never take your walking cues from the locals.** Wait for walk signals, and always use crosswalks—don't cross in the middle of the block. Do otherwise, and you could quickly end up with a jaywalking ticket—or as a statistic.

Always pay attention to the traffic flow. Walk as if you're driving, staying to the right. Pay attention to what's happening in the street, even if you have the right of way. At intersections, keep an eye out for drivers who don't yield, turn without looking, or think yellow means "Hurry up!" as you cross. Unfortunately, most bicyclists seem to think that the traffic laws don't apply to them; they'll often blithely fly through red lights and dash the wrong way on one-way streets, so be on your guard.

For more important safety tips, see "Playing it Safe" later in this chapter.

BY SUBWAY

The much-maligned subway system is the best way to travel around New York. Some 3½ million people a day seem to agree with me, as it's their primary mode of transportation. The subway is quick, inexpensive, relatively safe, and pretty efficient, as well as being a genuine New York experience that you shouldn't miss.

The subway runs 24 hours a day, seven days a week. The rush-hour crushes are roughly from 8am to 9:30am and from 5pm to 6:30pm on weekdays; the rest of the time the trains are relatively uncrowded.

PAYING YOUR WAY The subway fare is $1.50 (half-price for seniors and those with disabilities), and children under 44 inches tall ride free (up to three per adult). **Tokens** still exist (although there is some talk of phasing them out altogether), but most people pay fares these days with the **MetroCard,** a magnetically encoded card that debits the fare when swiped through the turnstile, or the fare box on any city bus. Once you're in the system, you can transfer freely to any subway line that you can reach without exiting your station. MetroCards—not tokens—also allow you **free transfers** between the bus and subway within a 2-hour period.

The MetroCard can be purchased in a few different configurations:

Pay-Per-Ride MetroCards can be used for up to four people by swiping up to four times (bring the whole family). You can put anywhere from $3 (two rides) to $80 on your card. Every time you put $15 on your Pay-Per-Ride MetroCard, it's automatically credited 10%—that's one free ride for every 10 you pay for. You can buy Pay-Per-Ride MetroCards in any denomination at any subway station; an increasing number of stations now have automated MetroCard vending machines, which allow you to buy MetroCards using your major credit card. MetroCards are also available from shops and newsstands around town in $15 and $30 values (with the free ride or rides included). You can refill your card at any time until the expiration date on the card, usually about a year from the date of purchase, at any subway station.

Unlimited-Use MetroCards, which can't be used for more than one person at a time or more frequently than 18-minute intervals, are available in four values: the **daily Fun Pass,** which allows you a day's worth of unlimited subway and bus rides for $4; the **7-Day MetroCard,** for $17; and the **30-Day MetroCard,** for $63. 7- and 30-day Unlimited-Use MetroCards can be purchased at any subway station or a Metro-Card merchant. Fun Passes, however, cannot be purchased at token booths—you can only buy them from a MetroCard merchant or at a station that has a MetroCard vending machine. Unlimited-Use MetroCards go into effect the first time you use them—so if you buy a card on Monday and don't begin to use it until Wednesday, Wednesday is when the clock starts ticking on your MetroCard. A Fun Pass is good from the first time you use it until 3am the next day, while 7- and 30-day MetroCards run out at midnight on the last day. These MetroCards cannot be refilled; you throw the card out once it's been used up and buy a new one.

Tips for using your MetroCard: The MetroCard-swiping mechanisms at turnstiles have been the source of much consternation among subway riders ever since the MetroCard was introduced. If you swipe too fast or too slow, the turnstile will ask you to swipe again. If this happens, do not move to a different turnstile, or you may end up paying twice. If you've tried a bunch of times and really can't make your Metro-Card work, tell the token-booth clerk; chances are good, though, that you'll get the movement down after a couple of uses.

If you're not sure how much money you have left on your MetroCard, or what day it expires, use the station's MetroCard Reader, usually located near the station entrance or the token booth (on buses, the fare box will also provide you with this information).

To locate the nearest MetroCard merchant, or for any other MetroCard questions, call ☎ **212/METROCARD.**

USING THE SYSTEM   As you can see from the full-color subway map on the inside front cover of this book, the subway system basically mimics the lay of the land above ground, with most lines in Manhattan running north and south, like the avenues, and a few lines east and west, like the streets. To go up and down the East Side of Manhattan (and to the Bronx and Brooklyn), take the 4, 5, or 6 train. To travel up and down the West Side (and also to the Bronx and Brooklyn), take the 1, 2, 3, or 9 line; the A, C, E, or F line; or the B or D line. The N and R lines first cut diagonally across town from east to west and then snakes under Seventh Avenue before shooting out to Queens. The crosstown S line, the Shuttle, runs back and forth between Times Square and Grand Central Terminal. Farther Downtown, across 14th Street, the L line works its own crosstown magic.

Lines have assigned colors on subway maps and trains—red for the 1, 2, 3, 9 line; green for 4, 5, 6 trains; and so on—but nobody ever refers to them by color. Always refer to them by number or letter when asking questions. Within Manhattan, the distinction between different numbered trains that share the same line is usually that some are express and others local. Express trains often skip about three stops for each one that they make; express stops are indicated on subway maps with a white (rather than solid) circle. Regular stops usually come about 9 blocks apart.

Directions are almost always indicated using "Uptown" (northbound) and "Downtown" (southbound), so be sure to know what direction you want to head in. The outsides of some subway entrances are marked UPTOWN ONLY or DOWNTOWN ONLY; read carefully, as it's easy to head in the wrong direction. Once you're on the platform, check the signs overhead to make sure that the train you're waiting for will be traveling in the right direction. If you do make a mistake, it's a good idea to wait for an express station, like 14th Street or 42nd Street, so you can get off and change for the other direction without paying again.

The days of graffiti-covered cars are gone, but the stations—and an increasing number of trains—are not nearly as clean as they could be. Trains are air-conditioned

---

For More Bus & Subway Information

For additional transit information, call the **MTA/New York City Transit's Travel Information Center** at ☎ **718/330-1234.** Extensive automated information is available at this number 24 hours a day, and travel agents are on hand to answer your questions and provide directions daily from 6am to 9pm. For online information, visit **www.mta.nyc.ny.us**.

To request free system maps or the *Token Trips Travel Guide* brochure, which gives subway and bus travel directions to more than 120 popular sites, call the **Customer Assistance Line** at ☎ **718/330-3322** (Mon–Fri 9am–5pm). For transit info for riders with disabilities, call the **Accessible Line** at ☎ **718/596-8585** (daily 6am–9pm).

You can get bus and subway maps and additional transit information at most tourist information centers (see "Visitor Information" earlier in this chapter). Maps are sometimes available in subway stations (ask at the token booth), but rarely on buses.

Money-Saving Transit Tips: Free Transfers

If you pay your subway or bus fare with a **MetroCard,** you can freely transfer to another bus or to the subway (or from the subway to a bus) for up to 2 hours. You don't need to do anything special: Just swipe your card at the token box or turnstile, and the automated system keeps track.

If you use a token or coins to board a bus and you expect to transfer to another line, you must request a free **transfer slip** that allows you to change to an intersecting bus route only (legal transfer points are listed on the transfer paper) within 1 hour of issue. Transfer slips cannot be used to enter the subway.

(move to the next car if yours isn't), though during the dog days of summer the platforms can be sweltering. In theory, all subway cars have PA systems to allow you to hear the conductor's announcements, but they don't always work well. It's a good idea to move to a car with a working PA system in case any sudden service changes are announced that you'll want to know about.

For **subway safety tips,** see "Playing It Safe" later in this chapter.

BY BUS

Less expensive than taxis and more pleasant than subways, buses are a good transportation option. They also kill two birds with one stone, since they provide you with a mobile sightseeing window on Manhattan for the price of a ride. Their very big drawback: They can get stuck in traffic, sometimes making it quicker to walk. They also stop every couple of blocks, rather than the 8 or 9 blocks that local subways traverse between stops. So for long distances, the subway is your best bet; but for short distances or traveling crosstown, try the bus.

PAYING YOUR WAY   Like the subway fare, the **bus fare** is $1.50, half-price for seniors and riders with disabilities, free for children under 44 inches (up to three per adult). The fare is payable with a **MetroCard, token** (for now, anyway), or **exact change.** Bus drivers don't make change, and fare boxes don't accept dollar bills or pennies. You can't purchase MetroCards or tokens on the bus, so you'll have to have them before you board; for details, see "Paying Your Way" under "By Subway," above.

USING THE SYSTEM   You can't flag down a city bus—you have to meet it at a bus stop. **Bus stops** are located every 2 or 3 blocks on the right-side corner of the street (facing the direction of traffic flow). They're marked by a curb painted yellow and a blue-and-white sign with a bus emblem and the route number or numbers. Guide-A-Ride boxes at most stops display a route map and a hysterically optimistic schedule.

Almost every major avenue has its own **bus route.** They run either north or south: Downtown on Fifth, Uptown on Madison, Downtown on Lexington, Uptown on Third, and so on. There are **crosstown buses** at strategic locations all around town: 8th Street (eastbound); 9th (westbound); 14th, 23rd, 34th, and 42nd (east- and westbound); 49th (eastbound); 50th (westbound); 57th (east- and westbound); 65th (eastbound across the West Side, through the park, and then north on Madison, continuing east on 68th to York Ave.); 67th (westbound on the East Side to Fifth Ave. and then south on Fifth, continuing west on 66th St. through the park and across the West Side to West End Ave.); 79th, 86th, 96th, 116th, and 125th (east- and westbound). Some bus routes, however, are erratic: The M104, for example, starts at the East River, then turns at Eighth Avenue and goes up Broadway. The buses of the Fifth Avenue line go up Madison or Sixth and follow various routes around the city. Most routes operate 24 hours, but service is infrequent at night. Some say that New York

---

Taxi-Hailing Tips

- When you're waiting on the street for an available taxi, look at the medallion light on the top of the coming cabs. If the light is out, the taxi is in use. When the center part (the number) is lit, the taxi is available—this is when you raise your hand to flag the cab. If all the lights are on, the driver is off duty.
- A taxi can't take more than four people, so expect to split up if your group is larger.

---

buses have a herding instinct: They come only in groups. During rush hour, main routes have "limited" buses, identifiable by the red card in the front window; they stop only at major cross streets.

To make sure the bus you're boarding goes where you're going, check the maps on the bus signs, get your hands on a route map (see "For More Bus & Subway Information," above), or **just ask.** The drivers are helpful, as long as you don't hold up the line too long.

While traveling, look out the window, not only to take in the sights but also to keep track of cross streets so you know when to get off. Signal for a stop by pressing the tape strip above and beside the windows and along the metal straps. Exit through the pneumatic back doors (not the front door) by pushing on the yellow tape strip; the doors open automatically—pushing on the handles is useless unless you're as buffed as Hercules. Most city buses are equipped with wheelchair lifts, making buses the preferable mode of public transportation for wheelchair-bound travelers; for more on this topic, see "Tips for Travelers with Special Needs" in chapter 2. Buses also "kneel," lowering down to the curb to make boarding easier.

BY TAXI

If you don't want to deal with the hustle and bustle of public transportation, finding an address that might be a few blocks from the subway station, or sharing your ride with 3½ million other people, then take a taxi. The biggest advantages are that cabs can be hailed on any street (providing you find an empty one—often simple, at other times nearly impossible) and will take you right to your destination.

Official New York City taxis, licensed by the Taxi and Limousine Commission, are yellow, with the rates printed on the door and a light with a medallion number on the roof. You can hail a taxi on any street. *Never* accept a ride from any other car except an official city yellow cab (private livery cars are not allowed to pick up fares on the street).

However, if you're planning to take extensive advantage of taxis, be prepared to pay. The **base fare** on entering the cab is $2 (a surcharge of 50¢ is added 8pm–6am). The cost is 30¢ for every ⅕ mile or 20¢ per minute in stopped or very slow-moving traffic (or for waiting time). There's no extra charge for each passenger or for luggage. However, you must pay bridge or tunnel tolls. (Sometimes the driver will front the toll and add it to your bill at the end; most times you pay the driver before the toll.) A 15% to 20% tip is customary.

Since it's going to cost you at least $2 just to get in the car, taxis are far more expensive than other forms of public transportation, and can really jack up your expenses quickly. Visitors on a limited travel budget are generally better off relying on subways and buses to get around town, using taxis only late at night (after 11pm or midnight, when buses and subway trains start getting fewer and farther between, and standing at a bus stop or a lonely platform may seem a little daunting), or to reach an out-of-the-way destination (maybe a bar or restaurant on the Lower East Side or the far East Village, neighborhoods not well served by the subway). You'll also get your money's worth out of a taxi at night, when there's little traffic to keep them from speeding you to your destination.

While taxis are generally far more expensive than taking the subway or a bus, consider taking cabs for short hauls if there's three or four in your group. A taxi may not actually save you money, but you'll get door-to-door service for about the same price: It costs four people $6 to take the subway, which is no less than you'd pay for a short taxi ride from Times Square to the West Village, say, or from Carnegie Hall to your Murray Hill hotel. Be aware that at rush hour, though, it still may be more convenient and cheaper to take the subway, since you won't end up stuck in traffic, delayed and paying for unnecessary wait time.

Forget about hopping into the back seat and having some double-chinned, cigar-chomping, all-knowing driver slowly turn and ask nonchalantly, "Where to, Mac?" Nowadays taxi drivers speak only an approximation of English and drive in engagingly exotic ways. Always wear your seat belt—taxis are required to provide them.

The TLC has posted a **Taxi Rider's Bill of Rights** sticker in every cab. Drivers are required by law to take you anywhere in the five boroughs, to Nassau or Westchester counties, or to Newark Airport. They are supposed to know how to get you to any address in Manhattan, and all major points in the outer boroughs. They are also required to provide air-conditioning and turn off the radio on demand, and they cannot smoke while you're in the cab. They are also required to be polite.

You are allowed to dictate the route that is taken. It's a good idea to look at a map before you get in a taxi. Taxi drivers have been known to jack up the fare on visitors who don't know better by taking a circuitous route between point A and point B. Know enough about where you're going to know that something's wrong if you hop in a cab at Sixth Avenue and 57th Street to go to the Empire State Building (Fifth Ave. and 34th St.), for instance, and you suddenly find yourself on Ninth Avenue.

On the other hand, listen to drivers who propose an alternate route. These guys spend 8 or 10 hours a day on these streets, and they know them well—where the worst midday traffic is or where Con Ed has dug up an intersection that should be avoided.

Another important tip: **Always make sure the meter is turned on at the start of the ride.** You'll see the red LED read-out register the initial $2 and start calculating the fare as you go. I've witnessed a good number of unscrupulous drivers buzzing unsuspecting visitors around the city with the meter off, and then overcharging them at drop-off time.

Always ask for the receipt—it comes in handy if you need to make a complaint or have left something in a cab. In fact, it's a good idea to make a mental note of the driver's four-digit medallion number (usually posted on the divider between the front and back seats) just in case you need it later. You probably won't, but it's a good idea to play it safe.

For driver complaints and lost property, call the 24-hour Consumer Hotline at ☎ 212/NYC-TAXI. For details on getting to and from the local airports by taxi, see "By Plane" under "Getting There" in chapter 2. For further taxi information—including a complete rundown of your rights as a taxi rider—visit **www.ci.nyc.ny.us/taxi**.

BY CAR

Forget driving yourself around the city. It's not worth the headache. Traffic is horrendous, the streets have all the civility of the Wild West, and street parking is nearly impossible (not to mention the security risks).

Impressions

Traffic signals in New York are just rough guidelines.

—David Letterman

Deals for Visitors with Wheels: Cheap Parking Tips

If you're driving into the city and you simply have to find somewhere to put your car, don't despair. Even under the best of circumstances, you'll probably pay more for parking in New York than you would in other cities, but it doesn't have to break the bank.

When planning your trip, your best bet is to pick a hotel that has a favorable parking agreement with a nearby garage. This is common practice with city hotels, and the rate that management has negotiated will always be much better than the full rate you would pay on your own. Many hotels are able to negotiate daily rates between $15 and $22 in neighborhoods where the going rate is anywhere from $25 to $40. In chapter 5, "Accommodations You Can Afford," you'll see estimated parking rates in each of the listings, most based on existing agreements with nearby garages. There's even one hotel, **Travel Inn,** that provides garage parking to its guests for free.

If you have to find your own parking, your best bet is to choose a lot on the far west or far east fringes of Midtown, near the West Side Highway to the west or the FDR Drive to the east. You won't have easy access to your wheels, but you'll pay much lower daily rate—probably $15 as opposed to a minimum of $25—than in midtown.

If you'd rather have your car closer at hand, midtown west of Seventh Avenue is always cheaper than more eastern Midtown areas (about $25 as opposed to $45, which is what you'll pay near Fifth or Sixth aves.). Residential Murray Hill is also cheaper than more commercial Midtown East. If you're staying on the Upper West Side, you may be able to save a few dollars by garaging your car north of 96th Street, where garage parking is significantly cheaper than in the ritzy residential area between 59th and 86th streets.

If you drive into the city, I highly recommend garaging your car for the duration of your stay, using it again only when you're ready to leave the city. Most city garages do not provide in-and-out privileges, so expect to pay twice the daily rate, or a much higher hourly rate, if you plan to use your car and return it later that same day.

Also remember that a steep **parking garage tax** of 18.25% is added to every parking bill, so be sure to factor that in to your calculations. See why we recommend that you just leave your car at home?

One last note: Despite the fact that a few crazy New Yorkers risk it every day, don't try street parking. You don't know the arcane alternate-side-of-the-street parking regulations (in fact, precious few New Yorkers do). You don't want to find out the monstrous price of parking violations or the Kafkaesque tragedy of liberating a vehicle from the tow pound. And your car is sure to come home with a new dent or two (at minimum) if you leave it on the street for a few days. As expensive as garaging it may be, trust me—it's cheaper in the long run.

If you do arrive in New York City by car, park it in a garage (expect to pay in the neighborhood of $20 to $30 per day) and leave it there for the duration of your stay; see "Deals for Visitors with Wheels: Cheap Parking Tips" on the this page for advice on how to pay as little as possible to park. If you drive a rental car in, return it as soon as you arrive and rent another on the day you leave. Just about all of the major car-rental companies, including **Hertz** (☎ 800/654-3131), **National** (☎ 800/227-7368), and **Avis** (☎ 800/230-4898), have airport and Manhattan locations.

FROM THE CITY TO THE SUBURBS

The **PATH** (☎ **800/234-7284;** www.panynj.gov/path) system connects urban communities in New Jersey, including Hoboken and Newark, to Manhattan by subway-style trains. Stops in Manhattan are at the World Trade Center, Christopher and 9th streets, and along Sixth Avenue at 14th, 23rd, and 33rd streets. The fare is $1.

New Jersey Transit (☎ **973/762-5100;** www.njtransit.state.nj.us) operates commuter trains from Penn Station, and buses from the Port Authority at Eighth Avenue and 42nd Street, to points throughout New Jersey.

The **Long Island Rail Road** (☎ **718/217-5477;** www.mta.nyc.ny.us/lirr) runs from Penn Station, at Seventh Avenue between 31st and 33rd streets, to Queens (ocean beaches, Shea Stadium, Belmont Park) and Long Island.

Metro North (☎ **800/638-7646** or 212/532-4900; www.mta.nyc.ny.us/mnr) departs from Grand Central Terminal, 42nd Street and Lexington Avenue, for areas north of the city, including Westchester County, the lovely Hudson Valley, and Connecticut.

If you'd like to investigate the areas beyond the city, check out *Frommer's Wonderful Weekends from New York City.*

3 Playing It Safe

Thanks to Hollywood films, political posturing in Washington, and sensationalistic journalism, many out-of-towners believe creepy characters leer from every doorway waiting to attack every unsuspecting passerby. Sure, there's crime in New York City, but millions of people spend their lives here without being robbed and assaulted. In fact, New York is safer than any other big American city, and it's listed by the FBI as somewhere around 150th in the nation for total crimes. The booming economy and gentrification of neighborhoods from Times Square to the Lower East Side has made the city safer in recent years than it has been in decades. While that's great news for all of us, it's still important to take precautions. Visitors should especially remain vigilant, as swindlers and criminals are expert at spotting disoriented or vulnerable newcomers.

Men should carry their wallets in their front pockets and women should keep constant hold of their purse straps. Cross camera and purse straps over one shoulder, across your front, and under the other arm. Never hang a purse on the back of a chair or on a hook in a bathroom stall; keep it in your lap or between your feet with one foot through a strap and up against the purse itself. Avoid carrying large amounts of cash. You might carry your money in several pockets so if one is picked, you're not left penniless. Skip the flashy jewelry and keep valuables out of sight when you're on the street.

Panhandlers are seldom dangerous, but it's best to ignore them altogether (more aggressive pleas should firmly be answered, "Not today"). I hate to be cynical, but experience teaches that if a stranger walks up to you on the street with a long sob story ("I live in the suburbs and was just attacked and don't have the money to get home") it should be ignored, too—it's a scam. If someone approaches you with any kind of elaborate tale, it's most definitely a confidence game. Walk away and don't feel bad. Be wary of an individual who "accidentally" falls in front of you or causes some other commotion, because he or she may be working with someone else who will take your wallet when you try to help. And remember: You *will* lose if you place a bet on a sidewalk card game or shell game.

Avoid certain areas late at night. I don't recommend going to the Lower East Side or the East Village unless you know where you're going; head straight for your destination and don't wander onto side streets. It's probably best to avoid Alphabet City, in the far East Village, altogether at night. The areas above 96th Street aren't the best, either, although it's generally fine on the Upper West Side along Broadway up to Columbia University (at 116th St.). Times Square isn't as bad as it once was; it's been cleaned up quite a bit, and there'll be crowds around until 11pm or midnight, when theatergoers leave the area. Still, stick to the main streets, such as Broadway. The areas west of Ninth Avenue and south of Times Square are best avoided after dark. Take a cab or bus when visiting the Jacob Javits Center on 34th Street and the Hudson River. Don't go wandering the parks after dark, unless you're going to a performance; if that's the case, stick with the crowd.

If you plan on visiting the outer boroughs, go only during the daylight hours. If the subway doesn't go directly to your destination (such as the Bronx Zoo or the Brooklyn Museum of Art), your best bet is to take a taxi, and don't wander the side streets. Many areas in the outer boroughs are perfectly safe, but neighborhoods change quickly, and it's easy to get lost.

All this said, don't panic. Remember that New York has experienced a dramatic drop in crime and is generally safe these days, especially in the neighborhoods of interest to visitors. There's a good police presence on the street, so don't be afraid to stop an officer, or even a friendly looking New Yorker (trust me—you can tell), if you need help getting your bearings.

SUBWAY SAFETY TIPS   In general, the subways are safe, especially in Manhattan. There are panhandlers and questionable characters like anywhere else in the city, but subway crime is down to 1960s levels. Still, stay alert and trust your instincts. Always keep a hand on your personal belongings.

When using the subway, don't wait for trains near the edge of the platform or at their extreme ends. During non-rush hours, wait for the train in view of the token booth clerk or under the yellow DURING OFF HOURS TRAINS STOP HERE signs, and ride in the train operator's or conductor's car (usually in the center cars of the train; you'll see his or her head stick out when the doors open). Choose crowded cars over empty ones—there's safety in numbers.

Avoid subways late at night, and splurge on a cab after about 10 or 11pm—it's money well spent to avoid a long wait on a deserted platform. Or take the bus.

Fast Facts: New York City

Ambulance & Emergencies   Dial ☎ **911.**

American Express   Travel service offices are at many Manhattan locations, including the New York Hilton, 1335 Sixth Ave., at 53rd Street (☎ 212/664-7798); the New York Marriott Marquis, 1535 Broadway, in the 8th floor lobby (☎ 212/575-6580); on the mezzanine level at Macy's Herald Square, 34th Street and Broadway (☎ 212/695-8075); and 65 Broadway, between Exchange Place and Rector Street (☎ 212/493-6500). A bank of phones at the NYCVB Visitor Information Center, 810 Seventh Ave. (between 52nd and 53rd streets), will connect you directly with American Express card-member services. Contact American Express at ☎ **800/AXP-TRIP** or visit **www.americanexpress.com** for other city locations or general information.

Area Codes   By the time you arrive, there'll be three area codes in the city: two in Manhattan, **212** and **646,** and one in the outer boroughs, **718** (it was undetermined at press time when the outer boroughs would start using their second, already designated area code, **347**). Dialing procedures for local calls hadn't been determined at this writing; for now, if the number you're dialing is in the same area code you're calling from, you only have to dial the seven digits. This may change in the future—you may be asked to dial 11 digits (1, the area code, and the number) even when making a call within the same area code. Check the phone book or dial 0 and ask the operator if you want to confirm before you dial.

Business Hours   In general, **retail stores** are open Monday to Saturday 10am to 6pm or 7pm, Thursday 10am to 8:30 or 9pm, and Sunday noon to 5pm (see chapter 8). **Banks** tend to be open Monday to Friday 9am to 3pm and sometimes Saturday mornings.

Dentists   See "Health & Insurance" in chapter 2.

Doctors   For medical emergencies requiring immediate attention, head to the nearest emergency room (see "Hospitals," below). For less-urgent health problems, see "Health & Insurance" in chapter 2 for walk-in medical centers and offices that will accept appointments.

Embassies/Consulates   See "Fast Facts: For the Foreign Traveler" in chapter 3.

Emergencies   Dial ☎ **911** for fire, police, and ambulance. The **Poison Control Center** is at ☎ **212/764-7667** or 212/340-4494.

Fire   Dial ☎ **911.**

Hospitals   Downtown: New York Downtown Hospital, 170 William St., at Beekman Street (☎ **212/312-5000**); St. Vincent's Hospital, Seventh Avenue and 11th Street (☎ **212/604-7000**); and Beth Israel Medical Center, First Avenue and 16th Street (☎ **212/420-2000**). **Midtown:** Bellevue Hospital Center, 462 First Ave. and 27th Street (☎ **212/562-4141**); New York University Medical Center, 560 First Ave. and 33rd Street (☎ **212/263-7300**); and Roosevelt Hospital Center, Tenth Avenue and 59th Street (☎ **212/523-4000**). **Upper West Side:** St. Luke's Hospital Center, Amsterdam Avenue and 114th Street (☎ **212/523-4000**). **Upper East Side:** New York Hospital's Emergency Pavilion, York Avenue and 70th Street (☎ **212/746-5050**), and Lenox Hill Hospital, 77th Street between Park and Lexington avenues (☎ **212/434-2000**). Don't forget your insurance card.

Hot Lines   The 24-hour **Crime Victims Hot Line** is ☎ 212/577-7777; **Alcoholics Anonymous** is ☎ 212/870-3400 for general information, 212/647-1680 for intergroup (for alcoholics who need immediate counseling from

The Top Safety Tips

Trust your instincts; they're usually right. You'll rarely be hassled, but it's always best to walk with a sense of purpose and self-confidence, and don't stop in the middle of the sidewalk to pull out and peruse your guidebook or map. Anywhere in the city, if you find yourself on a deserted street that feels unsafe, it probably is; leave as quickly as possible. If you do find yourself accosted by someone with or without a weapon, remember to keep your anger in check and that the safest response (maddening though it may be) is not to resist.

a sober alcoholic); the **Sex Crimes Report Line** ☎ 212/267-7273; **Suicide Prevention Help Line** ☎ 212/532-2400; **Samaritans' Suicide Prevention Line** ☎ 212/673-3000; local **police precincts** ☎ 212/374-5000; **Department of Consumer Affairs** ☎ 212/487-4444 or 718/286-2994; **taxi complaints** ☎ 212/NYC-TAXI.

Internet Access   The **Times Square Visitors Center,** 1560 Broadway, between 46th and 47th streets (☎ **212/768-1560**), has computer terminals with free Internet access. The **Internet Cafe,** 82 E. 3rd St., between First and Second avenues in the East Village (☎ **212/614-0747;** www.bigmagic.com), offers direct Internet access at $10 per hour; students get a 10% discount with ID. **Cybercafe,** 273 Lafayette St., at Prince Street in SoHo (☎ **212/334-5140;** www.cyber-cafe.com), is more expensive at $12.80 an hour, but offers much speedier access.

Libraries   The main research branch of the **New York Public Library** is on Fifth Avenue at 42nd Street (☎ **212/340-0849**). More efficient and modern, if less charming, is the mid-Manhattan branch at 40th Street and Fifth Avenue, across the street from the main library. There are other branches in almost every neighborhood; you can find a list online at **www.nypl.org**.

Liquor Laws   The minimum legal age to purchase and consume alcoholic beverages in New York is 21. Liquor and wine are sold only in licensed stores, which are closed on Sundays, holidays, and election days while the polls are open. Beer can be purchased in grocery stores and delis 24 hours, except Sundays before noon.

Newspapers/Magazines   There are three major daily newspapers: the *New York Times,* the *Daily News,* and the *New York Post.* For details on where to find arts and entertainment listings, see "Publications" under "Orientation" earlier in this chapter.

For foreign newspapers and magazines, see "Fast Facts: For the Foreign Traveler" in chapter 3.

Pharmacies   There are two 24-hour pharmacies, both branches of **Duane Reade:** one at Broadway and 57th Street (☎ **212/541-9708**) and the other at Third Avenue and 74th Street (☎ **212/744-2668**).

Police   Dial ☎ **911** in an emergency; otherwise, call ☎ **212/374-5000** for the number of the nearest precinct.

Post Office   The main New York City post office is on 421 Eighth Ave., between 31st and 33rd streets and is open 24 hours (☎ **212/967-8585**). There's a second branch with extended hours (Mon–Fri 7am–midnight, Sat 7am–4pm) just north of the World Trade Center at 90 Church St., between Barclay and Vesey streets (☎ **212/330-5313**). There are branches and drop boxes throughout the city. Call ☎ **800/275-8777** to locate the nearest post office. Most branches are open Monday to Friday from 8am to 5 or 6pm, and Saturday from 9am to 3pm. For information on receiving general delivery mail in the city, see "Mail" under "Fast Facts: For the Foreign Traveler" in chapter 3.

Rest Rooms   Public rest rooms are as hard to come by as an empty taxi in a downpour. The visitors centers in Midtown (1560 Broadway, between 46th and 47th streets; and 810 Seventh Ave., between 52nd and 53rd streets) have facilities. Grand Central Terminal, at 42nd Street between Park and Lexington avenues, has cleaned up its rest rooms. But only out of desperation should you take your chances with the facilities at places like Penn Station and the Port

Authority bus terminal, where cleanliness is not highly regarded. Your best bet is to head to hotel lobbies (especially the big midtown ones) and department stores like Macy's and Bloomingdale's. Restaurants often post intimidating signs like REST ROOMS FOR CUSTOMERS ONLY, but if you look clean-cut and ask nicely (or beeline it to the john), you shouldn't have a problem; better yet, just pay for a Coke to avoid a problem. On the Lower East Side, stop into the Lower East Side BID visitor center, 261 Broome St., between Orchard and Allen streets (open Sun–Fri 10am–4pm). There's a program to install pay toilets in the parks, but I wouldn't count on it anytime soon.

Smoking　Smoking is prohibited on all public transportation, in the lobbies of hotels and office buildings, in taxis, and in most shops. Smoking also may be restricted or not permitted in restaurants; for more on this, see chapter 6.

Taxes　**Sales tax** is 8.25% on meals, most goods, and some services, though there has been political chatter about reducing or eliminating it, especially on clothing under $500 (more on this in chapter 8). **Hotel tax** is 13.25% plus $2 per room per night (including sales tax). **Parking garage tax** is 18.25%.

Transit Information　For information on getting to and from the airport, see "Getting There" in chapter 2 or call **Air-Ride** at ☎ **800/247-7433.** For information on subways and buses, see "Getting Around" earlier in this chapter.

Traveler's Assistance　Travelers Aid is an organization that helps distressed travelers with all kinds of problems, including accidents, sickness, and lost or stolen luggage. The Manhattan office is on the second floor of 1451 Broadway, at 41st Street (☎ **212/944-0013**), although it was in danger of becoming the victim of budget cuts at press time. There is also an office (scheduled to remain open) in the international arrivals building at JFK Airport (☎ **718/656-4870**).

Telephone Information　Dial ☎ **411,** or the area code of the area you wish to reach plus 555-1212.

5 Accommodations You Can Afford

As you're probably well aware, New York is more popular than it's been in decades. On one hand, that's terrific: This popularity makes the city feel vital and self-assured; you can practically feel the excitement and energy as you walk down the street. From a more practical standpoint, it has also made the city safer and more visitor friendly than ever.

Now the downside: With increased demand comes higher prices—Econ 101. Occupancy rates are higher than they've been since the prewar years, and rates have responded accordingly. Average room rates are now hovering around $195, higher than ever before in the city's history, and out of reach of many budget travelers. But don't get discouraged yet—there are still a few remarkable bargains to be had if you know where to look. In the pages that follow, I'll tell you about some truly wonderful places to stay that won't break your bank account.

Nevertheless, keep in mind that this is the land of $200-a-night Holiday Inns and HoJos—so forget about calling up one of the chains and booking a reliable $75 motel room like you could in any other U.S. city. To stay in New York, you must carefully weigh what you're willing to afford versus what you're willing to put up with. If you only want to spend 100 bucks a night—a very budget-basic rate in this city—you're going to have to live with some inconveniences.

First and foremost, don't expect much in the way of **space.** Space is New York's most coveted commodity, its most precious resource, and most of it doesn't go to visitors on tight budgets. Don't be surprised if your hotel room isn't much bigger than the bed that's in it, the closet is just a rack screwed to the wall, and/or the bathroom is the smallest you've ever seen.

Also, you may have to stay in a residential district rather than your first-choice **neighborhood.** In general, it's more expensive to stay in the heart of the Theater District than in Murray Hill. But this can be a good thing, especially if you like peace and quiet. Staying in a residential area will also give you better access to affordable restaurants where locals eat rather than at places in tourist-heavy neighborhoods, which tend to jack up their prices. If you have the kids in tow (or even if you don't), be sure to look to the larger-than-average rooms on the residential Upper West Side. For more help in choosing a location, take a close look at "Manhattan's Neighborhoods in Brief" in chapter 4 before you delve into the hotel listings.

Last but not least, be aware that many of New York's budget hotel rooms have **shared bathrooms.** There are a few exceptions to the rule, but in general don't count on scoring a double room with a private bathroom for less than $100 a night. If your budget is extra-tight, you may want to seriously consider one of the city's shared-bathroom hotels, some of which are very nice—akin to European-style B&Bs rather than threadbare hotel rooms. I recommend the best of these below.

For an easy-to-scan introduction to the best of what the city has to offer, take a moment to check out **Best Affordable Hotel Bets** in chapter 1, if you haven't already.

HOW TO SAVE ON YOUR HOTEL ROOM

The rates quoted in the listings below are the **rack rates**—the maximum rates that a hotel charges for rooms. It's the rate you'd get if you walked in off the street and asked for a room for the night without bargaining. In the listings below, I've also tried to give you an idea of the kind of deals that may be available at particular hotels: which ones have the best discounted packages, which ones offer AAA and other discounts, which ones allow kids to stay with Mom and Dad for free, and so on. But rates in New York can change dramatically depending on demand, and demand is high these days—so be prepared for sticker shock. There's no way of knowing what the market will hold, or what the offers will be when you're booking.

Before you even start calling, be sure to review the **60 Money-Saving Tips** in chapter 2, where you'll find terrific time-tested advice on how to get the most for your accommodations dollar. You'll also find contact information on reservations services and B&B and homestay networks that may be able to book you into a room for better than you could do on your own.

STAYING "OUT"   One of the wonderful things about New York is its tolerance for alternative lifestyles. Indeed, in a city with one of the world's largest, loudest, and most powerful gay and lesbian populations, homosexuality is hardly seen as an "alternative" these days—it's squarely in the urban mainstream. As a result, city hotels tend to be neutral on the issue, and gay couples shouldn't have a problem. (If you do, please don't hesitate to let me know.) Nonetheless, some gays and lesbians might wish to seek out particularly gay-friendly accommodations. Two recommendable ones are the **Colonial House Inn,** a charming 1850 brownstone in the heart of gay-friendly Chelsea (p. 95); and the **Incentra Village House,** 32 Eighth Ave. (☎ **212/206-0007**), a moderately priced inn housed in two 1841 red-brick Greenwich Village town houses listed with the National Trust for Historic Places.

PET POLICIES   If you're traveling on a budget, your best bet is to leave Bowser or Fluffy at home. None of New York's budget-minded hotels accepts pets. If you have a small pet in tow, your best is to call the **Holiday Inn Broadway,** 49 W. 32nd St., at Broadway (☎ **888/NYHOLIDAY** or 212/736-3800; www.holiday-inn.com), a fine branch of this reliable chain but more expensive than you might think (usually around $200). However, pet acceptance may have limitations, such as weight and breed restrictions (25 pounds or less at the Holiday Inn); may require a deposit and/or a signed waiver against damages; and may be revoked at any time. At any hotel, always inquire when booking, and *never* just show up with pet in tow.

1 TriBeCa

✪ **Cosmopolitan Hotel–Tribeca.** 95 W. Broadway (at Warren St., 1 block south of Chambers St.), New York, NY 10007. ☎ **888/895-9400** or 212/566-1900. Fax 212/566-6909. www.cosmohotel.com. 104 units. A/C TV TEL. $109 double. AE, CB, DC, JCB, MC, V. Parking $20 (with validation) 1 block away. Subway: 1, 2, 3, 9, A, C, E to Chambers St.

Hiding behind a plain-vanilla TriBeCa awning is the best hotel deal in Manhattan for budget travelers who don't want to sacrifice the luxury of a private bathroom. Every room comes with its own small but spotless bathroom, telephone with data port, air-conditioning, satellite TV, alarm, and ceiling fan. Everything is strictly budget, but nice: The modern IKEA-ish furniture includes an armoire and a work desk; for a few extra bucks, you can have a loveseat, too. Beds are comfy, and sheets and towels are better quality than in many more expensive hotels. Rooms are small but well organized, and the whole place is pristine. The two-level mini-lofts have lots of character, but expect to duck on the second level: Downstairs is the bathroom, TV, closet, desk, and club chair, while upstairs is a low-ceilinged bedroom with a second TV and phone. The neighborhood is safe, hip, and subway-convenient, and the Financial District is just a walk away. There's no room service, but a range of great restaurants will deliver. All services are kept at a bare minimum to keep costs down, so you must be a low-maintenance guest to be happy here. If you are, this place is a smokin' deal.

2 The Lower East Side

Off SoHo Suites. 11 Rivington St. (btw. Chrystie St. and the Bowery), New York, NY 10002. ☎ **800/OFF-SOHO** or 212/979-9808. Fax 212/979-9801. www.offsoho.com. 38 units (28 with bathroom). A/C TV TEL. $97.50 economy suite (2 people maximum); $179 deluxe suite (4 people maximum). AE, MC, V. Parking $14, 3 blocks away. Subway: F to Second Ave.; J, M to Bowery.

The good news: Here's a hotel with clean, welcoming rooms with full kitchen facilities at surprisingly low prices. The bad news: When they say "Off SoHo," they mean it. This edge-of-Chinatown neighborhood is primarily industrial, and while close to Downtown dining, shopping, and nightlife (trendy Elizabeth St. is just 2 blocks away), it doesn't exactly scream Downtown chic. Still, if you're willing to dispense with the old real-estate bromide "location, location, location," you'll get well-rounded if Spartan spaces for a bargain rate. The deluxe suites have a living and dining area with a pullout sofa, fully stocked kitchen (with microwave), private bathroom, and separate bedroom. In the economy suites, a kitchen and bathroom are shared with another room; if four of you are traveling together, you can combine two economy suites into a sizable apartment. Everything is pretty basic and the beds are a bit harder than I like, but the whole place is well kept. Telephones have voice mail and data port, and satellite TV was in the plans at press time. The neighborhood isn't unsafe, just desolate; it's a good idea to take a cab back later in the evening. There's a workout room, a cafe serving breakfast and lunch, and self-service laundry.

3 The East Village

East Village Bed & Coffee. 110 Ave. C (btw. 7th and 8th sts.), New York, NY 10009. ☎/fax **212/533-4175.** www.citysearch.com/nyc/eastvillagebed. 6 rooms (all with shared bathroom). A/C. $45 single; $65 double. Rates include tax. AE, ER, MC, V. Nearby street parking. Subway: L to First Ave.; 6 to Astor Place.

Fair warning: This funny little guest house isn't for everyone. If you're turned off by the idea of staying behind a graffiti-covered facade in a space that's still a work in progress, set in a scruffy neighborhood that's also an ongoing project, skip this one. But if you're a young, adventurous, easy-going traveler who likes a communal vibe, who's willing to put up with a few eccentricities and a way-off-the-beaten-path location for a rock-bottom deal, read on.

Committed to providing affordable accommodations to budget travelers from around the globe, friendly innkeeper Carlos Delfin has created a series of private guest rooms on two floors. All are small, basic, and hostel-like, with little more than a bed and a loose

Downtown Accommodations

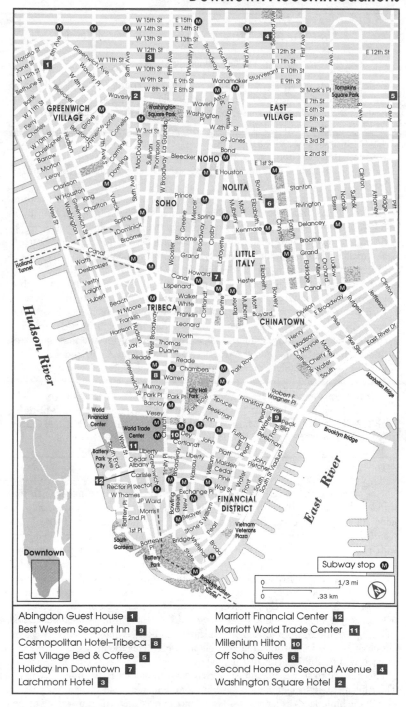

Abingdon Guest House **1**

Best Western Seaport Inn **9**

Cosmopolitan Hotel–Tribeca **8**

East Village Bed & Coffee **5**

Holiday Inn Downtown **7**

Larchmont Hotel **3**

Marriott Financial Center **12**

Marriott World Trade Center **11**

Millenium Hilton **10**

Off Soho Suites **6**

Second Home on Second Avenue **4**

Washington Square Hotel **2**

Getting the Most for Your Money, Part I:
Weekend Packages

Believe it or not, there is a way to stay in New York coddled in the lap of luxury without blowing your middle-class budget: weekend packages. The best weekend deals are available at hotels that cater primarily to a business clientele, in business-oriented neighborhoods that tend to empty out at the end of Friday's workday. There's no guarantee of what the offers will be when you come to town, but if you're visiting New York on a short weekend trip, or you don't mind temporarily moving up to luxury accommodations, see what's being offered at the following hotels:

Without a doubt, the city's best weekend values are available at the **Millenium Hilton,** across from the World Trade Center at 55 Church St. (☎ 800/ 835-2220 or 212/693-2001; www.hilton.com). This Mobil 4-star, AAA 4-diamond hotel is the top choice in the Financial District for bulls and bears. It also makes a great perch for vacationers on weekends, when its $300-a-night doubles go for just $120 to $199 (depending on the season). The extremely comfortable rooms are light and bright (most have glorious Manhattan or harbor views), and the services and facilities (which include an excellent fitness center with pool) are first rate. Continental breakfast is usually included in weekend packages, and corporate, senior, and other promotions may make the deeply discounted rates even more enticing. There's even a bonus for families, since kids under 18 stay free in mom and dad's room. This neighborhood goes from bustling to near-desolate on weekends, but multiple subway lines are nearby, ready to whisk you Uptown in no time.

If you don't mind the idea of a super-quiet Lower Manhattan base, you might also check with the **Marriott Financial Center,** 85 West St. (☎ 800/242-8685 or 212/385-4900), and the **Marriott World Trade Center,** 3 World Trade Center (☎ 800/228-9290 or 212/938-9100), both excellent branches of the reliable

"theme" that you may miss if you don't look carefully. Best is the sunlit French room, with a high-quality mattress on the queen bed and a chest of drawers. Also on the second floor are some very petite futon-bedded rooms, including the cute Mexican room (painted in a pretty South-of-the-Border palette), plus a common kitchen, living room with TV, and bathroom. Downstairs is a large loftlike space with Carlos's workroom up front; a living area with TV, stereo, and VCR; an office space where you can send and receive faxes and make free local calls; another kitchen with a big farmstead dining table; a second bathroom; and two more Japanese-style bedrooms (with low ceilings and low platform beds) built as enclosed lofts over the main space. These are for heavy sleepers only, as they're subject to noise from above and below. Furnishings are a hodge-podge collection assembled from junk shops and street finds; everything I saw was well worn, but clean, and a wonderful ethnic art collection brightens the mix. Carlos lives in the space as well (with his shepherd Fang, whose fierce name belies her sweet disposition), so he's on hand to answer questions; he even cooks dinner for guests from time to time. The Alphabet City neighborhood has improved dramatically in the last few years, but it's still the hinterlands as far as most New Yorkers are concerned. Subways are a significant walk away, so use the money you save on your room to take cabs back at night.

chain that offer similarly discounted weekend rates and promotions. Particularly recommendable is the Marriott World Trade Center, which boasts an excellent location, connected to the Twin Towers, and a great health club with a pool, jogging track, racquetball court, and saunas. The Financial Center location also features a health club with pool and sauna, plus Roy's New York, the first East Coast restaurant by venerable Hawaiian chef Roy Yamaguchi. You can find Marriott online at **www.marriott.com**.

If you're intrigued by the promise of weekend discounts but would prefer a Midtown location, check with **Crowne Plaza at the United Nations,** 304 E. 42nd St., just east of Second Ave. (☎ **800/227-6963,** 800/879-8836 or 212/986-8800; www.crowneplaza-un.com or www.crowneplaza.com). The lovely neo-Tudor building boasts newly renovated guest rooms with all the creature comforts, plus a surprising amount of individual flair for a chain hotel. It becomes a real steal on most weekends, when U.N. delegates head out of the city. Rack rates are generally $229 to $379 double, but I found rooms going for just $169 on a number of weekends throughout 1999. If you find yourself being offered such a deal, book it—you won't be disappointed.

Finally, if you're Web savvy, it's worth taking a moment to surf over to the site for the **Millennium Broadway,** 145 W. 44th St. (☎ **800/622-5569** or 212/768-0847; www.millenniumbroadway.com), and click on SPECIAL DEALS. Without question, the Millennium offers the best weekend packages in the Theater District: This terrific luxury high-rise sometimes offers its spacious and comfy art-deco–ish rooms, which normally go for $295–$345 double, to Internet customers for as little as $160 to $179 a night. No doubt pricey for some budget travelers, but an excellent deal if you're splurging. Weekend bunch is often included, and children under 13 stay can free in their parents' room.

Second Home on Second Avenue. 221 Second Ave. (btw. E. 13th and 14th sts.), New York, NY 10003. ☎/fax **212/677-3161.** www.citysearch.com/nyc/secondhome. 7 units (2 with private bathroom). A/C TV TEL. $65–$110 double with shared bathroom; $130 double with private bathroom; $155 suite. Extra person $25. 3-night minimum stay required. AE, ER, MC, V. Parking about $20 nearby. Subway: L to 3rd Ave.; N, R, 4, 5, 6 to Union Sq.

Here's another guest house run by Carlos Delfin, this one a big step up in quality, location, and price from his East Village Bed & Coffee, above. It's quite a find for independent-minded travelers who'd prefer the restaurant- and club-heavy East Village over more touristy 'hoods. The rooms are large and decently, if eclectically, furnished, with some surprisingly nice touches here and there. Each is outfitted with two full beds, good closet space, and a large TV with VCR and a CD player in every room (otherwise unheard of in this price category). If there's more than two of you, the suite, which has a separate living room with a nice leather sofa that pulls out into a queen bed and a big private bathroom, is a good bet. Bathrooms are older but clean. The fully outfitted common kitchen, with full stove and fridge, toaster oven, coffeemaker, and dishwasher, has free coffee and tea on hand at all times. A few words of caution, though: Don't expect lots in the way of service; you're really on your own here. Rooms are on the third and fourth floors, so this isn't the place for visitors with mobility issues. And the guest house is popular with European travelers, who like to smoke, so stay elsewhere if a slight odor will bother you.

4 Greenwich Village

۞ Abingdon Guest House. 13 Eighth Ave. (btw. W. 12th and Jane sts.), New York, NY 10014. ☎ **212/243-5384.** Fax 212/807-7473. www.abingdonguesthouse.com. 9 units (7 with private bathroom). A/C TV TEL. Low season (Jan–Apr, July–Aug) $95–$120 double with shared bathroom, $135–$175 with private bathroom; high season (May–June, Sept–Dec) $110–$135 double with shared bathroom, $155–$195 double with private bathroom. $10–$15 less for single travelers. Extra person $25. 4-night minimum on weekends, 2-night minimum on weekdays; longer minimum stays may be required for holidays. AE, DC, DISC, MC, V. Parking $20 nearby. Subway: A, C, E to 14th St.; 1, 2, 3, 9 to 14th St.

Steve Austin, who has a Hotel Management degree, and his partner, Zachary Stass, educated in interior design, now run this lovely guest house (and its downstairs coffee bar, Brewbar) in a wonderful West Village neighborhood. Both men have an eye for style and take the guest-house business seriously, and their commitment shows—the Abingdon is beautifully outfitted and professionally run. All the rooms are done in bold colors and outfitted with well-chosen art and furnishings; each can be previewed on the Web site. I suggest opting for one with a new bathroom, which are large and well done. But no matter which one you choose, you'll get a superior quality mattress and linens (better than at most hotels that cost more), hair dryer, soft polyfleece bathrobes, alarm, a small TV, and telephone with your own answering machine (a splitter can be provided for your laptop); five rooms also have ceiling fans. The neighborhood is terrific, especially for those who want to be close to good restaurants and boutiques, but it's a bit off the beaten path if you're planning on lots of Midtown sightseeing. And the Abingdon is best for independent-minded travelers since there's no regular staff on site. No smoking is allowed.

۞ Larchmont Hotel. 27 W. 11th St. (btw. Fifth and Sixth aves.), New York, NY 10011. ☎ **212/989-9333.** Fax 212/989-9496. www.citysearch.com/nyc/larchmonthotel. 55 units (none with bathroom). A/C TV TEL. $70–$80 single; $90–$109 double. Rates include continental breakfast. Children under 13 stay free in parents' room. AE, CB, DC, DISC, MC, V. Parking $20 nearby. Subway: 4, 5, 6, N, R, L to Union Square; A, C, E, B, D, F, Q to West 4th St. (use 8th St. exit); F to 14th St.

Excellently located on a beautiful tree-lined block in a quiet residential part of the village, this European-style hotel is simply a gem. If you're willing to put up with the inconvenience of shared bathrooms, you can't do better for the money. The entire place has a wonderful air of warmth and sophistication; the butter-yellow lobby even *smells* good. Each bright guest room is tastefully done in rattan and outfitted with a writing desk, a wash basin, a mini-library of books, an alarm clock, cotton bathrobes, and ceiling fans. Every floor has two shared bathrooms and a small, simple kitchen. The management is constantly renovating, so everything feels clean and fresh. The free continental breakfast, including fresh-baked goods, is the crowning touch that makes the Larchmont an unbeatable deal. And with some of the city's best shopping, dining, and sightseeing, plus your choice of subway lines, just a walk away, you couldn't be better situated. As you might expect, the hotel is always full, so book well in advance (the management suggests 6 to 7 weeks' lead time).

Washington Square Hotel. 103 Waverly Place (btw. Fifth and Sixth aves.), New York, NY 10011. ☎ **800/222-0418** or 212/777-9515. Fax 212/979-8373. www.wshotel.com. 180 units. A/C TV TEL. $116 single; $136–$146 double; $167 quad. Rates include continental breakfast. AE, MC, JCB, V. Parking $22. Subway: A, B, C, D, E, F, Q to W. 4th St.

The best thing about this hotel is its great location, right in the heart of Greenwich Village overlooking Washington Square Park. The pretty facade and marble-and-brass lobby comes as quite a surprise—not exactly what you expect from a budget hotel. Recent rate hikes have made the tiny, plain rooms not quite the deal they used to be, but they're still a decent value. Each comes with a private bathroom, a deposit-activated phone with voice mail and data port, and a small closet with a pint-sized safe; irons and hair dryers are available from the front desk. Beds are firm but the pillows are flat, and a little more elbow grease could go into the petite bathrooms. Still, for the money, you could do worse. It's worth paying a few extra dollars for a south-facing room on a high floor, since others can be dark. There's a basic gym and a very good restaurant, CIII, that even draws locals with its well-priced bistro fare, friendly staff, two-for-one happy hours, and Sunday jazz brunch that Zagat's calls "marvelous." However, the hotel staff can be terse and we've received complaints about their unresponsiveness to guest requests, so be on your guard and let me know if you have any problems.

5 The Flatiron District & Gramercy Park

✪ Gershwin Hotel. 7 E. 27th St. (btw. Fifth and Madison aves.), New York, NY 10016. ☎ 212/545-8000. Fax 212/684-5546. www.gershwinhotel.com. 94 doubles, 31 4-person dorms. TV TEL (in doubles only). $109–$139 double; $119–$149 triple; $129–$159 quad, depending on season; $22 per person in dorm. Check Web site for seasonal deals. AE, MC, V. Parking $20 nearby. Subway: N, R, 6 to 28th St.

If you see glowing horns protruding from a lipstick-red facade, you're in the right place. An upscale version of the Carlton Arms (see below), this budget-conscious, youth-oriented hotel caters to up-and-coming artistic types with its bold modern art collection and wild style. The lobby is a colorful, postmodern cartoon of kitschy furniture and pop art by Lichtenstein, Warhol, de Koonig, and others. The standard rooms are clean and saved from the budget doldrums by bright colors, Picasso-style wall murals, Starck-ish takes on motel furnishings, and more modern art. All have private bathrooms; none of the bathrooms are bad, but try to nab one of the new ones. The cheapest accommodations are four- and eight-bedded dorms: They're basic rooms with IKEA bunk beds sharing a bathroom, but better than a hostel, especially if you're traveling with a group and can claim one as your own.

One of the best things about the Gershwin is its great, Factory-esque vibe, sort of like an artsy frat or sorority house. The hotel is more service oriented than you usually see at this price level, and there's always something going on, whether it's live comedy or jazz in the beer and wine bar, a film screening or barbecue on the rooftop garden, or an opening at the hotel's own art gallery. At press time, a new vendor had just taken over the funky Gallery Cafe, and room service was in the works. Air-conditioning was also in the planning stage, but make sure before you book an August stay.

Hotel 17. 225 E. 17th St. (btw. Second and Third aves.), New York, NY 10003. ☎ 212/475-2845. Fax 212/677-8178. www.citysearch.com/nyc/hotel17. 130 units (all with shared bathroom). AC TV TEL. $75–$85 single; $98–$130 double; $200 3-person suite. Rates include tax. Weekly rates available. No credit cards. Parking $25. Subway: 4, 5, 6 to 14th St.; L to Third Ave.

In the last couple of years, Hotel 17 has managed to garner a reputation as the hippest budget hotel in Manhattan—Madonna, David Bowie, and Maxwell have all been photographed in the eclectic, eccentric rooms. But it's not all hype—Hotel 17 has a lot to recommend it: The neighborhood is great, the block peaceful, and the individually decorated rooms surprisingly attractive. Look beyond the stylish veneer, though, and you'll find rooms that are small, dark, and basic—definitely not for travelers looking for creature comforts. Each has its own sink; the shared bathrooms are older but kept very clean. Recent renovation has softened the edge, adding air-conditioning, TVs, hair dryers, and alarm clocks to all rooms. The lobby has a funky streamline, modern feel to it, but the security glass separating you from the front-desk staff detracts. There's a roof garden and self-service laundry. All in all, a good deal for the money, especially if you like some individuality in your hostelry. Expect lots of young and international travelers, who don't mind the inconveniences.

SUPER-CHEAP SLEEPS

Travelers on a shoestring budget should be sure to consider the dorm-style rooms at the **Gershwin Hotel,** above, which go for just $22 per person per night.

WORTH A SPLURGE

Gramercy Park Hotel. 2 Lexington Ave. (btw. 21st and 22nd sts.), New York, NY 10010. ☎ **800/221-4083** or 212/475-4320. Fax 212/505-0535. 360 units. A/C TV TEL. $165–$170 single; $180 double; from $210 suite. Extra person $10. Children under 12 stay free in parents' room. AE, CB, DC, DISC, EC, JCB, MC, V. Parking $20 nearby. Subway: 6 to 23rd St.

Opened in 1924, this appealing Old World hotel has one of the best settings in the city. It's in one of New York's loveliest neighborhoods, ideally located on the edge of the private park—restricted to just a few area residents and to hotel guests, who can also get a key—that gives Gramercy Park the air of a quiet London square. The hotel has been plagued by claims of neglect in recent years, but management seems to be responding well, and the old place is looking really good these days. You'll still have to overlook the finer details—expect a smoky lobby, chipped paint here and there, *Ice Storm*–era carpet in some halls, mix-and-match baths that have been updated haphazardly, and ancient TVs—but rooms are huge by city standards, decently furnished, and comfortable. Standard doubles have a king or two doubles, and some suites have pullout sofas that make them large enough to sleep six; all have big closets, unstocked minifridges, and hair dryers and fluffy towels in the roomy bathrooms. Request a park-facing room, which cost no more but feature great views and small kitchenettes. There's a continental restaurant and a lounge with nightly entertainment off the bustling lobby, plus a beauty salon and newsstand. Dry cleaning/laundry service and limited room service are available.

6 Chelsea

Chelsea Inn. 46 W. 17th St. (btw. Fifth and Sixth aves.), New York, NY 10011. ☎ **212/640-6469.** Fax 212/645-8989. www.chelseainn.com. 25 units (17 with bathroom). A/C TV TEL. $99–$119 double with shared bathroom; $139–$159 double with private bathroom; $179–$239 suite for up to 4. Check Web site for available specials. AE, DC, MC, V. Parking $20 nearby. Subway: 4, 5, 6, N, R to Union Sq.

The Chelsea Inn may be housed in two 19th-century landmark brownstones, but don't expect much. Staying here is sort of like living in your own bad New York City tenement for a few days: The rooms feature an eclectic mix of well-worn thrift-shop antiques, plus a hot plate, minifridge, and coffeemaker along with a cheap set of cups and utensils. Everything's faded and overpainted, and nothing matches. The beds in the twin rooms are little more than rollaways. So why am I telling you about this place? Because it's clean and cheap, and the location is good, especially for club-hoppers and shoppers. On the upside, closets are big, and all rooms feature a safe, voice mail, and free coffee; those without private bathroom have their own sink, too. If there's more than two of you, you can pair up two doubles that share a bathroom, creating a family-sized unit, and usually negotiate a discount on it. In fact, deals are often available, and rates can go as low as $79. Still, you can probably do better for the money; stay here only as a last resort.

☉ Chelsea Savoy Hotel. 204 W. 23rd St. (at Seventh Ave.), New York, NY 10011. ☎ **212/929-9353.** Fax 212/741-6309. www.citysearch.com/nyc/chelseasavoy. 90 units. A/C TV TEL. $99–$115 single; $125–$155 double; $155–$185 quad. Children under 13 stay free in parents' room. Rates include continental breakfast. AE, MC, V. Parking $16 nearby. Subway: 1, 9 to 23rd St.

This 2-year-old hotel is our top choice in Chelsea, a neighborhood abloom with art galleries, restaurants, and weekend flea markets but formerly devoid of nice, affordable hotels. The hallways are attractive and wide, the elevators are swift and silent, and the generic but cheery rooms are good-sized and have big closets and roomy, immaculate bathrooms with tons of counter space. Creature comforts abound: The rooms boast high-quality mattresses, furniture, textiles, and linens, plus hair dryers, minifridges, alarm clocks, irons and boards, in-room safes, and toiletries (VCRs were scheduled to be added at press time). Most rooms are street facing and sunny; corner rooms tend to be brightest and noisiest. Ask for a darker, back-facing room if you crave total silence. There's a plain but pleasant sitting room off the lobby where you can relax and enjoy your morning coffee over a selection of newspapers and magazines. The staff is young and helpful, and the increasingly hip neighborhood makes a good base for exploring both Midtown and Downtown.

Colonial House Inn. 318 W. 22nd St. (btw. Eighth and Ninth aves.), New York, NY 10011. ☎ **800/689-3779** or 212/243-9669. www.colonialhouseinn.com. 20 rooms (12 with shared bathroom). A/C TV TEL. $80–$99 single or double with shared bathroom; $125–$140 with private bathroom. Rates include continental breakfast. 2-night minimum on weekends. 5% discount for bookings of 7 nights or more. No credit cards. Nearby street parking. Subway: C, E to 23rd St.

This charming 1850 brownstone, on a pretty residential block in the heart of gay-friendly Chelsea, was the first permanent home of the Gay Men's Health Crisis. The four-story walk-up caters to a largely gay and lesbian clientele, but the friendly staff welcomes everybody equally, and straight couples are a common sight. The whole place is beautifully maintained and professionally run. Rooms are small and basic but clean; those that share a hall bathroom (at a ratio of about three rooms per bathroom) have in-room sinks. Both private and shared bathrooms are basic but nice. Rooms with private bathrooms also have minifridges, and a few have fireplaces that accommodate Duraflame logs. A terrific, mostly abstract art collection brightens the public spaces. At parlor level is a cute breakfast room where a continental spread is put out from 8am to noon daily, and coffee and tea is available all day. There's a nice roof deck split by a privacy fence; the area behind the fence is clothing-optional. The neighborhood is chock-full of great restaurants and shopping, and offers easy access to the rest of the city. Book at least a month in advance for weekend stays, as the inn regularly sells out.

WORTH A SPLURGE

Hotel Chelsea. 222 W. 23rd St. (btw. Seventh and Eighth aves.), New York, NY 10011. ☎ **212/243-3700.** Fax 212/675-5531. www.hotelchelsea.com. 400 units, 100 available to travelers (most with private bathroom). A/C (in most rooms) TV TEL. $150–$285 double or junior suite; from $300 suite. AE, JCB, MC, V. Valet parking $18. Subway: 1, 9, C, E to 23rd St.

If you're looking for dependable, predictable comforts, book a room next door at the Chelsea Savoy. But if it's Warhol's New York you're here to discover—or Sarah Bernhardt's or Eugene O'Neill's or Lenny Bruce's—the Hotel Chelsea is the only place to

Midtown Accommodations

Americana Inn **19**
Belvedere Hotel **34**
Best Western Manhattan **16**
Best Western President **35**
Best Western Woodward **37**
Broadway Inn **33**
Carlton Arms **7**
Chelsea Inn **4**
Chelsea Savoy Hotel **3**
Colonial House Inn **1**
Comfort Inn Manhattan **18**
Comfort Inn Midtown **29**
Crowne Plaza
  at the United Nations **20**
Gershwin Hotel **8**
Gramercy Park Hotel **6**
Habitat Hotel **24**
Herald Square Hotel **14**
Holiday Inn Broadway **15**
Hotel Chelsea **2**
Hotel Edison **30**
Hotel Grand Union **12**
Hotel Metro **17**
Hotel 17 **5**
Hotel 31 **11**
Hotel Wolcott **13**
Loews New York **23**
Millennium Brodway **28**
Murray Hill Inn **9**
Park Savoy Hotel **38**
Pickwick Arms Hotel **22**
Portland Square Hotel **27**
Quality Hotel Eastside **10**
Quality Hotel & Suites Midtown **25**
Ramada Inn Milford Plaza **32**
Travel Inn **31**
Vanderbilt YMCA **21**
Washington Jefferson Hotel **36**
The Wyndham **26**

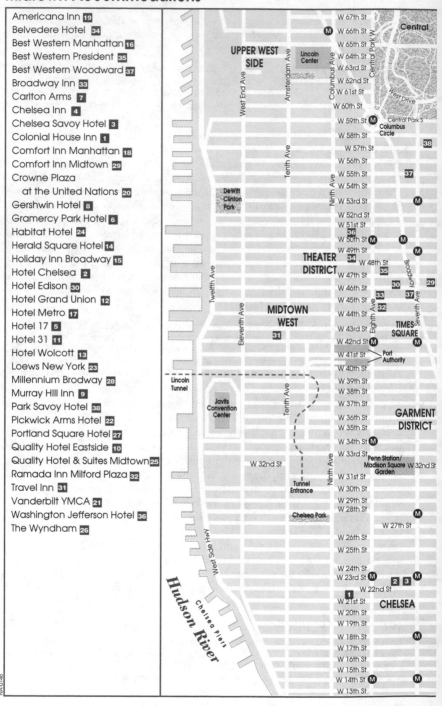

NA-0146

stay. Thomas Wolfe wrote *You Can't Go Home Again* at the Chelsea; Arthur Miller penned *After the Fall* in its welcoming arms; William Burroughs moved in to work on *Naked Lunch;* and in a defining moment of punk history, Sid Vicious killed girlfriend Nancy Spungeon here. No other hotel boasts so much genuine atmosphere. Currently, most of the 400 rooms are inhabited by long-term residents of the creative bent, so the bohemian spirit and sense of community are as strong as ever.

A designated landmark, the 1884 red-brick Victorian boasts graceful cast-iron balconies and a bustling lobby filled with museum-quality works by prominent current and former residents. A recent renovation has taken the seediness out of the allure—these days, the hotel is looking very nice. It's still very quirky, mind you, and not for everybody: Most of the individually decorated rooms and suites have air-conditioning, and they tell me that all have TVs and telephones now, but otherwise it's a crapshoot. The accommodations tend to be sparsely furnished, but they're almost universally large and virtually soundproof (you can see how this would be a plus for unbridled creation). I loved no. 520, a pretty purple-painted junior suite with two double beds, a ceiling fan, sofa, and a pantry kitchenette. Everything is clean, but don't expect new. The hotel is service oriented, but in an appropriately fluid way: There's no room or valet service, but the bellmen will be happy to deliver takeout to your room or run your dirty clothes to the cleaners.

7 Times Square & Midtown West

If you're visiting in winter or spring, seriously consider the terrific **Belvedere Hotel** (under "Worth a Splurge," below), where rates can go as low as $125 in these slower seasons. The Belvedere is worth checking out at any time of year if you're a AAA member who can qualify for the 10% discount, or if you catch one of their frequent Internet specials.

Americana Inn. 69 W. 38th St. (at Sixth Ave.), New York, NY 10018. ☎ **888/HOTEL58** or 212/840-2019. Fax 212/840-1830. www.newyorkhotel.com/americana. 50 units (all with shared bathroom). A/C TV. $75–$105 double. Extra person $10. AE, DC, DISC, MC, V. Parking $18–$22 nearby. Subway: B, D, F, Q to 42nd St.; N, R to 34th St.

The cheapest hotel from the Empire Hotel Group—the people behind the Belvedere, the Lucerne, and the Newton among other top-notch properties—is a winner in the budget-basic category. Linoleum floors give the rooms an unfortunate institutional quality, but the hotel is professionally run and immaculately kept. Rooms are mostly spacious, with good-size closets and private sinks, and the beds are the most comfortable I've found at this price. A few can accommodate three guests in two twin beds and a pullout sofa. There's one hall bathroom for every three rooms or so, and all are spacious and spotless. Every floor has a common kitchenette with microwave, stove, and fridge (BYO utensils, or go plastic). The five-story building has an elevator, and four rooms are handicap accessible. The Garment District location couldn't be more convenient for Midtown sightseeing and shopping. Ask for a back-facing room away from the street noise.

✪ Broadway Inn. 264 W. 46th St. (at Eighth Ave.), New York, NY 10036. ☎ **800/ 826-6300** or 212/997-9200. Fax 212/768-2807. www.broadwayinn.com. 40 units. A/C TV TEL. $85–$95 single; $115–$170 double; $195 suite. Extra person $10. Rates include continental breakfast. AE, DC, DISC, MC, V. Parking $16 3 blocks away. Subway: 1, 2, 3, 7, 9, S to 42nd St./Times Square; A, C, E to 42nd St.; N, R to 49th St.

More like a San Francisco B&B than a Theater District hotel, this lovely, welcoming inn is a real charmer. The second-floor lobby sets the homey, easy-going tone with stocked bookcases, cushy seating, and cafe tables where breakfast is served. The rooms are basic but comfy, outfitted in an appealing neo-deco style with firm beds. The whole place is impeccably kept. Two rooms have king beds and Jacuzzi tubs, but the standard doubles are just fine. If there's more than two of you, or you're looking to stay awhile, the suites—with pullout sofa, microwave, minifridge, and lots of closet space—are a great deal. The location can be noisy, but double-paned windows keep the peace; still, ask for a back-facing one if you're extra-sensitive.

The inn's biggest asset is its terrific staff, who go above and beyond to make guests happy and at home in New York. And thanks to Mayor Giuliani's quality-of-life campaign, this corner of the Theater District is now porn-free; it makes a great home base, especially for theatergoers. The inn has inspired a loyal following, so reserve early. However, there's no elevator in the four-story building, so overpackers and travelers with limited mobility should book elsewhere.

✪ **Comfort Inn Midtown.** 129 W. 46th St. (btw. Sixth Ave. and Broadway), New York, NY 10036. ☎ **800/567-7720** or 212/221-2600. Fax 212/790-2760. www.applecorehotels. com. 80 units. A/C TV TEL. $109–$249 double, depending on season. Children under 14 stay free in parents' room. Rates include continental breakfast. Ask about senior, AAA, corporate, and promotional discounts; check www.comfortinn.com for online booking discounts. AE, DC, DISC, MC, V. Parking $20 nearby. Subway: 1, 2, 3, 9 to 42nd St./Times Sq.; N, R to 49th St.; B, D, F, Q to 47–50th sts./Rockefeller Center.

A major 1998 renovation brightened the former Hotel Remington's public spaces and small guest rooms, which now boast nice floral patterns, neo-Shaker furnishings, and marble and tile baths (a few have showers only, so be sure to request a tub if it matters). Everything's fresh, comfortable, and new. In-room extras include hair dryers, coffeemakers, blackout drapes, pay movies, and voice mail. Other plusses include a small fitness center (stairmaster, treadmill, bike) and a business center; a coffee shop was in the works at press time. This one's considerably cheerier than the Comfort Inn Manhattan (below), but stay there if you need your space. The location is excellent, steps from Times Square, Rockefeller Center, and the Theater District. We're not thrilled with Apple Core Hotels' (the management company that handles this Comfort Inn franchise) wide-ranging price schedule, but we found that it was relatively easy to get a well-priced room ($150 or less) even around holiday time, and rates drop as low as $79 in the off-season.

Herald Square Hotel. 19 W. 31st St. (btw. Fifth Ave. and Broadway), New York, NY 10001. ☎ **800/727-1888,** 800/643-9208 or 212/279-4017. Fax 212/643-9208. www.heraldsquare hotel.com. 123 units (112 with bathroom). A/C TV TEL. $55–$125 single; $110–$125 double. AE, DISC, JCB, MC, V. Parking $21. Subway: N, R to 28th St.; B, D, F, Q, N, R to 34th St.

Presiding regally over the entrance, Philip Martiny's gilded sculpture *Winged Life* is certainly emblematic of the new life the Puchall family has breathed into this older Manhattan hotel. They took the Carriere and Hastings beaux-arts building that was once home to *Life* magazine and reinvented it as a budget hotel with a sense of history. *Life* covers decorate the lobby, hallways, and some of the rooms. The rooms themselves are small and Spartan, with laminated furniture, florescent lighting, and good-size but older bathrooms; some rooms I saw were worn-looking and in need of a fresh paint job, but voice mail and in-room safes soften the blow. Still, if you're looking for a great location on a shoestring, this is a good bet (although I'd try booking in at the Portland Square, the Herald Square's sister hotel, first; see below). The friendly staff can arrange bus tours and airport transportation. The hotel is popular with Europeans and other visitors who love the nearby shopping (Macy's, Lord & Taylor, the Manhattan Mall) and sightseeing (the Empire State Building).

✪ **Hotel Edison.** 228 W. 47th St. (btw. Broadway and Eighth Ave.), New York, NY 10036. ☎ **800/637-7070** or 212/840-5000. Fax 212/596-6850. www.edisonhotelnyc.com. 869 units. A/C TV TEL. $125 single; $140 double; $155–$170 triple or quad; $160–$200 suite. Extra person $15. AE, CB, DC, DISC, MC, V. Valet parking $22. Subway: N, R to 49th St.; 1, 9 to 50th St.

There's no doubt about it—the Edison is one of the Theater District's best hotel bargains, if not the best. No other area hotel is so consistently value-priced. About 90% of the rooms were refurbished in 1998 (the rest should be done by the time you arrive), and they're *much* nicer than what you'd get for just about the same money at the nearby Ramada Inn Milford Plaza (which ain't exactly the "Lullabuy of Broadway!" these days). Don't expect much more than the basics, but you will find a firm bed (flat pillows, though), motel decor that's more attractive than most, a phone with data port, and a clean, perfectly adequate tile bathroom. Most double rooms feature two twins or a full bed, but there are some queens; request one at booking and show up early in the day for your best chance at one. Triple/quad rooms are larger, with two doubles.

Off the attractive deco-ish lobby is Cafe Edison, a hoot of an old-style Polish deli that's a favorite among ladder-climbing theater types and downmarket ladies who lunch; Sofia's, an Italian restaurant; a homey tavern with live entertainment most nights; and a gift shop. Services are kept at a bare minimum to keep rates down, but there is a beauty salon and a guest-services desk where you can arrange tours, theater tickets, and transportation. The hotel fills up with tour groups from the world over, but with nearly 1,000 rooms, you can carve out some space if you call early enough.

Hotel Wolcott. 4 W. 31st St. (at Fifth Ave.), New York, NY 10001. ☎ **212/268-2900.** Fax 212/563-0096. www.wolcott.com. 250 units. A/C TV TEL. $120 double; $140 triple; $170 suite. Discounted AAA, AARP, and promotional rates may be available. AE, JCB, MC, V. Parking $16 next door. Subway: B, D, F, Q, N, R to 34th St.

The Wolcott was one of the grande dames of Manhattan hotels at the start of the 20th century. Somewhat less than that now, it has been reinvented as a good-value option for bargain-hunting travelers. Only the lobby hints at the hotel's former grandeur; these days, the rooms are motel-standard, but they're well kept and quite serviceable. Plusses include spacious bathrooms and voice mail, plus minifridges in most rooms. On the downside, some of the mattresses aren't as firm as I might like, and the closets are small. And some of the triples are poorly configured—the front door to one I saw hit up right against a bed—but they're plenty big enough for three, and come with two TVs to avoid before-bedtime conflicts (as do the suites). All in all, you get your money's worth here. The hotel's has a basement coin-op laundry, a rarity for Manhattan. There's also a tour desk and a snack shop where you can get your morning coffee; an Internet center was in the works at press time.

Park Savoy Hotel. 158 W. 58th St. (btw. Sixth and Seventh aves.), New York, NY 10019. ☎ **212/245-5755.** Fax 212/765-0668. www.neon.net/parksavoy. 70 units. A/C TV TEL. $70 single; $85–$155 double/quad. Rates include tax. AE, MC, V. Parking $20 nearby. Subway: A, B, C, D, 1, 9 to 59th St./Columbus Circle; N, R to 57th St.

The Park Savoy isn't quite as nice as its sister hotel, the Chelsea Savoy (see above), but the lower prices reflect the quality difference, making it a good deal nonetheless. The hotel has been renovated recently so that all rooms have nice new black-and-white–tiled private baths, which are petite (with showers only) but attractive and clean. If your budget is tight, two of you can make do in the smallest rooms; the biggest ones can accommodate three or four in two double beds. Rooms are basic and a few I saw were in need of a fresh coat of paint, but they do the job. All have voice mail on the telephones, most have walk-in closets, and a few have minifridges. Services are kept to a minimum to keep rates low, but there's a good Pasta Lovers restaurant in the building that gives guests 10% off and will deliver to your room. Best if all is the attractive and convenient location—a block from Central Park and a stone's throw from Carnegie Hall, Lincoln Center, and the Columbus Circle subway lines.

Portland Square Hotel. 132 W. 47th St. (btw. Sixth and Seventh aves.), New York, NY 10036. ☎ **800/388-8988** or 212/382-0600. Fax 212/382-0684. www.portlandsquarehotel. com or www.citysearch.com/nyc/portlandsquare. 145 units (30 with shared bathroom). A/C TV TEL. $60-$70 single or double with shared bathroom; $95-$109 single with private bathroom; $109-$119 double with private bathroom; $130-$140 triple or quad (in two double beds). Extra person $10. AE, JCB, MC, V. Parking $24. Subway: B, D, F, Q to Rockefeller Center.

Another Puchall family project (see the Herald Square Hotel, above), the Portland Square is a good Theater District bet for budget travelers. I like this hotel slightly better than the Herald Square: The public spaces have been nicely renovated, and everything seems to be in pretty good shape. The rooms are small, simple, and cheaply furnished (think laminated furniture, fluorescent lighting), but clean. Ask for one with an extra-large bathroom; some are almost as big as the bedroom. Avoid the shared-bathroom rooms if you can: The ratio is a high four rooms to a bathroom, the hall bathrooms I saw were on the crusty side, and most of the shared-bathroom rooms I visited had a smoky odor. But the private-bathroom rooms are a decent deal if money's tight. Every room has its own safe, voice mail on the phone, and air-conditioning year-round (many hotels take window units out in the winter). The staff is friendly and cooperative, but don't expect much in the way of service (that's one way they keep rates low). Luggage lockers are available.

Quality Hotel & Suites Midtown. 59 W. 46th St. (btw. Fifth and Sixth aves.), New York, NY 10036. ☎ **800/567-7720** or 212/719-2300. Fax 212/921-8929. www.applecorehotels. com. 193 units. A/C TV TEL. $109-$249 double; $149-$299 suite, depending on the season. Rates include continental breakfast. Children under 19 stay free in parents' room. Ask about senior, AAA, corporate, and promotional discounts. AE, DC, DISC, MC, V. Parking $20 nearby. Subway: B, D, F, Q to 47th-50th sts./Rockefeller Center.

Here's a fine choice for those looking for your basic, clean, well-outfitted hotel room for not too much money. Nice extras include coffeemaker with free coffee; decent closets with iron, ironing board, and safe; a smallish but fine bathroom with hair dryer; and phone with voice mail, data port, and free local calls (an excellent plus). The suites are great for families, with king bed, pullout sleeper sofa in the living room, and two TVs. The 1902 landmark building, with a beaux-arts facade and an attractive lobby, has been recently renovated to include a nice exercise room with cardio machines, two meeting rooms, and a business center with credit-card–activiated Internet access and fax and copy machines, as well as an ATM. The location, in the diamond district between Rockefeller Center and Times Square, is great for both business and pleasure. We're not thrilled with the management's wide-ranging price schedule, but we found that it was relatively easy to negotiate a good rate ($139 or less) even around holiday time, and rates drop as low as $79 in the off-season. (You might even be able to get a suite for 99 bucks if your timing is right.)

Ramada Inn Milford Plaza. 270 W. 45th St. (at Eighth Ave.). ☎ **800/2-RAMADA,** 800/221-2690 or 212/869-3600. Fax 212/398-6919. www.ramada.com. 1,310 units. A/C TV TEL. $109-$129 single; $124-$194 double. Corporate and AAA discounts available. AE, CB, DC, DISC, EC, JCB, MC, V. Parking $14 nearby. Subway: A, C, E to 42nd St.

Don't be surprised if this place sounds familiar—throughout the 1970s and 1980s, the Milford Plaza ran TV adds around the country declaring themselves "The Lullabuy of Broadway!" Well, it isn't exactly a bargain anymore—you'll get a much nicer room for your money at the nearby Hotel Edison (see above). But it's worth considering for a short stay if your timing is good and you can lock in a lower-than-rack rate. But you have to be lucky, because airline layover crews and international tour groups keep this place hopping despite its mediocrity. The rooms feature two twins, two doubles (for triples or quads only), or a queen; some of them are so small that there's hardly room to walk around the bed. The worn decor is plug-ugly, a fact accented by bad flourescent lighting, but the beds are firm, the towels surprisingly plush, and phones boast voice mail and data ports. Other hotel features include ice and soda machines on every floor, a decent fitness room, an international telephone room, limited room service, dry cleaning and laundry service, two on-site restaurants, a huge gift shop and newsstand, a game room with pool table and video games, and a guest-services desk that can arrange tours, theater tickets, and transportation.

Travel Inn. 515 W. 42nd St. (just west of Tenth Ave.). ☎ **888/HOTEL58,** 800/869-4630, or 212/695-7171. Fax 212/265-7778. www.newyorkhotel.com/travel. 160 units. A/C TV TEL. $125–$175 double; $250 executive suite. Extra person $15. Children under 16 stay free. AAA discounts available; check Web site for special Internet deals. AE, DC, DISC, MC, V. Free parking. Subway: A, C, E to 42nd St.–Port Authority Bus Terminal.

This hotel may be a bit on the expensive side for some budget travelers in the high-season or during show time at the nearby Javits Convention Center, but extras like a huge outdoor pool and sundeck, an up-to-date fitness room, and free parking (otherwise unheard of in Manhattan) make Travel Inn well worth the money even in busy seasons. It may not be loaded with personality, but it does offer the clean, bright regularity of a good chain hotel. Rooms are oversized and comfortably furnished, with extra-firm beds, a work desk (no data ports yet, though), alarm clock, full-length mirrors, iron and board, and almost all new bathrooms (ask for one when booking to be on the safe side) with hair dryers. Some of the furnishings are slightly worn at the edges, but everything else is new and fresh. Even the smallest double is sizable and has a roomy bathroom. There's an on-site coffee shop with room service (daily 6am–8pm), a gift shop run by Gray Line that can book tours and airport transfers, a well-equipped conference room, and a lifeguard on duty at that terrific pool in season. The neighborhood has gentrified nicely and isn't as far-flung as you might think: Off-Broadway theaters and great affordable restaurants are at hand, and it's just a 10-minute walk to the Theater District.

Washington Jefferson Hotel. 318 W. 51st St. (just west of Eighth Ave.), New York, NY 10019. ☎ **888/567-7550** or 212/246-7550. Fax 212/246-7622. www.citysearch.com/nyc/washingtonjeff. 150 units (35 with private bathroom). A/C (in summer) TV TEL. $68–$99 double with shared bathroom; $109–$149 double with private bathroom; $129–$169 suite, depending on season. Ask about special deals. AE, MC, V. Parking $15–$20 nearby. Subway: C, E to 50th St.

Here's a good choice in gentrifying Hell's Kitchen, just west of the Theater District. The lobby is warm and welcoming, the old-time staff service oriented, and the leafy, bistro-lined block one of the nicest in the neighborhood. The no-frills, mix-and-match rooms aren't anything special—expect small and K-mart quality and you won't be disappointed—but they do the job. The private-bathroom rooms have tiny tiled bathrooms with shower stalls, while the shared-bathroom rooms have older but larger in-hall bathrooms at a room-to-bathroom ratio of about 3 to 1. All rooms have clock radios, and shared-bathroom rooms have private sinks. Minifridges, microwaves, hair dryers, irons, and coffee-makers are available on request. The hotel has just hired the

PR man behind the successful, arts-oriented Gershwin (see above), hoping to appeal to young travelers and up-and-coming actors, so expect a move in that direction.

✪ **The Wyndham.** 42 W. 58th St. (btw. Fifth and Sixth aves.), New York, NY 10019. ☎ **800/257-1111** or 212/753-3500. Fax 212/754-5638. 140 units. AC TV TEL. $125–$140 single; $140–$155 double; $180–$225 1-bedroom suite; $320–$365 2-bedroom suite. AE, DC, MC, V. Parking $35 next door. Subway: N, R to Fifth Ave.; B, Q to 57th St.

This family-owned charmer is one of Midtown's best hotel deals—and it's perfectly located to boot, on a great block steps away from Fifth Avenue shopping and Central Park. The Wyndham is stuck in the 1970s on all fronts—don't expect so much as an alarm clock or hair dryer in your room, much less a data port—but its guest rooms are enormous by city standards, comfortable, and loaded with character. The entire hotel is papered with a wild collection of wallpaper, from candy stripes to crushed velvets, and some rooms definitely cross the tacky line. But others are downright lovely, with such details as rich oriental carpets and well-worn libraries, and the eclectic art collection that lines the walls boasts some real gems. Most importantly, the Me decade rates mean you get a lot for your money: The rooms all feature huge walk-in closets (the biggest I've ever seen); the surprisingly affordable suites also have full-fledged living rooms, dressing areas, and cold kitchenettes (fridge only). If you're put in a room that's not to your taste, just ask politely to see another one; the loyal staff is usually happy to accommodate. Dry cleaning and laundry service are available, as is limited room service (the restaurant should be in full swing by the time you arrive).

WORTH A SPLURGE

Belvedere Hotel. 319 W. 48th St. (btw. Eighth and Ninth aves.), New York, NY 10036. ☎ **888/HOTEL58** or 212/245-7000. Fax 212/265-7778. www.newyorkhotel.com/belvedere. 350 units. A/C TV TEL. $125–$240 double, depending on season. AAA discounts available; check Web site for special Internet deals. AE, DC, DISC, MC, V. Parking $17 on next block. Subway: C, E to 50th St.

If the Upper West Side's Lucerne is appealing but just a tad too pricey for you, or if you'd just rather not be Uptown, go with the Belvedere, another excellent hotel from the Empire Hotel Group. Public spaces, with a sharp retro-modern deco flair, lead to sizable, comfortable, and attractive rooms with smallish but very nice bathrooms with hair dryer and pantry kitchenettes with fridge, sink, and microwave (BYO utensils). Beds are nice and firm, and you'll find voice mail and data ports on the telephones. Ask for a renovated room, where you'll get good-quality cherry-wood furnishings, plus an alarm clock and work desk (in all but a few). Also ask for a high floor (8 and above) for great views; usually they'll cost no more (ask when booking).

　　On-site extras that make the Belvedere one of the city's top values include dry cleaning and laundry service, a self-serve Laundromat, electronic luggage lockers, fax and Internet-access machines, a brand-new and stylish breakfast room and light-bites cafe for guests, and the terrific Churrascaria Plataforma Brazilian restaurant (see chapter 6). At press time, two change rooms for guests with late flights and a cocktail lounge were in the works. On the edge of the Theater District, the neighborhood is loaded with terrific affordable restaurants along Ninth Avenue, and fancier places two blocks south on Restaurant Row.

Hotel Metro. 45 W. 35th St. (btw. Fifth and Sixth aves.), New York, NY 10001. ☎ **800/356-3870** or 212/947-2500. Fax 212/279-1310. 175 units. A/C TV TEL. $165–$250 double; $200–$325 suite. Extra person $25. Rates include continental breakfast. Off-season discounts may be available; check with airlines and other package operators for package deals. AE, DC, MC, V. Parking $20 nearby. Subway: B, D, F, Q, N, R to 34th St.

The Metro is the best choice in central Midtown for those who don't want to sacrifice either style or comfort for affordability. This lovely art-deco–ish jewel has larger rooms than you'd expect for the price, outfitted with smart retro furnishings, playful textiles, and extras like voice mail and data port on the phone and hair dryers and huge mirrors in the small but well-appointed bathroom. A great collection of black-and-white photos, from Man Ray classics in the halls to Garbo and Dietrich portraits in the lobby, adds to the glamorous vibe. Only about half the bathrooms have tubs, but the others have shower stalls big enough for two. One of the really nice things about this hotel is its welcoming public spaces: The comfy lounge area off the lobby, where buffet break-fast is laid out and the coffeepot's on all day, is a popular hangout; and the well-fur-nished rooftop terrace (a great place to order up room service) boasts one of the most breathtaking views of the Empire State Building. Dry cleaning and laundry service, room service from the stylish Metro Grill, and a sizable fitness room add to the great value.

8 Midtown East & Murray Hill

Carlton Arms. 160 E. 25th St. (btw. Lexington and Third aves.), New York, NY 10010. ☎ **212/679-0680** (reservations) or 212/684-8337 (guests). 54 units (20 with private bath-room). $57–$90 single–triple with shared bathroom; $68–$101 single–triple with private bathroom. Discounts for students and foreign visitors. 10% discount on seven-night stays paid upon arrival. MC, V. Parking $16 nearby. Subway: 6 to 23rd St.

The motto at the Carlton Arms is THIS AIN'T NO HOLIDAY INN—and boy, ain't that the truth. The true spirit of bohemianism and artistic freedom reigns in this back-packer's delight of a hotel, where every room is a work of art executed by an edgy artist given full license to go hog wild. Some spaces are sublime, such as Robin Banks' Car-toon Room (#5B), Thias Charbonet's Underwater Room (#1A), the ocean-blue lobby (complete with fish in the TV), and the stunning first-floor mosaic bathroom; others are simply bizarre. Whether you end up with a mermaid mural or a wall of teddy bears, you'll see why this is the most extraordinary hotel in the city.

But if you're looking for creature comforts and modern conveniences, this is *not* the place for you. The cramped rooms are basic—*very* basic. The beds are lumpy, there's no air-conditioning, and everything's old and on the crusty side. Each room has a sink, but you'll most likely end up sharing a hallway bathroom with your fellow travelers: mainly students, foreign travelers, and fellow existentialists. The place is kept clean, but there's no maid service during your stay. On the upside, the staff is super-friendly, and they'll be happy to take phone messages for you in the office (there's a pay phone in the lobby for outgoing calls). Reserve 1 to 2 months in advance, because despite the inconveniences this place is almost always full.

Habitat Hotel. 130 E. 57th St. (at Lexington Ave.), New York, NY 10022. ☎ **800/ 255-0482** or 212/753-8841. Fax 212/829-9605. www.stayinny.com. 300 units (about 60 with private bathroom). A/C TV TEL. $95–$105 single or double with shared bathroom; $110–$120 single or double with semi-private bathroom; $130–$170 single or double with private bathroom. AE, DC, MC, V. Parking $25 nearby. Subway: 4, 5, 6 to 59th St.; E, F to Lex-ington Ave.

This brand-new hotel is being marketed as "upscale budget," with rooms dressed to appeal to travelers who are short on funds but big on style. They're well designed in a natural palette that's accented with black-and-white photos. Everything is better quality and more attractive than I usually see in this price range, from the firm mat-tresses to the plush towels to the pedestal sinks in every room. The bathrooms—shared (one for every three to four rooms), semi-private (two rooms sharing a adjacent bath-room), and private—are all brand-new. The only downside—and it may be a big one for romance-seeking couples—are the sleeping accommodations: The double rooms consist of a twin bed with a pullout trundle, which takes up most of the width of the narrow room when it's open. (A few larger doubles with full-size beds and private bathrooms are scheduled to be available, but they were just in the planning stages at press time.) I think the prices are a tad high on the private-bathroom rooms considering the setup, but they're good for the shared-bathroom rooms; I would definitely choose the Habitat over the similarly accommodated Murray Hill and Amsterdam inns.

The neighborhood is excellent, especially for shoppers, since Bloomingdale's is just 2 blocks away. The public spaces were under the renovation when I visited (they should be completed by the time you arrive), but even the temporary lobby was more impressive than most. There's a glass-enclosed veranda looking down Lexington Avenue (where continental breakfast will be served), a bar, and a library lounge. Ask about guests-only deals such as 10% off one item at Bloomie's and reduced-rate access to nearby fitness centers.

Hotel Grand Union. 34 E. 32nd St. (btw. Madison and Park aves.), New York, NY 10016. ☎ 212/683-5890. Fax 212/689-7397. 95 units. A/C TV TEL. $110 double; $125 twin or triple; $150 quad. Rates increase during the holiday season. AE, DISC, MC, V. Parking $20. Subway: 6 to 33rd St.

This centrally located hotel is big with budget-minded international travelers. The rooms are spacious and clean and come with nice extras like voice mail, minifridges, and free HBO—but bad florescent lighting, cheap furniture and textiles, and an utter lack of natural light. The bathrooms vary greatly in quality, from almost-new to disco-era grim. Still, the prices are good, the staff is helpful, the lobby is pleasant, and there's an adjacent coffee shop for convenient meals. If asked to choose, I prefer the nearby Wolcott (see above). I suggest trying there first, and booking here only if you need to save the few dollars' difference.

Hotel 31. 120 E. 31st St. (btw. Park and Lexington aves.), New York, NY 10016. ☎ 212/685-3060. Fax 212/532-1232. www.citysearch.com/nyc/hotel31. 90 units (about half with private bathroom). A/C TV TEL. $85–$130 double. Rates include tax. No credit cards. Parking about $20 on next block. Subway: 6 to 33rd St.

This sister hotel to trendy Hotel 17 (see "The Flatiron District & Gramercy Park" above) is situated in a quiet, mostly residential neighborhood that's not quite as lovely as the 17th Street location, but fine nonetheless. The former SRO (the hotel still houses a number of permanent single-room-occupancy tenants) has been reinvented along the same lines as Hotel 17, with quirkily attractive but very basic rooms. They're dark and downright miniscule, but come with air-conditioning, alarm clocks, hair dryers, and voice mail. About half have private bathrooms; if you choose to save a few dollars and share, you'll have access to nice, newish bathrooms. Not all of the no-bathrooms have their own sinks, so be sure to request one when booking. Ask for a recently renovated room, as I spotted a few beginning signs of wear in the older ones. Since the hotel is most popular with—and most suited to—younger travelers and Europeans, there's lots of smoking going on; as a result, the narrow hallways tend to smell like cigarettes. Avid non-smokers may want to book elsewhere.

Murray Hill Inn. 143 E. 30th St. (btw. Lexington and Third aves.), New York, NY 10016. ☎ 888/996-6376 or 212/683-6900. Fax 212/545-0103. www.murrayhillinn.com. 50 units (39 with shared bathroom). A/C TV TEL. $75–$95 single or double with shared bathroom; $115–$135 single or double with private bathroom. Extra person $20. Ask about discounts and packages. No credit cards. Parking about $20 nearby. Subway: 6 to 33rd St.

Housed in a renovated five-story walk-up, the Murray Hill Inn (like its Upper West Side sibling, the Amsterdam Inn) offers very basic accommodations for those who want a bit more in terms of amenities and service than they'd get at a hostel. Frankly,

Getting the Most for Your Money, Part II: Dealmaking with the Chains

As you consider hotels, keep in mind that most—particularly those in the Times Square area, where most visitors want to stay, and particularly ones with recognizable names, like Comfort Inn, Holiday Inn, and Best Western—are highly sensitive to the market, in both directions. Because they hate to see rooms sit empty, they'll often negotiate astounding rates at the last minute and in the off-season.

Also keep in mind that the chains are where you're able to pull out all the stops for discounts, from auto club membership to senior status. AAA or AARP membership is well worth the annual fee for the 10% off it will garner you at most of the chains. And you may be able to take advantage of corporate rates or highly discounted weekend stays (more on that in the box earlier in this chapter). Most chain hotels will let the kids stay with mom and dad for free, and some even offer a special family rate for you and the kids. Always ask for every possible kind of discount; if you find that you get an unhelpful reservation agent at the main number, dial back and you're likely to get a more helpful one. And it's worth calling the hotel direct, where the front-desk staff will wheel and deal to keep their occupancy rate (the badge of honor among city hotels these days) high.

Of course, there's no guarantee what you'll be offered. Even if you're traveling in the off-season, you could stumble on a big convention or some other event that drives rates up. And your chances of getting a deal aren't great if you're visiting in a busy season. But if you're willing to make a few extra phone calls, or spend some time surfing online reservations systems, you may find that you can get a lot for your money at some very comfortable hotels that would otherwise be out of your price range.

Best Western (☎ **800/528-1234;** www.bestwestern.com) is one of the most reliable hotel chains in the nation, but the rack rates for their New York City hotels are higher than you'd expect—largely in the $200 range. At the **Best Western Seaport Inn,** 33 Peck Slip at South Street Seaport (☎ **800/HOTEL-NY** or 212/766-6600), doubles go for $169 to $209, but corporate rates and other seasonal discounts can drop to $149. Since rates include continental breakfast, that's a great deal on a very comfortable and well-kept hotel. At Midtown's **Best Western Woodward,** 210 W. 55th St. (☎ **800/336-4110** or 212/247-2000), and the **Best Western President,** 234 W. 48th St. (☎ **800/826-4667** or 212/246-8800), rack rates go well into the $200s, but I've found both hotels to offer rates as low as

both are highly priced for what you get; call here only if places like the Americana Inn, the Larchmont, the Newton, or the Cosmopolitan are booked up. Accommodations are no-frills: Rooms are small, with not much more than a bed or two (most have either two twins or a full size) with flat pillows, fluorescent lighting, a wall rack, and a TV. Some of the carpets are new, but others are old and stained. On the up side, most rooms with shared bathrooms have private sinks (request one when booking), the place is kept clean, and the residential neighborhood is quiet and nice. Rooms with private bathrooms are nicest; most have new bathrooms and sofas. The Euro-style rooms share the in-hall bathrooms at a ratio of about 8 rooms to 3 bathrooms—not bad. Don't let them book you into one of the few bunk-bed rooms left—monks live

$119 double ($107 to seniors and AAA members) in slower periods, such as Thanksgiving and just after the New Year.

Frankly, I'm not thrilled with the wide-ranging pricing policy at **Apple Core Hotels** (☎ 800/567-7720; www.applecorehotels.com) a small management company that handles three chain hotels reviewed in this chapter: the **Comfort Inn Midtown** (p. 99), the **Quality Hotel & Suites Midtown** (p. 101), and the **Quality Hotel Eastside** (p. 108), as well as the **Best Western Manhattan,** 17 W. 32nd St. (☎ 800/551-2303 or 212/736-1600). All have modest but comfortable and well-kept rooms with rack rates ranging from $109 to $249. If you can get a room on the lower end of that scale, it's always a good deal, especially when free continental breakfast and small business and fitness centers sweeten the pie in all but the Quality Hotel Eastside. You may even be able to do better depending on the season in which you visit—I've heard them negotiate rates as low as $79 a night more than once, which is a smokin' deal.

Comfort Inn Manhattan, at 42 W. 35th St. (☎ 800/228-5150 or 212/947-0200; www.comfortinnmanhattan.com), is not run by Apple Core, but it can offer some great deals on comfortable rooms nonetheless. The best time to stay here is between January and July, when standard rates run $129 to $189 double (including a substantial continental breakfast), and you may be able to do better with discounts and a little negotiation.

Like Best Western, **Holiday Inn** (☎ 800/HOLIDAY; www.holiday-inn.com) has also upped the ante on their New York City hotels, with rack rates hovering perilously close to $200. If you can negotiate a room down to $150 or so, it's well worth it. Unfortunately, both at the very nice **Holiday Inn Downtown,** on the edge of Chinatown and close to SoHo at 138 Lafayette St. (☎ 212/966-8898), the **Holiday Inn Broadway,** 49 W. 32nd St. (☎ 888/NYHOLIDAY or 212/736-3800), it's difficult to do better than $189 in all but the slowest seasons. Still, it's worth a try.

If you want something a bit on the nicer side, see what's on offer at **Loews New York,** 569 Lexington Ave. (☎ 800/836-6471 or 212/752-7000; www.loewshotels. com/newyork), a very nice chain hotel with business and fitness centers. Rack rates start at $189 here, but you can often do markedly better, especially if you ask for corporate, AAA, or senior discounts. Free cribs and rollaways for the kids can make this hotel a particularly good deal.

---

better. The public spaces are freshly redone, and there's a pleasant little lobby, plus a downstairs lounge and luggage storage area. The personable staff can book airport transfers and tours.

Pickwick Arms Hotel. 230 E. 51st St. (btw. Second and Third aves.), New York, NY 10022. ☎ 800/PICKWIK in the United States, 800/874-0074 in Canada, or 212/355-0300. Fax 212/755-5029. 320 units (200 with bathroom). A/C TV TEL. $70–$99 single; $125–$160 double. AE, CB, DC, MC, V. Parking $28 nearby. Subway: 6 to 51st St.

For a Midtown hotel in prime East Side territory, staying at the Pickwick is like entering an economic time warp. Set in one of the city's most prestigious neighborhoods, the hotel's location couldn't be better. The older, sometimes astoundingly small rooms are spare, some might even say monklike, but they're well kept, and the entire place is safe and well run. This former SRO has a few doubles and twins with private bathrooms (the larger deluxe twins can accommodate a rollaway for a third person), but the majority of rooms are singles with private, semi-private, or shared hall bathrooms. Two friends traveling together can take advantage of the semi-private situation: Two singles—each with its own sink, TV, desk, small closet, and telephone—share a bathroom, for the same price as a twin room. All of the bathrooms are worn looking and have showers only, but they're clean. A renovation is spiffing up the halls and some rooms a bit. On site is a rooftop patio with skyline views; Scarabee, a good but pricey French-Mediterranean restaurant; and a wine bar that also serves breakfast.

Quality Hotel Eastside. 161 Lexington Ave. (at 30th St.), New York, NY 10016. ☎ **800/ 567-7720** or 212/545-1800. Fax 212/790-2760. www.applecorehotels.com. 79 units (59 with private bathroom). A/C TV TEL. $109–$249 double, depending on the season. AE, DISC, MC, VISA. Parking $17 2 blocks away. Subway: 6 to 33rd St.

This hotel is nothing special—just some small, standard rooms done in a vaguely early-American style with older bathrooms. The property's recommendable features are its location, in a nice, quiet residential neighborhood, and its amenities, which include a business center (with copy and fax machines, plus Internet access) and a fitness room (with treadmill, lifecycle, and nordic track). In-room extras include coffeemaker, iron and board, data port, alarm clock, voice mail, and hair dryer. There's an affordable pasta joint next door, plus an adjacent coffee shop for your morning joe. Though it doesn't exactly excite me, I'm including this place because it can be a real deal—rates have been known to drop to as low as $79 on occasion. Don't bother if rates are higher than $139—you can do better for the money. And skip the shared bathrooms altogether.

Vanderbilt YMCA. 224 E. 47th St. (btw. Second and Third aves.), New York, NY 10017. ☎ **212/756-9600.** Fax 212/752-0210. www.ymcanyc.org. 374 units with shared bathroom, 5 with private bathroom. A/C TV. $65–$75 single; $78–$85 twin; $125–$135 suite. AE, MC, V. Parking about $20 nearby. Subway: S, 4, 5, 6, 7 to Grand Central.

This YMCA boasts a friendly, youthful atmosphere and a fashionable East Side location that's also convenient: It's within walking distance of the United Nations, Rockefeller Center, and Grand Central Terminal, as well as lots of good shopping and restaurants. The rooms are Spartan and tiny—I repeat, tiny—but the beds do somehow fit, as do the TVs, dressers, and desks. The more expensive rooms have sinks, and the suites have private bathrooms. The communal bathrooms and showers are well kept. A state-of-the-art fitness center—with two pools, a sauna, and sundeck, plus a full calendar of classes—is free to Y guests. The sports facilities and reasonably priced meals at the on-site cafe alone make the Y a worthwhile choice; other extras include room service from the cafe, luggage storage, safe-deposit boxes, and a self-service Laundromat. The rooms are booked far in advance, so call well ahead.

9 The Upper West Side

Amsterdam Inn. 340 Amsterdam Ave. (at 76th St.), New York, NY 10023. ☎ **212/ 579-7500.** Fax 212/579-6127. www.amsterdaminn.com. 20 units (about half with private bathroom). A/C TV TEL. $75–$95 single or double with shared bathroom; $115–$135 single or double with private bathroom. Packages and group discounts may be available. Cash or traveler's checks only. Parking $25 at adjacent lot. Subway: 1, 9 to 79th St.

Housed on the top three floors of a newly renovated five-story walk-up, the Amsterdam Inn offers very basic accommodations for those who want a bit more in terms of amenities and service than they'd get at a hostel. The inn's biggest assets are its prime Upper West Side location and its newness. Accommodations are no-frills: Rooms are small and narrow, with not much more than a bed, a wall rack to hang your clothes on, a cheap set of drawers with a TV on top, a side table with a lamp and a phone that requires a deposit to activate, and a sink if there's no private bathroom. The Euro-style rooms share the in-hall bathrooms at a ratio of about 2½-to-1. All the bathrooms are brand new and have showers only. Frankly, I think the rates are too high for what you get, but the friendly management seems willing to negotiate, so try to talk them down; if $135 for a double with private bathroom is the best they can do, you can probably do better elsewhere. If you book a double, make sure it's a *real* double, with a double bed, not a single with a trundle. The singles with trundles can accommodate two, but don't expect to have much space left over.

✪ **Hotel Newton.** 2528 Broadway (btw. 94th and 95th sts.), New York, NY 10025. ☎ 888/HOTEL58 or 212/678-6500. Fax 212/678-6758. www.newyorkhotel.com/newton. 120 units (10 with shared bathroom). A/C TV TEL. $85 single or double with shared bathroom; $99–$135 single or double with private bathroom; $150 suite. Extra person $15. Children under 17 stay free. AAA discounts available; check Web site for special Internet deals. AE, DC, DISC, MC, V. Subway: 1, 2, 3, 9 to 96th St.

Finally—a budget hotel that's actually *nice*. Unlike many of its peers, the Newton doesn't scream "budget!" at every turn, or require you to have the carefree attitude of a college student to put up with it. As you enter the pretty lobby, you're greeted by a uniformed staff that's attentive and professional. The rooms are generally large, with good, firm beds, a work desk, and a sizable new bathroom, plus roomy closets in most (a few of the cheapest have wall racks only). About 36 rooms are big enough to accommodate families on a budget in two doubles or two queen beds. The suites feature two queens, a sofa in the sitting room, plus niceties like a microwave, minifridge, iron and board, and hair dryer, making them well worth the few extra dollars. The bigger rooms and suites have been upgraded with cherry-wood furnishings, but even the older laminated furniture is much nicer than I usually see in this price range. Travelers on a shoestring can opt for one of the few doubles that share a hall bathroom with one other room. The AAA-approved hotel is impeccably kept, and there was lots of sprucing up going on—new drapes here, fresh paint there—during my last visit. The nice neighborhood boasts lots of affordable restaurants, and a cute diner on the same block provides room service from 6am to 1am. The 96th Street express subway stop is just a block away, providing convenient access to the rest of the city. A great bet all the way around.

Hotel Riverside. 350 W. 88th St. (btw. West End Ave. and Riverside Dr.), New York, NY 10024. ☎ 888/HOTEL58 or 212/724-6100. Fax 212/873-5808. www.newyorkhotel. com/riverside. 82 units (37 with shared bathroom). A/C TV TEL. $90–$100 single or double with shared bathroom; $100–$140 single or double with private bathroom. Extra person $10. Children under 16 stay free. Check Web site for special Internet deals. Parking about $29 nearby. Subway: 1, 9 to 86th St.

The Hotel Riverside is another good choice from the Empire Hotel Group, the same people behind the Newton (above) and the Lucerne (below). I prefer the Newton over the Riverside for the money, but the Riverside is also nicely kept and boasts a very quiet location, just steps from Riverside Park in one of the city's most desirable residential neighborhoods. Some rooms even have Hudson River views. All have firm beds and work desks, and those with private bathrooms sport fresh tile and new fixtures. The private-bathroom rooms are the best deal here; some of the shared-bathroom rooms (and shared bathrooms themselves) are a tad crusty for the relatively high price tag. Management is friendly and professional, and the public spaces are much finer than what I usually see in hotels in this price range. On-site coin-operated laundry for guests' use is another plus.

Uptown Accommodations

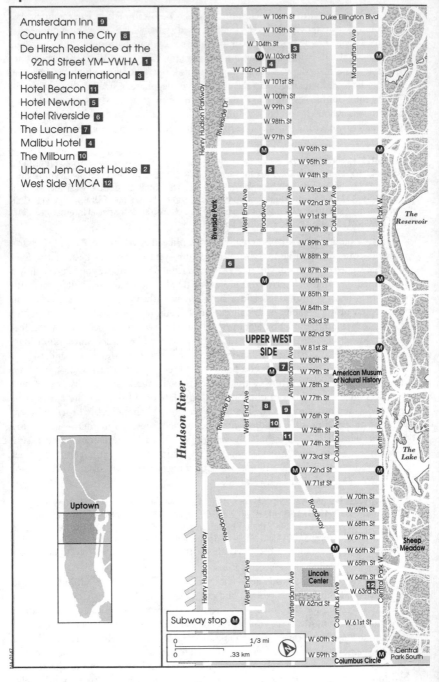

Amsterdam Inn **9**
Country Inn the City **8**
De Hirsch Residence at the
   92nd Street YM–YWHA **1**
Hostelling International **3**
Hotel Beacon **11**
Hotel Newton **5**
Hotel Riverside **6**
The Lucerne **7**
Malibu Hotel **4**
The Milburn **10**
Urban Jem Guest House **2**
West Side YMCA **12**

Uptown

Henry Hudson Parkway
Riverside Dr
Riverside Park
West End Ave
Broadway
Amsterdam Ave
Columbus Ave
Central Park W

W 106th St
W 105th St
Duke Ellington Blvd
W 104th St **3**
W 103rd St
W 102nd St **4**
W 101st St
W 100th St
W 99th St
W 98th St
W 97th St
W 96th St
W 95th St
W 94th St **5**
W 93rd St
W 92nd St
W 91st St
W 90th St
W 89th St
W 88th St
W 87th St
W 86th St
W 85th St
W 84th St
W 83rd St
W 82nd St
W 81st St
W 80th St
W 79th St **7**
W 78th St
W 77th St
W 76th St **9**
W 75th St **10**
W 74th St **11**
W 73rd St
W 72nd St
W 71st St
W 70th St
W 69th St
W 68th St
W 67th St
W 66th St
W 65th St
W 64th St
W 63rd St **12**
W 62nd St
W 61st St
W 60th St
W 59th St

Manhattan Ave

UPPER WEST
SIDE

6 **8**

The
Reservoir

American Musum
of Natural History

The
Lake

Sheep
Meadow

Hudson River

Riverside Dr
West End Ave
Freedom Pl
Henry Hudson Parkway
West End Ave
Amsterdam Ave
Columbus Ave
Broadway
Central Park W

Lincoln
Center

Subway stop **M**

0   1/3 mi
0   .33 km

Columbus Circle
Central
Park South

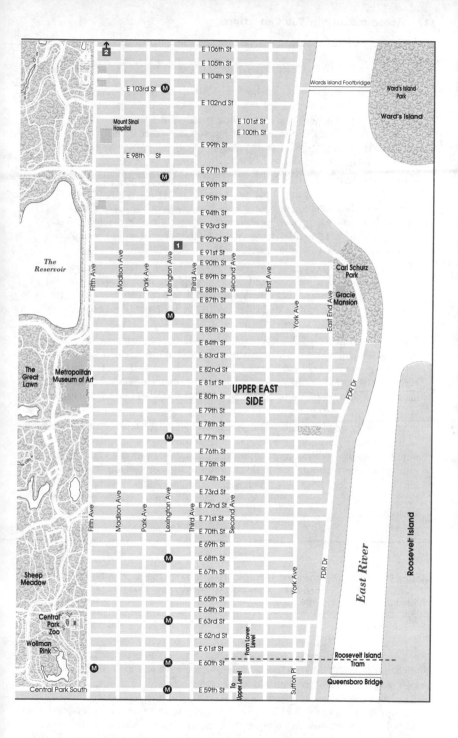

Affordable Family-Friendly Hotels

Now that New York has been reborn as a family-friendly city, a number of hotels now make it attractive for parents to take along the kids. The best way for families on a budget to save is to bunk together in a larger room with two double or queen beds. However, some hotels have wallet-friendly suite deals that allow the kids to sleep on a pullout sofa, thus giving everybody a little well-deserved privacy.

Money-saving tip: Most hotels add a surcharge to the nightly rate—anywhere from $10 to $25 per person, per night—for each extra person beyond two sharing a hotel room. Ten bucks may seem like a drop in the bucket, but it can really add up. So if you're traveling with the kids, choose a hotel that lets kids stay free. Even if the hotel usually charges for kids, they may be willing to drop this extra charge to draw you in, so always ask.

Chelsea Savoy Hotel *(p. 95)*   This 2-year-old Chelsea hotel boasts attractive, affordable rooms that are large and comfy enough to accommodate four. Big closets and roomy, immaculate bathrooms with tons of counter space make sharing even easier. Children under 13 stay free and complimentary continental breakfast is served.

Broadway Inn *(p. 98)*   This lovely, welcoming Theater District inn has a dozen suites—with pullout sofa, microwave, minifridge, and lots of closet space—that are a great deal for small families who want more home-style comforts than an average hotel room can offer. Rates include continental breakfast. This is a walk-up, however, so be prepared to carry pre-walkers and strollers up and down stairs.

Hotel Edison *(p. 100)*   The freshly renovated Edison is one of the Theater District's best hotel bargains. Quads can accommodate four in two double beds, and value-priced suites with pullout sofas offer even more space to spread out. The nearly 1,000-room hotel bustles around the clock with families and tour groups from around the world, so you can feel comfortable allowing the kids to act like kids here. Services are kept to a minimum to keep rates low, but there's a guest-services desk, plus a coffee shop/delicatessen that serves wallet-friendly meals.

Malibu Hotel. 2688 Broadway (at 103rd St.), New York, NY 10025. ☎ **800/647-2227** or 212/222-2954. Fax 212/678-6842. www.malibuhotelnyc.com. 150 units (40 with shared bathroom). TV. $39–$69 single or double with shared bathroom; $79–$109 deluxe single or double with private bathroom; $109–$149 quad (2 doubles) with private bathroom. Inquire about discounts for stays of a week or more. MC, V. Parking $20 nearby. Subway: 1, 9 to 103rd St.

If you're committed to finding a private-bathroom room for less than $100, it's hard to do better than this walk-up hotel. The rooms are small and basic, with little more than a moderately firm bed with a colorful spread (or two in the bigger rooms), an alarm clock on the bedside table, black metal shelving for the TV and your belongings (some rooms also have a wall rack for hanging clothes), and a newish bathroom that's small but slightly roomier than most in the budget category. Those with private bathrooms also have air-conditioning. The shared-bathroom rooms have private sinks and

Quality Hotel & Suites Midtown *(p. 101)* It's well worth a call to price a suite at this clean, well-outfitted hotel—especially if you're traveling in the off-season, when rates can drop dramatically. We've even seen suites go for as low as $99, but don't count on a deal like that—even $159 is a great deal on one of these spacious accommodations, which feature a king bed, a sleeper sofa in the living room, and two TVs. No charge for kids under 19, and local phone calls are value-added freebies.

Travel Inn *(p. 102)* If you're driving the family into the city, seriously consider Travel Inn, where free garage parking (otherwise unheard of in New York) saves you a minimum of $25 a day (probably more). In summer, the kids will love the huge outdoor pool and sundeck, and you'll love the freedom to relax while they play. No suites are available (the one executive suite isn't outfitted for families), but rooms are oversized and comfortably furnished (some with two queens, another rarity in New York), and almost all new, spacious bathrooms. Yet another plus: Children under 16 stay free.

The Milburn *(p. 113)* This budget-minded Upper West Sider is a real suite deal for any visitor to the city, but their kids-under-12-stay-free policy makes it a particularly stellar choice for families. Every room has a fully outfitted kitchenette (with microwave!) and a comfortable dining area, which can really save you money on meals. The one-bedroom suites are a bargain, and a pullout queen sofa in the living room makes them plenty comfortable for families. The terrific residential neighborhood is extremely kid friendly, and both Riverside and Central parks are an easy walk away.

Hotel Beacon *(p. 115)* There's no more splurge-worthy choice than the Beacon. Ideally located in the same kid-friendly neighborhood as the Milburn, the Beacon is one the best deals in town for families. Fitted with two double beds, virtually all of the spacious standard rooms are big enough for a family of four. Every room has a fully stocked kitchenette that makes breakfast and snacktime a cinch, and a Laundromat on site makes life even easier. The one- and two-bedroom suites give families plenty of room to spread out. Children under 17 stay free, which softens the blow.

share hall bathrooms at a ratio of one to every three or four rooms. I saw dust along the carpet edges and other maintenance issues here and there, and a hint of cigarette smoke pervaded the halls—but I've seen much worse for more money. (The rooms with private bathrooms seem to be somewhat better maintained.) The clientele is mostly young, with a good number of Europeans in the mix. The neighborhood has really come up in the last few years; it's safe, nice, and filled with lots of affordable restaurants. The front desk can book tours, airline transfers, and Atlantic City bus trips, but don't expect much more in the way of service.

✪ **The Milburn.** 242 W. 76th St. (btw. Broadway and West End Ave.), New York, NY 10023. ☎ 800/833-9622 or 212/362-1006. Fax 212/721-5476. www.milburnhotel.com. 111 units. A/C TV TEL. $119–$145 studio double; $149–$175 1-bedroom suite, depending on season. Extra person $10. Children under 12 stay free in parents' room. AE, CB, DC, MC, V. Parking $16–$20. Subway: 1, 2, 3, 9 to 72nd St.

On a quiet side street a block from the Hotel Beacon (see below), the Milburn also offers rooms with kitchenettes in the same great neighborhood for less. The Milburn may not be quite as nice as the Beacon, but it is arguably better in the less busy seasons, when a double studio goes for just $119. Every room is rife with amenities: dining area, safe, iron and ironing board, hair dryer, two-line phone with data port, alarm, nice newish bathroom, and kitchenette with minifridge, microwave, coffeemaker (with free coffee!), hot plate on request, and all the necessary equipment. The one-bedroom suites also boast a pullout queen sofa and a work desk. Don't expect much from the decor, but everything is attractive and in good shape. In fact, the whole place is spotless. But what makes the Milburn a real find is that it's more service oriented than most hotels in this price range. The friendly staff will do everything from providing free copy, fax, and e-mail services to picking up your laundry at the dry cleaners next door. Additional facilities include a self-serve Laundromat, VCR rentals, wheelchair-accessible rooms, discount dining programs at local restaurants, and use of the nearby Equinox health club for a special $15 fee (usually $35). At press time, a small workout room was in the works.

West Side YMCA. 5 W. 63rd St. (btw. Broadway and Central Park West), New York, NY 10023. ☎ **212/875-4100.** Fax 212/875-1334. www.ymcanyc.org. 550 units (25 with private bathroom). A/C TV. $65 single with shared bathroom; $75 double with shared bathroom; $95 single with private bathroom; $110 double with private bathroom. AE, MC, V. Parking about $25 nearby. Subway: 1, 9, A, B, C, D to Columbus Circle.

Another Y with a stellar location (see the Vanderbilt YMCA, above, and the 92nd Street Y, below), this one is housed in a National Historic Landmark building just steps from Lincoln Center and Central Park. A multimillion-dollar renovation of the public areas and guest rooms has made it more attractive and modern than the typical Y—but it's still a Y, so don't expect more than basic. The rooms are small and most share bathrooms down the hall, but they're well kept and outfitted like a real hotel room. Frankly, the Y is no cheaper than staying at a private hotel, but what makes it worth the money are the excellent health and fitness facilities, which include two pools, gyms, an indoor running track, handball and racquetball courts, exercise classes, and much more. There's also a cafe, luggage storage, and use of safe-deposit boxes. While not the equal of the 92nd Street Y, the West Side Y does offer a busy slate of arts and cultural programs. It's also a good bet for older travelers since the fitness center gives exercise and aqua-therapy classes for seniors, and hosts an extensive Elderhostel Program from September through May. The location and price keep the Y filled to capacity virtually every night, so book well in advance.

SUPER-CHEAP SLEEPS

Hostelling International–New York. 891 Amsterdam Ave. (at 103rd St.), New York, NY 10025. ☎ **800/909-4776, code 01** or 212/932-2300. Fax 212/932-2574. www.hinewyork. org. 624 beds, 4 units with private bathroom. A/C. $22–$24 AYH members, $3 extra nonmembers; private rooms $100 for up to 4 guests. Stays limited to 7 days (length of stay may be negotiable). Individual travelers must be 18 or older. JCB, MC, V. Parking $20 nearby. Subway: 1, 9 to 103rd St.

This landmark building is home to American Youth Hostels' largest hostel. Staying here is like going back to college—a very international college, with clocks set for six different time zones behind the front desk and a young, backpack-toting clientele from around the globe. Beds are incredibly cheap, but expect to bunk it (upper or lower?) with people you don't know in rooms of 4, 6, 8, or 12. Everything is extremely basic, but the mattresses are firm and the shared bathrooms are nicely kept. There are also four rooms with one double and two bunk beds that have private bathrooms. The well-managed hostel feels like a student union, with bulletin boards and listings of events posted; a coffee bar with an ample menu and pleasant seating; two TV rooms; a sundries shop; a game room; and a smoky library with bill- and credit-card–operated computers with Internet access. (An ATM and electronic luggage lockers were to be added during the renovation of the public spaces, which was ongoing at press time.) There's also a common kitchen, vending machines on each floor, a nice coin-op laundry, a second-floor terrace, and a really nice, big yard with picnic tables and barbecues in summer. There's a nice school spirit to the place. The neighborhood has improved over the years, but it's still a little sketchy over here on Amsterdam Avenue; one block over is much nicer Broadway, lined with affordable restaurants and shops.

WORTH A SPLURGE

Country Inn the City. W. 77th St. (btw. Broadway and West End Ave.), New York, NY 10024. (Exact address omitted by request of owner.) ☎ **212/580-4183.** Fax 212/874-3981. www.countryinnthecity.com. 4 units. A/C TV TEL. $160–$185 double. No sales tax added for stays of 7 nights or more. No credit cards. 3-night minimum. Maximum 2 per apartment; no children under 12 allowed. Parking $25 nearby. Subway: 1, 9 to 79th St.

If this marvelous gem fits your budget, book now—it's well worth every penny, and then some. This charming town house features four beautifully outfitted guest rooms that are rich with original details, impeccable Americana-style decor, and more homey comforts than you'll find anywhere else for the price. Each is actually a full studio apartment, with a cozy sofa, table and chairs for two, a private phone with answering machine, and a gorgeous, supremely comfortable queen bed in the large, high-ceilinged bedroom; a big galley kitchenette with a coffeemaker and everything you'll need to prepare a full meal; and a spacious, pretty bathroom. The whole place is bright and elegant, and the appointments—from the Oriental carpets covering the hardwood floors to the (nonworking) fireplaces that grace every room—couldn't be finer. Wonderful portraits, tasteful collectibles, and brandy and fresh fruit enhance the homey atmosphere. My favorite is no. 4, done in soft yellow with a high poster bed and whitewashed floorboards. Everything is immaculate, thanks to resident housekeeper Abigail, who provides maid service every other day. A quiet, peaceful air pervades the house, and the neighborhood couldn't be nicer. An excellent choice in every respect. No smoking is allowed.

Hotel Beacon. 2130 Broadway (at 75th St.), New York, NY 10023. ☎ **800/572-4969** or 212/787-1100. Fax 212/724-0839. www.beaconhotel.com. 210 units. A/C TV TEL. $145–$165 single; $170–$185 double; $205–$450 suite. Extra person $15. Children under 17 stay free in parents' room. AE, DC, DISC, MC, V. Parking $25 nearby. Subway: 1, 2, 3, 9 to 72nd St.

Ideally located in one of the city's most desirable neighborhoods, a few blocks from Lincoln Center, Central Park, and the Museum of Natural History, the Beacon is one the best deals in town, especially for families. Every generously sized room features a fully stocked kitchenette (with cooktop, coffeemaker, minifridge, and microwave), roomy closet, alarm, voice mail on the phone, and new marble bathroom with hair dryer. Rooms won't win any personality awards, but they're freshly done in muted florals. Virtually all standard rooms feature two double beds, and they're spacious enough to sleep a family on a budget. The big one- and two-bedroom suites are some of the best bargains in the city; each has two closets and a pullout sofa in the well-furnished living room. The two-bedrooms have a second bathroom. Another great family-friendly extra is the self-service Laundromat. There's no room service, but with gourmet markets like Zabar's and Fairway nearby, cooking is an attractive alternative, and there are plenty of restaurants nearby. Concierge and dry cleaning/laundry service are available, plus access to a terrific nearby health club for a daily fee. All in all, a great place to stay—and a great value to boot.

The Lucerne. 201 W. 79th St. (at Amsterdam Ave.), New York, NY 10024. ☎ **800/ 492-8122**, 888/HOTEL58, or 212/875-1000. Fax 212/579-2408. www.newyorkhotel.com/ lucerne. 250 units. AC TV TEL. $150–$230 double; $190–$240 junior (queen) suite; $220–$450 1-bedroom suite. AE, DC, DISC, MC, V. Parking $16 nearby. AAA discounts offered; check Web site for special Internet deals. Subway: 1, 9 to 79th St.

Want top-notch comforts and service without paying top-dollar prices? Then book into this Mobil 4-star, AAA 3-diamond hotel, one of the best values in the city. As soon as the morning-suited doorman greets you at the entrance to the 1903 landmark building, you'll know you're getting more for your money than you expected. The bright marble lobby leads to comfortable guest rooms done in a tasteful Americana style. The standard rooms are big enough for a king, queen, or two doubles (great for those traveling with kids). All rooms have Nintendo, coffeemakers, alarm, two-line phones with voice mail and data port (although not always near the work desk), iron and board, and very nice bathrooms with hair dryer, spacious travertine counters, and good toiletries. Everything is fresh and immaculate. The suites also boast a very nice kitchentte with microwave and minifridge, terry robes, and a sitting room with a sofa and an extra TV and Nintendo set. The queen suites are a great deal for couples willing to spend a few extra dollars, while the larger suites with two queens or a king and pullout sofa give families the room they need (although Mom and Dad might get more space for their money at the Beacon).

The Lucerne prides itself on its excellent service record. Amenities include a better-than-average fitness center with cardio machines and free weights, room service (7am–midnight), laundry and dry-cleaning service, secretarial services (a business center was in the works at press time), and meeting space with a terrific rooftop sundeck. On-site is Wilson's, a Upper West Side hotspot featuring good continental fare and even better live jazz 3 or 4 nights a week.

10 The Upper East Side

De Hirsch Residence at the 92nd Street YM–YWHA. 1395 Lexington Ave. (at 92nd St.), New York, NY 10128. ☎ **888/699-6884**, or 212/415-5650. Fax 212/415-5578. www. 92ndsty.org. 372 units (all with shared bathroom). A/C. $69 single; $90 double; long-term stays (2 months or more) $795/month single; $1,100–$1,300/month double. Must be at least 18 and no older than 30 for long-term stays. AE, MC, V. Parking $20 nearby. Subway: 4, 5, 6 to 86th St.; 6 to 96th St.

Contact the 92nd Street Y well in advance, because its good value and its unparalleled cultural programs mean it's always booked up. The de Hirsch Residence offers basic but comfortable rooms, each with either one or two single beds, a dresser, and bookshelves. Each floor has a large communal bathroom, a fully equipped kitchen/dining room with microwave, and laundry facilities. The building is rather institutional looking, but it's well kept and secure, the staff is friendly, and the location is terrific. This high-rent Upper East Side neighborhood is just blocks from Central Park and Museum Mile, and there's plenty of cheap eats and markets within a few blocks. Daily maid service and use of the Y's state-of-the-art fitness facility (pool, weights, racquetball, aerobics) is included in the daily rates. This is a great bet for lone travelers in particular, since the 92nd Street Y is a community center in a true sense of the word, offering a real sense of kinship and a mind-boggling slate of top-rated cultural happenings (see chapter 9 for details).

11   Harlem

Urban Jem Guest House. 2005 Fifth Ave. (btw. 124th and 125th sts.). ☎ **212/831-6029.**
Fax 212/831-6940. www.urbanjem.com. 4 units (2 with shared bathroom that can be combined into a suite). A/C TV TEL. $105 double with shared bathroom; $120 double with private bathroom; $200 suite. 2-night minimum. Rates include continental breakfast upon
request. Extra person $15. Rates $15 less for single travelers. 10% off 7–13 nights, 15% off 14
days or more. AE, DISC, MC, V. Parking $15 nearby. Subway: 2, 3 or 4, 5, 6 to 125th St.

This B&B is Harlem's best place to stay. It's run by Jane Alex Mendelson, a refugee
from the corporate world who has successfully reinvented herself as an innkeeper.
Located in the Mount Morris Historic District, her renovated 1878 brownstone is
graced with fine woodwork and beautiful original (nonworking) fireplaces. The house
is a work in progress, so don't expect perfection—there's still plenty to be done, and
the furnishings are largely an odds-and-ends mismatch. But the accommodations offer
good value. The second floor has two guest rooms with firm queen beds, new private
bathrooms, and spacious kitchenettes with stove, minifridge, and the basic tools for
preparing and serving a meal. On the third floor are two nice rooms that share a hall
bathroom and kitchen: one a pretty bedroom with a queen bed, the other a spacious
room with two foldout futon sofabeds. They can also be combined into a two-
bedroom suite, which gives you a whole floor to yourself.

You can pay an extra $7.50 for daily maid service (the trash is taken out daily);
otherwise, sheets and towels are changed weekly. There's also a washer and dryer for
use ($3). Jane is friendly and helpful, and can provide lots of neighborhood infor-
mation. The predominately African-American community isn't a regular home base
for tourists, but the bustling urban neighborhood has welcomed the inn, and it
makes a good starting point for exploring jazz-, gospel-, and history-rich Harlem.
Midtown is about a half-hour subway ride away, but Jane recommends taking a cab
back after 11pm or so.

6

Great Deals on Dining

Attention foodies: Welcome to mecca. Without a doubt, New York is the best restaurant town in the country, perhaps tops in the world. Other cities might have particular specialties—Paris has better bistros, of course, Hong Kong better Chinese, Los Angeles better Mexican, Austin better barbecue—but no culinary capital spans the globe so successfully as the Big Apple.

The sheer variety of eating places is astounding. That's due in part to New York's vibrant immigrant mix. Let a newcomer arrive and see that his or her native foods aren't being served and *zap!*—there's a new restaurant, cafe, or grocery to fill the void. Yet we New Yorkers can be fickle: One moment a restaurant is hot; the next it's passé. So restaurants close with a frequency we wish applied to the arrival of subway trains. Always call ahead.

But there's one thing we all have to face sooner or later: Eating in New York just ain't cheap. The primary cause? The high cost of real estate, which is reflected in what you're charged. Wherever you're from, particularly if you're from the reasonably priced American heartland, New York's restaurants will seem *expensive.* Yet, as you peruse the chapter that follows, you'll see that good values abound—especially if you're willing to eat ethnic, and venture beyond tourist zones into the neighborhoods where budget-challenged real New Yorkers eat, like Chinatown, the Upper West Side, and the East Village, which is particularly good for getting a lot of bang for your buck. But even if you have no intention of venturing beyond Times Square, don't worry: I've included inexpensive restaurants in every neighborhood in the list below—including some of the city's best-kept secrets.

For the absolute best of what the city has to offer, take a moment to check out "Best Low-Cost Dining Bets" in chapter 1, if you haven't already. Also take a quick look at the dining section in chapter 2's "60 Money-Saving Tips" for general advice on how to save while you're in the city. Frommer's Online Directory, in the back of the book, lists several Web sites that offer extensive listings and reviews of New York restaurants.

RESERVATIONS Reservations are always a good idea in New York, and a virtual necessity if your party is bigger than two. Do yourself a favor and make them so you won't be disappointed. If you're booking dinner on a weekend night, it's a good idea to call a few days to a week in advance if you can. In some cases—you want to score a bargain prix-fixe lunch, say, or dinner at TV chef Mario Batali's perennial hotspot Pó—calling a month ahead isn't too soon.

But What If They Don't *Take* **Reservations?**   Lots of city restaurants, especially at the affordable end of the price continuum, don't take reservations at all. One of the ways they're able to keep prices down is by packing people in as quickly as possible. This means that the best cheap and midpriced restaurants often have a wait. Again, your best bet is to go early. Often, you can get in more quickly on a weeknight. Or just go knowing that you'll have to wait if you head to a popular spot like Boca Chica. There are worse ways to wait than sipping a margarita at the festive bar.

THE LOWDOWN ON SMOKING   Following the national trend, New York City enacted strict no-smoking laws a few years back that made the majority of the city's dining rooms blessedly smoke-free. However, that doesn't mean that smokers are completely prohibited from lighting up. Here's the deal: Restaurants with more than 35 seats cannot allow smoking in their dining rooms. They can, however, allow smoking in their bar or lounge areas, and most do.

Restaurants with fewer than 35 seats—and there are more of those in the city than you'd think, especially in the budget category—can allow or prohibit smoking as they see fit. This ruling has turned some of the city's restaurants (like NoLiTa's Cafe Gitane, for instance) into particularly smoker-friendly establishments, which might be a turn-off for nonsmokers.

Whether you're a smoker or nonsmoker, your best bet is to call ahead and ask if it matters to you. If you're hell-bent on enjoying an after-dinner cigarette indoors, make sure that the restaurant has a bar or lounge that allows smoking. Some restaurants even offer dinner tables in their bar areas, such as Bar Pitti and Clementine (a pricey restaurant that offers an affordable late-night menu in their sleek lounge), where you can puff away during the meal if you so choose. And smoking is usually allowed in alfresco dining areas, but never assume—always ask. If you're a nonsmoker who doesn't want to be bothered by second-hand smoke, make sure your seat is well away from the bar.

TIPPING   Tipping is easy in New York. The way to do it: Double the 8¼% sales tax and voilà! Happy waitperson. In fancier venues, another 5% is appropriate for the captain. If the wine steward helps, hand him or her 10% of the bottle's price.

In the restaurant reviews below, I've made notes about what you can expect in terms of service. However, keep in mind that it all depends on the luck of the draw, and your waitperson's personality. Remember: No matter where you eat, if you get good service, reward your waitperson accordingly. But if you genuinely feel like you were short shrifted, feel free to let the tip reflect it.

If you check your coat, leave a dollar per item, no matter how small, for the checkroom attendant.

1 Restaurants by Cuisine

AMERICAN

America (p. 148)
B Bar & Grill (p. 136)
Bendix Diner (p. 152)
Big Nick's Burger Joint (p. 169)
Brooklyn Diner USA (p. 162)
Cafeteria (p. 153)
Chat 'n' Chew (p. 149)
Coffee Shop (p. 149)
Corner Bistro (p. 144)
EJ's Luncheonette (p. 174)
Ellen's Stardust Diner (p. 163)

Empire Diner (p. 153)
Fanelli's Cafe (p. 132)
Gray's Papaya (p. 147)
Hamburger Harry's (p. 154)
Hard Rock Cafe (p. 162)
Harley-Davidson Cafe (p. 162)
Hi-Life Restaurant & Lounge (p. 174)
Jekyll & Hyde Club (p. 163)
Kitchenette (p. 125)
Manhattan Chili Co. (p. 158)
Mars 2112 (p. 163)
Motown Cafe (p. 163)

The Odeon (p. 126)
Old Town Bar & Restaurant
   (p. 150)
Official All-Star Cafe (p. 163)
Papaya King (p. 175)
Planet Hollywood (p. 163)
Popover Cafe (p. 172)
Prime Burger (p. 166)
Riverrun Cafe (p. 126)
Serendipity 3 (p. 174)
SoHo Kitchen & Bar (p. 134)
Tom's Restaurant (p. 172)
"21" Club (p. 129, 164)
Walker's (p. 126)
Wall Street Kitchen & Bar (p. 122)

BELGIAN

B. Frites (p. 161)
Cafe de Bruxelles (p. 144)

BRAZILIAN SOUTH AMERICAN

Boca Chica (p. 136)
Churrascaria Plataforma (p. 164)
Coffee Shop (p. 149)
Rice 'n' Beans (p. 159)

BRITISH

The British Open (p. 165)
North Star Pub (p. 122)
Tea & Sympathy (p. 147)

CHINESE

Evergreen Shanghai (p. 165)
Grand Sichuan Chinese Restaurant
   (p. 127)
Hunan Park (p. 169)
Joe's Shanghai (p. 127)
New York Noodletown (p. 128)
Sammy's Noodle Shop (p. 146)

CONTEMPORARY AMERICAN

Alley's End (p. 154)
Bridge Cafe (p. 124)
Clementine (p. 149)
Drovers Tap Room (p. 148)
Home (p. 147)
Sarabeth's Kitchen (p. 173)
The Tavern Room at Gramercy
   Tavern (p. 152)
Time Cafe (p. 139)

ETHIOPIAN

Meskerem (p. 158)

FRENCH

Alison on Dominick Street (p. 135)
Cafe Gitane (p. 132)
Florent (p. 145)
Franklin Station Cafe (p. 125)
French Roast (p. 145)
La Bonne Soupe (p. 155)
Les Sans Culottes (p. 158)
Payard Pâtisserie & Bistro (p. 176)
Steak Frites (p. 152)
Tartine (p. 146)

GREEK

Molyvos (p. 164)

GOURMET SANDWICHES/ DELI/CAFE

Bread & Butter (p. 134)
Canova Market (p. 160)
Devon & Blakely (p. 124)
Ecce Panis (p. 124)
Emerald Planet (p. 141)
Ess-A-Bagel (p. 165)
Housing Works Used Books Cafe (p. 134)
Island Burgers & Shakes (p. 154)
Mangia (p. 122)
Paradise & Lunch (p. 161)
Yura & Company (p. 175)

INDIAN

Bombay Dining (p. 137)
Cafe Spice (p. 148)
Gandhi (p. 137)
Haveli (p. 137)
Mitali East (p. 137)
Passage to India (p. 137)
Salaam Bombay (p. 125)

ITALIAN

Bar Pitti (p. 142)
Caffe Grazie (p. 175)
Carmine's (p. 162)
Cucina di Pesce (p. 137)
Frutti di Mare (p. 138)
Gemelli (p. 122)
Il Bagatto (p. 138)
Il Cortile (p. 130)
Pó (p. 146)
San Domenico (p. 164)

JAPANESE

Dosanko (p. 165)
Haru (p. 173)

Iso (p. 138)
Menchenko-Tei (p. 122)
Sapporo (p. 159)
Shabu Tatsu (p. 139)
Village Yokocho (p. 141)

JEWISH
Carnegie Deli (p. 140)
Fine & Shapiro (p. 122)
Katz's Delicatessen (p. 140)
Second Avenue Deli (p. 140)
Stage Deli (p. 140)

KOREAN
Bop (p. 142)
Hangawi (p. 159)
Village Yokocho (p. 141)
Won Jo (p. 159)
Woo Chon (p. 159)

LATIN AMERICAN
La Caridad 78 (p. 172)
Cafe Habana (p. 132)
La Taza de Oro (p. 153)

MALAYSIAN
Franklin Station Cafe (p. 125)

MEDITERRANEAN
Layla (p. 126)
Medusa (p. 150)
Sam's Falafel (p. 124)

MEXICAN/TEX-MEX
Burritoville (p. 124)
Gabriela's (p. 169)
Los Dos Rancheros Mexicanos
  (p. 158)
Manhattan Chili Co. (p. 158)
Taco & Tortilla King (p. 166)

PAN-ASIAN
Cafe Asean (p. 144)
Kelley & Ping (p. 133)
Republic (p. 150)
Rice (p. 133)

PIZZA
California Pizza Oven (p. 151)
John's Pizzeria (p. 155)
Lombardi's (p. 133)
Patsy Grimaldi's Pizzeria (p. 176)
Pintaile's Pizza (p. 151, 175)

Sofia's Fabulous Pizza (p. 175)
Totonno's Pizzeria Napolitano
  (p. 175)
Two Boots to Go (p. 147)

SCANDINAVIAN
The Cafe at Aquavit (p. 161)

SEAFOOD
Oyster Bar (p. 168)
Pisces (p. 138)

SOUP
Soup Kitchen International
  (p. 161)

SOUL FOOD
Sylvia's (p. 176)

SOUTHERN/BARBECUE
Acme Bar & Grill (p. 135)
Virgil's Real BBQ (p. 160)

SPANISH
La Paella (p. 138)

SWISS
Roetelle A.G. (p. 139)

THAI
Chanpen (p. 160)
Pongsri Thai Restaurant (p. 160)
Siam Inn Too (p. 160)
Thailand Restaurant (p. 129)

TURKISH
Bereket (p. 130)

UKRANIAN
Veselka (p. 141)

VEGETARIAN/
HEALTH-CONSCIOUS
Angelica Kitchen (p. 136)
Dojo (p. 144)
Josie's Restaurant & Juice Bar
  (p. 169)
The Pump (p. 168)
Spring Street Natural Restaurant
  (p. 134)
Zen Palate (p. 151)

VIETNAMESE
Nha Trang (p. 129)

2 South Street Seaport & the Financial District

If you're want to rub elbows with Wall Street's after-work crowd, head to the **Wall Street Kitchen & Bar,** which, like its sister restaurant **SoHo Kitchen & Bar** (p. 134), serves up affordably priced bar food along with 50 beers on tap and "flight" of wines and microbrews for tasting. Housed in a spectacular former bank building in the heart of the Financial District at 70 Broad St. (☎ 212/797-7070; www.citysearch.com/nyc/wallstkitchen), it's worth a stop for a beer and a burger.

Mangia. 40 Wall St. (btw. Nassau and William sts.). ☎ **212/425-4040** or 212/363-9536. Main courses $5.95–$9.95. AE, DC, MC, V. Mon–Fri 7am–8pm. Subway: 4, 5 to Wall St.; J, M, Z to Broad St. GOURMET DELI.

This big, bustling gourmet cafeteria is an ideal place to take a break during your day of Financial District sightseeing. Between the giant salad and soup bars, the sandwich and hot entrée counters, and an expansive cappucino-and-pastry counter at the front of the cavernous room, even the most finicky eater will have a hard time deciding what to eat. Everything is prepared fresh and beautifully presented. The soups and stews are particularly good (there are always a number of daily choices), and a cup goes well with a fresh-baked pizzette (a mini-pizza). Pay-by-the-pound salad bars don't get any better than this, hot meal choices (such as grilled mahi-mahi or cumin-marinated lamb kabob) are cooked to order, and sandwiches are made to order. This place is packed with Wall Streeters between noon and 2pm, but things move quickly and there's enough seating that usually no one has to wait. Come in for a late breakfast or an afternoon snack, and you'll virtually have the place to yourself.

In addition to the Wall Street location, Mangia also has two cafeteria-style cafes in Midtown that offer similar, if not so expansive, menus: at 50 W. 57th St., between Fifth and Sixth avenues (☎ 212/582-5882); and at 16 E. 48th St., just east of Fifth Avenue (☎ 212/754-7600).

North Star Pub. At South Street Seaport, 93 South St. (at Fulton St.). ☎ **212/509-6757.** Main courses $7.50–$12.95. AE, CB, DC, MC, V. 11:30am–10:30pm. Subway: 2, 3, 4, 5 to Fulton St. BRITISH.

This friendly place right at the entrance to the seaport is a refreshing bit of authenticity in this mallified, almost theme park–like historic district. It's the spitting image of a British pub, down to the chalkboard menus boasting daily specials like kidney pie and the Guinness, Harp, and Fullers ESB on tap. I love the ale-battered fish 'n' chips (not too greasy); the excellent golden-browned shepherd's pie (just like grandma used to make); the bangers 'n' mash, made with grilled Cumberland sausage; and the traditional Ploughman's, including very good pâté, a sizable hunk of cheddar or stilton, fresh bread, and all the accompaniments (even Branston pickle!). All in all, a fun, relaxing place to hang out and eat and drink heartily (and cheap). In keeping with the theme, there's also an expansive menu of single-malt scotches and Irish whiskeys.

QUICK BITES

The Twin Towers and environs abound with places to nosh. After all, those on-the-go bankers and traders have to eat lunch, don't they? But with so many options at hand, the trick is knowing where to go.

On the main concourse of the World Trade Center (WTC) is **Gemelli**, a fine Italian cafeteria-style restaurant serving up affordable pastas and the like (there's also a pricier full-service branch of Gemelli in WTC4, upstairs on the plaza, if you're looking to take a load off for awhile). **Sbarro Pizza, Menchenko-Tei** for authentic Japanese, and **Fine & Shapiro** are also on the main concourse, right in a row between Borders and

Lower Manhattan, TriBeCa & Chinatown Dining

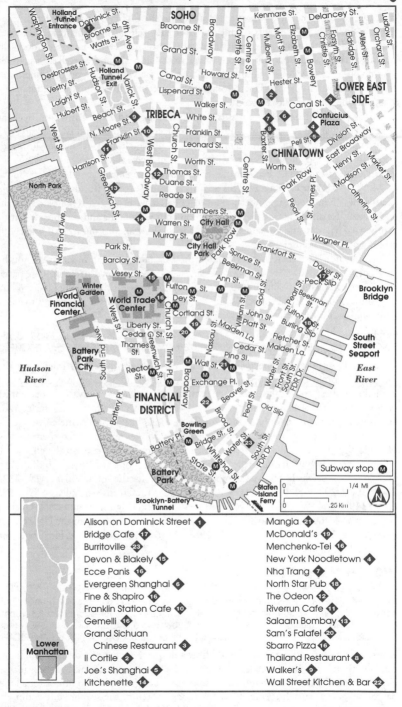

Alison on Dominick Street ◆1
Bridge Cafe ◆17
Burritoville ◆23
Devon & Blakely ◆15
Ecce Panis ◆16
Evergreen Shanghai ◆6
Fine & Shapiro ◆16
Franklin Station Cafe ◆10
Gemelli ◆16
Grand Sichuan
   Chinese Restaurant ◆3
Il Cortile ◆2
Joe's Shanghai ◆5
Kitchenette ◆14

Mangia ◆21
McDonald's ◆19
Menchenko-Tei ◆16
New York Noodletown ◆4
Nha Trang ◆7
North Star Pub ◆18
The Odeon ◆12
Riverrun Cafe ◆11
Salaam Bombay ◆13
Sam's Falafel ◆20
Sbarro Pizza ◆16
Thailand Restaurant ◆8
Walker's ◆9
Wall Street Kitchen & Bar ◆22

the center of the concourse (where the escalators to the PATH trains are). Menchenko-Tei is actually two restaurants in one: in front they sell Japanese bento box lunches with teriyakis and relatively cheap sushi, which are perfect for taking outdoors in warm weather; in the back are steam tables with Chinese food as well as a counter where you can order hearty udon and soba noodle bowls, which you can dine on at tables in back and upstairs. Fine & Shapiro has two entrances, one for full table service and one for the "only-to-go" deli.

Across the hall from those three is the recently opened **Ecce Panis,** an excellent bakery with a small selection of sandwiches, focaccias, breakfast and sweet treats, two daily soups, and tons of variations on the staff of life, including an amazing little creation: the ham and cheese brioche, which is sort of like a filled popover.

Just outside the WTC, between the north concourse entrance and Borders Books & Music, is **Devon & Blakely.** This appealing gourmet shop features lots of yuppie sandwiches (ham and camembert; smoked chicken with roasted tomatoes, spinach, and Caesar dressing), a few daily soups, a good chili with fixins and cornbread, British candy bars, pastries, and an espresso bar. The wide sidewalk just out front is lined with tables when the weather's nice.

Last but not least, there's **Sam's Falafel,** the best falafel cart in town, at the southwest corner of Broadway and Liberty Street. Sam's a well-known name in these parts, so the line can be long at lunchtime, but it always moves quickly. Nearby Liberty Plaza or Trinity Churchyard, two blocks south at Wall Street, both make great spots to enjoy your pita-wrapped lunch on a lovely day.

Burritoville. 36 Water St. (at Broad St.). ☎ **212/747-1100.** Main courses $4.25–$9.95. AE, DISC, MC, V. Daily 11am–midnight. Subway: 2, 3 to Wall St.; 1, 9 to South Ferry. TEX-MEX.

For a quick, healthy, and inexpensive lunch in the Seaport area, Burritoville fits the bill. These storefront taco shops serve up forward-thinking Mexican fare, all prepared with the freshest and healthiest ingredients, using no lard, preservatives, or canned goods—even the tortillas are pressed every day. Options range from well-stuffed taco and burrito standards to only-at-Burritoville creations like a spicy white chicken chili with cumin and a number of choice veggie wraps. As you might expect, there are lots of choices for vegetarians as well as anyone looking for a quick bite on the go.

There are a whole handful of Burritovilles throughout the city, including 141 Second Ave., between St. Mark's and 9th Street, in the East Village (☎ 212/260-3300); 298 Bleecker St., at Seventh Avenue, in Greenwich Village (☎ 212/633-9249); 264 W. 23rd St., between Seventh and Eighth avenues, in Chelsea (☎ 212/367-9844); and 166 W. 72nd St., at Amsterdam Avenue, on the Upper West Side (☎ 212/580-7700). Call ☎ 212/964-1119 or consult the White Pages for additional locations.

WORTH A SPLURGE

Bridge Cafe. 279 Water St. (at Dover St., just north of South Street Seaport). ☎ 212/227-3344. Reservations recommended. Main courses $12–$22; prix-fixe Sun brunch (until 4pm) $14.95; prix-fixe Sun dinner $19.95. AE, CB, DC, MC, V. Sun–Mon 11:45am–10pm; Tues–Fri 11:45am–midnight; Sat 5pm–midnight. Subway: 4, 5, 6 to Brooklyn Bridge–City Hall. Free parking after 6pm at the Edison parking lot, 1 block south. CONTEMPORARY AMERICAN.

It just isn't easy to find a decent and affordable place to eat in Lower Manhattan. Luckily, there's the Bridge Cafe. Housed in the oldest woodframe building in the city (built in 1794), this romantic little restaurant is a great place to dine after a long day of Seaport area sightseeing. It's a few blocks north of the seaport but definitely worth the couple of minutes' walk (take a cab if you're not good with maps). The room is a brick-walled charmer, and the service attentive and friendly. The menu changes seasonally, but expect variations on chicken (the fall version was marinated with chanterelles), roast duck, a few well-prepared fish dishes, and a few additional choices, such as a brisket of beef or a smoked chop. There's always a vegetarian choice, plus a wallet-friendly pasta or two. The all-American wine list boasts lots of good values, especially on **Wine Discovery Tuesdays,** when every bottle is 30% off.

3 TriBeCa

Franklin Station Cafe. 222 W. Broadway (at Franklin St.). ☎ **212/274-8525.** Sandwiches and noodle bowls $6–$9; house specials $10.50–$16.50. AE, DC, MC, V. Daily 8am–11pm. Subway: 1, 9 to Franklin St. FRENCH-MALAYSIAN.

This charming brick-walled cafe is a winner for affordable Malaysian noodle bowls and French-inspired sandwiches. All the dishes on the cute-as-a-button handwritten and illustrated menu are prepared by the health-minded kitchen with all-natural ingredients. Sandwiches are simple but satisfying creations like home-baked ham with honey mustard, lettuce, and tomato; fresh mozzarella with leafy basil, vine-ripened tomato, and extra-virgin olive oil; smoked salmon with mascarpone and chives; and old-fashioned tuna salad with jalapeno. For warm and cozy, you can't do better than one of Franklin Station's noodle bowls, such as tom yum shrimp, with sprouts, pineapple, and cucumber in a pleasingly hot-and-sour broth; or seafood udon, with generous helpings of squid, shrimp, and salmon in a milder vegetable broth. For a more substantial meal, check the blackboard for such house specials as Chilean sea bass in cardamom sauce, French- or Malaysian-style mussels, and grilled salmon with turmeric. Service is friendly and efficient, wine and beer is available, and the desserts (a fresh-baked tart, crème caramel, and home-baked banana or carrot-raisin cake are usually among the choices) are well priced and pleasing.

Kitchenette. 80 W. Broadway (at Warren St.). ☎ **212/267-6740.** Main courses $3.75–$6.50 at breakfast; $5.75–$7.50 at lunch and brunch; $8.50–$16 at dinner. AE ($20 minimum). Mon–Fri 7:30am–10pm; Sat–Sun 9am–10pm (soups and desserts only 4–5pm). Subway: 1, 2, 3, 9 to Chambers St. AMERICAN.

This unpretentious TriBeCa luncheonette has become a prime contender on the comfort-food circuit thanks to Hungry Man–sized breakfasts and just-like-home cooking. The little room has the feel of a New England country diner, with rough-edged folk art on the walls and mismatched country-rustic chairs at the tables. Expect high-cholesterol farmhouse breakfasts and hearty salads and sandwiches during the day. Weekly lunchtime blue-plate specials include excellent shepherd's pie with mashed potato crust on Tuesday, and gooey and delicious four-cheese mac and cheese on Friday (specials are always subject to change). In addition to salads and burgers, the nighttime menu features more sophisticated entrees like chicken pot pie with a cheddar biscuit crust, pot roast with pan potatoes and carrots, grilled pork chops (with Kitchenette's secret herb rub), and roast turkey with cornbread stuffing and sweet potato mashies. Everything is well prepared and filling (skip the prepackaged sandwiches at lunch, though). Service is sit-down at breakfast and dinner, but lunch is more cafeteria style, with orders taken at the counter. No wine or beer is served, but your welcome to BYO.

TriBeCa Meal Deal

At attractive **Salaam Bombay,** 317 Greenwich St., between Duane and Reade streets (☎ **212/226-9400**), the pan-Indian food is a cut above the standard fare, and the $10.95 all-you-can-eat lunch buffet, offered weekdays from noon to 3pm, is a steal.

Riverrun Cafe. 176 Franklin St. (btw. Greenwich Ave. and Hudson St.). ☎ **212/996-3894.** Most main courses $7.25–$14.25. AE, DC, DISC, MC, V. Daily 11:30am–midnight. Subway: 1, 9 to Franklin St. AMERICAN.

Down-to-earth as ever, this neighborhood pioneer is now a refreshing find in an increasingly haute 'hood. Before Nobu, before Chanterelle, before Miramax, before Sean Lennon grew up and moved Downtown, there was quiet, unpretentious, unassuming Riverrun, trying hard to feed the few savvy pioneers who thought it would be cool to live in a section of town known only for its egg merchants. Like a lot of vintage joints, the decor is more clutter than clean lines, but the menu is dependable: good burgers and salads, great sandwiches, plus a few satisfying entries like chicken pot pie. There's gratis chips for the bar crowd, a sensible wine list, a good selection of beers on tap, and a respectable single-malt selection. Not necessarily worth a special trip from Uptown, but a relaxing stop for those tired of New York's high prices and lofty pretensions.

Nearby **Walker's,** 16 North Moore St., at Varick Street (☎ 212/941-0142), is another old holdout from pre-fabulous TriBeCa. This pub and restaurant is surprisingly charming, with a tin ceiling, a long wooden bar, oldies on the sound system, friendly bartenders, and cozy tables where you can dine on affordable meat-and-potatoes fare. Prices are about the same no matter which one you choose, but Walker's has the advantage of being open later: from 11:45am to 4am daily, with the kitchen closing at 1am.

WORTH A SPLURGE

Layla. 211 W. Broadway (at Franklin St.). ☎ **212/431-0700.** Reservations recommended. Mezzes $6–$13; main courses $20–$27; $42 prix-fixe Layla's feast; $2 entertainment charge for belly-dancing show. AE, DC, MC, V. Mon–Thurs 5:30–11pm; Fri noon–2:30pm and 5:30–11:30pm; Sat 5:30–11:30pm; Sun 5:30–9:30pm. Subway: 1, 9 to Franklin St. MEDITERRANEAN/MIDDLE EASTERN.

Here's another wonderful TriBeCa restaurant from Drew Nieperont's Robert DeNiro–backed Myriad Group, the brains behind such wallet-busting spots as Nobu, Montrachet, and TriBeCa Grill. Unlike the others, though, which generally eschew themes, this one is like a page out of the *Arabian Nights*—there's even a belly dancer to entertain. A stylized take on a sultan's den, the fanciful dining room is the perfect setting for Layla's modern-meets–Middle East cuisine. Dinner can be expensive, but I wouldn't dream of coming here and ordering a traditional (and too pricey) appetizer-and-entree meal. The fun, high-energy setting and expansive, affordable mezze menu are made for family-style sharing. In fact, this is such a popular option that there's a $20 per person food minimum in the dining room, which you can circumvent if you wish by eating at the bar. The beautifully presented cuisine has a strong Greek influence, so expect well-prepared hummus, taramasalata, and babaganoush. But the mezzes quickly get more creative, with excellent coriander-crusted scallops over chickpeas and grilled flatbread topped with spicy lamb. The Moroccan couscous with braised lamb and the vegetable pastilla, are ideal entrees for sharing.

The Odeon. 145 W. Broadway (at Thomas St.). ☎ **212/233-0507.** Reservations recommended for parties of 4 or more. Main courses $9–$25. AE, DC, MC, V. Mon–Wed noon–2am; Thurs–Fri noon–3am; Sat 11:30am–3am; Sun 11:30am–2am. Subway: 1, 2, 3, 9 to Chambers St. (walk 3 blocks north). AMERICAN/FRENCH.

The Odeon is always the first place that comes to mind when I crave a late-night meal, but this attractive hotspot is satisfying at any time of day. The striking deco-ish room is perennially trendy but universally welcoming—no velvet ropes here. The restaurant crosses budget and culture lines: It's easy to eat cheap here if you stick to the burgers, vegetarian chili, and sandwiches, or you can spend a little more and go for excellent steak frites, roasted free-range chicken, braised lamb shank, and other top-notch brasserie-style fare. The prices are lower than they have to be for food like this, and the wine list is equally reasonable. With rich wood paneling, Formica-topped tables, and leather banquettes, the Odeon even manages to be swanky and comfortable at the same time. As proof of its egalitarianism, there's even a kid's menu—and the chocolate pudding is scrumptious.

4 Chinatown & Little Italy

In addition to the choices below, you might also want to consider the original Chinatown branch of **Evergreen Shanghai,** at 63 Mott St., south of Canal Street (☎ 212/571-3339), which accepts cash only.

Grand Sichuan Chinese Restaurant. 125 Canal St. (at Chrystie St.). ☎ 212/334-3323. Main courses $3.95–$15.95. No credit cards. Daily 11am–10pm. Subway: B, D, Q to Grand St. SZECHUAN CHINESE.

Attention spicy food lovers: Here's the Chinese restaurant for you. This plain Jane spot excels at dishes that are intensely spiced without being palate numbing—a brilliant culinary balance that few other Chinatown kitchens can achieve. The flavors are complex and strong, especially in such top choices as szechuan wontons in red oil, Chairman Mao's pork with chestnuts, and my favorite, boneless whole fish with pinenuts in a modified sweet-and-sour sauce. The house bean curd in spicy sauce is another winner, but only for those with a high tolerance for hot. Other terrific surprises include the sauteed loofah, a squashlike vegetable served in a variation on an oyster sauce—excellent. If some in your party shy away from hot and spicy, never fear: The friendly staff will be more than happy to recommend milder dishes.

There's now a second location at in Chelsea at 229 Ninth Ave., at 24th Street (☎ 212/620-5200; open daily 11am–11pm), which may even be a better bet than the original Chinatown location, since this is where the owner is focusing all of his attention these days.

☼ Joe's Shanghai. 9 Pell St. (btw. Bowery and Mott sts.). ☎ 212/233-8888. Reservations recommended for 10 or more. Main courses $4.25–$12.95. No credit cards. Sun–Thurs 11am–10pm; Fri–Sat 11am–10:30pm. Subway: N, R, 6 to Canal St.; B, D, Q to Grand St. SHANGHAI CHINESE.

Tucked away on a little elbow of a side street just off the Bowery, this Chinatown institution serves up authentic cuisine to enthusiastic crowds nightly. The stars of the huge menu are the signature soup dumplings, quivering steamed pockets filled with hot broth and your choice of pork or crab, accompanied by a side of seasoned soy. Listed on the menu as "steamed buns" (item numbers 1 and 2), these culinary marvels never disappoint. Neither does the rest of the authentic Shanghai-inspired menu, which boasts such main courses as whole yellowfish bathed in spicy sauce; excellent "mock duck," a saucy bean-curd dish similar to Japanese yuba that's a hit with vegeterians and carnivores alike; and lots of well-prepared staples. The room is set mostly with round tables of ten or so, and you'll be asked if you're willing to share. I encourage you to do so; it's a great way to watch and learn from your neighbors (many of whom are Chinese), who are usually more than happy to tell you what they're eating. If you want a private table, expect a wait.

Joe's Shanghai now has a second Manhattan location, in Midtown at 24 W. 56th St., just west of Fifth Avenue (☎ 212/333-3868). The Chinatown location remains

Bargain Alert—Great Prix-Fixe Lunch Deals

You walk the wide streets of TriBeCa, Midtown East, or the Upper East Side and gaze longingly past lace-curtained windows, behind which the barkeep is called a sommelier, menu items are so famous they're trademarked, and chocolate tortes are more artfully constructed than your home. Welcome to the world of fine dining, New York City style.

New York has one of the finest—and most expensive—dining scenes on the planet. But despite the fact that so many of them will think nothing of charging you upwards of $35 or $40 an entree, these restaurants are not entirely off limits. You just have to be a little creative about it. And the best time to be creative is at lunch.

Restaurant Week   In the last few years, many of New York's best restaurants started offering special summer prix-fixe lunches for a full week in late June (exact dates vary from year to year) at a cost mimicking the year ($20 even in 2000). It's an exceptional value, especially considering that lunch alone at some of these places can run upwards of $50 per person (or more with wine). The list of participating restaurants changes from year to year, but past participants have included such top-flight spots as **Jean Georges** (☎ 212/299-3900), **Union Square Cafe** (☎ 212/243-4020), **Chanterelle** (☎ 212/966-6960), **Gramercy Tavern** (☎ 212/477-0777), **Aureole** (☎ 212/319-1660), **Le Cirque 2000** (☎ 212/303-7788), **Daniel** (☎ 212/288-0033), and other *New York Times* 3- and 4-star winners.

There are catches. The offer applies only for lunch, and most restaurants limit your selection to three choices per course. At some restaurants, you must eat at the bar, or in a subsidiary room. Wine, tip, and tax are extra; occasionally you'll have to dine at a late hour, like after 2pm.

If you think you might be visiting during Restaurant Week, be on the lookout for this year's schedule as early as mid-April. There's always a full spread in the *New York Times,* as well as announcements on the restaurant pages of online sources like **www.newyork.sidewalk.com** and **www.newyork.citysearch.com**. Or just start calling the restaurants you're interested in and ask; many will even start taking reservations before the official announcement. Start dialing at least a

the better bargain, however; dishes are $2 to $5 more at the Midtown branch, which accepts reservations.

✪ **New York Noodletown.** 28½ Bowery (at Bayard St.). ☎ **212/349-0923.** Main courses $3.95–$10.95. No credit cards. Daily 9am–4am. Subway: N, R, 6 to Canal St. SEAFOOD/ CHINESE.

This just may be the best Chinese food in New York City. Among its fans are Ruth Reichl, restaurant critic for the *New York Times,* who constantly puts it at the top of the heap. But don't expect fancy—this is two-star food served in no-star ambiance. So what if the room is reminiscent of a school cafeteria? The food is fabulous. The mushroom soup is a lunch in itself, with earthy chunks of shiitakes, vegetables, and thin noodles. Another filling appetizer is the hacked roast duck in noodle soup. The kitchen excels at seafood, so be sure to try at least one: Looking like a snow-dusted plate of meaty fish, the salt-baked squid is sublime. The Chinese broccoli or the crisp sautéed baby bok choy make great accompaniments. Unlike most of its neighbors, New York Noodletown keeps very long hours, which makes it the best late-night bet in the neighborhood, too.

month in advance, because most restaurants—particularly the most popular ones—book up instantly.

But What If I'm Going to Miss Restaurant Week?   Don't worry—there are plenty of midday deals to be had for visitors who won't be here for that particular week in June.

A number of superb restaurants—many in Downtown districts—maintain their Restaurant Week deal all summer long. Though the list changes from year to year, among them are usually stellar **Chanterelle, Nobu** (☎ 212/219-0500), **Aquavit** (☎ 212/307-7311), **Gotham Bar & Grill** (☎ 212/620-4020), and **Tavern on the Green** (☎ 212/873-3200).

Even others simply offer a wallet-friendly lunchtime prix-fixe year-round. Upscale taverna **Molyvos** (p. 164) has a stellar $20 three-course meal that even includes their wonderful baklava. Favorite Miramax hangout **TriBeCa Grill** (☎ 212/941-3900), also features a $20 midday feast with limited but excellent choices.

While not quite that inexpensive, the midday prix-fixe meal at soaring Pacific Rim newcomer **Union Pacific** (☎ 212/995-8500) is well worth the $29 to $35 tariff. Ditto for **Gramercy Tavern,** where the stellar three-course lunch is $33, and the legendary caviar house **Petrossian** (☎ 212/245-2214), where it's $22 (a still-bargain-basement $39 with caviar). The midday deal is just $28 at the legendary **"21" Club** (☎ 212/582-7200). You can enjoy celebrity chef Jean-Georges Vongerichten's celebrated cuisine for just $28 midday at French/Thai fusion stalwart **Vong** (☎ 212/486-9592), or in the casual cafe Nougatine at his four-star French **Jean Georges** (☎ 212/299-3900). The prix-fixe lunch at top-rated **Aureole** (see "Restaurant Week" above) is always $20 after 2pm (earlier diners pay $32 each). Lastly, there's renowned chef Daniel Boulud's **Café Boulud** (☎ 212/772-2600), probably my favorite spot in the city for a ladies-who-lunch lunch, where the prix-fixe deal is well worth $28 to $35.

So, for foodies whose palettes are broader than their bank accounts, the lesson is this: get on the horn and start calling, preferably before you come to town.

Nha Trang. 87 Baxter St. (btw. Canal and Bayard sts.). ☎ **212/233-5948.** Reservations recommended for large parties. Main courses $4–$12.50. No credit cards. Daily 10:30am–9:30pm. Subway: N, R, 6 to Canal St. VIETNAMESE.

The decor may be standard-issue, no-atmosphere Chinatown (glass-topped tables, linoleum floors, mirrored walls), but this friendly, bustling place serves up the best Vietnamese in Chinatown. A plate of crispy, finger-sized spring rolls is a nice way to start, as the slightly spicy pork-and-shrimp filling is nicely offset by the wrapping of lettuce, cucumber, and mint. The pho noodle soup comes in a quart-sized bowl brimming with bright vegetables and various meats and seafood. But my favorite dish is the simple barbecued pork chops—sliced paper-thin, soaked in a soy/sugar-cane marinade, and grilled to utter perfection. Everything is well prepared, though, and your waiter will be glad to help you design a meal to suit your tastes. If there's a line, stick around; it won't take long to get a table.

Thailand Restaurant. 106 Bayard St. (at Baxter St.). ☎ **212/349-3132.** Reservations recommended. Main courses $4.95–$12.95. AE. Daily 11:30am–11pm. Subway: N, R, 6 to Canal St. THAI.

Thai has also been added to the expanding menu in Chinatown, and this kitchen turns out first-rate dishes—aromatic, searing, full of zest and colors. When you say spicy you'd better mean it, because your tongue will sizzle like a Midtown sidewalk in August. The sliced charcoal steak with onions, hot pepper, lemon juice, and mint is a fabulously fiery, flavorful appetizer. The tasty green curry with coconut milk, eggplant, bamboo shoots, and green chilies comes with your choice of chicken, beef, pork, lamb, or shrimp. Sautéed rice noodles are a good choice to offset the tangier dishes. The whole fish, especially sea bass, are delicately crispy outside, moist and flaky inside. The coconut-milk dessert, with slices of ice cubes, is the perfect finish.

WORTH A SPLURGE

Il Cortile. 125 Mulberry St. (btw. Canal and Hester sts.). ☎ **212/226-6060.** Reservations recommended. Pastas $8.50–$22; meats and fish $16.50–$32. AE, DC, DISC, MC, V. Sun–Thurs noon–midnight; Fri–Sat noon–1am. Subway: 6, N, R to Canal St. NORTHERN ITALIAN.

The best restaurant in Little Italy stands out on Mulberry Street thanks to its warm, sophisticated demeanor amid the bright lights and bold decor of its lesser neighbors. The interior has a dramatic skylit atrium; I prefer the cozier front room. You know you're out of the Little Italy ordinary when the warm basket of focaccia, crusty small loaves, golden-brown crostini, and crunchy breadsticks arrive. The Northern Italian fare is well prepared and pleasing: The greens fresh and crisp, the sauces appropriately seasoned, the pastas perfectly al dente. This is traditional cuisine, but not without a few welcome twists: The filet mignon carpaccio is rolled with onions and parsley, thick cut, and seared; shiitakes give an unexpected flair to the rigatoni. Fish and meat dishes can get expensive, but it's easy to keep the bill down with pastas or vegetarian plates. On my last visit, the best dish at our table was polenta with mushrooms in a savory white-wine sauce, a bargain at $10.50. The staff, made up of career neighborhood waiters, is attentive and reserved in an appealing Old World style. The extensive wine cellar contains a good number of well-priced selections.

5 The Lower East Side

Deli lovers should also consider **Katz's Delicatessen,** 205 E. Houston St., at Ludlow Street (☎ **212/254-2246**). All their traditional eats are first-rate, particularly their beloved all-beef hot dogs. For details, see "The New York Deli News" box later in this chapter.

Bereket. 187 Houston St. (at Orchard St.). ☎ **212/475-7700.** Reservations not accepted. Main courses $4–$10. No credit cards. Open 24 hours. Subway: F to Second Ave. TURKISH.

This popular Turkish kebab house is little more than a hole in the wall, but there's no arguing with the excellent quality of their grilled meats. Order at the counter, where you'll see the freshly skewered kebabs displayed behind glass, and then try to snare one of the few tables as your plate is being prepared. The kofte, ground lamb mixed with spices, is a favorite, but you won't go wrong with any of the choices. Complete dinners— which come with two skewers of your choice, rice, and salad—are a steal at $8, or $10 for the mixed grill, which features chicken, shish (beef), and doner (lamb) kebabs. Vegetarians have a lot to choose from as well, including excellently herbed hummus, falafel, great piyaz (white bean salad with chopped onions and parsley), and babaganoush. The counter staff is much more friendly and accommodating than I've come to expect from a place like this. No alcohol is served, but Turkish coffee should provide the necessary jolt. (Or consider getting your order to go and walking a couple of blocks up to dba, on First Avenue between 2nd and 3rd streets, where you can match your takeout meal with any number of fine brews; see chapter 9).

East Village & SoHo Area Dining

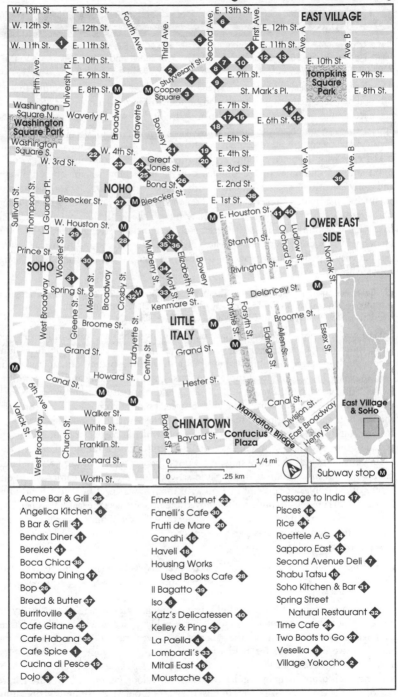

W. 13th St. | E. 13th St.
W. 12th St. | E. 12th St.
W. 11th St. | E. 11th St.
Fifth Ave. | E. 10th St.
E. 9th St.
E. 8th St.
Washington Square N.
Washington Square Park
Washington Square S.
W. 4th St.
W. 3rd St.

E. 13th St.
EAST VILLAGE
E. 12th St.
E. 11th St.
E. 9th St.
St. Mark's Pl.
Tompkins Square Park
E. 9th St.
E. 8th St.
E. 7th St.
E. 6th St.
E. 5th St.
E. 4th St.
E. 3rd St.
E. 2nd St.

Fourth Ave. · Third Ave. · Second Ave. · First Ave. · Ave. A · Ave. B

Stuyvesant St. · Cooper Square · Bowery

NOHO
Bleecker St. · Bleecker St.
W. Houston St.
Great Jones St.
Bond St.
E. 1st St.
E. Houston St.

SOHO
Prince St.
Spring St.
Broome St.
Grand St.
Howard St.
Canal St.
Walker St.
White St.
Franklin St.
Leonard St.
Worth St.

Sullivan St. · Thompson St. · La Guardia Pl. · Wooster St. · Greene St. · Mercer St. · Broadway · Crosby St. · Lafayette St. · Centre St. · Baxter St. · Church St. · West Broadway · Varick St. · 6th Ave.

Mulberry St. · Elizabeth St. · Mott St. · Bowery · Christie St. · Forsyth St. · Eldridge St. · Allen St. · Orchard St. · Ludlow St. · Essex St. · Norfolk St.

LITTLE ITALY
Kenmare St.
Grand St.
Hester St.
Canal St.

CHINATOWN
Bayard St. · **Confucius Plaza**
Baxter St.

LOWER EAST SIDE
Stanton St.
Rivington St.
Delancey St.
Broome St.
Division St.
East Broadway
Henry St.
Manhattan Bridge

Ave. A · Ave. B

East Village & SoHo

0   1/4 mi
0   .25 km

Subway stop **M**

Acme Bar & Grill **25**
Angelica Kitchen **6**
B Bar & Grill **21**
Bendix Diner **11**
Bereket **41**
Boca Chica **38**
Bombay Dining **17**
Bop **26**
Bread & Butter **37**
Burritoville **8**
Cafe Gitane **35**
Cafe Habana **36**
Cafe Spice **1**
Cucina di Pesce **19**
Dojo **3** **22**

Emerald Planet **23**
Fanelli's Cafe **30**
Frutti de Mare **20**
Gandhi **16**
Haveli **18**
Housing Works
  Used Books Cafe **28**
Il Bagatto **39**
Iso **5**
Katz's Delicatessen **40**
Kelley & Ping **29**
La Paella **4**
Lombardi's **43**
Mitali East **16**
Moustache **13**

Passage to India **17**
Pisces **15**
Rice **34**
Roettele A.G **14**
Sapporo East **12**
Second Avenue Deli **7**
Shabu Tatsu **10**
Soho Kitchen & Bar **31**
Spring Street
  Natural Restaurant **32**
Time Cafe **24**
Two Boots to Go **27**
Veselka **9**
Village Yokocho **2**

6 SoHo & NoLiTa

Cafe Gitane. 242 Mott St. (at Prince St.). ☎ 212/334-9552. Reservations not accepted. Main courses $4.50–$6 at breakfast; $7.50–$9.25 at lunch and dinner. AE, MC, V. Daily 9am–midnight. Subway: B, D, F, Q to Broadway–Lafayette St.; 6 to Spring St. FRENCH CAFE.

This NoLiTa cafe feels like it came straight out of the Latin Quarter, complete with lithe French-accented waiters, black-clad bohemian hipsters, and clouds of imported cigarette smoke. It's quite an affected place, alright, but somehow the attitude is the appeal—not to mention the good, cheap eats. The short, internationally accented menu is mainly comprised of sandwiches and noodle bowls. Appealing choices include baked eggs with baguette; noodles with shrimp and white beans in curried coconut milk; smoked salmon with red onions, capers, and lemon wasabi on sourdough; and—my favorite—roasted chicken with chipotle mayo, fresh Parmesan, and anchovies on a toasted baguette. In true French style, all the breads are admirable and ultra-fresh. Meals are well worth the money but on the small side; big appetites will have plenty of room for dessert. Beverage choices include strong coffee drinks and French wines by the glass or bottle. The servers may not have found their true calling yet, but they're polite and helpful. Don't miss the petite bathroom, which boasts some gorgeous mosaic work.

✪ **Cafe Habana.** 17 Prince St. (at Elizabeth St.). ☎ 212/625-2001. Reservations not accepted. Main courses $4.95–$12.50. AE, DISC, MC, V. Daily 9am–midnight. Subway: B, D, F, Q to Broadway–Lafayette St.; 6 to Spring St. LATIN AMERICAN.

Lots of new low-priced restaurants have taken root over the past year, but I've enjoyed none more than Cafe Habana, a sleek update on a typical Latin American luncheonette. It manages to be hip without being the least bit pretentious, and what the food may lack in authenticity it more than makes up for in quality and flavor: shrimp are big and hearty, pork is moist and flavorful, and cilantro and other spices are fresh and aromatic. Winning starters include pozole, hominy corn stew with shredded chicken or pork in a clear broth that you season to taste with oregano, chili, and lime; and the hugely popular Mexican corn on the cob, which is coated with lime juice and grated cheese, sprinkled with chili powder, and grilled into a messy but sweet treat. Main courses include the ultra-moist roast pork (perfect with a squeeze of lime) and *camarones al Ajillo*, shrimp in spicy garlic sauce. Most everything comes with your choice of red or black beans and rice; go with the yellow rice. Wine and a handful of Mexican beers are served, but I really enjoyed the not-too-sweet red Hibiscus tea. The room is narrow and tables are petite (especially those for two), but a middle aisle keeps the place from feeling too crowded, and service is easygoing and friendly. Don't be surprised if there's a wait for a table.

Fanelli's Cafe. 94 Prince St. (at Mercer St.). ☎ 212/226-9412. Reservations not accepted. Main courses $5–$12. AE, MC, V. Mon–Wed 10am–2am, Thurs–Sat 10am–4am; Sun noon–2am. Subway: N, R to Prince St. AMERICAN.

Once upon a time, SoHo consisted of a few daring galleries, a gaggle of artists living illegally in loft space that no one wanted, a few Italian bakeries, and Fanelli's. Matters couldn't be more different now: the galleries have given way to Banana Republic, the bakeries have moved over for Balthazar, and absolutely everyone wants those lofts. Thankfully, however, Fanelli's, remains the same. This place is classic New York pub: the long bar is propped up by regulars, and its corner door and pressed-tin ceiling have locked in the 1847 atmosphere (this is the second-oldest continuously operating establishment in the city, after Bridge Cafe). If smoke bothers you, ask to be seated in the back. There's not much point in getting fancy with your order: The burgers are great, the pastas fresh, the beer served in pint glasses. The daring will give the mussels a shot. Wine? House red. No kidding. If you're coming for dinner, especially on a weekend, your best bet is to arrive before 7pm, when the noise level really starts to escalate.

Kelley & Ping. 127 Greene St. (btw. Houston and Prince sts.). ☎ **212/228-1212.** Reservations not accepted. Main courses $3.95–$7.50 at lunch; $7.95–$16.95 at dinner. AE, MC, V. Daily 11:30am–11pm. Subway: N, R to Prince St. PAN-ASIAN.

At the northern edge of SoHo lies this convivial noodle restaurant, which is almost unbelievably low priced for the neighborhood and hipness quotient. The dark wood–and–glass decor, which evokes a sort of Shanghai-market look, is an ideal setting for the Pan-Asian cuisine, which crisscrosses the continent from Korea to Malaysia to Japan, with a little fusion thrown in for good measure. The menu is heavy on spicy soups, dumplings, and noodle dishes; I particularly like the shrimp-and-peanut Pad Thai, a traditionalist's delight; the excellent wonton and roast duck soup; and the flavorful curries. In keeping with the menu and the ambiance, there's an exhaustive tea selection. Expect lots of Downtown gallery and aspiring model types, who practically consider this their second home. Unfortunately, this place can be a little too popular—don't be surprised if you have to wait for a table at dinnertime. Things move a little faster at lunch, when you belly up to the kitchen counter, cafetcria-style, to place your order.

Lombardi's. 32 Spring St. (btw. Mott and Mulberry sts.). ☎ **212/941-7994.** Reservations accepted for parties of 6 or more. Small pies (6 slices) $10.50–$16; large pies (8 slices) $12.50–$20. No credit cards. Mon–Thurs 11:30am–11pm; Fri–Sat 11:30am–midnight; Sun 11:30am–10pm. Subway: 6 to Spring St.; N, R to Prince St. PIZZA.

Lombardi's is a living gem in the annals of the city's culinary history. First opened in 1905, "America's first licensed pizzeria" still cooks some of New York's best pizza in its original coal brick oven. The wonderful, crispy-thin crust (a generations-old family recipe that Gennaro Lombardi brought from Naples at the turn of the century) is topped with fresh mozzarella, basil, and tomatoes; Pecorino romano cheese; and virgin olive oil—from there, the choice is yours. Toppings are suitably old-world (pancetta, calamata olives, Italian sausage, and the like), but Lombardi's specialty is the fresh clam pie, with hand-shucked clams, oregano, garlic, romano, and pepper (no sauce). The main dining room is narrow but pleasant, with the usual checkered tablecloths and exposed brick walls. A big draw is the garden out back: walk past the kitchen and up a flight of stairs to reach this lovely second-floor deck, where tables sport Cinzano umbrellas and a flowering tree shoots up through the concrete. Another plus: In a city where rudeness is a badge of honor, Lombardi's waitstaff is extremely affable.

Rice. 227 Mott St. (btw. Prince and Spring sts.). ☎ **212/226-5775.** Reservations not accepted. Starters and sides $1–$6; main courses $6–$8. No credit cards. Daily noon–midnight. Subway: 6 to Spring St. PAN-ASIAN.

This sleek little restaurant has a cool Japanese vibe and a super-affordable seasonal menu built around—you guessed it—rice. You pick your grain from the seven choices, which range from healthy brown to Bhutanese red to Thai black, and pair it with any one of ten toppings. Vietnamese-grilled lemongrass chicken goes well with either short-grain Japanese or sticky rice, while Jamaican jerk chicken wings are an ideal match for yellow rice and peas. Basamati is a must for the warm lentil salad or Indian curry. If you're just not sure, go with the pairing suggestions on the short but appealing menu. Thick Portuguese soup, flavored with potatoes and distinctive caroway-flavored rice, is a vegan's delight; it pairs up well with grilled eggplant maki or rice balls topped with tomato cumin sauce for a complete vegetarian meal for about $10. Rice bowls come small or large, but all portions tend to be on the daintier side, so big appetites should order accordingly. Beer, wine, and sake are available. Like so many affordable Downtown restaurants, the space is petite; your best bet is to come early to snag a table along the comfortable banquette. Otherwise, duos may end up perched at postage stamp–sized high tables on the opposite wall. A takeout outlet is in the adjacent store-front.

SoHo Kitchen & Bar. 103 Greene St. (btw. Spring and Prince sts.). ☎ **212/925-1866.** Reservations are accepted for parties of 6 or more. Main courses $7.75–$18.50. AE, MC, V. Mon–Thurs 11:30am–midnight; Fri–Sat 11:30am–2am; Sun 12:30–11pm. Subway: N, R to Prince St.; C, E to Spring St. AMERICAN.

Even though the food is nothing special, the fun, easygoing atmosphere makes SoHo Kitchen a regular stop for me. This large, lofty space attracts an animated after-work and late-night crowd to its central bar, which dispenses more than 21 beers on tap, a whole slew of microbrews by the bottle, and more than 100 wines by the glass, either individually or in "flights" for comparative tastings. The menu offers predictable but affordable bar fare: buffalo wings, oversize salads, good burgers, and a variety of sand-wiches and thin-crust pizzas. You won't spend more than 12 bucks or so on your main meal unless you graduate to entrees like the New York sirloin, which makes this a great bet for wallet-watchers.

If you're in lower Manhattan and you're looking for similar fare, head to the **Wall Street Kitchen & Bar,** housed in a spectacular former bank building in the heart of the Financial District at 70 Broad St. (☎ **212/797-7070**).

Spring Street Natural Restaurant. 62 Spring St. (at Lafayette St.) ☎ **212/966-0290.** Main courses $7–$16. AE, DC, MC, V. Sun–Thurs 11:30am–midnight; Fri–Sat 11:30am–1am. Subway: 6 to Spring St. HEALTH-CONSCIOUS.

This 25-year-old spot is as comfortable and easygoing as your old college hangout—and just about as affordable, too. The large brick-walled room is filled with leafy greenery and anchored by an old oak bar. This is the kind of place that you can set yourself down at a table and camp awhile, poring over a good book while you nosh on a farm-fresh entree-sized salad or a terrific tempeh burger; the staff will happily refill your coffee mug as you relax. But while the cuisine is all natural, it's not strictly vegetarian: there's fresh-off-the-boat seafood and free-range chicken and turkey as well as creative and organic vegetarian dishes. Unlike many other health-minded restau-rants, however, the menu isn't restricted to soups, sandwiches, and salads; you can come for a full meal, dining on such entrees as broiled New England bluefish with shi-itake mushrooms, roasted chicken with pommery mustard glaze, or any number of pastas and stir-frys. Everything is well prepared and satisfying. The kitchen can also satisfy sugar, dairy, and other dietary restrictions. Brunch is served on weekends until 4pm, and there's pleasant outdoor seating along Lafayette Street in the good weather.

QUICK BITES

If you need a coffee break, skip Starbuck's and head instead to **Housing Works Used Books Cafe,** 126 Crosby St. (one block east of Broadway), just south of Houston Street (☎ **212/334-3324**). This attractive and airy used-book shop (whose proceeds support AIDS charities) has an appealing cafe in back that serves up coffee and tea, sandwiches, sweets, and other light bites. There are plenty of tables to pull up a chair at, and you're welcome to pull anything off the shelves to peruse as you snack.

✪ **Bread & Butter.** 229 Elizabeth St. (just north of Prince St.). ☎ **212/925-7600.** Soups and salads $3.75–$8; sandwiches $3.50–$10.50. AE, MC, V. Mon–Fri 8am–4pm; Sat–Sun 9am–5pm. Subway: B, D, F, Q to Broadway–Lafayette St.; 6 to Spring St. SANDWICHES.

New York's Top Early-Bird Meal Deal

It's bound to happen: You're on Varick looking for little Dominick Street, home to **Alison on Dominick Street,** at no. 38 (☎ 212/727-1188), and you think, "This can't be the right place." This is far west SoHo but it looks like warehouse-filled TriBeCa on a *really* quiet night, except for the cars with Jersey plates trying to shoehorn their way into the Holland Tunnel. It's not the kind of place you'd expect to find a sophisticated restaurant—but that's only the first of the surprises, the best of which is the pre-theater dinner, one of the best dining values in town. Sit down between 5:15 and 6pm and you can enjoy two stellar courses for just $20 (dessert is an extra $10–still a steal). There are three starters and three entrees to choose from, usually a market-fresh fish, a terrific roast chicken, and an excellent braised lamb with aromatic vegetables, white beans, and basil. The light, modern French fare is irresistible. The room is the epitome of gorgeous simplicity, from the midnight blue-velvet drapes to the long mahogany bar. Perfect for an off-the-beaten-track romantic rendezvous.

Reservations are highly recommended. To reach the restaurant from Varick Street, turn west onto Dominick Street at the Manhattan Mini-Storage facility.

This charming NoLiTa storefront serves up what just might be the best sandwiches in the city. All are made with top-quality ingredients—think fresh mozzarella, pan-roasted peppers, thick-sliced pastrami, stone-ground mustard—and served on homemade bread. Arugula is ever present and creations get pretty sophisticated (the grilled vegetables with goat cheese is excellent), but simple favorites are enough to make you swoon—witness the iconic BLT. Choices like egg salad, PBJ, and nutella and banana on grilled white bread will bring back your best kid memories. Salads, homemade fries, chocolate chip cookies, and other sweets will round out the perfect lunch. In the AM you'll find good coffee, fresh bagels, and baked goods, as well as thick, hot oatmeal with maple syrup (topped with raisins and cranberries, if you like). Bread & Butter is strictly takeout, but benches out front make a perfect perch in nice weather.

7 The East Village & NoHo

In addition to the choices below, also consider the East Village branch of **Bendix Diner** (p. 152), 167 First Ave., between 10th and 11th streets (☎ 212/260-4220) for home-style favorites. Try the East Village branch of **Dojo** (p. 144) at 24–26 St. Marks Place, between Second and Third avenues (☎ 212/674-9821), for super-cheap, super-healthy fare. A great choice for wallet-friendly Middle Eastern fare is **Moustache** (p. 145), at 265 E. 10th St., between First Avenue and Avenue A (☎ 212/228-2022). There's also an East Village branch of **Sapporo** (p. 159) at 245 E. 10th St., at First Avenue (☎ 212/260-1330), for cheap Japanese eats.

Acme Bar & Grill. 9 Great Jones St. (at Lafayette St.). ☎ **212/420-1934.** Reservations not taken. Main courses $5.95–$13.50 at lunch; $9.95 at weekend brunch (including one cocktail, juice, and coffee or tea); $6.95–$15.95 at dinner. DC, DISC, MC, V. Sun–Thurs 11:30am–midnight; Fri–Sat 11:30am–12:30am. Subway: 6 to Bleecker St.; B, D, F, Q to Broadway–Lafayette St. SOUTHERN/BARBECUE.

Acme's motto is AN OKAY PLACE TO EAT—a witty bit of clear-eyed candor in this best-obsessed town. This easygoing NoHo joint is divey in a pleasing way, with a good-natured staff, a Louisiana roadhouse theme, and the comfortable vibe of a well-worn neighborhood favorite. Acme serves up heaping platters of Southern home cooking and barbecue: po-boys, jambalaya, seafood gumbo, thick-cut pork chops, chicken-fried steak, baby-back ribs—not gourmet grub, but good, cheap, filling eats. The restaurant is a hot-sauce lover's delight, with dozens of bottles lining the walls so you can douse your dish with the perfect measure of heat. Yummy fresh-baked cornbread starts the meal, and a range of beers are available. Downstairs is **Acme Underground,** a small, low-cover, live music venue that books a broad range of hopeful rock and blues acts.

✪ **Angelica Kitchen.** 300 E. 12th St. (just east of Second Ave.). ☎ **212/228-2909.** Reservations accepted for six or more Mon–Thurs. Main courses $5.95–$14.25; lunch deal (Mon–Fri 11:30am–5pm) $6.75. No credit cards. Daily 11:30am–10:30pm. Subway: L, N, R, 4, 5, 6, to 14th St./Union Sq. ORGANIC VEGETARIAN.

If you like to eat healthy, take note: This cheerful restaurant is serious about vegan cuisine. The kitchen prepares everything fresh daily; they guarantee that at least 95% of all ingredients are organically grown, with sustainable agriculture and responsible business practices additionally required. But good-for-you (and good-for-the-environment) doesn't have to mean boring—this is flavorful, beautifully prepared cuisine served in a lovely country kitchen–style setting. Salads spill over with sprouts and crisp veggies and are crowned with homemade dressings. The Dragon Bowls, a specialty, are heaping portions of rice, beans, tofu, and steamed vegetables. The daily specials feature the best of what's fresh and in season, and may include fiery three-bean chili; baked tempeh nestled in a sourdough baguette and dressed in mushroom gravy; and lemon-herb baked tofu layered with roasted vegetables and fresh pesto on mixed-grain bread. Breads and desserts are fresh baked and similarly wholesome (and made without eggs, of course).

B Bar & Grill. 40 E. 4th St. (at Bowery). ☎ **212/475-2220.** Reservations suggested. Main courses $6–$16 at lunch and brunch; $9–$21 at dinner. AE, CB, DC, MC, V. Mon–Fri 11:30am–4am; Sat–Sun 10:30am–4am. Subway: 6 to Bleecker St. AMERICAN/ECLECTIC.

As Bowery Bar, this place was *the* celebrity hot spot a few years back. Reincarnated a year or so ago as B Bar, it managed to survive the limelight, and now makes an appealing spot for a casual meal and a cocktail. Originally a Gulf gas station, the cavernous dining room is 1960s modern and attractive, with high ceilings, comfy booths, retro-style mood lighting, and a large central bar. But it's the giant tree-filled courtyard that's the biggest draw, especially on warm nights and for weekend brunch. Don't expect gourmet fare, but the food's surprisingly good. I was thrilled with the freshness of the autumn vegetable and warm goat cheese salad, and you can't go wrong with the crispy calamari, steak frites, or a Bowery burger (beef, turkey, or veggie). The brunchtime egg dishes are also a good bet. Oddly, bread is only supplied on request, but it's bakery-fresh and addictive. Beware the self-important staff, whose impending stardom can sometimes distract them from their current duties. The bar offers a regular selection of signature drinks, including an excellent Ketel One martini. The hip crowd is on the Gen X side and the latest alterna-hits are usually playing over the sound system, but B Bar is suitable for anybody who likes a lively scene.

Boca Chica. 13 First Ave. (at 1st St.). ☎ **212/473-0108.** Reservations accepted for parties of 6 or more Mon–Thurs only. Main dishes $7.50–$19.75 (most less than $13). AE, MC, V. Sun–Thurs 6–11pm; Fri–Sat 6pm–midnight. Subway: F to Second Ave. SOUTH AMERICAN.

This lively, colorful joint is always packed with a gleefully mixed crowd working its way through a round of margaritas or a few pitchers of beer. The cuisine is a down-market version of the Pan-Latino favorites that have captivated palates farther Uptown. The food at Boca Chica is a little closer to its hearty South American roots:

well-prepared pork, beef, fish, and vegetarian dishes, pleasingly heavy on the sauce and spice, and accompanied by plantains, rice, and beans. There's also a bevy of interesting appetizers, including black bean soup, well seasoned with lime juice, and terrific coconut-fried shrimp. While this approach to cooking now tends to be well out of reach of the under-$25 crowd, Boca Chica keeps things at an affordable level. *Be fore-warned:* The place is packed on weekends.

Cucina di Pesce. 87 E. 4th St. (at Second Ave.). ☎ **212/260-6800.** Main dishes $6.95–$10.95 (specials may be slightly higher); 3-course early bird dinner (offered daily 3:30–6:30pm) $9.95. No credit cards. Daily 4pm midnight. Subway: F to Second Ave. ITALIAN.

This crowded East Village Italian is legendary for its good value—and it's surprisingly charming, too, if a little on the loud side. The focus is on Old World basics like hearty beef lasagna, marinara-topped pasta, shrimp scampi, and veal marsala. Every once in a while somebody in the kitchen goes too far with a shellfish-and-mollusk combo, but by and large the offerings really satisfy. The wide selection of basic pastas (fettuccine primavera, linguine with clam sauce—you get the picture) are always fresh and properly sauced, the veal nicely tender, and the fried calamari well seasoned and perfectly crisp. The great meal/low price combo means that the place can be a mob scene, but free mussels marinara at the bar makes the sometimes-long wait easier to take. The only disappointment is the wine list, which leaves a lot to be desired; your best bet is to stick with the house red, or opt for beer instead.

Dining Zone: Little India

The stretch of East Sixth Street between First and Second avenues in the East Village is known as "Little India" thanks to the dozen or more Indian restaurants that line the block (subway: F to Second Avenue). Dining here isn't exactly high style, but Little India's restaurants do offer decent Indian food at discount prices, sometimes accompanied by live sitar music. It's loads of fun to grab a bottle of wine or a six pack from one of the corner stores on Second Avenue (many of Little India's restaurants don't serve alcohol, but even those who do will often let you bring in your own) and cruise the strip, deciding which one most appeals to you. In the warm weather, each usually stations a hawker out front to help convince you that theirs is *so* much better than the competition.

Some people speculate that there's one big kitchen in the alley behind East 6th, but a few of Little India's restaurants deserve special attention. **Bombay Dining,** at 320 E. 6th St. (☎ 212/260-8229), is a standout, serving excellent *samosa* (crisp vegetable-and-meat patties), *pakora* (banana fritters), and *papadum* (crispy bean wafers with coarse peppercorns). Also satisfying are **Gandhi,** 344 E. 6th St. (☎ 212/614-9718), for a touch of low-light romance; **Mitali East,** 336 E. 6th St. (☎ 212/533-2508), the king of curry; and **Passage to India,** 308 E. 6th St. (☎ 212/529-5770), for North Indian tandoori. The Phyllis Diller of Little India, Christmas-light-bedecked **Rose of India,** 308 E. 6th St. (☎ 212/533-5011), used to be a kitschy favorite, but the food has been disappointing the last few times out.

Around the corner—and a giant step up in quality—from Little India is ✪ **Haveli,** 100 Second Ave. (☎ 212/982-0533), where the authentically prepared dishes, setting, and service are far superior to what you'll find on East 6th Street. Prices are a little steeper—solidly in the $10 to $16 range—but the Haveli experience is worth the extra dough if you can afford the tab.

If the wait is just too excruciatingly long, head across the street to **Frutti de Mare,** 84 E. 4th St. (☎ 212/979-2034), which offers up basically the same schtick, minus the mussels at the bar.

Il Bagatto. 192 E. 2nd St. (btw. aves. A and B). ☎ **212/228-0977.** Reservations recommended. Main courses $6–$20. Tues–Thurs 6:30–11:30pm; Fri–Sat 6:30pm–12:30am; Sun 6–10:30pm. No credit cards. Subway: F to Second Ave. ITALIAN.

After opening in late 1995, this cozy trattoria fast became a neighborhood favorite for its high-end Italian at next-to-nothing prices. Its out-of-the-way Alphabet City location kept Uptown gourmets away, until *New York* magazine voted its lasagna, offered only on Sunday, the best in town. Now the place is perpetually packed, and reservations don't mean much—make one, but be prepared to wait. Fortunately, the cozy bar downstairs provides the perfect parking space for a few pre-dinner cocktails. Daily specials are always a good bet—Thursday is the traditional day for gnocchi, and Friday (of course) is fish day—but wallet-watchers beware, because they'll run up your bill more quickly than ordering from the main menu. The wine list is well chosen and affordable, and the tiramisu is divine.

Iso. 175 Second Ave. (at 11th St.). ☎ **212/777-0361.** Reservations not taken. A la carte sushi $2.50–$6; sushi rolls $4.50–$12.50; sushi combos and main courses $13.50–$21. AE, MC, V. Mon–Sat 5:30pm–midnight. Subway: 6 to Astor Place. SUSHI.

Iso is the top choice in town for fresh and beautifully presented sushi at affordable prices. The sushi and sashimi combos are a good-value starting point; supplement with your favorites or a few of the daily special fish, which may include blue fin toro (tuna belly) or Japanese aji (horse mackerel). The menu also features light, greaseless tempura and entrees like chicken teriyaki and beef negamaki for the sushiphobes in your party. The attractive Keith Haring–themed room is tightly packed but relatively comfortable, and service is better than at other sushi joints in this price range. Unless you arrive before 6pm, expect a line—but the high-quality sushi and wallet-friendly pricing makes Iso worth the wait.

La Paella. 214 E. 9th St. (btw. Second and Third Aves.). ☎ **212/598-4321.** Reservations accepted for 6 or more. Tapas $4.50–$9; paella for 2 $22–$36. MC, V. Sun–Thurs 5–11pm; Fri–Sat 5–11:30pm. Subway: 6 to Astor Place. SPANISH.

La Paella's tapas are the best in town, and the paella can hardly be outdone. This is fun eating, the kind of place where patrons return again and again to wash down fish croquettes, chorizos, and green olives with bottles of chilled Negro Modela, a dark Mexican beer that goes perfectly with the flavorful menu of (primarily) grilled delights, or the terrific sangria, served in generous pitchers by a lively waitstaff, many of whom seem as though they just blew in from Madrid. Tapas here are more generously apportioned than at many other places; the grilled calamari is a perfectly sized appetizer without being overwhelming. The tapas and paellas are well priced, but it's easy to run up a tab in the festive setting, which tends to attract large parties after 8pm. There are two dining rooms: Upstairs is baroque-lite and smoky, with walls glazed to a gentle, earthen tone; a funkier, moodier, and more masculine vibe rules the nonsmoking downstairs.

✪ **Pisces.** 95 Ave. A (at 6th St.). ☎ **212/260-6660.** Reservations recommended. Main courses $8.95–$19.95; 2-course prix-fixe dinner (Mon–Thurs 5:30–7pm; Fri–Sun 5:30–6:30pm) $14.95. AE, CB, DC, MC, V. Mon–Thurs 5:30–11:30pm; Fri 5:30pm–1am; Sat 11:30am–3:30pm and 5:30pm–1am; Sun 11:30am–3:30pm and 5:30–11:30pm. Subway: 6 to Astor Place. SEAFOOD.

This excellent fish house serves up the best moderately priced seafood in the city. All fish is top quality and fresh daily, and all smoked items are prepared in the restaurant's own smoker. But it's the creative kitchen, which shows surprising skill with vegetables as well as fish, that makes Pisces a real winner. The mesquite-smoked whole trout in sherry oyster sauce is sublime, better than trout I've had for twice the price. Great starters include the phyllo-fried shrimp or the tuna ceviche with curried potato chips and roasted pepper coulis. There are daily specials in addition to the menu; last time we dined here, I feasted on an excellent grilled mako shark with chard in cockle stew. The wine list is appealing and very well priced, the decor suitably nautical without being kitschy, and the service friendly and attentive. For wallet-watchers, the early-bird prix-fixe can't be beat. The Alphabet City locale attracts a cool crowd, but it's laid-back enough that even grandma will be comfortable here. Tables spill out onto the sidewalk on warm evenings, giving you a ringside seat for the funky East Village show.

Roettele A.G. 126 E. 7th St. (btw. First Ave. and Ave. A). ☎ **212/674-4140.** Reservations recommended, especially on weekends. Main courses $7–$16; fondue for two $30–$34. AE, DC, DISC, MC, V. Tues–Sat noon–3pm and 5:30–11:30pm; Sun 5:30–10pm. Subway: L to First Ave.; 6 to Astor Place. SWISS.

This chalet hideaway is New York's only authentic Swiss restaurant, and it's a winner. The cheese fondue, a hearty dinner for two or a generous appetizer for four, is perfectly smooth and beautifully presented with crusty bread and fresh vegetables. Build your meal around it by supplementing with other Alpine and house specialties, such as air-dried beef, classic raclette and wienerschnitzl, duck liver mousse, and terrific sauteed wild mushrooms over fresh herbs and polenta—spaetzle on the side, of course. They stock Swiss and German wines and beers, plus a few French bottles; try the medium-bodied Spatenlager to wash down all that cheese. In keeping with the theme, a wide selection of tempting French and German pastries are available. The only thing that keeps me from awarding a star to this East Village fave is the harried service, which is friendly but seems stymied by the kitchen. It's not a big problem—just come armed with a little patience.

✪ Shabu Tatsu. 216 E. 10th St. (btw. First and Second aves.). ☎ **212/477-2972.** Reservations accepted for parties of 4 or more. Full shabu-shabu dinners for two $28–$34. AE, DC, MC, V. Sun–Thurs 5–11:45pm; Fri–Sat 3pm–2am. Subway: L to First Ave., 6 to Astor Place. JAPANESE SHABU-SHABU.

This casual place features shabu-shabu, a dish you prepare yourself in the hotpot of boiling water built into the center of your table. The interactive fun begins when the waiter brings a plate piled high with raw beef (turkey is also available) and vegetables and gives an introductory lesson on how to make "shabu." It's lots of fun poking into the pot with your chopsticks, watching your piece of meat or veggies cook to your satisfaction, then dipping them in a peanut or vinegar and soy sauce. After you're done, noodles are piled in and the broth is turned into a yummy after-dinner soup. The food is fresh, high quality, and palate-friendly even to those who otherwise don't care for Japanese food. The pure entertainment value makes this a great place to take kids or a group. The restaurant is always busy, so it's best to go early or late.

Other locations are on the Upper East Side at 1414 York Ave. and 75th Street (☎ 212/472-3322), and on the Upper West Side at 483 Columbus Ave., between 83rd and 84th streets (☎ 212/874-5366).

Time Cafe. 380 Lafayette St. (at Great Jones St.). ☎ **212/533-7000.** Reservations recommended on weekends. Main courses $4–$13.50 at breakfast and brunch; $7.50–$13.75 at lunch; $7.50–$22 at dinner. AE, MC, V. Mon–Wed noon–midnight; Thur noon–1am; Fri noon–2am; Sat 10:30am–2am; Sun 10:30am–midnight. Subway: 1, 9 to Christopher St.–Sheridan Sq. CONTEMPORARY AMERICAN.

The New York Deli News

There's simply nothing more Noo Yawk than hunkering down over a mammoth pastrami sandwich or a lox-and-bagel plate at an authentic Jewish deli, where anything you order comes with a bowl of lip-smacking sour dills and a side of attitude. All of the following are the real deal—you gotta problem wid'dat?

Opened in 1937, the **Stage Deli,** 834 Seventh Ave., between 53rd and 54th streets (☎ 212/245-7850), may be New York's oldest continuously run deli. The Stage is noisy and crowded and packed with tourists, but it's still as authentic as they come. Connoisseurs line up to sample the 36 famous specialty sandwiches named after many of the stars whose photos adorn the walls. The celebrity sandwiches, ostensibly created by the personalities themselves, are jaw-distending mountains of top-quality fixings: The Tom Hanks is roast beef, chopped liver, onion, and chicken fat, while the Dolly Parton is—drumroll, please—twin rolls of corned beef and pastrami.

For the quintessential New York experience, head to the **Carnegie Deli,** 854 Seventh Ave., at 55th Street (☎ 212/757-2245), where it's worth subjecting yourself to surly service, tourist-targeted pricing, and elbow-to-elbow seating for the best pastrami and corned beef in town. Even big eaters may be challenged by mammoth sandwiches with names like "fifty ways to love your liver" (chopped liver, hard-boiled egg, lettuce, tomato, onion). Main courses range from goulash to roasted chicken, and the heavenly blintzes come stuffed with cheese or fruit. Cheesecake can't get more divine, so save room!

The ✪ **Second Avenue Deli,** 156 Second Ave., at 10th Street (☎ 212/677-0606), is the best kosher choice in town (for all you goyem out there, that means no milk, butter, or cheese is served). There's no bowing to tourism here—this is old school. The service is brusque, the decor is nondescript, and the sandwiches don't have cute names, but the dishes served here are true New York classics: gefilte fish, matzoh ball soup, chicken livers, potato knishes, nova lox and eggs. And for $11 to $13—several bucks cheaper than Midtown's Carnegie—you get a monster triple-decker sandwich (try wrapping your gums around the corned beef, tongue, and salami) with a side of fries. The crunchy dills are to die for. Keep an ear tuned to the Catskills-quality banter among the crusty waitstaff. It don't get more Noo Yawk than this.

✪ **Katz's Delicatessen,** 205 E. Houston St., at hot Ludlow Street on the Lower East Side (☎ 212/254-2246), is another first-rate deli choice, beloved for their all-beef hot dogs. Their mammoth deli sandwiches are even less expensive than the Second Avenue Deli—in the $6–$10 range—and the proprietors dare you to even try to finish one. Lest you think that lower prices mean poorer quality, forget it: Katz's has been slicing pastrami on the Lower East Side since 1888, and they're the only ones who still do it by hand. Despite the nostalgic kitsch value of the metal sign that implores you to SEND A SALAMI TO YOUR BOY IN THE ARMY, home-shipped salami, pastrami, corned beef, knockwurst, and knishes still make great gift ideas for the folks at home—talk about a real taste of New York!

This easygoing, affordable spot can provide a night's entertainment or the perfect sidewalk brunch. The kitchen features a large selection of contemporary fare with a healthy bent, such as a grilled rare tuna sandwich with organic daikon sprouts and sesame wasabi on seven-grain bread; herb-roasted free-range chicken with roasted garlic hominy grits and sauteed spinach; and a host of creative thin-crust pizzas. The food isn't the best in town but it's fine, and I like the health-minded preparations and the casual, laid-back vibe. This branch has a wonderful Moroccan lounge called Fez (see chapter 9 for details).

In addition to this one, there's also the new Upper West Side variation at 2330 Broadway, at 85th St. (☎ 212/ 579-5100).

Veselka. 144 Second Ave. (at 9th St.). ☎ **212/228-9682.** Sandwiches $1.95–$6.50; main courses $5–$12. AE, MC, V. Daily 24 hours. Subway: 6 to Astor Place. UKRAINIAN DINER.

Whenever the craving hits for substantial Eastern European fare at old-world prices, Veselka fits the bill with *pierogi* (small doughy envelopes filled with potatoes, cheese, or sauerkraut), *kasha varnishkes* (cracked buckwheat and noodles with mushroom sauce), stuffed cabbage, grilled polish kielbasa, fresh-made potato pancakes, and classic soups like borscht, voted best in the city by the *New York Times* and *New York* magazine. Try the buckwheat pancakes for a perfect breakfast or brunch. The diner is comfortable and appealing, with an artsy slant. Thanks to Veselka's we-never-close policy, it's a favorite after-hours hangout for club kids and other night owls.

✪ **Village Yokocho.** 8 Stuyvesant St. (at Third Ave. and E. 9th St.), 2nd floor. ☎ **212/ 598-3041.** Reservations not taken. Main courses $3.75–$11.50. AE, MC, V. Sun–Wed 5pm–3am; Thurs–Sat 5pm–4am. JAPANESE/KOREAN BBQ.

Village Yokocho is about as authentic as Japanese restaurants get. Entering this casual second-floor spot feels just like stepping into a Tokyo yakitori bar, complete with a hip, young clientele that's a mix of Japanese and in-the-know Americans. Between the regular menu and the many handwritten sheets taped to the wall advertising the current specials, the choices are vast. Dishes run the gamut from familiar dumplings and yakisoba noodles to exotica like deep-fried squid eggs. The generous broiled eel bowl is finer quality than eel you'll get at many sushi restaurants, and a deal at $8. The barbecued yakitori skewers, both meat and veggie choices grilled over an open flame just behind the counter, are excellent. Korean dishes include flavorful oxtail soup and bibinbop, a hearty rice bowl topped with veggies, ground beef, and a fried egg. The specials change depending on what's in season and available, but you might find soft-shell crab in ponzu sauce, broiled yellowtail with teriyaki sauce, and any number of sashimi appetizers. There's a big, affordable sake menu as well as a choice of beers. At press time, late-nighters benefited from 50% off Korean barbecue Sunday through Wednesday between midnight and 3am; call to see if this or any other after-hours specials are on while you're in town (they're also posted on the street-level front door).

QUICK BITES

There's also **Burritoville** (p. 124), at 141 Second Ave., between St. Mark's and 9th Street (☎ 212/260-3300), which is great for a quick bite.

Emerald Planet. 2 Great Jones St. (at Broadway). ☎ **212/353-9727.** Wraps $4–$8; smoothies $2–$5. AE, MC, V. Mon–Fri 9am–10pm; Sat noon–10pm; Sun noon–8pm. Subway: 6 to Bleecker St.; N, R to 8th St. AMERICAN.

This San Francisco import has lead the charge to bury the sandwich and replace it with the wrap, a phenomenon that has reached every mall in America by now. The Emerald Planet ideology is simple: You can eat wraps at every meal, from bacon and eggs (the Omaha) in the AM to fresh grilled veggies with goat cheese (the Sonoma) at noon to Jerk chicken, mango salsa, and jasmine rice (the Kingston) at dinner. The tortilla-like wrapping changes depending on the ingredients, from flour to whole wheat to tomato to spinach. All ingredients are fresh, and the emphasis is on healthy. Supplement your wrap with one of the champion smoothies; my favorite is the Maui, a tropical blend of bananas, coconut, and passion fruit–guava juice. Or opt for one of the fresh-brewed iced teas, a latte from the espresso bar, or one of the international bottled beers on offer. The decor is haute NoHo—wee dangling halogen lights, clean woody surfaces, rain forest–green walls—but don't be put off. This is one of Downtown's best stops for quick, quality chow—just ask Madonna, an Emerald Planet regular.

WORTH A SPLURGE

✪ Bop. 325 Bowery (at 2nd St.). ☎ **212/254-7887.** Reservations accepted for parties of 4 or more. Main courses $12.95–$18.95. AE, MC, V. Mon–Sat 6pm–midnight; Sun 6–11pm; bar open daily from 5pm. Subway: 6 to Bleecker St.; F to 2nd Ave. KOREAN.

Bop may be on the fringes of Chinatown, but don't expect your average, brightly lit, ethnic restaurant serving up the staples. The brainchild of restaurateur Brad Kelley, also of **Kelley & Ping** in SoHo (p. 133) among other hot spots, Bop is a gorgeous space, dimly lit for ultimate effect. The friendly, attentive staff serves wonderful modern Korean cuisine with Pan-Asian twists. The signature dish is bi bim bop, rice served either sizzling in a hot stone bowl or warm in a wooden bowl with wild mountain vegetables, kimchee, and raw tuna or shredded beef. We prefer the sizzling variety, which actually cooks as you mix the ingredients with chili paste (you define the temperature by how much you add). For an even more interactive meal, dine at one of the tabletop barbecues, where you can have such specialties as short ribs brushed with sake and soy or squid marinated in chili sauce cooked right in front of you. Cocktail lovers shouldn't pass on the soju, a yummy, lightly sweet Korean vodka made from sweet potatoes that's beautifully served in a martini glass with cucumber slices.

8 Greenwich Village

In addition to the choices below, there's also a branch of the retro all-American diner, **EJ's Luncheonette** (p. 174), at 432 Sixth Ave., between 9th and 10th streets (☎ 212/ 473-5555).

Aggie's. 146 W. Houston St. (at MacDougal St.). ☎ **212/673-8994.** Main courses $7–$12.95. MC V. Mon–Wed 8am–10pm; Thurs–Fri 8am–11pm; Sat 10am–11pm; Sun 10am–4pm. Subway: A, B, C, D, E, F, Q to W. 4th St. ECLECTIC.

This funky diner on the southern outskirts of the Village dishes up sandwiches, pastas, and simple American comfort food with a healthful gourmet bent—crab cakes, meat loaf, grilled portabellos, and duck stroganoff with black pepper sauce are favorites. Some complain that portions are not as generous as they were before Aggie's became hip, but they're still plenty big. The hearty breakfasts are especially pleasing; go early or expect a line on weekends.

✪ Bar Pitti. 268 Sixth Ave. (btw. Bleecker and Houston sts.). ☎ **212/982-3300.** Reservations accepted only for 4 or more. Main courses $5.50–$12.50 (some specials may be higher). No credit cards. Daily noon–midnight. Subway: A, B, C, D, E, F, Q to W. 4th St. (use 3rd St. exit). TUSCAN ITALIAN.

This indoor/outdoor Tuscan-style trattoria is a perennially hip sidewalk scene, and one of Downtown's best dining bargains. Waiting for a table can be a chore (the wait list never seems very organized), but all soon forgiven thanks to authentic, affordably priced cuisine and some of the friendliest waiters in town. Despite the tightly packed seating, Bar Pitti wins you over with its rustic Italian charm. Peruse the menu, but don't get your heart set on anything until you see the well-worn board, which boasts the best of what the kitchen has to offer; last time we dined here, they wowed us with a fabulous veal meatball special. Winners off the regular menu, which focuses heavily on pastas and panini, include excellent rare beef carpaccio; grilled country bread with

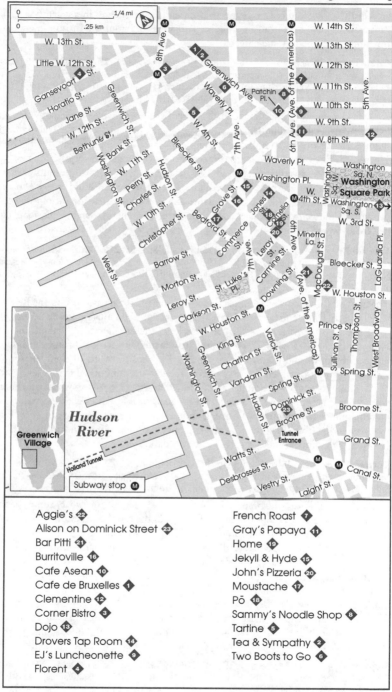

Greenwich Village Dining

Aggie's 22
Alison on Dominick Street 23
Bar Pitti 21
Burritoville 16
Cafe Asean 10
Cafe de Bruxelles 1
Clementine 12
Corner Bistro 3
Dojo 13
Drovers Tap Room 14
EJ's Luncheonette 9
Florent 4
French Roast 7
Gray's Papaya 11
Home 19
Jekyll & Hyde 15
John's Pizzeria 20
Moustache 17
Pō 18
Sammy's Noodle Shop 8
Tartine 5
Tea & Sympathy 2
Two Boots to Go 6

143

prosciutto, garlic, and olive oil; and spinach and ricotta ravioli in a creamy sage and Parmesan sauce. The all-Italian wine list is high priced compared to the menu, but you'll find a few good value choices.

Cafe Asean. 117 W. 10th St. (btw. Sixth and Greenwich aves.). ☎ **212/633-0348.** Reservations recommended. Main courses $6–$7 at lunch, $8–$14 at dinner; prix-fixe dinner $13–$15. No credit cards. Sun–Thurs noon–10:30pm; Fri–Sat noon–11pm. Subway: A, B, C, D, E, F, Q to W. 4th St. (use 8th St. exit). PAN–SOUTHEAST ASIAN.

If you're looking for old-fashioned enchantment and inventive Asian cooking, head to this affordable Village spot, which serves top-notch Vietnamese, Thai, Malaysian, and Indonesian cooking in an attractively simple dining room and a lovely small garden. The place is tiny but exudes charm, the service is friendly, and the prices are a real bargain. The beef-and-vermicelli appetizer salad, topped with crushed peanuts and surrounded by basil, is nearly as big as a dinner salad. The curried squid (*gaeng kheow*) is plentiful and blessed with the right texture and powerful taste. The shrimp dishes— particularly the *tom xao cari*, sauteed with vegetables and herbs—and the flavorful curries are all worth trying.

Cafe de Bruxelles. 118 Greenwich Ave. (at Horatio St.). ☎ **212/206-1830.** Reservations recommended. Main courses $10.95–$19.50. AE, DC, MC, V. Tues–Thurs noon–11:30pm; Friday and Sat noon–midnight; Sun and Mon noon–10:30pm. Subway: A, C, E, 1, 2, 3, 9 to 14th St. BELGIAN.

This wonderfully low-key, lace-curtained restaurant is the city's top stop for Belgian-style mussels, frites, and beers. Yummy starters include wild mushrooms in puff pastry, thick-cut country pate, and escargot in rich Roquefort sauce. You might want to follow with the *carbonade flamande,* beef stew made with dark Belgian beer; boudin blanc with apples and onions; Belgian seafood casserole; or one of eight varieties of mussels, the best of which is the simple mariniere—nothing more than a large bowl of the mollusks cooked in onion, garlic, and white wine. No matter what you choose, your order is accompanied by a metal tin of excellent crispy fries with the traditional accompaniment, mayonnaise. Winning choices from the excellent selection of Trappist ales and lambics include the Affligem Abbey, smooth, rich, and fruity; and my favorite, the Chimay Rouge, a great choice for dark beer lovers.

Corner Bistro. 331 W. 4th St. (at Jane St., near Eighth Ave.). ☎ **212/242-9502.** Reservations not taken. Burgers and sandwiches $2.50–$5. No credit cards. Daily 11am–3:30am. Subway: A, C, E to 14th St. (go 2 blocks south on Eighth Ave.). BURGERS.

This unpretentious, old-time neighborhood bar serves up what some people (including Jon Stewart) consider the best burger in the city. I don't know if I can stand by that claim (I really *love* the burgers at the Old Town), but the Corner Bistro's well-charred, beefy burgers are deservedly famous—and you'd be hard-pressed to dine so well for so little anywhere else in the city. The top of the line is the bistro burger, with bacon, cheese, lettuce, and tomato, for all of five bucks. The thin, crispy fries, served up on a crimped paper plate, are an appropriate accompaniment. Head elsewhere if you want anything else, because the other offerings are limited to a grilled chicken sandwich, grilled cheese, a BLT, and some chunky chili—all half-hearted at best, except for the chili. Beers on tap include Sam Adams, local McSorley's, and good ol' Bud. Service can be slow, but who's ever in a rush at a neighborhood local like this?

Dojo. 14 W. 4th St. (at Mercer St.). ☎ **212/505-8934.** Reservations not taken. Main courses $2–$7. No credit cards. Sun–Thurs 11–12:45am; Fri–Sat 11–1:45am. Subway: N, R to 8th St.; 6 to Bleecker St. HEALTHY PAN-ASIAN.

For New York's college students, the whole city is their campus. And, it would seem, Dojo is their cafeteria. This casual, tightly packed eatery in the heart of NYU territory attracts them in droves with its super-cheap healthy eats. While the emphasis is on Asian fare, don't expect traditional preparations; the miso soup, for example, is prepared with extra-dark miso paste and features potatoes and carrots as well as tofu. The big menu features hearty traditional and Japanese breakfasts, extremely tasty salads (try the carrot-ginger dressing), burgers (beef, turkey, and veggie), pita sandwiches, noodle dishes, and brown-rice platters and stir frys. Dojo isn't going to set the culinary world on fire, but you'd be hard pressed to find cheaper, healthier coffee-shop fare—and since this place virtually alternates as a study hall, you won't be rushed out the door. A full bar is available, as well as an extensive slate of coffee drinks to keep the crowd well fueled.

There's also an East Village location at 24–26 St. Marks Place, between Second and Third avenues (☎ 212/674-9821).

✪ **Florent.** 69 Gansevoort St. (2 blocks south of 14th St. and 1 block west of Ninth Ave., btw. Greenwich and Washington sts.). ☎ **212/989-5779.** Reservations recommended for dinner. Main courses $7.95–$17.95; 3-course prix-fixe dinner $16.50 before 7:30pm, $18.50 7:30pm–midnight. No credit cards. Mon–Fri 9–5am, Sat–Sun 24 hours. Subway: A, C, E, L to 14th St. FRENCH BISTRO/DINER.

So you get a craving at 3am for homemade rillettes, boudin noir, or steak frites and can't decide whether you'd like to eat with club kids, partying celebrities, cross-dressed revelers, truckers from Jersey, or the odd stockbroker? Then get thee down to Florent, the nearly 24-hour French bistro dressed up as a 50s-style diner, where you can have it all. Located in the far West Village area known as the Meat Packing District, Florent is a perennial hotspot no matter what the time of day. But it's after the clubs close when the joint really gets hoppin'. Tables are tightly packed, almost uncomfortably so in some cases, but it's all part of the late-night festivities. This place has a real sense of humor about it (check out the menu boards above the bar) and a CD catalog full of the latest indie sounds. The food's not half-bad, either: The grilled chicken with herbs and mustard sauce is a winner, moist and flavorful, as is the French onion soup crowned with melted gruyere. There are always diner faves like burgers and chili to choose from in addition to Gallic standards like moules frites, and comfort food specialties such as chicken pot pie. Try not to miss the fries, which are light, crispy, and addictive.

French Roast. 456 Sixth Ave. (at 11th St.). ☎ **212/533-2233.** Reservations accepted. Main courses $8–$13.95. AE, MC, V. Daily 24 hours. Subway: A, B, C, D, F, Q to W. 4th St. (use 8th St. exit). FRENCH CAFE.

Overwhelmingly popular with college students, writers working on their novels, and assorted others, this 24-hour Village corner spot went from zero to Mach speed before most of us could say, "Have you heard about . . . ?" The food has taken critical knocks, but it's fine for the money, and it sure hasn't kept the crowds away. You'll have lots of salads to choose from (arugula and fennel, baby mixed greens, grilled leeks vinaigrette) and some hot appetizers, like wild mushroom timbale and mussels Provençal. Entrees include roasted herb chicken, vegetable plates, beef pot au feu, and trout, as well as steak, pastas, and burgers. But I like French Roast best for a relaxing breakfast or brunch, or as a late coffee-and-dessert spot.

Moustache. 90 Bedford St. (btw. Barrow and Grove sts.). ☎ **212/229-2220.** Reservations not taken. Main dishes $5–$12. No credit cards. Daily noon–11:30pm. Subway: 1, 9 to Christopher St. MIDDLE EASTERN.

Moustache is the sort of exotic neighborhood spot that's just right. On a quiet side street in the West Village, this charming hole-in-the-wall boasts a cozy Middle Eastern vibe and authentic fare that's both palate-pleasing and wallet-friendly. Delicately seasoned dishes bear little resemblance to the food at your average falafel joint. Expect subtly flavored hummus, tabbouleh, and spinach-chickpea-tomato salad (or a large plate of all three); excellent oven-roasted "pitzas," thin, matzoh-like pita crusts topped with spicy minced lamb and other savory ingredients; and—best of all—fluffy, hot-from-the-oven homemade pita bread, which puts any of those store-bought Frisbees to shame. Moustache is hugely and justifiably popular, so don't be surprised if there's a line—but it's well worth the wait. A second Manhattan location is in the East Village at 265 E. 10th St., between First Avenue and Avenue A (☎ 212/228-2022).

✪ Pó. 31 Cornelia St. (btw. Bleecker and W. 4th sts.). ☎ **212/645-2189.** Reservations recommended well in advance. Main courses $8–$10 at lunch, $12–$15 at dinner; tasting menu $35. Tues–Sat 11am–2pm and 5–11pm; Sun 11am–2pm and 5–10pm. AE. Subway: A, B, C, D, E, F, Q to W. 4th St. (use W. 3rd St. exit). ITALIAN.

He may not be Emeril (yet), but chef Mario Batali has become quite the entrepreneur. His zesty Italian food has attracted a lot of attention since he began appearing on TV's Food Network. Well, kudos to Mario for keeping Pó real despite his burgeoning fame; it's well priced and justifiably popular. One of the nice things about Pó is that it's the kind of place where you'd enjoy celebrating a special occasion, yet you can still keep things affordable. Batali's pastas are unparalleled; even a simple white-bean ravioli in balsamic vinegar and browned butter takes on new, remarkable life in his kitchen. Other winning entrees include cavatelli with sage and three mushrooms (including stellar porcinis), and beautifully tender veal picatta with baby artichokes. The wine list is surprisingly affordable, and the service appealingly old world despite the hip address. The only downsides are that the pretty, narrow room is too tightly packed and smoking is allowed at the bar (a little too close to some dining tables in my view). Call well ahead—a month if you can—because Pó is perpetually booked.

Sammy's Noodle Shop. 453–461 Sixth Ave. (at 11th St.). ☎ **212/924-6688.** Main courses $6.95–$14.95. AE, DC, MC, V. Sun–Thurs 11:30am–midnight; Fri–Sat 11:30am–1am. Subway: F to 14th St. CHINESE.

This big, colorful, brightly lit noodle shop is perpetually packed with neighborhood regulars and NYU students, but it's large enough that there's rarely a wait for a table. Cantonese wonton and Mandarin noodle soups, barbecue roasted meats (pork, ribs, duck, and chicken), and dim sum are all well done—especially the dumplings—and the choice of Chinese mains is typically encyclopedic. But if you don't see something you like, Sammy's offers a create-your-own meal: pick four vegetables, a meat (optional), and a type of sauce (garlic, black bean, etc.), and the kitchen will whip it up for you for just $7.50 to $11. Service is friendly and efficient. The cuisine isn't Chinatown authentic, but you're unlikely to be disappointed. Next door is a Sammy's-owned bakery, where you can buy Asian sweet treats baked fresh daily.

Tartine. 253 W. 11th St. (at W. 4th St.). ☎ **212/229-2611.** Reservations not accepted. Main courses $8–$16. No credit cards. Tues–Fri and Sun 9am–10pm; Sat 9am–10:30pm. Subway: 1, 2, 3, 9 to 14th St. FRENCH BISTRO.

Authentic French isn't just for rich New Yorkers anymore thanks to the half-dozen or so affordable spots that have opened in recent years. The best of the bunch, by far, is Tartine. Tucked well west in Greenwich Village, this BYOB stalwart (no corkage fee) has been cooking up chicken pot pies and croque monsieurs for a friendly crowd for more than a decade. Packed at lunch, then packed again from 7pm until closing, Tartine is famous for its mignonettes of beef, served with a mountain of delectable golden frites. The food (including made-on-the-premises bread and baked goods) is so good that crowds are willing to put up with long lines and harried service. The only way to avoid the wait is to arrive early; otherwise, be prepared to hang around for an hour.

Tea & Sympathy. 108 Greenwich Ave. (btw. 12th and 13th sts.). ☎ **212/807-8329.** Reservations not taken. Main courses $5.50–$11.95 at lunch and brunch, $10.50–$16.95 at dinner; full afternoon tea $16.50. No credit cards. Mon–Fri 11:30am–10:30pm; Sat 10:30am–10:30pm; Sun 10:30am–10pm. Subway: 1, 2, 3, 9 to 14th St. BRITISH.

When Londoner Nicky Perry moved to New York, she was disappointed to find no proper British tearoom where she could get a decent cup, so she opened her own in the heart of the West Village. Tea & Sympathy seems as if it was transplanted wholesale from Greenwich or Highgate, complete with oddball collection of creamers and teapots, snappy British waitstaff, and plenty of old-time charm. Elbow room is at a minimum and the place is perpetually packed, but it's worth the squeeze for the full afternoon tea, which comes on a tiered tray with crust-off finger sandwiches like hearty chicken salad and egg and 'cress, scones with jam and Devonshire cream, and cakes and cookies for a sugary finish. The menu also features such traditional British comforts as shepherd's pie, bangers and mash, and a savory chicken and leek pie. Anglophiles line up for the Sunday dinner—roast beef and Yorkshire pudding, of course. For dessert, try the treacle pudding, warm ginger cake, or the yummy sherry trifle. Next door is a cute shop selling Cadbury Flake bars, Hob Nob biscuits, and other imported English groceries and trinkets.

QUICK BITES

Ask any New Yorker—one of the cheapest, most satisfying meals to be had in the city is the $1.95 two-dogs-and-drink deal from ✪ **Gray's Papaya,** 402 Sixth Ave., at 8th Street (☎ **212/260-3532**). This legendary storefront hot-dog stand hawks nothing but all-beef dogs (50¢ each), crispy thin fries, and your choice of tropical-flavored fruit drinks ranging from piña colada to Orange Julius–style OJ. Best of all, you can indulge in a Gray's frank and juice at any hour, since they never close. There's a second location on the Upper West Side at 2090 Broadway, at 72nd Street (☎ **212/799-0243**), also open around the clock.

There's also a nice branch of **Burritoville** (p. 124) at 298 Bleecker St., at Seventh Avenue (☎ **212/633-9249**).

WORTH A SPLURGE

Home. 20 Cornelia St. (btw. Bleecker and W. 4th sts.) ☎ **212/243-9579.** Reservations highly recommended. Main courses $14–$18 at dinner, $7–$10 at lunch. AE. Mon–Fri 9–11am, 11:30am–3pm, 6–11pm; Sat–Sun 11am–4pm and 6–11pm. Subway: A, B, C, D, E, F, Q to W. 4th St. (use W. 3rd St. exit). CONTEMPORARY AMERICAN HOME COOKING.

I love Home. This cozy restaurant is the domain of a husband-and-wife team, chef David Page and co-owner Barbara Shinn, who have made home-style cooking

Pizza! Pizza!

In the mood for a slice or two . . . or three? The village is the perfect place to be. The original location of **John's Pizzeria** (p. 155), 278 Bleecker St. between Sixth and Seventh avenues (☎ **212/243-1680**), is a New York original and still one of the city's best. The pies are thin-crusted, properly sauced, and served up piping hot in an authentic old-world setting. Sorry, no slices.

For something a little more funky, head to **Two Boots to Go,** 201 W. 11th St. (at Seventh Avenue; ☎ **212/633-9096**), and 74 Bleecker St. (btw. Broadway and Crosby St.; ☎ 212/777-1033), where creative variations on the traditional pie are precisely the point. Both are predominately takeout and delivery locations, but there are a few tiny tables for in-house eaters.

something to celebrate. Page and Shinn keep things fresh, popularly priced, and welcoming; as a result, their narrow, tin-roofed dining room is always packed. The menu changes regularly, but look for such signature dishes as the rich-and-creamy blue cheese fondue; an excellent cumin-crusted pork chop on a bed of homemade barbecue sauce; a filleted-at-your-table brook trout accompanied by an apple fig pancake and smoked bacon shallot dressing; and perfectly moist roasted chicken with a side of spicy onion rings. Chocolate lovers should save room for the silky-smooth pudding. Weekend brunch is another great time to visit, with fluffy pancakes and excellent egg dishes. This is a quintessential Village restaurant, loaded with sophisticated charm, but it is tiny. Seating isn't uncomfortable and you won't feel intruded upon by your neighbors, but the tight room isn't built for large parties or those who want to spread out. The lovely garden is heated year-round, but is most charming in the warm weather; book an outside table well ahead.

Page and Shinn also run **Drovers Tap Room,** around the corner at 9 Jones St. (☎ 212/627-1233), their Midwest-comes-to-Manhattan take on the small-town tavern. The all-American comfort food is delicious, reservations tend to be easier to come by, and the comfortable room is more suited to larger parties.

9　The Flatiron District, Union Square & Gramercy Park

America. 9 E. 18th St. (btw. Fifth Ave. and Broadway). ☎ **212/505-2110.** Reservations recommended. Main courses $6.95–$18.95. AE, DC, DISC, MC, V. Sun–Thurs 11:30am–midnight; Fri–Sat 11:30am–1am. Subway: L, N, R, 4, 5, 6 to 14th St./Union Sq. AMERICAN.

This attractive, kid-friendly restaurant is nearly as large as a continent, with a seemingly mile-high ceiling. The menu is eclectic (soups, omelets, pancakes, pastas, sandwiches, poultry, salads, meats, fish, burgers, pizza), with prices you're more likely to see in the heartland than in New York. Each dish is inspired by the state or city listed next to it: Texas five-way chili, Long Island duck pot pie, Mississippi fried catfish, New England clam chowder, and so on. (Get it?) The food isn't exactly gourmet fare, but so what? It does the job, and at the right price. America also offers a family brunch with a balloon maker and a magician on Saturdays and Sundays from noon to 4pm as well as a late kitchen Friday and Saturday nights.

Cafe Spice. 72 University Place (at 11th St.). ☎ **212/253-6999.** Full dinners $13.50–$18. Mon–Wed 11:30am–3pm and 5–10:30pm; Thur–Fri 11:30am–3pm and 5–11:30pm; Sat and Sun 1–11:30pm. AE, MC, V. Subway: L, N, R, 4, 5, 6 to Union Sq. INDIAN FUSION.

The owners of Dawat have opened an edgy, affordably priced restaurant that many (including yours truly) consider to be even better than their haute Indian Uptowner. Two steps up from Little India and more well developed than fusion hotspots like Surya, Cafe Spice is a terrific bet. The restaurant has a funky modern style—the room is all geometric shapes and vibrant colors, and each dish is artfully displayed and presented—that's a telltale sign of the not-quite-there-yet Indian fusion rage that has taken Manhattan this year. But, thankfully, the only thing that's really fusion about this menu is that it crisscrosses the sub-continent itself, from Punjab to Goa and back again, with a substantial side trip to southern India for spicy vegetarian along the way. The dishes are classic and confident. A great way to start is with the *palak papri chaat,* a well-spiced blend of spinach crisps, potatoes, and chickpeas in yogurt and tamarind; or with stuffed samosas, seasoned chicken or potatoes (skip the spiced tuna) in a light pastry shell. The tandooris (chicken, assorted veggies, or catch of the day) are all well prepared and pleasing, as are the other Indian basics: paneers, tikkas, and so on. All

Late-Night Meal Deal

Reminiscent of an elegant art-deco ocean liner with porthole-like sconces, circular mohair booths, and a long bar with a brass rail dominating the swanky but comfortable front-room lounge, **Clementine,** 1 Fifth Ave., at 8th Street (☎ 212/253-0003), attracts a stylish mix of trendsetters and devoted foodies. With most entrees squarely in the $20 range, John Schenk's daring New American cooking is normally out of reach for those of us on tight budgets—unless you don't mind eating late-night, that is. After regular dinner service is done for the evening, the kitchen reverts to a casual, more affordable menu that features dishes in the $7 to $13 range. Pair a few dishes with a cocktail, and you'll be living the good life. This smart move has transformed Clementine into a real hotspot on the lounge scene. Late-night menu service is offered Sunday through Thursday from 11:30pm to 1:30am, and Friday and Saturday from 12:30 to 2:30am.

dinners come with basmati rice, fluffy naan, lentils, and a seasonal vegetable of the day, making this an all-around great deal.

Chat 'n' Chew. 10 E. 16th St. (btw. Fifth Ave. and Union Sq. W.). ☎ 212/243-1616. Reservations not taken. Sandwiches $5.75–$10.50; main courses $6.95–$12.50. AE, MC, V. Mon–Thurs 11:30am–11pm; Fri 11:30am–11:30pm; Sat 10am–11:30pm; Sun 10am–10pm. Subway: L, N, R, 4, 5, 6 to Union Sq. AMERICAN.

Looking for a decent place to get an honest square meal that won't break the bank or leave you hungry? Then head to Chat 'n' Chew, a cute little hole in the wall that excels at down-home American cooking. In fact, the space is so down-homey that it's on the brink of becoming a theme restaurant, but the chow's the real thing. Look for honey-dipped fried chicken, roast turkey with all the fixin's, BBQ pork chops with skin-on mashed potatoes, and mac 'n' cheese that's as crispy on the outside and gooey on the inside as it should be. There are a few unnecessary nods to contemporary tastes—if you're looking for grilled tuna, you don't belong here!—but the only real misstep I can see is the meat loaf, which was a bready disappointment. Weekend brunch sees such standards as hot oatmeal with brown sugar and hearty three-egg omelettes with honey-baked ham on the side. Portions are all hungry man–sized, service is snappy, and beer's available to wash it all down. Desserts are of the Dunkin Hines layer-cake variety (just like ma used to make!), and the soda fountain serves up everything from egg creams to Haagen Dazs shakes. The crowd is mainly comprised of the very young and hip (the kind that can afford to throw caution to the wind when it comes to calories), but everyone will fill perfectly welcome.

Coffee Shop. 29 Union Sq. W. (at 16th St.). ☎ 212/243-7969. Reservations accepted for 6 or more. Main courses $7.95–$16.95. AE, DC, MC, V. Wed–Fri 6:30am–5:30am; Sat 8am–5:30am; Sun 8am–2am; Mon 6:30am–2am; Tues 6:30am–4am. Subway: L, N, R, 4, 5, 6 to 14th St.–Union Sq. AMERICAN/BRAZILIAN.

There are worse ways to spend a sunny afternoon than sitting at a sidewalk table at the Coffee Shop, watching the world (the beautiful world) go by while chowing down on a Brazilian feijoada (pork and bean stew), a churrasquino carioca (steak sandwich topped with peppers and onions), a Sonia Braga sandwich (chicken salad in a flour tortilla with papaya and cashews), or a good old burger (beef, turkey, or veggie—your choice) with a side of excellently crisped fries. The barbecued chicken sandwich with nonfat cilantro-lime mayonnaise will keep you trim and satisfied. The just-fine food isn't anything special, but it's not hard to see why this spirited perch, situated just across the street from super-popular Union Square Park, is a magnet for models, club kids, and scores of celebrities. Of course, its own celebrity can make it hard to get a seat here on a balmy summer day. But the inside space is pleasant as well, with funky 1950s lamps and sleek chrome touches. The service can be a roll of the dice, so come with a nonchalant attitude and just enjoy the affordable food and the pretty scene. Also inside is the World Room, which serves up exotic cocktails and becomes quite a party scene in the wee hours.

Medusa. 239 Park Ave. South (btw. 19th and 20th sts). ☎ **212/477-1500.** Reservations recommended. Pastas $10–$13; seafood and meat main courses $14–$19. Subway: L, N, R, 4, 5, 6 to 14th St.–Union Sq. MEDITERRANEAN.

If Medusa was just a little more expensive, there would be nothing special about it. It would be lost in the sea of overpriced Mediterranean boites that regularly come and go in the city. But what Medusa has going for it is *value.* In the increasingly high-rent, high-profile Flatiron District, Medusa has managed to keep its prices down to earth while still maintaining all the trappings of a Downtown see-and-be-seen hotspot. And what's more, the food is good. The grilled octopus with baby greens, tomatoes, and steamed potatoes is a great way to start, and a bargain at $9. Or go with the attention-grabbing toasted herbed Medusa bread, topped with kefalotyri cheese flambeed in sambuca. All the pastas are fresh and well prepared, as are mostly seafood mains like oven-roasted Chilean sea bass. We've always been pleased with our meals at romantic, stylish Medusa; this is a place that manages to feel grown-up without the requisite high tab. There are a few concessions, such as cheap cafe chairs, but they're all but unnoticeable in the candlelit tomato-red space.

۞ Old Town Bar & Restaurant. 45 E. 18th St. (btw. Broadway and Park Ave. South). ☎ **212/529-6732.** Main courses $6–$15. AE, MC, V. Mon–Sun 10am–midnight. Subway: 4, 5, 6, L, N, R to 14th St./Union Sq. AMERICAN.

If you've watched TV at all over the last couple of decades, this place should look familiar: It was featured nightly in the old *Late Night with David Letterman* intro, stars as Riff's Bar in *Mad About You,* and appeared in too many commercials to count as well as in such movies as *The Devil's Own,* Woody Allen's *Bullets Over Broadway,* and, most recently, Whit Stillman's *The Last Days of Disco.* But this is no stage set—it's a genuine tin-ceilinged, 19th-century bar serving up good pub grub, lots of beers on tap, and a real sense of New York history. Sure, there are healthy salads on the menu, but everybody comes for the burgers. Whether you go low-fat turkey or bacon-chili-cheddar, they're perfect every time. You have your choice of sides, but go with the shoestring fries—what else in a traditional place like this? Other good choices include spicy Buffalo wings with blue cheese, fiery bowls of chili with cheddar cheese and a dollop of sour cream, and a Herculean Caesar salad slathered with mayo and topped with anchovies. Food comes up from the basement kitchen courtesy of ancient dumbwaiters behind the bar, where equally crusty bartenders would rather *not* make you a cosmopolitan, thank you very much. If you want to escape the cigarettes and the predatory singles scene on weekends, head upstairs to the blissfully smoke-free dining room.

Republic. 37 Union Sq. W. (btw. 16th and 17th sts.). ☎ **212/627-7172.** Reservations not accepted. Main courses $6–$9. AE, DC, MC, V. Sun–Wed noon–11pm; Thurs–Sat noon–midnight. Subway: L, N, R, 4, 5, 6 to 14th St./Union Sq. PAN-ASIAN NOODLES.

Proving once and for all that you don't have to sacrifice high style for wallet-friendly prices, this ultra-chic, minimalist noodle joint serves up affordable fast food in an area where it's getting harder and harder to find a deal. Customers slurp up the Chinese-, Vietnamese-, and Thai-inspired noodle dishes while sitting on cushionless, backless benches pulled up to pine-and-steel refectory tables that don't encourage lingering: This is the kind of place that knows how to make you feel hip and happy while getting you out the door efficiently. For a one-bowl meal, try the spicy coconut chicken (chicken slices in coconut milk, lime juice, lemongrass, and galangal) or spicy beef (rare beef and wheat noodles spiced with chilies, garlic, and lemongrass). The long curving bar is perfect for solitary diners.

There's a second location on the Upper West Side at 2290 Broadway, between 82nd and 83rd streets (☎ **212/579-5959**).

Zen Palate. 34 Union Sq. E. (at 16th St.). ☎ **212/614-9345.** Reservations recommended. Main courses $6–$16. Mon–Thurs 11am–11pm; Fri–Sat 11am–midnight; Sun noon–10:30pm. AE, DC, MC, V. Subway: L, N, R, 4, 5, 6 to 14th St./Union Sq. PAN-ASIAN VEGETARIAN.

The hallmark of Asian dining has long been the health factor, particularly in the vegetarian dishes (the MSG controversy notwithstanding). This is certainly true of Zen Palate, which has adopted the less-is-more approach to Asian cuisine. Each location shares the same Japanese-influenced postmodern decor, with teak and patinated copper governing the aesthetic; the flagship Union Square location is a standout, with a long counter downstairs for on-the-run eaters and a warren of spare but attractive dining rooms upstairs, including some with Japanese-style seating. Tofu is king here, but you're not limited to it. Stars on the wide-ranging menu include taro spring rolls and basil moo-shu rolls, with steamed veggie dumplings and buns for a more traditional choice. Despite the good-for-you approach, mains like Rose Petals (homemade soy pasta in a sweet rice ginger sauce with garden vegetables) and Curry Supreme (with tofu, potatoes, and carrots) are very flavorful, even for spicy food lovers. All in all, a good bet for health-minded diners. Lest it all sound too healthy, you're welcome to BYOB for no corkage fee in the upstairs dining room.

There are two additional locations: in Midtown at 663 Ninth Ave., at 46th Street (☎ **212/582-1669**), and on the Upper West Side at 2170 Broadway (☎ **212/501-7768**).

QUICK BITES

A great choice for a yummy pastry (I just love the tea cake) or a well-made salad or sandwich is **Eureka Joe,** 168 Fifth Ave., at 22nd Street (☎ **212/741-7500**). One of my favorite coffeehouses in the city, Eureka Joe boasts comfy sofa nooks and a loungey, stay-as-long-as you want vibe, plus a wine and beer bar and live music or readings in the evenings.

Pizza! Pizza!

Pintaile's Pizza, 124 Fourth Ave., between 12th and 13th streets (☎ **212/475-4977**), dresses their daintily crisp organic crusts with layers of plum tomatoes, extra-virgin olive oil, and other fabulously fresh ingredients. This new Union Square–area sibling of the Upper East Side favorite even has lots of seating for in-house eating.

Also in the Union Square neighborhood is **California Pizza Oven,** at 122 University Place, between 13th and 14th streets (☎ **212/989-4225**), which cooks their thin-crust brick-oven pizzas over hickory and cherry wood, imbuing them with a rich, smoky flavor. The California-style pies come with a wealth of toppings, from pepperoni and Italian sausage to goat cheese and baby eggplant. A line of tables near the hearth make a cozy spot to enjoy a quick slice.

WORTH A SPLURGE

Steak Frites. 9 E. 16th St. (btw. Fifth Ave. and Broadway/Union Sq. W.). ☎ **212/463-7101.** Reservations recommended. Main courses $8.50–$17.50 at lunch; $13.95–$21.95 at dinner. AE, DC, MC, V. Mon–Thurs noon–11:30pm; Fri–Sat noon–12:30am; Sun noon–10pm. Subway: L, N, R, 4, 5, 6 to 14th St./Union Sq. FRENCH BISTRO.

Meat lovers, arm yourselves. The menu offers other choices (pasta, chicken, salads), but the thing to ask for is the steak frites for two—certified black Angus perfectly grilled, pink inside, blackened outside. Or go with the mussels—the best come in white wine and fresh herbs or hearty Belgian beer. The frites are better at Cafe de Bruxelles, but they're good here, too, served with ketchup on the side rather than Euro-style mayo. The big room is loud and the service isn't quite as attentive as I might like, but the food is well priced (especially the steak frites, a deal at $21.95) and well prepared. And I love the bustling, slice-of-St. Germain atmosphere, complete with mahogany-and-brass bar and Toulouse Lautrec–style murals on the walls. There's a good selection of wines and Belgian beers to choose from, as you'd expect from a French brasserie.

✪ The Tavern Room at Gramercy Tavern. 42 E. 20th St. (btw. Broadway and Park Ave. South). ☎ **212/477-0777.** Reservations not taken. Starters $6–$9.50; main courses $12.50–$18. AE, DC, MC, V. Mon–Thurs and Sun noon–11pm; Fri–Sat noon–midnight. Subway: 6, N, R to 23rd St. CONTEMPORARY AMERICAN.

Unquestionably, Gramercy Tavern's main dining room is one of the finest in town. However, dining there requires reservations weeks in advance, and deep, deep pockets. Not so in the front Tavern Room, a friendly, informal bistro-style alternative where you can decide to eat at the last minute and still dine on some of the best food in town—without breaking the bank in the process. The compact but immensely appealing menu offers a lighter, more casual take on chef Tom Colicchio's excellent, creative American fare. I love the perfectly roasted baby chicken with butternut squash succotash—nobody in town does chicken better. And where else are you going to get a filet mignon this good for less than $20? There's a good selection of salads, a terrific tomato garlic-bread soup, and a handful of fish dishes and sandwiches for lighter eaters, plus the restaurant's signature selection of cheeses and desserts. The room is very comfortable, with well-spaced tables and a pleasant energy that still allows for conversation; and owner Danny Meyer has a blanket no-smoking policy. Service is top-notch, too. All in all, one of the best dining values in town.

10 Chelsea

In addition to the choices below, there's a dazzling new branch of **Grand Sichuan** (p. 127) at 229 Ninth Ave., at 24th Street (☎ **212/620-5200**), which has been garnering rave reviews from restaurant reviewers throughout the city.

Bendix Diner. 219 Eighth Ave. (at 21st St.). ☎ **212/366-0560.** Main courses $5–$15. Daily 8am–midnight. AE, MC, V. Open 24 hours. Subway: C, E to 23rd St. AMERICAN DINER/THAI.

For the same reason that it's just plain wrong to order healthy at Bob's Big Boy when you're on a road trip, it's nutty to go for the gentler side of the menu at this funky Chelsea stalwart. Ignore the bizarro Thai dishes (head to a real Thai restaurant for pad thai and curries) and indulge in the big, patriotic, all-American grub. The burgers are served deluxe with a heap of French fries, the chili con carne (over rice with onions, peppers, and cheese) is heavy with beef and beans, the meat loaf and mashed potatoes are better than ma used to make. I love the chicken noodle soup, which is the best I've had in the city thanks to richer-than-usual broth (no bouillon cubes here, brother). Breakfast is available any time of day, and it's as hearty and wholesome as you'd expect. Sunday brunch gets alarmingly crowded, so bring a chunk of the *Times* to tide you over.

Bendix has a second, less worn location in the East Village at 167 First Avenue, between 10th and 11th streets (☎ **212/260-4220**).

Cafeteria. 119 Seventh Ave. (at 17th St.). ☎ **212/414-1717.** Reservations recommended. Sandwiches $7.50–$12.95; main courses $10.95–$18.95. AE, DISC, MC, V. Open 24 hours. Subway: 1, 9 to 18th St. AMERICAN.

The greasy spoon goes glam at this round-the-clock Chelsea hotspot. More über-diner than automat, Cafeteria is all about high style, from the white-leather ban-quettes to the waifish waitstaff. Luckily, there's follow-through: Both the food and the service are better than they have to be in this veneer-happy town. The menu fea-tures modern takes on blue-plate classics—meat loaf, chicken pot pie, fried chicken and waffles, and killer mac and cheese made with both cheddar and fontina (yum!)—as well as surprisingly successful neo-American fare, including a well-seared, thick cut tuna loin. On the downside, seating is tight—but that just puts you that much closer to the latest It-girls and boys, right? A great choice for those who want a dose of Downtown cool; just put on your best basic black and you'll fit right in. Cafeteria is at its best after 10pm or so, but be sure to call ahead or you may be turned away at the door.

Empire Diner. 210 Tenth Ave. (at 22nd St.). ☎ **212/243-2736.** Reservations not accepted. Main courses $9.95–$16.95. AE, CB, DC, DISC, MC, V. Daily 24 hours. Subway: C, E to 23rd St. AMERICAN DINER.

Used to be that the Empire was the only thing doing this far west in Chelsea, but the emergence of an alternative-to–SoHo gallery scene in the west 20s has raised the neigh-borhood's profile a notch. Not that it matters in this throwback shrine to the slicked-up all-American diner. This classic joint, which looks suspiciously like an Airstream camper plunked down on the corner, boasts a timeless Art Deco vibe, honest coffee, and supreme mashed potatoes, Manhattan's best. The food is all basic and good: eggs, omelets, burgers, overstuffed sandwiches, and a very nice turkey platter. There's live piano music courtesy every day at lunch and dinner, and at weekend brunch. If you want quiet, go early. If you want an eyeful, wait for the after-hours crowd; the hours between 1 and 3am offer the best people-watching, when Prada and Gucci meld with Phat Farm and Levi's. When the weather's warm, a sidewalk cafe appears, and the lim-ited traffic this far over—mostly aiming for the Lincoln Tunnel—keeps the soot-and-fumes factor down.

La Taza de Oro. 96 Eighth Ave. (btw. 14th and 15th sts.). ☎ **212/243-9946.** Main courses $5–$9.50. No credit cards. Mon–Sat 6am–11:30pm. Subway: A, C, E to 14th St. PUERTO RICAN.

This brightly lit luncheonette serves up some of the best and most authentic Latin American food in the city. Tuned-in locals know you won't find better, or better-priced, *chutelas fritas* (fried pork chops—and say yes to the garlic). *Mondongo* is a deli-cious rendering of traditional tripe soup. If that's just a bit too adventurous for you, try the beef stew (*carne guisada*), which is slow-cooked until meltingly tender. The squid and shrimp dishes are always supple, never rubbery, and the chicken is perfectly roasted. All the dishes are super flavorful without being overwhelming. Portions are huge, and most come with huge portions of red beans and yellow rice. Service is exu-berant and efficient. The desserts are limited and there's no beer, just soda; the cafe con leche is great. *¡Que bien!*

QUICK BITES

At Chelsea Market, 75 Ninth Ave., between 15th and 16th streets, a second branch of **Amy's Bread** (p. 161) has cafe tables where you can enjoy a light bite for breakfast or lunch. And there's another **Burritoville** (p. 124), at 264 W. 23rd St., between Seventh and Eighth avenues (☎ 212/367-9844), good for a quick bite.

WORTH A SPLURGE

Alley's End. 311 W. 17th St. (btw. Eighth and Ninth aves.). ☎ **212/627-8899.** Reservations recommended. Main courses $15–$20. DC, MC, V. Mon–Sat 6–11pm; Sun 11am–3pm and 6–11pm. Subway: A, C, E, L to 14th St. CONTEMPORARY AMERICAN.

Alley's End is a top pick of Chelsea residents and other Manhattanites, who consider it one of the city's few affordable restaurants where they feel safely cosseted from the hustle and bustle outside. To find the nearly secret entryway down an alleyway just west of Eighth Avenue, look for the neon knife and fork, the only indication that there's a restaurant here. At the end you'll find a warren of charming brick-walled dining rooms that are perfect for peaceful conversation. The menu changes frequently depending on what's fresh and in season, but past winning dishes have included heirloom beefsteak tomatoes with grilled chicory and roasted garlic aioli; grilled center-cut pork chop with summer succotash, pancetta, and chipotle sauce; and Coach Farm aged goat cheese ravioli in pumpkin seed pesto with roasted wild fennel. The prices have gone a bit higher than I like in the past year, but everything is carefully prepared, and the soothing setting (an increasing rarity in Manhattan) makes the prices more than palatable. A reasonable wine list, with most choices under $30, also helps.

11 Times Square & Midtown West

Even uninitiated palates will appreciate the Asian-nouvelle vegetarian cuisine at stylish **Zen Palate** (p. 151), at 663 Ninth Ave., at 46th Street (☎ 212/582-1669). **Joe's Shanghai** (p. 127) has a new Midtown branch at 24 W. 56th St., just west of Fifth Avenue (☎ 212/333-3868), but expect to pay $2 to $5 more per dish than you would at the Chinatown location; reservations are accepted at this one.

Hamburger Harry's. 145 W. 45th St. (btw. Sixth and Seventh aves.). ☎ **212/840-0566.** Reservations recommended for large groups. Burgers and burritos $7.25–$9.95; other main courses $10.95–$15.95. AE, CB, DC, DISC, MC, V. Mon–Thurs 11:30am–11pm; Fri–Sat 11:30am–11:30pm; Sun noon–8pm. Subway: N, R, S, 1, 2, 3, 7, 9 to 42nd St./Times Sq. AMERICAN/BURGERS.

Hamburger Harry's is the perfect stop for everyday refueling at the right price. The casual restaurant has distinguished itself by turning out delicious 7-ounce mesquite-grilled burgers that "may well be the best hamburger in New York City," according to the *New York Times.* I don't know if I can fully agree with that assessment, but they're definitely the best in Times Square. Served with curlicue fries, homemade potato salad, or Harry's coleslaw, burger platters are a belly-busting bargain. They come in a range of varieties, from plain and simple to the Ha Ha Burger, topped with Texas chili, cheddar cheese, onion, guacamole, and *pico de gallo.* There are turkey and veggie versions for waist-watchers, too, as well as chicken breast sandwiches, fajitas, southwest-style burritos, Cajun catfish, and New York steak. A great place to take the kids—you can even finish off with an old-fashioned hot fudge sundae.

✪ **Island Burgers & Shakes.** 766 Ninth Ave. (btw. 51st and 52nd sts.). ☎ **212/ 307-7934.** Main courses $5.50–$8.75. No credit cards. Sat–Thurs noon–10:30pm; Fri noon–11:15pm. Subway: C, E to 50th St. GOURMET BURGERS/SANDWICHES.

This excellent aisle-sized diner glows with the wild colors of a California surf shop. A small selection of sandwiches and salads are on hand, but as the name implies, folks come here for the Goliath-sized burgers—either beef hamburgers or, the specialty of the house, churascos (flattened grilled chicken breasts). Innovation strikes with the more than 40 topping combinations: choose anything from the horseradish, sour cream, and black pepper burger to the Hobie's (with black-pepper sauce, bleu cheese, onion, and bacon). Pick your bread from a wide selection, ranging from soft sour-dough to crusty ciabatta. Though Island Burgers serves fries now, you're meant to eat these fellows with their tasty dirty potato chips. Terrifically thick shakes and cookies are also available for those with a sweet tooth.

✪ John's Pizzeria. 260 W. 44th St. (btw. Broadway and Eighth Ave.). ☎ **212/391-7560.** Reservations accepted for ten or more. Pizzas $9–$12.50 (plus toppings); pastas $6–$8. AE, MC, V. Mon–Thurs 11:30am–11:30pm; Fri–Sat 11:30–1am; Sun noon–12:30am. Subway: A, C, E to 42nd St.–Port Authority; 1, 2, 3, 9, N, R, S, 7 to 42nd St.–Times Sq. PIZZA.

Thin-crusted, properly sauced, and fresh, the pizza at John's has long been one of New York's best—some even consider it the best pie New York has to offer. Housed in the century-old Gospel Tabernacle Church, the split-level dining room is vast and pretty, with a gorgeous stained-glass ceiling and chefs working at classic brick ovens right in the room. More importantly, it's big enough to hold pre-theater crowds, so there's never too long of a wait despite the place's popularity. Unlike most pizzerias, whole pies are made to order, so come with friends or family. There's also a good selection of traditional pastas to choose from, such as baked ziti, and well-stuffed calzones. This Theater District location is my favorite, but the original Bleecker Street location, at 278 Bleecker St., between Sixth and Seventh avenues (☎ 212/243-1680), is loaded with old-world atmosphere. The locations near Lincoln Center, 48 W. 65th St. (☎ 212/721-7001), and on the Upper East Side, 408 E. 64th St. (☎ 212/ 935-2895), are also worth checking out.

La Bonne Soupe. 48 W. 55th St. (btw. Fifth and Sixth aves.). ☎ **212/586-7650.** Reservations recommended. Main courses $8.95–$18.25; "les bonnes soupes" prix fixe $12.95; lunch and dinner prix-fixe $19.95. AE, DC, MC, V. Mon–Sat 11:30am–midnight; Sun 11:30am–11pm. Subway: E, F to Fifth Ave.; B, Q to 57th St. FRENCH BISTRO.

This little slice of Paris has been around forever; I remember discovering the magic of fondue here on a high school French Club field trip that took place more years ago than I care to think about. But for gourmet at good prices, it's still hard to best this authentic bistro, where you'll even see French natives seated elbow-to-elbow in the newly renovated dining room. "Les bonnes soupes" are satisfying noontime meals of salad, bread, a big bowl of soup (mushroom and barley with lamb is a favorite), dessert (chocolate mousse, crème caramel, or ice cream), and wine or coffee—a great bargain at just $12.95. The menu also features entree-sized salads (including a good niçoise), high-quality steak burgers, and traditional bistro fare like omelets, quiche Lorraine, croque monsieur, as well as fancier fare like steak frites and filet mignon au poivre. Rounding out the menu are those very French fondues: emmethal cheese, beef, and yummy, creamy chocolate. Bon appetit!

Lemon Tree Cafe. 769 Ninth Ave. (btw. 51st and 52nd sts.). ☎ **212/245-0818.** Main courses $2.50–$10. DISC, MC, V ($20 minimum). Daily 11am–10:45pm. Subway: C, E to 50th St. MIDDLE EASTERN.

Lemon Tree Cafe is bare-bones decor-wise, with institutional furnishings and just a few posters of Egypt or Syria distracting you from the fake wood paneling and worn linoleum floor, but the food is fresh, tasty, and more than plentiful. Skip those Mid-town falafel carts—readers of the *New York Press* voted Lemon Tree's crispy, savory

Midtown Dining

Alley's End 58
America 68
Amy's Bread 40 59
B. Frites 43
Bendix Diner 57
The British Open 4
Brooklyn Diner USA 8
Burritoville 56
The Cafe at Aquavit 18
Cafe Spice 75
Cafeteria 61
California Pizza Kitchen 74
Canova Market 27
Carmine's 15
Carnegie Deli 10
Chanpen 29
Chat 'n' Chew 70
Churrascaria Plataforma 38
Coffee Shop 71
Dosanko 22
Ellen's Stardust Diner 35
Empire Diner 55
Ess-A-Bagel 21 64
Eureka Joe 62
Evergreen Shanghai 49
Grand Sichuan 54
Hamburger Harry's 26
Hangawi 52
Hard Rock Cafe 7
Harley-Davidson Cafe 14
Island Burgers & Shakes 30
Jekyll & Hyde Club 5
Joe's Shanghai 16
John's Pizzeria 1 2 44
La Bonne Soupe 17

Midtown

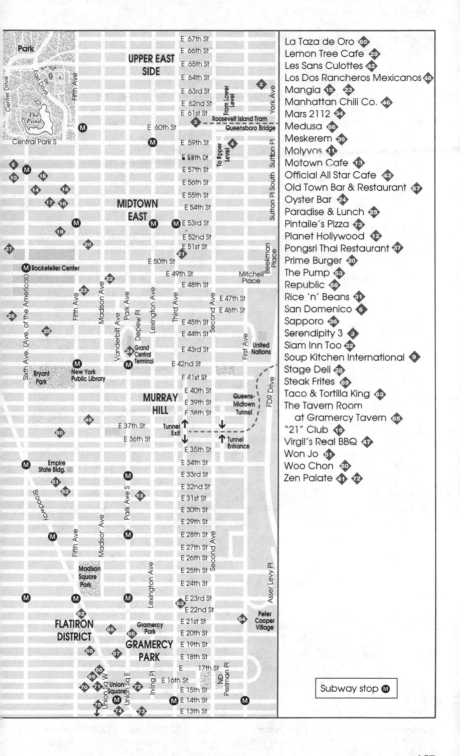

La Taza de Oro 60
Lemon Tree Cafe 29
Les Sans Culottes 42
Los Dos Rancheros Mexicanos 48
Mangia 15 23
Manhattan Chili Co. 46
Mars 2112 34
Medusa 66
Meskerem 39
Molyvos 11
Motown Cafe 13
Official All Star Cafe 43
Old Town Bar & Restaurant 67
Oyster Bar 24
Paradise & Lunch 25
Pintaile's Pizza 73
Planet Hollywood 12
Pongsri Thai Restaurant 37
Prime Burger 20
The Pump 53
Republic 68
Rice 'n' Beans 31
San Domenico 6
Sapporo 36
Serendipity 3 3
Siam Inn Too 32
Soup Kitchen International 9
Stage Deli 28
Steak Frites 69
Taco & Tortilla King 63
The Tavern Room
   at Gramercy Tavern 65
"21" Club 19
Virgil's Real BBQ 47
Won Jo 51
Woo Chon 50
Zen Palate 41 72

Subway stop Ⓜ

157

Looking for a good all-you-can-eat meal deal in the Theater District? Look no further: **Les Sans Culottes,** 347 W. 46th St., between Eighth and Ninth avenues (☎ 212/247-4284), is the place to go. This charming Restaurant Row eatery serves up just-fine French fare like boeuf bourguignon, chicken tarragon, shell steak au poivre, and filet mignon for $20 to $23. What makes Les Sans Culottes such a steal is that dinner is a three-course prix-fixe feast that includes a remarkable charcuterie basket as the appetizer course. It overflows with sausages, cheeses, and fresh fruits, from which you cut off chunks to nibble on as you please. Dessert is also included, and I dare you to save room for it. It's easy to fill up on just the charcuterie goodies; if you choose to pass on the other courses, you'll pay just $13. Reservations are recommended.

falafel sandwich best in the city. All pita sandwiches come overstuffed with lettuce, tomato, cabbage, onion, and tahini sauce. Veggie platters are light and delicious, particularly the lemony hummus, babaganoush, and tabouli. The grilled meat platters (served with salad and rice) could feed an army. Service can be slow and quirky (one day I was in, a 10-year-old girl served us), but it's worth putting up with for the great meal deal.

Los Dos Rancheros Mexicanos. 507 Ninth Ave. (at 38th St.). ☎ **212/868-7780.** Reservations not taken. Breakfast $1–$3; tacos $2; soups and sandwiches $3.50–$6; platters $7–$12. No credit cards. Daily 10:30am–11pm. Subway: A, C, E to 42nd St. MEXICAN.

This big, bright place is probably the most authentic Mexican restaurant in New York City. The decor is no-frills on every front—expect fluorescent lighting, tables with paper menus beneath the glass, plastic cups, and cheap dishes—but a neon-bright Wurlitzer jukebox pumping out Spanish-language pop adds genuine charm. The hearty Pueblo-style food isn't for the faint of heart: the justifiably famous moles are extra-rich; the housemade salsas are hot, hot, hot; and barbecued goat, tripe soup, and tongue tacos are among the specialties. But even the less adventurous will dig into the enchiladas (don't pass up the beef), burritos with your choice of fillings, and other, more familiar choices with gusto. Everything is extremely affordable and excellently prepared, and warm, soft, freshly made corn tortillas are served with just about every dish. Service is attentive, and Mexican beers are available. Check the wall behind the open kitchen for the specials. A few blocks south of gentrified Ninth Avenue, the neighborhood isn't unsafe but can be desolate at night, so I suggest going earlier rather than later.

Manhattan Chili Co. 1500 Broadway (entrance on 43rd St.). ☎ **212/730-8666.** Reservations accepted. Main courses $8.95–$14.95. AE, DISC, MC, V. Tues–Sat 11:30am–midnight; Sun–Mon 11:30am–11pm. Subway: N, R, S, 1, 2, 3, 7, 9 to 42nd St.–Times Sq. AMERICAN/TEX MEX.

This fun, cartoonish Theater District restaurant is a great choice if you have the kids in tow. The big, hearty chili bowls are geared to young palates, which tend to be suspicious of anything unfamiliar. The extensive list of chili choices is clearly marked by spice level, from the traditional Abilene with ground beef, tomatoes, basil, and red wine (mild enough for tenderfeet), to the Texas Chain Gang, which adds jalapenos to the mix for those who prefer hot. In addition, expect familiar favorites like nachos, chicken wings, big salads, and generous burritos and burgers. It's really hard to go wrong here—even vegetarians have lots to choose from.

Meskerem. 468 W. 47th St. (btw. Ninth and Tenth aves.). ☎ **212/664-0520.** Reservations recommended. Main courses $7–$11. DISC, MC, V. Daily 11:30am–midnight. Subway: C, E to 50th St. ETHIOPIAN.

Here's an exotic and affordable Theater District choice. Ignore the plain-Jane surroundings, get over the lack of silverware (you eat this African cuisine with your hands), and you'll enjoy a great dining experience here. Ethiopian stews of beef, lamb, chicken, and vegetables are served on communal platters and sopped up with spongy *injera* bread, made from fermented *tef,* an Ethiopian grain. The flavorful dishes range from the mild *doro alecha* (chicken seasoned with onions, garlic, and ginger in a butter sauce) to the spicy ribs dishes, simmered in a spicy berber sauce. The house specialty, *kitfo,* is Ethiopian-style steak tartare—less-adventurous eaters can ask for the beef rare instead of raw. For a little bit of everything, order a combination plate; two combos will easily feed three.

Rice 'n' Beans. 744 Ninth Ave. (btw. 50th and 51st sts.) ☎ **212/265-4444.** Reservations not taken. Full plates $5.95–$14.95. MC, V. Mon–Thurs 11am–10pm; Fri–Sat 11am–11pm; Sun 1–9pm. Subway: C, E to 50th St. BRAZILIAN.

This cool, dark, hallway-sized restaurant dishes up kick-ass, stick-to-your-ribs fare. Between the bold flavors and the bargain-basement prices, you'll want to stand up and samba. Among the Brazilian specialties they whip up here are *feijoada*—the national dish of Brazil—a hearty, brackish-looking stew of black beans, pork ribs, and linguiça (Portuguese sausage); and a lovely roasted chicken seasoned with tomato and cilantro. By far the best bargain is the eponymous dish: For a mere $9.25 you get a large oval plate mounded with rice, beans, mixed vegetables, collard greens, and sweet plantains—a vegetarian's delight. Portions are monstrous across the board. The weekday lunch specials—full meals with rice, beans, plantains, and your choice of roasted or sauteed chicken, beef stew, thin-cut sauteed pork chops, or the day's fried fish—are a steal at less than $9. Service can be slow at times and don't expect much in the way of ambiance—but at these prices, who cares?

✪ Sapporo. 152 W. 49th St. (btw. Sixth and Seventh aves.). ☎ **212/869-8972.** Reservations not taken. Main courses $6–$9. No credit cards. Subway: N, R to 49th St. JAPANESE.

In my world, comfort food doesn't get any better than a big ramen or fried rice bowl from Sapporo. This bustling, no-frills restaurant serves up good and cheap Japanese eats, and the mostly Japanese crowd is testimony to the food's authenticity. Sapporo is famous for their excellent *gyoza,* pork-filled dumplings that are pan fried and served with a soy, rice vinegar, and chili oil dipping sauce. Other winning choices include *chahan,* lightly fried Japanese rice with veggies, egg, fish cake, and your choice of pork or chicken; appealingly sweet beef and tofu sukiyaki; cleanly fried pork cutlets; and any of the gargantuan noodle bowls. Frankly, you can't really go wrong with anything—I've eaten here more times that I can count, and I've never been disappointed by a dish. Some of the servers speak little English, so feel free to just point to

Dining Zone: Koreatown

West 32nd Street between Fifth and Sixth avenues is neon lit like a block in Seoul, with reliable eateries serving exquisite, moderately priced food. ✪ **Won Jo,** 23 W. 32nd St. (☎ **212/695-5815**) is favored by many Koreans for its barbecue (sirloin, pork, chicken, or mushroom, accompanied by vegetables, kimchee, and noodles), which you cook yourself (each table has a small grill). Other top selections are **Hangawi,** 12 E. 32 St. (☎ **212/213-0077**), for a pricier but splendidly serene escape on the other side of Fifth; try the tempting pumpkin porridge and Korean vermicelli at this no meat, no fish, no dairy, Asian winner. Farther Uptown at 8–10 W. 36th St. is **Woo Chon** (☎ **212/695-0676**), open 24 hours and a good bet for first-timers.

your choice, and don't hesitate to ask for silverware if you prefer it over chopsticks. Beer and sake are served in addition to soft drinks.

If you're in the East Village, you'll find **Sapporo East** at 245 E. 10th St., at First Avenue (☎ 212/260-1330).

Siam Inn Too. 854 Eighth Ave. (btw. 51st and 52nd sts.). ☎ **212/757-4006.** Reservations accepted. Main courses $7.95–$15.95. AE, DC, MC, V. Mon–Fri noon–11:30pm; Sat 4–11:30pm; Sun 5–11pm. Subway: C, E to 50th St. THAI.

Situated on an unremarkable stretch of Eighth Avenue, Siam Inn is an attractive outpost of very good Thai food. All of your Thai favorites are here, well prepared and served by a brightly attired waitstaff. Tom kah gai soup (with chicken, mushrooms, and coconut milk), chicken satay with yummy peanut sauce, and light, flaky curry puffs all make good starters. Among noteworthy entrees are the masaman and red curries (the former rich and peanuty, the latter quite spicy), spicy sauteed squid with fresh basil and chilies, and perfect pad thai. And unlike many of the drab restaurants in this neighborhood, there's a semblance of decor—black deco tables and chairs, cushy rugs underfoot, and soft lighting. Another branch, Siam Inn, is just 3 blocks up at Eighth at no. 854 (☎ 212/489-5237).

Siam Inn is my favorite, but this neighborhood abounds with good Thai food. **Pongsri Thai Restaurant,** 244 W. 48th St. between Broadway and Eighth Avenue (☎ 212/582-3392), courteously serves lovingly cooked Thai specialties; the *tom yum goong* soup (loads of shrimp and straw mushrooms in a broth seasoned with lemongrass, lime juice, coriander, and exotic herbs) may be the best in town. Diners on a tight budget should head to **Chanpen,** 761 Ninth Ave., at 51st Street (☎ 212/ 586-6808), which serves bold Thai food at Chinatown prices; the lunch specials, in particular, are remarkable values.

Virgil's Real BBQ. 152 W. 44th St. (btw. Sixth and Seventh aves.). ☎ **212/921-9494.** Reservations recommended. Main courses $5.95–$24.95 (barbecue platters $12.95–$19.95). AE, DC, MC, V. Tues–Sat 11:30am–midnight; Sun–Mon 11:30am–11pm. Subway: 1, 2, 3, 7, 9, N, R to 42nd St./Times Sq. SOUTHERN/BARBECUE.

Virgil's may look like a comfy theme-park version of a down-home barbecue joint, but this place takes its barbecue seriously. The meat is house-smoked with a blend of hickory, oak, and fruitwood chips, and most every regional school is represented, from Carolina pulled pork to Texas beef brisket to Memphis ribs. You may not consider this contest-winning chow if you're from barbecue country, but we less-savvy Yankees are thrilled to have Virgil's in the 'hood. I love to start with the barbecued shrimp, accompanied by tasty mustard slaw, and a plate of buttermilk onion rings with blue cheese for dipping. The ribs are lip-smackin' good, and the chicken is moist and tender—go for a combo if you just can't choose. Burgers, sandwiches, and other entrees (chicken-fried steak, anyone?) are also available. And cast that cornbread aside for a full order of buttermilk biscuits, which come with maple butter so good it's like dessert. So hunker down, pig out, and don't worry about making a mess; when you're through eating, you get a hot towel for washing up. The bar offers a huge selection of on-tap and bottled brews.

QUICK BITES

Canova Market, 134 W. 51st St., between Sixth and Seventh avenues (☎ 212/ 969-9200), is a sprawling gourmet deli where your choices are only limited by your imagination (or your stomach). There's a fresh salad bar, an expansive deli counter, a soup bar, a sushi bar, and—my favorite—a pay-per-pound Mongolian grill, where you assemble your own concoction of fresh veggies, meats, seafood, rice, noodles, and seasonings to be grilled, and then watch the chefs do their stuff. There's a large dining area in the back where you can eat once you've paid. This place really bustles at lunch, but lines move fast. Canova Market is open around the clock, but don't expect all facilities (such as the Mongolian barbecue grill) to be going at all hours.

Over on Ninth Avenue, **Amy's Bread,** at no. 672, between 46th and 47th streets (☎ 212/977-2670), makes a great daytime stop. The cute, brick-walled bakery/cafe serves up fresh-baked breakfast pastries, sandwiches made on some of the city's best homemade bread, and excellent sweets as well as cappucino.

If you love French fries, don't miss **B. Frites,** 1657 Broadway, between 51st and 52nd streets (☎ 212/767-0858), purveyors of authentic Belgian fries. Little more than a jazzy, neon-lit storefront, B. Frites doles out their golden, thick-cut, crisped potatoes in hand-held cones, perfect for munching on the go.

Mangia (p. 122) also has a cafeteria-style cafe that's much smaller than the Wall Street location, but pleasing nonetheless: It's at 50 W. 57th St., between Fifth and Sixth avenues (☎ 212/582-5882). **Paradise & Lunch,** at 55 W. 44th St., between Fifth and Sixth avenues (☎ 212/944-5544), serves similar gourmet lunch fare in their sleek cafeteria-style cafe.

Soup Kitchen International. 259A W. 55th St. (at Eighth Ave.). ☎ **212/757-7730.** Soup $6–$16. Oct–June, Mon–Fri noon–6pm. Closed summer. Subway: C, E to 50th St. SOUP.

It's not hard to find Al Yeganeh, the famously dour soup vendor parodied on *Seinfeld*— just head for 55th Street, and walk to the end of the very long line. Many wait for the novelty, and even hope to be yelled at. (The real-life Kramer once posted a billboard next to the store with "behavior tips," but Yeganeh painted over the sign in red shortly after it appeared.) Here's the thing: It's ridiculously expensive for takeout soup, but it's really that good. Yeganeh labors fiercely, coddling the Hungarian goulash, mushroom barley, and mulligatawny, all subtly spiced and wonderful. The seafood bisque gets deserved kudos; I once found an entire lobster claw in mine. The 12 or so offered change daily, but don't call because he'll hang up on you. "Whatever soup you want, I have!" he snaps. Come after 2pm to minimize waiting; yes, have your money ready; and no, don't ask to take his picture, he finds that insulting.

WORTH A SPLURGE

۞ The Cafe at Aquavit. 13 W. 54th St. (btw. Fifth and Sixth aves.). ☎ **212/307-7311.** Reservations recommended. Main courses $13–$18; 3-course prix-fixe $25–$29. AE, DC, MC, V. Mon–Fri noon–2:30pm and 5:30–10:30pm; Sat 5:30–10:30pm; main dining room also open Sun noon–3pm (except summer). Subway. E, F to Fifth Ave. SCANDINAVIAN.

When Aquavit opened its doors, it opened the eyes of New Yorkers to what fine Scandinavian food could be: Its delicate elegance is reminiscent of Japanese refinement. But that doesn't mean that you have to spend a fortune to enjoy it. The main dining room space at Aquavit is soaring and sleek, with birch trees and an indoor waterfall; but I prefer to dine in the more casual upstairs cafe, a sophisticated modern space that also happens to be one of New York's best dining bargains. There's always a good-value fixed price meal available, but my favorite selections are well-prepared Scandinavian standards from the a la carte cafe menu: the smörgåsbord plate, an assortment of delicacies including perfectly smoked herring and zesty hot-mustard glazed salmon (which also comes as a full-size entree); and Swedish meatballs, a perfect realization of this traditional dish, accompanied by mashed potatoes and lingonberries. The Arctic char, served with cabbage salad, turkey bacon, and red-wine sauce, is another good choice. The bar offers a wide selection of aquavits, distilled liquors not unlike vodka flavored with fruit and spices and served Arctic cold, which have a smooth finish and are best accompanied by a full-bodied European brew like Carlsberg.

Theme Restaurant Thrills!

There's no doubt about it—New York's theme restaurant trend is on the wane. Sure, the Hard Rock, Planet Hollywood, and the All-Star Cafe are still going strong, but you won't see the legendary lines of the 80s forming outside these days. And thankfully, we're this close to losing the weakest of the bunch, the trouble-plagued **Fashion Cafe,** 51 Rockefeller Plaza, at 51st Street (☎ 212/765-3131), and **Comedy Nation,** 1626 Broadway, at 50th Street (☎ 212/757-4100), both officially "closed for renovations" at press time. This biz will prove to be Darwinist yet.

In addition to those listed below, there are some good ideas in the works. The best is **ESPN Zone,** which should be open at 42nd Street and Broadway by the time you read this. With 42,000 square feet of space slated to house a grill with set replicas from ESPN's hit shows (including *Sportscenter* and *Baseball Tonight*), a lounge with 13 massive TV screens and reclining leather chairs with speakers in the headrests, and a floor of sports-related arcade games, this upscale sports bar and restaurant should prove to be a sports fan's dream come true.

David Copperfield's **Copperfield Magic Underground** should magically appear at Broadway and 49th Street by the time you read this, the World Wrestling Federation has the **Raw Restaurant** in the works for Times Square (Stone Cold Steve cheeseburger, anyone?), and the **Rainforest Cafe** is planning to put down roots in the neighborhood. But until then:

✪ **Brooklyn Diner USA,** 212 W. 57th St., Broadway and Seventh Avenue (☎ 212/581-8900), looks like an old-fashioned diner on the outside, but inside you'll find linen tablecloths and mahogany touches instead of coffee-stained Formica tabletops. The food includes better-than-you'd-expect lump crabcakes, tenderloin steak, and Valrhona chocolate fudge sundae. To justify the name, there's a 15-bite Brooklyn hot dog and an Avenue U roast beef sandwich. Keep an eye on what you order, however, because the menu, while still affordable, is a tad pricier than at most theme restaurants.

Always the perennial favorite, New York's ✪ **Hard Rock Cafe,** 221 W. 57th St., between Broadway and Seventh Avenue (☎ 212/459-9320), is actually one of the originals of the chain, and a terrific realization of the concept. The memorabilia collection is terrific, with lots of great Lennon collectibles. The menu boasts all the Hard Rock standards, including a surprisingly good burger and fajitas, and the comfortable bar mixes up great cocktails.

Harley-Davidson Cafe, 1370 Sixth Ave., at 56th Street (☎ 212/245-6000), brings out the Hell's Angel in all of us. The just-fine munchies do the trick, and memorabilia documents 90 years of Hog history.

Carmine's. 200 W. 44th St. (btw. Broadway and Eighth Ave.). ☎ **212/221-3800.** Reservations recommended before 6pm, after 6pm accepted only for six or more. Family-style main courses $15–$47 (most under $21). AE, DC, MC, V. Tues–Sat 11:30am–midnight; Sun–Mon 11:30am–11pm. Subway: N, R, S, 1, 2, 3, 7, 9 to 42nd St./Times Sq.. SOUTHERN ITALIAN FAMILY STYLE.

Everything is done B-I-G at this rollicking, family-style Times Square mainstay. The dining room is vast enough to deserve a map, massive platters hold Brady Bunch–size portions of pasta, and large groups wait to join in the rambunctious atmosphere at this sibling of the original Upper West Sider. Don't let the price range quoted above scare

Something new to scare you with, my dear? You'll enter the **Jekyll & Hyde Club,** 1409 Sixth Ave., between 57th and 58th streets (☎ **212/541-9505**), through a small dark room with a sinking ceiling, where a corpse warns you of the oddities to come. There are five floors of bizarre artifacts, wall hangings that come to life, and other interactive bone chillers. Kids love it. There's a second, more publike location at 91 Seventh Ave. South, between Barrow and Grove streets, in Greenwich Village (☎ **212/989-7701**).

The subterranean red planet–themed restaurant, ✪ **Mars 2112,** 1633 Broadway, at 51st Street (☎ **212/582-2112**), is a hoot, from the simulated red-rock rooms to the Martian-costumed waitstaff to the silly "Man Eats on Mars!" newspaper-style menu. The eclectic food is better than you might expect, but skip the Star Tours–style simulated spacecraft ride at the entrance if you don't want to lose your appetite before you get to your table. The kids won't mind, though—they'll love it, along with the extensive video arcade.

Relive Berry Gordy's Detroit at the **Motown Cafe,** 104 W. 57th St., between Sixth and Seventh avenues (☎ **212/581-8030**). During lunch and dinner, a psuedo-Motown group slides and harmonizes its choreographed way through all your favorite tunes. The food isn't bad, but it's beside the point.

Superstar athletes Andre Agassi, Wayne Gretzky, Ken Griffey, Jr., Joe Montana, Shaquille O'Neal, Monica Seles, and Tiger Woods are the names behind the successful **Official All-Star Cafe,** 1540 Broadway, at 45th Street (☎ **212/840-8326**). At center court is a full-size scoreboard, on the sidelines are booths shaped like baseball mitts, and video monitors display the great plays of sports history. The food is straight from the ballpark—hot dogs and hamburgers, St. Louis ribs, Philly cheese steak sandwiches, and the like.

Ellen's Stardust Diner, 1650 Broadway, at 51st Street (☎ **212/956-5151**), is the quintessential 1950s-spoof diner, complete with singing waiters, outrageous lampshades, and Bobby Darin on the jukebox. The classic diner food is just fine—and how can you pass on a chocolate malt in a joint like this?

Bruce Willis, Sly Stallone, and Ah-nuld are the moneymongers behind **Planet Hollywood,** 140 W. 57th St., between Sixth and Seventh avenues (☎ **212/333-7827**). Frankly, the movie memorabilia doesn't hold the same excitement as the genuine rock 'n' roll goods over at the Hard Rock (didn't I see the R2D2 and C3PO robots at three *other* PHs?), but it's still plenty of fun for Hollywood buffs nonetheless. Watch for a 2000 move to the new Planet Hollywood hotel in Times Square.

you off; Carmine's is a value-priced restaurant where the bang for your buck increases for every person you add to your party, thanks to servings so monstrous that you can't avoid sharing (particularly if you show up with kids, who in no way could wrestle down these Herculean entrees). The waitstaff will often be able to size up your party and recommend how many dishes you should order. Caesar salad and a mound of fried calamari are a perfect beginning, followed by heaping portions of pasta topped with red or white clam sauce, mixed seafood, zesty marinara, and meatballs. The meat entrees include veal parmigiana, broiled porterhouse steak, chicken marsala, and shrimp scampi. The tiramisu is pie-size, thick and creamy, bathed in Kahlua and

Pre-Theater Meal Deals

Two of Midtown's best restaurants also offer two of its best pre-theater values. At elegant **San Domenico,** 240 Central Park South (☎ 212/265-5959), the room is swanky, the service impeccable, and the Bolognese-inspired Italian some of the best in the city—but you don't need a platinum card to enjoy it. The pre-theater prix fixe is just $32.50. Call well ahead, and specify that you're coming for the pre-theater deal when you book (if you're seated too late, you'll miss out).

For classic New York ambiance, there's no better place to dine than the landmark **"21" Club,** 21 W. 52nd St. (☎ 212/582-7200), favored dining room for the city's old-school business and celebrity power set. But you don't have to be a Broadway diva or a member of the Fortune 500 to enjoy this fascinating former speakeasy: the pre-theater prix fixe, served between 5:30–6:30pm, is just $33. Again, call well in advance—before you leave home, if possible.

---

marsala. Come early or late to avoid a long wait, and order half of what you think you'll need.

The original Carmine's, at 2450 Broadway (☎ 212/362-2200), is the same—but even B-I-G-G-E-R.

✪ **Churrascaria Plataforma.** 316 W. 49th St. (btw. Eighth and Ninth aves.). ☎ 212/245-0505. Reservations recommended. All-you-can-eat prix-fixe $27 at lunch, $31 at dinner. AE, DC, MC, V. Daily noon–midnight. Subway: C, E to 50th St. BRAZILIAN.

It's a carnival for carnivores at this upscale all-you-can-eat Brazilian rotisserie. A large selection of salad bar teasers like octopus stew, paella, and carpaccio may tempt you to fill up too quickly, but hold out for the never-ending parade of meat. Roving servers deliver beef (too many cuts to mention), ham, chicken (the chicken hearts are great, trust me), lamb, and sausage—more than 15 delectable varieties—and traditional sides like fried yucca, plantains, and rice right to your table until you cannot eat another bite. The food is excellent, and the service friendly and generous. A fun, festive family affair. The ideal accompaniment is a pitcher of Brazil's signature cocktail, a margarita-like blend of limes, sugar, crushed ice, and raw sugarcane liquor called *caipirinha* (grown-ups only, please); those in the know call Plataforma's the best in town.

Molyvos. 871 Seventh Ave. (btw. 55th and 56th sts.). ☎ 212/582-7500. Reservations recommended. Main courses $12.50–$20.50 at lunch, $18.50–$24.50 at dinner; prix-fixe lunch $20. AE, DC, DISC, MC, V. Mon–Fri noon–3pm and 5:30–11:30pm; Sat 5pm–midnight; Sun 5–11pm. Subway: N, R to 57th St.; B, D, E to Seventh Ave. GREEK.

Ruth Reichl of the *New York Times* was so thrilled with the high quality and authenticity of this cozy upscale taverna that she awarded Molyvos three stars (out of a possible four), and I concur wholeheartedly. The menu boasts beautifully prepared favorites—including superb taramosalata, tzatziki, and other traditional spreads—plus a few dishes with contemporary twists. The Greek country salad is generously portioned and as fresh as can be, while the baby octopus starter is grilled over fruit wood to tender, charred perfection. Among the main courses, the lemon and garlic-seasoned, roasted free-range chicken is right on the mark. More traditional tastes can opt for excellent moussaka; rosemary-skewered souvlaki; or the day's catch, wood grilled whole with lemon, oregano, and olive oil in traditional Greek style. Baklava fans shouldn't miss the restaurant's moist, nutty version, which is big enough to share. The room is spacious and comfortable, with a warm Mediterranean appeal that doesn't go overboard on the Hellenic themes, and service is attentive without being intrusive. The sommelier will be happy to help you choose from the surprisingly good list of

Greek wines, making Molyvos a winner on all counts. Well worth the splurge—and it's hard to find a better deal than the three-course $20 fixed-price lunch.

12 Midtown East & Murray Hill

The British Open. 320 E. 59th St. (btw. First and Second aves.). ☎ **212/355-8467.** Main courses $7.50–$19.75 (most under $13). AE, DC, DISC, MC, V. Mon–Sat noon–midnight; Sun noon–10pm. Subway: 4, 5, 6 to 59th St. BRITISH.

Here's the perfect pub for golf lovers, or anybody who pines for a pint and some good English grub. This charmer of an alehouse is more sophisticated than most, with a polished mahogany bar, a pretty dining room in back, and friendly, attentive service. Tartan carpet completes the theme and little blue lights create a romantic glow. This isn't a copy of a Brit pub—it's the real thing, bartender, malt vinegar, and all. The North Star at South Street Seaport is equally genuine, but it's more after-work local than Sunday dinner, if you know what I mean. The extensive menu serves well-prepared versions of the pub staples, plus steaks, chops, and the like. But go for the standards: light, well-battered fish with crispy chips; excellent cottage pie with veggies and perfectly browned mash; plus steak and kidney pie, bangers and mash, and so on. You'll find Guinness, Bass, Fullers ESB, and other British imports on tap, and golf and other sports on the telly at any hour.

Dosanko. 423 Madison Ave. (btw. 48th and 49th sts.). ☎ **212/688-8575.** Reservations not taken. Main courses $5–$9. No credit cards. Mon–Fri 11:30am–10pm; Sat–Sun noon–8pm. Subway: 6 to 51st St. JAPANESE.

This bright and simple sit-down eatery serves up the kind of affordable food that's eaten in cities throughout Japan every day: vegetable-heavy noodle bowls, gyoza (pan-fried dumplings stuffed with pork or shrimp), yakisoba (stir-fried noodles), and katsu (battered and fried pork cutlet). Everything is hearty, healthy, well prepared, and cheap. The yakisoba is a heaping plate, with thin-sliced beef and accompanied by a fresh green salad; it's a steal at $5.50. Flavored with your choice of soy, flavorful miso, or curry, the larmen (noodle soups) are meals unto themselves, especially when topped with chicken, beef, or pork cutlet. I prefer Sapporo (see "Times Square & Midtown West" above), but it's strictly personal taste—the menu is more limited here but Dosanko's food is just as good, the room itself is actually a little nicer, and the waitstaff tends to speak better English. Japanese beers and sake are available.

✪ Ess-A-Bagel. 831 Third Ave. (at 51st St.). ☎ **212/980-1010.** Sandwiches $1.35–$8.35. AE, DC, DISC, MC, V. Mon–Fri 6:30am–10pm; Sat–Sun 8am–5pm. Subway: 6 to 51st St.; E, F to Lexington Ave. BAGEL SANDWICHES.

Ess-A-Bagel turns out the city's best bagel, edging out rival H&H, who won't make you a sandwich. Baked daily on-site, the giant hand-rolled delicacies come in 12 flavors and are so plump, chewy, and satisfying it's hard to believe they contain no fat, cholesterol, or preservatives. Head to the back counter for a baker's dozen or line up for an overstuffed sandwich. Fillings can range from a generous schmear of cream cheese to smoked Nova salmon or chopped herring salad (both have received national acclaim) to sun-dried tomato tofu spread. There are also lots of deli-style meats to choose from, plus a wide range of cheeses and salads (egg, chicken, light tuna, and so on). The cheerful dining room has plenty of bistro-style tables.

There's a second, smaller location at 359 First Ave., at 21st St. (☎ 212/260-2252).

Evergreen Shanghai. 10 E. 38th St. (btw. Fifth and Madison aves.). ☎ **212/448-1199.** Reservations accepted. Most main courses $4.95–$16.95 (a few specialties are higher);

weekday lunch specials (including rice and soup) $5.95–$10.95. AE, MC, V. Mon–Fri 11:30am–10pm; Sat–Sun noon–10pm. Subway: 4, 5, 6, 7, S to 42nd St.–Grand Central. CHINESE.

If you'd like a true taste of Chinatown but don't feel like venturing Downtown, head to this Midtown branch of the Chinatown favorite. Featuring Szechuan, Cantonese, and Hunan dishes as well as Shanghai specialties, the mammoth menu is broad enough to appeal to conservative as well as adventurous tastes. But since the restaurant is so well known for its authentic regional specialties, I encourage you to indulge in at least one or two Shanghai-style dishes, such as the steamed soup dumplings (a close second to the dreamy pockets at Joe's Shanghai) or thick Shanghai noodles with flavorful, thin-sliced aromatic beef in broth; the helpful waitstaff will be glad to point you to other regional favorites. The only misstep is the sushi bar, which is just out of place (a common feeling, based on the inactivity of the sushi chef in the otherwise hopping restaurant on my last visit). The bi-level room is airy and pleasing, with large, well-spaced tables and a thoughtful decor that's much nicer than you usually find in Chinatown.

The original Chinatown location is at 63 Mott St., south of Canal Street (☎ 212/571-3339); this one accepts cash only.

Pamir. 1437 Second Ave. (btw. 74th and 75th sts.). ☎ 212/734-3791. Reservations recommended. Main courses $11.95–$16.95. MC, V. Tues–Sun 5–11pm. Subway: 6 to 77th St. AFGHAN.

Afghanistan's position astride the main western land route to India through the famed Khyber Pass has resulted in a culinary tradition marked by Middle Eastern and Indian influences. Peruse the menu while sipping *doodh*, a refreshing mix of yogurt, club soda, mint, and a touch of salt. You might start with the combination appetizer, one of which should be *bulanee kachalou*, a tasty turnover stuffed with mildly spiced potatoes and onions, with a tangy yogurt sauce. A favorite main course is *kormae-murgh*, a hearty stew of delicately seasoned chicken with tomatoes, onions, garlic, and Afghan spices. Or try *quabilli palaw*, aromatic pieces of lamb under a mound of brown rice topped with almonds, pistachios, carrot strips, and raisins. Though traditional dishes go well beyond kebabs, the ones served here are particularly tasty, with juicy meats marinated in a savory blend of spices. Afghan pudding with almonds and pistachios is the perfect finish.

Prime Burger. 5 E. 51st St. (btw. Fifth and Madison aves.). ☎ 212/759-4729. Main courses $3.25–$7.95. No credit cards. Mon–Fri 5am–7pm; Sat 6am–5pm. Subway: 6 to 51st St.; E, F to Lexington/Third aves. and 53rd St. AMERICAN/HAMBURGERS.

Just across the street from St. Patrick's Cathedral, this coffee shop is a heavenly find. The burgers and sandwiches are tasty, the fries crispy and generous. The front seats, which might remind you (if you're old enough) of old wooden grammar-school desks, are great fun—especially when ever-so-serious suited-up New Yorkers quietly take their places at these oddities. A great quickie stop during a day of Fifth Avenue shopping.

Taco & Tortilla King. 285 Third Ave. (btw. 22nd and 23rd sts.). ☎ 212/679-8882 or 212/481-3930. Tacos, burritos, and sandwiches $1–$6.79; fajitas $12.99–$13.99. No credit cards. Daily 11am–11:30pm. Subway: 6 to 23rd St. MEXICAN.

This place may be slightly off the tourist track, but if you're jonesing for some good, cheap Mexican, it's well worth the walk. This low-profile sleeper is little more than a lunch counter with a few tables and chairs, but the authentic Mexican food can't be beat. Sit down to a couple of tacos and you'll think you've been temporarily transported to one of those super-cheap, gourmet Mexican joints your friends in southern California

ⓘ Affordable Family-Friendly Restaurants

The increasing kid-friendliness of New York City has resulted in a growing number of restaurants that warmly welcome families. While it's always a smart move to call ahead to make sure the restaurant you're interested in can accommodate kids with such amenities as kids' menus and high chairs, you can always count on the following restaurants.

America *(p. 148)*   This kid-friendly Flatiron District restaurant is nearly as large as a continent, with a menu almost equally as big—even the fussiest kid will find something they like here. America's weekend family brunch features a balloon maker and a magician along with the good grub.

Carmine's *(p. 162)*   This rollicking, family-style Italian was created with kids in mind. Expect Brady Bunch–size portions of all the favorites, including Caesar salad, veal parmigiana, and pasta topped with zesty marinara and little fist-sized meatballs. The bigger the group, the better the bargain.

EJ's Luncheonette *(p. 174)*   These pleasing retro-1950s diners do what they're supposed to do best: serve up great burgers, fries, and blue plate specials. There's even a kids' menu featuring peanut butter–and-jelly sandwiches along with downsized versions of the classics. Order your kid a milk shake and they'll be in hog heaven.

John's Pizzeria *(p. 155)*   What kid doesn't love pizza? The Times Square location is particularly well located and kid-friendly, with family-sized tables, chefs cooking up pies in brick ovens right in the cavernous room, and a bustling atmosphere where kids are welcome to be kids.

Manhattan Chili Co. *(p. 158)*   This fun, cartoonish Theater District restaurant is geared for all-American tastes and palates. Expect kid-friendly nachos, chicken wings, not-too-hot bowls of thick and meaty chili, and other faves like burritos and burgers. It's really hard to go wrong here.

Serendipity 3 *(p. 174)*   Kids will love this whimsical restaurant and ice cream shop, which serves up a huge menu of American favorites, followed up by colossal ice-cream treats. This irony-free charmer even makes grown-ups feel like kids again.

Virgil's Real BBQ *(p. 160)*   This pleasing Times Square barbecue joint welcomes kids with open arms—and Junior will be more than happy, I'm sure, to be *allowed* to eat with his hands.

In addition to these choices, also consider the city's many theme restaurants. For details on all the choices, see "Theme Restaurant Thrills!" earlier in this chapter.

---

keep raving about. The kitchen won me over with the basics: Chunky fresh-made guacamole infused with lime, and flour tortillas made from scratch and baked on premises. All the Mexican staples, from well-stuffed burritos to sizzling fajitas, are authentically prepared, hearty, and satisfying; a good portion of the offerings can be prepared meatless for vegetarians. An all-around winner for a fast meal at an unbeatable price.

QUICK BITES

Mangia (p. 122) has a third cafeteria-style cafe that's much smaller than the Wall Street location, but pleasing nonetheless: at 16 E. 48th St., just east of Fifth Avenue (☎ 212/ 754-7600).

The Pump. 113 E. 31st St. (btw. Park and Lexington aves.). ☎ **212/213-5733.** Breakfast $2.50–$7; sandwiches and salads $3–$7; full plates $6.50–$12. AE, MC, V. Mon–Thurs 9:30am–9:30pm; Fri 9:30am–6:30pm; Sat 11am–7pm. Subway: 6 to 33rd St. HEALTH-CONSCIOUS.

This little storefront is a terrific stop for diners who are watching their figures as well as their wallets. An appealing mix of retro-cute and future-chic, with just a counter in back and a few high tables with stools, the Pump espouses a philosophy that eating right doesn't have to mean boring. Everything on the menu is low in fat and high in protein, but doesn't sacrifice flavor for healthfulness. This is casual food made with all-natural ingredients that's easy to enjoy as a quick meal: salads, sandwiches, "super-charged" combo platters, fresh juices, high-protein and health shakes. Although they serve up a great nature burger (a pleasing blend of brown rice, sunflower seeds, herbs, and veggies), the Pump isn't a vegetarian restaurant—lean beef, turkey, and chicken are served. And since they cater to a big workout crowd that needs energy, portions are substantial. Salad dressings are all fat-free creations, like tahini and honey mustard, and guilt-free pizzas are prepared with non-fat mozzarella, low sodium tomato sauce, and whole wheat crust. At breakfast, eggs, pancakes, and potatoes are all baked, never fried—which is precisely why you can indulge in the steak and eggs sandwich (served on a whole wheat pita) and feel not the least bit sinful.

WORTH A SPLURGE

✪ **Oyster Bar.** In Grand Central Terminal, lower level (btw. Vanderbilt and Lexington aves.). ☎ **212/490-6650.** Reservations recommended. Main courses $9.45–$34.95. AE, CB, DC, DISC, JCB, MC, V. Mon–Fri 11:30am–9:30pm (last seating). Subway: 4, 5, 6, 7, S to 42nd St./Grand Central. SEAFOOD.

Here's one New York institution housed within another: the city's most famous seafood joint in the world's greatest train station, newly renovated Grand Central Terminal. Fully recovered from a 1997 fire, the restaurant is looking spiffy, too, with a main dining room sitting under an impressive curved and tiled ceiling, a more casual luncheonette-style section for walk-ins, and a wood-paneled saloon-style room for smokers. If you love seafood, don't miss this place. A new menu is prepared every day, featuring only the freshest fish. The oysters are irresistible: Kumomoto, Bluepoint, Malepeque, Belon—the list goes on and on. The list of daily catches, which can range from arctic char to mako shark to ono (Hawaiian wahoo), is equally impressive. Most dinners go for between $19.95 and $24.95, and it's easy to jack up the tab by ordering live lobster (flown in directly from Maine) or one of the rarer daily special-ties. But it's just as easy to keep the tab down by sticking with hearty fare like one of the excellent stews and pan roasts (from $9.45 for oyster stew to $19.95 for a combo pan roast rich with oysters, clams, shrimp, lobster, and scallops) or by pairing the New England clam chowder (at $4.50, an unbeatable lunch) with a smoked starter to make a great meal.

13 The Upper West Side

In addition to the choices below, there's also a branch of the retro all-American diner, **EJ's Luncheonette** (p. 174), at 447 Amsterdam Ave., between 81st and 82nd streets (☎ 212/873-3444). More retro vibes can be had at the **Hi-Life Bar & Grill,** at Amsterdam Avenue and 83rd Street (☎ 212/787-7199). Near Lincoln Center, 48 W. 65th St. between Columbus Avenue and Central Park West, there's a nice **John's Pizzeria** (☎ 212/721-7001), serving up one of the city's best pies (p. 155). There's also **Time Cafe North,** 2330 Broadway, at 85th St. (☎ **212/579-5100**), a brand-new Uptown version of Time Cafe (p. 139), complete with the Moroccan-themed lounge,

Fez. You'll also find healthful **Zen Palate** (p. 151) at 2170 Broadway, between 76th and 77th streets (☎ **212/501-7768**); and affordable noodles at **Republic** (p. 150), 2290 Broadway, between 82nd and 83rd streets (☎ **212/579-5959**).

Big Nick's Burger Joint. 2175 Broadway (at 77th St.). ☎ **212/362-9238.** Main courses $3.50–$11. No credit cards. Open 24 hours. Subway: 1, 9 to 79th St. AMERICAN.

A neighborhood legend since 1962, Big Nick's is one of the best spots in the city for a midnight snack. They offer a full menu 24 hours a day, which includes everything from killer French toast and pancakes to Nick's infamous gourmet beefburgers. The classic char-broiled burgers come in a whole host of varieties, from your all-American cheeseburger to the Mediterranean, stuffed with herbs, spices, and onions and topped with anchovies, feta, and tomato. Or how 'bout a Texasburger, with an egg on top for "egg-stra" energy (Nick's joke, not mine). There's also a good selection of Big Nick–style pizzas, like the Gyromania, topped with well-seasoned gyro meat and onions. As the name suggests, Nick's is a real joint, specializing in homegrown Noo Yawk fare; however, the kitchen gets kudos for developing a diet-watchers menu, with pizzas prepared with skim cheese and lean-ground veal and turkey burgers. The atmosphere is suitably lively, with waiters and busboys scrambling about, cooks calling out orders, and crowded tables happily chowing down.

✪ Gabriela's. 685 Amsterdam Ave. (at 93rd St.). ☎ **212/961-0574.** Reservations accepted. Main courses $5–$12.95. AE, MC, V. Mon–Thurs 11:30am–11pm; Fri–Sat 11:30am–midnight; Sun noon–10pm. Subway: 1, 2, 3, 9 to 96th St. MEXICAN.

If you love roast chicken, trust me: it's well worth the trip Uptown for Gabriela's. A blend of Yucatan spices and a slow-roasting rotisserie results in some of the most tender, juiciest chicken in town—and at $6.95 for a half-chicken with two sides (plenty for all but the biggest eaters) and $12.95 for a whole, it's one of the city's best bargains, too. All of the Mexican specialties on the extensive menu are well prepared, generously portioned, and satisfying, from the monster tacos to the well-sauced enchiladas. The fresh, chunky, perfectly limed guacamole should please even Southwest natives. The dining room is large, bright, and pretty, with a pleasing South-of-the-Border flair, and the service is affable if a little slow at times. Mexican beers and wine are available, but you may want to consider one of Gabriela's yummy fruit shakes (both mango and papaya are good bets) or tall agua frescas (fresh fruit drinks), which come in a variety of tropical flavors.

Hunan Park. 235 Columbus Ave. (btw. 70th and 71st St.). ☎ **212/724-4411.** Reservations accepted for groups of 5 or more. Main courses $5.25–$10.50 (Peking Duck $24). AE, MC, V. Sun–Thurs noon–11:30pm; Fri–Sat noon–12:30am. Subway: B, C, 1, 2, 3, 9 to 72nd St. HUNAN CHINESE.

This casual place has been earning broad-sweeping kudos for years from Zagat's to *New York* magazine to Alan Alda for its well-prepared, inexpensive Chinese standards. Everything about it—quality, service, decor—is a cut above the standard. Expect all the familiar favorites, plus satisfying specialties like ginger chicken, spicy four-flavor beef, and crispy sea bass in a rich Hunan sauce. Service is quick and efficient, and the convenient location makes this a cheap and easy post–Central Park or pre–Lincoln Center stop.

If you're farther Uptown, there's a second location at 721 Columbus Ave., at 95th St. (☎ **212/222-6511**).

Josie's Restaurant & Juice Bar. 300 Amsterdam Ave. (at 74th St.). ☎ **212/769-1212.** Reservations recommended. Main courses $8–$16. AE, DC, MC, V. Mon 5:30–11pm; Tues–Fri 5:30pm–midnight; Sat 5pm–midnight, Sun 5–11pm. Subway: 1, 2, 3, 9 to 72nd St. HEALTH-CONCIOUS.

Uptown Dining

Big Nick's Burger Joint **27**
Burritoville **31**
Caffe Grazie **10**
Carmine's **5**
EJ's Luncheonette **15** **24**
Gabriela's **4**
Gray's Papaya **32**
Haru **16** **20**
Hi-Life Bar & Grill **14**
Hi-Life Restaurant & Lounge **23**
Hunan Park **3** **33**
John's Pizzeria **34** **35**
Josie's Restaurant & Juice Bar **30**
La Caridad **28**
Pamir **22**
Papaya King **9**
Payard Patisserie & Bistro **25**
Pintaile's Pizza **8**
Popover Cafe **11**
Republic **13**
Sarabeth's Kitchen **6** **17** **26**
Serendipity 3 **36**
Shabu Tatsu **21**
Sofia Fabulous Pizza **19**
Sylvia's **1**
Time Cafe North **12**
Tom's Restaurant **2**
Totonno's Pizzeria Napolitano **18**
Yura & Company **7**
Zen Palate **29**

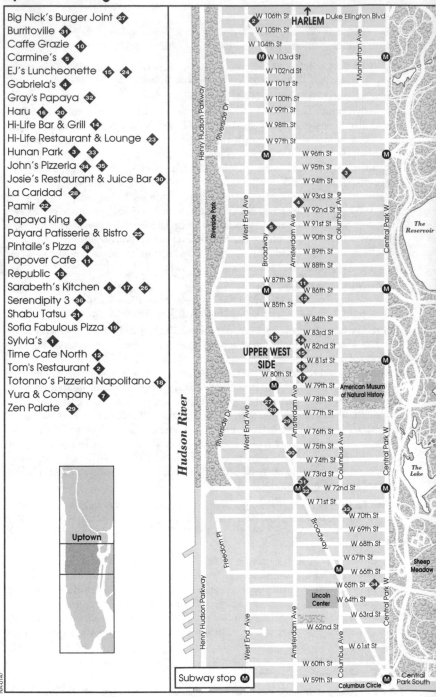

You have to admire the sincerity of an organic restaurant that uses chemical-free milk paint on its walls. Chef/owner Louis Lanza doesn't stop there: His adventurous menu shuns dairy, preservatives, and concentrated fats. Free-range and farm-raised meats and poultry augment vegetarian choices like baked sweet potato with tamari brown rice, broccoli, roasted beets, and tahini sauce; eggless Caesar salad; and a great three-grain vegetable burger with homemade ketchup and caramelized onions. The yellowfin tuna wasabi burger with pickled ginger is another signature. Everything is made with organic grains, beans, and flour as well as organic produce when possible. You don't have to be a health nut to enjoy Josie's; Lanza's eclectic cuisine really satisfies. If wheat grass isn't your thing, a full wine and beer list is served in this pleasing modern space, which boasts enough *Jetsons*-style touches to give the room a playful, relaxed feel.

La Caridad 78. 2197–2199 Broadway (at 78th St.). ☎ **212/874-2780** or 212/874-8001. Reservations not taken. Main courses $6–$11.25. No credit cards. Mon–Sat 11:30–1am; Sun 11:30am–10:30pm. Subway: 1, 9 to 78th St. LATIN AMERICAN/CHINESE.

This Upper West Side stalwart is the best of a string of uniquely New York institutions: the Chinese-Latin hybrid restaurant (supposedly the result of cultural intermarrying between Chinese and Hispanic immigrants). The cuisine isn't a cross; rather, the menu features both Latino and Chinese sections, so you could conceivably start with an egg roll, move on to Cuban-style fried pork with black beans and yellow rice, and follow up with moo goo gai pan if you were still hungry. Atmosphere is not the point here, so ignore the bare-bones interior and fluorescent lighting. Instead, line up with the rest of the crowd for the huge portions of good, cheap eats. The lemon pork chops, shrimp in tomato sauce, and stir-fried chicken are all recommendable choices. No beer or wine is served. If you're staying in the neighborhood, they'll deliver (until 11pm Monday through Saturday, until 10pm on Sunday).

Popover Cafe. 551 Amsterdam Ave. (btw. 86th and 87th sts.). ☎ **212/595-8555.** Reservations not taken. Main courses $5.75–$15.50 at breakfast and lunch; $11.95–$17.95 at dinner. AE, MC, V. Mon–Thurs 8am–10pm; Fri–Sat 8am–11pm; Sun 9am–10pm. Subway: 1, 9 to 86th St. AMERICAN.

The first thing people usually call Popover's is kid-friendly. Not that it isn't—there's the child-size burger, peanut butter and jelly sandwiches, and, of course, cutesy decor chock-a-block with teddy bears—but grownups will like it just as much. Everybody gets addicted to the namesake item: big, fluffy popovers served with strawberry butter or preserves. Popover's supplements their basic menu with full entrees at dinnertime that are a bit on the pricey side, but their real forte is the kind of comfort food that makes a hearty, and affordable, lunch or brunch: three-egg omelets and scrambles, savory home-style chili and soups, and generous salads and sandwiches. A bowl of one of the day's homemade soups (vegetarian three-bean, split pea, and chicken noodle are some of the possible options) accompanied by a popover makes a more-than-satisfying lunch. Service is appropriately warm and welcoming. In fact, eating here feels like stepping into somebody's big old, hospitable New England home. Well worth a stop.

Tom's Restaurant. 2880 Broadway (at 112th St.). ☎ **212/864-6137.** Main courses $3–$10. No credit cards. Mon–Wed 6–1:30am; Thurs–Sat 24 hours; Sun 6–1:30am. Subway: 1, 9 to Cathedral Pkwy. (110th St.). AMERICAN.

Tom's would be just any other diner if it weren't for its famous connections: This is the restaurant that served as the exterior for Monk's on *Seinfeld* and inspired a young Suzanne Vega to write "Tom's Diner." It's worth a pilgrimage if you're a diehard Jerry fan, or worth a stop if you're in the neighborhood. Tom's is hugely popular with Columbia University students thanks to its long hours and super-cheap coffee-shop fare. Expect all the standards, from three-egg omelettes to burgers to Virginia ham dinners with apple sauce. The circa-'72 waitstaff emits the requisite Noo Yawk attitude and won't think twice of rushing you when it's crowded.

QUICK BITES

For one of the cheapest, most satisfying meal deals in New York, head to the Uptown branch of ✪ **Gray's Papaya** (p. 147), 2090 Broadway, at 72nd Street (☎ 212/799-0243), where first-rate all-beef dogs are just 50¢ each around the clock. Pair your franks with some crispy fries and a tropical juice drink.

And what would the Upper West Side be without its own **Burritoville** (p. 124)? This one's at 166 W. 72nd St., at Amsterdam Avenue (☎ 212/580-7700).

WORTH A SPLURGE

Haru. 433 Amsterdam Ave. (btw. 80th and 81st sts.). ☎ **212/579-5655.** Reservations not taken. A la carte sushi and rolls $3–$8 (special rolls may be higher); sushi combos and main courses $14–$24.50. AE, DC, MC, V. Mon–Thurs 5–11:30pm; Fri 5pm–midnight: Sat–Sun 11:30am–midnight. Subway: 1, 9 to 79th St. SUSHI.

This attractive, sophisticated little restaurant arrived on the Upper West Side, a neighborhood desperately in need of high-quality sushi, like a breath of fresh air. Expect generous, super-fresh cuts of all the classics, plus a good number of vegetable choices (shiitake and cucumber, vegetable tempura) among the hand and cut rolls. I recommend starting with the seaweed salad, king crab shumai, a couple of grilled kushi yaki skewers, or a bowl of miso before launching into your raw meal. The attractive blond-wood room fills up quickly, so don't be surprised if there's a wait; but we've found that it's rather quiet in the pre-theater hour, and Lincoln Center is just a brisk 10- or 15-minute walk away. The outdoor seating is wonderful when it turns warm.

If you're on the east side, Haru has a second location at 1329 Third Ave., at 76th Street (☎ **212/579-5655**).

✪ **Sarabeth's Kitchen.** 423 Amsterdam Ave. (btw. 80th and 81st sts.). ☎ **212/496-6280.** Reservations accepted for dinner only. Main courses $5–$11 at lunch and brunch; $10–$22 at dinner. AE, CB, DC, DISC, JCB, MC, V. Mon–Thurs 8am–10:30pm; Fri 8am–11pm; Sat 9am–11pm; Sun 9am–9:30pm. Subway: 1, 9 to 79th St. CONTEMPORARY AMERICAN.

Its 200-year-old family recipe for orange-apricot marmalade first rooted Sarabeth's Kitchen into New York's consciousness, but its fresh-baked goods, award-winning preserves, and creative American cooking with a European touch keep the clientele loyal. This charming country restaurant with a distinct Hamptons feel is best known for its breakfast and weekend brunch, when the menu features such treats as porridge with wheatberries, fresh cream, butter, and brown sugar; pumpkin waffle topped with sour cream, raisins, pumpkin seeds, and honey (a sweet tooth's delight); and a whole host of farm-fresh omelets. But lunch is just as good and a lot less crowded. Offerings might include a generous Caesar salad with aged Parmesan, brioche croutons, and a tangy anchovy dressing accompanied by a hearty from-scratch soup, or some beautifully built country-style sandwiches.

Dinner is more sophisticated—with such specialties as hazelnut-crusted halibut in an aromatic seven-vegetable broth and oven-roasted lamb crusted in black mushrooms, with grilled leeks and Vidalia onion rings on the side—but a splurge, albeit a worthy one. No matter what time you come, leave room for the scrumptious desserts—Sarabeth Levine was just named James Beard Award for Best Pastry Chef recently, an honor well deserved. Or feel free to stop in just for dessert, as many New Yorkers do.

There are also two East Side locations: 1295 Madison Ave. (☎ **212/410-7335**) and inside the Whitney Museum at 945 Madison Ave. (☎ **212/570-3670**).

14   The Upper East Side

In addition to the choices below, also consider the local branch of **Shabu Tatsu** (p. 139), at 114 York Ave., at 75th Street (☎ 212/472-3322), which is well worth the trip to the far east side of town.

If you're in the mood for sushi, consider the eastside branch of **Haru** (p. 173), at 1329 Third Ave., at 76th Street (☎ 212/579-5655). If it's an excellent contemporary meal or a sweet treat you're after, head to **Sarabeth's Kitchen** (p. 173), which has two eastside locations: 1295 Madison Ave., at E. 92nd St. (☎ 212/410-7335), and at the Whitney Museum, 945 Madison Ave. (☎ 212/570-3670).

EJ's Luncheonette. 1271 Third Ave. (at 73rd St.). ☎ 212/472-0600. Main courses $3.95–$12. No credit cards. Mon–Thurs 8am–11pm; Fri–Sat 8am–11:30pm; Sun 8am–10:30pm. Subway: 6 to 77th St. AMERICAN DINER.

This retro diner is popular with Uptown yuppies and their kids who come for hearty American fare in a 1950s setting: turquoise vinyl booths, Formica tabletops, a soda fountain, and a lunch counter with stools that spin. The menu features a large selection of breakfasts so good that you shouldn't be ashamed of indulging in a stack of banana-pecan pancakes for dinner. There's also a terrific selection of burgers (including a great veggie version), well-stuffed sandwiches, hearty green salads, and blue-plate specials like meat loaf with mashed potatoes. Everything is well prepared—better than you'd expect from a joint like this, in fact—and service is friendly. Don't miss the amazing sweet-potato fries.

There are two other locations in addition to this one: On the Upper West Side at 447 Amsterdam Ave., between 81st and 82nd streets (☎ 212/873-3444); and in Greenwich Village at 432 Sixth Ave., between 9th and 10th streets (☎ 212/473-5555). Weekend brunch is a big deal at all three locations, so expect a wait.

Hi-Life Restaurant & Lounge. 1340 First Ave. (at 72nd St.). ☎ 212/249-3600. Reservations accepted. Main courses $4.95–$8.50 at lunch; $8.95–$16.50 (including soup or salad) at dinner. AE, DC, DISC, MC, V. Mon–Fri 11am–4pm and 5pm–midnight; Sat–Sun 11:30am–4pm and 5pm–midnight. Subway: 6 to 68th St. AMERICAN/ECLECTIC.

Here's a page out of the days when men wore gray flannel suits, women looked like Myrna Loy, and everybody had a few pre-dinner cocktails. Although it's a product of the 1990s, the Hi-Life was designed in the tradition of pre-war restaurant and lounges, with a mahogany bar, comfy leather banquettes, neon signs, and stainless steel touches throughout. The bar prides itself on its excellent classic cocktails, particularly its martinis, which are terrific. The food's not bad either—good all-American fare at reasonable prices, with a little Asian flair here and there. The flame-grilled burgers, steaks, and chops are satisfying and fit the mood perfectly. The seafood also tends to Sinatra-era preparations such as grilled tuna in teriyaki and jumbo shrimp scampi, and is better than I expected it to be. The menu also features a few pastas, entree-sized salads, and hearty noodle bowls for lighter tastes. There's a sushi and raw bar as well, but you can do better elsewhere in this department; stick with the standard menu.

The Hi-Life also has a more casual bar and grill on the Upper West Side at 477 Amsterdam Ave., at 83rd Street (☎ 212/787-7199).

Serendipity 3. 225 E. 60th St. (btw. Second and Third aves.). ☎ 212/838-3531. Reservations recommended for dinner. Main courses $5.50–$17.95; sweets and sundaes $4.50–$10. AE, DC, DISC, MC, V. Sun–Thurs 11:30am–midnight; Fri 11:30–1am; Sat 11:30–2am. Subway: 4, 5, 6 to 59th St.; N, R to Lexington Ave. AMERICAN.

You'd never guess that this whimsical place was once a top stop on Andy Warhol's agenda. Wonders never cease—and neither does the confection at this delightful restaurant and sweet shop. Tucked into a cozy brownstone a few steps from Bloomingdale's, Serendipity's small front-room curiosity shop overflows with odd objects, from jigsaw puzzles to silly jewelry. But the real action is in back, where the quintessential American soda fountain still reigns supreme. Remember Farrell's? This is the better version (complete with candy to tempt the kids on the way out). Happy people gather at marble-topped ice-cream parlor tables for burgers and foot-long hot dogs, country meat loaf with mashed potatoes and gravy, and salads and sandwiches with cute names like "The Catcher in the Rye" (their own twist on the BLT, with chicken and Russian dressing—on rye, of course). The food isn't great, but the main courses aren't the point—they're just an excuse to get to the desserts. The restaurant's signature is Frozen Hot Chocolate, a slushy version of everybody's cold weather favorite, but other crowd pleasers include dark double devil mousse, celestial carrot cake, lemon ice-box pie, and anything with hot fudge. So cast that willpower aside and come on in—Serendipity is a ironic-free charmer to be appreciated by adults and kids alike.

QUICK BITES

Papaya King, 179 E. 86th St., at Third Avenue (☎ **212/369-0648**), is the originator of the two-franks-and-a-fruit-drink combo that Gray's Papaya (p. 147) has popularized in other 'hoods. Papaya King isn't quite so cheap as Gray's, but close enough. Open daily from 8:30am to midnight.

For more refined tastes, there's **Yura & Company,** 6045 Third Ave., at 92nd Street (☎ **212/860-8060**), one of the Upper East Side's best-kept secrets. This quaint gourmet bakery/cafe serves good coffee, superlative scones and muffins, and a nice selection of prepared gourmet foods that are perfect for a Central Park picnic (the 90th Street pedestrian entrance is just a few blocks away). Or you can opt for table service in the country-style dining room, a cute spot for a quick breakfast or well-made sandwich. Good angel-food cake, too.

WORTH A SPLURGE

Caffe Grazie. 26 E. 84th St. (at Madison Ave.). ☎ **212/717-4407.** Reservations recommended. Main courses $12.50–$19.50; Sun brunch $12.95. AE, DC, MC, V. Mon–Sat 11:30am–11pm; Sun 11:30am–10pm. Subway: 4, 5, 6 to 86th St. ITALIAN.

This cheery, unpretentious Italian cafe is most notable for its convenient location near the Metropolitan Museum of Art, a neighborhood short on moderately priced, recommendable eats. It's perfect for sipping espresso between museum hops or lingering over an elegant dinner. Appetizers like the bruschetta assortment served with a small

---

Pizza! Pizza!

Leave it to the chi-chi Upper East Side to specialize in designer pizza. **Sofia Fabulous Pizza,** 1022 Madison Ave., at 79th Street (☎ 212/734-2676), serves pricey but terrific Tuscan-style pizza, and there's even wonderful alfresco rooftop dining. **Pintaile's Pizza,** at 26 E. 91st St., between Fifth and Madison avenues (☎ 212/722-1967), dresses their crisp organic crusts with layers of plum tomatoes, extra-virgin olive oil, and other fabulously fresh ingredients.

For something more traditional, head to **Totonno's Pizzeria Napolitano,** 1544 Second Ave., between 80th and 81st streets (☎ 212/327-2800), for killer coal-oven pies. Some naysayers consider this a pale comparison to the Coney Island original, but I think they're just hung up on the fancier digs. A little farther afield, at 408 E. 64th St. between First and York avenues, is a branch of **John's Pizzeria** (☎ 212/935-2895) that's worth checking out (p. 155).

salad and the warm white-bean salad over prosciutto are generous enough to be a light meal. The pasta selection mixes staples (satisfying penne pomodoro and linguini pesto) with standouts (lasagna layered with grilled chicken, fresh tomatoes, cheese, and pesto). The entrees, including veal stuffed with prosciutto and spinach and jumbo shrimp with lemon-caper sauce, are fresh and flavorful. All in all, a hidden treasure in a needy neighborhood.

Payard Pâtisserie & Bistro. 1032 Lexington Ave. (at 73rd St.). ☎ 212/717-5252. Reservations recommended. Main courses $10–$25. AE, DC, MC, V. Mon–Sat noon–2:30pm and 6–11pm; tea Mon–Sat 3:30–5pm. Subway: 6 to 77th St. FRENCH BISTRO.

From Daniel Boulud, celebrity chef and owner of the highly acclaimed Daniel, and his former pastry chef, François Payard, comes this grand turn-of-the-century, Parisian-style cafe. Elegant cakes, pastries, and handmade chocolates fill glass cases in the pastry shop up front, while mirrors, mahogany, and straightforward bistro fare entice patrons to the cafe in back. The menu is unabashedly classic, with homemade duck confit, thick slabs of foie gras terrine, wonderful steak frites, and fragrant bouillabaisse. The biggest problem with Payard? Choosing among the fabulous, beautifully presented desserts, which rank among the city's best. Everything is house-made, from the signature cakes, breads, and pastries to the delicate candies. Whether you go with the classic crème brulee or something more decadent (anything chocolate is to die for), you're sure to be wowed. If your sweet tooth is bigger than your bank balance, feel free to come just for dessert.

15 Harlem

Sylvia's. 328 Lenox Ave. (btw. 126th and 127th sts.). ☎ 212/996-0660. Reservations accepted for 10 or more. Main courses $8–$16. AE, DISC, MC, V. Mon–Thurs 8am–10:30pm; Fri–Sat 7:30am–10:30pm; Sun 11am–8pm. Subway: 2, 3 to 125th St. SOUL FOOD.

South Carolina–born Sylvia Woods is the last word in New York soul food. The place is so popular with both locals and visitors that the dining room has spilled into the building next door. Since 1962, her Harlem institution has dished up the southern-fried goods: Turkey with down-home stuffing; smothered chicken and pork chops; fried chicken and baked ham; collard greens and candied yams; cavity-inducing sweet tea; and "Sylvia's World Famous, Talked About, Bar-B-Que Ribs Special"—the sauce is sweet, with a potent afterburn. This Harlem landmark is still presided over by 72-year-old Sylvia, who's likely to greet you at the door herself. Some naysayers claim that Sylvia's just isn't what it used to be, but chowing down here is still a one-of-a-kind New York experience. Sunday gospel brunch is a joyous time to go, if you're not put off by the tour buses out front.

16 Waterfront Dining in Brooklyn

✪ **Patsy Grimaldi's Pizzeria.** 19 Old Fulton St. (btw. Front and Water sts.), Brooklyn Heights. ☎ 718/858-4300. Reservations not taken. Pies $14 and up, depending on toppings. No credit cards. Mon–Fri 11:30am–11pm; Sat–Sun 2–11pm. Subway: 2, 3 to Clark St. (use Henry St. exit); A, C to High St. PIZZA

Here's New York's best pizza. You don't have to take it from me—just check Zagat's, which gives this Brooklyn classic a whopping 26 (out of 30) for food, a rating usually reserved for the likes of Lutèce. Thin coal-oven crust, crisp and smoky, is topped with perfectly seasoned red sauce, leafy basil, and only the freshest mozzarella. Crown this perfect pie with your choice of traditional toppings, including meaty pepperoni and house-roasted red peppers. And you don't have to suffer a greasy pizza joint to enjoy this sublime pizza: Grimaldi's is a surprisingly pleasant place, with red-checked table-cloths, photos of Sinatra covering the walls, and the Chairman of the Board crooning out of the jukebox. Patsy is likely to greet you himself, warmly, with stogie in hand (despite the NO SMOKING signs). Otherwise, the service can be gruff, but that's how you'll know you've arrived—in Brooklyn, that is. The best time to come is in summer, when the restaurant sets up tables on the wide sidewalk outside, where you'll have spectacular views of the Brooklyn Bridge and twinkling Lower Manhattan.

7

Exploring New York City

Face facts, newcomers: It will be impossible to take in anything close to the entire city on your first visit. Because the city is almost unfathomably big and constantly changing, you could live your whole life here and still make fascinating daily discoveries—we New Yorkers do. First-time visitors shouldn't find this daunting.

This chapter is designed to give you an overview of what's available in this multifaceted city, so you can narrow your choices to an itinerary that's digestible for the amount of time you'll be here—be it a day, a week, or something in between.

So don't try to tame New York—you can't. Decide on a few must-see attractions, and then let the city take you on its own ride. Inevitably, as you schlep around the city you'll be blown off course by unplanned diversions that are just as alluring as what you meant to see. After all, the true New York is in the details. As you dash from sight to sight, take time to admire a lovely detail on a prewar building, linger over a cup of coffee at a sidewalk cafe, or just idle away a few minutes on a bench watching New Yorkers parade through their daily lives.

Before you start planning your time and money, be sure to check out the sightseeing advice under "60 Money-Saving Tips" in chapter 2. Frommer's Online Directory, in the back of the book, provides information on the best Web sites featuring information and listings of New York attractions.

LET'S GET LOST   One of the best ways to experience New York is to pick a neighborhood and just stroll it. Bring a map for reference, but put it in your pocket—let yourself get lost. Walk the prime thoroughfares, poke your head into shops, park yourself on a bench or at an outdoor cafe and just watch the world go by. For tips on where to go, how to get there, and what highlights to be on the lookout for, see the "Manhattan's Neighborhoods in Brief" in chapter 4.

If getting lost isn't your style—or even if it is—you might consider taking an organized tour. That doesn't have to mean a big bus with an out-of-work-actor pointing out the Empire State Building (although general introductory tours are available, too). Many wonderful walking tours that really let you get to know a neighborhood or a particular aspect of New York are offered throughout the city. Walking tours are cheap, they're fun, and there's no better way to get to know a neighborhood than with an expert at the helm. For a complete rundown of operators and the kinds of tours they offer, see "Affordable Sightseeing Tours" later in this chapter.

1 Sights & Attractions by Neighborhood

MANHATTAN

CHELSEA

Chelsea Piers Sports &
  Entertainment Complex (p. 250)

EAST VILLAGE & NOHO

Merchant's House Museum (p. 208)

THE FINANCIAL DISTRICT

American Museum of Financial
  History (p. 196)
Battery Park (p. 248)
Bowling Green Park (p. 196)
Brooklyn Bridge (p. 185)
Castle Clinton National Monument
  (p. 248)
City Hall & City Hall Park (p. 201)
Cunard Building (p. 197)
Ellis Island (p. 181)
Federal Hall National Memorial
  (p. 198)
Fraunces Tavern & Fraunces Tavern
  Museum (p. 197)
Group of Four Trees (p. 199)
Kalikow Building (p. 200)
Liberty Plaza (p. 199)
The Municipal Building (p. 202)
Museum of Jewish Heritage (p. 215)
National Museum of the American
  Indian (p. 216)
New York Stock Exchange (p. 185)
The Red Cube (p. 199)
South Street Seaport & Museum
  (p. 193)
Staten Island Ferry (p. 184)
Statue of Liberty (p. 181)
St. Paul's Chapel (p. 200)
Surrogate's Court (The Hall of
  Records) (p. 202)
Trinity Church (p. 198)
Tweed Courthouse (p. 202)
U.S. Customs House (p. 196)
Wall Street (p. 198)
Woolworth Building (p. 201)

World Financial Center (p. 200)
World Trade Center (p. 194)

THE FLATIRON DISTRICT

Center for Jewish History (p. 210)
Flatiron Building (p. 224)
Theodore Roosevelt Birthplace (p. 218)
Union Square Park (p. 249)

GREENWICH VILLAGE

Forbes Magazine Galleries (p. 212)
Washington Square Park (p. 249)

LOWER EAST SIDE

Lower East Side Tenement Museum
  (p. 213)

MIDTOWN EAST

Chrysler Building (p. 219)
Dahesh Museum (p. 211)
Ford Foundation Building (p. 224)
Grand Central Terminal (p. 220)
Japan Society (p. 213)
Lever House (p. 223)
Morgan Library (p. 214)
New York Skyride (p. 220)
Roosevelt Island Tramway (p. 225)
Seagram Building (p. 223)
Sony Building (p. 223)
Sony Wonder Technology Lab
  (p. 255)
St. Patrick's Cathedral (p. 225)
United Nations (p. 222)
Whitney Museum of American Art
  at Philip Morris (p. 207)

MIDTOWN WEST

American Craft Museum (p. 210)
Bryant Park (p. 248)
Empire State Building (p. 219)
International Center of
  Photography—Midtown (p. 212)
Intrepid Sea-Air-Space Museum
  (p. 212)
Madison Square Garden (p. 263)

Impressions

If you're bored in New York, it's your own fault.

—Myrna Loy

Museum of Modern Art (p. 204)
Museum of Television & Radio
(p. 215)
New York Public Library (p. 224)
Rockefeller Center (p. 221)
Times Square (p. 229)

SoHo

The Alternative Museum (p. 210)
Children's Museum of the Arts
(p. 254)
Guggenheim Museum SoHo (p. 207)
Museum for African Art (p. 214)
New Museum of Contemporary Art
(p. 217)

TRiBeCa

New York City Fire Museum (p. 254)

UPPER EAST SIDE

Abigail Adams Smith Museum &
Gardens (p. 209)
Asia Society (p. 210)
Central Park (p. 243)
Central Park Wildlife Center/Tisch
Children's Zoo (p. 246)
Cooper-Hewitt National Design
Museum (p. 211)
El Museo del Barrio (p. 211)
The Frick Collection (p. 212)
Gracie Mansion (p. 208)
International Center of Photography
(p. 212)
The Jewish Museum (p. 213)
Metropolitan Museum of Art (p. 203)
Museum of the City of New York
(p. 215)
Solomon R. Guggenheim Museum
(p. 205)
Temple Emanu–El (p. 225)
United Nations (p. 222)
Whitney Museum of American Art
(p. 207)

UPPER MANHATTAN

Abyssinian Baptist Church (p. 183)
The Cloisters (p. 210)
Dyckman Farmhouse Museum
(p. 208)
First Corinthian Baptist Church
(p. 183)
Morris-Jumel Mansion (p. 208)

Schomburg Center for Research in
Black Culture (p. 218)
Studio Museum (p. 218)

UPPER WEST SIDE

American Museum of Natural
History (p. 202)
The Ansonia (p. 223)
Cathedral of St. John the Divine
(p. 223)
Central Park (p. 243)
Children's Museum of Manhattan
(p. 254)
The Dakota (p. 223)
Museum of American Folk Art
(p. 214)
New-York Historical Society (p. 218)
Spanish & Portuguese Synagogue
(p. 225)

THE OUTER BOROUGHS
THE BRONX

Bronx Zoo Wildlife Conservation
Park (p. 256)
Edgar Allan Poe Cottage (p. 255)
New York Botanical Garden (p. 256)
Wave Hill (p. 257)
Yankee Stadium (p. 262)

BROOKLYN

Brooklyn Bridge (p. 185)
Brooklyn Botanic Garden (p. 258)
Brooklyn Heights Historic District
(p. 260)
Brooklyn Museum of Art (p. 258)
Brooklyn Public Library (p. 257)
Coney Island (p. 259)
Grand Army Plaza (p. 257)
New York Aquarium (p. 258)
New York Transit Museum (p. 259)
Prospect Park (p. 260)

QUEENS

American Museum of the Moving
Image (p. 261)
Flushing Meadows–Corona Park
(p. 255)
New York Hall of Science (p. 254)
P.S. 1 Contemporary Art Center
(p. 261)
Queens Museum of Art (p. 262)
Shea Stadium (p. 262)

2 In New York Harbor: Lady Liberty, Ellis Island & the Staten Island Ferry

✪ **Statue of Liberty.** On Liberty Island in New York Harbor. ☎ **212/363-3200** (general info) or 212/269-5755 (ticket/ferry info). www.nps.gov/stli. Ferry ticket/admission to Statue of Liberty and Ellis Island $7 adults, $6 seniors, $3 children under 17. Daily 9am–5pm; extended hours in summer. Subway: 4, 5 to Bowling Green; 1, 9 to South Ferry (the platform at this station is shorter than the train, so ride in the first five cars). From the station, walk south through Battery Park to Castle Clinton, the fort housing the ferry ticket booth

For the millions who first came by ship to America in the last century—either as privileged tourists or needy, hopeful immigrants—Lady Liberty, standing in the Upper Bay, was the first thing they saw of this country. No monument so embodies the nation's, and the world's, notion of political freedom and economic potential. Even if you don't make it out to Liberty Island, you can get a spine-tingling glimpse from Battery Park, from the New Jersey side of the bay, or during a free ride on the Staten Island Ferry (see below). Its always reassuring to see her torch lighting the way.

This gift from the French was designed by sculptor Frédéric-Auguste Bartholdi with the engineering help of Alexandre-Gustave Eiffel (responsible for the famed Paris tower), and unveiled on October 28, 1886. Despite the fact that Joseph Pulitzer had to make a mighty effort to attract donations on this side of the Atlantic for her pedestal, more than a million people watched as the French tricolor veil was pulled away. After nearly 100 years of wind, rain, and exposure to the harsh sea air, Lady Liberty received a resoundingly successful $70-million face-lift (including the replacement of the torch's flame) in time for its centennial celebration on July 4, 1986. Feted in fireworks, Miss Liberty became more of a city icon than ever before.

Touring Tips: Ferries leave daily every half hour to 45 minutes from 9:30am to 3:15pm, with more frequent ferries in the morning and extended hours in summer. Try to go early on a weekday to avoid the crowds that swarm in the afternoon, on weekends, and on holidays. Be sure to arrive by noon if your heart's set on experiencing everything; go later, and you may not have time to make it to the crown. A stop at Ellis Island (see below) is included in the fare, but if you catch the last ferry, you can only visit the statue or Ellis Island, not both.

The ferry deposits you, in about 20 minutes, on Liberty Island, a short distance from the statue. Once on the island, you'll start to get an idea of the statue's immensity: She weighs 225 tons and measures 152 feet from foot to flame. Her nose alone is 4½ feet long, and her index finger is 8 feet long. You may have to wait as long as 3 hours to walk up into the crown (the torch is not open to visitors). If it's summer, or if you're just not in shape for it, you may want to skip it: It's a grueling 354 steps (the equivalent of 22 stories) to the crown. Although you can cheat and take the elevator the first 10 stories up (an act I wholeheartedly endorse), the interior is still stifling once the temperature starts to climb. However, you don't have to go all the way to the crown; there are a number of **observation decks** at different levels, including one at the top of the pedestal reachable by elevator. Even if you don't go inside, a stroll around the base is an extraordinary experience, and the views of the Manhattan skyline are stellar.

Note: If you're driving into the city to visit Lady Liberty, know that a much less crowded ferry departs from Liberty State Park in Jersey City, New Jersey. Ferry fares are the same as from Battery Park. To get there, take the New Jersey Turnpike to exit 14B. Parking is available at that site. For more information, call ☎ **201/435-9499.**

✪ **Ellis Island.** Located in New York Harbor. ☎ **212/363-3200** (general info) or 212/269-5755 (ticket/ferry info). www.ellisisland.org. For subway, hours, and ferry ticket details, see the Statue of Liberty directly above (ferry stops at both sights).

Cheap Thrills: What to See & Do for Free

I won't kid you—New York can be an expensive city. But the good news is that it doesn't have to be. The Big Apple offers more freebies than you might think:

- **Ride the Staten Island Ferry.** This iconic ride into the world's biggest harbor has many charms, not the least of which is that it's absolutely free. The hour-long excursion offers the same brilliant Lower Manhattan skyline views as private harbor cruises with high price tags. And if you want to see the Statue of Liberty from the water but prefer to skip the tourist crowds, the ferry will take you gliding right by Lady Liberty.

- **Promenade Across the Brooklyn Bridge.** This is one of my favorite activities in the entire city. The easy walk from end to end offers a remarkable, up-close perspective of the marvelous Gothic-inspired stone pylons and intricate steel-cable webs that established the first physical connection between Brooklyn and Manhattan in 1883. Start at the Brooklyn end for the best views, and consider pairing your walk with a stroll through historic Brooklyn Heights—a leafy, lovely, and absolutely free afternoon.

- **Take a Walking Tour.** The best way to get to know New York is to pick one or two of its distinctive neighborhoods and meet them on a human scale. I recommend a number of very good guides that offer affordable walks later in this chapter, but there's no need to spend a dime on one if you don't want to. Two self-guided walking tours are included in this chapter, one focusing on historic Lower Manhattan and the other on lovely, literary Greenwich Village. If you'd rather go with a guide, consider one of the freebies offered by a local business improvement district, or arrange in advance to take a walk through the neighborhood of your choice with Big Apple Greeter (see "Show Me, Show Me, Show Me: Free Walking Tours" later in this chapter). Or just take out a map and chart a route for yourself.

- **Visit Museums.** Many museums are charging upwards of 10 bucks to get in the door these days—but the culture vulture who plans ahead can enjoy a whole vacation's worth of museum going for absolutely free. Every week many of the city's top museums and lesser-known gems set aside an afternoon, evening, or even an entire day when you can donate what you like or explore at no charge. Some are even free every day. See the "Free Culture at Big Apple Museums" box, below.

- **Ogle the City's Architecture.** New York boasts such a wealth of architectural treasures that this one could easily keep you busy for a full day or more. It doesn't cost a penny to admire such works of art and engineering as the neo-Gothic Woolworth Building; Rockefeller Center, an art-deco delight; regal Uptown apartment buildings like the legendary Dakota; paragons of the International Style such as the Lever House; and majestic Grand Central Terminal, recently restored to its original glory. See "Skyscrapers & Other Architectural Marvels," below.

- **Spend Saturday Afternoon Gallery Hopping.** You don't have to be carting a big fat checkbook to peruse New York's world-class art galleries. Virtually all are open free to the public—and most people who come through the door don't buy, so nobody will be expecting you to whip out the gold card, either. Consider going on Saturday afternoon, a particularly popular time for gallery hopping. For tips on where to look, see "Art for Art's Sake: The Gallery Scene."

- **Go to the Park.** Lots of travelers don't bother with Central Park—and they're making a huge mistake. An urban miracle, this massive verdant playground forms the backbone of the city, both physically and socially. This is where New Yorkers come year-round to relax, play, commune with nature, and get to know one another. Don't skip the chance to enjoy its many wonders. Or, if you like things on a smaller scale, head to one of the city's other green spaces, each of which has its own winning personality, from memorial-heavy Battery Park to the pleasing social scene at Union Square.
- **Attend a TV Show Taping.** With some advance planning—or just the right amount of luck on tape day—you can be an audience member at your favorite morning gabfest, network sitcom, or late-night talk show for absolutely free. I can't guarantee that you'll score tickets to Dave, Rosie, or Regis and Kathie Lee for the date of your choice (Maury or Ricki are much surer bets), but who knows? For tips on getting tix, see "Talk of the Town: Free TV Tapings."
- **Celebrate Sunday Morning in Harlem.** In a mixed blessing for local congregations, Sunday-morning gospel services have become so popular that tour groups sometimes outnumber parishioners. At **Abyssinian Baptist Church,** 132 W. 138th St., between Seventh and Lenox avenues (☎ 212/862-7474), services are held at 9 and 11am. Another resounding service takes place at the **First Corinthian Baptist Church,** 1912 Adam Clayton Powell Blvd., at West 116th Street (☎ 212/864-5976), at 11am. Just keep in mind that these are religious services first, not gospel shows.
- **Hear Some Classical Music.** Juilliard is one of New York's greatest cultural bargains. The nation's premier music school sponsors excellent-quality performances, ranging from classical concerts to opera to drama to dance, throughout the year—and most are free. The best way to learn about the wide array of productions is to call (☎ 212/769-7406) or visit the school's Web site (www.juilliard.edu). Watch for master classes and discussions open to the public featuring celebrity guest teachers. For further details, see chapter 9.
- **Or Head to Brooklyn for Some Livelier Tunes.** The renowned cultural institution known as the **Brooklyn Academy of Music** offers free live music every Friday and Saturday night at **BAMcafé.** Offerings can range from atmospheric electronica to jazz poetics to Harlem-style swing. Call ☎ 718/636-4100 or visit www.bam.org to see what's on while you're in town. Performances are in the evening, but come early (between 4 and 6pm) for happy hour, when all drinks are half-price. For more on BAM, see chapter 9.
- **Take Advantage of Summer's Outdoor Events.** New York's parks burst with freebies in the warm months. The city's most famous freebie is **Shakespeare in the Park,** a quintessential New York activity that can feature such names as Patrick Stewart and Andre Braugher taking on the Bard under the stars. Central Park also hosts a full slate of concerts at **SummerStage** that can range from James Brown to Verdi opera, as well as the **Metropolitan Opera** and **New York Philharmonic** beneath the stars. Lower Manhattan's excellent public spaces offer a full calendar of events, and Midtown hosts the free Monday-night **Bryant Park Film Festival.** See "Park It! Shakespeare & Other Free Fun" in chapter 9 for details.

Lost amid the hoopla of the Statue of Liberty reopening in 1986 was the fact that a much more fitting tribute to our nation was under renovation just next door. One of New York's most moving sights, the restored Ellis Island opened in 1990, slightly north of Liberty Island. Roughly 40% of Americans can trace their heritage back to an ancestor who came through here (myself included). For the 62 years when it was America's main entry point for immigrants (it closed in 1954), Ellis Island processed some 12 million people. The greeting was often a little rushed—especially in the early years of the century, when as many as 12,000 came through in a single day. The statistics and their meaning can be overwhelming, but the **Immigration Museum** skillfully relates the story of Ellis Island and immigration to America by putting the emphasis on personal experience.

Today you enter the Main Building's baggage room, just as the immigrants did, and then climb the stairs to the **Registry Room,** with its dramatic vaulted tiled ceiling, where millions waited anxiously for medical and legal processing. A step-by-step account of the immigrants' voyage is detailed in the **"Through America's Gate"** exhibit, with haunting photos and touching oral histories. What might be the most poignant exhibit is **"Treasures from Home,"** 1,000 objects and photos donated by descendants of immigrants, including family heirlooms, religious articles, and rare clothing and jewelry. Outside, the **American Immigrant Wall of Honor** commemorates the names of more than hundreds of thousands of immigrants and their families who have been commemorated by their descendants, including George Washington's great-grandfather, John F. Kennedy's great-grandparents, Rudolph Valentino, Harry Houdini, and Marlene Dietrich (all catalogued on a computer registry as well). You can even research your own family's history at the **American Family Immigration History Center.** It's difficult to leave the museum unmoved.

Touring Tips: Ferries run daily to Ellis Island and Liberty Island from Battery Park and Liberty State Park at frequent interval; see the Statue of Liberty (above) for details.

Staten Island Ferry. Departs from the Staten Island Ferry Terminal at the southern tip of Manhattan. ☎ **718/815-BOAT**. www.SI-Web.com/transportation/dot.htm. Free (fee charged for car transport). 24 hours; every 15–30 min weekdays, less frequently on off-peak and weekend hours. Subway: 1, 9, N, R to South Ferry.

Here's New York's best freebie—especially if you just want to glimpse the Statue of Liberty and not climb her steps. You get an enthralling hour-long excursion (round-trip) into the world's biggest harbor. This is not strictly a sightseeing ride, but commuter transportation to Staten Island (remember Melanie Griffith, in big hair and sneakers, heading to work in *Working Girl?*). As a result, during business hours, you'll share the boat with working stiffs reading papers and drinking coffee inside, blissfully unaware of the sights outside.

You, however, should go on deck and enjoy the busy harbor traffic. The old orange-and-green boats usually have open decks along the sides or at the bow and stern (try to catch one of these boats if you can; the newer white boats don't have decks). Grab a seat on the right side of the boat for the best view. On the way out of Manhattan, you'll pass the Statue of Liberty (the boat comes closest to Lady Liberty on the way to Staten Island), Ellis Island, and (from the left side of the boat) Governor's Island; you'll se the Verranzano Narrows Bridge linking Brooklyn to Staten Island in the distance.

When the boat arrives at St. George, Staten Island, everyone must disembark. Follow the boat loading sign on your right as you get off; you'll circle around to the next loading dock, where there's usually another boat waiting to depart for Manhattan. The skyline views are simply awesome on the return trip. Well worth the time spent—and the fare simply can't be beat.

3 Historic Lower Manhattan's Top Attractions

✪ **Brooklyn Bridge.** Subway: 4, 5, 6 to Brooklyn Bridge–City Hall; A, C to High St.

Its Gothic-inspired stone pylons and intricate steel-cable webs have moved poets like Walt Whitman and Hart Crane to sing the praises of this great span, the first to cross the East River and connect Manhattan to Brooklyn. Begun in 1867 and ultimately completed in 1883, the beautiful Brooklyn Bridge is now the city's best-known symbol of the age of growth that seized New York during the late 19th century. Walk across the bridge, and imagine the awe that New Yorkers of that age felt at seeing two boroughs joined by this monumental engineering feat. It's still awesome.

Designed by John Roebling, this massive project was plagued by death and disaster at its birth. Roebling was fatally injured in 1869 when a ferry rammed a waterfront piling on which he stood. His son, Washington, who was subsequently put in charge, contracted the bends in 1872 while working underwater on the bridge's towers, and oversaw the rest of the construction with a telescope from his bed at the edge of the East River in Brooklyn Heights (his wife relayed his instructions to the workers). Despite being declared the "Eighth Wonder of the World" upon its completion, the bridge's troubles were not over: Twelve pedestrians were killed in a stampede when panic about its eminent collapse spread like wildfire on the day it opened to the public. Things are usually calmer now.

Walking the Bridge: Walking the Brooklyn Bridge is one of my all-time favorite New York activities. A wide wood-plank pedestrian walkway is elevated above the traffic, making it a relatively peaceful, and popular, walk. It provides a great vantage point from which to contemplate the New York skyline and the East River.

There's a sidewalk entrance on Park Row, just across from City Hall Park (take the 4, 5, or 6 train to Brooklyn Bridge–City Hall). But why do this walk *away* from Manhattan, toward the far less impressive Brooklyn skyline? For gorgeous Manhattan skyline views, take an A or C train to High Street, one stop into Brooklyn. Come above ground, then walk through the little park to Cadman Plaza East and head downslope (left) to the stairwell that will take you up to the footpath. (Following Prospect Place under the bridge, turning right onto Cadman Plaza East, will also take you directly to the stairwell.) It's a 20- to 40-minute stroll over the bridge to Manhattan, depending on your pace, the amount of foot traffic, and the number of stops you make to contemplate the spectacular views (there are benches along the way). The footpath will deposit you right at City Hall Park.

If you'd like to extend this walk a bit, I highly recommend pairing it with a quick tour of Brooklyn Heights and its wonderful Promenade; see "Highlights of the Outer Boroughs" later in this chapter for exact directions.

New York Stock Exchange. 20 Broad St. (btw. Wall St. and Exchange Place). ☎ **212/ 656-5165.** www.nyse.com. Free admission. Mon–Fri 9am–4:30pm (ticket booth opens at 8:45am). Subway: 2, 3, 4, 5 to Wall St.; J, M, Z to Broad St.

Wall Street—it's an iconic name, and ground zero for bulls and bears everywhere. This narrow 18th-century lane (you'll be surprised at how little it is) is appropriately monumental, lined with neoclassic towers that reach as far skyward as the dreams and greed of investors who built it into the world's most famous financial market. At the heart of the action is the New York Stock Exchange, the world's largest securities trader, where you can watch billions change hands and get a fleeting idea of how the money merchants work.

While NYSE is on Wall Street, the ticket kiosk is around the corner at 20 Broad St., where you'll be issued a ticket with a time on it; you must enter during the window

Downtown Attractions

The Alternative Museum **4**

American Museum
  of Financial History **28**

Battery Park **17**

Brooklyn Bridge **23**

Children's Museum of the Arts **8**

Circle Line Sightseeing Cruises **25**

City Hall & City Hall Park **11**

Federal Hall National Memorial **21**

Forbes Magazine Galleries **1**

Fraunces Tavern Museum **29**

Fulton Fish Market **24**

Guggenheim Museum SoHo **7**

Lower East Side
  Tenement Museum **10**

Merchant's House Museum **3**

Museum for African Art **5**

Museum of Jewish Heritage **16**

National Museum
  of the American Indian **27**

New Museum
  of Contemporary Art **6**

New York City Fire Museum **9**

New York Stock Exchange **20**

Pioneer **25**

Pier 17 **24**

St. Paul's Chapel **13**

South Street Seaport Ice Rink **22**

South Street Seaport & Museum **22**

Staten Island Ferry **30**

Statue of Liberty
  & Ellis Island Ferries **18**

Top of the World
  Observation Deck **14**

Trinity Church **19**

Wall Street **26**

Washington Square Park **2**

Woolworth Building **12**

World Financial Center **15**

World Trade Center **14**

NA-0148

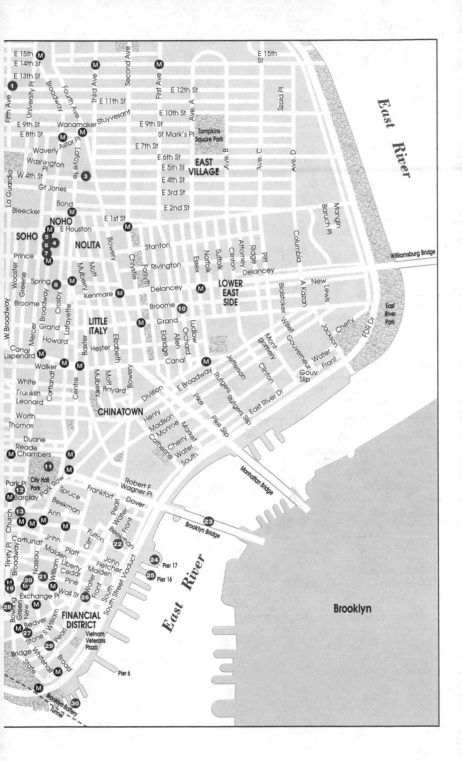

Midtown Attractions

Bryant Park **㉑**
Carnegie Hall **❷**
Central Synagogue **❹**
Center for Jewish History **㊱**
Chelsea Piers Sports
  & Entertainment Complex **㊲**
Chrysler Building **⑰**
Circle Line Sightseeing Cruises **㉕**
Dahesh Museum **⑬**
Empire State Building **㉜**
Flatiron Building **㉝**
Ford Foundation Building **⑯**
Grand Central Terminal **⑱**
Gray Line New York Tours **㉗**
International Center of
  Photography–Midtown **㉒**
Intrepid Sea-Air-Space
  Museum **㉔**
Jacob Javits
  Convention Center **㉙**
Japan Society **⑭**
Lever House **❻**
Madison Square Garden **㉚**
Morgan Library **㉛**
Museum of Modern Art **❼**
Museum of Television & Radio **❽**
New York Apple Tours **❺** **㉘**
New York Double-Decker Tours **㉜**
New York Public Library **⑳**
New York Skyride **㉜**
New York Waterway **㉖**
Radio City Music Hall **❾**
Rockefeller Center **❿**
Roosevelt Island Tramway **❶**
St. Patrick's Cathedral **⑪**
Seagram Building **❺**
Sony Building **❸**
Sony Wonder Technology Lab **❸**
Spirit Cruises **㊳**
Theodore Roosevelt Birthplace **㉞**
Union Square Park **㉟**
United Nations **⑮**
Villard Houses **⑫**
Whitney Museum of
  American Art at Philip Morris **⑲**

Uptown Attractions

Abagail Adams Smith
  Museum & Gardens **23**
American Museum
  of Natural History **10**
The Ansonia **13**
Asia Society **16**
Beacon Theater **12**
Central Park Wildlife Center **21**
Children's Museum
  of Manhattan **9**
Cooper-Hewitt
  National Design Museum **5**
Dakota Apartments **14**
El Museo del Barrio **1**
The Frick Collection **17**
Gracie Mansion **7**
International Center
  of Photography **3**
The Jewish Museum **4**
Lincoln Center
  for the Performing Arts **20**
Metropolitan Museum of Art **8**
Museum of American Folk Art **19**
Museum of the
  City of New York **2**
New-York Historical Society **11**
Roosevelt Island Tramway **24**
Solomon R. Guggenheim
  Museum **6**
Spanish & Portuguese
  Synagogue **18**
Temple Emanu-El **22**
Whitney Museum
  of American Art **15**

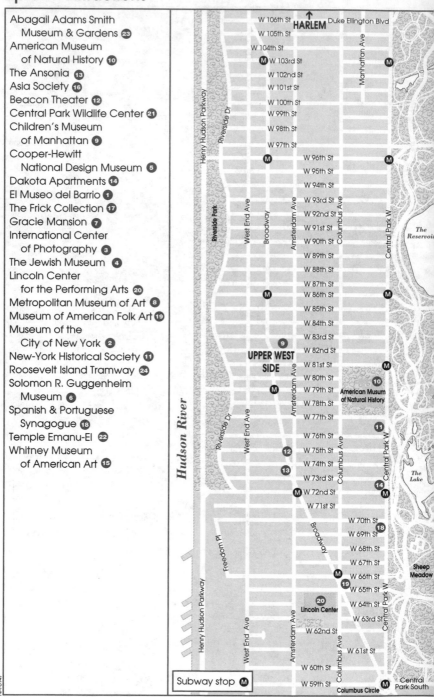

Upper Manhattan Attractions

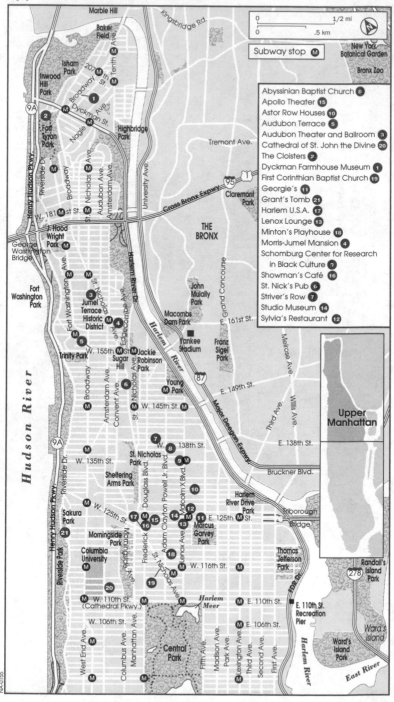

Abyssinian Baptist Church **8**
Apollo Theater **15**
Astor Row Houses **10**
Audubon Terrace **5**
Audubon Theater and Ballroom **3**
Cathedral of St. John the Divine **20**
The Cloisters **2**
Dyckman Farmhouse Museum **1**
First Corinthian Baptist Church **19**
Georgie's **11**
Grant's Tomb **21**
Harlem U.S.A. **17**
Lenox Lounge **13**
Minton's Playhouse **18**
Morris-Jumel Mansion **4**
Schomburg Center for Research
   in Black Culture **9**
Showman's Café **16**
St. Nick's Pub **6**
Striver's Row **7**
Studio Museum **14**
Sylvia's Restaurant **12**

of opportunity specified on your ticket. The staff starts handing out tickets at 8:45am, but get on line early if you want to be inside to see all hell break loose at the 9:30am opening bell. The 3,000 tickets issued per day are usually gone by noon; plan on having to return unless you're one of the first in line. Despite the number of visitors, things move pretty quickly.

Don't expect to come out with a full understanding of the market; if you didn't have one going in, you won't come out any more enlightened. Still, it's fun watching the action on the trading floor from the glass-lined, mezzanine-level **observation gallery** (look to the right, and you'll see the Bloomberg people sending their live reports back to the newsroom). You can stay as long as you like, but it doesn't really take more than 20 minutes or so to peruse the rather self-congratulatory exhibits ("NYSE—our hero!"), which include a rather oblique explanation of the floor activities, interactive exhibits, and a short film presentation of the Exchange's history and present-day operations.

South Street Seaport & Museum. At Water and South sts.; museum is at 12–14 Fulton St. ☎ 212/748-8600 or 212/732-7678. www.southstseaport.org. Museum admission $6 adults, $5 seniors, $3 children. Museum, Apr–Sept Fri–Wed 10am–6pm, Thurs 10am–8pm; Oct–Mar Wed–Sun 10am–5pm. Subway: 2, 3, 4, 5 to Fulton St. (walk east, or downslope, on Fulton St. to Water St.)

This landmark district on the East River encompasses 11 square blocks of historic buildings, a maritime museum, several piers, shops and restaurants (including the authentically Old World North Star Pub; see chapter 6), and even a Best Western hotel (see chapter 5).

You can explore most of the seaport on your own. It's an odd place. The 18th- and 19th-century buildings lining the cobbled streets and alleyways are beautifully restored but nevertheless have a theme-park air about them, no doubt due to the J. Crews, Brookstones, and Body Shops housed within. The height of the seaport's cheesiness is **Pier 17,** a historic barge converted into a mall, complete with food court and cheap jewelry kiosks.

Despite its rampant commercialism, the seaport is worth a look. There's a good amount of history to be discovered here. At the gateway to the seaport, at Fulton and Water streets, is the *Titanic* **Memorial Lighthouse,** a monument to those who lost their lives when the ocean liner sank on April 15, 1912. It was erected overlooking the East River in 1913, and moved to this spot in 1968. The **South Street Seaport Museum** is a fitting tribute to the sea commerce that once thrived in this area. Including the galleries—which display paintings and prints, ship models, scrimshaw, and nautical designs, as well as frequent changing exhibitions—there are a number of historic ships berthed at the pier to explore, including the 1911 four-masted *Peking* and the 1893 Gloucester fishing schooner *Lettie G. Howard.* A few of the boats are living museums and restoration works in progress; others are available for private charters. You can actually hit the high seas on the 1885 cargo schooner *Pioneer* (☎ 212/748-8786), which offers 2-hour sails daily from early May through September. Tickets are $20 for adults, $15 for seniors and students, and $12 for children. Advance reservations are recommended and can be made up to 14 days in advance; always call ahead to confirm sailing times.

Even **Pier 17** has its merits. Head up to the third-level deck overlooking the East River. From this level, you can see south to the Statue of Liberty, north to the Brooklyn Bridge, and Brooklyn Heights on the opposite shore.

Just to the north of Pier 17 is the famous **Fulton Fish Market,** on Fulton Street at the East River, the nation's largest wholesale fish market. If you're willing to come back down here at 4am, you can watch the catch of the day from all over the globe being tossed, traded, and sold the old-fashioned way.

A variety of events take place in summer, ranging from street performers and concerts to fireworks. In winter, a petite but charming **ice rink** is erected on the waterfront, overlooking the historic ships and the river beyond. The rink is generally open from November to March; two hours of skating is $8 for adults, $6 for kids, and skate rentals are $5. Call ☎ 212/SEA-PORT or 212/809-6080 for this year's schedule.

✪ **World Trade Center.** Bounded by Church, Vesey, Liberty, and West sts. ☎ 212/323-2340 for observation deck, 212/435-4170 for general information. www.wtc-top.com. Admission to observation deck $12 adults, $9 seniors, $6 children under 12. Sept–May, daily 9:30am–9:30pm; June–Aug, 9:30am–11:30pm. Subway: C, E to World Trade Center; 1, 9, N, R to Cortlandt St.

Nowhere near as romantic as the Empire State Building (see "Skyscrapers & Other Architectural Marvels" later in this chapter), the World Trade Center is nevertheless just as heroic, having withstood a bombing in its basement garage in 1993 without so much as a flinch. Built in 1970, the center is actually an immense complex of seven buildings on 16 acres housing offices, restaurants, a hotel, an underground shopping mall, and an outdoor plaza with fountains, sculptures, and summer concerts and performances. But the part you'll be interested in are the Twin Towers, which surpassed the Empire State to become New York's tallest structures.

The boxlike buildings are so nondescript that local Channel 11 once used them to represent that number in their commercials. Each is 110 stories and 1,350 feet high. The **Top of the World** observation deck is on the 107th floor of 2 World Trade Center, to the south. Like a mini theme park, it has a 6-minute simulated helicopter tour over Manhattan, high-tech kiosks, a food court, and a nighttime light show. But the reason to come is for those incredible views. The enclosed top floor offers incredible panoramas on all sides, with windows reaching right down to the floor. Go ahead, walk right up to one, and look down—*scaaary.*

Come on a clear day. If you're lucky, you'll be able to go out on the **rooftop promenade,** the world's highest open-air observation deck. (It's only open under pristine conditions; I've only been able to go out once in a lifetime of visits.) You thought inside was incredible? Wait 'til you see this. While you're up here, look straight down and wonder what Frenchman Philippe Petit could've been thinking when in August 1974 he walked across to tower no. 1 on a tightrope, stopping to lie down for a moment in the center.

A Walking Tour of Wall Street & the Financial District

by Reid Bramblett

Start: Battery Park/U.S. Customs House.
Subway: Take the 5 to Bowling Green, the 1 or 9 to South Ferry, or the N or R to Whitehall Street.
Finish: The Municipal Building.
Time: Approximately 3 hours.
Best Time: Any weekday, when the wheels of finance are spinning and lower Manhattan is a maelstrom of frantic activity.
Worst Time: Weekends, when most buildings and all the financial markets are closed.

The narrow, winding streets of the Financial District occupy the earliest-settled area of Manhattan, where the Dutch established the colony of Nieuw Amsterdam in the early 17th century. Before their arrival, Downtown was part of a vast forest, a lush hunting ground for the Native Americans, inhabited by mountain lions, bobcats, beavers, white-tailed deer, and wild turkeys. A hunting path—which later evolved into Broadway—extended from the Battery to the present City Hall Park.

Walking Tour: Wall Street & the Financial District

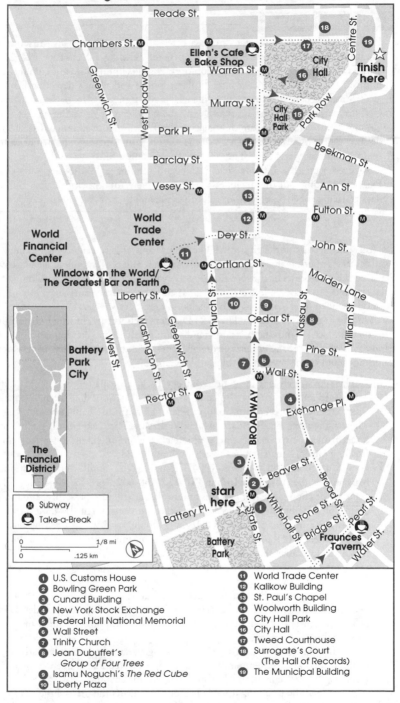

1. U.S. Customs House
2. Bowling Green Park
3. Cunard Building
4. New York Stock Exchange
5. Federal Hall National Memorial
6. Wall Street
7. Trinity Church
8. Jean Dubuffet's
   Group of Four Trees
9. Isamu Noguchi's *The Red Cube*
10. Liberty Plaza
11. World Trade Center
12. Kalikow Building
13. St. Paul's Chapel
14. Woolworth Building
15. City Hall Park
16. City Hall
17. Tweed Courthouse
18. Surrogate's Court
    (The Hall of Records)
19. The Municipal Building

The Money Museum

Real money buffs may want to make a brief stop at the **American Museum of Financial History,** 28 Broadway, just north of Bowling Green Park (☎ 212/908-4110 or 212/908-4519; www.mafh.org). Exhibits in this little museum include numismatic and vintage ticker-tape displays; murals and photos depicting historic Wall Street scenes; and interactive financial news terminals, in partnership with CNNfn, so little bulls and bears can learn how to keep up with the market. The Crouch & Fitzgerald briefcase that Jackie gave JFK on their wedding day is also on display. Open Monday through Friday from 11:30am and 3:30pm, with limited hours on summer weekends. The suggested admission is $2.

At press time, the museum had just begun offering a Wall Street "World of Finance" walking tour that includes a visit to the New York Stock Exchange on Fridays at 10am, for $15 per person; call to reserve one to 2 days in advance.

Today this section of the city, much like Nieuw Amsterdam, centers on commerce. Wall Street is America's most cogent symbol of money and power; bulls and bears have replaced the wild beasts of the forest, and conservatively attired lawyers, stockbrokers, bankers, and businesspeople have supplanted the Native Americans and Dutchmen who once traded otter skins and beaver pelts on these very streets.

A highlight of this tour is the Financial District's architecture, in which the neighborhood's modern manifestations and grand historical structures are dramatically juxtaposed: Colonial, 18th-century Georgian/Federal, and 19th-century neoclassical buildings stand in the shadow of colossal skyscrapers.

The subways all exit in or near **Battery Park,** an expanse of green at Manhattan's tip resting entirely upon landfill—an old strategy of the Dutch to expand their settlement farther into the bay. The original tip of Manhattan ran somewhere right along Battery Place, which borders the north side of the park. State Street flanks the park's east side, and stretched along it, filling the space below Bowling Green, squats the beaux-arts bulk of the old:

1. **U.S. Customs House,** since 1994, home to the Smithsonian's **National Museum of the American Indian** (☎ **212/668-6624** or 212/514-3700). The giant statues lining the front of this granite 1907 structure personify *Asia* (pondering philosophically), *America* (bright-eyed and bushy-tailed), *Europe* (decadent, whose time has passed), and *Africa* (sleeping), and were carved by Daniel Chester French of Lincoln Memorial fame. The most interesting, if unintentional, sculptural statement—keeping in mind the building's new purpose—is the giant seated woman to the left of the entrance representing America. The young, upstart America is surrounded by references to Native America: Mayan pictographs adorning her throne, Quetzalcoatl under her foot, a shock of corn in her lap, and the generic plains Indian scouting out from over her shoulder. Look behind her throne for the stylized crow figure—an important animal in many native cultures and myths.

   The free museum hosts a roster of interesting exhibits highlighting Native cultures, history, and contemporary issues in sophisticated and thought-provoking ways; see "More Manhattan Museums" later in this chapter.

   As you exit the building, directly in front of you sits the pretty little oasis of:

2. **Bowling Green Park.** This is probably the spot, or at least near enough, where in 1626 Dutchman Peter Minuit gave glass beads and other trinkets worth about

60 Guilders ($24) to a group of Indians, and then claimed he had thereby bought Manhattan. Now the local Indians didn't consider that they owned this island—not because they didn't believe in property (that's a colonial myth), as they did have their own territories nearby. But Manhattan (which in local language means "hilly island") was considered communal hunting ground, shared by several different groups. So it isn't clear what the Indians thought the trinkets meant. Either (a) they just thought the exchange was a formal way, one to which they were accustomed, of closing an agreement to extend the shared hunting use of the island to this funny-looking group of pale people with yellow beards, or (b) they were knowingly selling land that they didn't own in the first place, thus performing the first shrewd real-estate deal of the Financial District.

Today this is just another lunch spot for stockbrokers, but when King George III repealed the hated Stamp Act in 1770, New Yorkers magnanimously raised a statue of him here. The statue lasted 5 years, until the day the Declaration of Independence was read to the public in front of City Hall (now Federal Hall) and a crowd rushed down Broadway to topple the statue, chop it up, melt it down, and transform it into 42,000 bullets, which they later used to shoot the British.

The park also marks the start of Broadway. Walk up the left side of Broadway. At no. 25 is the:

3. Cunard Building, now a post office but in 1921 the ticketing room for Cunard, one of the world's most glamorous shipping and cruise lines and proprietors of the *QEII*. In this still-impressive Great Hall, you once could book passage on any one of Cunard's famous, fantastically unfortunate ships, from the *Lusitania* (blown up by the Germans) to the *Titanic*.

As you exit the building, cross to the traffic island to pat the enormous bronze **bull,** symbol of a strong stock market, ready to charge up Broadway. This instant icon began as a practical joke by Italian sculptor Arturo DiModica, who originally stuck it in front of the New York Stock Exchange building in the middle of the night. The unamused brokers had it promptly removed, and it eventually got placed here.

🍵 **TAKE A BREAK   Fraunces Tavern,** 54 Pearl St. (☎ 212/269-0144), is a great spot for a break, but it's also a legitimate stop on the tour. To reach Fraunces Tavern, head south again, around the left side of the U.S. Customs House on Whitehall Street. Take a left onto Pearl Street; just past Broad Street stretches a historic block lined with (partially rebuilt) 18th- and 19th-century buildings.

The two upper stories house the **Fraunces Tavern Museum,** where you can view the room in which Washington's historic farewell took place (today set up to represent a typical 18th-century tavern room) and see other American history exhibits. In late 1999–2000 new exhibits will include "Washington in Glory, American in Tears: The death of George Washington" and "Taverns, Coffeehouses and politics in Colonial New York." A small admission is charged. Hours are Monday through Friday from 10am to 4:45pm and Saturdays from noon to 4pm.

The main floor contains a posh, oak-paneled dining room with a working fireplace. The menu features steaks, seafood, pasta dishes, and colonial fare such as Yankee pot roast. Or you can opt for pub fare in the more moderately priced Tap Room, which has plush burgundy leather furnishings and walls hung with hunting trophies. Reservations are suggested for both. The restaurant is open weekdays for breakfast 7 to 10am, lunch 11:30am to 4pm, and dinner from 5 to 9:30pm; the Tap Room is open daily from 11:30am to 9:30pm.

From Fraunces Tavern, head straight up Broad Street. At no. 20, on the left, is the visitor's entrance to the:

4. New York Stock Exchange (☎ **212/656-5165**), which came into being in 1792, when merchants met daily under a nearby buttonwood tree to try and pass off to each other the U.S. bonds that had been sold to fund the Revolutionary War. By 1903, they were trading stocks of publicly held companies in this Corinthian-column, beaux-arts "temple" designed by George Post. More than 3,000 companies are listed on the exchange, trading 253 billion shares valued around $11 trillion.

Inside you can watch the frenzied action on the trading floor, where color-coded capitalists oversee the changing of hands of more than 200 million stocks daily. The observation platform has been glassed in since the 1960s when Abbie Hoffman and Jerry Rubin created chaos by tossing dollar bills onto the exchange floor. Admission is free; for more information, see "Lower Manhattan's Top Attractions" directly above.

After your visit, continue north (left) up Broad Street. At the end of the block you'll see the Parthenon-inspired:

5. Federal Hall National Memorial. 26 Wall St. at Nassau Street (☎ **212/ 825-6888**). Fronted by 32-foot, fluted, marble, Doric columns, this imposing 1842 neoclassical temple is most famous as the spot of the old British City Hall building, later called Federal Hall, that once stood here. Peter Zenger, publisher of the outspoken *Weekly Journal,* stood trial in 1735 for "seditious libel" against Royal Govenor William Cosby. Defended brilliantly by Alexander Hamilton, Zenger's eventual acquittal (based on the grounds that anything you printed that was true, even if it wasn't very nice, couldn't be construed as libel) set the precedent for freedom of the press, later guaranteed in the Bill of Rights, which was drafted and signed inside this building.

New York's first major rebellion against British authority occurred here when the Stamp Act Congress met in 1765 to protest King George III's policy of "taxation without representation." J. Q. A. Ward's 1883 statue of George Washington on the steps commemorates the spot of the first presidential inauguration, in 1789. Congress met here after the Revolution, when New York was briefly the nation's capital.

Exhibits within (open daily 9am–5pm mid-June to Sept, weekdays only Oct to mid-June) elucidate these events along with other aspects of American history. Admission is free; call ahead if you'd like to hook up with one of the short guided tours, which usually take place on the half hour between 12:30 and 3:30pm.

Facing Federal Hall, turn left up the road that has become the symbol of high finance the world over:

6. Wall Street. This short and narrow street started out as a service road that ran along the fortified wall erected in 1653 by the Dutch to defend against Indian attack.

Wall Street hits Broadway across the street from:

7. Trinity Church (☎ **212/602-0800**). Serving God and Mammon, this Wall Street house of worship—with neo-Gothic flying buttresses, beautiful stained-glass windows, and vaulted ceilings—was designed by Richard Upjohn and consecrated in 1846. At that time, its 280-foot spire dominated the skyline. Its main doors, embellished with biblical scenes, were inspired in part by Ghiberti's famed doors on Florence's Baptistery.

The church runs a brief tour daily at 2pm. There's a small museum at the end of the left aisle displaying documents (including the 1697 church charter from King William III), photographs, replicas of the Hamilton-Burr duel pistols, and other items.

Surrounding the church is a **churchyard** with monuments that read like an American history book: a tribute to Martyrs of the American Revolution; Alexander Hamilton (against the south fence, next to steamboat inventor Robert Fulton); Capt. James Lawrence, whose famous last words were "Don't give up the ship"; and many more. The oldest grave dates from 1681. Lined with benches, this makes a wonderful picnic spot on warm days.

The church is open to the public weekdays 7am to 6pm, Saturday 8am to 4pm, and Sunday 7am to 4pm. Services are held weekdays at 8am and 12:05 and 5:15pm, Saturday at 9am, and Sunday at 9 and 11:15am. Trinity holds its Noonday Concert series of chamber music and orchestral concerts Thursdays at 1pm. Call ☎ 212/602-0747 or visit **www.trinitywallstreet.org** for details.

Take a left out of the church and walk 2 short blocks up Broadway. As you pass Cedar Street, look (don't walk) to your right, across Broadway, and down Cedar and you'll see, at the end of the street:

8. **Jean Dubuffet's** *Group of Four Trees,* installed in 1972 in the artist's patented style: amorphous mushroom-like white shapes traced with undulating black lines. Dubuffet considered these drawings in three dimensions "which extend and expand into space."

Closer at hand, in front of the tall black Marine Midlank Bank building on Broadway between Cedar and Liberty streets, is:

9. **Isamu Noguchi's 1967** *The Red Cube,* another famed outdoor sculpture of Downtown Manhattan. Noguchi fancied that this rhomboid "cube"—balancing on its corner and shot through with a cylinder of empty space—represented chance, like the "rolling of the dice." It's appropriately located in the gilt-edged gambling den that is the Financial District.

As you're looking at the Cube across Broadway, behind you is the tiny square called:

10. **Liberty Plaza,** a block off Liberty Street with some benches and shade for lunching CEOs. Turn left and walk through the park, heading east toward Trinity Place. Mingling among the flesh-and-blood office workers seated here is one in bronze, called *Double Check* (1982), by realist American sculptor J. Seward Johnson, Jr.

At Trinity Place, take a right. A short block up on the left will open the grand plaza of the:

11. **World Trade Center (WTC),** bounded by Vesey, West, Liberty, and Church streets and best known for its famous 110-story twin towers. Still intact despite a terrorist bombing in early 1993, the WTC is an immense complex. Its 12 million square feet of rentable office space house more than 350 firms and organizations. About 50,000 people work in its precincts, and some 70,000 others (tourists and businesspeople) visit each day.

The plaza, like much of Downtown, is rich in outdoor sculpture, including the polished black-granite miniature mountains as you enter crafted by Japanese artist Masayuki Nagare (1972). Fritz Keonig's 25-foot-high bronze morphing sphere (1971) forms the centerpiece of the plaza's wide fountain. Hang a right here between two of the squat black glass buildings to get a glance of Alexander Calder's *Three Wings.*

Do an about-face to return to the central plaza. The left-hand of the twin towers is 2 World Trade Center. As you enter on the mezzanine level, to your left, you'll see a 1974 tapestry by Spanish artist Joan Miró and a TKTS booth if you want to pick up half-price tickets to one of tonight's Broadway or off-Broadway shows (see chapter 9 for details). The real thing to do, of course, is head around the elevator banks to the right to buy tickets and whiz up to the 107th-floor **Top of the World** observation deck, where you're treated to a 1,377-foot perspective of the city and New York Harbor; for details, see "Historic Lower Manhattan's Top Attractions" directly above.

☕ **TAKE A BREAK**   To enjoy those 107th-floor views to the fullest, consider dining "a quarter mile high in the sky" at the **Greatest Bar on Earth,** 1 World Trade Center (☎ **212/524-7000**), a casually conservative spot (no jeans or sneakers) with airy spaces, a trio of bars serving everything from wine to sushi, and a sweeping view of the East River. It serves a relatively affordable lunch Monday to Friday noon to 3pm, with continuous bar and food service (mostly munchies) also until midnight Monday and Tuesday, to 1am Wednesday through Saturday, and to 10pm on Sunday; see chapter 9 for details.

For a quicker and cheaper meal, there's a **Sbarro's** snack bar on the **107th-floor observation deck of WTC2.** There are also a number of casual, affordable sit-down restaurants and take-out joints scattered throughout the mall that is the first level of the World Trade Center. In summer, you might want to bring your own lunch as there are outdoor cafes with tables under trees and umbrellas on the plaza.

Alternatively, you might want to explore the varied dining choices offered under the enormous, 120-foot-high glass-and-steel atrium of the Winter Garden (featuring 45-foot palms from the Mojave Desert) in the **World Financial Center.** Options here tend to be slightly pricier than at the nearby World Trade Center, but the setting is fabulous: The atrium overlooks a yacht harbor and a pleasant cement park, with outdoor tables available in good weather. The World Financial Center is behind the WTC complex. As you exit WTC2 (the twin tower with the observation deck), walk straight, keeping the front side of WTC1 (the other twin tower) on your left, then turn left at its corner. To your right, tucked between the back corners of WTC1 and the squat black office building next door, are a set of doors. These open onto a long, glassed-in corridor running off to your left, suspended over the highway, that leads into the Financial Center's atrium.

Walk out the front side of WTC plaza again the way you came in, cross Church Street, and head straight down Dey Street, which is in front of you, back to Broadway. Take a left, and on your left is the:

12. Kalikow Building, at 195 Broadway. This 1915–22 neoclassic tower, formerly AT&T headquarters, has more exterior columns than any other building in the world. The 25-story structure rests on a Doric colonnade, with Ionic colonnades above. The lobby evokes a Greek temple with a forest of massive fluted columns. The building's tower crown is modeled on the Mausoleum of Halicarnassus, the great Greek monument of antiquity. The bronze panels over the entranceway by Paul Manship (sculptor of Rockefeller Center's *Prometheus*) symbolize wind, air, fire, and earth.

Continue south on Broadway. The next block contains the small:

13. St. Paul's Chapel, between Vesey and Fulton streets, New York's only surviving pre-Revolutionary church, and now a transition shelter for homeless men. Under the east portico is a 1789 monument to General Richard Montgomery, one of the first Revolutionary patriots to die in battle. During the 2 years that New York was the nation's capital, George Washington worshipped at this Georgian chapel belonging to Trinity Church and dating from 1764; his "pew" is on the right side of the church. Built by Thomas McBean, with a temple-like portico and fluted Ionic columns supporting a massive pediment, the chapel resembles London's St. Martin's-in-the-Fields. Explore the small **graveyard** where 18th- and early-19th-century notables rest in peace and modern businesspeople sit for lunch. Trinity's Noonday Concert series is held here on Mondays at noon; call the concert hotline at ☎ 212/602-0747 for details, or visit www.trinitywallstreet.org.

Continue up Broadway, crossing Vesey and Barclay streets, and at 233 Broadway is the:

14. **Woolworth Building.** This soaring "Cathedral of Commerce" cost Frank W. Woolworth $13.5 million worth of nickels and dimes in 1913. Designed by Cass Gilbert, it was the world's tallest edifice until 1930, when it was surpassed by the Chrysler Building. At its opening, President Woodrow Wilson pressed a button from the White House that illuminated the building's 80,000 electric light bulbs. The neo-Gothic architecture is rife with spires, gargoyles, flying buttresses, vaulted ceilings, 16th-century-style stone-as-lace traceries, castlelike turrets, and a churchlike interior.

Step into the lofty marble entrance arcade to view the gleaming mosaic, Byzantine-style ceiling and gold-leafed, neo-Gothic cornices. The corbels (carved figures under the crossbeams) in the lobby include whimsical portraits of the building's engineer, Gunwald Aus, measuring a girder (above the staircase to the left of the main door), Gilbert holding a miniature model of the building, and Woolworth counting coins (both above the left-hand corridor of elevators). Stand near the security guard's central podium and crane your neck for a glimpse at Paul Jennewein's murals of *Commerce* and *Labor,* half hidden up on the mezzanine.

To get an overview of the Woolworth's architecture, cross Broadway. On this side of the street, you'll find scurrying city officials and greenery that together make up:

15. **City Hall Park,** a 250-year-old green surrounded by landmark buildings. A Frederick MacMonnies statue near the southwest corner of the park depicts Nathan Hale at age 21, having just uttered his famous words before execution: "I only regret that I have but one life to lose for my country."

It is the setting for:

16. **City Hall,** the seat of municipal government, housing the offices of the mayor and his staff, the city council, and other city agencies. City Hall combines Georgian and French Renaissance styles, designed by Joseph F. Mangin and John McComb Jr. in 1803–11. Later additions include the clock and 6,000-pound bell in the cupola tower. The cupola itself is crowned with a stately, white-painted copper statue of *Justice* (anonymously produced in a workshop).

Barring days when there are demonstrations or special hearings that draw large crowds, you can enter the building between 10am and 4pm, Monday to Friday. If you'd like to take a tour, call ☎ 212/788-6865; they're offered daily between 9am and 3pm, but you should call ahead to reserve.

☕ **TAKE A BREAK** Grab a pastry or a diner meal at **Ellen's Cafe and Bake Shop,** 270 Broadway, at Chambers Street (☎ 212/962-1257). Owner Ellen Hart won the Miss Subways beauty pageant in 1959, and her restaurant walls are lined with her own and other Miss Subways posters, plus photographs of all the politicians who have eaten here, from Bella Abzug to Rudy Giuliani. Muffins, biscuits, and pastries are all oven fresh, and cheap 'n' cheerfully served full breakfasts of eggs, bacon, pancakes, and Belgian waffles are available. Open weekdays 6am to 7pm, Saturday 8am to 5pm.

Along the north edge of City Hall Park, on Chambers Street, sits the now-shabby:

17. Tweed Courthouse (New York County Courthouse, 52 Chambers St.). This 1872 Italianate courthouse was built during the tenure of William Marcy "Boss" Tweed, who, in his post on the board of supervisors, stole millions in construction funds. Originally budgeted as a $250,000 job in 1861, the courthouse project escalated to the staggering sum of $14 million. Bills were padded to an unprecedented extent—Andrew Garvey, who was to become known as the "Prince of Plasterers," was paid $45,966.89 for a single day's work! The ensuing scandal wrecked Tweed's career; he died penniless in jail.

Across Chambers Street and to the right, at the corner of Elk Street, lies the turn-of-the-century:

18. Surrogate's Court (The Hall of Records), 31 Chambers St. Housed in this sumptuous beaux-arts structure are all the legal records relating to Manhattan real-estate deeds and court cases, some dating from the mid-1600s. Heroic statues of distinguished New Yorkers (Peter Stuyvesant, De Witt Clinton, and others) front the mansard roof, and the doorways, surmounted by arched pediments, are flanked by Philip Martiny's sculptural groups portraying *New York in Revolutionary Times* (to your left) and *New York in Its Infancy* (to your right). Above the entrance is a three-story Corinthian colonnade.

Step inside to see the vestibule's beautiful barrel-vaulted mosaic ceiling, embellished with astrological symbols, Egyptian and Greek motifs, and figures representing retribution, justice, sorrow, and labor. Continue back to the two-story skylit neoclassical atrium, clad in honey-colored marble with a colonnaded second-floor loggia and an ornate staircase adapted from the foyer of the Grand Opera House in Paris.

Exiting the Surrogate's Court from the front door, you'll see to your left, at the end of the block, that Chambers Street disappears under:

19. The Municipal Building, a grand civic edifice built between 1909 and 1914 to augment City Hall's government office space. It was designed by the famed architectural firm of McKim, Mead, and White (as in Stanford White), who used Greek and Roman design elements. A triumphal arch, its barrel-vaulted ceiling adorned with relief panels, forms a magnificent arcade over Chambers Street; it has been called the "gate of the city." Sculptor Adolph Weinman created many of the building's bas-reliefs, medallions, and allegorical groupings of human figures (they symbolize civic pride, progress, guidance, prudence, and executive power). Manhattan's largest statue, the heroic hammered-copper statue of *Civic Fame* that tops the structure 582 feet above the street, was also designed by Weinman; it holds a crown whose five turrets represent New York's five boroughs.

See many lovey-dovey couples walking in and out? The city's marriage license bureau is on the second floor, and a wedding takes place about every 20 minutes.

4 The Top Museums

✪ **American Museum of Natural History.** On Central Park W., btw. 77th and 81st sts. ☎ 212/769-5100. www.amnh.org. Suggested admission $8 adults ($13 with 1 IMAX movie, $16 with 2), $6 seniors and students ($7 with 1 IMAX movie, $12 with 2), $4.50 children 2–12 ($13 with 1 IMAX movie, $9 with 2). Sun–Thurs 10am–5:45pm, Fri–Sat 10am–8:45pm. Subway: B, C to 81st St.; 1, 9 to 79th St.

This 4-block-square museum houses the world's greatest natural-science collection in a group of buildings made of towers and turrets, pink granite, and red brick—a mishmash of architectural styles, but overflowing with neo-Gothic charm. The diversity of the holdings is astounding: some 36 million specimens ranging from microscopic organisms to the world's largest cut gem, the Brazilian Princess Topaz (21,005 carats). If you spent the whole day in the museum, you still wouldn't get to everything. If you don't have a lot of time, you can see the best of the best on free **highlights tours** offered daily every hour at 15 minutes after the hour from 10:15am to 3:15pm. Free daily **spotlights tours,** thematic tours that change monthly, are also offered; stop by an information desk for the day's schedule. **Audio Expeditions,** high-tech audio tours that allow you to access narration in the order you choose, are also available to help you make sense of it all.

If you only see one exhibit, see the ✪ **dinosaurs,** which take up the entire fourth floor. Recent restorations and redesigns put new life in the old bones, making this the best of what the museum has to offer by far. Start in the **Orientation Room,** where a short video gives an overview of the 500 million years of evolutionary history that led to you. Continue to the **Vertebrate Origins Room,** where huge models of ancient fish and turtles hang overhead, with plenty of interactive exhibits and kid-level displays on hand to keep young minds fascinated. Next come the great **dinosaur halls,** with mammoth, spectacularly reconstructed skeletons and more interactive displays. **Mammals and Their Extinct Relatives** shows how yesterday's prehistoric monsters have evolved into today's modern animals. Simply marvelous—you could spend hours in these halls alone.

Many other areas of the museum pale in comparison. The **animal habitat dioramas** and **halls of peoples** seem a bit dated but still have something to teach, especially the Native-American halls. Other than peeking in to see the giant whale (viewable from the cafe below) skip the **Ocean Life** room altogether; let's hope this is next on the restoration agenda, because the current exhibit makes Disneyland's submarine ride look high-tech. The new **Hall of Biodiversity** is an impressive multimedia exhibit, but the doom-and-gloom story it tells about the future of rain forests and other natural habitats may be too much for the little ones. Kids 5 years and older should head to the **Discovery Room,** with lots of hands-on exhibits and experiments. (Be prepared, Mom and Dad—there seems to be a gift shop overflowing with fuzzy, overpriced stuffed animals at every turn.)

The museum excels at **special exhibitions,** so I recommend checking to see what will be on while you're in town. Highlights of the past year have included the magical Butterfly Conservatory, a walk-in enclosure housing nearly 500 free-flying tropical butterflies.

In addition, an **IMAX Theater** shows neat films like *Cosmic Voyage* and *Africa's Elephant Kingdom* on a four-story screen that puts you right in the heart of the action; you can buy tickets to screenings as part of your admission package (see above). IMAX tickets can also be ordered separately and in advance by calling ☎ **212/769-5200** or online at the museum's Web site. The **Hayden Planetarium** closed in 1997 for demolition and reconstruction that should be completed in 2000, but Beavis and Buttheads (and I say that fondly) can still see **laser light shows**—including U2 and Laser Zeppelin in 3D—Friday and Saturday at 9 and 10pm. Tickets are $9; call ☎ **212/769-5200** to reserve.

✪ **Metropolitan Museum of Art.** Fifth Ave. at 82nd St. ☎ **212/535-7710.** www. metmuseum.org. Suggested admission (includes same-day entrance to the Cloisters) $10 adults, $5 students and seniors, free for children under 12 when accompanied by an adult. Tues–Thurs and Sun 9:30am–5:15pm, Fri–Sat 9:30am–8:45pm. No strollers allowed Sun (back carriers available at 81st St. entrance coat-check area). Subway: 4, 5, 6 to 86th St.

Home to blockbuster after blockbuster exhibitions, the Metropolitan Museum of Art attracts some 5 million people a year, more than any other spot in New York City. And it's no wonder—this place is magnificent. At 1.6 million square feet, this is the largest museum in the Western Hemisphere. Nearly all the world's cultures are on display through the ages—from Egyptian mummies to ancient Greek statuary to Islamic carvings to Renaissance paintings to Native-American masks to 20th-century decorative arts—and masterpieces are the rule. You could go once a week for a lifetime and still find something new on each visit.

So unless you plan on spending your entire vacation in the museum (some people do), you cannot see the entire collection. My recommendation is to give it a good day—or better yet, 2½ days so you don't burn out. One good way to get an overview is to take advantage of the little-known **Highlights Tour.** Even some New Yorkers who've spent many hours in the museum could profit from this once-over. Call ☎ 212/570-3711 (Mon–Fri 9am–5pm) or visit the museum's Web site for a schedule of this and subject-specific tours (French Impressionists, Arts of Japan, and so on).

The least overwhelming way to see the Met on your own is to pick up a map at the round desk in the entry hall and choose to concentrate on what you like, whether it's 17th-century paintings, American furniture, or the art of the South Pacific. Highlights include the American Wing's **Garden Court,** with its 19th-century sculpture, the lower-level **Costume Hall,** and the **Frank Lloyd Wright Room.** The **Roman and Greek galleries** are overwhelming, but in a marvelous way, as is the collection of later **Chinese art.** The setting of the **Temple of Dendur** is dramatic, in a specially built glass-walled gallery with Central Park views. But it all depends on what your interests are. Don't forget the marvelous **special exhibitions,** which can range from "Jade in Ancient Costa Rica" to "Cubism and Fashion." If you'd like to plan your visit ahead of time, the museum's Web site is a useful tool; there's also a list of current exhibitions in the Friday and Sunday editions of the *New York Times.*

Special exhibits and programs abound. To purchase tickets for concerts and lectures, call ☎ 212/570-3949 (Mon–Sat 9:30am–5pm). The museum contains several dining facilities, including a **full-service restaurant** serving continental cuisine (☎ 212/570-3964 for reservations) as well as less-expensive options that need no advance planning. The roof garden is worth visiting if you're here from spring to autumn, offering wide and peaceful views over Central Park and the city.

On **Friday and Saturday evenings,** the Met stays open late not only for art viewing but also for cocktails in the Great Hall Balcony Bar (4–8:30pm) and classical music by a string quintet or trio. A slate of after-hours programs (gallery talks, walking tours, family programs) changes by the week; call for this week's schedule. The restaurant stays open until 10pm (last reservation at 8:30pm), and dinner is usually accompanied by piano music.

If you're interested in the medieval age, head to the **Cloisters,** a branch of the Met in Uptown Manhattan (see "More Manhattan Museums," below).

✪ **Museum of Modern Art.** 11 W. 53rd St. (btw. Fifth and Sixth aves.). ☎ **212/ 708-9400.** www.moma.org. Admission $9.50 adults ($13.50 with audio tour), $6.50 seniors and students ($10.50 with audio tour), free for children under 16 accompanied by an adult;

Avoid the Crowds

Many of the city's top museums—including the Natural History Museum, the Met, and MoMA—have late hours on Friday and/or Saturday nights. Take advantage of them. Most visitors run out of steam by dinnertime, so even on jam-packed weekends you'll largely have the place to yourself by 5 or 6pm—which, in most cases, leaves you hours left to explore, unfettered by crowds or screaming kids.

pay as you wish Fri 4:30–8:15pm. Sat–Tues and Thurs 10:30am–5:45pm, Fri 10:30am–8:15pm. Subway: E, F to Fifth Ave.; B, D, F, Q to 47–50th sts./Rockefeller Center.

The Museum of Modern Art (or MoMA, as it's usually called) boasts the world's greatest collection of painting and sculpture ranging from the late 19th century to the present, including everything from van Gogh's *Starry Night,* Picasso's early *Les Demoiselles d'Avignon,* Monet's *Water Lilies,* and Klimt's *The Kiss* to later masterworks by Frida Kahlo, Edward Hopper, Andy Warhol, Robert Rauschenberg, and many others. Top that off with an extensive collection of modern drawings, photography, architectural models and furniture (including the Mies van der Rohe Collection), iconic design objects ranging from tableware to sports cars, and film and video, and you have quite a museum. If you're into modernism, this is the place.

While not quite Met-sized, MoMa is probably still more than you can see in a day. In true modern style, the museum is efficient and well organized, so it's easy to focus on your primary interests; just grab a museum map after you pay your admission. For an overview, take the **self-guided tour** that stops at the collection's highlights, chosen by the different departments' curators. Be sure to check out the sculpture garden—an island of trees and fountains containing works by Calder, Moore, and Rodin. In addition, there's usually at least one beautifully mounted special exhibition in house that's worth a trip, whether it be the works of Finnish master architect Alvar Aalto, Julia Margaret Cameron's remarkable 19th-century photographs of women, or a celebration of sight gags in contemporary art.

MoMa boasts a host of special programs. Hour-long family-oriented **gallery talks,** with such titles as "Music to My Eyes: Matisse and More," take place Saturdays at 10am. There's live jazz three evenings a week in **Sette MoMA** (☎ 212/708-9710), the museum's notable Italian restaurant overlooking the sculpture garden, or the affordable **Garden Cafe.** A full slate of symposiums, gallery talks by contemporary artists, interactive family programs, and brown-bag lunches are always on offer; call ☎ 212/708-9781 or visit the museum's Web site to see what's on while you're in town. Additionally, there's always a multifaceted film and video program on the schedule; call the main number to see what's on. Films are included in the price of admission, but arrive early to make sure you get a seat.

Setting course for the 21st century, the Modern has embarked on a major expansion overseen by Japanese architect Yoshio Taniguchi that will attract worldwide attention and comparison to other recent museum projects, like Richard Meier's stunning Getty Center in Los Angeles and Frank Gehry's Guggenheim Museum in Bilbao, Spain. Don't look for this ambitious project to be completed anytime soon; but since it's expanding into adjacent space, it shouldn't appreciably affect your experience.

Solomon R. Guggenheim Museum. 1071 Fifth Ave. (at 88th St.). ☎ **212/423-3500.** www.guggenheim.org. Admission $12 adults, $7 seniors, children under 12 free; Fri 6–8pm pay what you wish. Two-museum pass, which includes one admission to the SoHo branch valid for 1 week, $16 adults, $10 seniors. Sun–Wed 10am–6pm, Fri–Sat 10am–8pm. Subway: 4, 5, 6 to 86th St.

It has been called a bun, a snail, a concrete tornado, and even a giant wedding cake; your kids will dream of skateboarding down it. Whatever descriptive you choose to apply, Frank Lloyd Wright's only New York building, completed in 1959, is undeniably a brilliant work of architecture—so impressive that it competes with the art for your attention. If you're looking for the city's best modern art, head to MoMA or the Whitney first; come to the Guggenheim to see the house.

It's easy to see the bulk of what's on display in 2 to 4 hours. Inside, a spiraling rotunda circles over a slowly inclined ramp that leads you past changing exhibits, which can range from modern masterworks from the Centre Pompidou to the Art of

Free Culture at Big Apple Museums

New York's gargantuan stash of museums, galleries, and attractions makes this city one of the cultural capitals of the world. But the cost of absorbing all this culture can get pretty high, especially since many museums are now asking around $10 to get in the door. But don't get discouraged; as you'll see from the list below, there are plenty of ways around these steep admission fees.

Some city attractions are free all the time. Some set aside an afternoon, evening, or even an entire day during the week when you can explore at no charge. Others offer "pay what you wish" times, which allow you to determine what contribution you make upon entering, be it $1 or the full admission price.

Most museums keep pretty solid schedules, but it's always a good idea to call ahead and confirm free and "pay as you wish" times—because these, like everything else, are always subject to change.

Always Free

- **Dahesh Museum** (p. 211)
- **Federal Hall National Memorial** (p. 198)
- **Forbes Magazine Galleries** (p. 212)
- **Museum of American Folk Art** (p. 214)
- **National Museum of the American Indian** (p. 216)
- Exhibitions at the **New York Public Library** (p. 224)
- **New York Stock Exchange** (p. 185)
- Exhibitions at the **Schomburg Center for Research in Black Culture** (p. 218)
- **Sony Wonder Technology Lab** (p. 255)
- **St. Patrick's Cathedral** (p. 225)
- The **Bernard Museum** at **Temple Emanu–El** (p. 225)
- **Whitney Museum of American Art at Phillip Morris** (p. 207)

Sometimes Free

- **Bronx Zoo Wildlife Conservation Park:** All day Wednesday; regular admission $7.75 April through October, $6 November to January, $4 January through March (p. 256).
- **Brooklyn Botanic Garden:** All day Tuesday and Saturday from 10am to noon; regular admission $3 (p. 258).

the Motorcycle. Usually the progression is counterintuitive: from the first floor up, rather than from the sixth floor down. If you're not sure, ask a guard before you begin. Permanent exhibits of 19th- and 20th-century art, including strong holdings of Kandinsky, Klee, Picasso, and French impressionists, occupy a stark annex called the **Tower Galleries,** an addition accessible at every level that some critics claim makes the original look like a toilet bowl backed by a water tank (judge for yourself—I think there may be something to that view).

The Guggenheim runs some interesting special programs, including free docent tours (there's a 1-hour highlights tour daily at noon), a limited schedule of lectures, free family films (*The Red Balloon* and *Babar: The Movie* were among the choices at press time), avant-garde screenings for grown-ups, and the World Beat Jazz Series, which resounds through the rotunda on Friday and Saturday evenings from 5 to 8pm.

- **Brooklyn Museum of Art:** First Saturday of every month from 5 to 11pm; regular admission $4 (p. 258).
- **Cooper-Hewitt National Design Museum:** Tuesday from 5pm to 9pm; regular admission $5 (p. 211).
- **New Museum of Contemporary Art:** Thursday 6 to 8pm; regular admission $5 (p. 217).
- **New York Botanical Garden:** All day Wednesday and Saturday from 10am to noon; regular admission $3 (p. 256).
- **New York Hall of Science:** Thursday and Friday from 2pm to 5pm; regular admission $6 (p. 254).
- **New York Transit Museum:** Wednesday from noon to 4pm; regular admission $3 (p. 259).
- **Wave Hill:** Every day in winter, on Saturday morning and all day Tuesday in summer; regular admission $4 (p. 257).

"Pay as You Wish" Evenings

- **American Craft Museum:** Thursday from 6 to 8pm; regular admission $5.
- **International Center of Photography** and **ICP—Midtown.** Tuesday from 5 to 8pm; regular admission (includes both locations) $6.
- **The Jewish Museum:** Tuesday from 5 to 8pm; regular admission $8 (p. 213).
- **Museum of Modern Art:** Friday from 4:30 to 8:15pm; regular admission $9.50 (p. 204).
- **Solomon R. Guggenheim Museum:** Friday from 6 to 8pm; regular admission $12 (p. 205).
- **Whitney Museum of American Art:** Thursday from 6 to 8pm; regular admission $9 (p. 207).

Almost Free (admission of $2 or less)

- **American Museum of Financial History:** $2 (p. 196)
- **Cathedral of St. John the Divine:** $2 (p. 223)
- **Theodore Roosevelt Birthplace:** $2 (p. 218)

There's also a trendier Downtown branch, the **Guggenheim Museum Soho,** 575 Broadway, at Prince Street (☎ 212/423-3500), that generally houses temporary installations of high-tech multimedia works. However, this location has been suffering from financial troubles of late, and at press time had closed for renovations that included the shrinking of its square footage. It should reopen by the time you arrive, and postmodern enthusiasts might want to check it out.

۞ Whitney Museum of American Art. 945 Madison Ave. (at 75th St.). ☎ 212/570-3600 or 212/570-3676. www.echonyc.com/~whitney. Admission $9 adults, $7 seniors and students, free for children under 12; pay as you wish Thurs 6–8pm. Wed and Fri–Sun 11am–6pm, Thurs 11am–8pm. Subway: 6 to 77th St.

What is arguably the finest collection of 20th-century American art in the world belongs to the Whitney thanks to the efforts of Gertrude Vanderbilt Whitney. A sculptor herself, she organized exhibitions by American artists shunned by traditional

In Search of Historic Homes

New York's voracious appetite for change often means that older residential architecture is torn down so that money-earning high-rises can go up in its place. Surprisingly, however, the city maintains a truly fine collection of often overlooked historic houses that are more than a tale of architecture—they're the stories of the people who passed their ordinary or extraordinary lives in buildings that range from humble to magnificent.

The **Historic House Trust of New York City** preserves 19 houses, located in city parks in all five boroughs. Those particularly worth seeking out include the **Morris-Jumel Mansion** (☎ 212/923-8008), built circa 1765 and Manhattan's oldest surviving house. The **Dyckman Farmhouse Museum** (☎ 212/304-9422) is the only Dutch-Colonial farmhouse remaining in Manhattan, stoically and stylishly surviving the urban development that grew up around it. Built in 1809, Federal-style **Gracie Mansion** (☎ 212/570-4751) is now the official residence of Hizzoner, the mayor of New York. The **Edgar Allan Poe Cottage** (☎ 718/881-8900) was the last home of the brilliant but troubled poet and author, who moved his wife to the Bronx because he thought the "country air" would be good for her tuberculosis. And the **Merchant's House Museum** (☎ 212/777-1089) is a rare jewel: a perfectly preserved 19th-century Greenwich Village home, complete with intact interiors, whose last resident is said to be the inspiration for Catherine Sloper in Henry James's *Washington Square*. Each of the 14 others has its own fascinating story to tell.

A brochure listing the locations and touring details of all 19 of the historic homes is available by calling ☎ **212/360-8282,** and recorded information on special events at the houses is available at ☎ **212/360-3448.** You'll also find complete information online at **www.ci.nyc.ny.us/html/dpr/html/nav.html**; click on HISTORIC HOUSES.

academies, assembled a sizable personal collection, and founded the museum in 1930 in Greenwich Village.

Today's museum is an imposing presence on Madison Avenue—an inverted three-tiered pyramid of concrete and gray granite with seven seemingly random windows designed by Marcel Breuer, a leader of the Bauhaus movement. The rotating permanent collection consists of an intelligent selection of major works by Edward Hopper, George Bellows, Georgia O'Keeffe, Roy Lichtenstein, Jasper Johns, and other significant artists. A pleasing new fifth-floor exhibit space, the museum's first devoted exclusively to works from its permanent collection from 1900 to 1950, opened in 1998.

There are usually several simultaneous shows, usually all well curated and more edgy than what you'd see at MoMA or the Guggenheim (despite recent controversy swirling around the museum's new curator, Maxwell Anderson). Topics range from topical surveys, such as "American Art in the Age of Technology" and "The Warhol Look: Glamour Style Fashion" to in-depth retrospectives of famous or lesser-known movements (such as Fluxus, the movement that spawned Yoko Ono, among others) and artists (Mark Rothko, Keith Haring, Duane Hanson, Bob Thompson). From April 1999 to February 2000, a substantial mulitmedia exhibition called "The American Century: Art and Culture 1900–2000" showcases the Whitney's innovative cultural-technological partnership with Intel as it explores the changing nature of American identity.

The next Whitney Biennial is scheduled for spring 2000. A major event on the national museum calendar, the Biennials serve as the premier launching pad for new American artists working in the vanguard of every media. The first to fall under Anderson's stewardship, the millennial edition promises to be an exciting and much-talked-about event.

The Whitney also has the best museum restaurant in town: **Sarabeth's at the Whitney** (☎ **212/560-3670**), open for lunch Tuesday through Sunday and worth a visit in its own right (see chapter 6).

Free **gallery tours** are offered daily; call ☎ **212/570-3676** for the current schedule, or check at the Information desk when you arrive.

A Midtown branch, the **Whitney Museum of American Art at Philip Morris,** 120 Park Ave., at 42nd Street opposite Grand Central Terminal (☎ **212/875-2550;** free admission; Mon–Wed and Fri 11am–6pm, Thurs 11am–7:30pm), features an airy sculpture court and a small gallery that hosts changing exhibits, usually the works of living contemporary artists. Free hour-long gallery tours are offered Wednesday and Friday at 1pm.

5 More Manhattan Museums

In 1978, New York's finest cultural institutions located on Fifth Avenue between 82nd and 104th streets formed a consortium called **Museum Mile,** the name New York City officially gave to the stretch several years later. The "mile" begins at the **Metropolitan Museum of Art** (see "Top Museums," above) and moves north to **El Museo del Barrio.** However, even the smallest museums along this stretch require some time, so don't plan on just popping into a few as you stroll along, or you'll be sorely disappointed by what you're able to see. Your best bet is to head directly to the museum that's tops on your list first, and then proceed to your second choice along the mile if you have time. If you're heading to the Metropolitan, forget trying to squeeze in anything else—as it is, you'll only see a portion of the collection there in a full day.

For details on **Federal Hall National Memorial** and **Fraunces Tavern Museum,** see the walking tour earlier in this chapter. For the **Brooklyn Museum of Art,** the **New York Transit Museum,** the **American Museum of the Moving Image,** the **Queens Museum of Art,** and the **P.S. 1 Contemporary Art Center,** see "Highlights of the Outer Boroughs" later in this chapter.

If you're traveling with the kids, also consider the museums listed under "Especially for Kids" later in this chapter, which include the **Children's Museum of Manhattan,** the **Sony Wonder Technology Lab,** the **Liberty Science Center,** the **New York Hall of Science,** and the **New York City Fire Museum.**

Abigail Adams Smith Museum & Gardens. 421 E. 61st St. (btw. First and York aves.). ☎ **212/838-6878.** Admission $3 adults, $2 seniors, children under 12 free. Tues–Sun 11am–4pm; June and July, to 9pm Tues. Closed Aug. Subway: 4, 5, 6 to 59th St.; N, R to Lexington Ave.

It's a shock, a very pleasant one, to find such a little-known jewel on this otherwise modern block. This rare survivor from early American was built as a carriage house for Abigail Adams Smith, daughter of President John Adams, and her husband, William Stephens Smith, in 1799. It was painstakingly restored by the Colonial Dames of America to its early 19th-century condition, when the house served as the Mount Vernon Hotel—a country hotel for bucolic overnights away from the city, if you can believe it. You can explore nine period rooms, outfitted in authentic Federal style, as well as the grounds.

The Alternative Museum. 594 Broadway (btw. Houston and Prince sts.), 4th floor. ☎ **212/966-4444.** Suggested admission $3. Tues–Sat 11am–6pm. Subway: N, R to Prince St.; B, D, F, Q to Broadway–Lafayette St.

Here's the sharpest edge on the New York museum scene. This upstart (actually founded on the Lower East Side in 1975) focuses on lesser-known and emerging artists with high-concept or issue-oriented works, including many working in new media. Expect lots of explorations of race, class, and gender. What you see might not always be good, but it will be thought provoking. There's also a jazz and new music program that has showcased such notables as the Kronos Quartet.

American Craft Museum. 40 W. 53rd St. (btw. Fifth and Sixth aves.). ☎ **212/956-3535.** $5 adults, $2.50 students and seniors, free for children under 12; pay as you wish Thurs 6–8pm. Tues, Wed, and Fri–Sun 10am–6pm, Thurs 10am–8pm. Subway: E, F to Fifth Ave.

This small but aesthetically pleasing museum is the nation's top showcase for contemporary crafts. The collection focuses on prime examples of form and function, ranging from jewelry to baskets to vessels to furniture. You'll see a strong emphasis on material as well as craft, whether it be fiber, ceramics, or metal. Special exhibitions can range from hand-blown glassworks to fine bookbinding. The gorgeous shop is worth checking out even if you don't make it into the museum, especially if you have some gift buying to do.

Asia Society. 725 Park Ave. (at 70th St.). ☎ **212/517-ASIA.** Gallery admission $4 adults, $2 seniors, children under 13 free; free Thurs 6–8pm. Tues–Sat 11am–6pm (to 8pm Thurs), Sun noon–5pm. Subway: 6 to 68th St.–Hunter College.

The Asia Society was founded in 1956 by John D. Rockefeller III with the goal of increasing understanding between Americans and Asians through art exhibits, lectures, films, performances, and international conferences. The society is a leader in presenting contemporary Asian and Asian-American art; recent exhibits have included "Bamboo Masterworks," and "Sheer Realities: Body, Power and Clothing in the 19th-Century Philippines" was on the schedule for late 1999 at press time.

Center for Jewish History. 17 W. 16th St. (btw. Fifth and Sixth aves.). ☎ **212/588-1253.** www.cjh.org. Admission and hours not determined at press time. Subway: L, N, R, 4, 5, 6 to 14th St./Union Sq.

Scheduled to open in fall 1999, the Center for Jewish History will occupy a new $40-million four-building complex. The Center brings together four of America's leading institutions of Jewish history: the **American Jewish Historical Society** (40 million documents and 30,000 books on Jewish Americana), the **Leo Baeck Institute** (documents, memoirs, and photos documenting German-speaking Jews), the **Yeshiva University Museum** (general-interest exhibits, plus a renowned collection of Judaica objects confiscated by the Nazis), and the **YIVO Institute for Jewish Research** (an academic institution concentrating on Eastern European Jewry before the Holocaust). Besides offering public exhibits, the center will feature special events and a kosher eatery.

✪ The Cloisters. At the north end of Fort Tryon Park. ☎ **212/923-3700.** www. metmuseum.org/htmlfile/gallery/cloister/cloister.html. Suggested admission (includes same-day entrance to the Metropolitan Museum of Art) $8 adults, $4 seniors and students, free for children under 12. Nov–Feb Tues–Sun 9:30am–4:45pm; Mar–Oct Tues–Sun 9:30am–5:15pm. Subway: A to 190th St., then a 10-minute walk north along Margaret Corgan Dr., or pick up the M4 bus at the station. Bus: M4 Madison Ave. (FORT TRYON PARK–THE CLOISTERS).

If it weren't for this branch of the Metropolitan Museum of Art, many New Yorkers would never get to this northernmost point in Manhattan. This remote yet lovely spot is devoted to the art and architecture of medieval Europe. Atop a magnificent cliff overlooking the Hudson River you'll find a 12th-century chapter house, parts of five cloisters from medieval monasteries, a Romanesque chapel, and a 12th-century Spanish apse brought intact from Europe. Surrounded by peaceful gardens, this is the one place on the island that can even approximate the kind of solitude suitable to such a collection. Inside you'll find extraordinary works that include the famed Unicorn tapestries, sculpture, illuminated manuscripts, stained glass, ivory, and precious metalwork. Despite its remoteness, the Cloisters are extremely popular, especially in fine weather, so try to schedule your visit during the week rather than on a crowded weekend afternoon. A free guided tour is offered Tuesday through Friday at 3pm and Sunday at noon.

○ Cooper-Hewitt National Design Museum. 2 E. 91st St. (at Fifth Ave.). ☎ 212/849-8300. www.si.edu/ndm. Admission $5 adults, $3 seniors and students, free for children under 12; free to all Tues 5–9pm. Tues 10am–9pm, Wed–Sat 10am–5pm, Sun noon–5pm. Subway: 4, 5, 6 to 86th St.

Part of the Smithsonian Institution, the Cooper-Hewitt is housed in the Carnegie Mansion, built by steel magnate Andrew Carnegie in 1901. The museum underwent an ambitious $20-million renovation in 1996 that gave the building new vitality. Some 11,000 square feet of gallery space is devoted to changing exhibits that are invariably well conceived, engaging, and educational. Shows are both historic and contemporary in nature, and topics range from "Graphic Design in the Mechanical Age" to "The Architecture of Reassurance: Designing the Disney Theme Parks." Many installations are drawn from the museum's own vast collection of industrial design, drawings, textiles, wall coverings, books, and prints. Exhibitions scheduled for late 1999–2000 include a retrospective on the work of Charles and Ray Eames and the National Design Triennial, featuring the work of both well-known and emerging talents as they address the pressing design issues of today.

On your way in, note the fabulous art-nouveau–style copper-and-glass canopy above the entrance. And be sure to visit the garden, ringed with Central Park benches from various eras.

Dahesh Museum. 601 Fifth Ave. (at 48th St.). ☎ 212/759-0606. www.daheshmuseum. org. Free admission. Tues–Sat 11am–6pm. Subway: B, D, F, Q to 47–50th sts./Rockefeller Center.

If you consider yourself a classicist, this small museum is for you. It's dedicated to 19th- and early-20th-century European academic art, a continuation of Renaissance, Baroque, and Rococo traditions that were overshadowed by impressionism. If you're not familiar with the academic school, expect lots of painstaking renditions of historical subjects and pastoral life. Artists represented include Jean-Léon Gérôme, Lord Leighton, and Edwin Long, whose *Love's Labour Lost* is a cornerstone of the permanent collection.

El Museo del Barrio. 1230 Fifth Ave. (at 104th St.). ☎ 212/831-7272. www.elmuseo.org. Suggested admission $4 adults, $2 seniors and students, children under 12 free. Wed–Sun 11am–5pm. Subway: 6 to 103rd St.

What started in 1969 with a small display in a local school classroom in East Harlem is today the only museum in America dedicated to Puerto Rican, Caribbean, and Latin American art. The northernmost Museum Mile institution has a permanent exhibit ranging from pre-Columbian artifacts to historic photographs and handicrafts to a variety of paintings and sculpture. The display of *santos de palo*, wood-carved religious figurines, is especially worth noting. The well-curated changing exhibitions tend to focus on 20th-century artists and contemporary subjects.

Forbes Magazine Galleries. 62 Fifth Ave. (at 12th St.). ☎ **212/206-5548.** Free admission. Tues, Wed, Fri, Sat 10am–4pm. Subway: L, N, R, 4, 5, 6 to 14th St./Union Sq.

The late publishing magnate Malcolm Forbes may have been a self-described "capitalist tool," but he had esoteric, almost childish, tastes. He also had the altruism to share what he collected with the public for free. With its model boats, toy soldiers, old Monopoly game sets, presidential papers and memorabilia, and jewel-encrusted Fabergé eggs, this is a great museum for both you and the kids. Personal anecdotes explain why certain objects attracted Forbes's attention and turn the collection into an oddly interesting biographical portrait.

✪ The Frick Collection. 1 E. 70th St. (at Fifth Ave.). ☎ **212/288-0700.** www.frick.org. Admission $7 adults, $5 seniors and students. Children under 10 not admitted; children 10–16 must be accompanied by an adult. Tues–Sat 10am–6pm, Sun and minor holidays 1–6pm (closed all major holidays). Subway: 6 to 68th St./Hunter College.

Henry Clay Frick could afford to be an avid collector of European art after amassing a fortune as a pioneer in the coke and steel industries at the turn of the century. To house his treasures and himself, he hired architects Carrère & Hastings to build this 18th-century-French–style mansion (1914), one of the most beautiful remaining on Fifth Avenue.

This is a living testament to New York's vanished Gilded Age: The interior still feels like a private home (albeit a really, really rich guy's home) graced with beautiful paintings, rather than a museum. Come here to see the works of the world's most famous painters: Titian, Bellini, Rembrandt, Turner, Vermeer, El Greco, and Goya, to name only a few. A highlight of the collection is the **Fragonard Room,** graced with the sensual rococo series *The Progress of Love.* The portrait of Montesquieu by Whistler is also stunning. Sculpture, furniture, Chinese vases, and French enamels complement the paintings and round out the collection. Included in the price of admission, the AcousticGuide audio tour is particularly useful, because it allows you to follow your own path rather than a proscribed route.

In addition to the permanent collection, the Frick regularly mounts small, well-focused temporary exhibitions. Free **chamber music concerts** are held twice a month, generally every other Sunday at 5pm; call or visit the Web site for the current schedule and ticket information.

International Center of Photography & ICP—Midtown. Uptown branch: 1130 Fifth Ave. (at 94th St.) ☎ **212/860-1777.** Midtown branch: 1133 Sixth Ave. (at 43rd St.). ☎ **212/768-4682.** www.icp.org. Admission (includes both Uptown and Midtown locations) $6 adults, $4 seniors, $1 children under 13; Tues 5–8pm pay what you wish. Tues–Thurs 10am–5pm, Fri 10am–8pm, Sat and Sun 10am–6pm. Subway: 6 to 96th St. to ICP Uptown; B, D, F, Q to 42nd St. to ICP Midtown.

The ICP is one of the world's premier collectors and exhibitors of photographic art, mounting some of the most interesting changing art exhibits in the city. The original ICP is also worth a look, but the Midtown branch is twice the size of the original and usually has two mounted exhibitions rather than just one. The emphasis is on contemporary photographic works, but historically important photographers aren't ignored. Topics can range from "Man Ray: Photography and its Double" to "Soul of the Game: Images and Voices of Street Basketball." A must on any photography buff's list. Call or check the Web site for current exhibitions.

***Intrepid* Sea-Air-Space Museum.** Pier 86 (W. 46th St. at Twelfth Ave.). ☎ **212/245-0072.** www.intrepid-museum.com. Admission $10 adults; $7.50 veterans, seniors, and students; $5 children 6–11; first child under 6 free, each extra child $1. May–Sept, Mon–Sat 10am–5pm (last admission 4pm), Sun 10am–6pm (last admission 5pm); Oct–Apr, Wed–Sun 10am–5pm (last admission 4pm). Subway: A, C, E to 42nd St. Bus: M42 crosstown.

The most astonishing thing about the aircraft carrier USS *Intrepid* is how it can be simultaneously so big and so small. It's a few football fields long, holds 40 aircraft, and sometimes doubles as a ballroom for society functions. But stand there and think about landing an A-12 jet on the deck and suddenly, it's minuscule. Now a National Historic Landmark, the entire exhibit also includes the destroyer USS *Edison*, the submarine USS *Growler*, and the lightship *Nantucket*, as well as a collection of vintage and modern aircraft, including the A-12 Blackbird, the world's fastest spy plane. Special exhibits are often mounted, such as 1998's tribute to 200 years of naval service by African-Americans. Kids just love this place. But think twice about going in winter—it's almost impossible to heat an aircraft carrier.

Japan Society. 333 E. 47th St. (btw. First and Second aves.). ☎ **212/832-1155**. Suggested admission to gallery $5. Tues–Sun 9am–5:30pm. Subway: 6 to 51st St.; E, F to Lexington Ave.

In a striking modern building by Junzo Yoshimuro (1971), the U.S. headquarters of the Japan Society mounts highly regarded exhibits of Japanese art in a suitably serene gallery, plus changing displays whose subjects have included "Japanese Theater in the World." The society also hosts a wide variety of lectures, films, concerts, and classes throughout the year.

The Jewish Museum. 1109 Fifth Ave. (at 92nd St.). ☎ **212/423-3230**. www. jewishmuseum.org. Admission $8 adults, $5.50 seniors and students, free for children under 12; pay as you wish Tues 5–8pm. Check Web site for special online admission discounts (50% off at press time). Sun, Mon, Wed, Thurs 11am–5:45pm, Tues 11am–8pm. Subway: 4, 5 to 86th St.; 6 to 96th St.

Housed in a Gothic-style mansion renovated in the early 1990s by AIA Gold Medal winner Kevin Roche, this wonderful museum now has the world-class space needed to showcase its remarkable collections, which chronicle 4,000 years of the Jewish experience. The two-floor permanent exhibit, "Culture and Continuity: The Jewish Journey," is the museum's centerpiece. Artifacts range from ancient daily objects from biblical days to a wonderful collection of classic TV programs (as any fan of television's Golden Age knows, its finest comic moments were Jewish comedy). There's also a great assemblage of intricate Torahs. The scope of the exhibit is phenomenal, and its story an enlightening—and intense—one. In addition, there's a rotating calendar of special exhibitions that range from antiquities to contemporary Jewish art, plus a design store showcasing contemporary Jewish crafts.

✪ Lower East Side Tenement Museum. Visitors' Center at 90 Orchard St. (at Broome St.). ☎ **212/431-0233**. www.wnet.org/tenement. $8 adults, $6 seniors and students for 1 tenement tour; $14 adults, $10 seniors and students for any 2 tours; $20 adults, $14 seniors and students for all 3 tours. Tenement tours depart Tues–Fri every half hour 1–4pm; Thurs hourly 6pm–9pm; Sat–Sun every half hour 11am–4:30pm. Subway: F to Delancey St.; B, D, Q to Grand St.

Awarded the prized designation just last year, this decade-old museum is the first-ever National Trust for Historic Preservation site that was not the home of someone rich or famous. This one is something quite different: A five-story tenement that 10,000 people from 25 countries called home between 1863 and 1935—people who had come to the United States looking for the American dream, and made 97 Orchard St. their first stop. This living history museum tells the story of the great immigration boom of the late 19th and early 20th centuries, when the Lower East Side was considered the

"Gateway to America." A visit here makes a good follow-up to an Ellis Island trip—what happened to all the people who passed through that famous waystation?

The only way to see the museum is by guided tour. At press time, three tours, each lasting about 1 hour, were on offer: two tenement tours, each showcasing the tenement during different decades, and one neighborhood walking tour. One tenement tour and the neighborhood tour are only offered on weekends, so it's wise to plan ahead if you'd like to see and do everything. However, the primary tenement tour, offered on all open days, might be enough. A knowledgeable guide leads you into the dingy urban time capsule, where several apartments have been faithfully restored to their exact lived-in condition, and recounts the real-life stories of the families who occupied them in fascinating detail. Tours are limited in number, so it pays to reserve ahead. The Visitors' Center has several small exhibits, including photos, videos, and a model tenement.

○ Morgan Library. 29 E. 36th St. (at Madison Ave.). ☎ **212/685-0008.** www.shop. morganlibrary.org. Admission $7 adults, $5 seniors, children under 12 free. Tues–Thurs 10:30am–5pm, Fri 10:30am–8pm, Sat 10:30am–6pm, Sun noon–6pm. Subway: 6 to 33rd St.

Here's an undiscovered New York treasure, boasting one of the world's most important collections of original manuscripts, rare books and bindings, master drawings, and personal writings. Among the remarkable artifacts on display are stunning illuminated manuscripts (including Guttenberg bibles); a working draft of the U.S. Constitution bearing copious handwritten notes; Voltaire's personal household account books; and handwritten scores by the likes of Beethoven, Mozart, and Puccini. The collection of mostly 19th-century drawings—featuring works by Seurat, Degas, Rubens, and other great masters—have an excitement of immediacy about them that the artists' more well-known paintings often lack. This rich repository originated as the private collection of turn-of-the-century financier J. Pierpont Morgan and is housed in a landmark Renaissance-style palazzo building (1906) he commissioned from McKim, Mead & White. Morgan's library and study are preserved virtually intact, and worth a look. The special exhibitions are particularly well chosen and curated; those scheduled for the coming year include "The Great Experiment: George Washington and the American Republic," tracing the first U.S. president's development from loyal British subject to radical revolution leader. A reading room is available by appointment.

Museum for African Art. 593 Broadway (btw. Houston and Prince sts.). ☎ **212/ 966-1313.** www.africanart.org. Admission $5 adults, $2.50 seniors and children. Tues–Fri 10:30am–5:30pm, Sat noon–8pm, Sun noon–6pm. Subway: N, R to Prince St.

This captivating museum (whose interior was designed by architect Maya Lin, best known for her Vietnam Veterans Memorial in Washington, D.C.) is a leading organizer of temporary exhibits dedicated to historic and contemporary African art and culture. Exhibitions on the calendar for late 1999–2000 include "Liberated Voices: Contemporary Art from South Africa," focusing on post-Apartheid works; an intricate look at hair and hair dressing in African art and culture; and a look at great African dynasties in "African Nobility and Their Objects of Power." In addition, an excellent museum shop showcases contemporary African crafts.

Museum of American Folk Art. 2 Lincoln Sq. (Columbus Ave. btw. 65th and 66th sts.). ☎ **212/977-7298** or 212/595-9533. www.folkartmuse.org. Free admission. Tues–Sun 11:30am–7:30pm. Subway: 1, 9 to 66th St.

This museum displays a wide range of works from the 18th century to the present reflecting the breadth and vitality of the American folk-art tradition. The textiles collection is the museum's most popular, highlighted by a splendid variety of quilts. The gift shop is filled with one-of-a-kind objects.

In 1998, the museum started construction on its new larger home on West 53rd Street, just down the block from the Museum of Modern Art. The new building, four times larger than the current space, is scheduled to open in 2001.

Museum of Jewish Heritage—A Living Memorial to the Holocaust. 18 First Place (at Battery Place), Battery Park City. ☎ **212/968-1800**. www.mjhnyc.org. Admission $7 adults, $5 seniors and students, children under 5 free. Sun–Wed 9am–5pm, Thurs 9am–8pm, Fri and evenings of Jewish holidays 9am–2pm. Subway: 1, 9 to South Ferry; 4, 5 to Bowling Green.

The Museum of Jewish Heritage was dedicated in fall 1997, more than 50 years after the idea was first proposed. Located in the south end of Battery Park City, it occupies a strikingly spare six-sided building designed by award-winning architect Kevin Roche, with a six-tier roof evoking the Star of David and the 6 million murdered in the Holocaust. The permanent exhibits—"Jewish Life a Century Ago," "The War Against the Jews," and "Jewish Renewal"—recount the daily pre-war lives, the unforgettable horror that destroyed them, and the tenacious renewal experienced by European and immigrant Jews. Their stories are powerfully told through the objects, photographs, documents, and, most poignantly, through the videotaped testimonies of Holocaust victims, survivors, and their families, all chronicled by Steven Spielberg's Survivors of the Shoah Visual History Foundation.

Advance tickets are highly recommended to guarantee admission, and can be purchased by calling ☎ **212/786-0820, ext. 111** or Ticketmaster (☎ **800/307-4007** or 212/307-4007; www.ticketmaster.com).

Museum of the City of New York. 1220 Fifth Ave. (at 103rd St.). ☎ **212/534-1672**. www.mcny.org. Suggested admission $5 adults, $4 seniors, students and children, $10 families. Wed–Sat 10am–5pm, Sun noon–5pm. Subway: 6 to 103rd St.

A wide variety of materials—costumes, photographs, prints, maps, dioramas, and memorabilia—traces the history of New York City from its beginnings as a humble Dutch colony in the 16th century to its present-day prominence. Two outstanding permanent exhibits are the re-creation of John D. Rockefeller's master bedroom and dressing room, and the space devoted to the history of New York theater. The permanent "Furniture of Distinction, 1790–1890" displays 33 elegant pieces that will have you eyeing your IKEA with new contempt. Kids will love "New York Toy Stories," a permanent exhibit showcasing toys and dolls owned and adored by centuries of New York children.

Museum of Television & Radio. 25 W. 52nd St. (btw. Fifth and Sixth aves.). ☎ **212/621-6800**. Admission $6 adults, $4 seniors and students, $3 children under 13. Tues, Wed, and Fri–Sun noon–6pm, Thurs noon–8pm. Subway: B, D, F, Q to 47–50th sts./Rockefeller Center; N, R to 49th St.

If you can resist the allure of this museum, I'd wager you've spent the last 70 years in a bubble. You can watch and hear all the great personalities of TV and radio—from Uncle Miltie to Johnny Carson to Jerry Seinfeld—at a private console (available for 2 hours). And amazingly, you can also conduct computer searches to pick out the great moments of history, viewing almost anything that made its way onto the airwaves, from the Beatles' first appearance on *The Ed Sullivan Show* to the crumbling of the Berlin Wall (the collection consists of 75,000 programs and commercials). The museum was founded by former CBS head William Paley, in a building designed by Philip Johnson. Selected programs are also presented on large screens, which can range from "Barbra Streisand: The Television Performances" to little-seen Monty Python episodes; check to see what's on while you're in town.

Art for Art's Sake: The Gallery Scene

The biggest news in the art-gallery world has been the SoHo exodus. With the increasing commercialization of SoHo as a trendy shopping district, major showrooms have fled either Uptown or to far West Chelsea. But all this commotion may just be the result of natural cycles of change, evidence of which is SoHo's rising prominence on the museum scene. Now that lower Broadway has turned into a veritable museum row—with the Museum of African Art, the Guggenheim SoHo, the Alternative Museum, and the New Museum of Contemporary Art—it may be simply that art has taken root in SoHo. So those opposed to such permanence—namely, cutting-edge artists—have fled elsewhere.

All this movement only serves to underline that Manhattan is the undisputed capital of art—or, more significantly, art sales. The island has more than 500 private art galleries, selling everything from old masters to tomorrow's news. Galleries are open free to the public, generally Tuesday through Saturday from 10am to 6pm. Saturday-afternoon gallery hopping, in particular, is a favorite pastime—nobody will expect you to buy, so don't worry. It's all about looking.

The best way to winnow down your gallery choices is by perusing the Friday and Sunday *New York Times, Time Out New York, New York* magazine, or the *New Yorker*. I suggest picking a neighborhood and just browsing. But if you want to plan your gallery visits before you arrive, go online at **www.gallery-guide. com/content/current/ny** for the latest exhibition listings. You can also pick up a hard copy of the *Gallery Guide* at most galleries around town.

Although Uptown tends to be more traditional and Downtown more contemporary, there are constant surprises in both neighborhoods. Several important dealers showing contemporary painting and sculpture are playing both sides of the deck, with galleries in more than one location: **Gagosian** is at 980 Madison Ave. (☎ 212/744-2313) and 136 Wooster St. (☎ 212/228-2828); **Pace-Wildenstein** is at 32 E. 57th St. (☎ 212/421-3292) and 142 Greene St. (☎ 212/431-9224); and **Leo Castelli** is at 420 W. Broadway (☎ 212/431-5160) and 578 Broadway (☎ 212/941-9855).

UPTOWN Uptown galleries are clustered in and around the glamorous crossroads of Fifth Avenue and 57th Street as well as on and off stylish Madison

National Museum of the American Indian, George Gustav Heye Center. 1 Bowling Green (btw. State and Whitehall sts.). ☎ **212/668-6624.** www.si.edu/nmai. Free admission. Sun–Wed and Fri–Sat 10am–5pm, Thurs 10am–8pm.Subway: 1, 9 to South Ferry; 4, 5 to Bowling Green.

Part of the Smithsonian Institution, this collection is the oldest of its kind in the country. It's housed in the beautiful 1907 beaux-arts U.S. Customs House, a National Historic Landmark that's worth a look in its own right. The bulk of the extensive collection is due to move yet again, in 2002, to the new Museum on the Mall in Washington, D.C. Until then, enjoy items from the spiritual to the quotidian, collected mainly by New York banking millionaire George Gustav Heye in the beginning of this century. Despite the wealth of material here, it's poorly organized and that curse of modern museums—video displays—vie for your attention when the exhibits themselves would suffice. Exhibitions scheduled for late 1999–2000 include "Spirit Capture: Native Americans and the Photographic Image." The museum also hosts interpretive programs plus free storytelling, music, and dance presentations. For a calendar of current programs, call ☎ **212/514-3888** or 212/825-6922.

Avenue in the 60s, 70s, and 80s. Unlike their upstart West Chelsea counterparts, these blue-chip galleries maintain their quiet white-glove demeanor. They include **Mitchell-Innes & Nash,** 1018 Madison Ave. (☎ 212/744-7400); **Richard Gray,** 1018 Madison Ave. (☎ 212/472-8787); **Winston Wachter Fine Art,** 39 E. 78th St. (☎ 212/327-2526); and **James Danziger,** 851 Madison Ave. (☎ 212/734-5300), a dealer in fine photographs who left SoHo after 8 years. Other major galleries include **Mary Boone,** 745 Fifth Ave. (☎ 212/752-2929), a major relocation from SoHo, known for her success with Ross Bleckner, Eric Fischl, and Malcolm Morley; **Hirschl & Adler,** 21 E. 70th St. (☎ 212/535-8810), 18th- to 20th-century European and American painting; **Kennedy,** 730 Fifth Ave., 2nd floor (☎ 212/541-9600), 18th- to 20th-century American painting; **Knoedler & Co.,** 19 E. 70th St. (☎ 212/794-0550), Helen Frankenthaler, Nancy Graves, David Smith, Frank Stella; **Wildenstein,** the classical big brother of PaceWildenstein, 19 E. 64th St. (☎ 212/879-0500), old master and Renaissance paintings and drawings.

DOWNTOWN Don't count **SoHo** out yet. The neighborhood does remain colorful, if less edgy than it used to be, and centered on West Broadway between Houston Street and Chinatown. In far **West Chelsea,** north and south of West 23rd Street and mostly between Tenth and Eleventh avenues, are a number of galleries, often in former garages and abandoned warehouses. If you're interested in the cutting edge, it's worth coming down just to browse around.

O. K. Harris, 383 W. Broadway (☎ 212/431-3600), shows a wide and fascinating variety of contemporary painting, sculpture, and photography; **Louis K. Meisel,** 141 Prince St. (☎ 212/677-1340), photorealism and other contemporary works; **Holly Solomon,** 172 Mercer St. (☎ 212/941-5777), mixed-media pieces and works by emerging artists. Other dealers in contemporary art from Cy Twombly to Nan Goldin include **Paula Cooper,** 534 W. 21st St. (☎ 212/255-1105); **Morris Healey,** 530 W. 22nd St. (☎ 212/243-3753); **Matthew Marks**, 522 W. 24th St. (☎ 212/243-1650); **Barbara Gladstone**, 515 W. 24th St. (☎ 212/206-9300); and **Alexander & Bonin**, 132 Tenth Ave. (☎ 212/367-7474).

New Museum of Contemporary Art. 583 Broadway (btw. Houston and Prince sts.). ☎ 212/219-1222. www.newmuseum.org. $5 adults, $3 seniors, students, and artists; free Thurs 6–8pm. Thurs–Sat noon–8pm, Sun and Wed noon–6pm. Subway: N, R to Prince St.; B, D, F, Q to Broadway–Lafayette St.

With 33,000 new square feet of space on Broadway, SoHo's burgeoning museum row (also home to the Guggenheim SoHo, the Museum of African Art, and the Alternative Museum), and the former curator of contemporary art at the Whitney as its brand-new director, the New Museum is now a prime contender on the museum scene. This contemporary arts museum has moved closer to the mainstream in recent years, but it's still close to the edge as far as most of us are concerned, so expect some adventurous and well-curated exhibitions. Subject matter on the schedule for late 1999–2000 includes "The Time of Our Lives," examining the concept of age and aging in Western society; "Picturing the Modern Amazon," a show devoted to representations of hypermuscular and physically strong women; and retrospectives of Brazilian artist Cildo Meireles and video artist/feminist Martha Rosler.

New-York Historical Society. 2 W. 77th St. (at Central Park W.). ☎ **212/873-3400.** www. nyhistory.org. Admission $5 adults, $3 seniors and students, free for children 12 and under. Tues–Sun 11am–5pm. Subway: B, C to 81st St.; 1, 9 to 79th St.

Launched in 1804, the New-York Historical Society is a major repository of American history, culture, and art, with a special focus on the New York region. The grand neo-classical edifice is undergoing major renovations, expected to be complete in early 2000, that will transform the fourth floor into a state-of-the-art study facility and gallery displaying highlights from the fine- and decorative-arts collections. In the meantime, check the schedule of temporary exhibits, which has featured subjects as wide-ranging as "New York's Finest: A History of the NYPD" to "Secrets of a Beautiful Face: Beauty Product Advertisements." On the second floor, a small selection of colorful Tiffany lamps is on display, and paintings from Hudson River School artists such as Thomas Cole, Asher Durand, and Frederic Church hang in the Luman Reed Gallery.

Schomburg Center for Research in Black Culture. 515 Malcolm X Blvd. (btw. 135th and 136th sts.). ☎ **212/491-2200.** www.nypl.org. Free admission. Mon–Wed noon–8pm, Thurs–Sat 10am–6pm, Sun 1–5pm. Subway: 2, 3 to 135th St.

The Schomburg Center is a research branch of the New York Public Library (see "Skyscrapers & Other Architectural Marvels," below), and it played a central role in the Harlem Renaissance. Arthur Schomburg, a Puerto Rican black, set himself to accumulating materials about blacks in America, and his collection is now housed and preserved here. The center hosts changing exhibits such as "Black New York Artists of the 20th Century," and performing arts events. Make an appointment—it'll be worth your while—to see the 1930s murals by Harlem Renaissance artist Aaron Douglas.

Studio Museum. 144 W. 125th St. (btw. Malcolm X [a.k.a. Lenox Ave.] and Adam Clayton Powell blvds.). ☎ **212/864-4500.** Admission $5 adults, $3 seniors and students, $1 children under 12. Wed–Fri 10am–5pm, Sat–Sun 1–6pm. Subway: 2, 3 to 125th St.

This museum is devoted to the historical and contemporary works of black artists. It also exhibits historic photographs of Harlem and has in its permanent collection fascinating works by James VanDerZee of the Harlem Renaissance. The museum offers a variety of special concerts, readings, and the like.

Theodore Roosevelt Birthplace. 28 E. 20th St. (btw. Broadway and Park Ave. S.). ☎ **212/ 260-1616.** Admission $2 adults, free for children under 17. Wed–Sun 9am–5pm. Subway: 6 to 23rd St.; N, R to Broadway/23rd St.

The present building is a faithful reconstruction, inside and out, on the same site of the brownstone where Theodore Roosevelt was born on October 27, 1858. The powder-blue parlor is in the rococo-revival style popular at the time, the stately green dining room boasts horsehair-covered chairs, and the children's nursery has a window that leads to a small gymnasium built to help the frail young Teddy become more "bully." About 40% of the furniture is original (another 20% belonged to family members). Tours are given every hour until 3:30pm. There's also a collection of Roosevelt memorabilia.

6 Skyscrapers & Other Architectural Marvels

For details on the World Trade Center, see p. 194; for details on the Brooklyn Bridge, see p. 185.

Impressions

It's the nearest thing to heaven we have in New York.

—Deborah Kerr to Cary Grant in
An Affair to Remember, on the Empire State Building

THE TOP BUILDINGS

Chrysler Building. 405 Lexington Ave. (at 42nd St.). Subway: 4, 5, 6, 7, S to 42nd St.–Grand Central.

Built as Chrysler Corporation headquarters in 1930 (they moved out decades ago), this is perhaps the 20th century's most romantic architectural achievement, especially at night, when the lights in its triangular openings play off its steely crown. A recent cleaning added new sparkle. As you admire the facade, be sure to note the gargoyles reaching out from the upper floors.

There's a neat tale behind this building. While it was under construction, its architect, William Van Alen, hid his final plans for the spire that now tops it. Working at a furious pace in the last days of construction, the workers assembled in secrecy the elegant pointy top—and then they raised it right through what people had assumed was going to be the roof, and for one brief moment it was the world's tallest tower (a distinction stolen by the Empire State Building only a few months later). Its exterior chrome sculptures are magnificent and spooky. The lavish ground-floor interior, which you can visit, is art deco to the max. The ceiling mural depicting airplanes and other early marvels of the 20th century evince the bright promise of technology. The elevators are works of art, masterfully covered in exotic woods (especially note the lotus-shaped marquetry on the doors). Although the observation deck closed long ago, developers have tossed around plans to turn the upper floors into a luxury hotel.

☺ Empire State Building. 350 Fifth Ave. (at 34th St.). ☎ **212/736-3100.** www. esbnyc.com. Observatory admission $6 adults, $3 seniors and children under 12, free for children under 5. Daily 9:30am–midnight (tickets sold until 11:30pm). Subway: B, D, F, Q, N, R to 34th St.; 6 to 33rd St.

King Kong climbed it in 1933. A plane slammed into it in 1945. The World Trade Center superseded it in 1970 as the island's tallest building. And in 1997, a gunman ascended it to stage a deadly shooting. But through it all, the Empire State Building has remained one of the city's favorite landmarks, and its signature high-rise. Completed in 1931 on what had been the site of the first Waldorf Astoria and, before that, Caroline Astor's mansion, it climbs 102 stories (1,454 feet) and now harbors the offices of fashion firms and, in its upper reaches, a jumble of high-tech broadcast equipment.

Always a conversation piece, the Empire State Building glows every night, bathed in colored floodlights to commemorate events of significance (red, white, and blue for Independence Day; green for St. Patrick's Day; red, black, and green for MLK Day; even lavender and white for Gay Pride Day). The familiar silver spire can be seen from all over the city; my favorite view is from 23rd Street, where Fifth Avenue and Broadway converge. On a lovely day, stand at the base of the Flatiron Building (see below) and gaze up Fifth: the crisp, gleaming deco tower jumps out, soaring above the office buildings that surround it.

But the views that keep nearly 3 million visitors coming every year are the ones from the 86th- and 102nd-floor **observatories.** The lower one is best—you can walk

Empire State Ticket-Buying Tip

Lines can be frightfully long at the concourse-level ticket booth, so be prepared to wait. Or, if time is more precious than money to you, consider purchasing **advance tickets** online using a credit card at **www.esbnyc.org**. You'll pay a $2 service charge for the service, but it's well worth it, especially if you're visiting during a busy season. You're not required to choose a time or date for your tickets in advance; they can be used on any regular open day. However, order them well before you leave home, because they'll take 7 to 10 days to reach you (longer if you live out of the country). With tickets in hand, you're allowed to proceed directly to the second floor—past everyone who didn't plan as well as you did!

out on a windy deck and look through coin-operated viewers (bring quarters!) over what, on a clear day, can be as much as an 80-mile visible radius. The citywide panorama is magnificent. The higher observation deck is glass-enclosed and cramped.

Light fog can create an admirably moody effect, but it goes without saying that a clear day is best. Dusk brings the most remarkable views, and the biggest crowds. Consider going in the morning, when the light is still low on the horizon, keeping glare to a minimum. Starry nights are pure magic.

In your haste to go up, don't rush through the beautiful three-story-high marble **lobby** without pausing to admire its features.

In case you haven't had enough of the real thing, **New York Skyride** (☎ 888/ SKYRIDE** or 212/279-9777; www.skyride.com) offers a short, motion-flight simulation sightseeing tour of New York on the second floor of the building. You sit on a platform that tilts and lurches to thunderous sound effects while the film takes you around and "through" New York's major landmarks (just like Star Tours). A high point: It lets you feel what it's like to fall from the building—what fun! Tickets are $11.50 for adults, $9.50 for kids, and the ride is open daily from 10am to 10pm— but unless the kids insist, skip it. There are far better ways to spend your hard-earned dollars in this city.

✪ **Grand Central Terminal.** 42nd St. at Park Ave. www.grandcentralterminal.com. Subway: 4, 5, 6, 7, S to 42nd St.–Grand Central.

After more than 2 years and $175 million, Grand Central Terminal has come out from under the tarps and scaffolding. Rededicated with all the appropriate pomp and circumstance on October 1, 1998, the 1913 landmark (originally designed by Warren & Wetmore with Reed & Stem) has been reborn as one of the most magnificent public spaces in the country. The restoration, by the New York firm of Beyer Blinder Belle, is an utter triumph. Their work has reanimated the genius of the station's original intent: to inspire those who pass through this urban meeting point with lofty feelings of civic pride and appreciation for Western architectural traditions. In short, they've put the "grand" back into Grand Central.

By all means, come and visit, even if you're not catching one of the subway lines or Metro North commuter trains that rumble through the bowels of this great place. And even if you arrive and leave by subway, be sure to exit the station, walking a couple of blocks south, to about 40th Street, before you turn around to admire Jules-Alexis Coutan's neoclassical sculpture *Transportation* hovering over the south entrance, with a majestically buff Mercury, the Roman god of commerce and travel, as its central figure.

The greatest visual impact hits when you enter the vast **main concourse.** Cleansed of decades of grime and cheezy advertisements, it is majestic. The high windows once again allow sunlight to penetrate the space, glinting off the half-acre Tennessee marble floor. The brass clock over the central kiosk gleams, as do the gold- and nickel-plated chandeliers piercing the side archways. The masterful **sky ceiling,** again a brilliant greenish blue, depicts the constellations of the winter sky above New York. The stars are surrounded by dazzling 24-karat gold and emit light fed through fiber-optic cables, their intensities roughly replicating the magnitude of the actual stars as seen from Earth. Look carefully, and you'll see a patch near one corner left unrestored as a reminder of the neglect once visited on this splendid overhead masterpiece. On the east end of the main concourse, a grand **marble staircase** has been built, as the original plans had always intended.

This dramatic beaux-arts splendor serves as a hub of social activity as well. New retail shops and restaurants have taken over the mezzanine and lower levels. The highlight of the mezzanine is **Michael Jordan's—The Steak House,** a gorgeous art-deco space; stop into the welcoming, comfortable bar, where you can enjoy the marvelous views for the price of a drink. Off the main concourse at street level there's a nice mix of specialty shops and national retailers, including **Banana Republic** and **Kenneth Cole.** The **lower concourse** houses newsstands, a food court, and the famous **Oyster Bar,** also restored to its original Old World glory (see chapter 6).

✪ Rockefeller Center. Between 47th and 50th sts., from Fifth to Sixth aves. ☎ **212/632-3975.** Subway: B, D, F, Q to 47th–50th sts./Rockefeller Center.

A streamline modern masterpiece, Rockefeller Center is one of New York's central gathering spots for visitors and New Yorkers alike. A prime example of the city's skyscraper spirit and historic sense of optimism, it was erected mainly in the 1930s, when the city was deep in a depression as well as its most passionate art-deco phase. Designated a National Historic Landmark in 1988, it's now the world's largest privately owned business-and-entertainment center, with 18 buildings on 21 acres.

For a dramatic approach to the entire complex, start at Fifth Avenue between 49th and 50th streets. The builders purposely created the gentle slope of the Promenade, known here as the **Channel Gardens** because it's flanked to the south by La Maison Française and to the north by the British Building (the Channel, get it?). You'll also find a number of attractive shops along here, including a big branch of the **Metropolitan Museum of Art Store.** The Promenade leads to the **Lower Plaza,** home to the famous ice-skating rink in winter (see next paragraph) and alfresco dining in summer in the shadow of Paul Manship's gilded bronze statue *Prometheus.* All around, the flags of the United Nations' member countries flap in the breeze. Just behind *Prometheus,* in December and early January, towers the city's official and majestic Christmas tree.

The **Rink at Rockefeller Plaza** (☎ 212/332-7654), is tiny but positively romantic, especially during the holidays, when the giant Christmas tree's multicolored lights twinkle from above. It's open from mid-October to mid-March, and you'll skate under the magnificent tree for the month of December.

The focal point of this "city within a city" is the **GE Building,** at 30 Rockefeller Plaza, a 70-story showpiece towering over the plaza. It's still one of the city's most impressive buildings; walk through for a look at the granite-marble lobby, lined with monumental sepia-toned murals by José Maria Sert. You can pick up a walking tour brochure highlighting the center's art and architecture at the main information desk in this building.

NBC television maintains studios throughout the complex. *Saturday Night Live,* the *Rosie O'Donnell Show,* and *Late Night with Conan O'Brien* are shot in the GE Building (see "Talk of the Town: Free TV Tapings" later in this chapter for tips on getting free tickets). If you're a fan of NBC's *Today* show, the glass-enclosed studio from which the show is broadcast live weekdays from 7 to 9am is on the southwest corner of 49th Street and Rockefeller Plaza; come early, and bring your HI MOM! sign. One-hour **NBC Studio Tours** (☎ 212/664-7174) run every 15 minutes daily from 9:15am to 4:30pm from Easter through Labor Day and Thanksgiving through New Year's, and every half hour Monday through Saturday at other times of the year. Tickets are $10 per person, and children under 6 are not admitted. The tours offer a moderately interesting look at the behind-the-scenes action at a TV studio; but if money's tight, yours is probably best spent elsewhere. (If you can get tickets to a free TV taping, you'll find it far more enlightening.)

Other notable buildings throughout the complex are the **International Building,** on Fifth Avenue between 50th and 51st streets, worth a look for its *Atlas* statue out front; and the **McGraw-Hill Building,** on Sixth Avenue between 48th and 49th streets, with its 50-foot sun triangle on the plaza. **Radio City Music Hall,** 1260 Sixth Ave., at 50th Street (☎ 212/247-4777), is perhaps the most impressive architectural feat of the complex. Designed by Donald Donald Deskey, it's one of the largest indoor theaters, with 6,200 seats. But its true grandeur is in its magnificent art-deco appointments. The crowning touch is the stage's great proscenium arch, which from the distant seats evokes a faraway sun setting on the horizon of the sea. The men's and women's lounges are also splendid. The theater is currently under renovation, but is scheduled to reopen in October 1999, in plenty of time for the season's **Christmas Spectacular,** starring the Rockettes. At that time, the illuminating 1-hour **Grand Tour** (☎ 212/632-4041) will also be reintroduced; call for the latest schedule and prices.

United Nations. At First Ave. and 46th St. ☎ **212/963-8687.** www.un.org. Guided tours $7.50 adults, $5.50 seniors, $4.50 students, $3.50 children (those under 5 not permitted). Daily tours every half hour 9:15am–4:45pm; closed weekends Jan–Feb. Subway: 4, 5, 6, 7, S to 42nd St.–Grand Central.

In the midst of what some consider the most cynical city is this working monument to world peace. U.N. headquarters occupies 18 acres of international territory—neither New York City nor the United States has jurisdiction here—along the East River from 42nd to 48th streets. Designed by an international team of architects (led by American Wallace K. Harrison and including Le Corbusier) and finished in 1952, the complex weds the 39-story glass slab Secretariat with the free-form General Assembly on beautifully landscaped grounds donated by John D. Rockefeller, Jr. One hundred eighty nations use the facilities to arbitrate worldwide disputes.

Guided 1-hour tours take you to the General Assembly Hall and the Security Council Chamber and introduce the history and activities of the United Nations and its related organizations. Along the tour you'll see donated objects and artwork, including charred artifacts from the atomic bombings of Hiroshima and Nagasaki, stained-glass windows by Chagall, a replica of the first *Sputnik,* and a colorful mosaic called *The Golden Rule* based on a Norman Rockwell drawing.

If you take the time to wander the beautifully landscaped **grounds,** you'll be rewarded with lovely views and some surprises. The mammoth monument *Good Defeats Evil,* donated by the Soviet Union in 1990, depicts a contemporary St. George slaying a dragon, made from parts of a Russian ballistic missile and an American Pershing missile.

The **Delegates' Dining Room** (☎ 212/963-7625), which has great views of the East River, is open to the public on weekdays for lunch 11:30am to 2:30pm (reserve in advance). The **gift shop** sells goodies from all over the world, and the **post office** sells unique U.N. stamps that can be purchased and posted only here.

OTHER NOTABLE STRUCTURES & ENGINEERING FEATS

In addition to the landmarks below, architecture buffs may also want to seek out these notable buildings: The **Lever House,** built in 1952 at 390 Park Ave., between 53rd and 54th streets, and the neighboring **Seagram Building** (1958), just west at 375 Park Ave., are the city's best examples of the form-follows-function, glass-and-steel International style, with the latter designed by master architect Mies van der Rohe himself. Also in Midtown East is the **Sony Building,** at 550 Madison Ave., designed in 1984 by Philip Johnson with a pretty rose-granite facade and a playful Chippendale-style top.

The Upper West Side is home to two of the city's prime examples of residential architecture. On Broadway taking up the block between 73rd and 74th streets is the **Ansonia,** looking for all the world like a flamboyant architectural wedding cake. This splendid beaux-arts building has been home to the likes of Stravinsky, Toscanini, and Caruso thanks to its virtually soundproof apartments; it was also featured prominently as the residence in *Single White Female.* Even more notable is the **Dakota,** at 72nd Street and Central Park West. Legend has it that the angular 1884 apartment house—accented with gables, dormers, and oriel windows that give it a brooding appeal—earned its name when its forward-thinking developer, Edward S. Clark, was teased by friends that he was building so far north of the city that he might as well be building in the Dakotas. The building's most famous resident, John Lennon, was gunned down outside the 72nd Street entrance on December 8, 1980, by Mark David Chapman; Yoko Ono still lives inside, while the all-grown-up Sean has since relocated to a Downtown loft.

For City Hall and the Woolworth Building, see the walking tour under "Historic Lower Manhattan's Top Attractions" earlier in this chapter.

✪ **Cathedral of St. John the Divine.** 1047 Amsterdam Ave. (at 112th St.). ☎ **212/ 316-7540,** or 212/932-7347 for tour information and reservations. www.stjohndivine.org. Suggested admission $2; tour $3; tower tour $10. Mon–Sat 8am–6pm, Sun 7am–7:30pm. Tours offered Tues–Sat 11am, Sun 1pm; tower tours 1st and 3rd Sat of the month at noon and 2pm. Services Mon–Sat 7:15am and 12:15 and 5:30pm; Sun 8, 9, and 11am and 7pm. Subway: 1, 9, B, C to Cathedral Pkwy.

The world's largest Gothic cathedral, St. John the Divine has been a work in progress since 1892. Its sheer size is amazing enough—a nave that stretches two football fields and a seating capacity of 5,000—but keep in mind that there is no steel structural support. The church is being built using traditional Gothic engineering; blocks of granite and limestone are carved out by master masons and their apprentices (some from the surrounding Harlem neighborhood). Construction is still going on, more than 100 years after it began, with no end in sight. But what makes this place so wonderful is that finishing isn't necessarily the point.

Though the seat of the Episcopal Diocese of New York, St. John's embraces an interfaith tradition. Internationalism is a theme found throughout; each chapel is dedicated to a different national or ethnic group. You can explore it on the **Public Tour,** offered six days a week, or on the twice-monthly **Vertical Tour,** which takes you up the 11-flight circular staircase to the top, for spectacular views. The cathedral is known for presenting outstanding musical events and important speakers. The free **New Year's Eve concert** draws thousands of New Yorkers; so, too, does its annual **Blessing of the Animals,** held in early October (see the "New York City Calendar of Events" in chapter 2). Call ☎ **212/662-2133** for event information and tickets.

If need a snack after your tour, stop into the lovely, worn **Hungarian Pastry Shop,** 1030 Amsterdam Ave., between 110th and 111th streets (☎ 212/866-4230), a favorite among Columbia University students. Order a plateful of crumbly, buttery cookies from the display case up front, then set up camp; this is another place you won't be rushed out of.

Flatiron Building. 175 Fifth Ave. (at 23rd St.). Subway: R to 23rd St.

This triangular masterpiece was one of the first skyscrapers. Its knife-blade wedge shape is the only way the building could fill the triangular property created by the intersection of Fifth Avenue and Broadway, and that happy coincidence created one of the city's most distinctive buildings. Built in 1902 and fronted with limestone and terra cotta (not iron), the Flatiron measures only 6 feet across at its narrow end. So called for its resemblance to the laundry appliance, it was originally named the Fuller Building, then later "Burnham's Folly." (Folks were certain that architect Daniel Burnham's 21-story structure would fall down. It didn't.) There's no observation deck, and the building mainly houses publishing offices, but a few shops do grace the ground floor. The building has given its name to the surrounding area—the Flatiron District, home to a bevy of smart new restaurants and shops (see "Manhattan's Neighborhoods in Brief" in chapter 4 for more on the surrounding 'hood).

Ford Foundation Building. 320 E. 43rd St. (at Second Ave.). ☎ **212/573-5000.** Subway: 4, 5, 6, 7, S to 42nd St.–Grand Central.

On your way to or from the United Nations, stop in the Ford Foundation Building for a stroll in its magnificent interior garden (open to the public weekdays from 9am to 5pm). The ⅓-acre landscape thrives with a small pond, greenery, and full-grown trees rising up under the 12-story glass-enclosed greenhouse. This is a fine example of what modern public spaces should be like. Even if the Kevin Roche design weren't so pleasing, a visit would be in order for the peace it affords.

New York Public Library. Fifth Ave. and 42nd St. ☎ **212/869-8089** (exhibits and events) or 212/661-7220 (library hours). www.nypl.org. Free admission to all exhibitions. Main Reading Room and exhibition halls, Mon and Thurs–Sat 10am–6pm, Tues–Wed 11am–6pm. Subway: B, D, F, Q to 42nd St.; 4, 5, 6, 7, S to Grand Central/42nd St.

The New York Public Library, adjacent to Bryant Park (see "Urban Oases: Central Park & Other Places to Play," below) and designed by Carrère & Hastings (1911), is one of the country's finest examples of beaux-arts architecture, a majestic structure of white Vermont marble with Corinthian columns and allegorical statues. Before climbing the broad flight of steps to the Fifth Avenue entrance, take note of the famous lion sculptures, Fortitude on the right, Patience on the left—so dubbed by whip-smart former mayor Fiorello La Guardia. At Christmastime they don natty wreaths to keep warm.

This library is actually the **Humanities and Social Sciences Library,** only one of the research libraries in the New York Public Library system. The fine interior features **Astor Hall,** with high arched marble ceilings and grand staircases. The stupendous **Main Reading Rooms** have reopened after a massive restoration and modernization that both brought them back to their stately glory and moved them into the computer age (goodbye, card catalogs!).

Even if you don't stop in to peruse the periodicals, you may want to check out one of the **exhibits,** which can range from "The Drawings of Charles Addams" to "Netherlandish Prints at the New York Public Library" to a private collection of 17th-century maps, atlases, charts, and globes. There's also a full calendar of **lecture programs,** with past speakers ranging from Tom Stoppard to Edward Ruscha to Cokie Roberts; popular speakers often sell out, so it's a good idea to purchase tickets in advance.

There are three other research libraries in the NYPL system: The **Schomburg Center for Research in Black Culture** (see "More Manhattan Museums," above); the high-tech **Science, Industry, and Business Library,** 188 Madison Ave., 34th Street (☎ 212/592-7700); and the **New York Public Library for the Performing Arts,** normally located at 40 Lincoln Center Plaza (☎ 212/870-1630), but the collection is currently housed in different locations as the building undergoes renovations. Call the general number or ☎ **212/621-0626,** or visit the Web site to locate branch libraries throughout the five boroughs.

Roosevelt Island Tramway. Departing Second Ave. at 60th St. ☎ **212/832-4543.** www. rioc.com. $1.50 each way; seniors and travelers with disabilities pay one-way only; children under 5 ride free. Sun–Thurs 6am–2am, Fri–Sat 6am–3:30am. Departures every 7½ minutes during rush hours; every 15 minutes at other times. Subway: 4, 5, 6 to 59th St.; N, R to Lexington Ave.

Gliding 250 feet over the East River, alongside the 59th Street Bridge, you have a unique view of Midtown Manhattan. On the other side of the 4- to 5-minute ride is Roosevelt Island, a small strip of land two miles in length and at most 800 feet wide. The eerie ruins of a hospital haunt the south end, where criminals, the insane, and other "undesirables" were exiled in the 19th and early 20th centuries. Today, the island is a planned community with spacious parks, city views, and a few historic buildings—and, on average, a much higher class of tenant.

St. Patrick's Cathedral. Fifth Ave. btw. 50th and 51st sts. ☎ **212/753-2261.** Free admission. Mon–Fri and Sun 7am–8:30pm, Sat 8am–8:30pm. Mass Mon–Fri 7, 7:30, 8, and 8:30am; noon and 12:30, 1, and 5:30pm. Sat 8 and 8:30am; noon and 12:30 and 5:30pm. Sun 7, 8, 9, and 10:15am; noon and 1, 4, and 5:30pm. Subway: B, D, F, Q to 47–50th sts./Rockefeller Center.

The largest Catholic cathedral in the United States is also the seat of the Archdiocese of New York. The congregation is still presided over by John Cardinal O'Connor, having received a special dispensation to continue past the age of retirement from Pope John Paul II. Designed by James Renwick, begun in 1858, and consecrated in 1878, St. Patrick's wasn't completed until 1906. Strangely, Irish Catholics picked one of the city's WASPiest neighborhoods for this Gothic church, constructed of white marble and stone. Look for Mother Elizabeth Seton, the first American-born saint, among the statues in the nave.

Spanish & Portuguese Synagogue (Congregation Shearith Israel). 2 W. 70th St. (at Central Park W.). ☎ **212/873-0300.** Free admission. Call synagogue for service schedule. Subway: 1, 2, 3, 9, B, C to 72nd St.

This is the oldest Jewish congregation in the United States, dating back to 1654, when the first refugees fleeing the Spanish Inquisition arrived in New Amsterdam. The interior of the 1897 classic-revival building is impressive, especially the Tiffany windows. The congregation follows Sephardic tradition.

Temple Emanu–El. 1 E. 65th St. (at Fifth Ave.). ☎ **212/744-1400.** www.emanuelnyc.org. Free admission. Daily 10am–5pm. Services Sun–Thurs 5:30pm, Fri 5:15pm, Sat 10:30am. Subway: 6 to 68th St.; N, R to Fifth Ave.

Many of New York's most prominent and wealthy families are members of this congregation, housed in the city's most famous synagogue. The largest Reform synagogue in the world is a blend of Moorish and Romanesque styles, symbolizing the mingling of Eastern and Western cultures. The **Bernard Museum** houses a small but remarkable collection of Judaica, including a collection of Hanukkah lamps from the 14th to the 20th centuries. There are also three galleries telling the story of the congregation Emanu–El from 1845 to the present.

7 Affordable Sightseeing Tours

Reservations are required on some of the tours listed below, but even if they're not it's always best to call ahead to confirm prices, times, and meeting places.

DOUBLE-DECKER BUS TOURS

Taking a narrated sightseeing tour is one of the best ways to see and learn quickly about New York's major sights and neighborhoods. However, keep in mind that the commentary is only as good as the guide, who is seldom an expert. Tour guides tend toward hyperbole, and might get a few of the facts wrong. Clyde Haberman of the *New York Times* recently found tour-bus guides spouting such inaccuracies as 65 people were killed in the World Trade Center blast (it was 6), New York has the oldest subway system in the world (third, behind London and Boston), Frank Sinatra was born in Jersey City (Hoboken), and Herald Square was named after the founder of the New York Herald Tribune (there was no Mr. Herald). But the idea is to see the highlights, not write a dissertation from this stuff. So enjoy the ride—and take the "facts" you hear along the way with a grain of salt.

○ **Gray Line New York Tours.** In the Port Authority Bus Terminal, Eighth Ave. and 42nd St. ☎ 212/397-2600. www.graylinenewyork.com. Hop-on, hop-off bus tours from $22 adults, $13 children 5–11; basic full-city tour $33 adults, $21 children. Check Web site for online booking discounts (10% at press time). Operates daily. Subway: A, C, E to 42nd St.

Gray Line offers just about every sightseeing tour option and combination you could imagine. There are double-decker bus tours by day and by night that run Uptown, Downtown, and all around the town; bus combos with Circle Line cruises, helicopter flights, museum entrances, and guided visits of sights. Two-day options are available, as are some out-of-town day trips (even a full day at Woodbury Commons, if the hardcore bargain hunters among you can't resist an opportunity for outlet shopping).

There's no real point to some of the combination tours—you don't need a guide to take you to the top of the World Trade Center or to the Statue of Liberty, and you don't save any money on admission by buying the combo ticket—but others are worth it—the Sunday Harlem Gospel tour, for example, which features a tour of Harlem's top sights and a gospel service, is worth the $33 price tag ($24 for kids 5–11). I've found Gray Line to put a higher premium on accuracy than the other big tour-bus operators, so this is your best bet among the biggies. There's also a sales office in the Times Square Visitors Center, 1560 Broadway, between 46th and 47th streets.

New York Apple Tours. Eighth Ave. at 53rd St.; tours also depart from three other stops in Midtown. ☎ 800/876-9868 (information) or 212/944-9200 (reservations). www.nyappletours.com. Hop-on, hop-off bus tours from $21 adults, $12 children under 12; full-city tour $35 adults, $22 children. 10% discount if tickets purchased in advance with major credit card. Multi-tour booking discounts available. Operates daily. Subway: C, E to 50th St.

This company operates a smaller slate of tours than competitor Gray Line, all aboard double-decker buses, but they do have a few twists, such as a tour of Brooklyn's major attractions. Most tours allow to hop on and off as much as you like along your purchased route for two days. New York Apple is the least reliable when it comes to the facts, so I suggest sticking with Gray Line instead.

New York Double-Decker Tours. In the Empire State Building, 350 Fifth Ave., Suite 4721 (at 34th St.). ☎ 800/692-2870 or 212/967-6008. www.nycdouble-decker.com. Hop-on, hop-off bus tours start at $20 adults, $12 children 12 and under; basic full-city tour $30 adults, $18 children. Visit Web site for online discount coupon (10% at press time). Operates daily. Subway: B, D, F, N, Q, R to 34th St.

Here's yet another variation on the theme, not really adding anything new or better to the mix. The basic routes are available on a 2-day hop-on, hop-off basis. They'll even take you to Niagra Falls, if you want. You can buy tickets to sights, including the Statue of Liberty and the World Trade Center observation deck, in the office before you board the bus so you won't have to wait in line later.

HARBOR CRUISES

If you'd like to sail the New York Harbor aboard the 1885 cargo schooner *Pioneer,* see the listing for South Street Seaport & Museum above under "Historic Lower Manhattan's Top Attractions."

✪ **Circle Line Sightseeing Cruises.** Departing from Pier 83, at W. 42nd St. and Twelfth Ave. and Pier 16 at South Street Seaport, 207 Front St. ☎ **212/563-3200** or 212/630-8888. www.circleline.com. Cruises from $12 adults, $6 children under 12; 3-hour Full Island cruise $22 adults, $12 children. Operates daily. Subway to Pier 83: A, C, E to 42nd St. Subway to Pier 16: J, M, Z, 2, 3, 4, 5 to Fulton St.

Circle Line is the only tour company that circumnavigates the entire 35 miles around Manhattan, and I love this ride. It takes 3 hours and passes by the World Trade Center, the Statue of Liberty, Ellis Island, the Brooklyn Bridge, the United Nations, Yankee Stadium, the George Washington Bridge, and more, including Manhattan's wild northern tip. The panorama is riveting, and the commentary isn't bad. The big boats are basic but fine, with lots of deck room for everybody to enjoy the view. Snacks, soft drinks, coffee, and beer are available onboard for purchase.

If 3 hours is more than you or the kids can handle, go for either the 1½-hour **Semi-Circle** or **Sunset** cruise ($18 adults, $10 kids), both of which show you the highlights of the skyline. There's also a 1-hour **Seaport Liberty** version ($12 adults, $6 kids) that sticks close to the south end of the island. But of all the tours, the kids might like **The Beast** best, a thrill-a-minute speedboat ride offered in summer only ($15 adults, $10 kids).

In addition, a number of adults-only **Music Cruises** are regularly offered in summer. Depending on the night of the week, you can groove to the sounds of jazz, Latin, gospel, or a DJ spinning dance tracks as you sail along the skyline. Call, check the Web site, or stop into the sales office in the Times Square Visitors Center, 1560 Broadway (between 46th and 47th streets), for details.

New York Waterway. Most tours departing from Pier 78, at W. 38th St. and Twelfth Ave. (Free bus pickup from 3 Midtown locations.) ☎ **800/533-3779.** www.nywaterway.com. Cruises from $11.50 adults, $5.50 children under 13. 90-min harbor cruises $18 adults, $9 children. Operates daily late Mar–Dec; limited service Jan–Mar. Subway: A, C, E to 42nd St.

New York Waterway offers similar 1½-hour narrated cruises to those offered by Circle Line. Their primary cruise is a **New York Harbor** trip showcasing the skyline's highlights. **Twilight** cruises are also offered from May to November, including Broadway show tune and disco versions where kids are welcome (unlike Circle Line's theme cruises). Additionally, New York Waterway offers a **Lower Harbor** cruise, a short-and-sweet, 45-minute tour around the Statue of Liberty, the Brooklyn Bridge, and lower Manhattan, from Pier 17 at South Street Seaport. Land-and-sea combo packages are also available with New York Apple Tours (see "Double-Decker Bus Tours," above).

Their city cruises may have little new to offer, but New York Waterway also has two exceptional day-long Hudson River cruises (May–Nov; $60 per person), which combine with historic sightseeing in the Hudson River Valley: The **Sleepy Hollow Cruise** features a working 17th-century Dutch-Colonial farm and then Sunnyside, the riverside home of Washington Irving; the **Kykuit Cruise** includes a tour of Kykuit, a Rockefeller family estate that's a Hudson Valley gem. There's also a 2-hour **North Hudson** river-only cruise ($15 adults, $8 kids) that's particularly wonderful in early autumn. The Kykuit Cruise is immensely popular and must be reserved well in advance. You can also spend the day on the beach at **Sandy Hook,** located in the Gateway National Recreation Area ($25 adults, $12.50 kids); this is a great way to beat the shore traffic.

Lastly, you can pair a cruise with a ball game by taking either the **Yankee Clipper** or the **Mets Express** from various points in Manhattan to the stadium; call or go online for details.

Spirit Cruises. Departing from Pier 61 (at Chelsea Piers), W. 23rd St. ☎ **212/727-2789.** 2 to 2½-hour lunch cruises $26.65–$33.80; 3-hour dinner cruises $50.70–$61.40. Inquire about children's rates. Operates daily May–Nov. Subway: C, E to 23rd St.

Spirit Cruises' three modern ships are floating cabarets that combine sightseeing in New York Harbor with freshly prepared meals, musical revues, and dancing to live bands. The atmosphere is festive and fun. The buffet meals are nothing special, but they're fine.

If you live or are staying outside the city, there's no need to drive into Manhattan. Cruises also depart from Lincoln Harbor Marina in Weehawken, New Jersey; call ☎ **201/867-6201** for details.

SPECIALTY TOURS
✪ MUSEUMS & CULTURAL ORGANIZATIONS

The **Municipal Art Society** (☎ 212/935-3960; www.mas.org) offers excellent historical and architectural walking tours aimed at intelligent, individualistic travelers, not the mass market. Each is led by a highly qualified guide who provides insights into the history and significance of buildings and neighborhoods. Topics range from the urban history of Greenwich Village to "Money Matters: The Interiors of Wall Street." Weekday walking tours are $10 for adults, $8 for students and seniors, and reservations are not usually necessary; prices for weekend walking tours vary, and reservations are highly recommended. A full schedule of upcoming tours is available online.

The **92nd Street Y** (☎ 212/415-5628 or 212/415-5420; www.92ndsty.org) offers a wonderful variety of **walking tours,** many featuring funky themes or behind-the-scenes visits. Subjects can range from "Diplomat for a Day at the U.N" to "Secrets of the Chelsea Hotel" to "Artists of the Meatpacking District" to "Jewish Harlem." Prices range from $18 to $60, but many include ferry rides, afternoon tea, dinner, or whatever suits the program. Guides are well-chosen experts, ranging from highly respected historians to an East Village poet, mystic, and art critic (for "Allen Ginsberg's New York" and "East Village Night Spots"), and many routes travel into the outer boroughs.

But Was There a *Real* Puffy Shirt?

Now that *Seinfeld* lives only in syndication, Kenny Kramer, former across-the-hall neighbor of show co-creator Larry David and the real-life inspiration for Cosmo Kramer ("Giddy-up!"), hopes his 3-hour **Kramer's Reality Tour for Seinfeld Fans** can fill the void. The tour starts out kind of hokey, but really gets going once you board the van (equipped with TV monitors showing clips of the show) and hit the road. Among the many stops are the real Monk's, Tom's Restaurant (also immortalized in song by Suzanne Vega); the office building where Elaine worked, Kramer had his coffee-table book published, and George had sex with the cleaning lady on his desk; and the vegetable stand where Kramer was banned for squeezing fruit. There's lots of trivia and anecdotes along the way, and Kenny does a good job keeping the crowd entertained. He's an official guide licensed by the city, so expect a good dose of general New York trivia, too. Tours are offered Saturday and Sunday at noon, and tickets are $37.50—pricey, but worth it for die-hard fans. Reservations are required (☎ 800/KRAMERS or 212/268-5525; www.kennykramer.com). *Tip:* Buy some soup if the Soup Nazi's open, because the pizza is less than inspiring.

Show Me, Show Me, Show Me: Free Walking Tours

A number of neighborhood organizations and business improvement districts (BIDs) offer free guided walks to highlight the new developments and hidden joys of their neighborhoods. For travelers on a budget, these introductory freebies are well worth taking advantage of:

The **34th Street Tour,** sponsored by the 34th Street Partnership (☎ 212/868-0521), reveals the stories behind the buildings under the guidance of architectural historian Francis Morron and architect Alan Neumann. Tours are offered Thursdays at 12:30pm; meet at the Fifth Avenue entrance to the Empire State Building.

The **Times Square Tour,** sponsored by the Times Square Visitors Center, 1560 Broadway, between 46th and 47th streets (☎ 212/768-1560; www.timessquarebid.org), offers a behind-the-scenes look at the Theater District's architecture, history, and current trends. Led by an actor, the tours are animated and enlightening. Be at the center Friday at noon.

The **Orchard Street Bargain District Tour,** sponsored by the Lower East Side Business Improvement District (☎ 888/VALUES-4-U or 212/226-9010), explores the general history and long-standing retail culture of this historic neighborhood. This is a particularly good bet for bargain-hunters, who will learn all about the famous Old World shops and newer outlet stores in this discount-shopping destination. The free tours are offered Sundays at 11am from April to December, rain or shine, and no reservation is required. Meet up with the guide in front of Katz's Delicatessen, 205 E. Houston St., at Ludlow Street.

Although none of the above tours require reservations, it's a good idea to call ahead to confirm meeting times and places, since life is always subject to change.

On Wednesdays at 12:30pm, the Municipal Art Society sponsors a free tour of **Grand Central Terminal** (although donations are accepted); call ☎ 212/935-3960 to confirm the schedule and meeting spot.

If you're looking to tour another neighborhood with an expert guide, call **Big Apple Greeter** (☎ 212/669-8159; www.bigapplegreeter.org). This non-profit organization is comprised of specially trained New Yorkers who volunteer to take visitors around town for a free 2- to 4-hour tour of a particular neighborhood. Reservations must be made in advance, preferably at least 1 week ahead of your arrival. Big Apple Greeter is also well suited to accommodate disabled travelers; see "Tips for Travelers with Special Needs" in chapter 2 for details.

The 92nd Street Y also offers a full range of day-long **bus tours** beyond Manhattan, which are equally compelling; prices generally range from $50 to $90. Advance registration is required for all tours. Schedules are planned out a few months in advance, so check the Web site for tours that might interest you.

INDEPENDENT OPERATORS

One of the most highly praised sightseeing organizations in New York is ✪ **Big Onion Walking Tours** (☎ 212/439-1090; www.bigonion.com). Enthusiastic Big Onion guides (all hold an advanced degree in American history from Columbia or New York universities) peel back the layers of history to reveal the city's inner secrets. The 2-hour tours are offered mostly on weekends, and subjects include the "The Bowery," "Presidential New York," "Irish New York," "Central Park," "Greenwich Village in Twilight," "Historic Harlem," and numerous historic takes on Lower Manhattan.

One of the most popular programs is the "Multi-ethnic Eating Tour" of the Lower East Side, where you munch on everything from dim sum to dill pickles to fresh mozzarella. Tour prices range from $10 to $16 for adults, $8 to $14 for students and seniors. No reservations are necessary, but Big Onion strongly recommends that you call to verify schedules.

All tours offered by ✪ **Joyce Gold History Tours of New York** (☎ 212/242-5762; www.nyctours.com) are led by Joyce Gold herself, an instructor of Manhattan history at New York University and the New School for Social Research, who has been conducting history walks of New York since 1975. Her tours can really cut to the core of this town; Joyce is full of fascinating stories about Manhattan and its people. Tours are arranged around themes like "The Colonial Settlers of Wall Street," "The Genius and Elegance of Gramercy Park," "Downtown Graveyards," and "TriBeCa: The Creative Explosion." Tours are offered most weekends March to December and last from 2 to 4 hours. The price is $12 per person; no reservations are required. Private tours are available if you're traveling with a group.

Alfred Pommer has conducted **New York City Cultural Walking Tours** (☎ 212/979-2388) of nearly every Manhattan neighborhood for more than 15 years. He focuses on history and architecture, making the past come alive via photographs and stories. A number of his tours concentrate on specific subjects, such as "Gargoyles in Manhattan" and "Rockefeller Center's Public Art." His 2- to 2½-hour tours take place Sundays at 2pm from March through December; the charge is $10 per person. Private tours are available at $15 per hour for one to three people or $25 per hour for four or more.

A landscape designer by trade, Patricia Olmstead offers **Urban Explorations** walking tours (☎ 718/721-5254). One of her best tours is "Hidden Gardens of New York," but her knowledge of art, architecture, history, and trivia makes each one engaging. Subjects run the gamut from "African-Americans in Colonial Times" to "Best-Decked Halls of the Holidays." Most tours are $12, $10 for students and seniors.

Behind the scenes is the focus of **Adventure on a Shoestring** (☎ 212/265-2663), a membership organization that offers 1¼-hour public walking tours on weekends year-round for just $5. One of the earliest entrants in the now burgeoning walking-tour market, Howard Goldberg has provided unique views of New York since 1963, exploring Manhattan's neighborhoods with a breezy, man-of-the-people style. Call for reservations.

Self-proclaimed "radical historian" Bruce Kayton leads unconventional **Radical Walking Tours** (☎ 718/492-0069) to conventional tourist sights. A tour of Harlem covers the Black Panthers, the Communist Party, and Malcolm X in addition to the Apollo Theater and the Schomburg Center. A Greenwich Village tour focuses on riots, folk singers, and prohibition, while a visit to the Lower East Side is incomplete without mention of radical Jews such as Abraham Cahan (founder of the influential newspaper *Forward* in 1897). Tour prices are $10, and tours last about 2½ hours; no reservations are required.

Harlem Spirituals (☎ 212/391-0900; www.munditickets.com/english/harlem. htm) specializes in gospel and jazz tours of Harlem. A variety of options is available, including a tour of Harlem and a gospel service, with a soul-food lunch (brunch on Sunday) as an add-on ($35 adults, $27 children 12 and under; $65 adults, $55 children with lunch or brunch). Evening tours of Harlem can be paired with visits to a jazz club and a "behind-the-scenes" gospel choir rehearsal. All tours leave from Harlem Spirituals' Midtown office (690 Eighth Ave., between 43rd and 44th), and all transportation is included.

For 18 years Larcelia Kebe, owner of **Harlem Your Way! Tours Unlimited** (☎ 212/ 690-1687; www.harlemyourway.com), has been leading visitors around Harlem on bus and walking tours that take you beyond the snapshot stops at major sights (though they're all included). She shares Harlem's distinct culture—peppered with her own social commentary—on spirited tours of brownstones, churches, jazz clubs, and soul-food restaurants. Walking tours are $25 to $48 per person, and bus tours are $35 to $55. Tours generally meet at the company's home base, an 1882 brownstone at 129 W. 30th St. Custom tours are also available.

A Self-Guided Walk
Through Greenwich Village's Literary Past

by Reid Bramblett

Start: Bleecker Street between La Guardia Place and Thompson Street.
Subway: Take the 6 to Bleecker Street, which lets you out at Bleecker and Lafayette streets. Walk west on Bleecker.
Finish: 14 West 10th St.
Time: Approximately 4 to 5 hours.
Best Time: If you plan to do the whole tour, start fairly early in the day (there's a breakfast break near the start).

The Village has always attracted rebels, radicals, and creative types—from earnest 18th-century Revolutionary Thomas Paine, to early 20th-century radicals such as John Reed and Mabel Dodge, to the Stonewall rioters who gave birth to the gay liberation movement in 1969. It was even a Village protest in 1817 that saved the area's colorfully convoluted lanes and byways when the city imposed a geometric grid system on the rest of New York's streets. Much of Village life centers around Washington Square Park, site of hippie rallies and counterculture demonstrations, as well as the former stomping ground of Henry James and Edith Wharton.

The 20th century saw this area transformed from a bastion of old New York families to a bohemian enclave of struggling writers and artists. But as early as the 19th century it was New York's literary hub, a venue for salons and other intellectual gatherings. Though skyrocketing rents made the Village less accessible to aspiring artists after the late 1920s, it remained a mecca for creative people—so much so that almost every building is a literary landmark. Today, the sheer cost of housing has seen to it that most modern Villagers are upwardly mobile professionals. There still are, however, plenty of resident throwbacks to the 1960s, latter-day bohemians of multiple body piercings, earnest NYU students, gawking tourists, funky shops, and great cafes that keep this one of the liveliest neighborhoods in town. And it remains one of Manhattan's most downright picturesque corners.

Though the focus of this tour is the Village's literary history, you'll also enjoy strolling along its quaint, tree-shaded streets lined with Federal and Greek-Revival buildings. This tour is a long one, and you may want to break it up into two visits, or just concentrate on the area that interests you most.

Begin on Bleecker Street at:
1. 145 Bleecker St., where James Fenimore Cooper, author of 32 novels, plus a dozen works of nonfiction, lived in 1833. Though he's primarily remembered for romantic adventure stories of the American frontier, Cooper also wrote political

Walking Tour: Greenwich Village's Literary Past

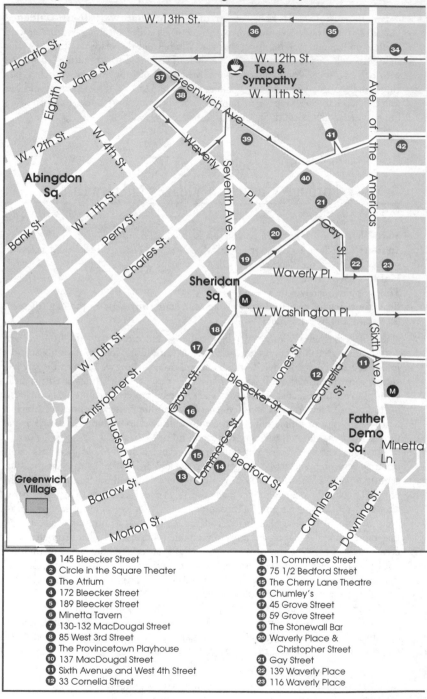

1 145 Bleecker Street
2 Circle in the Square Theater
3 The Atrium
4 172 Bleecker Street
5 189 Bleecker Street
6 Minetta Tavern
7 130-132 MacDougal Street
8 85 West 3rd Street
9 The Provincetown Playhouse
10 137 MacDougal Street
11 Sixth Avenue and West 4th Street
12 33 Cornelia Street

13 11 Commerce Street
14 75 1/2 Bedford Street
15 The Cherry Lane Theatre
16 Chumley's
17 45 Grove Street
18 59 Grove Street
19 The Stonewall Bar
20 Waverly Place & Christopher Street
21 Gay Street
22 139 Waverly Place
23 116 Waverly Place

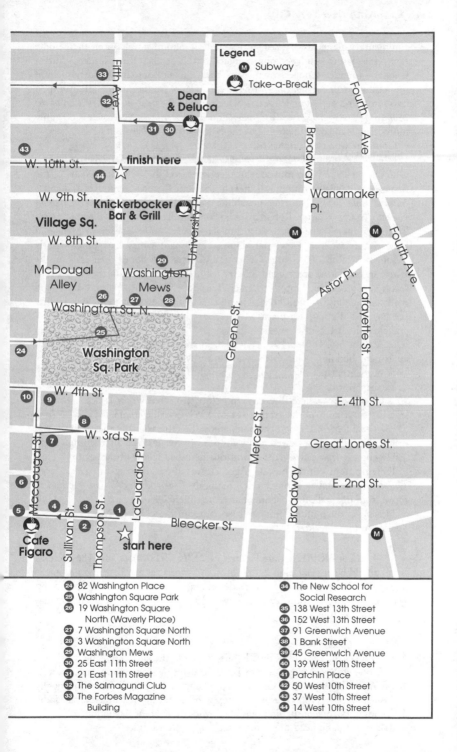

Legend
Ⓜ Subway
☕ Take-a-Break

Dean & Deluca ☕

Fifth Ave.

㉝
㉜
㉛ ㉚

㊸
W. 10th St.
㊹   **finish here** ☆

W. 9th St.
Knickerbocker Bar & Grill ☕

Village Sq.
W. 8th St.

McDougal Alley
Washington Mews   ㉙
㉖   ㉗   ㉘
Washington Sq. N.

㉕
㉔
Washington Sq. Park

W. 4th St.
⑩ ⑨
⑧
⑦   W. 3rd St.

⑥
⑤   ④ ③ ①
Cafe Figaro ☕   ②
☆ **start here**
Bleecker St.

Fourth Ave.
Broadway
Wanamaker Pl.
Ⓜ   Ⓜ
Astor Pl.   Lafayette St.   Fourth Ave.
University Pl.
Greene St.
E. 4th St.
Great Jones St.
Mercer St.   E. 2nd St.
Broadway
Ⓜ

Sullivan St.
Thompson St.
LaGuardia Pl.
McdougaI St.

㉔ 82 Washington Place
㉕ Washington Square Park
㉖ 19 Washington Square
   North (Waverly Place)
㉗ 7 Washington Square North
㉘ 3 Washington Square North
㉙ Washington Mews
㉚ 25 East 11th Street
㉛ 21 East 11th Street
㉜ The Salmagundi Club
㉝ The Forbes Magazine
   Building

㉞ The New School for
   Social Research
㉟ 138 West 13th Street
㊱ 152 West 13th Street
㊲ 91 Greenwich Avenue
㊳ 1 Bank Street
㊴ 45 Greenwich Avenue
㊵ 139 West 10th Street
㊶ Patchin Place
㊷ 50 West 10th Street
㊸ 37 West 10th Street
㊹ 14 West 10th Street

commentary, naval history, sea stories, and a group of novels about the Middle Ages. His father—judge, congressman, and Federalist Party leader William Cooper—founded Cooperstown, New York, the author's childhood home and the setting for *Leatherstocking Tales,* the epic tales of frontiersman Natty Bumppo (written over a period of 19 years), which includes *The Pioneers, The Last of the Mohicans, The Prairie, The Pathfinder,* and *The Deerslayer.* The town is certainly more famous today as the home of the Baseball Hall of Fame.

Continue west (walk right) to:

2. Circle in the Square Theater, 159 Bleecker St., founded by Ted Mann and Jose Quintero in 1951 (who moved it to Bleecker Street in 1959). It was one of the first arena, or "in-the-round," theaters in the United States. Tennessee Williams's *Summer and Smoke* (starring Geraldine Page), Eugene O'Neill's *The Iceman Cometh* (starring Jason Robards), Thorton Wilder's *Plays for Bleecker Street,* Truman Capote's *The Grass Harp,* and Jean Genet's *The Balcony* all premiered here. Actors Colleen Dewhurst, Dustin Hoffman, James Earl Jones, Cicely Tyson, Jason Robards, George C. Scott, and Peter Falk honed their craft on the Circle in the Square stage. And Sunday lectures and readings in the early 1950s featured Gore Vidal, Dorothy Parker, Tennessee Williams, Arthur Miller, and many other illustrious authors. The theater continues to present high-quality productions of important plays.

Across the street is:

3. The Atrium (no. 160), a 19th-century beaux-arts building that is today a posh apartment building. This former flophouse was Theodore Dreiser's first New York residence. (In 1895, he paid 25¢ a night for a cell-like room.)

Farther west is:

4. 172 Bleecker St., where film critic/poet/novelist/screenwriter James Agee lived in a top floor railroad flat from 1941 to 1951, after he completed *Let Us Now Praise Famous Men.* Though the book enjoyed a great vogue in the 1960s, it was originally scathingly reviewed and went out of print in 1948 after selling a mere 1,025 copies. *Time* called it "the most distinguished failure of the season."

Rallying from critical buffets, Agee created the screenplay for *The African Queen* and worked as a movie critic for both *Time* and the *Nation.* He had to move from this walk-up apartment after he suffered a heart attack.

Nearby, at the quintessential Village corner of Bleecker and MacDougal, is a good spot for a breakfast break.

☕ **TAKE A BREAK** Café Figaro (☎ 212/677-1100), at 184–186 Bleecker St., is an old beat-generation haunt. Stop in for pastries and coffee or an omelet and absorb the atmosphere. Sit at a sidewalk table to watch the Village parade by. It opens at 10:30am Monday to Friday and serves brunch Saturday and Sunday from 10am to 3pm.

On the opposite corner is:

5. 189 Bleecker St. For several decades, beginning in the late 1920s, the San Remo was a writer's hangout frequented by James Baldwin, William Styron, Jack Kerouac, James Agee, Frank O'Hara, Gregory Corso, Dylan Thomas, William Burroughs, and Allen Ginsberg. John Clellon Holmes wrote about this Italian restaurant in his 1952 novel, *Go,* one of the first published works of the beat generation.

Take a right and head north on MacDougal Street to the:

6. Minetta Tavern, 113 MacDougal St., at Minetta Lane (☎ 212/475-3850), which was a speakeasy called the Black Rabbit during Prohibition. The most unlikely event to take place here in those wild days was the founding of De Witt Wallace's very unbohemian *Reader's Digest* in 1923; the magazine was published in the basement in its early days. Since 1937, the Minetta has been a simpatico Italian restaurant and meeting place for writers and other creative folk, including Ezra Pound, e.e. cummings, Louis Bromfield, and Ernest Hemingway.

The Minetta still evokes the old Village. Walls are covered with photographs of famous patrons and caricatures (about 20 of which artist Franz Kline scrawled in exchange for drinks and food), and the rustic pine-paneled back room is adorned with murals of local landmarks. Stop in for a drink or a meal. **Minetta Lane** is named for the Minetta Brook that started on 23rd Street and flowed through here en route to the Hudson. The brook still runs underground.

A little farther up and across the street stands an 1852 house fronted by twin entrances and a wisteria-covered portico:

7. 130–132 MacDougal St. belonged to Louisa May Alcott's uncle and, after the Civil War, Alcott lived and worked here. Historians believe it was here she penned her best-known work, the autobiographical children's classic *Little Women*. Henry James called Alcott "The novelist of children . . . the Thackery, the Trollope, of the nursery and schoolroom."

Turn right onto West 3rd St. Walk 1 block, just beyond Sullivan Street, to:

8. 85 West 3rd St., where Edgar Allan Poe lived, on the third floor, in 1845 (last window on the right). He wrote *Facts in the Case of M. Valdemar* here, and *The Raven* was published during his tenancy. Today, it's part of NYU Law School, and the current residents claim Poe's rooms are haunted.

Double back down 3rd Street to MacDougal Street and turn right. On your left is:

9. The Provincetown Playhouse, 133 MacDougal St., first established in 1915 on a wharf in Provincetown, Massachusetts. Founders George Cram "Jig" Cook and his wife Susan Glaspell began by producing their own plays. One day, however, an intense 27-year-old named Eugene O'Neill arrived with a trunk full of plays, a few of which he brought for Cook and Glaspell to read. They immediately recognized his genius and were inspired to create a theater dedicated to experimental drama. It moved to this converted stable, where O'Neill managed it through 1927. Many of O'Neill's early plays premiered here—*Bound East for Cardiff, The Hairy Ape, The Long Voyage Home, The Emperor Jones,* and *All God's Chillun's Got Wings.* That last play was especially radical for its time, portraying a racially mixed couple; star Paul Robeson actually kissed white actress Mary Blair (literary critic Edmund Wilson's wife) on stage, prompting general outrage and Ku Klux Klan threats. Nevertheless, the play ran for 5 months.

Edna St. Vincent Millay, whose unlikely life plan was to support herself as a poet by earning her living as an actress, snagged both the lead in Fred Dell's *An Angel Intrudes* here, as well as Dell himself (their love affair inspired her poems *Weeds* and *Journal*). Millay's own work, *Aria da Capo,* was produced here in 1919. Katharine Cornell, Tallulah Bankhead, Bette Davis (who made her stage debut here), and Eva Le Gallienne appeared on the Provincetown stage in its early years. The theater was a great success, but instead of basking in their popularity, Cook and Glaspell disbanded the company in 1929 and moved to Greece, convinced that acceptance by the establishment signaled their failure as revolutionary artists.

Next door is:

10. **137 MacDougal St.** Jack London, Upton Sinclair, Vachel Lindsay, Louis Unter-
    meyer, Max Eastman, Theodore Dreiser, Lincoln Steffens, and Sinclair Lewis
    hashed over life theories at the Liberal Club, "A Meeting Place for Those Inter-
    ested in New Ideas," founded in 1913 on the second floor of the house that once
    stood here. Margaret Sanger lectured the club on birth control, an on-premises
    organization called Heterodoxy worked to promote feminist causes, and cubist
    art was displayed on the walls.

    Downstairs were **Polly's Restaurant,** run by Polly Holladay and Hippolyte
    Havel, and the radical **Washington Square Book Shop,** from which Liberal
    Club members more often borrowed than bought. Holladay, a staunch anarchist,
    refused to join even the Liberal Club, which, however bohemian, was still an
    "organization." In a previous incarnation, this building was the home of
    Nathaniel Currier (of Currier & Ives).

    Turn left onto West 4th Street and continue to the corner of:

11. **Sixth Avenue and West 4th Street.** Eugene O'Neill, a heavy drinker, nightly fre-
    quented a bar called the Golden Swan (more familiarly known as the "Hell Hole"
    or "Bucket of Blood") where the recycling center now stands, and later used it as
    a setting for his play *The Iceman Cometh,* a play that was 12 years in the writing
    (and recently revived, first on London's West End then on Broadway, with Kevin
    Spacey in the lead role). The bar was patronized by prostitutes, gangsters, long-
    shoremen, anarchists, and politicians as well as artists and writers. Eccentric
    owner Tom Wallace, on whom O'Neill modeled saloon proprietor Harry Hope,
    kept a pig in the basement and seldom ventured off the premises.

    Cross Sixth Avenue, angle up the continuation of West 4th Street, and make
    your first left onto Cornelia Street looking for:

12. **31 Cornelia St.** Here once stood the **Caffè Cino,** which opened in 1958, serving
    cappuccino in shaving mugs. In the early 1960s, owner Joe Cino encouraged
    aspiring playwrights, such as Lanford Wilson, Sam Shepard, and John Guare, to
    stage readings and performances in his cramped storefront space. Experimenta-
    tion in this tiny cafe gave birth to New York's off-Broadway theater.

    Continue down Cornelia Street to Bleeker Street and turn right. Cross Seventh
    Avenue and angle back to your left into Commerce Street. Near the corner stands:

13. **11 Commerce St.** Washington Irving wrote *The Legend of Sleepy Hollow* while
    living in this quaint three-story brick building. Born into a prosperous New York
    family, he penned biographies of naval heroes as an officer in the War of 1812.
    In 1819, under the name Geoffrey Crayon, he wrote *The Sketch Book,* which
    contained the stories of *The Legend of Sleepy Hollow, Westminster Abbey,* and *Rip
    Van Winkle.* Irving was one of the elite New Yorkers who served on the planning
    commission for Central Park, and, from 1842 to 1846, was ambassador to Spain.
    He coined the phrase "the almighty dollar," and once observed that "A tart
    temper never mellows with age, and a sharp tongue is the only tool that grows
    keener with constant use."

    Continue walking west on Commerce and turn left at Bedford Street to find:

14. **75½ Bedford St.** The narrowest house in the Village (a mere 9½ feet across), this
    unlikely three-story brick residence was built on the site of a former carriage alley
    in 1873. Pretty, red-headed, feminist poet Edna St. Vincent Millay, who arrived
    in the Village fresh from Vassar, lived here from 1923 (the year she won a Pulitzer
    Prize for her poetry) to 1925. Other famous occupants have included a young
    Cary Grant and John Barrymore.

    Return to Commerce Street, and turn left, where:

15. The Cherry Lane Theatre, nestled in a bend at 38 Commerce St., was founded in 1924 by Edna St. Vincent Millay. The playhouse presented works by Edward Albee, Samuel Beckett (*Waiting for Godot* and *Endgame* premiered here), Eugene Ionesco, Jean Genet, and Harold Pinter. In 1951, Judith Malina and Julian Beck founded the ultra-experimental Living Theatre on its premises. Before rising to megafame, Barbra Streisand worked as a Cherry Lane usher.

Continue around Commerce Street's bend to Barrow Street, where you turn right, then left back onto Bedford Street. A few doors up on the right is:

16. Chumley's, 86 Bedford St. (☎ 212/675-4449), opened in 1926 in a former blacksmith's shop. During Prohibition it was a speakeasy with a casino upstairs. Its convoluted entranceway with four steps up and four down (designed to slow police raiders), the lack of a sign outside, and a back door that opens on an alleyway are remnants of that era. Original owner Lee Chumley was a radical labor sympathizer who held secret meetings of the IWW on the premises. Chumley's has long been a writer's bar. Walls are lined with book jackets of works by famous patrons who, over the years, have included Edna St. Vincent Millay (she once lived upstairs), John Steinbeck, Eugene O' Neill, e.e. cummings, F. Scott Fitzgerald, Theodore Dreiser, William Faulkner, Gregory Corso, Norman Mailer, William Carlos Williams, Allen Ginsberg, Lionel Trilling, Harvey Fierstein, Calvin Trillin, and others. Even the elusive J. D. Salinger hoisted a few at the bar here, and Simone de Beauvoir came by when she was in town. With its working fireplaces (converted blacksmith forges), wood-plank flooring, old carved-up oak tables, and amber lighting, Chumley's lacks nothing in the way of mellowed atmosphere. Open nightly from 5:30pm.

Continue up Bedford to Grove Street, named in the 19th century for its many gardens and groves, and make a right to:

17. 45 Grove St. Originally a freestanding two-story building, this was, in the 19th century, one of the Village's most elegant mansions, surrounded by verdant lawns with greenhouses and stables. Built in 1830, it was refurbished with Italianate influences in 1870. In the movie *Reds,* based on the life of John Reed, 45 Grove was portrayed (inaccurately) as Eugene O'Neill's house.

Ohio-born poet Hart Crane rented a second-floor room at 45 Grove in 1923, and began writing his poetic portrait of America, *The Bridge* (Hart depicted the Brooklyn Bridge as a symbol of America's westward expansion). Crane was born in 1899 with "a toe in the 19th century." His parents' marriage was a miserably unhappy one, and his mother, an artistic beauty subject to depression, concentrated her energies on her son. Although constant traveling by his mother's side kept Crane from finishing school, he was a voracious reader and brilliantly self educated. By the time he was 17, his poetry had been published in prestigious New York magazines.

In later years, frustrated by frequent rejection from magazines and other exigencies of his craft, Crane would occasionally toss his typewriter out the window. Often moody and despondent, he was chronically in debt, plagued by guilt over homosexual encounters on the nearby docks, and given to almost nightly alcoholic binges. In 1932, returning by ship from Mexico (where, on a Guggenheim fellowship, he had been attempting to write an epic poem about Montezuma), Crane made sexual advances to a crew member, was badly beaten up, and jumped into the waters to his death at the age of 33.

Continue up the street to:

18. 59 Grove St. English-born American revolutionary/political theorist/writer Thomas Paine died here in 1809. Paine came to America (with the help of

Benjamin Franklin) in 1774, and in 1776 produced his famous pamphlet, *The Crisis,* which begins with the words: "These are the times that try men's souls." After fighting in the American Revolution, he returned to England to advocate the overthrow of the British monarchy. Indicted for treason, he escaped to Paris, becoming a French citizen; while imprisoned there during the Terror, he wrote *The Age of Reason.* He returned to the United States in 1802, where he was vilified for his atheism. Benjamin Franklin once said to Paine, "Where liberty is, there is my country." To which revolutionary Paine replied: "Where liberty is not, there is mine."

The downstairs space has always been a restaurant, today **Marie's Crisis** (☎ **212/243-9323**). Though the building Paine lived in burned down, some of the interior brickwork is original. In the 1920s, you might have spotted anyone from Eugene O'Neill to Edward VIII of England here. Today, Marie's is a lively piano bar; everyone sings along Monday through Friday from 9:30pm to 3:30am, to 4am Friday through Sunday.

At 7th Avenue, cross to the opposite side of the wide intersection, walk around to the left of the little park, and head half a block up Christopher Street, the hub of New York's gay community, to no. 53:

19. The Stonewall Bar (☎ **212/463-0950**). The current bar on this spot shares a name with its more famous predecessor, the Stonewall Inn. This was scene of the Stonewall riots of June 1969, when gay customers decided to resist the police during a routine raid. The event launched the lesbian and gay rights movement, and is commemorated throughout the country every year with gay pride parades (see the "New York City Calendar of Events" in chapter 2 for New York's annual June blowout).

Continue up the block to the corner of:

20. Waverly Place & Christopher Street. The wedge-shaped Georgian Northern Dispensary building dates from 1831. Edgar Allan Poe was treated for a head cold here in 1836, the year he came to New York with his 13-year-old bride for whom he would later compose the pain-filled requiems *Annabel Lee* and *Ulalume.*

Keep walking up Christopher Street to take a right onto:

21. Gay Street. Famous residents of this tiny street have included New York Mayor Jimmy Walker, who owned the 18th-century town house at no. 12. More recently, Frank Paris, creator of *Howdy Doody,* lived here. During Prohibition there were several speakeasies on the street.

At the end of the short street, take a left onto Waverly Place and look for:

22. 139 Waverly Place. Edna St. Vincent Millay lived here with her sister, Norma, in 1918. Radical playwright Floyd Dell, her lover, who found the apartment for her, commented: "She lived in that gay poverty which is traditional of the Village, and one may find vivid reminiscences of that life in her poetry."

Cross Sixth Avenue to check out:

23. 116 Waverly Place. Dating from 1891, the building has hosted William Cullen Bryant, Horace Greeley, Margaret Fuller, poet Fitz-Greene Halleck, and Herman Melville. Here Poe read his latest poem, *The Raven,* to assembled literati. Waverly Place, by the way, was named in 1833 for Sir Walter Scott's novel, *Waverley.*

Return to Sixth Avenue and turn left (south) down it. Take another left onto Washington Place to:

24. 82 Washington Place, residence from 1908 to 1912 of Willa Cather, whose books celebrated pioneer life and the beauty of her native Nebraska landscape. Cather came to New York in 1906 at the age of 31 to work at the prestigious *McClure's* magazine and rose to managing editor before resigning to write full time.

As her career advanced, and she found herself besieged with requests for lectures and interviews, Cather became almost a recluse, fiercely protective of her privacy.

Band leader John Philip Sousa owned the beautiful 1839 building next door (no. 80).

Washington Place ends at:

25. Washington Square Park, the hub of the Village. This area was once a swamp frequented largely by duck hunters (Minetta Brook meandered through it). In the 18th and early 19th centuries it was a potter's field (more than 10,000 people are buried under the park) and an execution site (one of the makeshift gallows survives—a towering English elm in the northwest corner of the park). The park was dedicated in 1826, and elegant residential dwellings—some of which have survived NYU's cannibalization of the neighborhood—went up around the square. Unlike the center of Bohemia that it later became, it was the citadel of stifling patrician gentility so evocatively depicted in the novels of Edith Wharton. She defined Washington Square society as "a little 'set' with its private catch-words, observances, and amusements" indifferent to "anything outside its charmed circle."

The white marble **Memorial Arch** (1892) at the Fifth Avenue entrance, which replaced a wooden arch erected in 1889 to commemorate the centenary of Washington's inauguration, was designed by Stanford White. One night in 1917, a group of Liberal Club pranksters climbed the Washington Square Arch, fired cap guns, and proclaimed the "Independent Republic of Greenwich Village," a utopia dedicated to "socialism, sex, poetry, conversation, dawn-greeting, anything—so long as it is taboo in the Middle West." Today, Washington Square Park would probably surpass any of this group's most cherished anarchist fantasies and might even lead them to question the philosophy altogether.

Along the square's north edge stand many of the surviving old homes, including, just west of Fifth Avenue:

26. 19 Washington Square North (Waverly Place). Henry James's grandmother, Elizabeth Walsh, lived at this now-defunct address. (The no. 19 that exists today is a different house, the numbering system having changed since James's day.) Young Henry spent much time at her house, the inspiration for his novel *Washington Square*.

Farther east is:

27. 7 Washington Square North, where Edith Wharton, age 20, and her mother lived in 1882. A wealthy aristocrat, born Edith Jones, Wharton maintained a close friendship with Henry James, and, like him, left New York's stultifying upper-class social scene for Paris in 1910, where she wrote the Pulitzer Prize–winning *The Age of Innocence.* Both she and James were immensely popular in Europe. Wharton wrote almost a book a year her entire adult life, while also finding time to feed French and Belgian refugees during World War I and take charge of 600 Belgian orphans. For these efforts she was awarded the Legion of Honor by the French government in 1915. No. 7 was also once the home of Alexander Hamilton.

Nearby is:

28. 3 Washington Square North (today the NYU School of Social Work). Critic Edmund Wilson, managing editor of the *New Republic,* lived here from 1921 to 1923. Another resident, John Dos Passos, wrote *Manhattan Transfer* here.

Make a left at University Place and another immediate left into:

29. Washington Mews. This picturesque 19th-century cobble-stoned street, lined with vine-covered two-story buildings (converted stables and carriage houses constructed to serve posh Washington Square town houses), has had several famous residents, among them John Dos Passos, artist Edward Hopper (no. 14A), and Sherwood Anderson (no. 54). The latter building dates from 1834.

Double back to University Place and turn left to head north to the southeast corner of 9th Street, where stands the first of two possible places to:

☕ **TAKE A BREAK**   At the southeast corner of 9th Street and University Place, the **Knickerbocker Bar and Grill** (☎ 212/228-8490) is a comfortable wood-paneled restaurant and jazz club. Harry Connick, Jr. got his start playing piano at the Knickerbocker, and Charles Lindbergh signed the contract for his transatlantic flight at the bar here. The restaurant is open daily from 11:45am to midnight (to 2am on Friday and Saturday).

For smaller appetites, head 2 blocks up to a branch of **Dean and Deluca,** 75 University Place, at 11th Street (☎ 212/473-1908), which offers superior light fare—pastries, croissants, ham and brie sandwiches, pasta salads—in a pristinely charming setting. Be sure to look up at the gorgeous plasterwork ceiling. Open Monday to Thursday 8am to 9pm, Friday and Saturday 8am to 10pm, and Sunday 9am to 8pm.

This address is also a stop on the tour. When Thomas Wolfe graduated from Harvard in 1923, he came to New York to teach at NYU and lived at the Hotel Albert (depicted as the Hotel Leopold in his novel *Of Time and the River*) at this address.

From University Place, turn left onto 11th Street to:

30. 25 East 11th St. The unhappy and sexually confused poet Hart Crane (whom we met at Stop 18) lived here for a short time. His neighbor at:

31. 21 East 11th St. was Mary Cadwaller Jones, who was married to Edith Wharton's brother. Her home was the setting for literary salons; Henry Adams, Theodore Roosevelt, Augustus Saint-Gaudens, and John Singer Sargent often came to lunch, and Henry James was a houseguest when he visited from Europe. Jones's daughter, landscape architect Baetrix Farrand, grew up here before designing such renowned outdoor spaces as the White House's East Garden and the New York Botanical Gardens' Rose Garden.

Continue to Fifth Avenue, cross it, and turn right. On your left is:

32. The Salmagundi Club, 47 Fifth Ave., which began as an artist's club in 1871 and was originally located at 596 Broadway. The name comes from the *Salmagundi* papers, in which Washington Irving mocked his fellow New Yorkers and first used the term *Gotham* to describe the city. Theodore Dreiser lived at the Salmagundi in 1897, when it was located across the street where today stands the First Presbyterian Church, and probably wrote *Sister Carrie* there, a work based on the experiences of his own sister, Emma.

Cross 12th Street. At the northwest corner is:

33. The Forbes Magazine Building, 60–62 Fifth Ave., with a museum housing exhibits from the varied collections of the late Malcolm Forbes, famous as a frequent Liz Taylor escort, financier, magazine magnate, and father of Presidential hopeful Steve Forbes. For details on the Forbes collection, see "More Manhattan Museums" earlier in this chapter.

Make a left on 12th Street and you'll see:

34. The New School for Social Research, 66 West 12th St., which was founded in 1919 as a forum for professors too liberal-minded for Columbia University's then stiflingly traditional attitude. In the 1930s it became a "University in Exile" for intelligentsia fleeing Nazi Germany. Many great writers have taught or lectured in its classrooms over the decades: William Styron, Joseph Heller, Edward Albee, W. H. Auden, Robert Frost, Nadine Gordimer, Max Lerner, Maya Angelou, Joyce Carol Oates, Arthur Miller, I. B. Singer, Susan Sontag, and numerous others.

Turn right up Sixth Avenue and left onto 13th Street to:

35. 138 West 13th St. Max Eastman and other radicals urged revolution in the pages of the *Liberator*, headquartered in this lovely building on a pleasant tree-lined street. The magazine published works by John Reed, Edna St. Vincent Millay, Ernest Hemingway, e.e. cummings (who later became very right-wing and a passionate supporter of Senator Joseph McCarthy's Communist witch hunts), John Dos Passos, and William Carlos Williams.

Farther west along the block is:

36. 152 West 13th St. Offices of the *Dial*, a major avant-garde literary magazine of the 1920s, occupied this beautiful Greek-Revival brick town house. The magazine dated from 1840 in Cambridge, MA, where transcendentalists Margaret Fuller and Ralph Waldo Emerson were its seminal editors. In the 1920s, its aim was to offer "the best of European and American art, experimental and conventional." Contributors included Hart Crane, Conrad Aiken, Ezra Pound, Theodore Dreiser (who once wrote an article claiming that American literature had to be crude to be truly American), and artist Marc Chagall. T. S. Eliot, who once grumbled of the *Dial* "there is far too much in it, and it is all second rate and exceedingly solemn," nevertheless published *The Waste Land* in its pages.

Continue west on 13th Street, and make a left on Seventh Avenue, a right on 12th Street, and then another right for some afternoon tea.

☕ **TAKE A BREAK** **Tea & Sympathy** (☎ 212/807-8329), at 108 Greenwich Ave., is straight out of the English countryside, a hole-in-the-wall crammed with a few tables (always crowded), a friendly British wait staff, and plenty of old-time charm. Elbow room is at a minimum here, but it's worth the squeeze for a full afternoon tea, shepherd's pie, bangers and mash, Welsh rarebit, or a traditional sweet such as treacle pudding or warm ginger cake. Open Monday through Friday 11:30am to 10:30pm, Saturday 10:30am to 10:30pm, and Sunday 10:30am to 10pm.

From Tea & Sympathy, turn left to walk back down Greenwich Avenue to the corner of 12th Street and:

37. 91 Greenwich Ave. At the beginning of the 20th century, Max Eastman was editor of a radical left-wing literary magazine called *The Masses* that published, among others, John Reed, Carl Sandburg, Sherwood Anderson, Upton Sinclair, Edgar Lee Masters, e.e. cummings, and Louis Untermeyer. John Sloan, Stuart Davis, Picasso, and George Bellows provided art for its pages. *The Masses* was suppressed by the Justice Department in 1918 because of its opposition to World War I (it called on Woodrow Wilson to repeal the draft and claimed that America's enemy was not Germany but "that 2% of the United States that owns 60% of all the wealth"). Reed, Eastman, political cartoonist Art Young, and writer/literary critic Floyd Dell were put on trial under the Espionage Act and charged with conspiracy to obstruct recruiting and prevent enlistment. Pacifist Edna St. Vincent Millay read poems to the accused to help pass the time while juries were out. The trials all ended in hung juries.

Continue another block down Greenwich Avenue; turn right on Bank Street, and look for:

38. 1 Bank St. In 1913, shortly after the publication of *O Pioneers!*, Willa Cather, age 40, moved to a seven-room, second-floor apartment in a large brick house here. Here she lived with her companion Edith Lewis and wrote *My Antonia* (the third of a trilogy about immigrants in the United States), *Death Comes to the Archbishop*, and several other novels. In 1920, H. L. Mencken called *My Antonia* "the best piece of fiction ever done by a woman in America . . . I know of no novel that makes the remote folk of the western farmlands more real than *My Antonia* makes them, and know of none that makes them seem better worth knowing." Cather's Friday afternoon at-homes here were frequented by D. H. Lawrence, among others. Unlike many Village writers of her day, Cather eschewed the radical scene and took little interest in politics.

From Bank Street, take a left onto Waverly Place, another left on Perry Street, and a final right back onto Greenwich Avenue, to:

39. 45 Greenwich Ave. In 1947, William Styron came to New York from North Carolina to work as a junior editor at McGraw-Hill. He moved here in 1951, after a stint in the Marines and the success of his first novel, *Lie Down in Darkness*. Styron originally showed manuscript pages from that novel, begun at age 23, to Hiram Haydn, a Bobbs-Merrill editor whose writing class he was taking at the New School. Haydn told Styron he was too advanced for the class and took an option on the novel.

Continue down Greenwich Avenue to West 10th Street and detour right to:

40. 139 West 10th St. It was at a former bar at this location that, in 1954, playwright Edward Albee saw graffiti on a mirror reading, "Who's afraid of Virginia Woolf?" and, years later, appropriated it.

Double back up West 10th Street, cross Greenwich Avenue, and walk a block where you will see the gated entry to:

41. Patchin Place. The gate closing off Patchin Place is never locked; feel free to pass through it. This tranquil, tree-shaded cul-de-sac has sheltered many illustrious residents: From 1923 to 1962, e.e. cummings lived at no. 4, where visitors included T. S. Eliot, Ezra Pound, and Dylan Thomas. The highly acclaimed but little-known Djuna Barnes (literary critics have compared her to James Joyce) lived in a tiny one-room apartment at no. 5. Reclusive and eccentric, she almost never left the premises for 40 years, prompting cummings to occasionally shout from his window, "Are you still alive, Djuna?"

Though they were usually elsewhere, John Reed and Louise Bryant maintained a residence at Patchin Place from 1895 until his death in 1920. It was during this time that he wrote his eyewitness account of the Russian Revolution, *Ten Days That Shook the World*. Theodore Dreiser was a Patchin Place resident in 1895, when he was still an unknown journalist.

Turn left out of Patchin Place to cross Sixth Avenue. Head east down West 10th Street to:

42. 50 West 10th St. After his great success with *Who's Afraid of Virginia Woolf?*, Edward Albee bought this late 19th-century converted carriage house in the early 1960s. It's a gem of a building, with highly polished wooden carriage doors. Albee wrote *Tiny Alice* and *A Delicate Balance* here, the latter a Pulitzer Prize winner. In 1994, he won a second Pulitzer Prize for *Three Tall Women*.

Now look for:

43. 37 West 10th St. Sinclair Lewis, already a famous writer by the mid-1920s, lived in this early-19th-century house from 1928 to 1929.

Our final stop is:

44. 14 West 10th St. When Mark Twain came to New York at the turn of the century (at the age of 65), he lived in this gorgeous 1855 mansion. An extremely successful writer, he entertained lavishly. Twain was famous for his witticisms, including a quip on the art of quipping: "How lucky Adam was. He knew when he said a good thing, nobody had said it before."

8 Urban Oases: Central Park & Other Places to Play

✪ CENTRAL PARK

Without this miracle of civic planning, Manhattan would be a virtual unbroken block of buildings. Instead, smack in the middle of Gotham, a 843-acre natural retreat provides a daily escape valve for millions of New Yorkers.

While you're in the city, be sure to take advantage of the park's many charms, not the least of which is its sublime layout. Frederick Law Olmstead and Calvert Vaux won a competition with a plan that marries flowing paths with sinewy bridges, integrating them into a rolling landscape with rocky outcroppings, man-made lakes, and wooded pockets. The park's construction, between 1859 and 1870, provided much-needed employment during an economic depression and drew the city's population into the upper reaches of the island, which at that time were still quite rural. Nevertheless, designers predicted the hustle and bustle to come, and tactfully built roads that are largely hidden from the bucolic view.

On just about any day, Central Park is crowded with New Yorkers and visitors alike. On nice days, especially weekends, it's the city's party central. Families play and picnic; rollerbladers fly around the park or twirl in front of the bandshell; couples come to stroll or paddle the lake; dogs and owners romp through the open space; and it seems that just about everybody is out sunbathing at the first sign of summer. On beautiful days, the crowds are part of the appeal—everybody comes here to peel off their urban armor and relax. Believe it or not, there's actually a feeling of camaraderie in the air. On these days, the people watching is more compelling than anywhere else in the city. But one of Central Park's great appeals is that even on the most crowded days, there's always somewhere to get away from it all—find a little peace and quiet, and commune with nature.

ORIENTATION & GETTING THERE   Look at your map—that great green swath in the center of Manhattan is Central Park. It runs from 59th Street (also known as Central Park S.) at the south end to 110th Street at the north end, and from Fifth Avenue on the east side to Central Park West (the equivalent of Eighth Ave.) on the west side. The 6-mile rolling **Central Park Drive** circles the park and has a lane set aside for bikers, joggers, and in-line skaters. A number of **transverse** (crosstown) **roads** cross the park at major points—at 65th, 79th, 86th, and 97th streets—but they're built down a level, largely out of view, so as not to intrude.

A number of subway stops and lines serve the park; which one you take all depends on where you want to go. To reach the southernmost entrance on the west side, take an A, B, C, D, 1, or 9 to 59th St.–Columbus Circle. To reach the southeast corner entrance, take the N, R to Fifth Avenue; from this stop, it's an easy walk into the park to the Information Center in the **Dairy** (☎ 212/794-6564; open daily 11am–5pm, to 4pm in winter), midpark at about 65th Street, where you can ask questions and pick up park information and a good park map. If your time for exploring is limited, I suggest entering the park at West 72nd or 79th streets for maximum exposure (subway: B, C to 72nd St. or 81st St.–Museum of Natural History). From here, you can pick up park information at the Visitor Center at **Belvedere Castle** (☎ 212/772-0210; open Wed–Sun 11am–4pm), midpark at 79th Street. There's also a third Visitor Center at the **Charles A. Dana Discovery Center** (☎ 212/860-1370; open daily 11am–5pm, to 4pm in winter), at the northeast corner of the park at Harlem Meer (subway: 2, 3 to Central Park North/110th St.). The Dana Center also hosts workshops, music programs, and park tours, and lends fishing poles for fishing in Harlem Meer (park policy is catch-and-release).

Food carts and vendors are set up at all of the park's main gathering points, selling hot dogs, pretzels, and ice cream, so finding a cheap bite to eat is never a problem. You'll also find a fixed food counter at the **Conservatory,** on the east side of the park north of the 72nd Street entrance.

GUIDED TOURS   Trolley tours of the park are offered weekdays from May through November; call ☎ 212/397-3809 for details. The Dana Center hosts ranger-guided tours on occasion (☎ 212/860-1370). Also consider a private walking tour; many of the companies listed under "Affordable Sightseeing Tours" earlier in this chapter offer guided tours.

FOR FURTHER INFORMATION   Call the main number at ☎ 212/360-3444 for recorded information, or 212/794-6564 to talk to a real person at the Dairy Information Center. The park also has a comprehensive Web site at **www.centralpark.org**.

SAFETY TIP   Even though the park has the lowest crime rate of any of the city's precincts, be wary, especially in the more remote northern end. It's a good idea to avoid the park entirely after dark, unless you're heading to one of the restaurants for dinner or to a SummerStage or Shakespeare in the Park event (see chapter 9), when you should stick with the crowds. For more safety tips, see "Playing It Safe" in chapter 4.

EXPLORING THE PARK

The best way to see Central Park is to wander along the park's 58 miles of winding pedestrian paths, keeping in mind the following highlights.

Before starting your stroll, stop by the Information Center in the Dairy, midpark in a 19th-century–style building overlooking Wollman Rink at about 65th Street, to get a good park map and other information on sights and events, and to peruse the kid-friendly exhibit on the park's history and design.

The southern part of Central Park is more formally designed and heavily visited than the relatively rugged and remote northern end. Not far from the Dairy is the carousel with 58 hand-carved horses (open daily 10:30am–6pm, to 5pm in winter; rides are 90¢), the zoo (see "Central Park Wildlife Center," below), and the Wollman Rink for roller- or ice skating (see "Activities" below).

The Mall, a long formal walkway lined with elms shading benches and sculptures of sometimes forgotten writers, leads to the focal point of Central Park, Bethesda Fountain (along the 72nd Street transverse road). Bethesda Terrace and its grandly sculpted entryway border a large lake where dogs fetch sticks, rowboaters glide by, and dedicated early-morning anglers try their luck at catching carp, perch, catfish, and bass. You can rent a rowboat at or take a gondola ride from Loeb Boathouse, on the eastern end of the lake (see "Activites," below). Boats of another kind are at Conservatory Water

---

Where's Balto

The people at Central Park say that the question they're asked almost more than any other these days is "Where is the statue of Balto?" The heroic dog is just northwest of the zoo, midpark at about 66th Street.

Central Park

American Museum of
  Natural History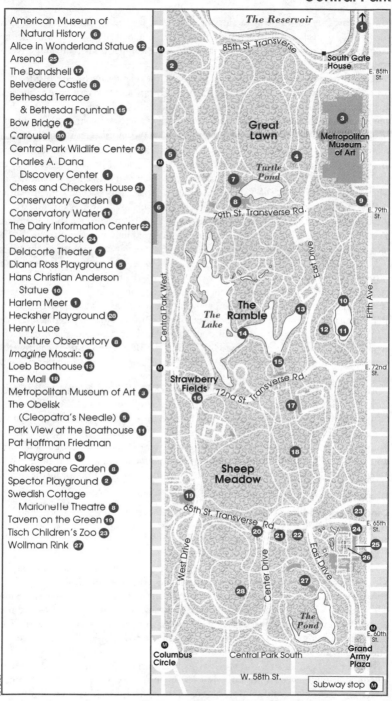
Alice in Wonderland Statue
Arsenal
The Bandshell
Belvedere Castle
Bethesda Terrace
  & Bethesda Fountain
Bow Bridge
Carousel
Central Park Wildlife Center
Charles A. Dana
  Discovery Center
Chess and Checkers House
Conservatory Garden
Conservatory Water
The Dairy Information Center
Delacorte Clock
Delacorte Theater
Diana Ross Playground
Hans Christian Anderson
  Statue
Harlem Meer
Hecksher Playground
Henry Luce
  Nature Observatory
Imagine Mosaic
Loeb Boathouse
The Mall
Metropolitan Museum of Art
The Obelisk
  (Cleopatra's Needle)
Park View at the Boathouse
Pat Hoffman Friedman
  Playground
Shakespeare Garden
Spector Playground
Swedish Cottage
  Marionette Theatre
Tavern on the Green
Tisch Children's Zoo
Wollman Rink

The Reservoir
85th St. Transverse
South Gate House
E. 85th St.
Great Lawn
Metropolitan Museum of Art
Turtle Pond
79th St. Transverse Rd.
E. 79th St.
Central Park West
East Drive
The Ramble
The Lake
Fifth Ave.
E. 72nd St.
Strawberry Fields
72nd St. Transverse Rd.
Sheep Meadow
65th St. Transverse Rd.
Center Drive
East Drive
E. 65th St.
West Drive
E. 60th St.
Columbus Circle
Central Park South
Grand Army Plaza
W. 58th St.
Subway stop

NA-0154

(on the east side at 73rd St.), a stone-walled pond flanked by statues of both Hans Christian Andersen and Alice in Wonderland. On Saturdays at 10am, die-hard yachtsmen race remote-controlled sailboats in fierce competitions following Olympic regulations. (Sorry, model boats aren't for rent.)

If the action there is too intense, Sheep Meadow on the southwestern side of the park is a designated quiet zone, where Frisbee throwing and kite flying are as energetic as things get. Another respite is Strawberry Fields, at 72nd Street on the West Side. This memorial to John Lennon, who was murdered across the street at the Dakota apartment building (72nd Street and Central Park W., northwest corner), is a gorgeous garden centered around an Italian mosaic bearing the title of the lead Beatle's most famous solo song: *Imagine.* In keeping with its goal of promoting world peace, the garden has 161 varieties of plants, donated by each of the 161 nations in existence when it was designed in 1985. This is a wonderful place for peaceful contemplation.

Bow Bridge, a graceful lacework of cast iron designed by Calvert Vaux, crosses over the lake and leads to the most bucolic area of Central Park, the Ramble. This dense 38-acre woodland with spiraling paths, rocky outcroppings, and a stream is the best spot for bird-watching and forgetting that you're actually in the middle of a huge city.

North of the Ramble, Belvedere Castle is home to the **Henry Luce Nature Observatory** (☎ **212/772-0210**), worth a visit if you're with children. From the castle, set on Vista Rock (the park's highest point at 135 feet), you can look down on the Great Lawn, which has emerged lush and green from renovations, and the Delacorte Theater, home to Shakespeare in the Park (see chapter 9). The small Shakespeare Garden south of the theater is scruffy, but it does have plants, herbs, trees, and other bits of greenery mentioned by the playwright. Behind the Belvedere Castle is the **Swedish Cottage Marionette Theatre** (☎ **212/988-9093**), hosting various marionette plays for children throughout the year; call to see what's on.

At the northeast end, Conservatory Garden (at 105th St. and Fifth Ave.), Central Park's only formal garden, is a magnificent display of flowers and trees reflected in calm pools. (The gates to the garden once fronted the Fifth Ave. mansion of Cornelius Vanderbilt II.) Harlem Meer and its boathouse were recently renovated, and look beautiful. The boathouse now berths the **Dana Discovery Center** (☎ **212/860-1370**), where children learn about the environment and borrow fishing poles at no charge; see "Orientation & Getting There" earlier in this section for further details.

GOING TO THE ZOO

Central Park Wildlife Center/Tisch Children's Zoo. In the park at Fifth Ave. and E. 64th St. ☎ **212/861-6030.** www.wcs.org/zoos. Admission $3.50 adults, $1.25 seniors, 50¢ children 3–12, free for children under 3. Apr–Oct, Mon–Fri 10am–5pm, Sat–Sun 10:30am–5:30pm; Nov–Mar, daily 10am–4:30pm. Subway: N, R to Fifth Ave.

It has been nearly a decade since the zoo in Central Park was renovated, making it in the process both more human and more humane. Lithe sea lions frolic in the central pool area. The gigantic but graceful polar bears (one of whom, by the way, made himself a true New Yorker when he began regular visits with a shrink) glide back and forth across a pool with glass walls. The monkeys seem to regard those on the other side of the fence with knowing disdain. In the hot and humid Tropic Zone, large colorful birds swoop around in freedom, sometimes landing next to nonplussed visitors.

Because of its small size, the zoo is at its best with its displays of smaller animals. The indoor, multilevel Tropic Zone is a real highlight, its steamy rainforest home to everything from black-and-white Colobus monkeys to Emerald tree boa constrictors to a leaf-cutter ant farm. So is the large penguin enclosure in the Polar Circle, which is better than the one at San Diego's Sea World. In the Temperate Territory, look for the Asian red pandas, which look like the world's most beautiful raccoons. Despite their pool and piles of ice, however, the polar bears still look sad.

The zoo is good for short attention spans; you can cover the whole thing in 1½ to 3 hours, depending on the size of the crowds and how long you like to linger. It's very kid friendly, with lots of well-written and -illustrated placards that older kids can understand. For the littlest ones, there's the $6-million **Tisch Children's Zoo.** With llamas, potbellied pigs, and more, this new (in fall 1997) petting zoo and playground is a real blast for the five-and-under set.

ACTIVITIES

The 6-mile rolling road circling the park, **Central Park Drive,** has a lane set aside for bikers, joggers, and in-line skaters. The best time to use it is when the park is closed to traffic: Monday to Friday 10am to 3pm (except Thanksgiving to New Year's) and 7 to 10pm. It's also closed from 7pm Friday to 6am Monday, but when the weather is nice, the crowds can be hellish.

BIKING   Off-road mountain biking isn't permitted; stay on Central Park Drive or your bike may be confiscated by park police.

You can rent 3- and 10-speed bikes as well as tandems in Central Park at the **Loeb Boathouse,** midpark near 74th Street and East Drive (☎ **212/861-4137** or 517-3623); at **Metro Bicycles,** 1311 Lexington Ave., at 88th Street (☎ **212/427-4450**); at **Pedal Pushers,** 1306 Second Ave., between 68th and 69th streets (☎ **212/288-5592**); and at **Toga Bike Shop,** 110 West End Ave., at 64th Street (☎ **212/799-9625**).

BOATING   From spring to fall, gondola rides and canoe rentals are available at the **Loeb Boathouse,** midpark near 74th Street and East Drive (☎ **212/517-3623**). Rentals are $10 for the first hour, $2.50 every 15 minutes thereafter, and a $30 deposit is required.

HORSE-DRAWN CARRIAGE RIDES   At the entrance to the park at 59th Street and Central Park South, you'll see a line of **horse-drawn carriages** waiting to take passengers on a ride through the park or along some of the city's streets. Horses belong on city streets as much as chamber pots belong in our homes. You won't need me to tell you how forlorn most of these horses look; if you insist, a ride is a whopping $50 for two for a half hour. I strongly suggest skipping it.

IN-LINE SKATING   Central Park is the city's most popular place for blading. See the top of this section for details on Central Park Drive, main drag for skaters. On weekends, head to West Drive at 67th Street, behind Tavern on the Green, where you'll find trick skaters weaving through an NYRSA slalom course at full speed, or the Mall in front of the bandshell (above Bethesda Foutain) for twirling to tunes. In summer, **Wollman Rink** converts to a hot-shot roller rink, with half-pipes and lessons available (see "Ice Skating," below).

You can rent skates for about $15 a day weekdays and $25 a day weekends from **Blades East,** 160 E. 86th St. (☎ **212/996-1644**), and **Blades West,** 120 W. 72nd St. (☎ **212/787-3911**). April to October. Wollman also rents in-line skates for park use at similar rates.

ICE SKATING   Central Park's **Wollman Rink,** at 59th Street and Sixth Avenue (☎ **212/396-1010**), is the city's best outdoor skating spot. It's open for skating generally from mid-October to mid-April, depending on the weather. Rates are $7 for adults, $3.50 for seniors and kids under 12, and skate rental is $3.50; lockers are available.

PLAYGROUNDS   Nineteen Adventure Playgrounds are scattered throughout the park, perfect for jumping, sliding, tottering, swinging, and digging. At Central Park West and 81st Street is the **Diana Ross Playground,** voted the city's best by *New York* magazine. Also on the west side is the **Spector Playground,** at 85th Street and Central Park West, and, a little farther north, the **Wild West Playground** at 93rd Street. On the east side, the **Rustic Playground,** at 67th Street and Fifth Avenue, is a delightfully landscaped space rife with islands, bridges, and big slides; and the **Pat Hoffman Friedman Playground,** right behind the Metropolitan Museum of Art at East 79th Street, is geared toward older toddlers.

RUNNING   Marathoners and wannabes regularly run in Central Park along the 6-mile **Central Park Drive,** which circles the park (run toward traffic to avoid being mowed down by wayward cyclists and in-line skaters). For a shorter loop, try the midpark 1.58-mile track around the **Reservoir,** recently renamed for Jacqueline Kennedy Onassis, who often enjoyed a jog here (keep your eyes peeled for Madonna and other famous bodies). It's safest to jog only during daylight hours and where everybody else does. Avoid the small walks in the Ramble and at the north end of the park.

TENNIS   Of the 50 or so municipal tennis courts maintained by the New York City Parks Department, Central Park's 30 Har-Tru outdoor courts are the best. The verdant setting is beautiful and the atmosphere friendly, making it easy to find a partner. Single-play is generally $5; call the **Central Park Tennis Center** at ☎ 212/280-0201 for more information. Courts are assigned on a first-come, first-serve basis by sign-up sheets put out every half hour for the next hour's play. When the U.S. Open is in town, stop by to try to catch the athletes warming up already hot backhands.

OTHER PARKS

For parks in Brooklyn and Queens, see "Highlights of the Outer Boroughs" later in this chapter. For more information on these and other city parks, visit **www. ci.nyc.ny.us/html/dpr**.

Battery Park. From State St. to New York Harbor. Subway: N, R to Whitehall St.; 1, 9 to South Ferry; 4, 5 to Bowling Green.

As you traverse Manhattan's concrete canyons, it's sometimes easy to forget you're actually on an island. But here, at Manhattan's southernmost tip, you can actually sense that just out past Liberty, Ellis, and Staten islands is the vast Atlantic Ocean.

The 21-acre park is named for the cannons built to defend residents after the American Revolution. **Castle Clinton National Monument** (the place to purchase tickets for the Statue of Liberty and Ellis Island Ferry; see section 2 earlier in this chapter) was built as a fort before the War of 1812, though it was never used as such. You'll likely recognize Battery Park for the prominent role it played in *Desperately Seeking Susan,* Madonna's first movie. Besides the requisite T-shirt vendors and hot-dog carts, you'll find several statues and memorials scattered throughout the park. This is quite the civilized park, with lots of STAY OFF THE GRASS! signs and Wall Streeters eating sandwiches on the many park benches. Find your own bench for a good view out across the harbor.

Bryant Park. Behind the New York Public Library, at Sixth Ave. btw. 40th and 42nd sts. Subway: B, D, F, Q to 42nd St.; 7 to Fifth Ave.

Another success story in the push for urban redevelopment, Bryant Park is the latest incarnation of a 4-acre site that was, at various times in its history, a graveyard and a reservoir. Named for poet and *New York Evening Post* editor William Cullen Bryant (look for his statue on the east end), the park actually rests atop the New York Public Library's many miles of underground stacks. Another statue is also notable: a squat and evocative stone portrait of Gertrude Stein, one of the few outdoor sculptures of women in the city.

This simple green swath, just east of Times Square, is welcome relief from Midtown's concrete, taxi-choked jungle, and good weather attracts brownbaggers from

We Can Work It Out

Your hotel doesn't have a gym, and walking around New York just isn't enough of a workout for you? Never fear: The city has a number of health clubs that are open to out-of-towners on a day-to-day basis.

Since many of the city's private gyms charge upwards of 40 bucks for day passes, the best bet for wallet-watching visitors is **Crunch Fitness,** 404 Lafayette St. (☎ 212/614-0120), 160 W. 83rd St. on the Upper West Side (☎ 212/875-1902), and at other locations throughout Manhattan (check the Yellow Pages). Down-to-earth Crunch charges a more reasonable per-day drop-in fee of $22, and the Lafayette Street location is open 24 hours.

Two favorites of Midtown office workers are the **Midtown YWCA,** 610 Lexington Ave. (☎ 212/755-4500; $15 drop-in fee), and **Vanderbilt YMCA,** 224 E. 47th St. (☎ 212/756-9600; $20 drop-in fee), both with pools.

---

neighboring office buildings. Just behind the library is **Bryant Park Grill** (☎ 212/840-6500), an airy bistro with New American food and service that doesn't live up to its fine setting (or high prices). Still, the casual, outdoor cafe is quite affordable.

Additionally, the park plays host to New York's **Seventh on Sixth** fashion shows, set up in billowy white tents (open to the trade only) in the spring and fall. If you're visiting in summer, bring a picnic supper to the free Monday-night **Bryant Park Film Festival,** where you'll see classic and kitschy flicks under the stars—just like a drive-in, but without the car. Call ☎ 212/512-5700 for this season's film schedule.

✪ **Union Square Park.** From 14th to 17th sts., btw. Park Ave. South and Broadway. Subway: L, N, R, 4, 5, 6 to 14th St.–Union Sq.

Here's a delightful place to spend an afternoon. Reclaimed from drug dealers and abject ruin in the late 1980s, Union Square Park is now one of the city's best assets. The seemingly endless subway work should no longer be disturbing the peace by the time you're here. This patch of green remains, with or without the construction, the focal point of the newly fashionable Flatiron and Gramercy Park neighborhoods. Don't miss the grand equestrian statue of George Washington at the south end or the bronze (by Bartholdi, who sculpted the Statue of Liberty) of the marquis de Lafayette at the eastern end, gracefully glancing toward France.

This charming square is now best known as the site of New York's premier **greenmarket.** Every Monday, Wednesday, Friday, and Saturday, vendors come down from upstate, Long Island, and as far away as Pennsylvania to hawk fresh veggies and fruits, organic baked goods, cider, wine, and even fresh fish and lobsters in booths that flank the north and west sides of the square. Fresh-cut flowers and plants are also for sale, as are books and postcards. During summer and fall, you can graze the bazaar and easily assemble a cheap and healthy lunch to munch under the trees, or at the picnic tables at the park's north end. Musical acts regularly play the small pavilion at the north end of the park, and in-line skaters take over the market space in the after-work hours. At the north end of the park, a small cafe, **Luna Park** (☎ 212/475-8464), is open in warm weather. A number of hip restaurants and superstores rim the small park—so on a nice day, pop in to **Barnes & Noble** superstore for a book or a magazine, browse the **Virgin Megastore** for some new tunes for you walkman, pick a bench in the park, and you'll be happy as a clam.

Washington Square Park. At the southern end of Fifth Ave. (where it intersects Waverly Place) btw. Macdougal and Wooster sts. Subway: A, B, C, D, E, F, Q to West 4th St.–Washington Sq.

You'll be hard-pressed to find much "park" in this mainly concrete square, but it's undeniably the focal point of Greenwich Village. Chess players, skateboarders, street musicians, New York University students, gay and straight couples, the occasional film crew, and not a few homeless people compete for attention throughout the day, and most of the night. For a look at the park's fascinating past, see the Greenwich Village walking tour earlier in this chapter.

Despite a city cleanup and increased police presence, it's a good idea to stay out of the park after dark.

CHELSEA PIERS

One of the city's biggest—and most successful—private urban development projects of the last few years has been the 30-acre **Chelsea Piers Sports and Entertainment Complex** (☎ 212/336-6666; www.chelseapiers.com). Jutting out into the Hudson River on four huge piers between 17th and 23rd streets, it's a terrific multi-functional recreational facility.

The **Sports Center** (☎ 212/336-6000), a three-football-fields-long megafacility, does health clubs one better. It offers not only the usual cardiovascular training, weights, and aerobics but also a four-lane, quarter-mile indoor running track, a boxing ring, basketball courts, a sand volleyball court, a gorgeous 25-yard indoor pool with a whirlpool and sundeck, the world's most challenging rock-climbing wall plus a bouldering wall, and the **Origins Feel-Good Spa** (☎ 212/336-6780), which offers massage, reflexology, facials, and the like. Day passes to the Sports Center are a pricey-but-worth-it $36 for nonmembers (spa treatments not included).

The **Golf Club** (☎ 212/336-6400), has 52 all-weather, fully automated hitting stalls on four levels, and a 200-yard net-enclosed turf fairway jutting out over the water. The Piers is the best place in the city to hit a few. It's $15 for 100 balls at off-peak hours, $15 for 68 balls at peak times; club rentals are $2 each, or $3 for five.

The **Sky Rink** (☎ 212/336-6100), the city's newest ice rink, has twin round-the-clock indoor rinks for recreational skating and pickup hockey games with Hudson River views. Skating is $10.50 for adults, $8 for seniors and kids; skate rental is $5.

If wheels are your thing, there are two outdoor **Roller Rinks** (☎ 212/336-6200) for in-line skating and roller hockey games. General skating is $5 for adults, $4 for kids; skate rentals are $13.50 for adults, $8 for kids, and a $150 cash or credit-card deposit is required. The **Skate School** offers lessons.

The **Field House** (☎ 212/336-6500) is mainly for team sports, but young rock climbers will enjoy the 30-foot indoor **climbing wall,** suitable for kids as well as grown-ups. Adult open climbs are $15, and children's lessons are available. **Batting cages** are also available ($1 per 10 pitches).

Feeling like a little 10-pin tonight? State-of-the-art **AMF Chelsea Piers Bowling** (☎ 212/835-2695) offers 40 lanes of fun. Games are $6.50 per person, and shoe rental is $4.

Beyond its athletic facilities, the complex is a destination in and of itself. The 1.2-mile **esplanade** has benches and picnic tables with terrific river views; they serve as the perfect vantage point for watching the *QEII* head out to sea, or Navy and Coast Guard ships sailing in for Fleet Week each May (see the "New York City Calendar of Events" in chapter 2). For waterfront dining, New York's largest microbrewery/restaurant, the **Chelsea Brewing Company** (☎ 212/336-6440), on Pier 59, serves up very good brews and okay food on a terrific waterfront terrace.

Getting There: Chelsea Piers is accessible by taxi and the M23 crosstown bus. The nearest subway is the C and E at 23rd Street and Eighth Avenue, then pick up the M23 or walk 4 long blocks west. Another option is to take the A, C, E to 14th Street or the L train to Eighth Avenue, walk to the river, then follow the walking/riding/running path along the river north.

9 Talk of the Town: Free TV Tapings

The trick to getting tickets for TV tapings in this city is to be from out of town. Producers are gun-shy about filling their audiences with obnoxious locals, and see everybody who's not from New York as being from the heartland—and therefore their target TV audience. Whatever—this means good news for you, as long as you don't live in the city. If you do, my best advice is use Uncle Phil's address in Boise when you send in your postcard for tickets.

If your heart's set on getting tickets to a show, be sure to request them as early as possible—6 months ahead isn't too early. You're usually asked to send a postcard. Always include the number of tickets you want, your preferred dates of attendance (be as flexible as you can with this one), and your address *and* phone number. Tickets are always free. The shows tend to be pretty good about trying to meet your specific date requests, but don't be surprised if Maury Povich is far more responsive than, say, Dave. And even if you send in your request extra early, don't be surprised if tickets don't show up at your house until 1 or 2 weeks before the tape date.

If you come to town without any tickets, all hope is not lost. Because they know that every ticket holder won't make it, many studios give out a limited number of standby tickets on the day of taping. If you can get up a little early and don't mind standing in line for a couple (or a few) hours, you have a good chance of getting one. Now, the bad news: Only one standby ticket per person is allowed, so everybody who wants to get in has to get up at the crack of dawn and stand in line. And even if you get your hands on a standby ticket, it doesn't guarantee admission; they usually only start seating standbys after the regular ticket holders are in. Still, chances are good.

For additional information on getting tickets to tapings, call ☎ **212/484-1222,** the New York Convention and Visitors Bureau's 24-hour hot line. And remember—you don't need a ticket to be on the *Today* show. *Good Morning America* will also have a street-facing studio, in Times Square on Broadway between 43rd and 44th streets, by the time you read this—but it will be on the second floor (just like the MTV studios across the street, at 1515 Broadway), so you won't be able to peer in.

If you do attend a taping, be sure to bring a sweater, even in winter. As anybody who watches Letterman knows, it's an icebox in those studios. And bring ID, as proof of age may be required.

Cosby Tapings of this legendary funnyman's CBS sitcom are Thursdays at 4 and 7:30pm at Kaufman-Astoria Studios in Queens, and you must be 16 or older to attend. Send a postcard requesting tickets to *Cosby* Tickets, c/o Kaufman Astoria Studios, 34–12 36th St., Astoria, NY 11106 (☎718/706-5389).

The Daily Show with Jon Stewart Comedy Central's boldly irreverent, often hilariously funny mock newscast tapes every Monday through Thursday at 5:45pm, at 513 W. 54th St. Call ☎ 212/586-2477 at least 2 months in advance (no postcards), or check with them on Fridays to see if cancellations have freed up any tickets for the upcoming week.

Late Night with Conan O'Brien Conan tix are a hot commodity—so start planning now. Tapings are Tuesday through Friday at 5:30pm (plan on arriving by 4:45pm if you have tickets), and you must be 16 or older to attend. Send your postcard to NBC Tickets/Late Night, 30 Rockefeller Plaza, New York, NY 10112 (☎ 212/664-3056, 212/664-3057, or 212/664-4000). Fifty same-day standby tickets are distributed at the page desk at NBC Studios at 30 Rockefeller Plaza at 9am, but come much earlier if you actually want to get one.

The Late Show with David Letterman   Here's the most in-demand TV ticket in town—so planning 9 months ahead isn't too soon. Tapings are Monday through Thursday at 5:30pm (arrive by 4:15pm), with a second taping Thursday at 8pm (arrive by 6:45pm). You must be 16 or older to attend. Send your postcard at least 6 months early (2 tickets max; one request only, or all will be disregarded), to *Late Show* Tickets, Ed Sullivan Theater, 1697 Broadway, New York, NY 10019 (☎ 212/ 975-5853). On tape days, call ☎ 212/247-6497 at 11am for standby tickets (no in-line standbys anymore); start dialing early, because the machine will kick in as soon as all standbys are gone.

Live! with Regis and Kathie Lee   Here's the *other* hot ticket in town. Tapings of this popular couple are Monday to Friday at 9am at the ABC Studios at 7 Lincoln Square (Columbus Ave. and West 67th St.) on the Upper West Side. You must be 10 or older to attend (under 18s must be accompanied by a parent). Send your postcard (4 tickets max) a *full year* in advance to *Live!* Tickets, Ansonia Station, P.O. Box 777, New York, NY 10023-0777 (☎ 212/456-3054 or 212/456-3537). Standby tickets are some-times available. Arrive at the studio no later than 8am and request a standby number; they're handed out on a first-come, first-serve basis. You might also have a chance at last-minute tickets by calling ☎ 212/456-2410 or 212/456-3055, but this is a longer shot than going standby.

The Maury Show   Tapings of Maury Povich's talkfest are generally Tuesday through Thursday at 8:30am and 11:30am, at 15 Penn Plaza, 33rd Street between Seventh Avenue and Broadway. You must be 18 or over to attend. Mr. Connie Chung doesn't exactly have the best ratings in town, so getting in isn't that difficult; just call ☎ 212/244-7545.

The Montel Williams Show   Tapings are generally Wednesday and Thursday at 10:30am and 1:30 and 3:30pm, at 356 W. 58th St. You must be 18 or older to attend. Order tickets by calling ☎ 212/989-8101.

The Ricki Lake Show   Tapings are generally Tuesday at 1pm, Wednesday and Thursday at 3 and 5:30pm, and Friday 1 and 3pm. You must be 18 or older to attend. Order tickets by sending a postcard 1 month in advance to the *Ricki Lake Show*, 226 W. 26th St. 4th Floor, New York, NY 10001 (☎ 800/GO-RICKI or 212/352-3322; e-mail requests: rltickets@aol.com). Standby tickets are usually available 1 to 1½ hours before taping; just show up at the studio, 26th Street and Seventh Avenue (call to con-firm that a taping is on first).

The Rosie O'Donnell Show   Rosie is so popular right now that ticket requests have been suspended at press time. Take heart, however, because they're scheduled to start up again by the time you read this. The schedule varies, but in general Rosie tapings are Monday through Thursday at 10am and Wednesday at 2pm. No children under 5 are allowed, and under 18s must be accompanied by an adult. Send your postcard a year in advance (2 per request) to NBC Tickets/ *The Rosie O'Donnell Show*, 30 Rocke-feller Plaza, Suite 800E, New York, NY 10112 (☎ 212/506-3288 or 212/664-4000). Standby tickets, if available, are distributed at 7:30am outside 30 Rockefeller Plaza, on the 49th Street side of the building; it's a random lottery system, so it doesn't help to show up too early.

The Sally Show   You can Sally Jessy Raphaël in action twice daily Monday through Wednesday (usually 10am and 3pm), at 15 Penn Plaza, 33rd Street between Seventh Avenue and Broadway. You must be 18 or older to attend. Call ☎ 800/411-7941 or 212/244-3595 for tickets.

Saturday Night Live   Everything about the show may change, but one thing remains the same—SNL's enduring popularity. This is another extremely hard ticket to come by. Tapings are Saturdays 11:30pm (arrival time 10pm); there's also a full dress rehearsal (arrival time 7pm). You must be 16 or older to attend. Send your postcard to arrive *in the month of August only* to NBC Tickets/*Saturday Night Live*, 30 Rockefeller Plaza, New York, NY 10112 (☎ **212/664-4000**). Lotteries for pairs of tickets are held during the season; if you're a winner, you'll be notified with only 1 to 2 weeks' advance notice. Standby tickets may be a better bet: They're available at 9:15am on Saturday morning of tape day at the 49th Street entrance to Rockefeller Plaza.

Spin City   Taping days vary for Michael J. Fox's hit sitcom, but filming always takes place at Pier 61 at Chelsea Piers, 23rd Street and the Hudson River. You must be 18 or older to attend. Send your request (2 tickets max) at least 4 weeks in advance to *Spin City* Tickets, London Terrace Post Office, P.O. Box 20241, New York, NY 10011-0003 (☎ **212/336-6993**). Since ticket requests are often suspended early in the season, standbys may be a better bet: Show up at the studio by 5pm on tape day; standby tix are handed out at 6:45pm. Taping begins at 7:30pm and generally lasts four hours. Call for the current taping schedule.

The *Today* Show   As most of you know, anybody can be on TV with Katie, Matt, and cuddly weatherman Al Roker. All you have to do is show up outside the *Today* show's glass-walled studio at Rockefeller Center, on the southwest corner of 49th Street and Rockefeller Plaza, with your very own HI, MOM! sign. Tapings are Monday through Friday at 7am sharp, but come at the crack of dawn if your heart's set on being in front. Who knows? If it's a nice day, you may even get to chat with Katie, Matt, or Al.

The *View*   ABC's girl power gabfest tapes live Monday through Friday at 11am, and you must be at least 18 to attend. Requests, which should be send about 3 to 4 months in advance, can be submitted online (**www.abc.go.com/theview**) or via postcard to Tickets, *The View*, 320 W. 66th St., New York, NY 10023 (☎ **212/579-1167**). Since date requests are not usually accommodated, try standby: Arrive before 10am and put your name on the standby list; earlier is better, since tickets are handed out on a first-come, first-serve basis.

10 Especially for Kids

You don't have to worry about how you'll keep your kids occupied in New York. This action-packed, neon-bright urban jungle has always kept kids enthralled. These days, it's better than ever for the under-16 set—just ask Disney, which has turned Times Square into a pint-sized person's paradise. For general tips and other resources for visiting the city with the kids, see "For Families" under "Tips for Travelers with Special Needs" in chapter 2.

Some of New York's sights and attractions are designed specifically with kids in mind, and I've listed those below. But many of those I've discussed in the rest of this chapter are terrific for kids as well as adults; I've also included cross-references to the best of them below.

Probably the best place of all to entertain the kids is in ✪ **Central Park**, which has kid-friendly diversions galore. For details on all of Central Park's delights, see the section earlier in this chapter.

MUSEUMS

In addition to the museums designed specifically for kids below, also consider the following, discussed elsewhere in this chapter: The **American Museum of Natural History** (p. 202), whose dinosaur displays are guaranteed to wow both you and the kids; the *Intrepid* **Sea-Air-Space Museum** (p. 212), on a real battleship with an amazing collection of vintage and high-tech airplanes; the **Forbes Magazine Galleries**

(p. 212), whose wacky collection includes a number of vintage toys and games; the **Museum of Television & Radio** (p. 215), where you and the kids can pull up episodes of *Sesame Street* and other classic kids' TV shows to watch; the **American Museum of the Moving Image** (p. 261), where you and the kids can learn how movies are actually made; the **Lower East Side Tenement Museum** (p. 213), whose living-history approach really intrigues school-age kids; the **New York Transit Museum** (p. 259), where kids can explore vintage subway cars and other hands-on exhibits; and the **South Street Seaport & Museum** (p. 193), which little ones will love for its theme-park–like atmosphere and old boats.

Children's Museum of the Arts. 182 Lafayette St. (btw. Broome and Grand sts.). ☎ 212/ 941-9198 or 212/274-0986. Admission $4 weekdays, $5 weekends for adults under 65 and children over 18 months. Wed noon–7pm, Thurs–Sun noon–5pm. Subway: B, D, F, Q to Broadway–Lafayette St.; 6 to Spring St.

Interactive workshop programs for children 18 months to 10 years are the attraction here. Kids dabble in puppet making and computer drawing or join in sing-alongs and live performances, which may include improvisational storytelling from "The Brothers Grin." Call for the current schedule.

✪ **Children's Museum of Manhattan.** 212 W. 83rd St. (btw. Broadway and Amsterdam Ave.). ☎ 212/721-1234. www.cmom.org. Admission $5 children and adults, $2.50 seniors. Wed–Sun 10am–5pm. Subway: 1, 9 to 86th St.

Here's a great place to take the kids when they're tired of being told not to touch. Designed for kids 2 to 12, this museum is strictly hands-on. Interactive exhibits and activity centers encourage self-discovery—and a recent expansion means that there's now more than ever before to keep the kids busy and learning. The Time Warner Media Center takes children through the world of animation and helps them produce their own videos. Brand-new in 1999 is the Body Odyssey, a zany, scientific journey through the human body. This isn't just a museum for the five-and-up set—there are exhibits especially designed for babies and toddlers, too. The busy schedule also includes daily art classes and storytellers, and a full slate of entertainment on weekends.

New York City Fire Museum. 278 Spring St. (btw. Varick and Hudson sts.). ☎ 212/ 691-1303. www.nyfd.com/museum.html. Suggested donation $4 adults, $2 seniors and students, $1 children under 12. Tues–Sun 10am–4pm. Subway: C, E to Spring St.; 1, 9 to Houston St.

What's better than fire trucks when you're a little kid? Not much. Housed in a real three-story 1904 firehouse, displays include vintage fire trucks and equipment all the way back to the horse-drawn days. Look for the leather hoses, fire boats, poles, bells, Currier & Ives prints, and even a stuffed firehouse dog. Tours with an emphasis on fire safety can be arranged in advance for small groups.

✪ **New York Hall of Science.** 4701 111th St., in Flushing Meadows–Corona Park, Queens. ☎ 718/699-0005. www.nyhallsci.org. Admission $6 adults, $4 children and seniors; free Thurs and Fri 2–5pm. Mon–Wed 9:30am–2pm, Thurs–Sun 9:30am–5pm. Subway: 7 to 111th St.

Children of all ages will love this huge, hands-on museum, which bills itself as New York's only Science Playground. This place is amazing for school-age kids—like Beakman's World come to life. Exhibits let them be engulfed by a giant soap bubble, float on air in an antigravity mirror, compose music by dancing in front of light beams, and explore the more-than-miniature world of microbes. There are video machines that kids can use to retrieve astronomical images, including pictures taken by the *Galileo* in orbit around Jupiter. There's even a Preschool Discovery Place for the really little ones. But probably best of all is the summertime Outdoor Science Playground for kids six and older—ostensibly a physics lesson, but really just a great excuse to laugh, jump, and play on jungle gyms, slides, seesaws, spinners, and more.

The museum is located in **Flushing Meadows–Corona Park,** where kids can enjoy even more fun beyond the Hall of Science. Not only are there more than 1,200 acres of park and playgrounds, but there's also a zoo, a carousel, an indoor ice-skating rink, an outdoor pool, and bike and boat rentals. Kids and grown-ups alike will love getting an up-close look at the Unisphere steel globe, which was not really destroyed in *Men in Black.* The park is also home to the Queens Museum of Art (see "Highlights of the Outer Boroughs," below) as well as Shea Stadium and the U.S. Open Tennis Center.

Sony Wonder Technology Lab. Sony Plaza, 550 Madison Ave. (at 56th St.). ☎ **212/ 833-8100.** Free admission. Tues, Wed, Fri, Sat 10am–6pm; Thurs 10am–8pm; Sun noon–6pm. Subway: 4, 5, 6 to 59th St.; E, F, to Fifth Ave.

Not as much of an infomercial as you'd expect. Both kids and adults love this high-tech science and technology center, which explores communications and information technology. You can experiment with robotics, explore the human body through medical imaging, edit a music video, mix a hit song, design a video game, and save the day at an environmental command center. The lab also features the first high-definition interactive theater in the United States.

OTHER KID-FRIENDLY DIVERSIONS

In addition to the choices below, don't forget New York's fabulous theme restaurants, which are all playgrounds unto themselves; see "Theme Restaurant Thrills!" in chapter 6.

ZOOS & AQUARIUMS Bigger kids will love the legendary **Bronx Zoo** (p. 256), while the **Central Park Wildlife Center** with its Tisch Children's Zoo (p. 246) is particularly suitable for younger kids. At the **New York Aquarium** at Coney Island (p. 258), kids can touch starfish and sea urchins and watch bottlenose dolphins and California sea lions stunt-swim in the outdoor aquatheater.

SKY-HIGH VIEWS Kids of all ages can't help but turn dizzy with delight taking in incredible views from atop the **Empire State Building** (p. 219) and the **World Trade Center** (p. 194). The Empire State Building also offers the **New York Skyride,** a stomach-churning virtual tour of New York—just in case the real one isn't enough for them.

THEATER FOR KIDS The kid-oriented theater scene is flourishing. The top venue is the **New Victory Theater,** 209 W. 42nd St. (☎ 212/382-4020), which reopened a few years back as the city's first full-time family-oriented performing-arts center. For events at the New Victory and all around the city, check the "Cue" section of *New York* magazine, *Time Out New York,* or the Friday *New York Times* for current listings. Also be on the lookout for the **Paper Bag Players,** called "the best children's theater in the country" by *Newsweek;* in winter only, at Hunter College's Sylvia and Danny Kaye Playhouse, 68th Street between Park and Lexington avenues (☎ 212/ 362-0431 or 212/772-4448).

SPECIAL EVENTS Children's eyes grow wide at the year-long march of **parades** (especially Macy's Thanksgiving Day Parade), **circuses** (Big Apple and Ringling Bros. Barnum & Bailey), and **holiday shows** (the Rockettes' Christmas and Easter performances). See the "New York City Calendar of Events" in chapter 2 for details.

11 Highlights of the Outer Boroughs

IN THE BRONX

In addition to the choices below, literary buffs might also want to consider the **Edgar Allan Poe Cottage,** at the Grand Concourse and East Kingsbridge Road

(☎ 718/ 881-8900), the final home for the brilliant but troubled author of *The Raven, The Tell-Tale Heart,* and other masterworks. For more information, see the box "In Search of Historic Homes" earlier in this chapter.

❂ Bronx Zoo Wildlife Conservation Park. At Fordham Rd. and Bronx River Pkwy., the Bronx. ☎ 718/367-1010. www.wcs.org. Admission Jan 4–Mar, $4 adults, seniors and children under 12 $2; Apr–Oct, $7.75 adults, $4 seniors and children under 12; Nov–Jan 3, $6 adults, $3 seniors and children under 12; free Wed year-round. There may be small additional charges for some exhibits. Jan–Mar daily 10am–4:30pm; Apr–Oct, Mon–Fri 10am–5pm, Sat–Sun 10am–5:30pm; Nov 1–Nov 20, daily 10am–4:30pm; Nov 20–Dec 31, Sun–Thu 10am–9pm, Fri and Sat 10am–9:30pm. Transportation: See "Getting There," below.

Founded in 1899, the Bronx Zoo is the largest metropolitan animal park in the United States, with more than 4,000 animals living on 265 acres. Most of the old-fashioned cages have been replaced by more natural settings, and this is quite a progressive zoo as zoos go.

One of the zoo's most impressive exhibits is the **Wild Asia Complex.** This zoo-within-a-zoo comprises the **Wild Asia Plaza** education center; **Jungle World,** an indoor re-creation of Asian forests with birds, lizards, gibbons, and leopards; and the **Bengali Express Monorail** (open May–Oct), which takes you on a narrated ride high above free-roaming Siberian tigers, Asian elephants, Indian rhinoceroses, and other non-native New Yorkers (keep your eyes peeled—the animals aren't as interested in seeing you). You might also catch a glimpse of the beautiful and extremely rare (estimates indicate fewer than 1,000 in nature) snow leopard, as the zoo has re-created a **Himalayan Highlands habitat** that's home to some 17 snow leopards, as well as red pandas and white-naped cranes.

The **Children's Zoo** (open Apr–Oct) allows youngsters to learn about their wildlife counterparts. Kids can compare their leaps to those of a bullfrog, slide into a turtle shell, climb into a heron's nest, see with the eyes of an owl, and hear with the acute ears of a fennec fox. There's also an area where children feed domestic animals.

A popular exhibit, open from spring to September, is the **Butterfly Zone,** aflutter with 1,000 colorful specimens flying all around you inside a 170-foot-long tent. Call ahead to check if it will be around when you get to the zoo. New in 1999 is the **Congo Gorilla Forest,** a 6½-acre exhibit that will be home to Western lowland gorillas, okapi, red river hogs, and other African rain forest animals.

If the natural settings and breeding programs aren't enough to keep zoo residents entertained, they can always choose to ogle the 2 million annual visitors. But there are ways to beat the crowds: Try to visit on a weekday or on a nice winter's day. In summer, come early in the day, before the heat of the day sends the animals back into their enclosures. And you can always schedule an **Insider's Hour** tour (Jan–Mar and July–Sept) by calling ☎ 718/220-5141.

Getting There: The easiest way to get to the Bronx Zoo is by Liberty Line's BxM11 express bus running from various stops on Madison Avenue to the park entrance; call ☎ 718/652-8400 for a schedule. By subway, take the no. 2 train to Pelham Parkway and then walk 2 blocks west.

New York Botanical Garden. At 200th St. and Southern Blvd., the Bronx. ☎ 718/817-8700. www.nybg.org. Admission $3 adults, $2 seniors and students, $1 children 2–12; free all day Wed and Sat 10am–noon. Extra charges for Everett Children's Adventure Garden, Enid A. Haupt Conservatory, and T. H. Everett Rock Garden and Native Plant Garden. Apr–Oct, Tues–Sun and Mon holidays 10am–6pm; Nov–Mar, Tues–Sun and Mon holidays 10am–4pm. Transportation: See "Getting There," below.

A National Historic Landmark, the 250-acre New York Botanical Garden was founded in 1891 and today is one of America's foremost public gardens. The setting is spectacular—a natural terrain of rock outcroppings, a river with cascading waterfall, hills, ponds, and wetlands.

Highlights of the Botanical Garden are the 27 **specialty gardens** (the Peggy Rockefeller formal rose garden, the Nancy Bryan Luce herb garden, and the restored rock garden are my favorites), an exceptional **orchid collection,** and 40 acres of **uncut forest.** Natural exhibits are augmented by year-round educational programs, musical events, bird-watching excursions, lectures, special family programs, and many more activities. Snuff Mill, once used to grind tobacco, has a charming cafe on the banks of the Bronx River.

A major beneficiary of capital improvements in 1997 was the **Enid A. Haupt Conservatory,** a stunning series of Victorian glass pavilions that recall London's former Crystal Palace, sheltering a rich collection of tropical, subtropical, and desert plants as well as seasonal flower shows. In 1998, a brand-new **Children's Adventure Garden** debuted.

There are so many ways to see the garden—tram, golf cart, walking tours—that it's best to call for more information.

Getting There: The easiest way is by Garden Shuttle that operates weekends, April through October, between the American Museum of Natural History, the Metropolitan Museum of Art, and the Botanical Garden; call ☎ **718/817-8700** for reservations and information. By train, take Metro North (☎ **212/532-4900**) from Grand Central Terminal to the New York Botanical Garden Station. By subway, take the D or 4 train to Bedford Park Boulevard and walk east 8 long blocks.

Wave Hill. 675 W. 252nd St. (at Independence Ave.), Bronx. ☎ **718/549-3200.** www.wavehill.org. Tues–Sun 9am–4:30pm; extended in summer (check ahead). Admission $4 adults, $2 seniors and students; free in winter, and on Sat mornings and Tues in summer. Transportation: See "Getting There," below.

Wave Hill has, at various times in its history, been home to a British UN ambassador as well as Mark Twain and Theodore Roosevelt. Its 28 acres were bequeathed to the city of New York for use as a public garden that is now one of the most beautiful spots in the city, with panoramic views of the Hudson River and the Palisades. Programs range from horticulture to environmental education, visual and performing arts, landscape history, and forestry—more than enough to justify a visit.

Getting There: Take the 1 or 9 subway to 231st Street., then take Bx7 or BX10 bus at the northwest corner of 231st Street; Wave Hill is a short walk from the 252nd Street stop. Metro-North trains (☎ 212/532-4900) to the Riverdale stop, then walk up 254th Street and turn right on Independence Avenue. Or take Liberty Lines' Manhattan-Riverdale Express (☎718/652-8400) bus BxM1 or BxM2 to 252nd Street and walk west across the parkway bridge, following the signs.

IN BROOKLYN

For details on walking the **Brooklyn Bridge,** see "Historic Lower Manhattan's Top Attractions" earlier in this chapter.

It's easy to link visits to the Brooklyn Botanic Garden, the Brooklyn Museum of Art, and Prospect Park, since they're all an easy walk from one another, just off **Grand Army Plaza.** Designed by Frederick Law Olmsted and Calvert Vaux as a suitably grand entrance to their Prospect Park, it boasts an impressive Civil War memorial arch designed by John H. Duncan (1892–1901) and the main **Brooklyn Public Library,** an art-deco masterpiece completed in 1941 (the garden and museum are just on the other side of the library, down Eastern Pkwy.). If you don't want to walk, a **free trolley** loops the area once an hour weekends and holidays noon to 5pm; for information, call ☎ **718/965-8967.** The entire area is a half-hour subway ride from Midtown Manhattan.

✪ **Brooklyn Botanic Garden.** 1000 Washington Ave. (at Eastern Pkwy.), Brooklyn. ☎ 718/623-7200. www.bbg.org. Admission $3 adults, $1.50 seniors and students, 50¢ children 6–16. Admission free Tues and Sat 10am–noon. Free tours Sat–Sun 1pm. Apr–Sept, Tues–Fri 8am–6pm, Sat–Sun 10am–6pm; Oct–Mar, Tues–Fri 8am–4:30pm, Sat–Sun 10am–4:30pm. Subway: 2, 3 to Eastern Pkwy.–Brooklyn Museum; D to Prospect Park.

Just down the street from the Brooklyn Museum of Art (below) is the most popular botanic garden in the city. This peaceful, 52-acre sanctuary is at its most spectacular in late April and May, when thousands of deep-pink cherry tree blossoms bloom. In addition to the **rose garden,** there is the **Shakespeare Garden** with plants mentioned in his writings, a **Children's Discovery Garden,** and the **Fragrance Garden** designed for the blind but appreciated by all noses. Inside the Steinhardt Conservatory is the world-renowned **Bonsai Museum.** Much-needed restoration was just beginning on the extraordinary **Japanese Hill-and-Pond Garden** at press time, and is scheduled to be completed in January 2000.

✪ **Brooklyn Museum of Art.** 200 Eastern Pkwy. (at Washington Ave.), Brooklyn. ☎ 718/638-5000. www.brooklynart.org. Suggested admission $4 adults, $1.50 seniors and students, children under 12 free. Free first Sat of the month 5–11pm. Wed–Fri 10am–5pm; Sat–Sun 11am–6pm; first Sat of the month 11am–11pm. Subway: 2, 3 to Eastern Pkwy.–Brooklyn Museum.

One of the nation's premier art institutions, the Brooklyn Museum of Art rocketed back into the public consciousness with a blockbuster a couple of years ago: "Monet and the Mediterranean" attracted 225,000 visitors. It's now best known for its consistently remarkable temporary exhibitions, as well as its excellent permanent collection. Among the exhibitions scheduled for late 1999–2000 are "Vital Forms: American Art in the Atomic Age, 1940–1960"; "Sensation: Young British Artists from the Saatchi Collection," featuring works from such innovative contemporary shockmasters as Damien Hirst and Marc Quinn; and "Masterpieces of Fashion," from the museum's outstanding costume collection.

The museum's grand beaux-arts building designed by McKim, Mead & White (1897) befits its outstanding holdings, most notably the Egyptian collection of sculpture, wall reliefs, and mummies. The distinguished decorative arts collection includes 28 American period rooms from 1675 to 1928. Other highlights are the African and Asian arts galleries, 58 works by Rodin, and a diverse collection of both American and European painting and sculpture that includes works by Homer, O'Keeffe, Monet, Cézanne, and Degas.

First Saturday is the museum's ambitious—and popular—program that takes place on the first Saturday of each month. It runs from 5 to 11pm and includes free admission and a slate of live music, films, dancing, and other wide-ranging entertainment (think karaoke, lesbian poetry, silent film, experimental jazz, and disco dancing). **Insider's Hour** gallery talks are offered on weekends; call for schedule.

New York Aquarium. West 8th St. and Surf Ave., Coney Island, Brooklyn. ☎ 718/265-3400. www.wcs.org. Admission $8.75 adults, $4.50 seniors and children 2–12, free for children under 2. Daily 10am–5pm. Subway: D, F to W. 8th St. in Brooklyn.

Because of the long subway ride (about an hour) and its proximity to the Coney Island boardwalk, this one is really for summer. The Aquarium is home to hundreds of sea creatures. Taking center stage are Atlantic bottlenose dolphins and California sea lions that perform daily during summer at the **Aquatheater.** Also basking in the spotlight are seven beluga whales, gangly Pacific octopuses, and Bertha the sand tiger shark. Black-footed penguins, California sea otters, and a variety of seals live at the **Sea Cliffs exhibit,** a re-creation of a Pacific coastal habitat. Children love the hands-on exhibits at **Discovery Cove.** There's an indoor ocean-view cafeteria and an outdoor snack bar, plus picnic tables.

Brooklyn Heights Attractions

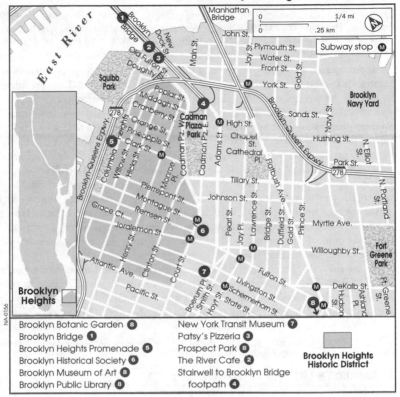

Brooklyn Botanic Garden 8	New York Transit Museum 7	
Brooklyn Bridge 1	Patsy's Pizzeria 3	
Brooklyn Heights Promenade 5	Prospect Park 8	
Brooklyn Historical Society 6	The River Cafe 2	**Brooklyn Heights Historic District**
Brooklyn Museum of Art 8	Stairwell to Brooklyn Bridge	
Brooklyn Public Library 8	footpath 4	

If you'd made the trip out, you simply must check out the human exhibits on nearby **Coney Island**'s 2.7-mile-long boardwalk. Not much is left from its heyday, and it can be a little eerie when the crowds aren't around, but you can still use the beach, drop some cash at the boardwalk arcade, and ride the famed wooden Cyclone roller coaster (still a terrifying ride, if only because it seems so . . . rickety). You can't leave without treating yourself to a **Nathan's Famous** hot dog (just off the boardwalk at Surf and Stillwell aves.)—this is the *original* location, where the term "hot dog" was coined back in 1906.

New York Transit Museum. Boerum Place and Schermerhorn St., Brooklyn. ☎ **718/ 243-8601.** www.mta.nyc.ny.us/museum. Admission $3 adults, $1.50 seniors and children under 18; free Wed noon–4pm. Tues–Fri 10am–4pm, Sat–Sun noon–5pm. Subway: 2, 3, 4, 5 to Borough Hall; C, F to Jay St.; N, R to Court St.

This underground museum, housed in a real decommissioned subway station, is a wonderful place to spend an hour or so, especially if you're a transit or social history buff. The museum is small but very well done, with good multimedia exhibits exploring the history of the subway from the first shovelful of dirt scooped up at groundbreaking (March 24, 1900) to the present. Kids and parents alike will enjoy the interactive elements—you even get to lift a wheelbarrow full of rocks just like the ones that the turn-of-the-century tunnel blasters had to move—as well as the vintage subway cars, old wooden turnstiles, and beautiful station mosaics of yesteryear. All in all, a minor but remarkable tribute to an important development in the city's history, and to a time when mass transit was a thing of sophistication and civic pride— a remarkable contrast for those of us who only know the grimy MTA of today.

Prospect Park. At Grand Army Plaza, bounded by Prospect Park W., Parkside Ave., and Flatbush Ave., Brooklyn. ☎ **718/965-8951.** www.prospectpark.org. Subway: 2, 3 to Grand Army Plaza (walk down Plaza St. W. 3 blocks to Prospect Park W. and the entrance) or Eastern Pkwy.–Brooklyn Museum.

Designed by Frederick Law Olmsted and Calvert Vaux after their great success with Central Park, these 562 acres of woodland, meadows, bluffs, and ponds are considered by many to be their masterpiece and the pièce de résistance of Brooklyn.

The best approach is from Grand Army Plaza, presided over by the monumental **Soldiers' and Sailors' Memorial Arch** (1892) honoring Union veterans. For the best view of the lush landscape, follow the path to Meadowport Arch, and proceed through to the Long Meadow, following the path that loops around it (it's about an hour's walk). Other park highlights include the 1857 Italianate mansion, **Litchfield Villa,** on Prospect Park West; the **Friends' Cemetery** Quaker burial ground (where Montgomery Clift rests—sorry, it's fenced off to browsers); the **carousel** with white wooden horses salvaged from a famous Coney Island merry-go-round; and **Lefferts Homestead** (☎ **718/965-6505**), a 1783 Dutch farmhouse with a museum of period furniture and exhibits geared toward children. There's a map at the park entrance that you can use to get your bearings.

On the east side of the park is the **Prospect Park Wildlife Conservation Center** (☎ **718/399-7339**). Major renovations completed in 1993 have made it a thoroughly modern children's zoo where kids can walk among wallabies, explore a prairie-dog town, and much more. Admission is $2.50 for adults, $1.25 for seniors, 50¢ for children under 12, free for those under 3. April through October, it's open Monday through Friday from 10am to 5pm, to 5:30 on weekends and holidays; November through March, hours are daily from 10am to 4:30pm.

✪ BROOKLYN HEIGHTS HISTORIC DISTRICT

Just across the Brooklyn Bridge is a peaceful neighborhood of tree-lined streets, more than 600 historic houses built before 1860, landmark churches, and restaurants. Even with its magnificent promenade providing sweeping views of Lower Manhattan's ragged skyline, it feels more like its own village than part of the larger urban expanse.

This is where Walt Whitman lived and wrote *Leaves of Grass;* where the 19th-century, fiery abolitionist Henry Ward Beecher railed against slavery at **Plymouth Church** of the Pilgrims on Orange Street between Henry and Hicks streets (his sister wrote *Uncle Tom's Cabin*). If you walk down **Willow Street** between Clark and Pierrepont, you'll see three houses (nos. 108–112) in the Queen Anne style that was fashionable in the late 19th century, as well as an attractive trio of Federal-style houses (nos. 155–159) built before 1829. Also visit lively **Montague Street,** the main drag of Brooklyn Heights, full of cafes and shops. And don't forget about **Patsy Grimaldi's Pizzeria,** nearby on historic Old Fulton Street, serving up the city's best pizza (see chapter 6).

Getting There: Bounded by the East River, Fulton Street, Court Street, and Atlantic Avenue, the Brooklyn Heights Historic District is one of the most outstanding and easily accessible sights beyond Manhattan. The neighborhood is reachable via a number of subway trains: the A, C, F to Jay St.; the 2, 3, 4, 5 to Clark Street or Borough Hall; and the N, R to Court Street.

It's easy to link a walk around Brooklyn Heights and along its Promenade with a walk over the **Brooklyn Bridge** (p. 185), a tour that makes for a lovely afternoon on a nice day. Take a 2 or 3 train to **Clark Street** (the first stop in Brooklyn). Turn right out of the station and walk toward the water, where you'll see the start of the waterfront **Brooklyn Promenade.** Stroll along the promenade bordered by stellar views of lower Manhattan to the left and gorgeous multi-million-dollar brownstones to the right, or park yourself on a bench for awhile to soak up the scene.

The promenade ends at Columbia Heights and Orange Street. To head to the bridge from here, turn left and walk toward the Watchtower Building. Before heading downslope, turn right immediately after the playground onto Middagh Street. After 4 or 5 blocks, you'll reach a busy thoroughfare, Cadman Plaza West. Cross the street and follow the walkway through little **Cadman Plaza Park;** veer left at the fork in the walkway. At Cadman Plaza East, turn left (downslope) toward the underpass, where you'll find the stairwell up to the Brooklyn Bridge footpath on your left.

IN QUEENS

For details on the **New York Hall of Science** and **Flushing Meadows–Corona Park** (also home to the Queens Museum of Art, below), see "Especially for Kids" earlier in this chapter.

✪ American Museum of the Moving Image. On 35th Ave. at 36th St., Astoria, Queens. ☎ **718/784-0077** or 718/784-4777. www.ammi.org. Admission $8.50 adults, $5.50 seniors and college students, $4.50 children 5–18. Tues–Fri noon–5pm, Sat–Sun 11am–6pm. Subway: R to Steinway St.

Here's the museum for all of us who truly love movies. Unlike the Museum of Television and Radio (see "More Manhattan Museums" earlier in this chapter), which is more of a library, this is a thought-provoking museum examining how moving images—film, video, and digital—are made, marketed, and shown; it encourages you to consider their impact on society as well. It's housed in part of the Kaufman Astoria Studios, once host to W. C. Fields and the Marx Brothers, and more recently used by Martin Scorsese (*The Age of Innocence*), Woody Allen (*Radio Days*), Bill Cosby (his *Cosby* TV series), and *Sesame Street*. (For details on getting tickets to a *Cosby* taping, see "Talk of the Town: Free TV Tapings" earlier in this chapter.)

The museum's core exhibit, **"Behind the Screen,"** is a thoroughly engaging two-floor installation that takes you step-by-step through the process of making, marketing, and exhibiting moving images. There are more than 1,000 artifacts on hand, from technological gadgetry to costumes, and interactive exhibits where you can try your own hand at sound-effects editing and create your own animated shorts, among others. Special-effects benchmarks from the mechanical mouth of *Jaws* to the blending of past and present in *Forrest Gump* are explained. And the collection of memorabilia should stir up some nostalgic silver-screen memories.

The museum hosts **film and video screenings,** usually accompanied by artist appearances, lectures, panel discussions, or live music. Free **exhibition tours** are offered Tuesday through Saturday at 3pm.

P.S. 1 Contemporary Art Center. 22–25 Jackson Ave., at 46th Ave., Long Island City, Queens. ☎ **718/784-2084.** www.queensmuse.org. Suggested admission $4 adults, $2 seniors and students. Wed–Sun noon–6pm. (Hours vary in summer, so call ahead.) Subway: E, F to 23rd St.–Ely Ave.; 7 to 45th Rd.–Court House Sq.

If you're interested in contemporary art that's too cutting edge for most museums, don't miss P.S. 1. Re-inaugurated in 1997 after a 3-year, $8.5-million renovation of the Renaissance-Revival building (originally a public school), this is the world's largest institution exhibiting contemporary art from America and abroad. You can expect to see a kaleidoscopic array of works from artists ranging from Jack Smith to Julian Schnabel; the museum is particularly well known for large-scale exhibitions by artists such as James Turrell. In early 1999 a high-profile merger with the Museum of Modern Art was announced, so P.S. 1 should start getting the kind of attention it so richly deserves.

Queens Museum of Art. Next to the Unisphere in Flushing Meadows–Corona Park, Queens. ☎ **718/592-9700.** www.queensmuse.org. Suggested admission $4 adults, $2 seniors and children, free for children under 5. Wed–Fri 10am–5pm, Sat–Sun noon–5pm. Subway: 7 to Willets Point–Shea Stadium.

One way to see New York in the shortest time (albeit without the street life) is to visit the Panorama, an enormous building-for-building architectural model of New York City complete with an airplane that takes off from La Guardia Airport. The 9,335-square-foot Gotham City is the largest model of its kind in the world, with 895,000 individual structures built on a scale of 1 inch = 100 feet. Constructed for the 1964–65 World's Fair, today it mirrors most of the current cityscape thanks to a 2-year rebuilding and refurbishing in the early 1990s.

12 Spectator Sports

For details on the **New York City Marathon,** see the "New York City Calendar of Events," in chapter 2. For all events at the Meadowlands Sports Complex in New Jersey, take the NJ Transit bus from Manhattan's Port Authority Bus Terminal, Eighth Avenue between 40th and 42nd streets (☎ **212/564-8484**).

BASEBALL With two baseball teams in town, you can catch a game almost any day from April to October (don't bother trying to get subway series tix, though—they're the hottest seats in town). Fans of the **New York Mets** and the **New York Yankees** are slightly nuts, and can't seem to understand why their team doesn't win every year (perhaps a by-product of the Yankees' winning ways, which produced a 24th World Championship in 1998). The Mets, playing at dreary **Shea Stadium** in Queens (subway: 7 to Willets Point–Shea Stadium), haven't been as productive, but their strong 1998 season and the signing of star catcher Mike Piazza bode well for the near future. For tickets and information, call the **Mets Ticket Office** at ☎ **718/507-8499,** or visit **www.mets.com.** The Yankees play at Yankee Stadium (Subway: 4, C, D to 161st St.–Yankee Stadium); get here quick, because with Steinbrenner at the helm, who knows how long the Yanks will be in residence in the Bronx? For tickets call **Ticket-Master** (☎ **212/307-1212** or 212/307-7171; www.ticketmaster.com) or **Yankee Stadium** (☎ **718/293-6000;** www.yankees.com).

You can decide to catch a game a couple of hours before game time, hop on the subway, and buy your tickets at the stadium. At Yankee Stadium, upper-tier box seats, especially those behind home plate, give you a great view of all the action. Upper-tier reserve seats are directly behind the box seats, and are significantly cheaper. Bleacher seats are even cheaper, and the rowdy commentary from that section's infamous crowd is absolutely free—a true New York experience. Most of the expensive seats (field

Year-Round Yankee Tip

For a taste of Yankee glory at any time of year, take the **Insider's Tour of Yankee Stadium** (☎ **718/579-4531**). This official tour of the House That Ruth Built will take you out onto the field, to monument park, into the press box and the dugout. You'll even learn how to run the scoreboard and—if you're lucky—take a peek inside the clubhouse. The guide peppers the tour with lots of Yankee history and anecdotes. And who knows? You might even spot that cutie Derek Jeter as you make the rounds. Tours are offered Monday through Saturday at noon (other times are available for groups of 12 or larger). Tickets are $8 for adults, $4 for seniors and kids under 14. No reservations are required; all you need to do is show up at the ballpark's press gate just before tour time, but it's still a good idea to call and confirm.

boxes) are sold out in advance to season-ticket holders. You can often purchase these very same seats from scalpers, but you'll pay a premium for them.

BASKETBALL   Three teams call **Madison Square Garden,** on Seventh Avenue between 31st and 33rd streets (☎ 212/465-6741 or www.thegarden.com; 212/307-7171 or www.ticketmaster.com for tickets; Subway: 1, 2, 3, 9, A, C, E to 34th St.), home court: Patrick Ewing and the **New York Knicks** (☎ **212/465-JUMP** or www.nba.com/knicks), who traded crowd-pleaser John Starks for Golden State bad boy Latrell Sprewell at the start of 1999's strike-shortened season; the **New York Liberty** (www.wnba.com/liberty), who have electrified fans with their tough-playing defense and star players—Rebecca Lobo, Richie Audubato, and Teresa Weatherspoon—since the WNBA's inaugural season; and, in college hoops, **St. John's Red Storm.** Knicks tickets are hardest to come by, of course, so plan ahead if you want a front-row seat near first fan Spike Lee.

The NBA's **New Jersey Nets** play at Continental Airlines Arena, Meadowlands Sports Complex, East Rutherford, New Jersey (☎ **800/7NJ-NETS** or www.nba.com/nets; 212/307-7171 or www.ticketmaster.com for tickets).

FOOTBALL   Though they both play in New Jersey, the **Jets** and the **Giants** are both claimed by New York, especially after the Jets came so close to snaring a Super Bowl berth in 1999. Their regular season schedules are played out at Giants Stadium, Meadowlands Sports Complex, East Rutherford, New Jersey (☎ **201/935-3900** or www.meadowlands.com; **212/307-7171** or www.ticketmaster.com for tickets). Chances are you'll have to catch these teams from a sports bar, as tickets are hard to come by.

ICE HOCKEY   The **New York Rangers** play at Madison Square Garden, Seventh Avenue between 31st and 33rd streets (☎ **212/308-NYRS** or www.newyorkrangers.com; Subway: 1, 2, 3, 9, A, C, E to 34th St.). The memories of the Mark Messier–led 1994 Stanley Cup team linger on, much to the chagrin of the present underachieving team, which suffered another serious blow when Wayne Gretzky retired in April 1999. Tickets are hard to get nevertheless, so plan well ahead.

The 1995 Stanley Cup champion **New Jersey Devils** play at Continental Airlines Arena, Meadowlands Sports Complex, East Rutherford, New Jersey (☎ **201/935-6050;** www.newjerseydevils.com).

For tickets to either Rangers or Devils games, call ☎ **212/307-7171,** or visit www.ticketmaster.com for online orders. If you'd rather head out to the Island to see the New York Islanders, call ☎**888/ETM-TIXS** or visit www.xice.com.

SOCCER   The **New York/New Jersey MetroStars** play at Giants Stadium, in the Meadowlands Sports Complex, East Rutherford, New Jersey (☎ **201/935-3900** for the box office, or 212/307-7171 for TicketMaster; www.metrostars.com or www.ticketmaster.com).

TENNIS   From late August to early September, the hottest ticket in town is to the **U.S. Open Tennis Championships** at the National Tennis Center in Flushing Meadows–Corona Park (☎ **718/760-6200** for information, or **888/673-6849** or 212/239-6200 for tickets; www.usopen.org; Subway: 7 to Willets Point/Shea Stadium). Tickets go on sale in June. While it's next to impossible to cop final-round tickets, early-round seats are relatively abundant and just as entertaining; for more ticket-scoring tips, see the "New York City Calendar of Events" in chapter 2.

The **Chase Championships of the Corel WTA Tour** at Madison Square Garden, Seventh Avenue between 31st and 33rd streets (☎ **212/465-6741**), in mid-November, attracts the top 16 singles players and top eight doubles teams.

8 Shopping for Big Apple Bargains

Calling New York a shopper's paradise is like saying you caught a little flick last night called *Lawrence of Arabia*—that is, something of an understatement.

At first glance, the size and breadth of the city's shopping scene seems more overwhelming than anything else. Even as more and more big chains lay down roots in the city (what New Yorkers like to refer to as the "mallification" of Manhattan), the world's most unique crop of specialty shops continues to thrive right alongside them. And while you can easily go broke trying to keep up with what's new and haute, there's no need to. New York draws bargain-hunters from around the globe with its wealth of good values, wide range of merchandise, and unparalleled sales. As with anything, you just have to know where to look.

OPEN HOURS   Keep in mind that open hours can vary significantly from store to store—even different branches of the Gap can keep different schedules depending on location and management. As a general rule of thumb, stores open at 10 or 11am from Monday through Saturday, and 7pm is the most common closing hour (although sometimes it's 6pm); both opening and closing hours tend to get later as you move downtown to SoHo and the Village. The department stores, and shops along major strips like Fifth Avenue, usually stay open late once a week (oftentimes Thursday) until 8 or 8:30pm, although not all shops may comply. Sunday hours are usually noon to 5 or 6pm. Most shops are open 7 days a week, but smaller boutiques may close 1 day a week, and sometimes whole neighborhoods virtually shut down—namely the Lower East Side on Saturday and most of the Financial District for the weekend. Your best bet is to call ahead if your heart's set on visiting a particular shop, especially late in the day or on Sunday. At holidaytime, anything goes: Macy's often stays open to midnight for the last couple of weeks before Christmas!

SALES TAX   New York City sales tax is 8.25%. For the last couple of years, however, the city has experimented with a few highly successful **tax-free weeks** on clothing purchases of less than $500—usually in January and again in late August or early September. There has been much talk about eliminating sales tax on such purchases altogether; discussions about killing the levy on book purchases have also recently surfaced. If you'd like to check on the state of the situation, or inquire as to when the next tax-free week is on the calendar, your best bet is to call the **Department of Consumer Affairs** (☎ 212/487-4444 or 718/286-2994).

Additional Sources for Serious Shoppers

If you're looking for a specific item, your best bet is to peruse the online shopping listings at **www.timeoutny.citysearch.com** or **www.newyork.citysearch.com** before you go. The Time Out shopping site is more limited, but it's unsullied by advertising compared to the more extensive main CitySearch site. (CitySearch takes payment for Web site space from shops, and lists advertisers first in any given shopping category, such as "Antiques" or "Children's Clothing.") There's also shopping coverage at **www.newyork.sidewalk.com**, but it's an odd mix of New York stores and net shopping that can be confusing to navigate.

For the latest sales, visit **www.inshop.com,** where you can search for sales by merchandise type, store name, or designer name. The information is extremely detailed, such as, "Kate Spade is having a 2-day sale at her SoHo store. All her fab handbags from the fall/winter collection will be 40% off." This tip comes accompanied by exact dates and store location and hours. An excellent source for bargain hunters.

Hard information about current sales, new shops, and special art, craft, and antique shows is best found in the "Check Out" section of *Time Out New York* or the "Sales & Bargains" and "Best Bets" sections of *New York* magazine (New York doesn't usually cover shows). And don't forget to check the front section of the daily edition of the *New York Times,* as that's where all of the big department stores advertise their seasonal sales, sometimes even including clip-out coupons for additional discounts.

If you're coming in search of sample sales, check out the box later in this chapter.

If you're visiting from out of state, consider having your purchases shipped directly home to avoid paying sales tax.

1 The Top Shopping Streets & Neighborhoods

Here's a rundown of New York's prime shopping areas, with some highlights of each to give you a feel for the neighborhood. If addresses and phone numbers are *not* given here, refer to the store's more expanded listing by category below under "Shopping A to Z."

DOWNTOWN
LOWER MANHATTAN

The Financial District and environs are home to two kinds of shopping: discount shopping a la Century 21 department store, and J&R for electronics galore; and mall-style retail shopping. National chains and standard mall stores are housed at **South Street Seaport** (☎ 212/732-7678; subway: 2, 3, 4, 5 to Fulton St.) on Pier 17 and on Fulton Street, the seaport's main cobbled drag; and on the ground level of the **World Trade Center** (☎ 212/435-4170; subway: 1, 9, N, R to Cortlandt St.; C, E to World Trade Center), a good bet for standards like the Gap, the Body Shop, Nine West for shoes, the Limited, and the neighborhood's only bookstore, a terrific branch of Borders Books & Music.

CHINATOWN

Don't expect to find the purchase of a lifetime on Chinatown's streets, but there's some fun browsing to be had. The fish markets along Canal, Mott, Mulberry, and Elizabeth streets are fun to explore for their bustle and exotica. Especially along Canal, you'll find an astounding (and sometimes astoundingly bad) collection of super-cheap knock-offs—mostly sunglasses, designer bags, and watches. **Mott Street** between Pell

Street and Chatham Square boasts the most interesting of Chinatown's off-Canal shopping, with an antique shop or two dispersed among the tiny storefronts selling blue-and-white dinnerware. But the definite highlight of Chinatown shopping is the three-story **Pearl River Mart** (see "The Department Stores," below).

THE LOWER EAST SIDE

The bargains aren't quite what they used to be in the **Historic Orchard Street Shopping District**—which basically runs from Houston to Canal along Allen, Orchard, and Ludlow streets, spreading outward along both sides of Delancey Street—but prices on leather bags, shoes, luggage, fabrics on the bolt, and men's and women's clothes are still quite good. Be aware, though, that the hard-sell on Orchard Street can be pretty hard to take. Still, the district is a nice place to discover a part of New York that's disappearing. Come during the week, since most stores are Jewish-owned, and therefore close Friday afternoon and all day Saturday. Sundays tend to be a madhouse. Stop in first at the **Lower East Side's Visitor Center,** 261 Broome St., between Orchard and Allen streets (☎ 888/825-8374 or 212/226-9010; open Sun–Fri 10am–4pm; subway: F to Delancey St. or B, D, Q to Grand St.) for a shopping guide to the bargain district.

The artists and other trendsetters who have turned this neighborhood into a hopping club scene have also added a cutting edge to its shopping scene. You'll find a handful of mainly kitschy alterna-shops tucked between the bars and clubs mostly along Ludlow Street—the couple of blocks south of Houston—and also on Rivington Street. Highlights include the funky junk at **Lucky Wang,** 100 Stanton St., between Orchard and Ludlow streets (☎ 212/353-2850); **Yu,** 151 Ludlow St., between Stanton and Rivington streets (☎ 212/979-9370), a consignment shop specializing in vintage wear and Japanese designer labels; and **Patch,** 155 Rivington St., between Suffolk and Clinton streets (☎ 212/533-9995), with witty new designs for young hipsters.

A little farther west, the stretch of the Bowery (Third Ave.) from Canal to Houston streets is considered the "light-fixture district" for its huge selections and great bargains on light fixtures, lamps, and ceiling fans. The best of the bunch is **Lighting by Gregory,** 158 Bowery, between Delancey and Broome streets (☎ 212/226-1276).

SOHO

People love to complain about super-fashionable SoHo—it's become too trendy, too tony, too Mall of America. True, **J. Crew,** 99 Prince St. (☎ 212/966-2739), is only one of many big names to have supplanted the galleries that used to inhabit the historic cast-iron buildings, but SoHo is still one of the best shopping neighborhoods in the city—and few are more fun to browse. You'll find few bargains here, as rents are too high for merchants to sell at anything but a premium. This is the epicenter of cutting-edge haute couture, with such designers as glammy Anna Sui, trend-busting British legend Vivienne Westwood, and golden boy Todd Oldham in residence. Most of these designer shops are likely to be *way* out of your price range (they're way outta mine, that's for sure), but the streets are chock-full of unique boutiques, some hawking more affordable wares, and the eye candy is tops. End-of-season sales, when racks are cleared for incoming merchandise, are the best bet for those who actually want to buy.

SoHo's prime shopping grid is from Broadway east to Sullivan Street, and from Houston down to Broome, although Grand Street, one block south of Broome, has been sprouting shops of late. Broadway is the most commercial strip, with such recognizable names as **Pottery Barn, Victoria's Secret,** and **Banana Republic.** Most compelling along here are gourmet supermarket **Dean and Deluca** and discount favorite **Canal Jean Co.**

The Lowdown on Sidewalk Vendors

New York has a very active street culture. Along main thoroughfares throughout the city, you'll see street merchants selling everything from fresh fruit to knapsacks to art books to baseball cards. Many are legitimate, licensed vendors, but some aren't. Chances are, if there's a suitcase involved or a blanket that can be rolled up and carted away quickly, or the collection of stuff for sale is a little too eclectic (like it could be the contents of somebody's apartment or a traveler's bag, say), the vendor shouldn't be there.

The museum streets of West 53rd and 54th are peppered with vendors selling their own art. Book vendors line Broadway on the Upper West Side, especially on weekends. If you encounter a vendor selling just-published hardcover books on the street, chances are they've been stolen. And paperback books sold without covers are considered returned goods and aren't meant for resale. Hawkers with faux Chanel and Prada handbags and "designer" watches are most prolific in Times Square. The quality is questionable, so don't even think about shelling out more than $20 for a counterfeit watch. Lower Fifth Avenue has become popular with vendors selling cheap knockoffs of current handbag styles. SoHo is popular with high-end street peddlers, mostly legitimate, hawking hand-crafted silver jewelry, coffee-table books, and their own art, mainly along Prince Street. St. Marks Place (8th St.) in the East Village is big on cheap sunglasses and goth jewelry.

At the city's immensely popular weekly outdoor flea markets, particularly those at 26th Street and Sixth Avenue, you'll find all kinds of stuff, from trash-worthy junk to highly collectible antiques. (See "Antiques & Collectibles" under "Shopping A to Z," below.) Most flea-market vendors are perfectly legitimate, but on occasion you'll run across one that's clearly hawking stolen goods.

When it comes to this type of alternative retail, the best rule of thumb is this: Use your best judgement, and let your conscience be your guide. But if you choose to buy what are clearly stolen goods, keep in mind that you're encouraging this kind of resale with your wallet—and the next set of stuff for sale on the street could be yours.

If you're less interested in designer fashions and more interested in unique mid-priced wearables, consider **Anthropologie,** 375 W. Broadway (☎ 212/343-7070), whose funky-chic, affordable clothes mix with fun gifts and home decorating items— much like Urban Outfitters for grown-ups. Hat lovers shouldn't miss the wonderful **Hat Shop,** 120 Thompson St. (☎ 212/219-1445), a full-service millener for women with some affordable ready-to-wear choices, too.

High-end home stores are another huge part of the SoHo scene, but **Global Table,** 107 Sullivan St. (☎ 212/431-5839), is a great source for beautiful, affordable tableware from around the world (including lots of Japanese stuff).

NOLITA

Less than a handful of years ago, Elizabeth Street was a nondescript adjunct to Little Italy and the no-man's land east of SoHo; today it's the grooviest shopping strip in town, star of the neighborhood known as NoLita. Elizabeth and neighboring Mott and Mulberry streets are dotted with an increasing number of shops between Houston and Spring streets, with a few pushing one more block south to Kenmare. It's an easy walk from the Broadway–Lafayette stop on the B, D, F, Q line.

This may be a burgeoning neighborhood, but don't expect cheap—NoLiTa is clearly a stepchild of SoHo. Its boutiques are largely the province of sophisticated shopkeepers specializing in high-quality, fashion-forward products and design. Still, this can be a good neighborhood to browse if you're looking for an exotic import or one-of-a-kind gift.

Prince Street is probably the best stretch for affordable treasures. There's **Dö Kham** at no. 51 (☎ 212/966-2404), for Tibetan bags, rugs, hats, and other Himalayan imports; **Cocoon & Co.** at no. 25 (☎ 212/966-8680) for a charmingly quirky mix of well-priced vintage housewares and contemporary gifts; and **Gates of Morocco,** at no. 8 (☎ 212/925-2650), for traditional Moroccan goodies.

While not exactly reaching SoHo standards yet, the boutique density is highest on Elizabeth. Some super-expensive vintage modern furniture dealers have taken roost here, but a few shops yield quirkier, more affordable gifts, particularly ✪ **Daily 235,** at no. 235 (☎ 212/334-9728), a cool candy and card store for artsy grown-ups that's terrific for under-$10 tchotchkes.

THE EAST VILLAGE

Despite the arrival of **Kmart** on the scene (a sure sign of the apocalypse, as far as some New York purists are concerned), the East Village remains the international standard of bohemian hip. It's one of the city's best neighborhoods for wallet-friendly shopping. The easiest subway access is the 6 train to Astor Place, which lets you out by Kmart and **Astor Wines & Spirits;** from here, it's just a couple blocks east to the prime hunting grounds. Note that some East Village shops don't open until 2pm, so your best bet is to come in the afternoon; most stay open until 8pm, some later.

✪ **East 9th Street** between Second Avenue and Avenue A has become one of my favorite shopping strips in the entire city. Lined with an increasingly smart collection of boutiques, it proves that the East Village isn't just for kids anymore. I'm happy to report that—so far, at least—prices have stayed within reach. Up-and-coming designers selling good-quality and affordably priced original fashions for women have set up shop along here, including **Lisa Tsai,** 436 E. 9th St. (☎ 212/529-8231), a bright, cheery shop with wonderful retro-inspired designs and accessories; **Mark Montano,** next door at no. 434 (☎ 212/505-0325), who harkens back to styles from Victoria to Jackie O. as inspiration for his line of wonderful clothes and handbags; **Between the Sheets,** at no. 315 (☎ 212/677-7586), for ultra-feminine lingerie; **Meghan Kinney Studio,** at no. 312 (☎ 212/260-6329), for gorgeous, figure-flattering separates in fabrics that cling just a bit, but not too much; plus the utterly fabulous **Jill Anderson,** and a small branch of **Eileen Fisher** that's great for bargain hunters since it basically serves as the burgeoning chain's outlet store.

Vintage stays affordable on East 9th, too, and runs the gamut from pristine wear-ables at **Argosy** to kitschy collectibles at **Cha Cha Tchatchka** and **Atomic Passion.**

For stylish gifts and little luxuries, there's **Paper Rock Scissors,** 436 E. 9th St. (☎ 212/358-1555), specializing in handmade treasures; **Ichak,** at no. 430 (☎ 212/673-0673), for funky, affordable handbags constructed from clear plastic, steel rivets, and images that range from Tide detergent box labels to vintage pulp fiction covers; **Mascot Studio,** whose remarkable one-of-a-kind picture frames are sold at no. 328 (☎ 212/228-9090); and ✪ **H,** at no. 335 (☎ 212/477-2631), with wonderful Japanese-inspired and other collectibles, from slinky vases to rice-paper coasters. There's also the factory store for super-hip **Manhattan Portage,** if you're looking for something to stash your booty in.

If you're really enjoying this 'hood, check out the offerings on surrounding blocks, too, which aren't quite as mature yet, but it won't take long. Among the hidden treasures are **Kimono House,** 93 E. 7th St. (☎ **212/505-0232**), for low prices on vintage kimono and yukata (cotton kimono, which make great bathrobes). The fabrics alone are worth the price.

If it's strange, illegal, or funky, it's probably available on **St. Marks Place,** which is 8th Street, running east from Third Avenue to Avenue A. This skanky strip is a permanent street market, with countless T-shirt and jewelry stands. The height of the action is between Second and Third avenues, which is prime hunting grounds for used-record collectors (see "Music" under "Shopping A to Z" later in this chapter).

LAFAYETTE STREET FROM SoHo TO NoHo

Lafayette Street has a retail character all its own, distinct from the rest of SoHo. It has grown into a full-fledged Antique Row, especially strong in mid-century modern furniture. The quality is high, but prices are even higher. Lafayette is great for browsing if you have a strong interest in design trends—the stretch to stroll is between Astor Place to the north and Spring Street to the south—but bargain hunters are better off elsewhere.

Dispersed among the furniture and design stores are a number of cutting-edge clothiers—this is where skateboard fashion moved from the street to the catwalks. Among the fashion outlets worth noting are **Daryl K.,** 21 Bond St. (☎ **212/777-0713**), for cool hiphugger pants and other groovy-sexy wear for men and women; **Spooly D's,** 51 Bleecker St., at Lafayette (☎ **212/598-4415**), featuring artfully displayed collections of classic vintage fashions and accessories; and **Screaming Mimi's,** the city's most famous—and maybe its best—vintage-clothing outlet. South of Houston is **X-Large,** 267 Lafayette St. (☎ **212/334-4480**), for upscale hip-hop wear (the Beasties' Mike D is a co-owner); and **Swell,** 240 Lafayette St. (☎ **212/966-0215**), for funky streetwear from L.A.-based designers as well as a terrific collection of Hush Puppies. And don't forget the wonderful **Pop Shop,** which sells cool casual wear emblazoned with Keith Haring's distinctive modern art (see "Logo Stores").

A block over from Lafayette in NoHo, on the **Bowery** just north of Houston Street, is the place to find restaurant-supply–quality kitchenware at low, low prices.

GREENWICH VILLAGE

The West Village is great for browsing and gift shopping. Specialty book- and record stores, antique and craft shops, and gourmet food markets dominate. The best **Tower Records** in the country is at West 4th Street and Broadway; there's even an outlet annex for committed bargain hunters.

Except for NYU territory—**8th Street** between Broadway and Sixth Avenue for trendy footwear and affordable fashions, and Broadway from 8th Street south to Houston, anchored by **Urban Outfitters** and dotted with skate and sneaker shops—the Village isn't much of a destination for fashion hunters. Clothes hounds looking for volume shopping are better off elsewhere.

The prime drag for strolling is bustling Bleecker Street, where you'll find lots of leather shops and record stores interspersed with a good number of interesting and artsy boutiques. Just a few of the highlights include **Old Japan,** 382 Bleecker St. (☎ **212/633-0922**), for Japanese gifts, including cool vests fashioned out of vintage kimonos; **Barr-Magill,** at no. 333 (☎ **212/741-0656**), whose moderately priced black-and-white photography—much of which features the city—makes a great souvenir; and **Condomania,** at no. 351 (☎ **212/691-9442**), everybody's favorite creative condom store. Newer on the scene is **Sleek on Bleecker,** at no. 361 (☎ **212/243-0284**), for fashionable but affordable clothes for working women with style.

Narrow Christopher Street is another fun street to browse, because it's loaded with genuine Village character. Here you'll find such highlights as **Amalgamated Home** for cool household goods; **Li-Lac Chocolates** for sweets made the old-fashioned way; and the **Oscar Wilde Bookshop,** which bills itself as the world's oldest gay and lesbian bookstore.

MIDTOWN
THE FLATIRON DISTRICT & UNION SQUARE

When 23rd Street was the epitome of New York Uptown fashion more than a hundred years ago, the major department stores stretched along **Sixth Avenue** for about a mile from 14th Street up. These elegant stores stood in huge cast-iron buildings that were long ago abandoned and left to rust. In the last few years, however, the area has been rezoned and turned into the city's discount shopping center, with superstores and off-pricers filling up the renovated spaces: **Filene's Basement, TJ Maxx,** and **Bed Bath & Beyond,** are all at 620 Sixth Ave., while **Old Navy,** the cheaper version of the Gap, is next door.

On Broadway just a few blocks north of Union Square is **ABC Carpet & Home,** a magnet for aspiring Martha Stewarts. Even if you can't afford anything, ABC is well worth a peek, and the first-floor gallery often boasts a gorgeous array of reasonably priced goodies.

Upscale retailers who have rediscovered the architectural majesty of **lower Fifth Avenue** include retro-inspired **Restoration Hardware,** at 22nd Street (☎ 212/ 260-9479), and national mainstays like **Kenneth Cole** and **Victoria's Secret**. You won't find too much that's new along here, but it's a pleasing, if pricey, stretch nonetheless.

HERALD SQUARE & THE GARMENT DISTRICT

Herald Square—where 34th Street, Sixth Avenue, and Broadway converge—is dominated by **Macy's,** the self-proclaimed world's biggest department store, and other famous-name shopping, like **Toys 'Я' Us** at 34th Street and Broadway (☎ 212/ 594-8697). At Sixth Avenue and 33rd Street is the **Manhattan Mall** (☎ 212/ 465-0500), anchored by unremarkable Stern's department store and home to mall standards like Foot Locker and Radio Shack.

A long block over on Seventh Avenue, not much goes on in the grimy, heavily industrial Garment District. This is, however, where you'll find that quintessential New York experience, the sample sale; see the box called "Scouring the Sample Sales," later in this chapter.

TIMES SQUARE & THE THEATER DISTRICT

This neighborhood has become increasingly family oriented: hence, **Disney** and **Warner Bros**. outposts at the crossroads of **Times Square,** and **Richard Branson's** rollicking **Virgin Megastore. The Gap** is already here at 42nd and Broadway, and word is that **Old Navy** is moving in, too.

West 47th Street between Fifth and Sixth avenues is the city's famous **Diamond District.** Apparently, more than 90% of the diamonds sold in the United States come through this neighborhood first, so there are some great deals to be had if you're in the market for a nice rock or another piece of fine jewelry. Be ready to wheel and deal with the largely Hasidic dealers. For a complete introduction to the district, including smart buying tips, visit **www.47th-street.com.** For semiprecious stones, head one block over to the **New York Jewelry Mart,** 26 W. 46th St. (☎ 212/575-9701). Virtually all of these dealers are open Monday through Friday only.

Shopper's Alert: You'll also notice a wealth of electronics stores throughout the neighborhood, many trumpeting GOING OUT OF BUSINESS sales. These guys have been going out of business since the Stone Age. That's the bait and switch; pretty soon you've spent too much money for not enough stereo. If you want to check out what they have to offer, go in knowing what going prices are on that PDA or digital camera you're interested in. You can negotiate a good deal if you know exactly what the market is—I've seen prices tumble precipitously the closer I got to the door—but these guys will be happy to suck you dry given half a chance. Trust me on this: The only way you'll do well is if you know your stuff.

FIFTH AVENUE & 57TH STREET

The heart of Manhattan retail is the corner of Fifth and 57th. Home to high-ticket names like Gucci, Chanel, Cartier, and Van Cleef & Arpels, this tony shopping neighborhood has long been the province of the über-rich. In recent years, however, both Fifth Avenue and 57th Street have become more accessible as wallet-friendlier retailers like the **Original Levi's Store,** the **Warner Bros. Studio Store, Niketown,** and the **NBA Store** have joined the fold. You'll also find kid wonderland **FAO Schwartz** here, as well as a number of national names, like **Banana Republic,** which have further democratized Fifth by setting up their flagships along the avenue.

Despite its more egalitarian profile, don't expect to find any bargains along these main drags. High traffic flow and real-estate costs keep prices up, and the flagship stores tend to send their sale merchandise to lower-profile shops around town. Still, the window shopping is classic. And if you, like Holly Golightly, always dreamed of shopping at **Tiffany & Co.,** 727 Fifth Ave., at 57th Street (☎ **212/755-8000**), the most famous jewelry store in New York (maybe the world) is well worth a stop. The multilevel showroom is so full of tourists at all times that it's easy to browse without having any intention of buying. If you do want to indulge, your best bet is to head upstairs to the gift level, where you'll find a number of gifts to suit a $50 budget.

UPTOWN
MADISON AVENUE

Welcome to Rich Man's Land. Madison Avenue from 57th to 79th streets has usurped Fifth Avenue as *the* toniest shopping stretch in the city. In fact, in 1998, it vaunted ahead of Hong Kong's Causeway Bay to become the most expensive retail real estate in the world. This strip is home to the world's most luxurious designer boutiques: Calvin, Prada, Versace, Valentino . . . the list goes on. Even the *sales* are ridiculous. ("This $1,200 sweater is on sale for just $575? I'll take it!" Yeah, right.)

For those of us with limited budgets, the good news is that stores like **Crate & Barrel,** at 59th Street (☎ **212/308-0011**), and the fabulous **Ann Taylor** flagship make untouchable Madison Avenue seem a little more approachable. Shoe freaks will want to check out wallet-friendly **Unisa,** 701 Madison Ave. (☎ **212/753-7474**); the luxury shoe shops along here, like Joan & David and Cole-Haan, also tend to have more accessible sales.

THE UPPER WEST SIDE

The Upper West Side's best shopping street is **Columbus Avenue.** Small shops catering to the neighborhood's white-collar mix of young professionals and families line both sides of the pleasant avenue from 66th Street (where you'll find an excellent branch of **Barnes & Noble**) to about 86th Street. For comfort over style (these city streets can be murder on the feet!), try **Aerosoles,** 310 Columbus Ave. (☎ **212/579-8659**), or **Sacco** for women's shoes that offer a bit of both. Other highlights include **Housing Works Thrift Shop,** an excellent not-for-profit thrift store; and **Maxilla & Mandible** for funky natural science–based gifts (see "Museum Stores").

There are also a few shops lining main drag Broadway, but it's most notable for its terrific gourmet edibles at **Zabar's** and **Fairway** markets, both legends in their own right.

2 The Department Stores

The stores I've outlined below are, to varying degrees, in keeping with the good-value mindset. There's also **Bergdorf Goodman,** 754 Fifth Ave., at 57th Street (☎ 212/753-7300), and **Barney's New York,** 660 Madison Ave., at 61st Street (☎ 212/826-8900), both temples of haute couture—Bergdorf's largely in the classic style and Barney's more on the cutting edge. Nothing comes cheap at either of these stores, and bargains are few and far between. Real fashion hounds may want to browse, but I feel like everything on the racks is just taunting me. (And Bergdorf's is too museum-like to even make it fun.)

All of the city's department stores are open 7 days a week. However, unlike those in suburban malls, most of these stores don't keep a regular 10am to 9pm schedule, so your best bet is to call ahead if you're planning on a late afternoon visit. Virtually all keep extended hours during the Christmas season, which tend to get longer as the holiday grows nearer.

✪ **Bloomingdale's.** 1000 Third Ave. (Lexington Ave. at 59th St.). ☎ 212/705-2000. Subway: 4, 5, 6 to 59th St.

This is my favorite of New York's big department stores. It's more accessible than Barneys or Bergdorf's and more affordable than Saks, but still has the New York pizzazz that Macy's and Lord & Taylor now largely lack. Taking up the space of a city block, Bloomie's has just about anything you could want, from clothing (both designer and everyday basics) and fragrances to a full range of housewares. Service is a step above increasingly lackluster Macy's. The frequent sales can yield unbeatable bargains; look for full-page advertisements in front section of the daily *New York Times.*

The main entrance is on Third Avenue, but pop up to street level from the 59th Street station and you'll be right at the Lexington Avenue entrance.

✪ **Century 21.** 22 Cortlandt St. (btw. Broadway and Church St.). ☎ 212/227-9092. Subway: 1, 9, N, R to Cortlandt St.; 4, 5 to Fulton St.; C, E to World Trade Center.

Just across from the World Trade Center, Century 21 long ago achieved legend status as *the* designer discount store. If you don't mind wrestling with the aggressive, ever-present throngs, this is where you'll find those $20 Todd Oldham pants or the $50 Bally loafers you've been dreaming of—not to mention underwear, hosiery, and ties so cheap that they're almost free. Don't see how $250 for an Armani blazer is a bargain? Look again at the tag—the retail on it is upwards of $800. The shoe department is an outlet-style madhouse, but the bargains can be incredible. The whole store's an utter hassle, but always worth it. To avoid the bulk of the crowds, avoid lunch hour, the after-work hours, and weekends; weekday mornings are best.

Henri Bendel. 712 Fifth Ave. (at 56th St.). ☎ 212/247-1100. Subway: N, R to Fifth Ave.

This beautiful Fifth Avenue store is a lot of fun to browse. It feels like you're shopping in the townhouse of a confident, old lady who doesn't think twice about throwing on a little something by Anna Sui and an outrageously wide-brimmed hat to go out shopping for the day. It's a super-stylish, high-ticket collection, but the sales are good, and there's always some one-of-a-kind accessories that make affordable souvenirs (and earn you one of their black-and-white striped shopping bags, the best in town) on the first floor. The pretty **tearoom** looks out on Fifth Avenue through Lalique windows.

Kmart. 770 Broadway (at Astor Place, btw. 8th and 9th sts.). ☎ **212/673-1540.** Subway: 6 to Astor Place.

Kmart is so out of place in the East Village that it has turned the mundane into marvelous camp: Japanese kids stare and marvel at gargantuan boxes of laundry detergent as if they were Warhol designed, while multi-pierced and mohawked locals navigate the name-brand maze alongside stroller-pushing housewives. U2 even held a press conference/performance here to announce their consumption-minded *Popmart* tour back in 1998. Kitsch value aside, this multilevel megastore is a great bet for discount prices on practicals, from socks to shampoo. You'll also find a pharmacy, a sizable food department where you can stock up on Cocoa Puffs and other kitchenette supplies (sale prices on snack foods are rock-bottom), and even a photography studio.

There's a second Kmart in midtown at 1 Penn Plaza, on 34th Street between Seventh and Eighth avenues (☎ **212/760-1188**).

Lord & Taylor. 424 Fifth Ave. (at 39th St.). ☎ **212/391-3344.** Subway: B, D, F, Q to 42nd St.

Okay, so maybe Lord & Taylor isn't the first place you'd go for a vinyl miniskirt. But I like Lord & Taylor's understated, elegant mien. Long known as an excellent source of women's dresses and coats, L&T stocks all the major labels for men and women. Their house-brand clothes (khakis, blazers, turtlenecks, and summer sportswear) are well-made and a great bargain. Sales, especially around holidays, can be stellar. The store is big enough to have a good selection, but doesn't overwhelm—I wish the lighting were better, though, but it's a minor complaint. The Christmas window displays are an annual delight.

Macy's. At Herald Square, W. 34th St. and Broadway. ☎ **212/695-4400.** Subway: 1, 2, 3, 9, B, D, F, Q, N, R to 34th St.

A four-story sign on the side of the building trumpets, MACY'S, THE WORLD'S LARGEST STORE—a hard fact to dispute, since the 10-story behemoth covers an entire city block, even dwarfing Bloomie's on the other side of town. Macy's is a hard place to shop: The size is unmanageable, the service is dreadful, and the incessant din from the crowds on the ground floor alone will kick your migrane into action. But they do sell *everything*. Massive renovation over the past few years has redesigned many departments into more manageable "mini-stores"—there's a Metropolitan Museum Gift Shop, a Swatch boutique, and cafes and make-up counters on several floors—but the store's one-of-a-kind flair that I remember so well from my childhood is just a memory now. Still, sales run constantly, so bargains are guaranteed. And because so many feel adrift in this retail sea, the store provides personal shoppers to serve as guides at absolutely no charge. My advice: Get the floor plan, and consult it often to avoid wandering off into the sportswear netherworld. At Christmastime, come as late as you can (the store is usually open until midnight in the final shopping days).

Tips for Sale Seekers: One-day sales usually occur on Wednesdays, and sometimes on Saturdays. Extended hours are common on sale days. Call the store when you arrive to find out if your visit overlaps with one. It's also a terrific idea to check the A (front) section of the *New York Times* any day of the week for full-page advertisements, which sometimes include clip-out coupons for additional 10 to 15% discounts.

✪ **Pearl River Mart.** 277 Canal St., at Broadway. ☎ **212/431-4770.** Subway: N, R to Canal St.

It doesn't look like much more than your average storefront from the street, but this three-floor Chinatown emporium overflows with affordable Asian exotica. Cool goods run the gamut from colorful paper lanterns to Chinese snack foods to Mandarin-collared silk pajamas to mah jongg sets to Hong Kong action videos. This fascinating place can keep you occupied for hours, and it's a great source for cheap, creative souvenirs.

Saks Fifth Avenue. 611 Fifth Ave. (btw. 49th and 50th sts.). ☎ **212/753-4000.** Subway: B, D, F, Q to 47–50th sts.–Rockefeller Center; E, F to Fifth Ave.

There are branches of Saks all over the country now, but this is it: Saks *Fifth Avenue.* This legendary flagship is well worth an hour or two for real department-store aficionados, and the smaller-than-most size makes it manageable in that amount of time. Saks carries a wide range of clothing; departments err on the pricey designer side (stay out of the lingerie department if you're looking for basics) but run the gamut to affordable house-brand basics. As department stores go, there's something for everyone, and every budget, here. The cosmetics and fragrance departments on the main floor are justifiably noteworthy, since they carry many hard-to-find and brand-new brands. And the store's location, right across from Rockefeller Center, makes it a convenient stop for those on the sightseeing circuit. Don't miss the holiday windows.

3 Shopping A to Z
ANTIQUES & COLLECTIBLES

New York has a wealth of antiques shops, covering everything from ancient to Americana to art deco to mid-century modern. The browsing almost qualifies as torture, however, because prices are astronomical across the board—much higher than virtually everywhere else in the country.

Those looking for kitschy 20th-century collectibles will enjoy a few of the shops on East 9th Street in the East Village, such as the charming **Cha Cha Tchatchka,** at no. 437 (☎ 212/674-9242), and **Atomic Passion,** across the street at no. 430 (☎ 212/533-0718). **Screaming Mimi's** also boasts a small but cute selection of vintage housewares (see "Clothing," below).

Collectibles hounds should also consider the regular calendar of antiques shows, the best of which is the twice-annual **Triple Piers Expo,** always in March and again in November; see the "Calendar of Events" in chapter 2 for details.

Antique Addiction. 436 West Broadway (just south of Prince St.). ☎ **212/925-6342.** Subway: N,R to Prince St.; C,E to Spring St.

This charming SoHo shop is chock full of vintage costume jewelry (including a great selection of cuff links), plus classic eyewear and lighters. Prices are decent, and collectors are bound to find something they like—or have lots of fun trying.

Chelsea Antiques Building. 110 W. 25th St. (btw. Sixth and Seventh aves.). ☎ **212/929-0909.** www.chelseaantiques.com. Subway: F to 23rd St.

Right around the corner from New York's best flea market, the Annex Antiques Fair and Flea Market, this 12-floor building filled with dealers is open not only during the weekend to coincide with the market but also during the week. Goods are priced more reasonably than at Uptown addresses, and shoppers are the type who love to prowl, touch everything, and sniff out a deal. Highlights include **Waves** (☎ 212/989-9284; www.wavesradio.com) for antique radios and phonographs, including a good selection of 78s and Edison cylinders; **Jerome Wilson** (☎ 212/352-1370) for fine vintage linens, porcelain, and glass; **Julian's Books** (☎ 212/929-3620; www.julianbook.com), for first, signed, and rare editions; **Retro-Metro/The Missing Link** (☎ 212/645-6928) for cuff links, handbags, and other vintage jewelry and accessories; and **Toys from the 50s** (☎ 212/352-9182; www.toys-50s.com), specializing in classic TV show toys and memorabilia.

Where the Fleas Are

When people refer to New York City as a shopping mecca, what usually pops to mind are images of glittering department stores and chic boutiques. But there's another side to the selling picture: For those in search of vintage treasures, the Big Apple is also a flea market bonanza. City fleas operate on weekends throughout the year, so even winter visitors can enjoy the prowl.

Usually called the 26th Street flea market, the famous **Annex Antiques Fair and Flea Market (☎ 212/243-5343)** is an outdoor emporium of nostalgia, filling a few parking lots along Sixth Avenue between 24th and 27th streets on weekends year-round. The assemblage is hit or miss—some days you'll find treasures galore, and others it seems like there's nothing but junk. A few quality vendors are almost always on hand, though, and prices are usually negotiable. The truly dedicated arrive at 6:30am, but the browsing is still good as late as 4pm. Sunday is always best, since there's double the booty on hand. One lot charges $1 admission both days, but the rest are free. Die-hards can continue the hunt at the **Garage,** an indoor two-story parking garage at 112 W. 25th St., between Sixth and Seventh avenues (☎ 212/647-0707), then proceed to 26th Street and Seventh Avenue, where another lot fills up with dealers on Sunday.

Another popular weekend market is the **SoHo Antiques and Collectibles Market,** at Broadway and Grand Street, on Saturdays and Sundays starting at 9am. Knowledgeable fleabees don't consider this the prime hunting ground it once was, but prices are reasonable and real finds surface every so often. The collections tend toward mid-century kitsch, vintage clothes, old records, old-fashioned kitchen appliances, furniture odds and ends, and the like.

Uptown, the **Greenflea Market (☎ 212/721-0900)** operates at two different venues: on the east side on East 67th Street, between First and York avenues, on Saturday from 6am to 6pm; and on the west side on Columbus Avenue at West 77th Street, Sundays from 10am to 6pm. Both markets operate as both green and flea markets (hence the name). I'm not a big fan, but some people just love the west side Sunday event, where goods run from used records to Turkish kilims to discount pet supplies. Costume jewelry hunters in particular should enjoy the east side Saturday event.

In April 1999, the people behind the Annex launched the year-round **South Street Seaport Outdoor Market,** at Burling Slip, John Street and South Street, 1 block north of Fulton Street (☎ 212/463-0200, ext. 225). This one is still finding its footing, but expect goods from furniture and textiles to books and prints to fruits and veggies. This market operates every Thursday through Saturday from 11:30am to 7pm, so it's a great place to start for those who want to get a jump on their weekend treasure hunting.

Manhattan Art & Antiques Center. 1050 Second Ave. (btw. 55th and 56th sts.). ☎ 212/355-4400. www.glenwoodmanagement.com/maac. Subway: N, R to Lexington Ave.

This three-floor antiques center represents just about every genre of collecting on the map, from perfume bottles and porcelain to arms and armor. Once you've toured the more than 100 stalls, stroll along 60th Street, where about two dozen dealers selling higher-end goods line both sides of the street.

ART

See "Art for Art's Sake: The Gallery Scene" in chapter 7.

BEAUTY & BATH

Cosmetics Plus. 1601 Broadway (at 48th St.). ☎ 212/757-3122. Subway: N, R to 49th St.

This chain sells a wide range of perfumes, health and beauty aids, cosmetics from Cover Girl to Lancome and Borghese, and high-end hair-care products, all at discounted prices. Check the Yellow Pages for additional locations throughout the city.

Kiehl's. 109 Third Ave. (at 13th St.). ☎ 212/475-3400. Subway: 4, 5, 6, N, R, L to 14th St.–Union Sq.

Kiehl's is more than a store: It's a virtual cult. Models, stockbrokers, foreign visitors, and just about everyone else stops by this always-packed old-time apothecary for its simply packaged, wonderfully formulated products for women and men. Lip Balm no. 1 is the perfect antidote to the biting winds of city or slope.

MAC. 113 Prince St. (btw. Mercer and Greene sts.). ☎ 212/334-4641. Subway: N, R to Prince St.

What began as a Canadian-based, custom-designed modeling makeup line has become a super-successful retail operation thanks to a chic color line, eco-friendly packaging, decent prices (considering the quality), and a downtown-chic, don't-hate-me-because-I'm-beautiful unisex staff dressed in all-black. Lighter and more sheer than most, the lipsticks are particularly popular; I buy Redwood practically by the gross. Another, smaller branch is in the Village at 14 Christopher St. (☎ 212/243-4150), plus counters at Saks, Bloomingdale's, and Henri Bendel.

BOOKS

THE BIG CHAINS

Barnes & Noble Booksellers. 22 E. 17th St. (at Union Sq.). ☎ 212/253-0810, or 212/727-4810 for New York–area B&N information. www.barnesandnoble.com. Subway: 4, 5, 6, N, R, L to Union Sq.

With locations throughout the city, B&N is the undisputed king of city bookstores. The Union Square location is my favorite: The selection is huge and well organized, the store is comfortable and never feels too crowded, and you're welcome to browse— or nab a comfy chair and read—for as long as you like. There's a cafe, of course, and an extensive magazine stand.

There's another superstore at 1972 Broadway, at 66th Street (☎ 212/595-6859), plus additional good-size locations at 4 Astor Place, between Broadway and Lafayette Street (☎ 212/420-1322); 675 Sixth Ave., near 22nd Street (☎ 212/727-1227); 160 E. 54th St. (☎ 212/750-8033); at Rockefeller Center, 600 Fifth Ave., at 48th St. (☎ 212/765-0590); 2289 Broadway, at 82nd Street (☎ 212/362-8835); and 240 E. 86th St., at Second Avenue (☎ 212/794-1962). Look for an extensive calendar of readings at most locations; recently featured luminaries have included Martin Amis, Peter Jennings, A. S. Byatt, and Elmore Leonard.

Borders Books & Music. 5 World Trade Center (at Church and Vesey sts.). ☎ 212/839-8049. www.bordersstores.com. Subway: 1, 9, N, R to Cortlandt St.; C, E to World Trade Center.

After several years with no decent bookstores anywhere in the 'hood, Borders is a welcome addition to the Financial District. The selection of both books and music is extensive, service is great, and the store hosts a wealth of in-store events, from best-selling authors to musicians like Lou Reed. There's a second location at 461 Park Ave., at 57th Street (☎ 212/980-6785), and, at press time, a third was scheduled to open soon on the city's east side.

SPECIALTY BOOKSTORES

New York has more terrific specialty bookstores than I can possibly recount here. These are just some of the best. In addition to these choices, also consider **Tower Books,** a branch of the mega-music chain (see "Music," below).

Academy Book Store. 10 W. 18th St. (btw. Fifth and Sixth aves.). ☎ 212/242-4848. Subway: 4, 5, 6, N, R, L to 14th St.–Union Square.

Academy is best known for its record store (see "Music," below), but adjacent is this friendly neighborhood used-book store. Their inventory is quite deep, focusing on literature, history, art, humanities, and philosophy. Best of all, the prices are scrupulously fair.

Archivia. 944 Madison Ave. (btw. 74th and 75th sts.). ☎ 212/439-9194. Subway: 6 to 77th St.

Here you'll find new, imported, and rare books on architecture, the decorative arts, gardening, and interior design. A book and design lover's dream.

If you like Archivia, you might also check out the Municipal Art Society's **Urban Center Books,** 457 Madison Ave., between 50th and 51st streets (☎ 212/935-3595), which has a terrific selection of books on architecture, design, and urban planning.

Argosy Books. 116 E. 59th St. (btw. Park and Lexington aves.). ☎ 212/753-4455. Subway: 4, 5, 6 to 59th St.

Rare and used-book hounds should check out this stately store, with high ceilings, packed shelves, a quiet intellectual air, and an outstanding collection of rarities, including 18th- and 19th-century prints.

Books of Wonder. 16 W. 18th St. (btw. Fifth and Sixth aves.). ☎ 212/989-3270. www.booksofwonder.com. Subway: 4, 5, 6, N, R, L to 14th St.–Union Sq.

You don't have to be a kid to fall in love with this charming bookstore, which served as the model for Meg Ryan's shop in *You've Got Mail* (Meg even worked here a spell to train for the role). Kids will love BOW's story readings, which take place every Sunday at 11:45am.

Coliseum Books. 1771 Broadway (at 57th St.). ☎ 212/757-8381. Subway: 1, 9, A, B, C, D to 59th St./Columbus Circle.

This big, well-stocked independent is a must on any book-lover's list—and it's well located for visitors, right on the edge of the Theater District, a stone's throw from Central Park. It may not be Barnes & Noble cozy, but you'll find an excellent selection of fiction and literature (both contemporary and the classics), along with great travel, art, and coffee-table books. Staff, poised atop a raised platform in the middle of the store, are on hand to answer questions or proffer a literary opinion. Coliseum also stocks a selection of note cards, greeting cards, and journals.

Complete Traveller. 199 Madison Ave. (at 35th St.). ☎ 212/685-9007. Subway: 6 to 33rd St.

Whether your destination is Texas or Tibet, you'll find what you need in this, possibly the world's best travel bookstore. There are maps and travel accessories, plus a rare collection of antiquarian travel books.

A Different Light Bookstore. 151 W. 19th St. (btw. Sixth and Seventh aves.). ☎ **212/ 989-4850.** www.adlbooks.com. Subway: 1, 9 to 18th St.

The city's largest gay and lesbian bookstore stocks just about every category—fiction, nonfiction, biography, travel, gay/lesbian studies, and more—plus cassettes, calendars, you name it. There's also a cafe. Check the Web site for a full calendar of readings and video nights.

Forbidden Planet. 840 Broadway (at 13th St.). ☎ **212/473-1576.** Subway: 4, 5, 6, N, R, L to 14th St.–Union Sq.

Here's the city's largest collection of sci-fi, comics, and graphic-illustration books. The prices aren't low, but the range of products can't be beat, and the proudly geeky staff really knows its stuff. Great sci-fi–themed toys, too.

✪ Gotham Book Mart. 41 W. 47th St. (btw. Fifth and Sixth aves.). ☎ **212/719-4448.** Subway: B, D, F, Q to 47–50th sts./Rockefeller Center.

Paris may have had Sylvia Beach, but New York was lucky enough to have Frances Steloff. She opened Gotham Book Mart in 1920, and quickly became a defender of First Amendment rights for authors. She championed such once-banned works as Henry Miller's *Tropic of Cancer,* and numbered among her admirers Ezra Pound, Saul Bellow, and Jackie Kennedy Onassis. Frances has since passed on, but here, her aura lives on. As always, the emphasis is on poetry, literature, and the arts. An undisputed literary landmark; look for the sign that says WISE MEN FISH HERE.

Hagstrom Map & Travel Center. 57 W. 43rd St. (btw. Fifth and Sixth aves.). ☎ **212/ 398-1222.** Subway: B, D, F, Q to 42nd St.

This bookstore sells travel guides and an incredible selection of cartography to meet just about any map need. There's a second location in lower Manhattan at 125 Maiden Lane, at Water Street (☎ 212/785-5343).

✪ Housing Works Used Books Cafe. 126 Crosby St. (south of Houston St.). ☎ **212/ 334-3324.** Subway: B, D, F, Q to Broadway–Lafayette St.

Like the idea of your hard-earned dollars benefiting both you and others? Then buy your reading material at this quietly cozy used-bookshop. It's part of Housing Works, a not-for-profit organization that provides housing, services, and advocacy for homeless people living with HIV and AIDS. The sizable collection is terrific and well organized, with lots of well-priced paperbacks, hardbacks, advance copies, and coffee-table books. There's a comfortable cafe in back that serves up coffee and tea, sandwiches, sweets, and other light bites, and you're welcome to pull anything off the shelves to peruse as you snack.

Kitchen Arts & Letters. 1435 Lexington Ave. (btw. 93rd and 94th sts.). ☎ **212/ 876-5550.** Subway: 6 to 96th St.

Foodies take note: Here's the ultimate cook's and food-lover's bookstore. You'll be wowed by the depth of the selection, which includes rare and out-of-print cookbooks. The staff will conduct free searches for hard-to-find titles. The shop is an overstuffed jumble, but if this is your bag, you'll be browsing for hours.

Murder Ink. 2486 Broadway (at 92nd St.). ☎ **212/362-8905.** www.murderink.com. Subway: 1, 9 to 96th St.

Murder, she wrote, he wrote, they wrote. This is the ultimate specialty bookstore—as much fun as a good mystery. They claim to sell every mystery in print, and also carry a huge selection of out-of-print paperbacks, hard-to-find imported titles, and rare signed first editions. You can even keep buying over the Web site or toll-free line (☎ 800/488-8123) from home; have your name added to the catalog mailing list.

Mystery and true-crime fans will also enjoy the **Mysterious Book Shop,** 129 W. 56th St., between Sixth and Seventh avenues (☎ **212/765-0900;** www.mysteriousbookshop.com), another store specializing in current and rare whodunits.

Oscar Wilde Bookshop. 15 Christopher St. (btw. Sixth and Seventh aves.) ☎ **212/255-8097.** www.OscarWildeBooks.com. Subway: 1, 9 to Christopher St.–Sheridan Sq.

The world's oldest gay and lesbian bookstore is still going strong. It's much smaller than A Different Light (above), but a recent renovation allows for more titles and ancillary merchandise than ever before, and the nice staff makes this landmark a pleasure.

Rand McNally Travel Store. 150 E. 52nd St. (btw. Lexington and Third aves.). ☎ **212/758-7488.** www.randmcnallystore.com. Subway: 6 to 51st St.; E, F to Lexington Ave.

Sheet maps, globe maps, city maps, international maps, laminated maps—so many maps, in fact, you might never get lost again. In addition to cartography, Rand McNally sells a wide range of travel guides, atlases, and such travelers' aids as voltage converters and inflatable pillows. There's a second location in the Garment District at 555 Seventh Ave. (☎ **212/944-4477**).

Rizzoli. 31 W. 57th St. (btw. Fifth and Sixth aves.). ☎ **212/759-2424.** Subway: N, R to Fifth Ave.

This clubby Italian bookstore is the classiest—and most relaxing—spot in town to browse for the best visual art and design books, plus quality fiction, gourmet cookbooks, and other upscale reading. There's also a decent selection of foreign-language, music, and dance titles as well. They're also in SoHo at 454 West Broadway, just south of Houston (☎ **212/674-1616**), and at 3 World Financial Center (☎ **212/385-1400**).

Revolution Books. 9 W. 19th St. (btw. Fifth and Sixth aves.). ☎ **212/691-3345.** Subway: 4, 5, 6, L, N, R to 14th St.–Union Sq.

If you're looking for an alternative viewpoint, you'll find quite a few of them at Revolution. Books on Marxism, feminism, black nationalism, and just about any other "ism" make up the bulk of this earnest store. But it's not just political tracts; fiction, poetry, magazines, and newspapers are on hand as well. Stock is organized by such provocative categories as "U.S. Imperialism, Past & Present" and "Women's Oppression/Women's Liberation." Flyers advertise rallies and get-togethers to support local and international labor and human-rights causes.

Shakespeare & Co. 716 Broadway (at Washington Place). ☎ **212/529-1330.** Subway: N, R to 8th St.

A boutique-like bookstore in the Village stocks the latest fiction (and non-) bestsellers, and has a generally well-rounded inventory. The displays are quite enticing if you're looking for something new to read. Another branch is Uptown, at 939 Lexington Ave., between 68th and 69th streets (☎ **212/570-0201**).

✪ **St. Mark's Bookshop.** 31 Third Ave. (at 9th St.). ☎ **212/260-7853.** Subway: 6 to Astor Place.

This left-of-center East Village bookshop is a great place to browse. You'll find lots of terrific alternative and small-press fiction and literature, plus cultural criticism and mainstream literature with an edge. You'll also find art and design books as well as an alternative 'zine rack.

✪ **The Strand.** 828 Broadway (at 12th St.). ☎ **212/473-1452.** Subway: 4, 5, 6, N, R, L to 14th St.–Union Sq.

Something of a New York legend, the Strand's worth a visit for its staggering "8 miles of books" as well as its extensive inventory of review copies and bargain titles at up to

85% off list price. It's unquestionably the city's best book deal—there's almost nothing marked at list—and the selection is phenomenal in all categories (there's even a rare-book department on the third floor). Still, you'll work for it: The narrow aisles mean you're always getting bumped; the books are only roughly alphabetized; and there's no air-conditioning in summer. Nevertheless, a used-book lover's paradise. There's a smaller Strand Downtown, at 95 Fulton St., between William and Gold streets (☎ 212/732-6070).

CLOTHING
RETAIL FASHIONS
Fashion hounds should be sure to check out "The Top Shopping Streets & Neighborhoods" earlier in this chapter for advice on prime hunting grounds for affordable original designs.

FASHION FLAGSHIPS   Some New York flagship stores of the major brands are an experience you won't catch in your nearest mall. These stores are display cases for the complete line of fashions, so you'll often find much more to choose from than in your at-home branch. Check out the gorgeous **Ann Taylor,** at 645 Madison Ave., at 60th Street (☎ 212/832-2010); **Banana Republic,** 655 Fifth Ave., at 52nd Street (☎ 212/644-6678); **Eddie Bauer,** 1976 Broadway, at 67th Street (☎ 212/877-7629), which also carries the AKA Eddie Bauer line and the sports and mountaineering line; the **Original Levi's Store** at 3 E. 57th Street, between Fifth and Madison (☎ 212/838-2125); and **Victoria's Secret,** 34 E. 57th St., between Madison and Park avenues (☎ 212/758-5592).

Occupying three floors right across the street from Macy's, the sprawling **Gap** at 60 W. 34th St., at Broadway (☎ 212/643-8960), is worth mentioning because many items sold here never make it to suburbia; this is one of the major test markets for new styles. **Old Navy** has a huge flagship at 610 Sixth Ave., at 18th St. (☎ 212/645-0663). **Diesel** sells its casual, youthful streetwear at its vibrant superstore across from Bloomingdale's, at Lexington and 60th Street (☎ 212/755-9200). **J. Crew** has a big bi-level SoHo store at 100 Prince St., between Mercer and Greene (☎ 212/966-2739).

For Men & Women
Canal Jean Co. 504 Broadway (btw. Spring and Broome sts.). ☎ **212/226-1130.** Subway: N, R to Prince St.; 6 to Spring St.

This big, bright store almost single-handedly started the SoHo shopping revolution nearly 2 decades ago. You'll find tons of well-priced jeans (low-riders, bellbottoms, and just plain regular), midriff-baring T-shirts, and flannels, with the requisite vinyl purses/backpacks, and clunky costume jewelry thrown in. Go downstairs for vintage wear, but know that the stuff they have is geared to the skateboard set and tends to be a tad shopworn.

Patricia Field. 10 E. 8th St. (btw. Fifth Ave. and University Place). ☎ **212/254-1699.** Subway: 6 to Astor Place.

The wildest club kids and trendsetters know Patricia Field as *the* place to shop. She has been the leading doyenne of cutting-edge chic and downtown cool for more than two decades now. Her shop sports the city's grooviest, most outrageous men's and women's clubwear. The store's wild makeup counter will appear tame once you see the outlandish 'dos in the wig and hair salon. There is nothing understated about this place—it's a great browse. Pat Field's SoHo location, **Hotel Venus,** 382 West Broadway, between Spring and Broome streets (☎ 212/966-4066), is a bit more upscale, but no less funky.

Scouring the Sample Sales

Welcome to the ultimate New York bargain: the sample sale. At a sample sale, top-notch designers recoup some losses by selling off the sample outfits they make to show to store buyers. Often, they throw in canceled orders, overstock, and discontinued styles as well. Prices are rock-bottom, even better than what you'd pay at TJ Maxx and other such discounters. What's the drawback? Sales aren't advertised, because fashion designers don't want to alienate the big retailers by stealing their customers.

So how do you get the inside scoop? The **weekly columns** "Sales & Bargains" in *New York* magazine and "Check Out" in *Time Out New York* list current and future sales. A Web site, **www.samplesale.com**, posts information on sales in New York City as well as other cities. And **www.newyork.sidewalk.com/ shopping** is a great source for the latest sales (click on "weekly sales sheet"); you can even register to be notified on a weekly basis. If you're in the Garment District (especially along Broadway and Seventh Ave.) in the morning or at lunchtime, you'll probably be handed several **flyers** advertising the sales going on that day.

A few tips as you venture into bargain land:

- Though some designers do accept credit cards, don't chance it; cash is the preferred method of payment.
- *Don't* go during lunch hour—you'll be elbow-to-elbow with harried, rushed office workers.
- Few, if any, of these spaces have dressing rooms, so be prepared to try things on over your clothes (or cross your fingers and hope it fits). Furthermore, since these garments are samples, they don't always come in a wide array of sizes. A man who is a 40 regular, for instance, is in like Flynn. If you're a 46 extra long, you're going to have rougher going.
- All items are sold "as is," and every sale is final, so inspect merchandise carefully before forking over your dough.

Phat Farm. 129 Prince St. (btw. West Broadway and Wooster St.). ☎ **212/533-PHAT.** Subway: N, R to Prince St.

For the most stylish hip-hop clothes on the market, head to music impresario Russell Simmons's SoHo boutique, which sells his label exclusively. Extra-puffy down jackets, extra-baggy pants, logo Ts—you'll find it all here.

Tristan & America. 1230 Sixth Ave. (at 49th St.). ☎ **212/246-2354.** Subway: B, D, F, Q to 47–50th sts./Rockefeller Center.

This Canadian retailer sells affordable, nicely tailored clothing in muted palettes to men and women who love Banana Republic's clothes, but need a break from the high prices there. Look for great men's sweaters, affordable women's suits, and nicely cut trousers and A-line skirts. Also in SoHo at 560 Broadway, at Prince Street (☎ **212/ 965-1810**).

Urban Outfitters. 628 Broadway (at Bleecker St.). ☎ **212/475-0009.** Subway: 6 to Bleecker St.

The store for basics is sort of a Gap for alternative guys and gals. Jeans, oversized and tiny T-shirts, and lots of bright velours and stretchy polyesters. There's a good selection of earrings and funky jewelry for women, as well as a wonderfully offbeat, affordable housewares section, with batik bedspreads, candles, glassware, and mod bathroom accessories. You'll also find lots of silly gifts, from *Mad Libs* books to boxes of genuine South Park Cheesy Poofs. Look for additional branches at 374 Sixth Ave., at Waverly Place (☎ 212/677-9350); 162 Second Ave., between 10th and 11th streets (☎ 212/375-1277); and 127 E. 59th St., between Park and Lexington avenues (☎ 212/688-1200).

Just Women

✪ **Eileen Fisher.** 314 E. 9th St., btw. First and Second aves. ☎ **212/529-5715**. Subway: C, E to Spring St.

Slowly making their way around the nation in her own shops and through outlets like Saks and the Garnet Hill catalog, Eileen Fisher's separates are a dream come true for stylish women looking for easy-to-wear classic pieces that transcend the latest fads. She designs fluid clothes in a pleasing neutral palette with natural fibers that don't sacrifice comfort for chic. The A-line styles look a bit droopy on shorter women, but otherwise suit all figures well. Prices are on the high side, but the superior quality, fabrics, and style make them worth every penny. The SoHo shop, at 395 West Broadway, between Spring and Broome streets (☎ 212/431-4567), is Fisher's prime showcase, but bargain hunters should head straight for this closet-sized East 9th Street location, which basically functions as an outlet store, with lots of sale merchandise and seconds on hand.

You'll find additional locations at 103 Fifth Ave., near 18th Street (☎ 212/924-4777); 521 Madison Ave., at 53rd Street (☎ 212/759-9888); and 341 Columbus Ave., near 77th Street (☎ 212/362-3000).

✪ **Jill Anderson.** 311 E. 9th St. (btw. First and Second aves.). ☎ **212/253-1747**. Subway: 6 to Astor Place.

Finally, a New York designer who designs affordable clothes for real women for real life—not just for 22-year-old size-2s to match with a pair of Pradas and wear out club-hopping. This narrow, peaceful shop and studio is lined on both sides with Jill's simple, clean-lined designs. They drape beautifully and accentuate a woman's form without clinging, making them wearable for all ages and many figure types (her small sizes are small enough to fit petites, and her larges generally fit a full-figured size 14). Her clothes are feminine without being frilly, retro-reminiscent but completely modern, understated but utterly stylish.

Liberty House. 2878A Broadway (at 112th St.). ☎ **212/932-1950**. Subway: 1, 9 to Cathedral Pkwy.–110th St.

This Columbia University–area boutique is a real find. It specializes in comfy womenswear in easygoing styles that transcend age lines and figure types. Great casual sweaters, Ts, cotton pants and skirts, linen separates, and much more, all at affordable prices. You'll also find affordable ethnic gifts at the front of the store, neat jewelry and accessories under the glass-topped counter, and a great kids' shop in the back specializing in unique styles that don't cost a fortune.

Nicolina. 247 W. 46th St. (btw. Broadway and Eighth Ave.). ☎ **212/302-NICO**. Subway: 1, 2, 3, 9, N, R, S to 42nd St.–Times Square.

This charming and sophisticated shop is a Theater District anomaly. Come for fashionable basics in high-quality natural materials: wide-legged linen pants, flowing A-line and princess-cut dresses in silk and cotton, sweaters from labels like Beyond Threads and Sarah Arizona. Great accessories, too, plus a small selection of contemporary and vintage gifts. A joy to browse.

Just Kids

If you need the basics, you'll find branches of **Gap Kids** and **Baby Gap** all over town—it's harder to avoid one than find one—including at 60 W. 34th St., at Broadway (☎ 212/643-8960). The department stores are also great sources, of course.

Also, don't forget **Liberty House,** which has a kids' boutique in back specializing in great styles at reasonable prices; see "Just Women," directly above. **Little O's** is the stop for vintage-minded kids; see "Vintage Clothing," below.

OshKosh B'Gosh. 586 Fifth Ave. (btw. 47th and 48th sts.). ☎ **212/827-0098.** Subway: E, F to Fifth Ave.

Wisconsin's most famous name in fashion has a store decked out with train compartments to display the clothes: infants in the rear, boys on the left, and girls on the right. Prices are affordable, especially for European shoppers who pay upward of $100 for overalls at home.

DISCOUNT FASHIONS

For details on discount mega-mart **Century 21,** see "The Department Stores" earlier in this chapter.

Burlington Coat Factory. 116 W. 23rd St. (at Sixth Ave.). ☎ **212/229-1300.** Subway: F to 23rd St.

Burlington also has a stash of off-price and slightly irregular designer togs, but I say don't bother—come for the coats. You'll find an exhaustive selection at excellent prices, as well as a fine selection of discounted leather bags.

Daffy's. 111 Fifth Ave. (at 18th St.). ☎ **212/529-4477.** Subway: 4, 5, 6, L, N, R, to 14th St.–Union Sq.

Long before any of these Johnny-come-lately discounters dropped anchor in Manhattan, Daffy's offered rock-bottom prices to the masses. They don't get the big-time brand names of Century 21, but you'll come across classic European sportswear (cashmere sweaters and the like) and reliable staples, especially for men. The kid's collection—much of it froufrou continental or trendy designer—is a well-kept secret among city moms. Also at 335 Madison Ave., at 44th Street (☎ 212/557-4422); right across the street from Macy's at 1311 Broadway, at 34th Street (☎ 212/736-4477); and 135 E. 57th St., between Park and Lexington avenues (☎ 212/376-4477).

Filene's Basement. 620 Sixth Ave. (btw. 18th and 19th sts.). ☎ **212/620-3100.** Subway: F to 14th St.

This Boston-based bargain institution's Manhattan satellites pale when compared to the mother store. The stock can be hit-or-miss, but you will find discounts on men's and women's clothing, handbags, accessories, shoes, and a few brands of perfume. Every now and then a big-time European label pops up, but don't count on finding the current season's goods, especially in the downstairs men's store. Inventory turns over lightning-quick here, though, so you never know what a trip through can yield. Also at 2222 Broadway, at 79th Street (☎ 212/873-8000).

✪ **Loehmann's.** 101 Seventh Ave. (btw. 16th and 17th sts.). ☎ **212/352-0856.** Subway: 1, 9 to 18th St.

This enormous outlet occupies a major chunk of the original Barneys, and it's really latched onto the stylish vibe. Unlike its progenitors, this Loehmann's is so fancy it even has its own personal shopper (at your service absolutely free!). Two chock-full floors of casual wear by makers like Liz Claiborne and Laundry lead to one of the city's best discount finds: The top-level "Back Room," where styles by some of fashion's biggest names—think Versace, D&G, Donna Karan, Max Mara—are offered at a fraction of retail. There's also a whole floor of men's fashions, the best you'll find in the discount realm. You'll find excellent shoes, too, with great prices on top-quality, high-fashion styles by the likes of Calvin Klein, Joan & David, and Cole-Haan.

TJ Maxx. 620 Sixth Ave. (btw. 18th and 19th sts.). ☎ 212/229-0875. Subway: F to 14th St.

Directly above Filene's Basement, in the same rehabbed building, TJ Maxx is yet another off-pricer of wearables for the entire family. If you're seriously into bargains, price check each store—there's some crossover merchandise between Filene's Basement and TJ Maxx—as prices at TJ Maxx can be lower.

VINTAGE & RESALE CLOTHING

✪ **Allan & Suzi.** 416 Amsterdam Ave. (at 80th St.). ☎ 212/724-7445. Subway: 1, 9 to 79th St.

Make it past the freaky windows and inside you'll find one of the best consignment shops in the city. Allan and Suzi have specialized in gently worn 20th-century designer wear for well more than a decade now, and their selection is marvelous. Their extensive vintage and contemporary couture collection—which ranges from conservative Chanel to over-the-top Halston—is so well priced that it's within reach of the average shopper looking for something extra-glamorous to wear.

Antique Boutique. 712 Broadway (btw. 4th St. and Astor Place). ☎ 212/460-8830. Subway: 6 to Astor Place.

With a techno soundtrack and a huge array of cheap duds like bowling shirts, Hawaiian shirts, and hiphuggers among the vintage wear, this store targets the teen and nightclubbing crowd who want to look retro-sharp when they make the scene.

Argosy. 428 E. 9th St. (btw. First Ave. and Ave. A). ☎ 212/982-7918. Subway: 6 to Astor Place.

This narrow shop offers a small but utterly pristine collection of 1960s and 1970s fashions, including an excellent collection of leather jackets. Prices are reasonable considering the quality.

Encore. 1132 Madison Ave. (at 84th St.). ☎ 212/879-2850. Subway: 6 to 86th St.

This is one of the city's best resale shops, with two floors of quality womenswear, plus a small men's department and some accessories. Periodic sales sweeten the deal even more: The Chanel suit I saw here for $650 was the buy of the century, but you don't have to bring that much cash to go home with a bargain.

Just a few blocks down is **Michael's,** at no. 1041 (☎ 212/737-7273), an upper-floor boutique boasting exclusively top-drawer designers at a fraction of their original cost. The bridal consignment department is a real find for brides looking for a top-quality dress at an off-the-rack price.

✪ **Housing Works Thrift Shop.** 143 W. 17th St. (btw. Sixth and Seventh aves.). ☎ 212/366-0820. Subway: 1, 9 to 18th St.

With consistently low prices (most pieces $25 or less), lots of designer names (Todd Oldham, Calvin Klein, Donna Karan, and friends), and clothes in excellent condition, why go anywhere else? Styles range from classic tweeds to funky pieces you could picture only RuPaul wearing. There's also a good used-jeans area and a mini-boutique selling couture-ish items at slightly higher prices. There's furniture, too, but good pieces go very fast. A great place to shop—not only will you get a bargain, but sales benefit homeless people living with HIV and AIDS. Additional locations are on the Upper East Side at 202 E. 77th St., between Second and Third avenues (☎ 212/772-8461), and across the park at 306 Columbus Ave., between 74th and 75th streets (☎ 212/579-7566).

Little O's. 1 Bleecker St. (btw. Bowery and Elizabeth St.). ☎ **212/673-0858.** Subway: 6 to Bleecker St.

New York's first vintage clothing shop for kids is overflowing with little fashions of yesteryear, from hand-embroidered pre-war christening dresses to Speed Racer pjs. Everything is freshly cleaned and in good condition, so expect to pay more than you would at the Salvation Army.

Love Saves the Day. 119 Second Ave. (at 7th St.). ☎ **212/228-3802.** Subway: 6 to Astor Place.

This is the store made famous in Madonna's big film break, *Desperately Seeking Susan* (she bought those groovy boots here). In the more than 10 years since the movie's release, LSD hasn't changed much, except the prices keep going up. In addition to the big and entertaining collection of tacky vintage clothes, there's one good reason to fall in Love here: the impressive assortment of Donny and Marie memorabilia and other collectible kitsch.

Metropolis. 43 Third Ave. (btw. 9th and 10th sts.). ☎ **212/358-0795.** Subway: 6 to Astor Place.

It's rumored that some of the biggest names in the fashion world scout this clean, orderly vintage shop for street-fashion ideas. With good reason, too: Some of the coolest old clothes in the world turn up here, from skater pants and micro-cords to gingham-checked Western shirts perfect for your very own hoe-down or hullabaloo.

✪ **Screaming Mimi's.** 382 Lafayette St. (btw. 4th and Great Jones sts.). ☎ **212/677-6464.** Subway: 6 to Astor Place.

Think you hate vintage shopping? Think again: Screaming Mimi's is as neat and well organized as any boutique. The clothes are a little pricier than in some competing shops but they're still within reach, and it's worth paying for the well-chosen selection and top-notch display. The vintage housewares department offers a cornucopia of kitschy old stuff, as does the selection of New York memorabilia. Good accessories, too.

EDIBLES

New York boasts the finest gourmet markets in the world. Below are my favorites, but foodies will also have a ball at **Chelsea Market,** a big, dazzling food mall at 75 Ninth Ave., between 15th and 16th streets (☎ 212/243-5678). The **Vinegar Factory,** 431 E. 91st St., between First and York avenues (☎ 212/987-0885), is a high-end food emporium from the Zabar family (see below), this time with a chic uptown vibe; a pleasant brunch is served on a loft overlooking the bustling store on weekends from 8am to 4pm. And don't forget about the **Union Square greenmarket;** see p. 249.

Balducci's. 424 Sixth Ave. (at 9th St.). ☎ **212/673-2600.** Subway: A, B, C, D, E, F, Q to W. 4th St. (use 8th St. exit).

This pricey gourmet grocery is a foodie's dream come true. It's relatively small (the shopping carts are even scaled down) and always packed, but the store overflows with imported foodstuffs; the best and freshest meats, fish, and breads; picture-perfect fruits and veggies, including international exotica like hard-to-find starfruit and enoki mushrooms; and deli, cheese, and dessert counters to die for. The knowledgeable staff manages to keep its collective cool even at the height of the holiday bustle.

Across the street is **Cafe Balducci,** at Sixth Avenue and West 10th Street, where you can order from the extensive selection of sandwiches, salads, and other prepared foods and enjoy your meal at one of the pleasant cafe tables.

Dean & DeLuca. 560 Broadway (at Prince St.). ☎ **212/431-1691.** Subway: N, R to Prince St.

Another in the gourmet supermarket field, though this one is a little too self-consciously hip, and even pricier than Balducci's. Still, it's hard to argue with quality.

In addition to the excellent butcher, cheese, and dessert counters (check out the stunning cakes and the great character cookies) and beautiful greens, you'll find a dried fruit and nut bar, a huge coffee-bean selection, gorgeous cut flowers, lots of imported waters and beers, and a limited but quality selection of kitchenware in back.

Up front is a small, affordable **cafe** with prepared sandwiches, cakes, cappucino, and other goodies. Other **cafe-only** locations include a roomy branch at 9 Rockefeller Center, across from the *Today* show studio, and at the Paramount hotel, 235 W. 46th St., between Broadway and Eighth Avenue.

✪ **Fairway Market.** 2127 Broadway (at 74th St.) ☎ **212/595-1888.** Subway: 1, 2, 3, 9 to 72nd St.

This completely unpretentious gourmet food market, just down the street from equally earthy Zabar's (below), is an excellent place to put together a sophisticated picnic for nearby Central Park or an eat-in meal. The fruits and vegetables are glorious, and prices are better than you'll find at similar quality markets. Fairway is in the process of doubling its size, so expect an expanded section of prepared and prepackaged foods.

Gourmet Garage. 453 Broome St. (at Mercer St.). ☎ **212/941-5850.** Subway: N, R to Prince St.

This SoHo store features a neighborhood-appropriate loft-like setting and some of the tastiest gourmet products in town (the produce is particularly impressive). The Garage supplies many of the city's best restaurants, including Le Cirque 2000, and sells to the public at wholesale, about 40% off the retail of fancier stores. You'll find additional locations at 301 E. 64th St., between First and Second avenues (☎ **212/535-6271**); and 2567 Broadway, between 96th and 97th streets (☎ **212/663-0656**), the latter featuring an extensive department of Kosher foods.

✪ **Zabar's.** 2245 Broadway (at 80th St.). ☎ **212/787-2000.** Subway: 1, 9 to 79th St.

More than any other New York gourmet food store, Zabar's is an institution. This giant deli sells prepared foods, packaged goods from around the world, coffee beans, excellent fresh breads, and much more. This is the place for lox, and the rice pudding is the best I've ever tasted. You'll also find an excellent selection of cooking and kitchen gadgets on the second floor, and a never-ending flow of Woody Allen film stock characters who shop here daily.

BAGELS

No one should visit New York without tasting a real New York bagel. They come in all flavors, from plain to "everything" (sesame, poppy seeds, garlic, onion, *and* salt). H&H, below, is my (and most New Yorkers') favorite, but for excellent bagels and sit-down service, head to **Ess-A-Bagel** (p. 165) instead.

✪ **H&H Bagel.** 2239 Broadway (at 80th St.). ☎ **212/595-8003.** Subway: 1, 9 to 79th St.

H&H is the king of New York bagel makers. Stop in to this bare-bones shop for a piping-hot bagel, which is so good it needs no accompaniment. If you prefer the traditional toppings—cream cheese, lox, and the like—they're sold in the refrigerator cases. Other locations: 639 W. 46th St., at Twelfth Avenue, across from the *Intrepid* (☎ **212/595-8000**); and 1551 Second Ave., between 80th and 81st streets (☎ **212/ 734-7441**). All locations are open around the clock, so come by for a bagel fix anytime. If you crave more H&H when you get home, call ☎ **800/NY-BAGEL** to order; they ship almost anywhere.

CHOCOLATES

Black Hound. 170 Second Ave. (btw. 10th and 11th sts.). ☎ **212/979-9505.** Subway: 6 to Astor Place; L to Third Ave.

This charming shop specializes in beautifully made truffles, cookies, and cakes. This is a terrific choice for those who like their chocolates not too frilly or too sweet. Just about everything comes packaged in a blond-wood box tied with a velveteen ribbon, making them simple but elegant gifts for chocolate lovers.

Li-Lac Chocolates. 120 Christopher St. (btw. Bleecker and Hudson sts.). ☎ 212/242-7374. Subway: 1, 9 to Christopher St.–Sheridan Sq.

Li-Lac is one of the few chocolatiers anywhere still making its sweets by hand. In business in the same location since 1923, this supremely charming Village shop whips up its chocolate and maple-walnut fudge fresh every day, and it's about the best this city has seen. If fudge isn't your bag, they also make pralines, caramels, and other hand-dipped chocolates, including specialty sweets for the holidays (hollow bunnies and chocolate eggs for Easter, chocolate Santas for Christmas, and so on).

Teuscher Chocolates of Switzerland. 620 Fifth Ave. (at the Channel Gardens in Rockefeller Center). ☎ 212/246-4416. Subway: B, D, F, Q to 47–50th sts./Rockefeller Center. Also at 25 E. 61st St. (just east of Madison Ave.). ☎ 212/751-8482. Subway: 4, 5, 6 to 59th St.; N, R to Lexington Ave.

At $49 a pound, you'd think they were selling gold boullion. Teuscher makes mints, pralines, and wondrous marzipan, but it's the truffles that folks write home about. Splurge on one or two justifiably famous champagne truffles, and you'll weep with joy.

ELECTRONICS

J&R Music World/Computer World. Park Row (at Ann St., opposite City Hall Park). ☎ 800/221-8180 or 212/238-9100. www.jandr.com. Subway: 2, 3 to Park Place.

Midtown may be overrun with electronics dealers, but it's the Financial District's J&R that's the city's top discount computer, electronics, and small appliance retailer. J&R takes up almost the whole block of Park Row, with separate storefronts for small appliances, computers, music (jazz, pop, and classical), audio and video, and office equipment. The sales staff is knowledgeable but can get pushy if you don't buy at once or know exactly what you want. Don't succumb—take your time and find exactly what you need. Or better yet, peruse the store's copious catalog or extensive Web site, both of which make advance research, mail order, and comparison shopping easy.

GIFTS

If you're looking for a special gift for a creative spirit, be sure to check out the shops that line ✪ **East 9th Street** between Second Avenue and Avenue A in the East Village; for details on what's available along this strip, see "The Top Shopping Streets & Neighborhoods" earlier in this chapter.

An American Craftsman. 790 Seventh Ave. (at 52nd St.) ☎ 212/399-2555. Subway: 1, 9 to 50th St.

This pleasing shop sells wood furniture and crafts, decorative glassware, silver jewelry, and other fine-quality gift items—all, as the name implies, hand-crafted by American artists. Their wooden jewelry box and humidor collection is stunning. Other branches: In the Village at 317 Bleecker St. (☎ 212/727-0841) and 478 Sixth Ave. (☎ 212/243-0245); in the Financial District at 60 Broad St. (☎ 212/480-3945); in Gramercy Park at 77 Irving Place (☎ 212/598-4248); and on the East Side at 1222 Second Ave. (☎ 212/794-3440).

And Bob's Your Uncle. 137 W. 22nd St. (btw. Sixth and Seventh aves.). ☎ 212/627-7702. Subway: 1, 9, F to 23rd St.

So who is Bob? He's a genius for whimsy, kitsch, and clutter, turning it into creative and eco-friendly gift items. Practically everything is artfully made from stuff that the rest of us throw away: lampshades from vintage clothing and electrical piping, mirrors framed in mosaics of broken bottle glass. Some pieces are surprisingly beautiful, and the whole vintage-meets-postmodernism take is tons of fun.

Kate's Paperie. 561 Broadway (btw. Prince and Spring sts.). ☎ **212/941-9816.** Subway: N, R to Prince St.

Three cheers to Kate's for keeping the art of letter writing alive in our computer age. I could browse for hours among this delightful shop's handmade stationery and wrap, innovative invitations and thank yous, imported notebooks, writing tools, and other creative paper products, including cool paper lampshades. Lovely art cards, too—perfect for writing the folks back home. A joy! Also at 8 W. 13th St., between Fifth and Sixth avenues (☎ **212/633-0570**), and 1282 Third Ave., between 73rd and 74th streets (☎ **212/396-3670**), but the SoHo location is best.

La Maison Moderne. 144 W. 19th St. (btw. Sixth and Seventh aves.). ☎ **212/691-9603.** Subway: 1, 9 to 18th St.

This lovely little shop is filled with a beautiful, affordable mix of both vintage and contemporary gift items. Lots of care went into assembling this charming Parisian-inspired store, and it shows. My favorite part is the basement, where you'll find one-of-a-kind homewares, such as handcrafted velvet pillows and the cutest collection of teapots in town.

Mxyplyzyk. 125 Greenwich Ave. (at 13th St., near Eighth Ave.). ☎ **212/989-4300.** Subway: 1, 2, 3, 9, A, C, E to 14th St.

Come to this unpronounceable Village shop for one of the city's coolest collections of one-of-a-kind housewares and gifts.

HOME FASHIONS & HOUSEWARES

✪ **ABC Carpet & Home.** 888 Broadway (at 19th St.). ☎ **212/473-3000.** www.abccarpet.com. Subway: N, R, 4, 5, 6, L to 14th St.–Union Sq.

This 10-floor emporium is the ultimate home fashions and furnishings department store, a dream come true for aspiring Martha Stewarts. Shopping ABC has often been compared to taking a fantasy tour of your ancestor's attic: The goods run the gamut from mosaic-tile end tables to hand-painted Tuscan pottery to Tiffanyish lamps to distressed bed frames made up with Frette linens to much, much more, all carefully chosen and exquisitely displayed. Prices aren't bad comparatively speaking, but these are high-end goods. Some of the smaller items are quite affordable, though, and their occasional sales yield substantial discounts. In back is the **ABC Parlour Cafe,** serving lunch fare, tea, and elegant desserts. Across the street is the multi-floor carpet store, which boasts a remarkable collection of area rugs.

Amalgamated Home. 9–19 Christopher St. (btw. Sixth and Seventh aves.). ☎ **212/255-4160** (furniture and lighting), 212/989-6538 (hardware), or 212/691-8695 (household sundries). Subway: 1, 9 to Christopher St.–Sheridan Sq.

This trio of home shops stocks eye-catching household goods you won't see anywhere else. Looking for brushed metal switch plates for your stainless-steel kitchen? How about a purple velvet love seat straight out of a Looney Tunes cartoon? Or the hippest rice bowls in town? You'll find it all and more at Amalgamated. Don't miss the terrific matte-white dinnerware shaped like Chinese takeout containers from Swid Powell.

✪ **Fishs Eddy.** 889 Broadway (at 19th St.). ☎ **212/420-9020.** Subway: N, R, 4, 5, 6, L to 14th St.–Union Sq.

What a great idea—selling remainders of kitschy, custom-designed china leftover from yesteryear. Ever wanted a dish that *really* says BLUE PLATE SPECIAL? Or how about a coffee mug with the terse logo CUP O' JOE TO GO? The store is Browse Heaven, and prices are low enough. Other items for sale include basic vintage and retro-inspired flatware, heavy crockery bowls, and classic restaurant-supply glassware that can be hard to find in regular stores, like soda-fountain and pint glasses. There's also a branch at 2176 Broadway, at 77th Street (☎ 212/873-8819).

LEATHER GOODS, HANDBAGS & LUGGAGE
Greenwich Village is the place to go for affordable leather looks, especially along Christopher and Bleecker streets in the West Village. Worth seeking out are **Bleecker House,** at 182 Bleecker St. (☎ 212/358-1442), for leather jackets, and the **Village Tannery,** at 173 Bleecker (☎ 212/673-5444), for bags, wallets, and organizers.

The Lower East Side's bargain district is a great source for discount handbags and luggage. The best of the bunch is **Fine & Klein,** 119 Orchard St., near Delancey (☎ 212/674-6720), offering good discounts (usually 20%) on name-brand handbags.

Jobson's. 666 Lexington Ave. (at 55th St.). ☎ 212/355-6846, or 800/221-5238 (outside New York state). Subway: 6 to 51st St.

Jobson's is a great discount source for name-brand luggage and small leather goods. Rather than just offering a cut off the retail price, management marks most items at just 10% above cost, which usually amounts to a whopping 40% to 60% break for the buyer. The shop also does a huge airline and professional flyers business, and they'll be happy to tell you what the pros buy.

Manhattan Portage Ltd. Store. 333 E. 9th St. (btw. First and Second aves.). ☎ 212/995-1949. www.manhattanportageltd.com. Subway: 6 to Astor Place.

Come here for the hippest nylon and canvas carry-alls in town. True to its name, Manhattan Portage manufactures all its bags right in the city, and they're made from durable materials that can stand up to an urban lifestyle. Popular styles include all-purpose messenger bags, DJ bags, and backpacks in a range of colors from iridescent yellow to camouflage. Manhattan Portage bags are also sold at a number of other stores in the city and throughout the world (all listed on the Web site), but you're unlikely to find such a complete selection elsewhere.

LOGO STORES
Coca-Cola Fifth Ave. 711 Fifth Ave. (btw. 55th and 56th sts.). ☎ 212/418-9261. Subway: E, F, N, R to Fifth Ave.

The one that began the Fifth Avenue theme-store invasion. If they can slap a Coke logo on it, it's probably for sale here. You'll also find vintage vending machines—and, of course, Coke.

Disney Store. 711 Fifth Ave. (at 55th St.). ☎ 212/702-0702. Subway: E, F or N, R to Fifth Ave.

Disney burst onto Manhattan's retail scene with this monster three-story emporium. Bring the kids, and just try and get out without buying something. As a corollary to the Disney-led Times Square redevelopment, you'll find another big branch at 210 W. 42nd St., at Seventh Avenue (☎ 212/221-0430). There's yet another on the Upper West Side at Columbus Avenue and 66th Street (☎ 212/362-2386), worth mentioning for its collection of ABC TV souvenirs (the studio is right next door).

NBA Store. 666 Fifth Ave. (at 52nd St.). ☎ 212/515-NBA1. Subway: B, D, F, Q to 47–50th sts./Rockefeller Center.

For all things NBA and WNBA, head to this three-level mega-store, a multimedia celebration of pro basketball, complete with a bleacher-seated arena for player appearances and signings.

Niketown. 6 E. 57th St. (btw. Fifth and Madison aves.). ☎ **212/891-6453.** Subway: N, R to Fifth Ave.

More multimedia advertorial than sportswear store, Niketown opened in the fall of 1996 with much to-do. It's actually surprisingly low-key and attractive, with five floors of shoes and athletic wear displayed in stark, Lucite-and-polished-metal surroundings. "Museum" cases display Sneakers of the Rich and Famous, and everywhere you're assailed by images of celebrity pitchmen and women, with his Airness above all others, of course (retirement? what retirement?). No sales or bargains here—plan on paying top dollar for the high-style athletic wear. Somebody's gotta pay for this place!

✪ The Pop Shop. 292 Lafayette St. (at Prince St.). ☎ **212/219-2784.** www.haring.com. Subway: B, D, F, Q to Broadway–Lafayette St.

For affordable and wearable art that makes super-cool souvenirs, come to the Pop Shop. This store is chock-full of items based on designs by artist Keith Haring, who died in 1990. T-shirts, posters, calendars, stationery, toys, notebooks, neat transparent backpacks—all sport the vivid primary colors and loopy stick-figure drawings that Haring made famous. Best of all, the Pop Shop is a non-profit offering continued support to the AIDS-related and children's charities that the young artist championed.

Warner Bros. Studio Store. 1 E. 57th St. (at Fifth Ave.). ☎ **212/754-0300.** Subway: N, R to Fifth Ave.

This mega–theme store sits right near both Van Cleef & Arpels and Tiffany—wouldn't Bugs have a field day in those joints! Another three-story shop with cartoon-character everything, including animation cells for sale. For the short-attention-span crowd, Looney Tunes play continuously on store monitors. There's now an equally monolithic branch at 1 Times Square, at 42nd Street between Broadway and Seventh Ave. (☎ **212/840-4040**).

Yankees Clubhouse Shop. 393 Fifth Ave. (btw. 36th and 37th sts.). ☎ **212/685-4693.** Subway: 6 to 33rd St.

For all your Bronx Bombers needs—hats, jerseys, jackets, and so on, including souvenirs from the 1996 and 1998 World Series wins. Tickets for regular-season home games are also for sale, and there's a limited selection of other New York team jerseys as well. Also at 110 E. 59th St., between Park and Lexington avenues (☎ **212/758-7844**); and at Fulton and South streets in the South Street Seaport (☎ **212/514-7182**).

MUSEUM STORES
American Craft Museum. 40 W. 53rd St. (btw. Fifth and Sixth Aves.). ☎ **212/956-3535.** Subway: E, F to Fifth Ave.

Unsurprisingly, the nation's top showcase for contemporary crafts boasts an impressive collection of crafts in its museum store, too. Come for exquisite hand-blown glassware, one-of-a-kind jewelry, and other artistic treasures, all beautifully displayed.

Metropolitan Museum of Art Store. Fifth Ave. at 82nd St. ☎ **212/570-3894.** www.metmuseum.org. Subway: 4, 5, 6 to 86th St.

Given the scope of the museum itself, it's no wonder that the gift shop is outstanding. Many treasures from the museum's collection have been reproduced as jewelry, china, and other objets d'art. The range of art books is dizzying, and upstairs is an equally comprehensive selection of posters and inventive children's toys. The note cards, calendars, and wrapping paper also make great gifts. And you don't even have to go uptown to indulge: Other branches can be found on the plaza at Rockefeller Center

(☎ 212/332-1360), in SoHo at 113 Prince St. (☎ 212/614-3000), and on the mezzanine level at Macy's (☎ 212/268-7266).

Maxilla & Mandible. 451–5 Columbus Ave. (btw. 81st and 82nd sts.). ☎ **212/724-6173.** Subway: B, C to 81st St.

This shop is not affiliated with the American Museum of Natural History, but a visit here makes a good adjunct to your trip to the museum (which is right around the corner). It may look like a freak-shop at first glance, but it's really fascinating. Inside you'll find unusual rocks and shells from around the world, luminescent butterflies in display boxes, even surprisingly affordable real fossils (some as cheap as $20) that come with details on their history and where they were excavated. There's also a good variety of natural history–themed toys for the kids.

✪ **MOMA Design Store.** 44 W. 53rd St. (btw. Fifth and Sixth aves.). ☎ **212/767-1050.** www.moma.org. Subway: E, F to Fifth Ave.; B, D, F, Q to 47–50th sts./Rockefeller Center.

Across the street from the Museum of Modern Art is this terrific shop, whose stock ranges from museum posters and clever toys for kids to *way* overpriced reproductions of many of the classics of modern design, including free-form Alvar Aalto vases and Eames recliners. Luckily, there are plenty of more affordable outré home accessories to choose from.

Even if you don't check out the permanent collection, also pop in at the museum's main gift shop for a stellar collection of gift books, artsy note cards, and the like, all with a modern twist.

Museum of American Folk Art. 2 Lincoln Sq. (Columbus Ave. btw. 65th and 66th sts.). ☎ **212/496-2966.** Subway: 1, 9 to 66th St.

This charming gift shop is filled with one-of-a-kind objects that make wonderful take-home gifts. It's especially good with gifts for children and homespun holiday ornaments at Christmastime.

MUSIC & VIDEO

In addition to the choices below, music buffs will find a wealth of new-and-used shops in the West Village on **Bleecker Street** between Sixth and Seventh avenues as well as on side streets like Carmine and Christopher. Standouts include **Rebel Rebel,** 319 Bleecker St. (☎ 212/989-0770), for British and Japanese imports and New Wave and glam classics. Unfortunately, **Bleecker Bob's Golden Oldies**, 118 W. 3rd St., between Sixth Avenue and MacDougal Street (☎ 212/475-9677), has outlived its legend; it's now a dirty little hole-in-the-wall with lots of worn, badly organized vinyl and a rude staff.

Grungy **St. Marks Place** between Third and Second avenues in the East Village is another great bet. **Venus Records** (☎ 212/598-4459) is a standout, as is **Sounds** (☎ 212/677-3444), the dirt-cheap grandaddy of the St. Marks shops. Farther down, just off of St. Marks at 131 Ave. A, is **Accidental Records and Tapes** (☎ 212/995-2224), a friendly junk-pile of a store known for its good, cheap collection of used CDs and "we never close" policy.

In the Financial District, **J&R Music World** has a big selection of classical, jazz, and rock, and brand-new releases are almost always on sale; see "Electronics" for details.

Academy Records & CDs. 12 W. 18th St. (btw. Fifth and Sixth aves.). ☎ **212/242-3000.** Subway: 4, 5, 6, N, R, L to 14th St.–Union Sq.

This Flatiron District shop has a cool intellectual air that's more reminiscent of a good used-book store than your average used-record store. Academy is always filled with classical, opera, and jazz junkies perusing the extensive and well-priced collection of used CDs and vinyl. In addition to the extensive classical and jazz collection is a variety of other favorites, from rare 1960s pop songsters to spoken word. Adjacent is the actual used-book store.

✪ **Bleecker St. Records.** 239 Bleecker St. (near Carmine St., just west of Sixth Ave.). ☎ **212/255-7899.** Subway: A, B, C, D, E, F, Q to W. 4th St.

This sizable, well-lit space is great for one-stop shopping. The clean, well-organized CD and LP collections run the gamut from rock, oldies, jazz, folk, and blues to Oi! punk. You'll find lots of imports, collectible, and out-of-print records (including singles), and a terrific collection of used CDs.

✪ **Colony Record & Tape Center.** 1619 Broadway (at 49th St.). ☎ **212/265-2050.** Subway: 1, 9 to 50th St.; N, R to 49th St.

This enduring Theater District shop is housed in the legendary Brill Building, the Tin Pan Alley of 1950s and 1960s pop, where legendary songwriters like Goffin and King and producers like Don Kirschner and Phil Spector crafted the soundtrack for a generation. It's the perfect home for Colony, a nostalgic store filled with a pricey but excellent collection of vintage vinyl and CDs. You'll find a great collection of Broadway scores and cast recordings, plus decades worth of recordings by pop song stylists both legendary and obscure. There's also one of the best collections of sheet music in the city (including some hard-to-find international stuff), and a great selection of original theater and movie posters. You can stock up your in-home karaoke machine here, too.

If you like Colony, also visit **Footlight,** 113 E. 12th St., between Third and Fourth avenues (☎ **212/533-1572**), whose collection of vintage vinyl is strong in jazz and pop vocalists, soundtracks, and show tunes.

Generation Records. 210 Thompson St. (btw. Bleecker and 3rd sts.). ☎ **212/254-1100.** Subway: A, B, C, D, E, F, Q to W. 4th St.

This tidy little store sells mostly CDs and is an excellent source for "import" live recordings. Originally specializing in hardcore, punk, and heavy metal, the new collection upstairs still has a heavy edge but has since diversified appreciably. Downstairs is a well-organized and well-priced used CD selection that's not as picked over as most and runs the genre gamut; there's also a good selection of used LPs. Despite the staff's tough look, they're actually quite friendly and helpful.

Jazz Record Center. 236 W. 26th St. (btw. Seventh and Eighth aves.), 8th floor. ☎ **212/ 675-4480.** Subway: 1, 9 to 28th St.

Jazz Record Center is *the* place to find rare and out-of-print jazz records. In addition to the extensive selection of CDs and vinyl (including 78s), videos, books, posters, and other memorabilia are available. Prices can be high, as befits the rarity of the stock. Owner Frederick Cohen is extremely knowledgeable, so come here if you're trying to track down something obscure (Cohen does mail-order business as well).

Kim's Video & Audio. Kim's Underground at 144 Bleecker St. (at LaGuardia Place). ☎ **212/260-1010.** Subway: A, B, C, D, E, F, Q to West 4th St. Kim's West at 350 Bleecker St. (at W. 10th St.). ☎ **212/675-8996.** Subway: 1, 9 to Christopher St.–Sheridan Square. Mondo Kim's at 6 St. Mark's Place (btw. Second and Third aves.). ☎ **212/598-9985.** Subway: 6 to Astor Place.

This funky mini-chain is New York's underground alternative to Blockbuster Video, but they also stock a decent selection of indie vinyl and CDs as well as books and 'zines. The staff at all three locations has a terrible reputation, but word is they're reforming themselves of late.

✪ **NYCD.** 426 Amsterdam Ave. (btw. 80th and 81st sts.). ☎ **212/724-4466.** Subway: 1, 9 to 79th St.

This neat, narrow little store is home to one of the city's best collections of used rock CDs. Downtown trollers simply don't make it this far Uptown to prune the selection, so it's easy to find lots of top titles among the pickings.

✪ **Other Music.** 15 E. 4th St. (btw. Broadway and Lafayette St.). ☎ **212/477-8150.** Subway: 6 to Astor Place; B, D, F, Q to Broadway–Lafayette St.

Head to Other Music for the wildest sounds in town. You won't find a major label here (that's what Tower is for across the street). This shop focuses exclusively on small international labels, especially those on the cutting edge (you can find records on the Knitting Factory label here). This is the place if you're looking for underground Japanese spin doctors or obscure Irish folk; needless to say, the world music selection is terrific. The sales staff really knows their stuff, so ask away.

Throb. 211 E. 14th (btw. Second and Third aves.). ☎ **212/533-2328.** Subway: L to Third Ave.

Throb is home to CDs and 12-inch vinyl of not-even-close-to-mainstream genres: house, ambient, jungle, drum-and-bass, trance, trip-hop. Imports are also big business here. Not surprisingly, considering the cutting-edge inventory, it's a popular stop for dance-club DJs. Test drive the trippy sounds in a listening booth. You'll also find record bags and T-shirts.

If the music at Throb is your thing, you might also want to hike out to **Temple Records,** 29A Ave. B, between 2nd and 3rd streets, in the East Village (☎ 212/ 475-7552).

Tower Records. 692 Broadway (at W. 4th St.). ☎ **212/505-1500.** Subway: N, R to 8th St.; 6 to Astor Place.

As mighty a chain as it may be, it's hard to complain about Tower. Both the Village location and the Upper West Side branch (2107 Broadway, at 66th St.; ☎ 212/ 799-2500), are huge multimedia superstores brimming with an encyclopedic collection of music—classical, jazz, rock, world, you name it. The Village location also stocks a very good selection of indie and alternative labels. Just behind it at West 4th and Lafayette is **Tower Books** (☎ 212/228-5100), where you'll find videos, books, and magazines; and the **Tower Clearance Outlet** (☎ 212/228-7317), sells out-of-print and cut-out CDs for a song. Look for in-store appearances by big names in music, usually advertised in *Time Out New York* and *Village Voice* music sections.

Virgin Megastore. 1540 Broadway (at 45th St.). ☎ **212/921-1020.** Subway: 1, 2, 3, 7, 9, N, R to 42nd St.–Times Sq.

Right in the heart of Times Square, this superstore bustles day and night. For the size of it, the selection isn't as wide as you'd think; still, you're likely to find what you're looking for among the two levels of domestic and imported CDs and cassettes (there's also a limited vinyl selection). Other plusses are an extensive singles department, a phenomenal number of listening posts, plus a huge video department. There's also a bookstore, a cafe, and multiplex movie theater, and you can even arrange airfare on Virgin Atlantic with the on-site travel agent. The new Union Square location, 52 E. 14th St., at Broadway (☎ 212/598-4666), is brand-new but equally hopping. As at Tower, look for a busy schedule of in-store appearances at both locations.

SHOES

Designer shoe shops are on **East 57th Street** and amble up **Madison Avenue,** becoming pricier as you move uptown. **SoHo** is an excellent place to search for the latest styles; the streets are overrun with terrific shoe stores. Cheaper copies of the trendiest styles are sold in the tiny shops along **8th Street** between Broadway and Sixth Avenue in the Village, which some people call Shoe Row. Most department stores have two sizable shoe departments—one for designer stuff and one for daily wearables. See "Discount Fashions," above; at both **Loehmann's** and **Century 21,** the women's shoe departments are well stocked and unbelievably priced. Also see "The Department Stores" earlier in this chapter. For **Niketown,** see "Logo Stores," above.

John Fluevog Shoes. 104 Prince St. (btw. Mercer and Greene sts.). ☎ **212/431-4484.** Subway: N, R to Prince St.

John Fluevog's funky, chunky footwear has proven stylish enough to make the brand a mainstay among usually fickle young trendsetters. Some of the styles border on the ridiculous (check out the super-silly space-age Lift-Offs, with lucite heels) but others, like the beautifully retro Buick loafers, are a dream. Offering a more stylized take on the Dr. Marten look, the longstanding Angels line are the ultimate in sturdy comfort for urban feet.

Make 10. 49 W. 8th St. (btw. Sixth Ave. and MacDougal St.) ☎ **212/254-1132.** Subway: A, B, C, D, E, F, Q to West 4th St.

Make 10 sells good leather shoes (with some designer names) in trendy, up-to-the-minute styles. They're quite affordable for what you're getting—in fact, name brands are often a fraction of what you'd pay at a store like Barneys. Also at 1227 Third Ave., at 71st Street (☎ **212/472-2775**); and 1386 Sixth Ave. between 56th and 57th streets (☎ **212/956-4739**).

Sacco. 324 Columbus Ave. (btw. 75th and 76th sts.). ☎ **212/799-5229.** Subway: B, C to 81st St.

This city shoe chain specializes in women's shoes that combine style with supreme comfort. I especially love their fall and winter boots, comfortable enough to carry me around the city on even the most arduous of research days. Lots of terrific basic blacks and browns. Good sales, too. Also at 111 Thompson St. in SoHo (☎ **212/925-8010**); 94 Seventh Avenue, at 16th Street, in Chelsea (☎ **212/675-5180**); and 2355 Broadway, at 86th Street (☎ **212/874-8362**).

Skechers. 592 Seventh Ave. (just south of 42nd St.). ☎ **212/354-8110.** Subway: 1, 2, 3, 7, 9, N, R, S to 42nd St.–Times Sq.

As final proof of the "new" family-friendly Times Square, stop into Skechers. This footwear retailer specializes in the chunky club-kid shoes and thick-soled teeny-bopping tennies that have wooed heartland mallrats by the thousands. Despite their flavor-of-the-month status, the shoes are well priced and comfortably made, and this big, colorful shop carries the entire line. Other locations include 150 Fifth Ave. (☎ **212/627-9420**); on the Upper West Side at 2169 Broadway (☎ **212/712-0539**); 55 W. 8th St. in the Village (☎ **212/253-5810**); and 530 Broadway in SoHo (☎ **212/431-8803**).

Stapleton Shoe Company. 68 Trinity Place (at Rector St., 3 blocks south of the World Trade Center). ☎ **212/964-6329.** Subway: N, R to Rector St.

If Imelda Marcos had been a man, her first stop would have been this shoe store, right near the American Stock Exchange. Stapleton sells men's brands like Bally, Timberland, and Johnston & Murphy, all at discounts so deep it'll feel like insider trading.

SPORTING GOODS

For **Niketown,** see "Logo Stores," above.

Eastern Mountain Sports. 611 Broadway (at Houston St.). ☎ **212/505-9860.** Subway: B, D, F, Q to Broadway–Lafayette St.

EMS is famous for all-weather, high-tech camping and hiking gear at prices well below those of Patagonia. An excellent source for Polartec pullovers, waterproof shells, and the like. You'll also find hardware like compasses, cookwear, and Swiss Army knives. Also at West 61st Street and Broadway (☎ **212/397-4860**).

Paragon Sporting Goods. 867 Broadway (at 18th St.). ☎ **212/255-8036.** Subway: 4, 5, 6, N, R, L to 14th St.–Union Sq.

Paragon is another excellent all-purpose sporting-goods store. The emphasis here is on equipment and athletic wear for virtually every sport, from tennis to biking to mountain climbing. End-of-season sales, especially on sneakers and outdoor clothing, bring serious discounts.

TOYS

If your kids love to read, don't miss **Books of Wonder;** see "Books" earlier in this chapter.

FAO Schwarz. 767 Fifth Ave. (at 58th St.). ☎ **212/644-9400.** Subway: N, R to Fifth Ave.

The best-loved toy store in America was designed with an eye for fun: The elevator is shaped like a huge toy soldier, and there are plenty of hands-on displays to keep the little ones occupied for hours. Entire areas are devoted to specific toy makers (Lego, Fisher Price, *Star Wars* action figures, Barbie). You and the kids will find plenty of affordable little gifts to take home as souvenirs (the front-left corner specializes in prewrapped gifts for Moms and Dads on business trips).

Tootsie's Children's Books. 554 Hudson St. (btw. Perry and 11th sts.). ☎ **212/242-0182.** Subway: A, C, E to 14th St.

Despite the name, books are only part of the inventory at Tootsie's. This cute as a button shop also carries a creative selection of toys (with an emphasis on learning toys) and games. Look for the Space Puppies, the coolest stuffed animals around.

WINE & SPIRITS

Astor Wines & Spirits. 12 Astor Place (at Lafayette St.). ☎ **212/674-7500.** Subway: 6 to Astor Place.

This large store is the source for excellent values on liquor and wine; their stock is deep, and ranges far and wide. The knowledgeable staff is always willing to recommend a vintage.

Acker Merrall & Condit Co. 160 W. 72nd St. (btw. Amsterdam and Columbus aves.). ☎ **212/787-1700.** Subway: 1, 2, 3, 9 to 72nd St.

This attractive little store is the Upper West Side's best wine source. There are no bad bottles here. The careful selection is well displayed, with opinionated cards attached to each bin to help you choose. A supremely knowledgeable staff is on hand if you'd like additional assistance.

✪ **Best Cellars.** 1291 Lexington Ave. (btw. 86th and 87th sts.). ☎ **212/426-4200.** Subway: 6 to 86th St.

Committed to stocking "great wines for everyday," Best Cellars succeeds with elan. I've never seen so many fine labels for less than $10. Interestingly, the wines are stocked by taste (not by grape or region); look for fizzy, fresh, juicy, and other descriptors. The staff is terrific, too.

9

New York City After Dark

New York's nightlife scene is an embarrassment of riches. There's so much to see and do in this city after the sun goes down that your biggest problem is likely going to be choosing among the many temptations.

There's no way that I can tell you what's going to be on the calendar while you're in town. For the latest, most comprehensive nightlife listings, from classic and cutting-edge theater and performing arts to live rock, jazz, and dance-club coverage, *Time Out New York* is my favorite weekly source; a new issue hits newsstands every Thursday. The free weekly *Village Voice,* the city's legendary alterna-paper, is available late Tuesday Downtown and early Wednesday in the rest of the city. The arts and entertainment coverage couldn't be more extensive, and just about every live music venue advertises its shows here. Other great weeklies are *New York* magazine (flip to the "Cue" section at the back for the latest happenings) and the *New Yorker,* whose "Goings on About Town" section is at the front. the *New York Times* features terrific nightlife coverage, particularly in the two-part Friday "Weekend" section. The cabaret, classical music, and theater guides are particularly useful. You might also want to pick up a copy of the pocket-sized *Shecky's Bar, Club & Lounge Guide,* available in most city bookstores (but check the copyright date before you buy).

Some of your best, most comprehensive and up-to-date information sources for what's going on about town are in cyberspace, of course. Excellent sources worth scanning are **www.newyork. sidewalk.com**, which is particularly good for nightlife—most club listings even feature day-to-day schedules, and there's a "Select-a-Bar" page to help you find the drink shop that's exactly right for you. Done in cooperation with the *Daily News* and *Time Out,* **www. newyork.citysearch.com** is another complete online source, while **www.nytoday.com** is an expanded version of the the *New York Times*'s already terrific cultural coverage. If you want to check the *Village Voice*'s extensive listings before you arrive, visit **www. villagevoice.com**. Hipster monthly the *Paper* boasts opinionated coverage of the Downtown club and bar scenes at **www.papermag. com**. Check out Frommer's Online Directory, in the back of this book, for more comprehensive descriptions of Web sites on New York's teeming nightlife.

Sponsored by the Theatre Development Fund and supported by American Express, **NYC/Onstage** at (☎ **212/768-1818;** www.tdf.org)

is a recorded and online service providing schedules, descriptions, and other details on theater and the performing arts. The bias is toward Broadway and off-Broadway plays, but NYC/Onstage is a good source for concerts, chamber and orchestral music (including all Lincoln Center events), dance, opera, cabaret, and family entertainment, too.

For more on these and other general information sources, see "Visitor Information" in chapter 2 and "Orientation" in chapter 4. I'll also discuss subject-specific information sources in the appropriate sections below.

1 All the City's a Stage: The Theater Scene

Nobody does theater better than New York. No other city—not even London—has a theater scene with so much breadth and depth, with so many wide-open alternatives. Broadway, of course, gets the most ink and the most airplay, and deservedly so: Broadway is where you'll find the big stage productions and the moneymakers, from crowd-pleasing war horses like *Cats* to phenomenal newer successes like *The Lion King*. But today's scene is thriving beyond the bounds of just Broadway—smaller, "alternative" theater has taken hold of the popular imagination, too. With bankable stars on stage, crowds lining up for hot tickets, and hits popular enough to generate major-label cast albums, off-Broadway isn't just for culture vultures anymore.

With such a vital scene, it's no wonder that it's the promise of the stage, more than anything else, that draws visitors from all over the world to New York City. Despite this vitality, plays and musicals close all the time, often with little warning. So I can't tell you precisely what will be on while you're in town. Your best bet is to check the publications and Web sites listed at the beginning of this chapter before you go, or even once you reach town to get an idea of what you might like to see. A particularly useful source is the **Broadway Line** (☎ **888/BROADWAY** or 212/302-4111; www. broadway.org) where you can obtain details and descriptions on current Broadway shows, hear about special offers and discounts, and then transfer to Tele-charge to buy tickets. There's also **NYC/Onstage** (☎ **212/768-1818;** www.tdf.org), providing the same kind of service for both Broadway and off-Broadway productions. (Don't buy tickets, though, until you read "Top Ticket-Buying Tips," below.)

Even though I can't guarantee what'll be on offer when you're visiting, the likelihood is good that you'll find lots of large-scale musicals and revivals on Broadway, and more original drama and offbeat musicals on the off-Broadway stage. If you find new drama on Broadway, it's likely to be the transcontinental transfer of a London stage hit, similar to Yasmina Reza's *Art* in 1998, and David Hare's *Amy's View,* starring recent Oscar winner Judi Densch, in 1999. If you're coming to see the big hits, chances are extremely good that you'll still find *Cats* (the longest-running show in Broadway history) at the Winter Garden, *Les Misèrables* at the Imperial, *Miss Saigon* at the Broadway Theater, and *Phantom of the Opera* at the Majestic. Kids will be enchanted by Disney's one-two punch of *Beauty and the Beast* and, if you can get tickets (call now!), *The Lion King.* Off-Broadway is more volatile, but you're likely to still find the ridiculously fun *Blue Man Group* at the Astor Place Theater, and the percussion sensation *Stomp* at the Orpheum Theatre; both are performance-art pieces that are more palatable than you'd expect, and have been pleasing kids and grown-ups alike for years now. And I'd pretty much stake my life on the fact that the legendary show *The Fantasticks* will still be alive and kicking at the Sullivan Street Playhouse—it opened on May 3, 1960, and is now the longest-running musical in the world. (For tickets, see "Top Ticket-Buying Tips," below.)

Keep in mind that while "Off-Broadway" may mean experimental, it doesn't have to mean lower-quality in any way. These days, the best off-Broadway shows don't need to move to Broadway to be legitimized and can charge lower ticket prices. Witness such recent powerhouse hits as Margaret Edson's Pulitzer Prize–winning *Wit,* and John Cameron Mitchell's *Hedwig and the Angry Inch* (step aside, *Rent*—here's a musical that really rocks!), plus the aforementioned long-runners *Blue Man Group* and *Stomp.* And remember—*Rent* is just one of many phenomenons that made its debut off-Broadway.

In addition to *Blue Man Group* and *Stomp* (see above), off-Broadway theaters that deserve a special look include **The Public Theater,** 425 Lafayette St. (☎ 212/ 260-2400), Joseph Papp's legacy, and home to the New York Shakespeare Festival as well as launching pad for such hits as *Bring in 'da Noise, Bring in 'da Funk.* (For details on the Public Theater's summertime **Shakespeare in the Park** in Central Park—probably the city's best outdoor arts event—see the box called "Park It! Shakespeare, & Other Free Fun" later in this chapter.)

THE BASICS

LOCATIONS   The terms **Broadway, Off-Broadway,** and **Off-Off-Broadway** refer to theater size, pay scales, and other arcane details, not location. Most of the Broadway theaters are in Times Square, huddled around the avenue the scene is named for, but not directly on it: Instead, you'll find them dotting the side streets that intersect Broadway, mostly in the mid-40s between Sixth and Eighth avenues (44th and 45th sts. in particular) but running north as far as 53rd Street. There's even a Broadway theater outside Midtown: The Vivian Beaumont in Lincoln Center, at Broadway and 65th Street.

Off-Broadway, on the other hand, is not that exacting an expression. Frankly, with the increasing popularization of off-the-beaten-track productions, the distinction between off- and off-off-Broadway productions has become fuzzier. Off-off-Broadway shows tend to be more avant-garde, experimental, and/or nomadic. Off- and off-off-Broadway productions tend to be based around Greenwich Village, but pockets show up in the East Village, around Midtown, in SoHo, and even on the Upper West Side. And there are Off Broadway theaters in Times Square and even *on* Broadway. Needless to say, carefully check the address where your production is playing.

TIMETABLES   Broadway shows tend to keep pretty regular schedules. There are usually eight performances a week: Evening shows Tuesday through Saturday, plus matinees on Wednesday, Saturday, and Sunday. Evening shows are usually at 8pm, while matinees are usually at 2pm on Wednesday and Saturday, and 3pm on Sunday. Schedules do vary, however; both *Cats* and *Les Misèrables,* for instance, also stage a Monday show to accommodate the seemingly endless tourist demand. And times often vary depending on the show's length. Shows usually start right on the dot, or within a few minutes of starting time; if you arrive late, you may have to wait until after the first act to take your seat, which can really be a drag.

Off-Broadway shows tend to follow a similar daily schedule and time clock, but you'll find more variation. Off-Broadway theaters usually stage an additional Sunday evening show. Some, such as the rock musical *Hedwig and the Angry Inch,* also stage 11:30pm shows on Friday and Saturday to accommodate the Downtown crowds who could care less about the late hour; this, however, is the exception, not the rule.

TICKET PRICES   Ticket prices for Broadway shows vary dramatically. Expect to pay for good seats; the high end for any given show is likely to be between $60 and $100. The cheapest end of the price range can be as low as $15 or as high as $50, depending on the theater configuration. If you're buying tickets at the very low end of

The Theater District

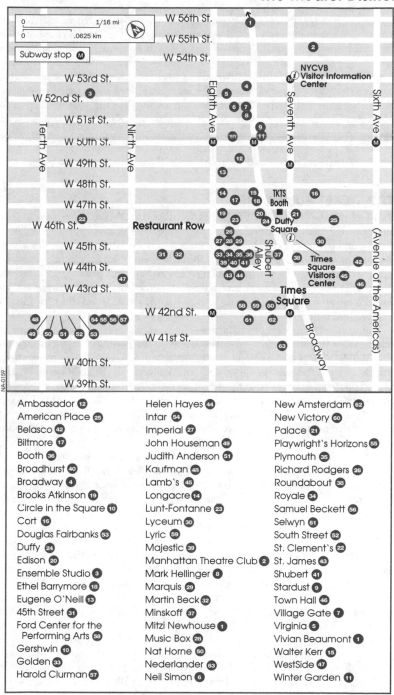

Ambassador 12	Helen Hayes 44	New Amsterdam 62
American Place 25	Intar 54	New Victory 60
Belasco 42	Imperial 27	Palace 21
Biltmore 17	John Houseman 49	Playwright's Horizons 55
Booth 36	Judith Anderson 51	Plymouth 35
Broadhurst 40	Kaufman 48	Richard Rodgers 26
Broadway 4	Lamb's 45	Roundabout 38
Brooks Atkinson 19	Longacre 14	Royale 34
Circle in the Square 10	Lunt-Fontanne 23	Samuel Beckett 56
Cort 16	Lyceum 30	Selwyn 61
Douglas Fairbanks 53	Lyric 59	South Street 52
Duffy 24	Majestic 39	St. Clement's 22
Edison 20	Manhattan Theatre Club 2	St. James 43
Ensemble Studio 3	Mark Hellinger 8	Shubert 41
Ethel Barrymore 18	Marquis 29	Stardust 9
Eugene O'Neill 13	Martin Beck 32	Town Hall 46
45th Street 31	Minskoff 37	Village Gate 7
Ford Center for the Performing Arts 58	Mitzi Newhouse 1	Virginia 5
Gershwin 10	Music Box 28	Vivian Beaumont 1
Golden 33	Nat Horne 50	Walter Kerr 15
Harold Clurman 57	Nederlander 63	WestSide 47
	Neil Simon 6	Winter Garden 11

a wide price range, be aware that you may be buying obstructed-view seats. If all tickets are the same price or the range is small, you can pretty much count on all of the seats being pretty good. Otherwise, price is your barometer. Note that leg room can be tight in these old theaters, and you'll usually get more in the orchestra seats.

Off-Broadway and off-off-Broadway shows tend to be cheaper, with tickets often as low as $10 or $15. However, seats for the most established shows (such as Margaret Edson's phenomenal *Wit*) and those with star power (like the 1999 production of Molière's *The Misanthrope* starring Uma Thurman and Roger Rees) can command prices as high as $50.

Don't let price be an automatic deterrent to enjoying the theater. There are ways to pay less if you're willing to make the effort and be flexible, with dates and productions. For details, read on.

TOP TICKET-BUYING TIPS

PURCHASING TICKETS BEFORE YOU LEAVE HOME   If you want to guarantee yourself a seat at a particular show by buying them in advance, there's almost no way around paying full price. (The only exception is the "Passport to Off-Broadway" discount program offered from February through April, which only some theaters will honor over the phone; see "Bargain Alert—How to Save on Theater Tickets," below.) Phone ahead or go online for tickets to the most successful or popular shows as far in advance as you can—in the case of shows like *The Lion King* and, thus far, *Cabaret*, it's never too early.

Buying tickets can be simple, if the show you want to see isn't sold out and you don't mind paying full price (plus a service charge). You need only call such general numbers as **Tele-Charge** (☎ 212/239-6200; www.telecharge.com), which handles most Broadway and off-Broadway shows and some concerts; or **TicketMaster** (☎ 212/307-4100; www.ticketmaster.com), which also handles Broadway and off-Broadway shows and most concerts. If you use the **Broadway Line** (☎ 888/411-BWAY or 212/302-4111) or **NYC/Onstage** (☎ 212/768-1818; www.tdf.org) services discussed above to select your show, you can be automatically transferred to the appropriate ticket agency.

If you're an American Express gold-card holder, see if tickets are being sold through **American Express Gold Card Events** (☎ 800/448-TIKS; www.americanexpress. com/gce). You'll pay full price just as you would through Tele-Charge or TicketMaster, but AmEx has access to blocks of preferred seating that are specifically set aside for gold-card holders.

Owned by Cameron Mackintosh (producer behind such megahits as *Cats, Phantom of the Opera, Les Misérables,* and *Miss Saigon*), **Theatre Direct International (TDI)** is a ticket broker that sells tickets to select Broadway and off-Broadway shows direct to individuals and travel agents. Check to see if they have seats to the shows you're interested in by calling ☎ 800/334-8457 or visiting www.theatredirect.com. (Disregard the discounted prices, unless you're buying for a group of 20 or more; tickets are full price for smaller quantities.) With a service charge of $12.50 per ticket, you're better off trying TicketMaster or Tele-charge first; but because they act as a consolidator, TDI may have tickets left for a specific show even if the major outlets don't.

Other reputable ticket brokers who may have tickets to the shows you want to see include **Keith Prowse & Co.** (☎ 800/669-8687; www.keithprowse.com) and **Edwards & Edwards Global Tickets** (☎ 800/223-6108). For a complete list of other licensed ticket brokers recommended by the NYCVB, get a copy of the "Big Apple Visitor's Kit" (see "Visitor Information" in chapter 2 for details). All kinds of ticket brokers list ads in the Sunday *New York Times* and other publications, but don't

Bargain Alert—How to Save on Theater Tickets

If you employ a little patience, flexibility, and know-how, there are ways to pay less than full price for your theater tickets—sometimes a lot less.

If you're visiting the city early in the year, be sure to look into the **Passport to Off Broadway.** The Alliance of Resident Theaters/New York sponsors this campaign, which offers 10% to 50% discounts on tickets to more than 200 off- and off-off-Broadway shows from February through April. You can download the discount coupon as many times as you want by visiting **www.newyork.sidewalk. com/passport**. Note, however, that restrictions may apply: For instance, some theaters don't accept the coupons for Friday or Saturday night performances, and some will accept them only for cash purchases. Still, the inconveniences are minimal, and it's a great deal.

Even blockbusters can have a limited number of cheaper tickets for **students and seniors,** and they may even be available at the last minute. In the past, the Roundabout Theater offered half-price tickets to those 17 and under, and *Rent* has offered all kinds of bargains to keep younger theatergoers coming. Your best bet is to call the box office direct to inquire.

The best deal in town on **same-day tickets** for both Broadway and off-Broadway shows is at the ✪ **Times Square Theatre Centre,** better known as the **TKTS booth,** run by the nonprofit Theatre Development Fund in the heart of the Theater District at Duffy Square, 47th Street and Broadway (open 3–8pm for evening performances, 10am–2pm for Wednesday and Saturday matinees, from 11am on Sunday for all performances). Tickets for that day's performances are usually offered at half price, with a few reduced only 25%, plus a $2.50 per ticket service charge. Boards outside the ticket windows list available shows; you're unlikely to find certain perennial or outsize smashes, but most other shows turn up. Cash and traveler's checks only are accepted. There's often a huge line, so show up early for the best availability and be prepared to wait—but frankly, the crowd is all part of the fun. If you don't care much what you see and you'd just like to go to a show, you can walk right up to the window later in the day and something's always available.

Run by the same group and offering the same discounts is the **TKTS Lower Manhattan Theatre Centre,** on the mezzanine of 2 World Trade Center (open Mon–Fri 11am–5:30pm and Sat 11am–3:30pm). All the same policies apply. The advantages to coming down here is that the lines are generally shorter; your wait is sheltered indoors; and matinee tickets are available a day in advance.

Many theater shows, particularly long-running shows like *Miss Saigon* and *Cats,* offer special coupons that allow you to buy **twofers**—two tickets for the price of one certain nights of the week. You can find these coupons at many places in the city: hotel lobbies, in banks, even at restaurant cash registers. A guaranteed bet is the Times Square Visitors Center, 1560 Broadway, between 46th and 47th streets; they're also likely to be available at the new NYCVB Visitor Information Center at 810 Seventh Ave., between 52nd and 53rd streets.

There are so many options for getting cut-rate tickets that virtually any visitor can fill up a week's vacation with shows seen on the cheap. But keep in mind that there is never any guarantee that last-minute tickets or discounts will be available to any given show, and they may not be. If your heart is set on seeing a specific show, save yourself the possible heartache and splurge on full-price advance-purchase tickets.

take the risk. Stick with a licensed broker recommended by the NYCVB. You should be aware that state law limits the premium brokers can charge to $5 or 10%, whichever is less, but if you believe they all stick to that, I know of this bridge to Brooklyn. . . .

If you want to secure tickets before you come to New York but don't want to pay a service charge, try calling the **box office** direct. Broadway theaters don't sell tickets over the telephone, but a good number of off-Broadway theaters do.

WHEN YOU ARRIVE Once you arrive in the city, getting your hands on tickets can take some street smarts—and failing those, good hard cash. Even if it seems unlikely that seats are available, always **call the box office** before attempting any other route. Single seats are often easiest to obtain, so people willing to sit apart may find themselves in luck.

You should also try the **Broadway Ticket Center,** run by the League of American Theaters and Producers (the same people behind the Broadway Line, above) at the Times Square Visitors Center, 1560 Broadway, between 46th and 47th streets (open daily 8am–8pm). They often have tickets available for otherwise sold-out shows, and only charge $4 extra per ticket.

If you want to deal with a licensed broker direct, **Global Tickets Edwards & Edwards** has a local office that accommodates drop-ins at 1270 Sixth Ave. between 50th and 51st streets on the 24th floor (☎ **212/332-2435;** open Mon–Sat 9am–9pm, Sun noon–7pm).

If you buy from one of the **scalpers** selling tickets in front of the theater doors, you're taking a risk. They may be perfectly legitimate—a couple from the 'burbs whose companions couldn't make it for the evening, say—but they could be swindlers passing off fakes for big money. It's a risk that's not worth taking.

One preferred **insiders' trick** is to make the rounds of Broadway theaters at about 6pm, when unclaimed house seats are made available to the public. These tickets—reserved for VIPs, friends of the cast, the press, or other hangers-on—offer great locations and are sold at face value.

Also, note that **Mondays** are often good days to cop big-name show tickets. Though most theaters are dark on that day, some of the most sought-after choices aren't. Locals are at home on the first night of the work week, so all the odds are in your favor. Your chances will always be better on weeknights, or for Wednesday matinees, rather than weekends.

2 Opera, Classical Music & Dance

While Broadway is the Big Apple's greatest hit, many other performing arts also flourish in this culturally rich and entertainment-hungry town.

In addition to the listings below, you may also want to see what's happening at **Carnegie Hall** and the **Brooklyn Academy of Music,** two of the most respected—and enjoyable—multifunctional performing arts venues in the city. The marvelous **92nd Street Y** also regularly hosts events that are well worth considering for both their excellence and affordability. For details on these venues, as well the complete offerings at **Lincoln Center,** see "Major Concert Halls & Landmark Venues" later in this chapter.

OPERA

New York has established itself as an important center in the opera world. Stars like Luciano Pavarotti, Kathleen Battle, and Roberto Alagna regularly take the city's stages, where they're warmly welcomed by a full house of passionate, knowledgeable fans. The season generally runs from September to May, but there's usually something going on at any time of year.

In addition to the choices below, fans with an ear for experimentalism may want to consider **American Opera Projects,** 463 Broome St., in SoHo (☎ 212/431-8102), a showcase for new American operas and other innovative projects. Recent performances have included the warmly received *Patience & Sarah,* and *Hidegurls Electric Ordo Virtutum,* Hildegard von Bingen's 12th-century morality play adapted for modern audiences.

Amato Opera Theatre. 319 Bowery (at 2nd St.). ☎ **212/228-8200.** www.amato.org. Subway: 6 to Bleecker St.; F to Second Ave.

This cozy, off-the-beaten-track venue for mostly Italian opera is run by husband-and-wife team Anthony and Sally Amato and functions as a showcase for talented young American singers. The intimate 100-plus-seat house celebrated its 50th season last year amid a rising reputation and increasing ticket sales. The staple is full productions of Italian classics—Verdi, Puccini, Rossini, Verdi, with an occasional Mozart tossed in—at great prices (usually $20 to $25). Performances, usually held on Saturday and Sunday, now regularly sell out, so it's a good idea to reserve 3 weeks in advance.

Once a month at 11:30am on Saturday, "Opera in Brief" offers fully costumed, kid-length versions of the classics interwoven with narration to introduce the little ones to the music form. At $12 or so per ticket, these matinees are wallet-friendly, too.

Metropolitan Opera. At the Metropolitan Opera House, Lincoln Center, Broadway and 64th St. ☎ **212/362-6000.** www.metopera.org. Subway: 1, 9 to 66th St.

Brace yourself, opera fans: Tickets can cost a small fortune (anywhere from $30 to $250). But for its full productions of the classic repertory and schedule packed with world-class grand sopranos and tenors, the Metropolitan Opera ranks first in the world. Millions are spent on fabulous stagings, and the venue itself is an acoustic wonder. To guarantee that its audience understands the words, the Met has outfitted its seat backs with screens for subtitles. James Levine continues his role as the brilliant and popular conductor of the orchestra. Associate conductor Valery Gergiyev helps fill in for the peripatetic Levine (who also conducts the Munich Philharmonic), bringing needed experience in the Russian repertory to the Met.

The Met Opera has a number of programs that allow access to cut-rate tickets to operagoers; for details, see "Last-Minute Discount Ticket-Buying Tips" on p. 305.

✪ **New York City Opera.** At the New York State Theater, Lincoln Center, Broadway and 64th St. ☎ **212/870-5570,** or 212/307-4100 for tickets (online purchases at www.ticketmaster.com). www.nycopera.com. Subway: 1, 9 to 66th St.

The New York City Opera is a superb company that's a wonderful choice for value-minded fans looking for first-class opera. The NYC Opera not only attempts to reach a wider audience than the Met with its more "human" scale and significantly lower prices—just $22 to $82—but it's also committed to adventurous premieres, newly composed operas, the occasional avant-garde work, American musicals presented as operettas (Stephen Sondheim's *Sweeney Todd* is an example), and even obscure works

Freebies for Opera Fans

The New York Grand Opera (☎ 212/245-8837; www.csis.pace.edu/newyork-grandopera) puts on free productions of Verdi operas at Central Park's SummerStage in July and August; for more on SummerStage, see the box called "Park It! Shakespeare & Other Free Fun" later in this chapter.

Bargain Alert—The Classical Learning Curve

The **Juilliard School,** Lincoln Center at Broadway and 65th Street (☎ 212/
769-7406; www.juilliard.edu), the nation's premier music education institution,
sponsors about 550 performances of the highest quality—at the lowest prices.
With most concerts free and $15 as a maximum ticket price, Juilliard is one of
New York's greatest cultural bargains. In addition to classical concerts, Juilliard
offers other music as well as drama, dance, opera, and interdisciplinary works. The
best way to find out about the wide array of productions is to call, visit the school's
Web site, or consult the bulletin board in the building's lobby. Watch for master
classes and discussions open to the public featuring celebrity guest teachers.

The well-regarded **Manhattan School of Music,** at Broadway and 122nd
Street (☎ 212/749-2802; www.msmnyc.edu), hosts regular student concerts as
well as daily recitals during the academic year. Most performances are absolutely
free, and the top ticket price is $20. In addition to orchestral and chamber music,
the school is highly regarded for its contemporary music and jazz as well as
musical theater programs, so performances run the gamut. Also look for free
master classes featuring distinguished artists. The concert hotline isn't always
active, so call the Music Concert office weekdays between 9am and 6pm or visit
the Web site for the complete schedule.

by mainstream or lesser-known composers. Its mix stretches from the "easy" works of
Puccini, Verdi, and Gilbert & Sullivan to the more challenging works of Arnold
Schönberg and Philip Glass.

A few years back, the company, then under the direction of the incomparable Bev-
erly Sills, was the first to introduce "supratitles," above the stage, so its audience could
follow the words as well as the music. Snickers were heard across the plaza at the Met,
which has since followed Bubbles's lead.

New York Gilbert and Sullivan Players. At Symphony Space, Broadway and 95th St.
☎ 212/864-5400 or 212/769-1000. www.nygasp.org. Subway: 1, 2, 3, 9 to 96th St.

If you're in the mood for light-hearted operetta, try this lively company, which specializes in Gilbert and Sullivan's 19th-century English comic works. Tickets are affordable, in the $25 to $50 range. This year's calendar, which generally runs from October
through April, is scheduled to include *The Pirates of Penzance, Princess Ida,* and *The
Mikado.*

CLASSICAL MUSIC

Just about any grand interpreter of the classics comes through New York. The many
concert halls throughout the city—ranging from the expected, like **Carnegie Hall,** to
the surprising, like the **92nd Street Y**—book the best of the best (see "Major Concert
Halls & Landmark Venues," below). Additionally, you might wish to see what's on at
the Metropolitan Museum of Art's **Grace Rainey Rogers Auditorium** (☎ 212/
570-3949), an elegant venue that presents recitals, chamber music, and orchestral
concerts throughout the year. Many other venues also offer performances, so be sure
to check one of the publications or Web sites mentioned at the start of this chapter
before you come to town.

✪ **Bargemusic.** At the Fulton Ferry Landing (just south of the Brooklyn Bridge), Brooklyn.
☎ 718/624-2083 or 718/624-4061. www.bargemusic.org. Subway: 2, 3 to Clark St.

Many thought Olga Bloom peculiar, if not deranged, when she transformed a 40-year-old barge into a chamber-music concert hall. More than 20 years later, Bargemusic is an internationally reputed recital room boasting more than 100 first-rate chamber music performances a year. Olga trawls from the pool of visiting musicians who love the chance to play in such an intimate setting, so the roster regularly includes highly respected international musicians as well as local stars like violinist Cynthia Phelps. There are two shows per week, on Thursday evening and Sunday afternoon; from June through August, there's also a Friday-evening performance.

The musicians perform on a small stage in a cherry-paneled, fireplace-lit room accommodating 130. Bloom herself places name cards on the red-velvet cushions of the folding chairs, and there's bread and cheese, cakes and cookies, and wine and coffee. The barge may creek a bit and an occasional boat may speed by, but the music rivals what you'll find in almost any other New York concert hall—and the panoramic view through the glass wall behind the stage can't be beat. Neither can the price: Tickets are just $23 ($20 seniors, $15 students). Reserve well in advance.

✪ **New York Philharmonic.** At Avery Fisher Hall, Lincoln Center, Broadway and 64th St. ☎ **212/875-5030,** or 212/721-6500 for tickets. www.newyorkphilharmonic.org, or www.lincolncenter.org for online purchases. Subway: 1, 9 to 66th St.

Symphony-wise, you'd be hard-pressed to do better than the New York Philharmonic. The country's oldest philharmonic orchestra is under the strict but ebullient guidance of music director Kurt Masur. Since he has announced that he'll retire in 2002, don't miss this chance to see the master conductor. Highlights of the 1999–2000 season include the Completely Copland Festival throughout December, Anne-Sophie Mutter

Last-Minute Discount Ticket-Buying Tips

The majority of seats at **New York Philharmonic** performances are sold to subscribers, with just a few left for the rest of us. But there are still ways to get tickets. When subscribers can't attend, they may turn their tickets back to the theaters, which then resell them at the last moment. These can be in the most coveted rows of the orchestra. The hopeful form "cancellation lines" 2 hours or more before curtain time for a crack at returned tickets on a first-come, first-serve basis. And periodically, a number of **same-day orchestra tickets** are set aside at the philharmonic, and sold first thing in the morning for $25 a pop (maximum 2). **Senior/student/ disabled rush tickets** may be available for $10 (maximum 2) on concert day, but never at Friday matinees or Saturday evening performances. To check availability for all **New York Philharmonic** performances, call the Audience Services Department at ☎ **212/875-5656.**

Note that Lincoln Center's **Alice Tully Hall** (where the Chamber Music Society performs and other concerts are held), the **Metropolitan Opera,** and **Carnegie Hall** offer similar last-minute and discount programs. It makes sense to call the box office first to check on same-day availability before heading to the theater—or, if you're willing to take to risk of coming away empty-handed, be there at opening time for first crack.

If all else fails and your heart is set on seeing a sold-out performance you can call or go to the box office to see if **standing room** is available (usually around $20). The best standing room is at the Met, where you get to lean against plush red bars. (Don't tell them I told you, but if subscribers fail to show, I've seen standees with eagle eyes fill the empty seats at intermission.)

in residence in January, an all-Mozart night led by guest conductor Sir Colin Davis in May, and Mahler's *Symphony no. 9* to close the season in early June. There's a summer season in July, when classics brighten the hall, as well as summer concerts in Central Park that are worth checking out.

Tickets range from $12 to $88; opt for a rush-hour concert or a matinee for the lowest across-the-board prices. The acoustics of the hall are such that, at midrange prices, I prefer the second tier (especially the boxes) over the more expensive rear orchestra seats. Go cheap if you have to; you're sure to enjoy the program from any vantage.

DANCE

In general, dance seasons run September to February and then March to June, but there's almost always something going on. For particularly innovative works, see what's on at the **Merce Cunningham Studio,** 55 Bethune St. (☎ 212/691-9751; www.merce.org); the **Dance Theater Workshop,** in the Bessie Schönberg Theater, 219 W. 19th St. (☎ 212/924-0077; www.dtw.org); and **Danspace Project,** at St. Mark's Church, 131 E. 10th St. (☎ 212/674-8194), whose performances lean toward the seriously avant garde. Ticket prices are quite affordable at all three of these forward-thinking venues: between $8 and $20, depending on the performance and venue.

In addition to regular appearances at City Center (below), the **American Ballet Theatre** (www.abt.org) takes up residence at Lincoln Center's Metropolitan Opera House (☎ 212/362-6000) for 8 weeks each spring. The Met also hosts such visiting companies as the **Kirov, Royal,** and **Paris Opéra ballets.** Budget-minded ballet fans should see "Last-Minute Discount Ticket-Buying Tips" on p. 305.

Some other names to keep in mind for dance are the **Brooklyn Academy of Music** (see "Major Concert Halls & Landmark Venues," below), and the **Dance Theatre of Harlem** (☎ 212/690-2800), which performs throughout the city and holds an open house one Sunday a month.

City Center. 131 W. 55th St. (btw. Sixth and Seventh aves.). ☎ **212/581-7907.** Subway: N, R or B, Q to 57th St.; B, D, E to Seventh Ave.

Modern dance usually takes center stage in this Moorish dome–topped performing arts palace, which regularly hosts the companies of Merce Cunningham, Martha Graham, Paul Taylor, Trisha Brown, Alvin Ailey, Twyla Tharp, and the American Ballet Theatre. Don't expect cutting edge—but do expect excellence. Tickets generally run $25 to $55; sightlines are terrific from all corners, so you won't lose with cheaper tickets.

✪ **Joyce Theater.** 175 Eighth Ave. (at 19th St.). ☎ **212/242-0800.** www.joyce.org. Subway: C, E to 23rd St.; 1, 9 to 18th St.

Housed in an old art-deco movie house, the Joyce has grown into one of the world's greatest modern dance institutions. You can see everything from Native-American ceremonial dance to the innovative works of Pilobolus. In residence annually is Eliot Feld's Ballet Tech, which WQXR radio's Francis Mason called "better than a whole month of namby-pamby classical ballets." The Joyce now has a second space, **Joyce SoHo,** at 155 Mercer St., between Houston and Prince streets (☎ 212/431-9233), where you can see rising young dancers and experimental works in the intimacy of a 70-seat performance space. Tickets are usually $28 to $35 at the main theater, and $10 to $20 at the SoHo space.

New York City Ballet. At the New York State Theater at Lincoln Center, Broadway and 64th St. ☎ **212/870-5570,** or 212/307-4100. www.nycballet.com or www.ticketmaster.com. Subway: 1, 9 to 66th St.

Highly regarded for its unsurpassed technique, the New York City Ballet is the world's best. The company renders with happy regularity the works of two of America's most important choreographers: George Balanchine, its founder, and Jerome Robbins. Under the direction of former dancer Peter Martins, the troupe continues to expand its repertoire and performs to a wide variety of classical and modern music. The cornerstone of the annual season is the Christmastime production of *The Nutcracker,* for which tickets usually become available starting in early October. Ticket prices for most events run $16 to $70.

3 Major Concert Halls & Landmark Venues

Apollo Theater. 253 W. 125th St. (btw. Adam Clayton Powell and Frederick Douglass blvds.). ☎ **212/749-5838** or 212/864-0372. Subway: 1, 9 to 125th St.

Built in 1914, the Apollo had its heyday in the 1930s when Count Basie, Duke Ellington, Ella Fitzgerald, and Billie Holiday were on the bill. By the 1970s it had fallen on hard times, but a 1986 restoration breathed new life into the historic Harlem landmark. Today the Apollo is again internationally renowned as a showcase for African-American music, from hip-hop acts to B. B. King to Wynton Marsalis' "Jazz for Young People" events. Wednesday's "Amateur Night at the Apollo" are loud, fun-filled nights that draw in young talents from all over the country with high hopes of making it big (a very young Lauryn Hill started out here—and didn't win!); tickets are $13 to $21, slightly higher for finalist shows.

✪ Brooklyn Academy of Music. 30 Lafayette Ave., Brooklyn. ☎ **718/636-4100.** www. bam.org. Subway: 2, 3, 4, 5, D, Q to Atlantic Ave.; B, M, N, R to Pacific Ave.

BAM, as it's known, is the city's most renowned contemporary arts institution, presenting cutting-edge theater, opera, dance, and music. Offerings have included historically informed presentations of baroque opera by William Christie and Les Arts Florissants; pop opera from Lou Reed; Marianne Faithfull singing the music of Kurt Weill; dance by Mark Morris and Mikhail Baryshnikov; music by Laurie Anderson and Philip Glass; the Royal Dramatic Theater of Sweden directed by Ingmar Bergman; and many more experimental works by both renowned and lesser-known international artists as well as visiting companies. Tickets run $15 to $50.

Of particular note is the **Next Wave Festival,** from September through December, this country's foremost showcase for new experimental works (see the "New York City Calendar of Events" in chapter 2). There's also free live music every Friday and Saturday night at **BAMcafé,** which can range from atmospheric electronica from coronetist Graham Haynes to Harlem-style swing by the Yallopin' Hounds.

Carnegie Hall. 881 Seventh Ave. (at 57th St.). ☎ **212/247-7800.** www.carnegiehall.org. Subway: N, R or B, Q to 57th St.

Perhaps the world's most famous performance space, Carnegie Hall offers everything from grand classics by visiting international orchestras to the sitar music of Ravi Shankar. The legendary 2,804-seat main hall is both visually and acoustically brilliant. There's also the intimate 284-seat **Weill Recital Hall,** used to showcase chamber music and vocal and instrumental recitals. Carnegie Hall has also reclaimed an ornate underground concert hall, occupied by a movie theater for 38 years, and plans to turn it into an intermediate-size third stage by the 2001–02 season. For last-minute discount ticket-buying tips, see p. 305.

✪ Lincoln Center for the Performing Arts. 70 Lincoln Center Plaza (at Broadway and 64th St.). ☎ **212/546-2656.** www.lincolncenter.org. Subway: 1, 9 to 66th St.

Park It! Shakespeare & Other Free Fun

As the weather warms, New York culture comes outdoors to play.

Shakespeare in the Park, held at Central Park's Delacorte Theater, is by far the city's most famous alfresco arts event. Organized by the Joseph Papp Public Theater, the schedule consists of summertime productions of usually two of the Bard's plays (although the 1997 season also saw a restaging of the 1944 musical *On the Town*). Productions often feature big names, and range from traditional interpretations (Patrick Stewart as Prospero, Andre Braugher as an armor-clad *Henry V*) to avant-garde presentations (Morgan Freeman, Tracey Ullman, and David Alan Grier in *Taming of the Shrew* as Wild-West showdown). The theater itself, next to Belvedere Castle near 79th Street and West Drive, is a dream—on a beautiful starry night, there's no better stage in town. Tickets are given out free on a first-come, first-serve basis (two per person), at 1pm on the day of the performance at the theater. Each of the 1,881 seats is a hot commodity, so people generally line up on the baseball field next to the theater about 2 to 3 hours in advance. You can also pick up tickets between 1 and 3pm at the Joseph Papp Public Theater, at 425 Lafayette St., where the Shakespeare Festival continues throughout the year. For more information, call the Public Theater at ☎ **212/539-8500** or the Delacorte at **212/861-7277,** or go online at www.publictheater. org.

With summer comes the sound of music to Central Park, where the **New York Philharmonic** and the **Metropolitan Opera** regularly entertain beneath the stars; for the current schedule, call ☎ **212/360-3444** or 212/875-5709. But the most active music stage in the park is **SummerStage,** at Rumsey Playfield, midpark around 72nd Street, which has featured everyone from the Godfather of Soul, James Brown, to the angel poet of punk, Patti Smith. Recent offerings have included concerts by Yoko Ono, Rocket from the Crypt, and Peter, Paul, and Mary; readings by authors Grace Paley, Paul Auster, and Tom Robbins; and "Viva, Verdi!" festival performances by the New York Grand Opera. The season usually lasts from mid-June to early August. Tickets aren't usually required, but donations are warmly accepted. For the latest concert and performance info, call the SummerStage hot line at ☎ **212/360-2777** or visit **www.summerstage.org**.

New York is the world's premier performing arts city, and Lincoln Center is its premier institution. On any given evening, the offerings can include opera, dance, symphonies, jazz, theater, film, and more, from the classics to the contemporary. Lincoln Center's many buildings serve as permanent homes to their own companies as well a major stops for world-class performance troupes from around the globe.

Resident companies include: The **Chamber Music Society of Lincoln Center** (☎ 212/875-5788; www.chamberlinc.org), which performs at Alice Tully Hall or the Daniel and Joanna S. Rose Rehearsal Studio, often in the company of such high-caliber guests as Anne Sofie Von Otter and Midori. The **Film Society of Lincoln Center** (☎ 212/875-5600; www.filmlinc.com), screens a daily schedule of movies at the Walter Reade Theater, and hosts a number of important annual film and video festivals as well as the Reel to Real program for kids, pairing silent screen classics with live performance. **Jazz at Lincoln Center** (☎ 212/875-5299; www.jazzatlincolncenter.org),

Central Park may be the most happening park in town, but the calendar of free events heats up throughout the city's parks in summertime. You can find out what's happening by calling ☎ **212/360-3456,** or by visiting www.ci.nyc.ny.us/ html/dpr.

The **Bryant Park Film Festival** takes place every Monday night throughout July and August, starting at sunset. This charming block-square park is blanket-to-blanket as crowds come to watch classic and family-friendly films such as *Breakfast at Tiffany's* under the stars. The crowds can get thick, especially for popular ones, so stake out your spot early. Rain dates are Tuesday. Call ☎ **212/ 512-5700** for this season's schedule.

A full slate of free concerts (Philip Glass and Robert Fripp have been recent performers), modern and classical dance, family events, and more are offered year-round in the Winter Garden and, in warm weather, on surrounding plazas of the **World Financial Center** (☎ **212/945-0505;** www.worldfinancial-center.com), on the Hudson River west of the World Trade Center in Battery Park City. Events are regularly held at the **South Street Seaport** (☎ **212/ 732-7678;** www.southstseaport.org) indoors at Pier 17 in winter, outdoors on Pier 16 in summer. You'll also find free lunchtime and after-work alfresco performances on the plaza at the **World Trade Center** (☎ **212/435-4170**) in July and August.

And keep in mind that Lower Manhattan is rife with free arts and entertainment during the daytime, too. Trinity Church, on Broadway at Wall Street, hosts a chamber music and orchestral Noonday Concert series each Thursday at 1pm, and each Monday at noon at nearby St. Paul's, on Broadway at Fulton Street. This excellent program isn't quite free, but almost: The suggested donation is just $2. Call the concert hot line at ☎ **212/602-0747** or visit www.trinitywallstreet.org.

Additionally, most of the city's top museums offer free music and other programs after regular hours on Friday, Saturday, and other nights of the week (although you'll have to pay the basic admission fee to enter the museum). The **Metropolitan Museum of Art,** in particular, has an extensive slate of offerings each week, but there's lots of fun to be had at others as well, including the **Museum of Modern Art** and the **Brooklyn Museum of Art,** which hosts the remarkably eclectic **First Saturday** program monthly. For details, see the museum listings in chapter 7.

is led by the incomparable Wynton Marsalis, with the orchestra usually performing at Alice Tully Hall; the new "Jazz at the Penthouse" program, where great jazz pianists like Ellis Marsalis and Tommy Flanagan play in a spectacular candlelit setting overlooking the Hudson River, is the hottest ticket in town. **Lincoln Center Theater** (☎ 212/501-3100; www.lct.org), consists of the Vivian Beaumont Theater, a modern and comfortable venue with great sightlines that has been the stage for good Broadway drama, and the Mitzi E. Newhouse Theater, a well-respected off-Broadway house. Past seasons have included excellent productions of Tom Stoppard's *Arcadia, Carousel* in revival, and David Hare's one-man show, *Via Dolorosa.* For details on the **Metropolitan Opera,** the **New York City Opera,** the **New York City Ballet,** the **Juilliard School,** the phenomenal **New York Philharmonic,** and the **American Ballet Theatre,** which takes up residence here every spring, see "Opera, Classical Music & Dance" earlier in this chapter.

Most of the companies' **major seasons** run from about October to May or June. **Special series** like Great Performers and the new American Songbook, showcasing classic American show tunes, round out the regular calendar. Indoor and outdoor events are held in the warmer months: Spring blooms with the **JVC Jazz Festival;** July sees **Midsummer Night's Swing** with partner dancing, lessons, and music on the plaza; **Mostly Mozart** attracts talents like Alicia de Larrocha and André Watts; the **Lincoln Center Festival** celebrates the best of the performing arts; free alfresco music and dance performances comprise **Lincoln Center Out-of-Doors** from August through September; and the **New York Film Festival** is a major showcase for new films. Check the "New York City Calendar of Events" in chapter 2 or Lincoln Center's Web site to see what's on while you're in town.

Tickets for all performances at Avery Fisher and Alice Tully halls can be purchased through **CenterCharge** (☎ 212/721-6500) or online at www.lincolncenter.org. Tickets for all Lincoln Center Theater performances can be purchased through **Tele-Charge** (☎ 212/239-6200; www.telecharge.com). Tickets for New York State Theater productions (New York City Opera and Ballet companies) are available through **Ticket-Master** (☎ 212/307-4100; www.ticketmaster.com), while tickets for films showing at the Walter Reade Theater can be bought via **Movie Phone** (☎ 212/777-FILM; www.777film.com; the theater code is 954). For last-minute discount ticket-buying tips, see p. 305.

Madison Square Garden. On Seventh Ave. from 31st to 33rd sts. ☎ **212/465-MSG1.** www.thegarden.com. Subway: 1, 2, 3, 9, A, C, E to 34th St.; B, D, G, F, N, R to Herald Sq.

Kiss, Springsteen, Smashing Pumpkins, Tina Turner, Lauryn Hill, Dave Matthews Band, and other monsters of rock and pop regularly fill this 20,000-seat arena. A cavernous concrete hulk, it's better suited to sports than to concerts (end up in back, and you better bring binoculars). The Garden is also home to the NBA's Knicks and the NHL's Rangers; see "Spectator Sports" in chapter 7.

You'll find far better sightlines at **The Theater at Madison Square Garden,** an amphitheater-style auditorium with 5,600 seats that has also played host to some major stars, from Barbra Streisand to Bob Dylan to Oasis. Watch for possibly annual stagings of *The Wizard of Oz,* which has starred Roseanne and Eartha Kitt in past productions; and *A Christmas Carol,* with Roger Daltrey as last season's Scrooge.

The box office is through the Seventh Avenue entrance (behind the shops). You can also purchase tickets via **TicketMaster** (☎ 212/307-7171; www.ticketmaster.com).

✪ 92nd Street Y. 1395 Lexington Ave. (at 92nd St.). ☎ **212/996-1100.** www.92ndsty. org. Subway: 4, 5, 6 to 86th St.; 6 to 96th St.

Just because you see "Y", don't think this place is small potatoes: This community center offers a phenomenal slate of top-rated cultural happenings. The greatest classical performers—Isaac Stern, Janos Starker, Nadja Salerno-Sonnenberg—give recitals here. In addition, the full concert calendar often includes musical programs from luminaries such as Max Roach, John Williams, and Judy Collins; Jazz at the Y from Dick Hyman and guests; the long-standing Chamber Music at the Y series; the new Music from the Jewish Spirit series; and regular cabaret programs. The lectures and literary readings calendar is unparalleled, with featured speakers ranging from Lorne Michaels to David Halberstam to Edgar Bronfman, Jr. to Ann Richards to Susan Sontag to Edward Albee to . . . the list goes on and on. Best of all, readings and lectures are usually priced between $10 and $15 for nonmembers (although select lectures can be priced as high as $30), and concert tickets generally go for $25 to $35—half or a third of what you'd pay at comparable venues.

Radio City Music Hall. 1260 Sixth Ave. (at 50th St.). ☎ **212/247-4777,** or 212/307-1000 for tickets. www.radiocity.com. Subway: B, D, F, Q to 49th St./Rockefeller Center.

Opened in 1932, this stunning 6,200-seat art-deco theater continues to be a choice venue, where the ambiance alone adds a dash of panache to any performance. Star of the Christmas season is the **Radio City Music Hall Christmas Spectacular,** with the legendary Rockettes. Visiting pop chart-toppers, from Stevie Nicks to Radiohead, also perform here. Thanks to perfect acoustics and uninterrupted sightlines, there's hardly a bad seat in the house. Radio City also hosts a number of annual awards shows—such as the ESPYs, the GQ Man of the Year Awards, and anything MTV is holding in town—so this is a good place to celeb-spot on show nights. The theater is currently under renovation, and is scheduled to reopen by October 1999. In the meantime, the box office remains open.

Town Hall. 123 W. 43rd St. (btw. Sixth and Seventh aves.). ☎ 212/840-2824. www. the-townhall-nyc.org. Subway: 1, 2, 3, 7, 9, N, R, S to Times Sq.; B, D, F, Q to 42nd St.

This intimate landmark theater is blessed with outstanding acoustics, making it an ideal place to enjoy many kinds of performances, including theater, dance, and pop and world music. The calendar regularly includes such offerings as American tap and Brazilian tango exhibitions; Native-American music and global rhythms; comedy from Chicago City Limits or Bill Maher; concerts by the likes of Sarah MacLachlan or the reunited Blondie; and much more. The grade is extremely steep, so unless Lurch sits in front of you, fellow audience members shouldn't block your view.

4 Live Rock, Jazz, Blues & More

For the latest goings-on at these top venues and others around town, be sure to check the publications and online sources discussed at the opening of this chapter.

For coverage of **Madison Square Garden,** the **Theater at MSG,** and **Town Hall,** see "Major Concert Halls & Landmark Venues," above. Another large venue that regularly hosts pop-music concerts as well as a smattering of other events is the 2,700-seat art-deco **Beacon Theatre,** 2124 Broadway, at 74th Street (☎ **212/496-7070**). General-admission halls that serve as popular stages for national rock, pop, and hip-hop acts are **Hammerstein Ballroom,** at the Manhattan Center, 311 W. 34th St., between Eighth and Ninth avenues (☎ **212/564-4882**); and **Roseland,** 239 W. 52nd St., between Broadway and Eighth Avenue (☎ **212/247-0200**).

MIDSIZE & MULTIGENRE VENUES

Expect to pay a little more for shows at these venues than you would at smaller clubs—anywhere from $10 to $25, depending on the venue and the act.

The Bottom Line. 15 W. 4th St. (at Mercer St.). ☎ **212/228-7880** or 212/228-6300. Subway: N, R to Astor Place.

The Bottom Line built its reputation on performances by the likes of Bruce Springsteen and the Ramones, and it remains one of the city's most well-respected venues. With table seating, waitress service, decent burgers and fries, and a no-smoking policy, it's one of the city's most comfortable, too. It's renowned for its excellent sound and bookings of the best rock and folk singer/songwriters in the business. Lucinda Williams, Jimmy Webb, Graham Parker, Emmylou Harris, Robyn Hitchcock, and David Johansen (and alter-ego Buster Poindexter) are among the many artists that make this their favored venue for area appearances. There are usually two shows nightly.

Ticket-Buying Tips

Tickets for events at all larger theaters as well as at Hammerstein Ballroom, Roseland, Irving Plaza, Coney Island High, S.O.B's, and Tramps can be purchased through **TicketMaster** (☎ 212/307-7171; www.ticketmaster.com).

Advance tickets for an increasing number of shows at smaller venues—including CBGB's (and CB's 313 Gallery), Bowery Ballroom, Mercury Lounge, Iridium, Knitting Factory, and Manny's Car Wash—can be purchased through **Ticketweb** (☎ 212/269-4TIX; www.ticketweb.com). Do note, however, that just because Ticketweb doesn't have tickets left for an event doesn't mean it's completely sold out, so be sure and check with the venue directly.

Many venues also have their own box offices for advance ticket purchases. Showing up in person to buy your tickets will save you a few dollars in service charge. It's best to call ahead for box-office hours, though, as they may be limited.

Even if a show is sold out doesn't mean you're out of luck. There's usually a number of people hanging around at showtime trying to get rid of extra tickets for friends who didn't show, and they're usually happy to pass them off for face value. You'll also see professional scalpers, who are best avoided—it doesn't take a rocket scientist to tell the difference. Be aware, of course, that all forms of resale are illegal.

☉ Bowery Ballroom. 6 Delancey St. (at Bowery). ☎ **212/533-2111.** Subway: F, J, M, Z to Delancey St.

New in 1998, this marvelous space is run by the same people behind the pleasing Mercury Lounge (below). The Bowery is bigger, accommodating a crowd of 500 or so, and even better. The stage is big and raised to allow good sightlines from every corner. The sound is excellent, and art-deco details give the place a sophistication that doesn't come easy to general-admission halls. It's quickly becoming a favorite with alt-rockers like Afghan Whigs, Cibo Matto, and Shudder to Think as well as more established acts (Neil Finn, Patti Smith) who thrive in an intimate setting. **Money-Saving Tip:** Save on the service charge by buying advance tickets at Mercury's box office.

Irving Plaza. 17 Irving Place (at 15th St.). ☎ **212/777-6800.** www.irvingplaza.com. Subway: 4, 5, 6, L, N, R to Union Sq.

This high-profile midsize music hall is the prime stop for national-name rock bands that aren't quite big enough yet (or anymore) to sell out Hammerstein, Roseland, or the Beacon. Think Shawn Mullins ("Lullaby"), Squirrel Nut Zippers, Kula Shaker, Run DMC, Cheap Trick, Maceo Parker. All in all, a great place to see a show, with a well-elevated stage and lots of open space even on sold-out nights. The upstairs balcony offers unparalleled views, but come early for a spot. You can also buy tickets to Roseland events at the box office here.

Knitting Factory. 74 Leonard St. (btw. Broadway and Church St.). ☎ **212/219-3006.** www.knittingfactory.com. Subway: 1, 9 to Franklin St.

New York's premier avant-garde music venue has four separate spaces, each showcasing performances ranging from experimental jazz and acoustic folk to spoken-word and poetry readings to out-there multimedia works. Regulars who use the Knitting Factory as their lab of choice include former Lounge Lizard John Lurie; around-the-bend experimentalist John Zorn; guitar gods Vernon Reid, Eliot Sharp, and David Torn; innovative sideman (to Tom Waits and Elvis Costello, among others) Marc Ribot; and Television's Richard Lloyd. (If these names mean nothing to you, chances are good that the Knitting Factory is not for you.) The schedule is peppered with edgy star turns from the likes of Yoko Ono, Taj Mahal, Faith No More's Mike Patton, and folky charmer Jill Sobule ("I Kissed a Girl"). There are often two showtimes a night in the remarkably pleasing main performance space. The Tap Bar offers an extensive list of microbrews and free live music, often soundtracking obscure silent films.

Tramps. 51 W. 21st St. (btw. Fifth and Sixth aves.). ☎ **212/544-1666.** Subway: F to 23rd St.; N, R to 23rd St.

This loft space is a happening spot for roots music, zydeco, reggae, funk, blues, and blues-tinged classic rock. Anything goes here, from Jerry Lee Lewis pounding out sets of oldies to Shawn Colvin singing her latest laments to George Clinton and the P-Funk All Stars rocking the house 'til dawn. This place gets packed, and the grown-up audience can really move when things get rocking. Stake out a spot behind the railing near the elevated bar if you'd like a view over the crowd.

ROCK & MIXED-MUSIC CLUBS

In addition to the choices below, you might also want to see what's happening at **Meow Mix,** a friendly lesbian bar that's been booking a quality local rock calendar of late (see "The Lesbian & Gay Scene" later in this chapter). Also see what's on at **Don Hill's,** a multidimensional party scene showcasing live bands on some nights, as well as the increasingly eclectic **Baby Jupiter,** which hosts live music in its back coffeehouse-like room; see "Dance Clubs & Party Scenes," below.

✪ **Arlene Grocery.** 95 Stanton St. (btw. Ludlow and Orchard sts.). ☎ **212/358-1633.** www.arlene-grocery.com. Subway: F to Second Ave.

Live music is always free at this Lower East Side club, which boasts a friendly bar and a good sound system. Arlene Grocery primarily serves as a showcase for hot bands looking for a deal or promoting their self-pressed record. On occasion, bigger names like Mark Eitzel and Richard X. Heyman take the stage to, but it's far more likely that the act on stage will be brand new to you. Still, there's little risk involved thanks to the no-cover policy, and bookers who know what they're doing. The crowd is an easygoing mix of club hoppers, rock fans looking for a new fix, and industry scouts looking for new blood.

The Bitter End. 147 Bleecker St. (btw. La Guardia Place and Thompson St.). ☎ **212/673-7030.** www.bitterend.com. Subway: A, B, C, D, E, F, Q to W. 4th St.

This old-time club has been a Village mainstay since the 1960s, when it launched many an early folk career. The Bitter End now features five rock, blues, and/or R&B bands a night at a cover charge that seldom tops $5. Expect a crowd chock full of students from nearby NYU.

Brownie's. 169 Ave. A (btw. 10th and 11th sts.). ☎ **212/420-8392.** Subway: L to First Ave.

This unpretentious bar has grown into a well-respected alt-rock club. The crowd is half music-savvy scenesters and half carefree college students, with a few A&R types in the mix. The sound system is very good, but the layout could be better. Still, expect a packed bill—and a full crowd—just about any night of the week. Shows generally start at 8 or 9pm, and a DJ cranks out tunes after 11pm on weeknights. The cover runs $6 to $10.

Cafe Wha? 115 MacDougal St. (btw. Bleecker and W. 3rd sts.). ☎ **212/254-3706.** Subway: A, B, C, D, E, F, Q to W. 4th St.

You'll find a carefree crowd dancing in the aisles of this casual basement club just about any night of the week. From Wednesday through Sunday, the stage features the house's own Wha Band, which does an excellent job cranking out crowd-pleasing covers of familiar rock-and-roll hits from the 1970s, 1980s, and 1990s. Monday night is the hugely popular Brazilian Dance Party, while Tuesday night is Funk Night. Expect to be surrounded by lots of Jersey kids and out-of-towners on the weekends, but so what? You'll be having as much fun as they are. Cover charges range from $5 to $10, and Wednesdays and Sundays are free.

CBGB's. 315 Bowery (at Bleecker St.). ☎ **212/982-4052**. www.cbgb.com. Subway: 6 to Bleecker St.; F to Second Ave.

The original Downtown rock club has seen much better days, but no other spot is so rich with rock-and-roll history. This was *the* launching pad for New York punk and New Wave—everybody from the Ramones to Blondie got started here—but you've never heard of most of the acts who perform here now. Never mind—CB's still rocks. Expect loud and cynical, and you're unlikely to come away disappointed. Come early if you have hopes of actually seeing the stage, and avoid the bathrooms at all costs. Covers run $3 to $10, or higher if a big name is in the house.

More today than yesterday is ✪**CB's 313 Gallery** (☎ 212/677-0455), a welcome spin-off that showcases alternative art on the walls and mostly acoustic singer/songwriters on stage. The music tends toward smoother rock, folk, blues, and acoustic. Within striking distance of the history, but much more pleasant.

Coney Island High. 15 St. Mark's Place (btw. Second and Third aves.). ☎ **212/674-7959**. www.coneyhigh.com. Subway: 6 to Astor Place.

If you're over 30, you're likely to just consider this place a trial—even if you still love rock shows—but younger fans looking for the East Village edge will be in heaven. Founded by Jesse Malin (lead singer for local heroes D Generation), Coney Island High is the star of the East Village's skankiest strip, St. Mark's. With two main spaces, expect lots of loud, obnoxious rock and neo-punk, plus an occasional alt-star (Spacehog, Alex Chilton) turn. A few theme nights pop up here and there, including the Green Door, a monthly Saturday-night glam-fest. The cover charge ranges from $5 to $15.

Continental. 25 Third Ave. (at St. Mark's Place). ☎ **212/529-6924**. Subway: 6 to Astor Place.

This dark, sweaty, basic East Village club hosts a rollicking crowd energized by the low cover (usually $5 or less), cheap beer, and loud music. Slumming stars like Iggy Pop and Joey Ramone take the stage on occasion, but most acts are local rockers paying their dues. Now that tribute showcase Rock 'n' Roll Cafe is no more, cover bands like Strawberry Fields and Tramps Like Us have been populating the weekend bills of late.

The Cooler. 416 W. 14th St. (btw. Ninth and Tenth aves.). ☎ **212/229-0785**. www.thecooler.com. Subway: A, C, E to 14th St.; L to Eighth Ave.

A former meat locker in the heart of the meat-packing district has been transformed into this marvelously moody alternative music club with a discriminating taste for the eclectic—anything goes, as long as it's good. Offerings can range from Afrika Bambaataa to the acid-jazz of Groove Collective to any number of local boy Thurston Moore's numerous side projects. DJ nights can range from ambient to hip-hop. There's no sign, so look for the metal doors and the staircase leading to the subterranean entrance. The cover can range from free to $10.

Fez Under Time Cafe. 380 Lafayette St. (at Great Jones St.). ☎ **212/533-2680**. Subway: 6 to Bleecker St.

You have to reserve a seat a few days ahead for the wildly popular Thursday-night Mingus Big Band, when the low-ceilinged basement performance space is filled with the cool sounds of mighty Mingus jazz. The rest of the week brings an eclectic live

Free Music

Arlene Grocery (see above) and **Rodeo Bar** (see below) are the city's top no-cover clubs, but they're far from the only free shows in town.

Others worth checking out include the **Living Room,** 84 Stanton St., at Allen Street (☎ 212/533-7235), an unpretentious bar/restaurant that's particularly good for acoustic acts (the sound system isn't great for electric acts). The pass-the-bucket policy allows you to contribute as much or as little as you want to the performers' earnings for the evening. Also on the Lower East Side is comfy **Luna Lounge,** 171 Ludlow St., between Houston and Stanton streets (☎ 212/260-2323), which usually hosts two bands per night, and is a popular venue for local record-release parties. Monday's comedy night, however, has become so popular that a $5 cover is now charged.

East Village stalwart **Sidewalk Cafe,** 94 Ave. A, at 6th Street (☎ 212/473-7373), hosts live bands in the back room most nights. Pretty good cheap eats and two-for-one drinks before 8pm serve as additional attractions for the monetarily challenged. **Manitoba's,** 99 Ave. B, between 6th and 7th streets (☎ 212/982-2511), is a new, easygoing East Village hangout from former Dictators frontman Dick Manitoba. The booker has been scoring top-flight entertainment, which include a weekly gig from country-pop faves Beat Rodeo at press time. Sibling club **Lakeside Lounge,** 162 Ave. B, between 10th and 11th streets (☎ 212/529-8463), is slightly more rollicking.

One of my favorite coffeehouses, **Eureka Joe,** 168 Fifth Ave., at 22nd Street (☎ 212/741-7500, or 212/741-7504 for recorded schedule information), hosts a mix of eclectic acoustic acts and readings in its cozy, velvet-curtained environs. The cappucino, sandwiches, and pastries are great, and there's also a beer and wine bar.

Jazz fans will want to try **Arthur's Tavern,** 57 Grove St., at Seventh Avenue South (☎ 212/675-6879), a comfortable club and piano bar attracting a mixed gay-and-straight crowd. Beware of the drinks, however, which can be pricey. Also in the Village is **55 Bar,** at 55 Christopher Street, 1 block south of Seventh Avenue and 10th Street (☎ 212/929-9883), which hosts free, high-quality jazz nightly (blues on Saturday); there's a two-drink minimum per set. The house guitar trio is definitely worth a listen, and if saxist Ed Palermo is on the bill, go.

World music fans should check out the spicy sounds at **Gonzalez y Gonzalez,** 625 Broadway, just north of Houston Street (☎ 212/473-8787), which regularly hosts Latin American acts. The gringo-friendly Mexican food is mediocre at best, but the frosty piña coladas are terrific.

Louisiana Community Bar & Grill, 622 Broadway, at Houston Street (☎ 212/460-9633), is a great place to do the swing thing for free. There's live music 7 nights a week, and acts like the Flipped Fedoras, the Harlem Jazz Legends, and George Gee and the Jump, Jive and Wailers have been dominating the bill of late.

Also keep in mind that a number of clubs offer free music one or more nights a week, such as **Cafe Wha?,** the **Continental,** the **Cooler, Chicago B.L.U.E.S.,** and the **Internet Cafe;** the **Knitting Factory** offers free music in its Tap Bar. The easiest way to check for free events while you're in town is to peruse the music calendar in the weekly *Time Out New York,* which announces no-cover shows with an easy-to-spot FREE! Sunday night, in particular, is a big night for freebies.

Remember that schedules and no-cover policies can change at any time, so it's a good idea to confirm in advance.

music/performance art mix, which can range from Combustible Edison to esoteric local acts. The stage is fronted by tightly packed picnic-style tables and a few coveted booths. Time Cafe's pleasing, well-priced menu is served during performances (see chapter 6). I would love this sophisticated space if it were just better ventilated; if you need to escape the cigarette smoke, head upstairs to the relaxing Moroccan-themed lounge and bar. The cover ranges from $5 to $18, and a two-drink minimum may be required.

✪ **Mercury Lounge.** 217 E. Houston St. (at Essex St./Ave. A). ☎ **212/260-4700.** Subway: F to Second Ave.

The Merc is everything a top-notch live music venue should be: unpretentious, extremely civilized, and outfitted with a killer sound system. The rooms themselves are nothing special: a front bar and an intimate back-room performance space with a low stage and a few tables along the wall. The calendar is filled with a mix of accomplished local rockers and national acts like Del Amitri and Art Alexakis from Everclear. The crowd is grown-up and easygoing. The only downside is that it's consistently packed thanks to the high quality of the entertainment and all-around pleasing nature of the experience. The cover can reach $15 for national acts, but seldom does; it's more likely to be around $8.

Rodeo Bar. 375 Third Ave. (at 27th St.). ☎ **212/683-6500.** www.rodeobar.com. Subway: 6 to 28th St.

Here's New York's oldest—and finest—honky-tonk. Hike up your Wranglers and head those Fryes inside, where you'll find longhorns on the walls, peanut shells underfoot, and Tex-Mex on the menu. But this place is really about the music: urban-tinged country, foot-stompin' bluegrass, swinging rockabilly, Southern-flavored rock. While bigger names like Rosie Flores and up-and-comers on the tour circuit occasionally grace the stage, regular acts like Dixieland swingers the Flying Neutrinos and Simon and the Bar Sinisters usually supply the free music, keeping the urban cowboys plenty happy.

Tonic. 107 Norfolk St. (btw. Delancey and Rivington sts.). ☎ **212/358-7503.** Subway: F to Delancey St.

This quirky Lower East Sider has become quite the avant-garde jazz spot in the Knitting Factory vein. Look for the "Klezmer Sundays at Tonic" series; Monday night is movie night, featuring cult classics. Tickets range from $4 to $15.

Wetlands. 161 Hudson St. (at Laight St.). ☎ **212/966-4225.** www.wetlands-preserve.org. Subway: 1, 9, A, C, E to Canal St.

This environmentally conscious club isn't just for Deadheads anymore. Sure, Phish is worshipped by most of the crowd and you'll still find Haight-Ashbury vets like Jorma Kaukonen on the schedule every once in awhile, but the club's musical focus has really broadened in recent years. Wetlands regularly offers hip-hop, global funk, and world music in addition to mind-bending, indie, and roots rock.

JAZZ, BLUES, LATIN & WORLD MUSIC

Be aware that a night at a top-flight jazz club can be expensive. For serious fans, it's worth splurging on a night at the **Blue Note,** the **Village Vanguard, Iridium,** or **Sweet Basil,** all world-class showcases for the top talents in the jazz world. However, cover charges can vary dramatically—from as little as $10 to as high as $65, depending on who's taking the stage—and there's likely to be an additional drink minimum (or a dinner requirement, if you choose an early show). Call ahead so you know what you're getting into; reservations are also an excellent idea at top spots.

For those of you who like your jazz with an edge, see what's on at the **Knitting Factory** (see "Midsize & Multigenre Venues") and **Tonic** (see "Rock & Mixed-Music Clubs"). Trad fans should also consider the Thursday Mingus Big Band Workshop at **Fez Under Time Cafe;** those wearing their dancing shoes should check out the Monday-night Brazilian big band and Tuesday-night funk at **Cafe Wha?;** and look for groovy world music at **Wetlands;** see "Rock & Mixed-Music Clubs," above. If swing's your thing, check out "It Might As Well Be Swing" later in this chapter. Also see **Arthur's Tavern** and the **55 Bar** in the "Free Music" box.

There's also **Jazz at Lincoln Center,** the city's—and the nation's—premier forum for the traditional and developing jazz canon; see "Major Concert Halls & Landmark Venues" earlier in this chapter.

Blue Note. 131 W. 3rd St. (at Sixth Ave.). ☎ **212/475-8592.** www.bluenote.net. Subway: A, B, C, D, E, F, Q to W. 4th St.

The Blue Note attracts the biggest names in jazz to its intimate setting, from Lionel Hampton to Manhattan Transfer to Oscar Peterson to B. B. King. The sound system is excellent, and every seat in the house has a sightline to the stage. Dinner is served (main courses are $19 to $29), as is Sunday brunch. **Money-Saving Tip:** If you'd like to experience this legendary club but can't stomach the high charges that can accompany standard shows, consider the Friday- and Saturday-night **Late Night Jam Sessions,** which require just a $5 cover and last until 4am.

Chicago B.L.U.E.S. 73 Eighth Ave. (btw. 13th and 14th sts.). ☎ **212/924-9755.** Subway: A, C, E, L to 14th St.

Here's the best blues joint in the city, with a genuine Windy City flair. The contrived decor makes the place feel more theme park than roadhouse, but the music is the real thing. The cover can go as high as $15 for acts like Carl Perkins, Buddy Miles, and Lonnie Brooks, but it's usually less than $10, and at least 2 nights a week are free.

Iridium. 44 W. 63rd St. (at Columbus Ave., below the Merlot Bar & Grill). ☎ **212/582-2121.** www.iridiumjazz.com. Subway: 1, 9 to 66th St.; 1, 9, A, B, C, D to Columbus Circle.

This well-respected and snazzily designed basement boîte features such top-flight acts as the Frank Foster Quintet and the excellent Jazz Messengers, plus the legendary Les Paul every Monday night. A $20 minimum cover (it may be higher) plus a $10

Take the A Train

Harlem's jazz scene has taken on new energy in recent years, serving up top-notch music without the high cover charges and drink/food minimums that Downtown clubs often require. **Showman's Cafe,** 2321 Frederick Douglass Blvd., between 124th and 125th streets (☎ **212/864-8941;** subway: A, B, C, D to 125th St.), has one of the few organ rooms left in the Harlem jazz scene; the nightly music ranges from soulful jazz to funky bebop. **Lenox Lounge,** 288 Lenox Ave., between 124th and 125th streets (☎ **212/427-0253;** subway: 2 or 3 to 125th St.), is a great art-deco bar with live jazz quintets on weekends, as well as a lively Monday-night jam session featuring trumpeter Roy Campbell. And **St. Nick's Pub,** 773 St. Nicholas Ave., at 149th Street (☎ **212/283-9728;** subway: A, B, C, D to 145th St.), is an older Sugar Hill closet that's being rediscovered by a younger crowd for its great jazz 5 nights a week. The Monday jazz jams attract music lovers and players from all walks of life, and the service is just as friendly whether you come from the neighborhood, Downtown, or out of town.

per-person drink minimum makes Iridium worth it only if you're a huge fan. **Money-Saving Tip:** Check the Web site for special coupons and student-discount offers.

Internet Cafe. 82 E. 3rd St. (btw. First and Second aves.). ☎ **212/614-0747.** Subway: F to Second Ave.

Those looking for an affordable jazz fix should visit this casual online cafe, which features well-regarded jazz from up-and-coming acts nightly, plus film screenings on Sunday. The cover charge is $5 to $7; there's no cover on Sunday.

The Jazz Standard. 116 E. 27th St. (btw. Park Ave. S. and Lexington Ave.) ☎ **212/576-2232.** Subway: 6 to 28th St.

Boasting a sophisticated retro-speakeasy vibe, this basement lounge is one of the city's largest jazz clubs, with well-spaced tables and a manageable $15 to $20 cover. The rule is straightforward, mainstream jazz by new and established musicians. You really can't go wrong here. Upstairs is 27 Standard, serving highly regarded, if pricey, New American cuisine that you can also enjoy downstairs.

Manny's Car Wash. 1558 Third Ave. (btw. 87th and 88th sts.). ☎ **212/369-BLUES.** www.mannyscarwash.com. Subway: 4, 5, 6 to 86th St.

Some come to this friendly Upper East Side joint for the top-notch blues, while others come for the scene (yuppie love seekers on Monday for ladies' night, frat-pack types on weekends). Fans know Manny's best for its excellent Windy City sounds, but the schedule also features Louisiana bayou blues and zydeco. Don't be surprised if you spot a star or two on the bill, such as Hiram Bullock. The cover is remarkably low for the quality of the music: Often less than $10, and I've never seen it go higher than $15. Look for the legendary free Sunday-night blues jam, and don't miss Popa Chubby's rockin' Blues Band if he's on the bill.

✪ **Small's.** 183 W. 10th St. (at Seventh Ave.). ☎ **212/929-7565.** Subway: 1, 2, 3, 9 to W. 14th St.

If you just don't want to stop grooving after the other jazz clubs close, grab a bottle of wine from a store and head to this cozy basement hideaway, which stays open all night. Scheduled performers, which often include cutting-edge unsigned acts or overlooked talents, play from around 10pm to 2am, followed by a nightly jam session (I once saw Joshua Redman sit in) until dawn or beyond. No alcohol is served, but that doesn't keep the crowds away—they're happy to come just for the jazz. Drinks (and sometimes snacks) are free with the $10 cover, and all ages are welcome.

✪ **S.O.B's.** 204 Varick St. (at W. Houston St.). ☎ **212/243-4940.** www.sobs.com. Subway: 1, 9 to Houston St.

This is the city's top world-music venue, specializing in Brazilian, Caribbean, and Latin sounds. The packed house dances and sings along nightly to calypso, samba, mambo, African drums, reggae, or other global grooves, united in the high-energy, feel-good vibe. Bookings include top-flight performers from around the globe; luminaries from Marc Anthony to Astrud Gilberto to King Sunny Ade have graced the stage. This place has real island-style pizzazz, and is so popular that you may want to book in advance if you'd like table seating. The cover ranges from $10 to $20. At press time, free before-show dance lessons were offered on Mondays.

Sweet Basil. 88 Seventh Ave. South (btw. Grove and Bleecker sts.). ☎ **212/242-1785.** www.sweetbasil.com. Subway: 1, 9 to Christopher St.–Sheridan Sq.

The choice runs from fusion to traditional at this intimate but excellent jazz club, featuring big-name talent nightly. Pricey—expect a $17.50 to $20 cover plus a $10 minimum—but you'll get your money's worth. The Sunday brunch is so popular that they've added a Saturday version.

The Village Vanguard. 178 Seventh Ave. S. (just below 11th St.). ☎ **212/255-4037.** Subway: 1, 2, 3, 9 to 14th St.

What CBGB's is to rock, the Village Vanguard is to jazz. Thankfully, this legendary club is just as vital as ever. Expect a mix of established names and high-quality local talent, including the Vanguard's own jazz orchestra. The sound is great but sightlines are terrible, so come early for a front table. The crowd can seem either overly serious or overly touristy, but don't let that stop you—you'll always find great music.

5 Comedy & Cabaret

STAND-UP & SKETCH COMEDY

Cover charges are generally in the $8 to $15 range, with all-star **Caroline's,** 1626 Broadway, between 49th and 50th streets (☎ 212/757-4100), going as high as $25 on occasion. Unless you're enamored with seeing a big name that's scheduled there, I suggest that those of you watching your wallets opt for a less-expensive club, where you're likely to enjoy just as many yuks. Keep in mind that many clubs have a two-drink minimum, and may raise their covers if a famous name is in the house; be sure to ask about the night's cover and requirements when you reserve. And ask about open-mike shows if you want to try to tickle some funny bones yourself.

If it's Monday, also consider the weekly comedy night at **Luna Lounge,** 171 Ludlow St., between Houston and Stanton streets (☎ 212/260-2323), which is a bargain at $5.

Boston Comedy Club. 82 W. 3rd St. (btw. Thompson and Sullivan sts.). ☎ **212/ 477-1000.** Subway: A, B, C, D, E, F, Q to W. 4th St. (use 3rd St. exit).

If you don't like the act here, wait a couple of minutes and it'll change. The M.O. here is to barrage the audience with a lineup of a dozen or so talents per set on the theory that someone will get a laugh. Jay Mohr is one of the Boston's breakthrough acts, and this is still his home club. The cover is $8 weekdays, $12 weekends.

✪ **Comedy Cellar.** 117 MacDougal St. (btw. Bleecker and W. 3rd sts.). ☎ **212/254-3480.** Subway: A, B, C, D, E, F, Q to W. 4th St. (use 3rd St. exit).

This intimate subterranean spot is the club of choice for stand-up fans in the know, thanks to the best, most consistently impressive lineups in the business. I'll always love the Comedy Cellar for introducing me to an uproariously funny unknown comic named Ray Romano a few years back. Just $5 weekdays, $12 weekends.

Comic Strip Live. 1568 Second Ave. (btw. 81st and 82nd sts.). ☎ **212/861-9386.** www.comicstriplive.com. Subway: 4, 5, 6 to 86th St.

This was *the* comedy club of the 1980s, launching the careers of Jerry Seinfeld, Eddie Murphy, Carol Leifer, Paul Reiser, Adam Sandler, and Chris Rock. The big, boisterous room is still a very well-respected forum for new talent, and grateful superstars often return to the old homestead for surprise appearances. The cover is $8 weekdays, $12 weekends.

✪ **Gotham Comedy Club.** 34 W. 22nd St. (btw. Fifth and Sixth aves.). ☎ **212/367-9000.** www.citysearch.com/nyc/gothamcomedy. Subway: N, R or F to 23rd St.

Here's the city's trendiest and most sophisticated comedy club. The young talent—Tom Rhodes, Jeff Ross, Paul Mercurio, Lynn Harris—is red-hot. Look for theme nights like the lovelorn laugh riot "Breakup Girl Live!" and "A Very Jewish Thursday." The cover is $8 cover weekdays, $12 weekends.

New York Comedy Club. 241 E. 24th St. (btw. Second and Third aves.). ☎ **212/ 696-5233.** Subway: 6 to 23rd St.

With a $5 cover charge on weekdays ($10 Friday and Saturday), this club offers the best laugh value for your money. Despite what the owners call their "Wal-Mart approach" to comedy, the club has presented Damon Wayans, Chris Rock, and Brett Butler, among others, in its two showrooms. Fridays feature African-American comics, while Saturdays save time for Hispanic comics.

Stand-Up New York. 236 W. 78th St. (at Broadway). ☎ **212/595-0850.** Subway: 1, 9 to 79th St.

The Upper West Side's premier stand-up comedy club hosts some of the brightest young comics in the business, and drop-in guests have included Dennis Leary, Robin Williams, and Mr. Upper West Side himself, Jerry Seinfeld. $7 weekdays, $12 weekends.

✪ **Upright Citizen's Brigade Theater.** 161 W. 22nd St. (btw. Sixth and Seventh aves.) ☎ **212/366-9176.** www.uprightcitizens.com. Subway: 1, 9 to 23rd St.

You've seen their twisted, highly original sketch comedy on Comedy Central—and now you can see New York's premier sketch comedy troupe live. The biggest success to come out of New York's late 1990s alternative comedy explosion, the UCB now has its very own showcase. The best of the non-stop hilarity is *A.S.S.S.C.A.T.*, the troupe's extremely popular long-form improv show. At press time, it was being offered twice on Sundays; make your reservations for the 7:30pm show well in advance. The 9:30pm show is free, but come extra early to stand in line. For everything else, you won't pay more than $5.

CABARETS

The city's top supper clubs and cabarets are not for the budget-minded. Places like **Cafe Carlyle,** in the Carlyle Hotel, 781 Madison Ave. (☎ **212/744-1600**), home to the legendary Bobby Short, and the Algonquin's **Oak Room**, 59 W. 44th St. (☎ **212/ 840-6800**), charge covers that are usually in the $50 range, plus two-drink or dinner-check minimums and other qualifications. Be sure to get the low down when you make reservations, and count on a $300 night on the town. Or try one of these more casual, less-expensive options.

Don't Tell Mama. 343 W. 46th St. (btw. Eighth and Ninth aves.). ☎ **212/757-0788.** Subway: A, C, E to 42nd St.

Singing waitresses go from tips to tunes when their turn in the spotlight comes. You'll find an evening of torch songs, comedy, and much more in a friendly, and affordable, atmosphere. The piano bar is particularly lively. There's a $3 to $15 cover, depending on the show, but the piano bar is free.

Duplex Cabaret. 61 Christopher St. (at Seventh Ave. S.). ☎ **212/255-5438.** Subway: 1, 9 to Christopher St.–Sheridan Sq.

Expect a high camp factor and lots of good-natured fun in this multilevel space. A mixed gay/straight crowd of locals and curious out-of-towners sit at outdoor tables for drinks, gather around the downstairs piano (sing-alongs from around 9pm), or head upstairs to the cabaret for shows that run from mini-musicals to drag revues to stand-up comedy ($3 to $12 cover).

Eighty Eights. 228 W. 10th St. (btw. Bleecker and Hudson sts.). ☎ **212/924-0088.** Subway: 1, 9 to Christopher St.–Sheridan Sq.

This attractive, informal spot offers affordable, top-quality cabaret that ranges from torch songs to musical comedy to stand-up; the cover is $8 to $15. Downstairs is a friendly piano bar where both patrons and staff aren't afraid to sing along loudly.

⭕ **Joe's Pub.** At the Joseph Papp Public Theater, 425 Lafayette St. (btw. Astor Place and 4th St.). ☎ **212/539-8777** or Telecharge at 212/239-6200 (for advance tickets). www. publictheater.org. Subway: 6 to Astor Place.

Named for the legendary Joseph Papp, the newest entry on the cabaret circuit is everything a New York cabaret should be: an elegant retro-style, multilevel space serving up a classic American menu (think burgers, shrimp cocktail, baked Alaska) and top-notch entertainers. The sophisticated crowd comes early (around 8:30pm) for music and spoken word that ranges from legendary Broadway duo Betty Comden and Adolph Green to fiery flamenco dancing to performance poets to pop golden-boy Duncan Sheik. Don't be surprised if Broadway actors show up on off-nights to exercise their substantial chops. Expect to blow a wad, though: There's a $10 to $30 cover, plus a two-drink minimum. Reservations are required.

6 Bars & Cocktail Lounges

SOUTH STREET SEAPORT & THE FINANCIAL DISTRICT

⭕ **The Greatest Bar on Earth.** 1 World Trade Center, 107th floor (on West St., btw. Liberty and Vesey sts.) ☎ **212/524-7000.** Subway: 1, 9, C, E to Church St.; N, R to Cortlandt St.

High atop the World Trade Center sits the Greatest Bar on Earth, whose name is only a slight exaggeration. This is a magical spot for cocktails, decent a la carte dining (finger foods and gourmet munchies mostly), and dancing. No matter how many times I come up here, I'm wowed by the incredible views, which are equal to those at the Top of the World observation deck atop the other tower. The place is huge, but intimate nooks and a separate back room bring the scale down to comfortable proportions. The crowd is a lively mix of locals and stylish out-of-towners. This is a great place to come with a group; the music is loud, and the joint really jumps as the night goes on. Quintessentially—and spectacularly—New York, GBOE is relatively affordable, too: The generous, top-shelf martinis are just $8.50. The same cocktail costs $10 to $12 at most trendy places about town. Look for swing on Friday and Saturdays, plus mambo, funk, and R&B other nights of the week. Wednesday is home to the hip Mondo 107 strato-lounge DJ party. The door charge ranges from $5 to $15 Thursday through Saturday, but there's no cover the rest of the week.

North Star Pub. At South Street Seaport, 93 South St. (at Fulton St.). ☎ **212/509-6757.** Subway: 2, 3, 4, 5 to Fulton St.

In addition to an excellent selection of bottled and on-tap brews, this genuine British pub boasts one of the finest single-malt scotch menus in the city. Owner Devon Black is very serious about his potables: He carries no fewer than 75 single malts, conducts regular tasting seminars, and specializes in British-style ales, bitters, ciders, and stouts. The North Star is warm, friendly, and affordable—a perfect place to linger over an Imperial pint or a wee dram. Great pub grub, too.

Wall St. Kitchen & Bar. 70 Broad St. (btw. Beaver and S. William sts., about 1½ blocks south of New York Stock Exchange). ☎ **212/797-7070.** Subway: 4, 5 to Bowling Green; J, M, Z to Broad St.

Want to rub elbows with some genuine bulls and bears after a hard day of Downtown sightseeing? Head to this surprisingly appealing and affordable bar, housed (appropriately enough) in a spectacular former bank in the heart of the Financial District. Wall St. Kitchen specializes in on-tap beers (around 50 are on offer at any given time) and "flight" menus of wines and microbrews for tasting. The familiar bar food is well prepared and reasonably priced. Come on a weekday to enjoy the crowd.

TRIBECA

El Teddy's. 219 W. Broadway (btw. Franklin and White sts.). ☎ **212/941-7070.** Subway: 1, 9 to Franklin St.

This upscale South-of-the-Border restaurant is a great place to pony up to the bar for a cocktail. The bathtub-sized margaritas ($7) are terrific, and you have about two dozen to choose from. All the fashionistas left years ago, but the kitschy decor is still retro-hip. You can't miss this place—just look for the enormous Statue of Liberty crown suspended over the sidewalk.

Riverrun. 176 Franklin St. (btw. Greenwich Ave. and Hudson St.). ☎ **212/996-3894.** Subway: 1, 9 to Franklin St.

Down-to-earth as ever, this neighborhood pioneer is now a refreshing find in an increasingly haute 'hood. Like a lot of vintage joints, the decor is more clutter than clean lines, but friendly bar does a great job of keeping the easygoing crowd happy. There's a sensible wine list, a good selection of beers on tap, a respectable single-malt selection, and satisfying comfort food. The crowd morphs from traders to locals as the evening wears on.

☼ The Sporting Club. 99 Hudson St. (btw. Franklin and Leonard sts.). ☎ **212/219-0900.** Subway: 1, 9 to Franklin St.

The city's best sports bar is a guy's joint if there ever was one. The space is as big as a linebacker, with giant TV screens at every turn tuned to just about every game on the planet. (Wall Streeters bring their international cohorts here to catch everything from English football to Japanese sumo.) The menu is what you'd expect: wings, burgers, club sandwiches, and *lots* of beer. There's no better place for sports fans to get crazy at Super Bowl time and during March Madness. When the big games are over, this turns into a surprisingly popular singles place.

Walker's. 16 North Moore St. (at Varick St.). ☎ **212/941-0142.** Subway: 1, 9 to Franklin St.

Like Riverrun, Walker's is an old holdout from pre-fabulous TriBeCa. It's surprisingly charming, with a tin ceiling, a long wooden bar, oldies on the sound system, and cozy tables where you can dine on affordable meat-and-potatoes fare. The bartenders are a friendly bunch, but do yourself a favor and don't get fancy with your drink orders.

CHINATOWN & LITTLE ITALY

☼ Double Happiness. 173 Mott St. (at Broome St.). ☎ **212/941-1282.** Subway: 6 to Spring St.; B, D, Q to Grand St.

This new kid on a new block has already shown itself to be quite a star. The only indicator to the subterranean entrance is a vertical WATCH YOUR STEP sign. Once through the door, you'll find a beautifully designed lounge with artistic nods to the neighborhood throughout. The space is large, but a low ceiling and intimate nooks enhance its romantic vibe (although the loud funkified music mix may deter true wooing). Don't miss the green-tea martini, an inspired house creation.

Mare Chiaro. 176½ Mulberry St. (at Broome St.). ☎ **212/226-9345.** Subway: 6 to Spring St.

This authentic corner of Little Italy now hosts a bizarro mix of slumming NoLiTa hipsters, Uptown singles, and neighborhood holdovers from an age when this was just a drinking-man's bar. But Mare Chiaro still works its crusty magic, transporting you back to another era with its gentrification-resistant vibe. A great place for a cheap beer at a crossroads of city life.

SOHO

Ear Inn. 326 Spring St. (btw. Greenwich and Washington sts.). ☎ **212/226-9060.** Subway: C, E to Spring St.

This historic far-west SoHo pub has always been a local fave since before the Civil War thanks to its casual ambiance, huge selection of beers, and old-style bartenders who aren't looking for their big break. This is the kind of place where tatooed bikers can pony up to the bar next to bankers, and everybody gets along. Live music and spoken-word events dot the not-too-ambitious calendar.

Ñ. 33 Crosby St. (btw. Grand and Broome sts.). ☎ 212/219-8856. Subway: 6 to Spring St.; N, R to Prince St.

On a charming cobbled street that somehow escaped gentrification, Ñ (pronounced like the Spanish letter, *enyay*) is long, narrow, candlelit, and hip. Despite its cool, the staff is warm, and the many sherries for sale are excellent. There's also a nice, fruity sangria, plus a full bar for non-Spanish tastes. You can order some of the city's best tapas, and flamenco dancers heighten the appeal on select Wednesday nights.

Pravda. 281 Lafayette St. (btw. Prince and Houston sts.). ☎ **212/226-4696** or 212/226-4944. Subway: B, D, F, Q to Broadway–Lafayette St.

If you were prowling New York's watering holes looking for Boris and Natasha, this is where you'd most likely find them. This Soviet-chic lounge makes pricey but perfect martinis for a classy crowd drawn in by the romantic pre-Gorbachev revolutionary vibe.

Soho Kitchen & Bar. 103 Greene St. (btw. Spring and Prince sts.). ☎ **212/925-1866.** Subway: N, R to Prince St.; C, E to Spring St.

This fun, easy-going bar and restaurant is a nice antidote to the standard SoHo pretensions. The large, lofty space attracts an animated after-work and late-night crowd to its central bar, which dispenses 21 beers on tap, a whole slew of microbrews by the bottle, and more than 100 wines by the glass or in "flights" for comparative tastings.

Veruka. 525 Broome St. (btw. Thompson St. and Sixth Ave.). ☎ **212/625-1717.** Subway: C, E to Spring St.

Lounges just don't get more 21st-century swellegant than this impeccably designed bi-level hotspot. The mark-ups on cocktails and the haute bar food are ridiculous, so normally I would tell you to avoid this place like the plague. But at press time, free Veruka Tuesdays allowed us regular folks to don our very best and rub elbows with the sleek, super-chic crowd. Check to see if it's still on while you're in town. Dress to impress and arrive early for your best chance of making it past the velvet rope.

LOWER EAST SIDE

Also consider the **Mercury Lounge,** 217 E. Houston St. (☎ 212/260-4700), which has a casual, comfortable bar up front; see p. 316. There's also **Baby Jupiter,** 170 Orchard St. (☎ 212/982-BABY), a hybrid coffeeshop/dance club/performance art space that has blossomed into a top-notch scene; see p. 332.

✪ **Idlewild.** 145 E. Houston St. (btw. First and Second aves.). ☎ **212/477-5005.** Subway: F to Second Ave.

It may look unapproachable from the street, with nothing but an unmarked stainless-steel facade, but inside you'll find a fun, easygoing bar that's perfect for lovers of retro-kitsch. The interior is a larger-scale repro of a jet airplane, complete with reclining seats, tray tables, and too-small bathrooms. There are booths in back for larger crowds, and an Austin Powers–style bar to gather around at center stage. The DJ spins a listener-friendly mix of light techno, lounge, disco in the funkadelic vein, and 1980s tunes from the likes of the Smiths and the Cure.

Lansky Lounge. 138 Delancey St. (entrance on Norfolk St., btw. Rivington and Delancey sts.). ☎ **212/677-9489.** Subway: F to Delancey St.

A doorman stands on the sidewalk to point patrons down a flight of stairs, through an alley, and back up a staircase into this faux speakeasy. Fashionistas lament that Lansky Lounge has been "discovered" (read: ruined), but it's still one of the Lower East Side's coolest scenes. The special martinis and infused vodkas are terrific. Come on a week-night, when the crowd is more local than bridge-and-tunnel. Note: The bar is closed on Friday night in observance of the Jewish Sabbath.

Ludlow Bar. 165 Ludlow St. (btw. Stanton and Houston sts.). ☎ **212/353-0536.** Subway: F to Second Ave.

This friendly little lounge manages to avoid the pretensions of its hipper-than-thou neighbors. Still, in keeping with the lounge trend, you'll find cozy furniture, a purple-felt pool table, and a DJ spinning funky jazz, house, and trip-hop for an artsy crowd that's slightly older than neighboring Max Fish's.

Max Fish. 178 Ludlow St. (at Houston St.). ☎ **212/529-3959.** Subway: F to Second Ave.

If grungy kitsch is more your style than loungey sleek, then Max Fish is the place for you. You'll find a great jukebox, video games, and a pool table that's best left to the locals unless you can live up to the challenge. The crowd is a curious mix of serious neighborhood artists (shows hang here periodically) and twentysomethings seriously on the make.

Orchard Bar. 200 Orchard St. (btw. Houston and Stanton sts.). ☎ **212/673-5350.** Subway: F to Second Ave.

This super-cool lounge is the best of the Lower East Side crop. The postmodern-goes-organic decor is at once funky and serene, the friendly barstaff knows how to mix a cocktail, and the crowd is more relaxed than at neighboring pickup spots. DJs spin a smart, eclectic mix that creates a nice backdrop without overwhelming. A terrific place for a casual drink on a weeknight, but skip it on the weekend unless you can stand the tight squeeze (I can't).

THE EAST VILLAGE & NOHO

In addition to the choices below, also consider the magical Moroccan lounge at **Fez,** 380 Lafayette St., at Great Jones St. (☎ **212/533-2680**), which I much prefer to the downstairs performance space (see p. 314).

Barmacy. 538 E. 14th St. (btw. aves. A and B). ☎ **212/228-2240.** Subway: L to First Ave.

Barmacy is just what you'd guess—a bar housed in a vintage pharmacy, complete with shelves of classic toiletries and a drugstore counter that would make Lana Turner smile. On an otherwise desolate stretch of East 14th, it's really a fun place to spend an evening, complete with a youngish party-hearty crowd and DJs spinning tunes in the back room that range from earnest Britpop to modern funk to makeout music, depending on the evening.

B Bar & Grill. 40 E. 4th St. (at Bowery). ☎ **212/475-2220.** Subway: 6 to Bleecker St.

Originally a Gulf gas station, B Bar is 1960s modern and attractive, with high ceilings, comfy booths, retro-style mood lighting, a large central bar, and the latest alterna-hits on the sound system. But it's the giant tree-filled courtyard that's the biggest draw, as well as the terrific menu of signature drinks. The reasonably priced food is better than you'd expect (see chapter 6). A real party scene later in the evening. The shallow, self-important

Spoken Word, Slams & More

Nuyorican Poets Cafe, 236 E. 3rd St., between avenues B and C (☎ 212/505-8183; www.nuyorican.org), is a neat performance-art space with a persistent boho spirit and a long history of showcasing fledgling creativity. The full calendar runs the gamut from experimental film to unstaged readings of original screenplays to live Latin-infused jazz. The Wednesday and Friday poetry slams can be a fun ride—a 1990s version of the *Gong Show*, where poets compete as audience members score the performances. The neighborhood gets dicey at night, so beware.

---

crowd isn't the type you'll find a best friend in, but they're fun to watch. Go on a weeknight to avoid the annoying velvet-rope policy that reigns on weekends.

○ **dba.** 41 First Ave. (btw. 2nd and 3rd sts.). ☎ 212/475-5097. Subway: F to Second Ave.

Along with Temple Bar (below), this is my other favorite bar in the city. It has completely bucked the lounge trend that has taken over the city by remaining firmly and resolutely an unpretentious neighborhood bar that's as comfy and welcoming as your favorite shirt. Most importantly, dba is a beer- and scotch-lover's paradise. Owner Ray Deter specializes in British-style cask-conditioned ales (the kind that you pump by hand) and stocks a phenomenal collection of 90 single-malt scotches. The relaxed crowd is a pleasing mix of connoisseurs and casual drinkers who like the unlimited choices and egalitarian vibe. Excellent jukebox, too.

Decibel. 240 E. 9th St. (btw. Second and Third aves.). ☎ 212/979-2733. Subway: N, R to 8th St.; 6 to Astor Place.

This subterranean sake bar is a genuine Japanese refuge. The warren of little, dimly lit rooms draws a hip crowd with its long, excellent list of sakes and affordable Japanese nibbles. The menu explains everything you ever wanted to know about sake and then some; feel free to ask the bar's wise and tolerant staff for suggestions. Japanese beers and saketinis (martinis made with sake—an excellent invention) are also available.

○ **KGB Bar.** 85 E. 4th St. (btw. Second and Third Aves.) ☎ 212/505-3360. Subway: 6 to Astor Place.

This former Ukranian social club still boasts its Soviet-themed decor, but it now draws creative intellectual types who like the low-key boho vibe. Sunday nights are the biggest draw thanks to the success of KGB's excellent reading series, where an increasingly talented pack of up-and-coming and published writers read their prose to a receptive crowd starting at 7pm. Past readers have included Rick Moody (*The Ice Storm*), Catherine Texier (*Breakup*), and Kathryn Harrison (*The Kiss*). The Red Room also stages theatrical productions regularly.

Korova Milk Bar. 200 Ave. A (btw. 12th and 13th sts.). ☎ 212/254-8838). Subway: L to First Ave.

Clockwork Orange fans will get a kick out of this eye-popping but ultimately unpretentious theme bar. The kitschy-cool vibe makes it more fun when the place is full, so go on a weekend night, when a DJ spins a trippy goth/funk/electronica mix.

Lucky Cheng's. 24 First Ave. (btw. 1st and 2nd sts.). ☎ 212/473-0516. Subway: F to Second Ave.

You gotta have a gimmick if you want to get ahead, according to *Gypsy*—so why not go the RuPaul route? The Asian fusion food is beside the point at this silly place, so come simply to be entertained by the fabulous drag queens in the brand-new six-screen, state-of-the-art karaoke lounge with a goldfish pond under the plexiglass stage. It's pure camp—like stepping into a production of *The King and I* cast in a New Orleans bordello. You'll find a mixed crowd, suits and jeans, yuppies and gays, with bemused out-of-towners spicing the brew.

McSorley's Old Ale House. 15 E. 7th St. (btw. Second and Third aves.). ☎ **212/ 473-9148.** Subway: 6 to Astor Place.

Shrine Time—and they want you to worship their way. In business for more than 140 years, McSorley's window proudly claims, WE WERE HERE BEFORE YOU WERE BORN. Only McSorley's Ale is served, light or dark, and two at a time. Come to bask in the old-time New York glory, not to nurse a Diet Coke. This is an ale-sodden madhouse most nights, and an Irish Armageddon on St. Patrick's Day. While it's also a McSorley's tradition to urinate on the wall outside, they prefer you honor that one in the breach, not in the commission.

✪ Temple Bar. 332 Lafayette St. (just north of Houston St.; look for the petroglyph-like lizards by the door). ☎ **212/925-4242.** Subway: B, D, F, Q to Broadway–Lafayette St.; 6 to Bleecker St.

Temple Bar is, hands down, my favorite lounge in the city. Members of the It crowd will tell you it's passe, which only serves to increase its appeal as far as I'm concerned— it's easy to get in now and, on weeknights at least, you can usually manage to find a comfy seat. One of the first comers to New York's lounge scene, Temple Bar is still a gorgeous art-deco hangout, with a long L-shaped bar leading to a lovely seating area with velvet drapes, romantic backlighting, and Sinatra softly crooning in the background. Cocktails simply don't get any better than the classic martini or the smooth-as–penoir silk Rob Roy. Pricey, but well worth the splurge. Bring a date—and feel free to invite me along anytime.

✪ Tom & Jerry's (288 Bar). 288 Elizabeth St. No phone. Subway: B, D, F, Q to Broadway–Lafayette St.; 6 to Bleecker St.

Here's an extremely pleasing neighborhood bar minus the grunge factor that usually plagues such joints. The place has an authentic local vibe, and the arty crowd is unpretentious and chatty. The beer selection is very good, and the mixed drinks are better than average. Flea-market hounds will enjoy the vintage collection of "Tom & Jerry" punchbowl sets behind the bar. There's no sign, but you'll spy the action through the plate-glass window on the east side of Elizabeth Street just north of Houston.

GREENWICH VILLAGE

Bar d'O. 29 Bedford St. (at Downing St.). ☎ **212/627-1580.** Subway: A, B, C, D, E, F, Q to W. 4th St. (use 3rd St. exit).

This intimate space is home to the Village's best lounge scene—which unfortunately makes it crowded, but still cozy and appealing. A different DJ sets the scene for the mixed gay/straight crowd nightly in this low-slung, candlelit space; but the real show is drag diva Joey Arias, who wows the crowd twice weekly (Tuesdays and Saturdays at press time) with her spot-on Billie Holliday renditions. Check for a cover charge on performance nights.

✪ Chumley's. 86 Bedford St. (btw. Grove and Barrow sts.). ☎ **212/675-4449.** Subway: 1, 9 to Christopher St.–Sheridan Sq.

A classic. Many bars in New York date their beginnings to Prohibition, but this former speakeasy still has the vibe. The circa college-age crowd doesn't date back nearly as far, however. Come to warm yourself by the fire and indulge in a once-forbidden pleasure: beer. The door is unmarked, with a metal grille on the small window. Another entrance is at 58 Barrow St., which takes you in through a back courtyard.

Peculier Pub. 145 Bleecker St. (btw. Thompson St. and La Guardia Place). ☎ **212/ 353-1327.** Subway: A, B, C, D, E, F, Q to W. 4th St.

This buzzy tavern is popular with NYU students and just-graduated professionals who come for the excellent beer selection—17 on tap and over 500 bottled beers from around the world—doled out by a staff that knows their stuff.

White Horse Tavern. 567 Hudson St. (at 11th St.). ☎ **212/989-3956.** Subway: 1, 9 to Sheridan Sq.

Poets and literary buffs pop into this 1880 wood-paneled pub to pay their respects to Dylan Thomas, who tipped his last jar here before shuffling off this mortal coil. Best enjoyed in the warm weather when there's outdoor drinking, or at happy hour for the cheap drafts.

THE FLATIRON DISTRICT, UNION SQUARE & GRAMERCY PARK

Heartland Brewery. 35 Union Sq. W. (16th St.). ☎ **212/645-3400.** Subway: 4, 5, 6, N, R, L to 14th St.–Union Sq.

The food leaves a bit to be desired, but the house-brewed beers are first-rate. Brewmaster Jim Migliorini's two-time award-winner, Farmer Jon's Oatmeal Stout, is always on hand, as are four other hand-crafted brews. The wood-paneled, two-level bar is big and appealing, but expect a loud, boisterous after-work crowd. There's now a Midtown location, too: 1285 Sixth Ave., at 51st Street (☎ 212/582-8244).

○ **Old Town Bar & Restaurant.** 45 E. 18th St. (btw. Broadway and Park Ave. S.). ☎ **212/ 529-6732.** Subway: 4, 5, 6, N, R, L to 14th St.–Union Sq.

This genuine tin-ceilinged, 19th-century bar is a terrific place to soak up some old New York atmosphere. You'll find lots of beers on tap, great pub grub, a youngish singles crowd packing the joint just about every night of the week, plus a blissfully smoke-free upstairs room. I like this place so much that I also listed it among my favorite restaurants; see chapter 6.

Pete's Tavern. 129 E. 18th St. (at Irving Place). ☎ **212/473-7676.** Subway: 4, 5, 6, N, R, L to 14th St./Union Sq.

Here's another old-timer. There's a sidewalk for summer imbibing, Guinness on tap, and a St. Patrick's Day party that make the neighbors crazy. But the best thing in Pete's (opened in 1864—while Lincoln was still president!) is the happy hour, where drinks are cheap and the crowd is a mix of locals from ritzy Gramercy Park and more down-to-earth types.

CHELSEA

Ciel Rouge. 176 Seventh Ave. (btw. 20th and 21st sts.). ☎ **212/929-5542.** Subway: 1, 9 to 23rd St.

Here's a haven for hip Francophiles in need of a shot of Left Bank lounging. Completing the red-hued scene are well-mixed drinks, decent food, and live music: either jazz piano, classical, or Piaf and Brel types conjuring up Gallic memories, depending on the night (no cover!).

Flight 151. 151 Eighth Ave. (16th and 17th sts.). ☎ **212/229-1868.** Subway: A, C, E to 14th St.; L to Eighth Ave.

This friendly bar is full of great deals: Monday launches the week with dollar drafts and $2.50 margaritas. On Tuesday night, the bartender flips a coin to see if you or the house is going to buy your next drink. Wednesday is "Let's Make a Deal" night: Pull a tab and pay what it says for your drink—full price, half price, or just 25¢. Thursday is trivia night: You be the first to call out the answer to a new trivia question every

15 minutes, and your drink is free. Weekend brunch is a $9.95 fete with unlimited champagne or mimosas. Even without the bargains, this popular aviation-themed hangout is affordable and very welcoming. There's now a second location, **Flight 1668,** on the Upper East Side at 1668 Third Ave., between 93rd and 94th streets (☎ 212/426-1416), offering the same bar specials.

Merchant's New York. 112 Seventh Ave. (at 17th St.). ☎ **212/366-7267.** Subway: 1, 9 to 18th St.

New York's young working crowd just loves this place, and for good reason: It's attractive, comfortable, and mixes a great martini. On the ground floor is an stylish bar, with a mezzanine for dinner. In the downstairs lounge a fireplace roars even in a heat wave, while air-conditioning delivers a polar blast. The crowd is a pleasing mix of yuppies looking for love, smart folks on dates, gays and straights, and friends chatting on the couches and chairs downstairs.

TIMES SQUARE & MIDTOWN WEST

Also consider the genuinely terrific bar at the original theme restaurant, **Hard Rock Cafe,** 221 W. 57th St., between Broadway and Seventh Avenue (☎ 212/459-9320), where you can groove to classic rock while you peruse a truly astounding collection of memorabilia (see "Theme Restaurant Thrills!" in chapter 6). There's also a second branch of **Heartland Brewery** (p. 327) at 1285 Sixth Ave., at 51st Street (☎ 212/582-8244).

✪ **The Algonquin.** 59 W. 44th St. (btw. Fifth and Sixth aves.), New York, NY 10036. ☎ **212/840-6800.** Subway: B, D, F, Q to 42nd St.

The past isn't just a memory anymore at this venerable literary landmark—a complete 1998 restoration returned the hotel to its full Arts-and-Crafts splendor. The oak-paneled lobby is the comfiest and most welcoming in the city, perfect for a pre- or post-theater cocktails. You'll feel the spirit of Dorothy Parker and the legendary Algonquin Round Table that pervades the room. Adjacent is the pubby, clubby **Blue Bar,** home to a rotating collection of Hirschfeld drawings.

Joe Allen. 326 W. 46th St. (btw. Eighth and Ninth aves.). ☎ **212/581-6464.** Subway: A, C, E to 42nd St.

An upscale pub peopled with Broadway types gives this atmospheric place the edge on Restaurant Row. More than 30 bottled beers are on the shelves and the walls are covered with posters from legendary Broadway flops. The bar is always hopping, but the American food is reliable and well-priced if you'd rather sit down at a table for a bite. Don't be surprised if you spot a star or two among the clientele.

Mickey Mantle's. 42 Central Park S. (btw. Fifth and Sixth aves). ☎ **212/688-7777.** Subway: B, Q to 57th St.

Of course, it's terribly sad that the Mick, who gave his life to the bottle, should have his name on a bar. But if you're a fan, it's definitely worth a visit to his sports bar and restaurant, which chronicles his life and career in photos. A great place to watch the game, too. Don Imus, a self-styled sports expert, has been known to wander in on occasion.

The Royalton. 44 W. 44th St. (btw. Fifth and Sixth aves.). ☎ **212/869-4400.** Subway: B, D, F, Q to 42nd St.

The Philippe Starck–designed lobby of this Ian Schrager hotel is still a major hangout for the fashionable crowd. The sunken lounge space features comfy seating nooks, an extensive martini list, and a light menu of excellent finger foods. Pricey but worth it if you want to see how the scenesters live. Come early to nab a seat in the marvelous

Round Bar, a 20-seat circular enclave done in high *Jetsons* style (on your right just past the invariably cute doorman).

The View Lounge. On the 48th floor of the New York Marriott Marquis, 1535 Broadway (btw. 45th and 46th sts.). ☎ **212/398-1900.** Subway: 1, 2, 3, 9, N, R to Times Sq.; N, R to 49th St.

If it's a clear night, head up to this aptly named three-story revolving rooftop bar for great views and decent cocktails. Grab a window seat if you can; it takes about an hour to see the 360-degree view of Times Square go by.

MIDTOWN EAST & MURRAY HILL

British Open. 320 E. 59th St. (btw. First and Second aves.). ☎ **212/355-8467.** Subway: 4, 5, 6 to 59th St.

Here's the perfect pub for golf lovers, or anybody who pines for a well-pulled pint and some good English grub. This charming local is more sophisticated than most, with a mahogany bar polished to a high sheen, a pretty dining room in back, and friendly, attentive service from an imported staff. I just love this place; last time I was in, the Scottish bartender and an English regular were debating the merits of Brad Pitt's Irish accent in *The Devil's Own.* You'll find Guinness, Bass, Fullers ESB, and other British imports on tap, and golf and other sports on the telly at all hours. (See chapter 6 for dining details.)

Divine Bar. 244 E. 51st St. (btw. Second and Third aves.). ☎ **212/319-9463.** Subway: 6 to 51st St.; E, F to Lexington Ave.

This glowing hacienda-style wine bar is a big hit with a cute and sophisticated under-40 crowd (think up-and-coming media types and you'll get the picture), with a few older patrons in the mix who come for the excellent selection of wines and microbrews rather than the pick-up scene. I prefer the more relaxed, fireplace-lit upstairs over the first floor bar. The DJ plays a radio-friendly mix, and there's live acoustic music on Sundays. Good tapas and an extensive humidor round out the appeal.

The Ginger Man. 11 E. 36th St. (btw. Fifth and Madison aves.). ☎ **212/532-3740.** Subway: 6 to 33rd St.

The big bait at this appealing and cigar-friendly beer bar is the 66 gleaming tap handles lining the wood-and-brass bar, dispensing everything from Sierra Nevada and Hoegaarden to cask-conditioned ales. The cavernous space has a clubby feel, as Cohiba-toking Wall Streeters lounge on sofas and chairs. The limited menu is well prepared, and prices are better than you'd expect from an upmarket place like this.

✪ King Cole Room. At the St. Regis hotel, 2 E. 55th St. (at Fifth Ave.). ☎ **212/339-6721.** Subway: E, F to 53rd St.

The birthplace of the Bloody Mary, this theatrical spot may just be New York's best hotel bar. The Maxfield Parrish mural alone is worth the high tab of a classic cocktail (ask the bartender to tell you about the "hidden" meaning of the painting). The sophisticated setting demands proper attire, so be sure to dress for the occasion. The *New York Times* calls the bar nuts "the best in town," but there's an elegant bar food menu if you'd like something more substantial.

✪ Mica Bar. 252 E. 51st St. (btw. Second and Third aves.). ☎ **212/888-2453.** Subway: 6 to 51st St.; E, F to Lexington Ave.

This cool, Japanese-inspired bar is one of my favorite places in the city for a romantic cocktail, or relaxed drinks with a small group of friends. You'll find comfortable, low-slung furniture and votives throughout the intimate bi-level space, with petite bonsai tucked into wall niches. The friendly staff serves up a terrific cocktail menu; try the saketini (Finlandia, sake, dry vermouth, cucumber) for a neat twist on the original. You'll also find good selections of beer, wine, sake, single malts, and brandies. Pan-Asian finger foods are also available. A bamboo open-air terrace adds extra appeal in warm weather.

Park Avenue Country Club. 381 Park Ave. S. (at 27th St.). ☎ **212/685-3636.** Subway: 6 to 28th St.

Despite the sophisticated name, this sports bar and restaurant is quite approachable, though a bit more polished than your average beer-and-pretzels sports bar. It's a very comfortable and wallet-friendly place to hunker down over a club sandwich and a beer to watch the game. There are TVs at every turn, and a nice mahogany bar serves up an extensive list of bottled and on-tap brews.

Top of the Tower. On the 26th floor of Beekman Tower, 3 Mitchell Place (First Ave. at 49th St.). ☎ **212/355-7300.** Subway: 6 to 51st St.

Location is everything, and this lounge has a great one overlooking glorious Manhattan. The art-deco room sets the mood for the view, which includes the romantic Empire State Building. A simply wonderful place to escape the urban bustle for a quiet, elegant drink. A pianist keeps the tone hushed and romantic after 9pm.

THE UPPER WEST SIDE

In addition to the choices below, also consider **Fez** at **Time Cafe North,** 2330 Broadway, at 85th St. (☎ **212/579-5100**), a second Moroccan-themed cafe from the people behind the ultra-groovy original Fez at Time Cafe in NoHo (see p. 314).

Boomer's Sports Club. 349 Amsterdam Ave. (btw. 76th and 77th sts.). ☎ **212/362-5400.** Subway: 1, 9 to 79th St.

Surprise, surprise: Jets quarterback Boomer Esiason's pub is a sports bar. Come here if you like to watch, talk, eat, and drink sports. The youngish yuppie crowd doesn't mind that the food is no great shakes, since the beer selection is extensive.

Hi-Life Bar & Grill. 477 Amsterdam Ave. (at 83rd St.). ☎ **212/787-7199.** Subway: 1, 9 to 86th St.

During the week, expect a few quiet drinks with a slightly older crowd in this casual retro-style bar and restaurant. Come the weekend, youth reigns, the volume cranks up, and the dating game zooms into full gear. The classic martinis couldn't be better.

O'Neal's. 49 W. 64th St. (btw. Broadway and Central Park W.). ☎ **212/787-4663.** Subway: 1, 9 to 66th St.

O'Neal's easy-going, old-time atmosphere makes it a favorite of the grown-up neighborhood crowd as well as students from nearby Juilliard. Only a stone's throw away from Lincoln Center, this is a great place for a pre-theater cocktail or a reasonably priced, if unremarkable, bite to eat.

Shark Bar. 307 Amsterdam Ave. (btw. 74th and 75th sts.). ☎ **212/874-8500.** Subway: 1, 2, 3, 9 to 72nd St.

This perennially popular spot is well known for its good soul food and even better singles' scene. It's also a favorite hangout for sports celebs, so don't be surprised if you spot a New York Knick or two.

THE UPPER EAST SIDE

There's also **Flight 1668,** 1668 Third Ave., between 93rd and 94th streets (☎ **212/426-1416**), offering the same big-drinking bar specials as sibling hangout **Flight 151** (p. 327).

Brandy's Piano Bar. 235 E. 84th St. (btw. Second and Third aves.). ☎ **212/650-1944.**
Subway: 4, 5, 6 to 86th St.

A mixed crowd—Upper East Side locals, waiters off work, gays, straights, all ages—
comes to this intimate, old-school piano bar for the friendly atmosphere and nightly
entertainment. The talented waitstaff does most of the singing while waiting for their
big break, but enthusiastic patrons join in on occasion.

Madison Pub. 1043 Madison Ave. (btw. 79th and 80th sts.). ☎ **212/650-1809.** Subway:
6 to 77th St.

Near the Metropolitan Museum of Art, Madison Pub is a neighborhood place that, if
it weren't for the tony address, you'd dismiss as a blue-collar bar. A fine place to nurse
a Rolling Rock and rest your museum-weary feet. The jukebox is a few decades out of
date, but that only adds to the appeal.

Subway Inn. 143 E. 60th St. (just east of Lexington Ave.). ☎ **212/223-8929.** Subway: 4,
5, 6 to 59th St.

Now, here's a dive bar if there ever was one—and that's precisely the Subway Inn's
charm. Every time I go to Bloomingdale's, I get a perverse joy at seeing this hole-in-
the-wall surviving in the shadow of the great department store, as the high-rent neighborhood around it grows more and more upscale and out-of-reach to the average Joes
inside. A great spot for hubbies to nurse a cheap beer while their wives exercise the
plastic next door. Note to film buffs: This was Montgomery Clift's local—he lived just
down the street for years.

7 Dance Clubs & Party Scenes

No slice of the New York nightlife pie is as mutable as the club scene. In this world,
hotspots don't even get 15 minutes of fame—their time in the limelight is usually
more like a commercial break.

First things first: Finding and going to the latest hotspot is not worth agonizing
over. Clubbers spend their lives obsessing over the scene. My rule of thumb is, if I
know about a place it must not be hip anymore. Even if I could tell you where the
hippest club kids were hangout today, chances are very good that they will have moved
on by the time you arrive in town. One big trend in recent years that makes the scene
so hard to chart is that "clubs" as actual, physical spaces don't mean much anymore.
The hungry-for-nightlife crowd now follows certain party "producers" who switch
venues and times each week. As the scene becomes more and more amorphous, venues
become less and less traditional. Lots of the bars and lounges listed in the previous section host "club" scenes on various nights of the week, such as—at press time, at least—
the super-popular Thursday night 1980s-themed BeavHer at **Coney Island High,** the
loungey Beige on Tuesdays at **B Bar,** the Mondo 107 strato-lounge party Wednesdays
at the **Greatest Bar on Earth,** and the Big 1980s–themed Reagan Death Watch at
Barmacy on Sundays.

The tracking game is best left to the perennial party crowd. Even if you manage to
make your way into the club du jour (after groveling to a meat-headed doorman, no
doubt), you'll find out that everyone looks supremely bored. Just find someplace that
amuses you, and enjoy the crowd that enjoys it with you.

In the listings below, I've concentrated on a wide variety of club scenes, from performance arty to perennially popular discos, most of which are generally easy to make
your way into. You can find listings for the most current hotspots and moveable parties in the sources listed at the start of this chapter. Another good bet is to cruise hip
boutiques in SoHo, the East Village, and the Lower East Side, where party planners

usually leave flyers advertising the latest goings-on. You might also check **www.models.com/night**, an online nightclubbing guide that can help you choose among current happenings; it's not comprehensive, but it can be useful if you're looking for a scene.

No matter what, **always call ahead,** because schedules change constantly, and can do so at the last minute.

MONEY MATTERS FOR NIGHTCLUBBERS Keep in mind that New York nightlife starts late. With the exception of places that have scheduled performances, it's almost useless to show up anywhere before about 11pm. Don't depend on plastic—bring cash, and plan on dropping a wad at most places. Cover charges start out high—anywhere from $10 to $25—and often get more expensive as the night wears on. Keep in mind that it's almost always cheaper to go clubbing on weeknights; cover charges are usually lower Sunday through Thursday, and some venues are free on select nights (often Sunday or Tuesday). *Time Out New York* is a great source to check, because it lists cover charges for the week's big events and clearly indicates which are free.

In addition to the choices below, lovers of Brazilian, Afro-Caribbean, and other world music should seriously consider ✪ **S.O.B's,** where top-notch live bands keep the party sizzling nightly. For S.O.B's and details on other club scenes with live music, see "Live Rock, Jazz, Blues & More" earlier in this chapter.

✪ **Baby Jupiter.** 170 Orchard St. (at Stanton St.). ☎ **212/982-BABY.** Subway: F to Second Ave.

This funny, funky place may look like a 1960s-style retro-diner restaurant, but it's actually becoming popular for its club scene. The weekly calendar features an ever-changing and increasingly eclectic mix of live music and DJ nights. At press time, the best of the bunch was Wednesday's Jungle Jazz, a wild mix of dub, jazz, jungle, and tap lines led by a high-BPM DJ and one-armed Italian trumpeter Fabio Morgera. You'd think the other nights would pale in comparison, but Thursday's funky soul and Saturday's tribal house offer equally esoteric fun. There's just a nominal cover charge—usually between $2 and $4—so you can afford to take the risk of arriving with just an open mind. Leave your Prada at home—this place caters to working arts and other edgy Lower East Side types.

China Club. 268 W. 47th St. (btw. Broadway and Eighth Ave.). ☎ **212/398-3800.** Subway: N, R to 49th St.

The China Club has been a top choice for club hoppers for years now, and it's still a great place to shake your booty. This huge club caters to both celebs and mere mortals drawn in by the top-flight sound system, high-style fiber-optic lighting, and a good, accessible dance music mix. Live acts perform once in awhile. Trendy types gravitate to the bar and VIP lounge, where Broadway hopefuls mix with famous faces like Christy Turlington and Rod Stewart on occasion. The cover is $20.

The Copacabana. 617 W. 57th St. (btw. Eleventh and Twelfth aves.). ☎ **212/582-2672.** Subway: 1, 9, A, B, C, D to 59th St.–Columbus Circle.

The Copa isn't exactly the hippest spot in town these days, but it does offer images of retro-glamour for the grown-up crowd that likes to groove to hot Latin sounds. There's a high cheese factor in the glittery Big 1980s vibe, but it's all part of the fun. The cover ranges from $5 to $20 (arrive early enough on Sunday and admission is free); men will usually pay slightly more than women. Take a cab to the far-west location.

Don Hill's. 511 Greenwich St. (at Spring St.). ☎ **212/219-2850.** Subway: 1, 9 to Canal St.; C, E to Spring St.

Getting Beyond the Velvet Rope

If your heart's set on getting into an exclusive club or lounge, here are a few pointers that may help to tip the scale in your favor:

- **Dress well and fashionably.** Like it or not, the doorman is sizing you up to decide if you're hip enough to make the scene. If you want to get in, you have to play along.
- **Arrive early.** Frankly, the bouncers are just not as vigilant at 9pm, when the place is half empty, as they are at 11pm—and once you're inside, you're in for the night if you wish. Weeknights are also a better bet.
- **Be polite.** No matter how obnoxious the doorman may be, giving attitude back won't help. And who knows? You might just charm him with your winning personality.
- **Don't try to talk your way in.** Don't drop names or make up some story to get in the door. These guys have heard it all. If you're not wanted, why bother? Take your business to a friendlier establishment, where you'll be happier in the long run.

This big and eclectic place changes faces constantly: Some nights it's a rock performance space featuring top-notch local talent, others it plays host to party nights. Look for Squeezebox (usually Thursday and Friday), a rollicking gay/straight party with a drag edge. The cover is usually $10.

Life. 158 Bleecker St. (Sullivan and Thompson sts.). ☎ **212/420-1999.** Subway: A, B, C, D, E, F, Q to W. 4th St.

A $12-million renovation of what used to be the venerable Village Gate jazz club instantly established this velvet-drenched, faux-deco nightclub as *the* clubbers' hotspot a few years back, and it just keeps on going (although it's a bit easier to get in these days). The formula changes nightly, from super-fashionable Lifestyle Fridays to 1980s retro-glammy Lust for Life on Wednesdays to Boy's Life Sundays, which draws beautiful Chelsea boys looking for the same. The cover ranges from $10 to $20, depending on the night.

✪ **Mother.** 432 W. 14th St. (at Washington St.). ☎ **212/366-5680.** Subway: A, C, E to 14th St.

Fabulous hipsters, both gay and straight, crowd this joint for a variety of hugely popular events. On Tuesday it's Jackie 60 (☎ 212/929-6060; www.echonyc.com/~interjackie), which *Paper* magazine calls "the mother of all freak fests." Boys and girls dress up in drag based on the night's theme, which can get pretty twisted (witness the recent "Daddy's Little Prostitute: The JonBenet Ramsey Story"), yet the party always manages an upbeat, enthusiastic vibe. Almost as popular is Saturday's Click + Drag, a futuristic techno-fetish party from the same team. Performance art, poetry readings, and other multimedia fun round out the goings-on. The cover ranges from $5 to $15; call to check if a strict dress code is being enforced the night you go.

✪ **Nell's.** 246 W. 14th St. (btw. Seventh and Eighth aves.). ☎ **212/675-1567.** Subway: 1, 2, 3, 9, A, C, E to 14th St.

Nell's was the first to establish a loungelike atmosphere years ago. It has been endlessly copied by restaurateurs and nightclub owners, who have since realized that if people wanted to stay home, why not make "out" just as comfy as "in?" Nell's attracts everyone from homies to Wall Streeters. Most of the parties have a soulful edge. Look

It Might As Well Be Swing

It may have taken some time for the swing thing to make its way to the right coast, but New York has taken to it with a vengeance.

Swing is a nightly affair at **Swing 46,** a jazz and supper club on the Theater District's Restaurant Row at 349 W. 46th St. (☎ **212/262-9554**). There's live swing every night at 10pm from big bands with names like the Flipped Fedoras and the Crescent City Maulers, as well as the club's own 15-piece Make-Believe Ballroom Orchestra. The young, enthusiastic crowd dresses to the nines, 1940s style, and really knows the moves. The cover is just $7 weeknights, $12 weekends, and free swing lessons (at 7 and 9pm) are part of the package.

On weekends, the best place to get jiggy is the **Supper Club,** 240 W. 47th St., between Broadway and Eighth Avenue (☎ **212/921-1940**), an ultra-plush dance hall that's been dressed and waiting for the swing trend to come along for a few years now. The 16-piece house band plays old-school swing every Friday and Saturday night early on for an older supper crowd. Later in the evening, around 11pm, the tables are cleared and the neo-swingers show up to strut their stuff to an ultra-hot visiting jump band like Zoot Suit Revue, Harlem's Yallopin' Hounds, or Swingerhead. Come after 11pm, when the $20 cover drops to $15.

Another terrific spot for swing is **The Greatest Bar on Earth,** high atop 1 World Trade Center on the 107th floor (☎ **212/524-7000**). The live jive from circuit bands like the Camaros and the Blue Saracens starts Friday and Saturday at 9pm; there's also a mambo party on Thursday for a little Latin-flavored swing. The dance floor is big enough for everybody to enjoy but small enough that you don't feel like you're on display. And no dance floor has more spectacular views. The cover runs $5 to $15.

For the latest on the local neo-swing scene from the man behind the Supper Club's success, "Lo-Fi" Lee Sobel, check out **www.nycswing.com.** Lo-Fi Lee always has a swing party going on, and at press time had just introduced swing to the tony **Tatou Supper Club,** 151 E. 50th St., between Lexington and Third avenues (☎ **212/753-1144**). Tatou Swings! features live first-rate bands and dance lessons every Thursday night for $15.

In the Village, do the swing thing for free at **Louisiana Community Bar & Grill,** 622 Broadway, at Houston Street (☎ **212/460-9633**), which is booking more and more swing bands on its weekly schedule.

Serious folks who know that swing transcends its fad status belong to the **New York Swing Dance Society** (☎ **212/696-9737**), which holds its weekly Savoy Sundays at Irving Plaza. This event is for all ages and abilities and there's no dress code, so you don't have to worry about impressing the cool cats around you. Free dance lessons are offered the first Sunday of the month. Tickets are $13 ($5 for seniors).

for the hugely popular laid-back Voices, sort of a sophisticated weekly *Star Search* that's a showcase for a surprising number of new talents. The cover runs $10 to $15.

Polly Esther's. 1487 First Ave. (btw. 77th and 78th sts.). ☎ **212/628-4477.** Subway: 6 to 77th St. Also at 186 W. 4th St. (btw. Sixth and Seventh aves.). ☎ **212/924-5707.** Subway: 1, 9 to Christopher St.–Sheridan Sq.

Here's the ultimate 1970s theme club, where you can groove to the sounds of K. C. and the Sunshine Band, Gloria Gaynor, the Bee Gees, Abba, and every other band you loved when you still listened to AM radio and turned the dial on the TV set. This cheesy place is geared to tourists, but who cares? Dig out those bellbottoms, tie on those platform shoes, and hustle on over to Polly Esther's for a nostalgic good time. Arrive before 10pm to avoid the $8 cover (no cover on Wednesday and Thursday).

If you're more Karma Chameleon than Dancing Queen, then head to the similarly silly **Culture Club,** 179 Varick St., between King and Charlton streets (☎ 212/ 243-1999), where the big 1980s come to life.

Roxy. 515 W. 18th St. (at Tenth Ave.). ☎ **212/645-5156.** Subway: 1, 9 to 18th St.

This club scene stalwart could be the single best place to see the Manhattan night mix, worth the (usually) $20 cover. You'll find fashion models, city club kids, wide-eyed kids from the 'burbs, straights and gays of every color, lights, sound, and action. At press time, the schedule featured in-line roller disco on Tuesday (predominantly gay) and Wednesday (mixed). Friday nights draw a big hetero Hispanic crowd with salsa and merengue, while Saturdays bring in a committed, mostly gay crowd in love with DJ Victor Calderone's tribal house mix. There's also a martini lounge, a cigar bar, and two VIP rooms.

✪ **13.** 35 E. 13th St. (btw. Broadway and University Place), 2nd floor. ☎ **212/979-6677.** Subway: 4, 5, 6, N, R, L to Union Sq.

This little lounge is a great place to dance the night away. It's stylish but unpretentious, with a steady roster of fun weekly parties. I'm thrilled that Sunday night's no-cover Britpop fest Shout! lives on, as popular as ever. Other regular highlights include Wednesday's Beep, a friendly progressive beat party (also free); and DJ Cadet spinning an appealing dance mix that ranges from 1970s disco to current hip-hop on Friday and Saturday. Monday is poetry and spoken-word night. If there's a cover, it's usually just $5. Arrive extra early, between 4 and 8pm, for two-for-one happy hour.

Twilo. 530 W. 27th St. (btw. Tenth and Eleventh aves.). ☎ **212/268-1600.** www. twiloclub.com. Subway: C, E to 23rd St.

Go west—way west—to this mega-size dance factory. Superstar DJ Junior Vasquez still spins pulsating dance music marathons, called Juniorverse, for an adoring, mostly gay crowd on Saturdays. Twilo Fridays draws an energized straight crowd with imported international DJs. Expect a hefty $25 cover; occasional Sunday dance parties are less.

XIT. 511 Lexington Ave. (btw. 47th and 48th sts.). ☎ **212/371-1600.** Subway: 4, 5, 6, 7 to Grand Central.

The former home of urban hoedown Denim & Diamonds has been transformed into a popular baby-boomer hangout, where thirty-, forty-, and fiftysomethings boogie to a mainstream mix of tunes from the 1960s to the top hits of today. Tuesday is country night, Wednesday is salsa night, and Thursday is reserved for swing. The owners have issued a "no attitude" promise to the press, so everyone should feel comfortable here. Admission is $10.

Vinyl. 6 Hubert St. (btw. Hudson and Collister sts.). ☎ **212/343-1379.** Subway: 1, 9 to Canal St.

This commodious TriBeCa club welcomes a big, mixed black/white, gay/straight crowd to hip-hop– and house-flavored party nights ruled by a terrific crop of DJs. Best of all is the long-lived Body and Soul, a Sunday afternoon acid-garage-house party that's on its way to becoming a legend. Also look for Planet V, a hugely popular monthly jungle party. Covers run $12 to $20.

Webster Hall. 125 E. 11th St. (btw. Third and Fourth aves.). ☎ **212/353-1600.** www. webster-hall.com. Subway: 6 to Astor Place.

Five floors and a seemingly endless warren of rooms mean that there's something for everyone at this old war horse of a nightclub. Even though it's dominated by a bridge-and-tunnel crowd, Webster Hall is still a plenty interesting place to hang on the weekends, especially if you're looking for a straightforward crowd and music mix. Expect to wait in line to get in. The standard cover is $22, but add your name to the guest list via the Web, and you can enter for as little as $5 before midnight. Ladies free on Thursdays.

8 The Lesbian & Gay Scene

To get a thorough, up-to-date take on what's happening in gay and lesbian nightlife, pick up a free copy of *Homo Xtra (HX)* or *HX for Her,* the best guides to the gay scene. They're available for free in bars and clubs or at the Lesbian and Gay Community Center (see "Tips for Travelers with Special Needs" in chapter 2). Both mags also have information online at **www.hx.com.** *Time Out New York* also boasts a notable gay and lesbian section, and the Web sites at the start of this chapter are also good sources.

These days, many bars, clubs, cabarets, and lounges are neither gay nor straight but a bit of both, either catering to a mixed crowd or to varying orientations on different nights of the week. In addition to the choices below, most of the clubs listed under "Dance Clubs & Party Scenes," above cater to a gay crowd, some predominately so; see what's happening at **Don Hill's, Life, Mother, Roxy, Twilo,** the **Tunnel,** and **Vinyl.** The **Duplex Cabaret** is at the heart of the gay cabaret scene (see "Comedy & Cabaret," above). Among bars and cocktail lounges, consider **Lucky Cheng's** and **Bar d'O** (particularly on nights the phenomenal Joey Arias is performing) if you're looking for a predominately gay crowd.

Axis. 17 W. 19th St. (btw. Fifth and Sixth aves.). ☎ **212/633-1717.** Subway: 1, 9 to 18th St.; F to 23rd St.

If your idea of masculine beauty is buffed bodies and beefed go-go boys, Axis is your ideal club. Very big, very popular, very cruisy. Watch for the weekly DJ parties, the best of which is Subliminal, probably the hottest house party in town.

✪ **Barracuda.** 275 W. 22nd St. (btw. Seventh and Eighth aves.). ☎ **212/645-8613.** Subway: 1, 9 or C, E to 23rd St.

This trendy, loungey place was voted "Best Bar" by *HX* and *New York Press* magazines, while *Paper* singles out the hunky bartenders. There's a sexy bar for cruising out front, and a comfy lounge in back. Look for the regular drag shows.

Boiler Room. 86 E. 4th St. (btw. First and Second aves.). ☎ **212/254-7536.** Subway: F to Second Ave.

This East Village dive is a serious cruising scene for well-sculpted beautiful boys who just love to pose. There's plenty of space to lounge, shoot pool, or just listen to the rock-heavy jukebox. Girls who like girls take over the house once a month, usually on a Sunday.

Crazy Nanny's. 21 Seventh Ave. South (at Leroy St.). ☎ **212/366-6312.** Subway: 1, 9 to Houston St.

This longstanding lesbian bar is huge and hugely popular with women on the make. There's two floors, two bars, dancing, and a variety of theme nights. Especially popular with out-of-towners.

g. 223 W. 19th St. (btw. Seventh and Eighth aves.). ☎ **212/929-1085.** Subway: 1, 9 to 18th St.

Big crowds of muscular, designer-dressed men have made this lovely lounge a popular style scene for meeting dream dates. Excellent DJs set the stage.

Hangar Bar. 115 Christopher St. (btw. Bleecker and Bedford sts.). ☎ **212/627-2044.** Subway: 1, 9 to Christopher St.–Sheridan Sq.

Across from Ty's (below), this easygoing men's hangout has a big window that lets you watch who's walking Christopher. Excellent happy-hour drink specials make this a pick-up scene from early in the evening.

Hell. 59 Gansevoort St. (btw. Washington and Greenwich sts.). ☎ **212/727-1666.** Subway: A, C, E to 14th St.

This glamorous lounge is a sexy haven for a predominately gay crowd in a sketchy section of the meat-packing district. The cocktails are well mixed, and plenty of comfy sofas are on hand for getting cozy. Do yourself a favor and take a cab.

Henrietta Hudson. 438 Hudson St. (at Morton St.). ☎ **212/924-3347.** Subway: 1, 9 to Houston St.

This friendly and extremely popular women's bar is known for drawing in an attractive crowd that comes for the great jukebox and videos as well as the pleasingly low-key atmosphere.

✪ **Meow Mix.** 269 E. Houston St. (btw. avenues A and B) ☎ **212/254-0688.** Subway: F to Second Ave.

This funky two-level East Villager is the city's best and most popular lesbian hangout. It draws in a young, attractive, arty crowd with nightly diversions like groovy DJs and the hugely popular Xena Night. Meow Mix is also booking an increasing number of good local bands, with most nights dedicated to the girls but one night set aside for all-boy bands.

Splash. 50 W. 17th St. (at Sixth Ave.). ☎ **212/691-0073.** Subway: 1, 9 to 18th St.; F to 14th St.

Preppy gays mix with gym bunnies to watch go-go guys get wet onstage. This recently redone bi-level place is most popular at happy hour—in fact, at all hours. The crowd includes lots of visitors as well as locals.

Stonewall. 53 Christopher St. (just east of Seventh Ave. South). ☎ **212/463-0950.** Subway: 1, 9 to Christopher St.–Sheridan Sq.

A new bar at the spot where it all started. A mixed male crowd—old and young, beautiful and interesting—makes this an easy place to begin.

Ty's. 114 Christopher St. (at Bedford St.). ☎ **212/741-9641.** Subway: 1, 9 to Sheridan Sq.

Here's a very friendly, unassuming gay bar that's been a part of the Christopher Street men's cruise scene for about a million years.

The Web. 40 E. 58th St. (btw. Madison and Park aves.) ☎ **212/308-1546.** Subway: 4, 5, 6, N, R to 59th/60th sts.

Formerly known as Club 58, this subterranean complex offers many different events throughout the week, sometimes with a door charge (call for specifics). You might find go-go boys, drag shows, and other diversions for the heavily Asian crowd. The dance floor gets crowded on weekends after midnight. Go late or it's Dullsville.

✪ **Wonder Bar.** 505 E. 6th St. (btw. avenues A and B). ☎ **212/777-9105.** Subway: 6 to Astor Place.

The "sofa look" has lent a loungier, more stylish tone to this packed-on-weekends East Village hangout. There's some male cruising, but fun-and-friendly Wonder Bar gets points for making straights feel welcome, too. DJs now spin a listener-friendly mix from the revamped back room.

Frommer's Online Directory

by Michael Shapiro

Michael Shapiro is the author of *Internet Travel Planning*
(The Globe Pequot Press).

Frommer's Online Directory is a new feature designed to help you take advantage of the Internet to better plan your trip. Part I lists some general Internet resources that can make any trip easier, such as sites for booking airline tickets. It's not meant to be a comprehensive list—it's a discriminating selection of useful sites to get you started. In Part II you'll find some top online guides specifically for New York, which cover local lodging, the top attractions, and getting around.

1 The Top Travel-Planning Web Sites

Among the most popular sites are online travel agencies. The top agencies, including Expedia, Preview Travel, and Travelocity, offer an array of tools that are valuable even if you don't book online. You can check flight schedules, hotel availability, car-rental prices, or even get paged if your flight is delayed.

While online agencies have come a long way over the past few years, they don't *always* yield the best price. Unlike a travel agent, for example, they're unlikely to tell you that you can save money by flying a day earlier or a day later. On the other hand, if you're looking for a bargain fare, you might find something online that an agent wouldn't take the time to dig up. Because airline commissions have been cut, a travel agent may not find it worthwhile spending half an hour trying to find you the best deal. On the Net, you can be your own agent and take all the time you want.

Online booking sites aren't the only places to book airline tickets—all major airlines have their own Web sites and often offer incentives, such as bonus frequent-flyer miles or Net-only discounts, for buying online. These incentives have helped airlines capture the majority of the online booking market.

Below are the Web sites for the major airlines serving New York's airports. These sites offer schedules and flight booking, and most have pages where you can sign up for e-mail alerts on weekend deals.

Aer Lingus. www.aerlingus.ie
Air Canada. www.aircanada.ca
America West. www.americawest.com
American. www.americanair.com
British Airways. www.british-airways.com
Canadian Airlines. www.cdair.ca
Continental. www.flycontinental.com
Delta. www.delta-air.com

Northwest. www.nwa.com
TWA. www.twa.com
US Airways. www.usairways.com
United. www.ual.com
Virgin Atlantic. www.fly.virgin.com

WHEN SHOULD YOU BOOK ONLINE?

Online booking is not for everyone. If you prefer to let others handle your travel arrangements, one call to an experienced travel agent should suffice. But if you want to know as much as possible about your options, the Net is a good place to start, especially for bargain hunters.

The most compelling reason to use online booking is to take advantage of last-minute specials, such as American Airlines' weekend deals or other Internet-only fares that must be purchased online. Another advantage is that you can cash in on incentives for booking online, such as rebates or bonus frequent-flyer miles.

Online booking works best for trips within North America; for international tickets, it's usually cheaper and easier to use a travel agent or consolidator.

Online booking is certainly not for those with a complex international itinerary. If you require follow-up services, such as itinerary changes, use a travel agent. Though Expedia and some other online agencies employ travel agents available by phone, these sites are geared primarily for self-service.

LEADING BOOKING SITES

Below are listings for the top travel-booking sites. The starred selections are the most useful and best designed sites.

Cheap Tickets. www.cheaptickets.com
Essentials: Discounted rates on domestic and international airline tickets and hotel rooms.

Sometimes discounters such as Cheap Tickets have exclusive deals that aren't available through more mainstream channels. Registration at Cheap Tickets requires inputting a credit-card number before getting started, which is one reason many people elect to call the company's toll-free number rather than booking online. Cheap Tickets actually regards this policy as a selling point, arguing that "lookers" who don't intend to buy will be scared off and won't bog down the site with their queries. If Cheap Tickets is serious about getting people to use its online booking service, it should abolish this credit card–first approach.

Despite its misguided credit-card policy, Cheap Tickets is worth the effort because its fares can be substantially lower than those offered by its competitors.

✪ Expedia. expedia.com
Essentials: Domestic and international flights, plus hotel and rental-car booking; late-breaking travel news, destination features, and commentary from travel experts; deals on cruises and vacation packages. Free registration is required for booking.

Factoid ————————————————————————————————————

Far more people look online than book online, partly due to fear of putting their credit cards through on the Net. Though secure encryption has made this fear less justified, there's no reason why you can't find a flight online and then book it by calling a toll-free number or contacting your travel agent. To be sure you're in secure mode when you book online, look for a little icon of a key (in Netscape) or a padlock (Internet Explorer) at the bottom of your Web browser.

Take a Look at Frommer's Site

We highly recommend Arthur Frommer's Budget Travel Online (**www. frommers.com**) as an excellent travel-planning resource. Of course, we're a little biased, but you will find indispensable travel tips, reviews, monthly vacation give-aways, and online booking.

Subscribe to Arthur Frommer's Daily Newsletter (**www.frommers.com/ newsletters**) to receive the latest travel bargains and inside travel secrets in your mailbox every day. You'll read daily headlines and articles from the dean of travel himself, highlighting last-minute deals on airfares, accommodations, cruises, and package vacations. You'll also find great travel advice by checking our Tip of the Day or Hot Spot of the Month.

Search our Destinations archive (**www.frommers.com/destinations**) of more than 200 domestic and international destinations for great places to stay, tips for traveling there, and what to do while you're there. Once you've researched your trip, you might try our online reservation system (**www.frommers.com/ booktravelnow**) to book your dream vacation at affordable prices.

Expedia makes it easy to handle flight, hotel, and car booking on one itinerary, so it's a good place for one-stop shopping. Expedia's hotel search offers crisp, zoomable maps to pinpoint most properties; click on the camera icon to see images of the rooms and facilities. But like many online databases, Expedia focuses on the major chains, such as Hilton and Hyatt, so don't expect to find too many one-of-a-kind boutique hotels or B&Bs here.

Once you're registered (it's only necessary to do this once from each computer you use), you can start booking with the Roundtrip Fare Finder box on the home page, which expedites the process. After selecting a flight, you can hold it until midnight the following day or purchase online. If you think you might do better through a travel agent, you'll have time to try to get a lower price. And you may do better with a travel agent because Expedia's computer reservation system does not include all airlines. Most notably absent are some leading budget carriers, such as Southwest Airlines, which doesn't serve New York's major airports, but has begun service to Long Island. (*Note:* At press time, Travelocity was the only major booking service that includes Southwest.)

Expedia's World Guide, offering destination information, is a glaring weakness; it takes lots of page views to get very little information. However, Expedia compensates by linking to other Microsoft Network services, such as its Sidewalk city guides, which offer entertainment and dining advice.

Preview Travel. www.previewtravel.com
Essentials: Domestic and international flights, plus hotel and rental-car booking; Travel Newswire lists fare sales; deals on cruises and vacation packages. Free (one-time) registration is required for booking. Preview offers express booking for members, but at presstime, this feature was buried below the fold on Preview's reservation page.

Preview features the most inviting interface for booking trips, though the wealth of graphics can make the site somewhat slow. Use Farefinder to quickly find the lowest current fares on flights to dozens of major cities. Carfinder offers a similar service for rental cars, but you can only search airport locations, not city pick-up sites. To see the lowest fare for your itinerary, input the dates and times for your route and see what Preview comes up with.

In recent years Preview and other leading booking services have added features such as Best Fare Finder, so after Preview searches for the best deal on your itinerary, it will check flights that are a bit later or earlier to see if it might be cheaper to fly at a different time. While these searches have become quite sophisticated, they still occasionally overlook deals that might be uncovered by a top-notch travel agent. If you have the time, see what you can find online and then call an agent to see if you can get a better price.

With Preview's Fare Alert feature, you can set fares for up to three routes and you'll receive e-mail notices when the fare drops below your target amount. For example, you could tell Preview to alert you when the fare from Chicago to New York drops below $250. If it does, you'll get an e-mail telling you the current fare.

Minor quibbles: When you search for a fare or hotel (at least when we went to press), Preview launches an annoying little "Please Wait" window that gets in the way of the main browser window, even when your results begin to appear. The hotel search feature is intuitive, but the images and maps aren't as crisp as those at Expedia. Also, all sorts of information that's irrelevant to travelers (such as NYC public school locations) is listed on the maps.

Note to AOL Users: You can book flights, hotels, rental cars and cruises on AOL at keyword: Travel. The booking software is provided by Preview Travel and is similar to Preview on the Web. Use the AOL "Travelers Advantage" program to earn a 5% rebate on flights, hotel rooms, and car rentals.

Priceline.com. www.priceline.com

Even people who aren't familiar with too many Web sites have heard of Priceline.com, which lets you "name your price" for domestic and international airline tickets. In other words, you select a route and dates, guarantee with a credit card, and make a bid for what you're willing to pay. If one of the airlines in Priceline's database has a fare that's lower than your bid, your credit card will automatically be charged for a ticket.

But you can't say when you want to fly—you have to accept any flight leaving between 6am and 10pm, and you may have to make a stopover. No frequent-flyer miles are awarded, and tickets are non-refundable and can't be exchanged for another flight. So if your plans change, you're out of luck. Priceline can be good for travelers who have to take off on short notice (and who are thus unable to qualify for advance-purchase discounts). But be sure to shop around first—if you overbid, you'll be required to purchase the ticket and Priceline will pocket the difference.

Travelocity. www.travelocity.com

Essentials: Domestic and international flight, hotel and rental-car booking; deals on cruises and vacation packages. Travel Headlines spotlights latest bargain airfares. Free (one-time) registration is required for booking.

Travelocity almost got it right. Its Express Booking feature enables travelers to complete the booking process more quickly than they could at Expedia or Preview, but Travelocity gums up the works with a page called "Featured Airlines." Big placards of several featured airlines compete for your attention. If you want to see the fares for *all* available airlines, click the much smaller box at the bottom of the page labeled "Book a Flight."

Some have worried that Travelocity, which is owned by American Airlines' parent company AMR, directs bookings to American. This doesn't seem to be the case—I've booked there dozens of times and have always been directed to the cheapest listed flight, for example on Tower or ATA. There are rewards for choosing one of the featured airlines. You'll get 1,500 bonus frequent-flyer miles if you book through United's site, for example, but the site doesn't tell you about other airlines that might be cheaper. If the United flight costs $150 more than the best deal on another airline, it's not worth spending the extra money for a relatively small number of bonus miles.

On the plus side, Travelocity has some leading-edge techie tools. Exhibit A is Fare Watcher E-mail, an "intelligent agent" that keeps you informed of the best fares offered for the city pairs (round-trips) of your choice. Whenever the fare changes by $25 or more, Fare Watcher will alert you by e-mail. Exhibit B is Flight Paging: If you own an alphanumeric pager with national access that can receive e-mail, Travelocity's paging system can alert you if your flight is delayed. Finally, though Travelocity doesn't include every budget airline, it does include Southwest, the leading U.S. budget carrier, which now flies into Long Island's Islip Airport.

FINDING LODGINGS ONLINE

While the services above offer hotel booking, it can be best to use a site devoted primarily to lodging; you may find properties that aren't listed on more general online travel agencies. Some lodging sites specialize in a particular type of accommodation, such as B&Bs, which you won't find on the more mainstream booking services. Other services, such as TravelWeb, offer weekend deals on major chain properties, which cater to business travelers and have more empty rooms on weekends.

All Hotels on the Web. www.all-hotels.com
Well, this site doesn't include *all* the hotels on the Web, but it does have tens of thousands of listings throughout the world. Bear in mind that each hotel listed has paid a small fee ($25 and up) for placement, so it's not an objective list but more like a book of online brochures.

Hotel Reservations Network. www.180096hotel.com
Bargains on room rates at hotels in more than two dozen U.S. cities. The cool thing is that HRN pre-books blocks of rooms in advance, so sometimes it has rooms—at discount rates—at hotels that are "sold out." Select a city, input your dates, and you'll get a list of best prices for a selection of hotels. Descriptions include an image of the property and a locator map (to book online, click the "Book Now" button). HRN is notable for some deep discounts, even in cities where hotel rooms are expensive. The toll-free number is printed all over this site; call it if you want more options than are listed online.

InnSite. www.innsite.com
B&B listings for inns in all 50 U.S. states and dozens of countries around the globe.

Find an inn at your destination, have a look at images of the rooms, check prices and availability, and then send e-mail to the innkeeper if you have further questions. This is an extensive directory of B&Bs, but only includes listings if the proprietor submitted one (note: it's free to get an inn listed). The descriptions are written by the innkeepers and many listings link to the inn's own Web sites, where you can find more information and images.

Places to Stay. www.placestostay.com
Mostly one-of-a-kind places in the United States and abroad that you might not find in other directories, with a focus on resorts. Again, listing is selective—this isn't a comprehensive directory, but can give you a sense of what's available at different destinations.

Quikbook. www.quikbook.com
Though Quikbook only lists hotels in seven U.S. cities (including New York), it offers some good rates on these properties, such as rooms for under $200 at Manhattan's Omni, where the rack rate is as high as $389. Lists of amenities and expandable images of the hotel, rooms, and lobby round out Quikbook's listings.

✪ TravelWeb. www.travelweb.com

TravelWeb lists more than 16,000 hotels worldwide, focusing on chains such as Hyatt and Hilton, and you can book almost 90% of these online. TravelWeb's Click-It Weekends, updated each Monday, offers weekend deals at many leading hotel chains. TravelWeb is the online home for Pegasus Systems, which provides transaction processing systems for the hotel industry.

LAST-MINUTE DEALS & OTHER ONLINE BARGAINS

There's nothing airlines hate more than flying with lots of empty seats. The Net has enabled airlines to offer last-minute bargains to entice travelers to fill those seats. Most of these are announced on Tuesday or Wednesday and are valid for travel the following weekend, but some can be booked weeks or months in advance. You can sign up for weekly e-mail alerts at airlines' sites (see above) or check sites such as WebFlyer (see below) that compile lists of these bargains. To make it easier, visit a site (see below) that will round up all the deals and send them in one convenient weekly e-mail. But last-minute deals aren't the only online bargains; some of the sites below can help you find value even if you can't wait until the eleventh hour.

✪ 1travel.com. www.1travel.com

Deals on domestic and international flights, cruises, hotels, and all-inclusive resorts such as Club Med.

1travel.com's Saving Alert compiles last-minute air deals so you don't have to scroll through multiple e-mail alerts. A feature called "Drive a little using low-fare airlines" helps map out strategies for using alternate airports to find lower fares. And Farebeater searches a database that includes published fares, consolidator bargains, and special deals exclusive to 1travel.com. *Note:* The travel agencies listed by 1travel.com have paid for placement.

BestFares. www.bestfares.com

Budget seeker Tom Parsons lists some great bargains on airfares, hotels, rental cars, and cruises, but the site is poorly organized. News Desk is a long list of hundreds of bargains, but they're not broken down into cities or even countries, so it's not easy trying to find what you're looking for. If you have time to wade through it, you might find a good deal. Some material is available only to paid subscribers.

Go4less.com. www.go4less.com

Specializing in last-minute cruise and package deals, Go4less has some eye-popping offers, such as off-peak Caribbean cruises for under $100 per day. The site has a clean design but the bargains aren't organized by destination. However, you avoid sifting through all this material by using the Search box and entering vacation type, destination, month, and price.

Moment's Notice. www.moments-notice.com

As the name suggests, Moment's Notice specializes in last-minute vacation and cruise deals. You can browse for free, but if you want to purchase a trip, you have to join Moment's Notice, which costs $25.

Smarter Living. www.smarterliving.com

Best known for its e-mail dispatch of weekend deals on 20 airlines, Smarter Living also keeps you posted about last-minute bargains on everything from Windjammer Cruises to flights to Iceland.

✪ WebFlyer. www.webflyer.com

WebFlyer is the ultimate online resource for frequent flyers and also has an excellent listing of last-minute air deals. Click on "Deal Watch" for a round-up of weekend deals on flights, hotels, and rental cars from domestic and international suppliers.

While most people learn about last-minute weekend deals from e-mail dispatches, it can be best to find out precisely when these deals become available and check airlines' Web sites yourself at this time. To find out when bargains will be announced, check the pages devoted to these deals on airlines' Web pages. Because these offerings are limited, seats can vanish within hours (sometimes even minutes), so it pays to log on as soon as they're available. An example: Southwest's specials are posted at 12:01am Tuesdays (Central time). So if you're looking for a cheap flight, stay up late and check Southwest's site to grab the best new deals.

TRAVELER'S TOOLKIT

○ CultureFinder. www.culturefinder.com
Up-to-date listings for plays, opera, classical music, dance, film, and other cultural events in more than 1,300 U.S. cities. Enter the dates you'll be in a city and get a list of events; you can also purchase tickets online.

Intellicast. www.intellicast.com
Weather forecasts for all 50 states and cities around the world.

○ MapQuest. www.mapquest.com
Specializing in U.S. maps, MapQuest enables you to zoom in on a destination, calculate step-by-step driving directions between any two U.S. points, and locate restaurants, hotels, and other attractions on maps.

○ Net café Guide. www.netcafeguide.com
Locate Internet cafes at hundreds of locations around the globe. Catch up on your e-mail, log onto the Web, and stay in touch with the home front, usually for just a few dollars per hour.

TheTrip: Airport Maps and Flight Status. www.thetrip.com
A business-travel site where you can find out when an airborne flight is scheduled to arrive. Click on "Guides and Tools" to peruse airport maps for more than 40 domestic cities.

Visa. www.visa.com/pd/atm/
MasterCard. www.mastercard.com/atm
Find Cirrus and Plus ATMs in hundreds of cities in the United States and around the world. Both include maps for some locations and both list airport ATM locations, some with maps. Remarkably, MasterCard lists ATMs on all seven continents (there's one at Antarctica's McMurdo Station). Tip: You'll usually get a better exchange rate using ATMs than exchanging traveler's checks at banks.

2 The Top Web Sites for New York City

CITY GUIDES

City guides are a good way to get acquainted with what's going on in New York. While some are geared toward residents, they can still be excellent for travelers who want to read a theatrical review, find out what's on at the Met, or get ideas about what to see and do.

○ CitySearch: New York. www.newyork.citysearch.com
Reviews and listings for arts and entertainment, restaurants, shopping, hotels, and attractions.

Check Your E-Mail While You're on the Road

Until a few years ago, most travelers who checked their e-mail while traveling carried a laptop, but this posed some problems. Not only are laptops expensive, but they can be difficult to configure, incur expensive connection charges, and are attractive to thieves. Thankfully, Web-based free e-mail programs have made it much easier to stay in touch.

Just open an account at a freemail provider, such as Hotmail (hotmail.com) or Yahoo! Mail (mail.yahoo.com), and all you'll need to check your mail is a Web connection, easily available at Net cafes and copy shops around the world. After logging on, just point the browser to www.hotmail.com, enter your username and password and you'll have access to your mail.

Internet cafes have become ubiquitous, so for a few dollars an hour you'll be able to check your mail and send messages back to colleagues, friends, and family. If you already have a primary e-mail account, you can set it to forward mail to your freemail account while you're away. Freemail programs have become enormously popular (Hotmail claims more than 10 million members), because they enable everyone, even those who don't own a computer, to have an email address they can check wherever they log on to the Web.

CitySearch is part of a national network of city guides, and has editorial reviews as well as paid Web pages from restaurants and other businesses. CitySearch clearly labels its links "editorial profile" or "advertiser's Web site." Use CitySearch's Event Finder to search for sports, opera, comedy, and much more—just choose a date and see what's available. The extensive shopping listings range from clothing to wine. Along with New York Sidewalk, CitySearch is the leading directory for arts and dining in New York (but New York Today, backed by the *New York Times,* is quickly catching up; see below).

MiningCo.com: New York City for Visitors. gonyc.miningco.com
The core of this site is its collections of New York links, on topics ranging from accommodations to zoos. Features (all with Net links) cover dining, dancing, and attractions, as well as unusual topics such as where to go when you gotta go.

New York City! www.nycvisit.com
The Web site for the New York Convention and Visitors Bureau. Fast Facts, fantastic photos, an events calendar, and online hotel booking. Boosterish, as expected, but not overdone.

New York City Reference. www.panix.com/clay/nyc
Almost 2,000 links to sites about the Big Apple, organized by category. Hunt for gems such as the quirky New York Trash (www.nytrash.com), a rant on everything trashy about New York.

✪ New York Today. www.nytoday.com
Arts, restaurant, and entertainment reviews and listings from the *New York Times.* At press time, New York Today was the only major city guide to offer an easy-to-use calendar format on its home page (don't be surprised if other sites soon emulate this). While much of NY Today's content comes from the *Times,* it also has content found only on this site, including some arts reviews.

✪ Time Out New York. www.timeoutny.com
Reviews and listings for restaurants, shops, and nightlife, with tips from TONY's critics. Time Out is a lively guide with a young, hip approach but has features for

everyone, such as "Got Beer," a roundup of the best microbreweries in town. See "Essential New York" for off-the-beaten-track suggestions, such as free kayaking or the Greater New York Orchid Show.

NEWSPAPERS & MAGAZINES

New York Magazine. www.newyorkmag.com
Insightful features on the city. But they don't give it all away—some articles are available only in the print magazine. Click on "Cue" for arts listings.

✪ The New York Times Online. www.nytimes.com
The authoritative scoop from the paper of record: sports, arts, restaurants, and much more.

The Village Voice. www.villagevoice.com
Features, columns, and reviews from New York's venerable, left-leaning alternative newspaper. Click on "Listings" for efficient searches of art, dance, music, and theater events by date and borough.

DINING GUIDES

Get a taste of the restaurants at your destination with online reviews.

CuisineNet. www.cuisinenet.com
Listings and reviews for New York and 15 other U.S. cities. Each restaurant has a capsule review compiled by CuisineNet and ratings based on survey responses from site users. For many restaurants, only two or three people have bothered to submit ratings, so they may not be statistically significant. However, comments can be instructive, as CuisineNet's readers discuss service, parking, free birthday desserts, and a host of other insightful observations.

Zagat Restaurant Survey. cgi.pathfinder.com/cgi-bin/zagat/homepage
Reviews of top restaurants for New York and dozens of U.S. cities. Zagat has made a name for itself as the people's choice, as its listings are based on extensive surveys. As this book went to press, Zagat (after several years on Pathfinder's site) was launching its own site at **www.zagat.com.**

THE TOP ATTRACTIONS

American Museum of Natural History. www.amnh.org
Exhibition information and an online tour of the one place on earth where massive dinosaur skeletons still rule.

Carnegie Hall. www.carnegiehall.org
A concert calendar, a box office, and a virtual tour.

Note to AOL Users

The keyword "New York" leads to **Digital City New York,** a site that's similar in scope to CitySearch and Sidewalk. You'll find reviews and listings for restaurants, arts, sports, and much more. If you search for the term "New York" in AOL's Find box, you'll come up with a list of other resources for New York, including an adventure/outdoor guide, B&B listings, New York vacation packages, and AOL's New York Message Board, an online bulletin board that's open to any AOL member who wants to browse or ask a question. Digital City: New York is also available on the Web at **newyork.digitalcity.com.**

Central Park. www.centralpark.org
Maps, upcoming events, and a tour of the park.

Circle Line. www.circleline.com
Tickets and information on how to see the world's most famous skyline in a 3-hour cruise around Manhattan Island.

Ellis Island. www.ellisisland.org
An online tour of the former immigration center that was the gateway to the United States for millions of immigrants.

Empire State Building. www.esbnyc.com
Tour information, facts, history, and kid stuff.

Lincoln Center. www.lincolncenter.org
A calendar of upcoming performances, plus online ticket purchasing for many events.

Madison Square Garden. www.thegarden.com
Home to the Knicks and Rangers, the Garden site lists upcoming games, concerts, the circus, and more, plus how to buy tickets.

Metropolitan Museum of Art. www.metmuseum.org
A taste of the million-plus works of art, plus a calendar of exhibitions.

Museum of Modern Art. www.moma.org
Calendar and exhibition information for one of the world's leading modern-art collections.

New York Mets. www.mets.com
New York Yankees. www.yankees.com
Tickets, schedules, stadium information, and player profiles.

NY.com: Museums in New York City. http://ny.com/nyc/museums/all.museums. html
An extensive listing of city museums.

NYC Museums. www.go-newyorkcity.com/museums/index.html
A guide to the city's leading museums and current exhibitions.

Radio City Music Hall. www.radiocity.com
A schedule of events and an online tour.

South Street Seaport. www.southstreetseaport.com
A guide to shopping, dining, and special events on Manhattan's waterfront.

Statue of Liberty. www.nyctourist.com/liberty1.htm
An online photo tour of America's enduring symbol of freedom.

Top of the World. www.wtc-top.com
Visitor information and sample views from atop the World Trade Center.

United Nations. www.un.org
Information on how to watch diplomats from dozens of nations try to keep the peace.

GETTING TICKETS
Remember, you can also buy tickets through the venues themselves, or through Culturefinder.com.

Ticket Depot. www.ticketdepot.com
A broker for tickets to Tri-state area sports, theater, concerts and more.

TicketMaster. events.ticketmaster.com
A national outlet, TicketMaster sells tickets for sports, theater, and concerts—all with a hefty service charge. You can also reach TicketMaster through CitySearch.

TicketWeb. www.ticketweb.com
TicketWeb also sells theater and concert tickets, but usually with a much lower service charge than TicketMaster. TicketWeb is best for events at smaller venues such as CBGB—many of the larger arenas and halls only sell through large ticket outlets.

GETTING AROUND

New York Transportation. www.newyorktransportation.com
A guide to the city's buses, subway, taxis, and airports. You'll also find information on ground transportation from the airports to Downtown.

✪ **Subway Navigator. metro.ratp.fr:10001/bin/cities/english**
An amazing site with detailed subway route maps for more than 60 cities around the world. Select a city and enter your departure and arrival points. Subway Navigator maps out your route and tells you how long the trip should take. It will even show your route on a subway map.

Index

See also Accommodations and Restaurant indexes, below.

GENERAL INDEX

Abigail Adams Smith Museum & Gardens, 209
Abyssinian Baptist Church, 183
Accommodations, 86–117. *See also* Accommodations Index
  best bets, 6–7
  hotel chains, 106–7
  money-saving tips, 15–18, 87
  reservations, 15–16, 343–44
Adams Smith, Abigail, Museum & Gardens, 209
Aerial Tramway, Roosevelt Island, 225
African Art, Museum for, 214
Agee, James, former residence of, 234
Airfares, 11–13, 52–53, 340–44
Airlines, 38–40, 51–52, 339–40
Airports, 11, 37–44, 51–52, 345
  transportation to/from, 14, 40, 42–44, 85
Albee, Edward, 242
  former residence of, 242
Alcott, Louisa May, former residence of, 235
Alternative Museum, 210
Amato Opera Theatre, 21, 303
American Art, Whitney Museum of, 206, 207–9
American Ballet Theatre, 306, 309
American Craft Museum, 207, 210, 290
American Express, 10–11, 23, 24, 50, 82, 300
American Folk Art, Museum of, 206, 214–15, 291
American Indian, National Museum of the, 196, 206, 216
American Jewish Historical Society, 210
American Museum of Financial History, 196, 207
American Museum of Natural History, 202–4, 253, 347
American Museum of the Moving Image (Queens), 209, 254, 261

Amtrak, 14, 36, 44, 52–54
Ansonia, the, 223
Antiques, 274–75
  fairs and shows, 25–26, 30–31, 274
Apollo Theater, 307
Aquarium, 255, 258–59
Architectural highlights, 218–25
Art, Brooklyn Museum of, 207, 209, 258, 309
Art, Metropolitan Museum of, 203–4, 209–10, 221, 290–91, 309, 348
Art, Museum of American Folk, 206, 214–15, 291
Art, Museum of Modern, 204–5, 207, 291, 309, 348
Art, New Museum of Contemporary, 207, 217
Art, Whitney Museum of American, 206–9
Art galleries, 69, 182, 216–17
Asia Society, 210
ATM machines, 23, 50–51
Atrium, the, 234
Auditoriums, 307–11

Baby-sitters, 34
Bagels, 286
Ballet, 31, 306–7, 309
Balto, statue of, 244
Bank Street, walking tour, 242
Bargemusic (Brooklyn), 21, 304–5
Barnes, Djuna, former residence of, 242
Bars, 321–31
  gay and lesbian, 336–38
Baseball, 5, 228, 262–63
Basketball, 263, 289
Battery Park, 64, 196, 248
Battery Park City, 64, 215
Beacon Theatre, 311
Beauty products, 276
Bed-and-breakfasts, 17
Bedford Street, walking tour, 236
Belvedere Castle, 244
Bernard Museum, 206, 225
Bicycling, 27, 247
Black Culture, Schomburg Center for Research in, 206, 218, 224
Bleecker Street, 69
  walking tour, 231, 234, 236
Bloomingdale's, 272

Blues music, 316–19
Boating, in Central Park, 247
Boat tours, 227–28. *See also* Ferries
Bonsai Museum (Brooklyn), 258
Bookstores, 276–80
Bowling, 250
Bowling Green Park, 196–97
Broadway on Broadway, 29
Broadway theater. *See* Theater
Bronx, 62, 255–57
  attractions index, 180
Bronx Zoo Wildlife Conservation Park, 206, 255–56
Brooklyn, 62, 257–61
  attractions index, 180
  waterfront restaurants, 176–77
Brooklyn Academy of Music (BAM), 30, 183, 302, 306–7
Brooklyn Botanic Garden, 206, 258
Brooklyn Bridge, 4, 64, 182, 185, 257, 260
Brooklyn Heights Historic District, 260–61
Brooklyn Museum of Art, 207, 209, 258, 309
Brooklyn Promenade, 260–61
Brooklyn Public Library, 257
Bryant Park, 248–49
  free Monday night movies, 183, 249, 309
Buses, 14, 77–78
  to/from airports, 14, 40, 42–43
  for disabled travelers, 36
  to New York City, 14, 44
  tours, 226

Cabarets, 320–21
Cabs. *See* Taxis
Calder, Alexander, *Three Wings*, 199
Calendar of events, 25–32
Canal Street, 66, 265–66
Carnegie Hall, 302, 304–5, 307, 347
Car rentals, 14, 52–53, 80
Car travel, 79–80
  to New York City, 45
  parking, 7, 14, 18, 56, 80
  safety tips, 51

Castle Clinton National Monument, 248
Cathedral of St. John the Divine, 30, 32, 207, 223
Cather, Willa, former residences of, 238–39, 242
Center for Jewish History, 210
Center of Photography, International, 207, 212
Central Park, 5, 183, 243–44, 246–48, 253, 348
  exploring, 244, 246–47
  free events, 308–9
    Shakespeare in the Park, 21, 28, 183, 298, 308
    SummerStage, 28, 183, 303, 308
  guided tours, 244
  ice skating, 30, 244, 247
  information, 243–44
  recreational activities, 247–48
  safety tips, 244
  traveling to, 243–43
Central Park Wildlife Center, 246–47, 255
Century 21, 272, 283
Channel Gardens, 221
Chelsea, 69
  accommodations, 94–95, 98
  art galleries, 69, 217
  attractions index, 179
  bars, 327–28
  restaurants, 152–54
Chelsea Market, 154, 285
Chelsea Piers Sports & Entertainment Complex, 69, 250
Cherry Lane Theatre, 237
Children
  accommodations, family-friendly, 7, 112–13
  restaurants, family-friendly, 167
  sights and activities, 253–55
  travel tips, 34
Children's Adventure Garden (Bronx), 257
Children's Museum of Manhattan, 209, 254
Children's Museum of the Arts, 254
Children's Zoo (Bronx Zoo), 256
Children's Zoo (Central Park), 246–47, 255
Chinatown, 66
  bars, 322
  restaurants, 127–30
  shopping, 265–66
Chinese New Year, 5, 25–26
Christopher Street, 69, 238, 270, 320, 337
Chrysler Building, 5, 72, 219
Chumley's, 237, 326
Churches and cathedrals, 30, 32, 72, 183, 198–99, 206–7, 223, 225, 260, 309

Circle in the Square Theater, 234
Circle Line Sightseeing Cruises, 227, 348
Circuses, 26, 31, 255
City Center, 306
City Hall, 64, 201
City Hall Park, 201–2
City of New York, Museum of the, 215
CityPass, 4, 20
Classical music, 304–6, 309. See also Concerts
Climate, 24–25
Cloisters, the, 74, 204, 210–11
Clothing, 280–85
  department stores, 272–74
  discount stores, 283–84
  sample sales, 20, 60, 71, 265, 281
  vintage, 20, 284–85
Coca-Cola Fifth Ave, 289
Collectibles, 274–75
Columbia University, 72, 82
Comedy clubs, 319–20
Commerce Street, walking tour, 236–37
Concert halls, 307–11
Concerts, free, 21, 28, 183, 199, 212, 304, 308–10
Coney Island (Brooklyn), 255, 258–59
Congregation Shearith Israel, 225
Consulates, 54–55
Contemporary Art, New Museum of, 207, 217
Contemporary Art Center, P. S. 1 (Queens), 209, 261
Cooper, James Fenimore, former residence of, 231, 234
Cooper-Hewitt National Design Museum, 207, 211
Cosby (TV show), 5, 251
Craft Museum, American, 207, 210, 290
Crane, Hart, former residences of, 237, 240
Cruises, 227–28. See also Ferries
Cunard Building, 197
Customs House, U. S., 196, 216
Customs regulations, 48–49, 52
Cybercafes, 84, 345

Dahesh Museum, 206, 211
Daily News, 22, 61, 84, 296
Daily Show with Jon Stewart (TV show), 251
Dakota Building, 73, 223, 246
Dana Discovery Center, 244, 246
Dance clubs, 331–36
  gay and lesbian, 336–38
Dance troupes, 31, 306–9
Delacorte Theater, 21, 28, 298, 308

Delis, 8, 121, 130, 140
Department stores, 31, 272–74
Design Museum, Cooper-Hewitt National, 207, 211
Diamond District, 270
Dining. See Restaurants
Dinosaurs, at American Museum of Natural History, 203, 253
Disabled travelers, 7, 34–36
Discos. See Dance clubs
Disney Store, 289
Doctors, 32–33, 83
Dos Passos, John, former residence of, 239
Double-decker bus tours, 226
Downtown, 62, 64, 66–69. See also specific neighborhoods
Dreiser, Theodore, former residence of, 240
Drugstores, 84
Dubuffet, Jean, Group of Four Trees, 199
Dyckman Farmhouse Museum, 208

Easter Parade, 27
East Side, 63. See also East Village; Gramercy Park; Midtown East; Murray Hill; Upper East Side
East Village, 68, 81
  accommodations, 88, 90–92
  attractions index, 179
  bars, 324–26
  restaurants, 135–42
  shopping, 268–69
8th Street, shopping, 269, 293
Ellis Island, 181, 184, 348
El Museo del Barrio, 209, 211
Emergencies, 32–33, 55, 82–83
Empire State Building, 5, 26, 72, 219–20, 255, 348
Entertainment. See Nightlife
Entry requirements, 46–47

Families. See Children
FAO Schwarz, 31, 295
Farmer's market, 70, 249, 285
Fashion. See Clothing
Feast of San Gennaro, 30, 66
Federal Hall National Memorial, 198, 206, 209
Ferries
  to Ellis Island, 181, 184, 348
  Staten Island Ferry, 182, 184
  to Statue of Liberty, 3–4, 181, 348
Festivals, 25–32, 255
Fifth Avenue, 31, 62
  Museum Mile, 4, 73, 209
  shopping, 271
57th Street
  shopping, 271
  theme restaurants, 162–63

Film festivals, 26–27, 30, 309–10

Financial District, 64, 185, 193
attractions index, 179
bars, 321
guided walking tours, 230
restaurants, 122, 124–25
shopping, 265
walking tour, 194–202

Financial History, American Museum of, 196, 207

Fire Museum, New York City, 209, 254

First Corinthian Baptist Church, 183

Fish markets, 193, 265

Flatiron Building, 224

Flatiron District, 69–70
accommodations, 93–94
attractions index, 179
bars, 327
restaurants, 148–52
shopping, 270

Flea markets, 275

Fleet Week, 27

Flushing Meadows-Corona Park (Queens), 255, 261–63

Folk Art, Museum of American, 206, 214–15, 291

Food. *See also specific foods*
festival, 27
shopping for, 285–87
greenmarket, 70, 249, 285

Football, 263

Forbes Magazine Galleries, 206, 212, 240, 253–54

Ford Foundation Building, 224

Foreign visitors, 46–58

Fort Tryon Park, 74, 210–11

Fragonard Room, 212

Fraunces Tavern Museum, 64, 197, 209

Frick Collection, 212

Fulton Fish Market, 193

Gardens, 206–7, 209, 221, 246, 256–58

Garment District, 71, 270, 281

Gay and lesbian travelers, 36–37, 238
accommodations, 87, 95
bookstores, 37, 278–79
nightlife, 336–38
special events, 27–29

Gay Street, 238

GE Building, 221

George Gustav Heye Center, 216

Giants (football team), 263

Gift stores, 287–88, 290–91

Golf, 250

Good Morning America (TV show), 251

Gracie Mansion, 208

Gramercy Park, 69–70
accommodations, 93–94
bars, 327
restaurants, 148–52

Grand Army Plaza (Brooklyn), 257, 260

Grand Central Terminal, 4, 32, 60, 72, 220–21, 229
restaurants, 8, 168

Gray Line New York Tours, 226

Greenmarket, Union Square, 70, 249, 285

Greenwich Avenue, walking tour, 241–42

Greenwich Village, 68–69, 231
accommodations, 92–93
attractions index, 179
bars, 326–27
guided walking tours, 229–30
Halloween Parade, 30
restaurants, 142, 144–48
shopping, 269–70
walking tour, 231–43

Group of Four Trees (Dubuffet), 199

Grove Street, walking tour, 237–38

Guggenheim Museum, 205–7
Soho, 207

Gyms, 249

Hall of Records, 202

Hall of Science, New York (Queens), 207, 209, 254–55, 261

Hanukkah Menorah, Lighting of, 31–32

Harbor. *See* New York Harbor

Harlem, 73–74
accommodations, 117
guided walking tours, 229–31
jazz scene, 317
restaurants, 176
Sunday morning services in, 183

Harlem Week, 29

Hayden Planetarium, 203

Health clubs, 249

Health concerns, 32–33

Henry Luce Nature Observatory, 246

Herald Square, 71, 270

Hockey, 263

Holidays, 5–6, 55

Holocaust Memorial, 215

Homestays, 17

Horse-drawn carriage rides, 247

Horse racing, 27

Hospitals, 83

Hostels, 17–18, 37, 114–15

Hotels. *See* Accommodations

Housewares, 288–89

Hudson River, cruises, 227–28

Ice hockey, 263

Ice skating, 30–31, 194, 221, 247, 250

Imagine mosaic, 246

IMAX Theater, 203

Immigration Museum, Ellis Island, 184

Information sources, 21–22, 59–60

Insurance, 32–33, 49

International Center of Photography, 207, 212
Midtown, 207, 212

Internet access, 84, 345

Intrepid Sea-Air-Space Museum, 27, 212–13, 253

Inwood, 74

Irving, Washington, former residence of, 236

Jacob K. Javits Convention Center, 25, 27

James, Henry, former residence of, 239

Japan Society, 213

Jazz, 28, 205, 308–10, 316–19

Jets (football team), 263

Jewish Heritage, Museum of, 215

Jewish History, Center for, 210

Jewish Museum, 207, 213

John F. Kennedy International Airport, 37–40, 42–44

Joyce Theater, 306

Juilliard School, 21, 183, 304, 309

Kalikow Building, 200

Kaufman-Astoria Studios (Queens), 251, 261

Kennedy International Airport, 37–40, 42–44, 51–52

Knicks (basketball team), 263, 310, 348

Koreatown, restaurants, 159

Kramer's Reality Tour, 228

Lafayette Street, shopping, 269

LaGuardia Airport, 37–40, 42–44

Late Night with Conan O'Brien (TV show), 221, 251

Late Show with David Letterman (TV show), 252

Leather goods, 289

Lefferts Homestead (Brooklyn), 260

Legal aid, 55

Lennon, John, 5, 223, 246

Lenox Lounge, 317

Leo Baeck Institute, 210

Lever House, 223

Lewis, Sinclair, former residence of, 242

Liberator, 241

Liberty (basketball team), 263

Liberty Island, 3–4, 181, 348

Liberty Plaza, 199

Liberty Science Center, 209

Libraries, 84, 206, 214, 224–25, 257

Lincoln Center for the Performing Arts, 307–10, 348
performance venues, 303–6
special events, 28–29, 310

Liquor stores, 295
Literary walking tour, 231–43
Little India, restaurants, 137
Little Italy, 66
  bars, 322
  restaurants, 127–30
Live music. *See*
  Concerts; Music
Live! with Regis and Kathie Lee
  (TV show), 252
Loeb Boathouse, 247
Logo stores, 289–90
Long Island Rail Road, 81
Lower East Side, 60, 66–67,
  81. *See also* Orchard Street
  accommodations, 88
  attractions index, 179
  bars, 323–24
  guided walking tours,
    229–30
  restaurants, 130
  shopping, 266
Lower East Side Tenement
  Museum, 213–14, 254
Lower Manhattan, 64, 185,
  193–94. *See also* Battery
  Park; Financial District;
  South Street Seaport; World
  Trade Center
  attractions index, 179
  shopping, 265
  walking tour, 194–202

MacDougal Street, walking
  tour, 234–36
McGraw-Hill Building, 222
Macy's, 71, 264, 270, 273
  Thanksgiving Day Parade,
    5–6, 31
Madison Avenue, shopping, 271
Madison Square Garden, 26,
  31, 71, 263, 310–11, 348
Magazines, 56, 60, 84,
  296, 347
Manhattan Mall, 19, 270
Manhattan School of
  Music, 304
Maps, street, 63
Marathons, 26, 30, 262
Markets. *See* Farmer's market;
  Fish markets; Flea markets
Maury Show (TV show), 252
Merchant's House
  Museum, 208
MetroCard, 14–15, 42,
  75–77
Metropolitan Museum of Art,
  203–4, 209–10, 221,
  290–91, 309, 348
Metropolitan Opera, 21, 28,
  183, 303, 305, 308–9
Mets (baseball team), 5, 228,
  262–63, 348
Midtown, 69–72
  shopping, 270–71
Midtown East, 72
  accommodations, 104–8
  attractions index, 179
  bars, 329–30
  restaurants, 165–68

Midtown West, 70–72. *See also*
  Times Square
  accommodations, 98–104
  attractions index, 179–80
  bars, 328–29
  restaurants, 154–55,
    158–65
Minetta Lane, 235
Minetta Tavern, 235
Modern Art, Museum of,
  204–5, 207, 291, 309, 348
Money, 22–24, 50–51
Money Museum, 196, 207
Money-saving tips, 10–21
Montel Williams Show
  (TV show), 252
Morgan Library, 214
Morris-Jumel Mansion, 208
Mostly Mozart, 28, 310
Moving Image, American
  Museum of the (Queens),
  209, 254, 261
Mulberry Street, 30, 66, 130,
  267, 322
Municipal Art Society, 228–29,
  277
Municipal Building, 202
Murray Hill, 72
  accommodations, 104–8
  bars, 329–30
  restaurants, 165–68
Museo del Barrio, 209, 211
Museum for African Art, 214
Museum Mile, 4, 73, 209
Museum of American Folk Art,
  206, 214–15, 291
Museum of Jewish
  Heritage, 215
Museum of Modern Art,
  204–5, 207, 291, 309, 348
Museum of Natural History,
  202–4, 253, 347
Museum of Television &
  Radio, 215, 254
Museum of the City of New
  York, 215
Museum of the Moving
  Image (Queens), 209,
  254, 261
Museums, 4, 182, 202–18,
  258, 261–62, 348. *See also*
  specific museums
  avoiding crowds, 204
  for children, 253–55
  gift stores, 290–91
  index of, 179–80
  money-saving tips, 206–7
Music, 311–19
  blues, 316–19
  cabarets, 320–21
  classical, 304–6, 309
  concerts, free, 21, 28,
    183, 199, 212, 304,
    308–10
  cruises, 227
  jazz, 28, 205, 308–10,
    316–19
  opera, 302–4
  shopping for, 291–93
  swing, 334

National Design Museum,
  Cooper-Hewitt, 207, 211
National Museum of the
  American Indian, 196,
  206, 216
National Tennis Center,
  29, 263
Natural History, American
  Museum of, 202–4,
  253, 347
NBA Store, 289
NBC Studios, 221–22
Neighborhoods, 4, 62–74. *See*
  also specific neighborhoods
  guided walking tours,
    228–31
  sightseeing by, 179–80
Nets (basketball team), 263
Newark International Airport,
  38–40, 42–44, 51–52
New Jersey Devils, 263
New Jersey Nets, 263
New Museum of
  Contemporary Art, 207, 217
New School for Social
  Research, 240–41
Newspapers, 56, 60, 296, 347.
  See also specific newspapers
  tabloids, 61, 84
New Year's Eve, 32
New York, Museum of the City
  of, 215
New York Apple Tours, 226
New York Aquarium
  (Brooklyn), 255, 258–59
New York Botanical Garden
  (Bronx), 207, 256–57
New York City Ballet, 31,
  306–7, 309
New York City Fire Museum,
  209, 254
New York City Marathon,
  30, 262
New York City Opera,
  303–4, 309
New York County
  Courthouse, 202
New York Double-Decker
  Tours, 226
New York Giants, 263
New York Hall of Science
  (Queens), 207, 209,
  254–55, 261
New York Harbor, 28, 181,
  184. *See also* Ferries
  cruises, 227–28
New-York Historical
  Society, 218
New York Jets, 263
New York Knicks, 263,
  310, 348
New York Liberty, 263
New York Mets, 5, 228,
  262–63, 348
New York Philharmonic, 183,
  305–6, 308–9
New York Post, 61, 84
New York Public Library, 84,
  206, 224–25
New York Rangers, 263

New York Skyride, 220, 255
New York Stock Exchange, 64, 185, 193, 196, 198, 206
New York Times, 22, 34, 56, 60–61, 84, 204, 216, 255, 265, 296, 346–47
New York Transit Museum (Brooklyn), 207, 209, 254, 259
New York Waterway, 227
New York Yankees, 5, 228, 262–63, 290, 348
Nightlife, 296–338. *See also* Bars; Comedy clubs; Dance clubs; Dance troupes; Music; Theater
  current schedule, 60, 296–97
  money-saving tips, 20–21
  tickets, 298, 300–302, 310, 312, 348–49
Niketown, 290, 294
92nd Street Y, 21, 116, 228–29, 302, 304, 310
Noguchi, Isamu, *The Red Cube,* 199
NoHo, 68
  attractions index, 179
  bars, 324–26
  restaurants, 135–42
  shopping, 269
NoLiTa, 67
  restaurants, 132–35
  shopping, 267–68
Nutcracker, The (ballet), 31, 307
Nuyorican Poets Cafe, 325

O'Neill, Eugene, 234–36, 238
  former residence of, 237
Opera, 302–4
Orchard Street, 60, 67, 213–14, 229, 266, 324, 332

Package deals, 7, 10, 32, 38–39, 90–91
Paine, Thomas, former residence of, 237–38
Paris, Frank, former residence of, 238
Parking, 7, 14, 18, 56, 80
Parks, 248–50, 260. *See also* Central Park
Passports, 47–48
Patchin Place, 242
Penn Station, 60, 81
Performing arts. *See also* Dance troupes; Music; Theater
  current schedule, 60, 296–97
  money-saving tips, 20–21
  tickets, 298, 300–302, 310, 312, 348–49
Pets, traveling with, 30, 87, 223
Pharmacies, 84
Photography, International Center of, 207, 212
Pier 17, 193, 265, 309

Pioneer, 193, 227
Pizza, 8, 19, 147, 151, 175
  index of, 121
Playgrounds, 247–48
Plymouth Church (Brooklyn), 260
Poe, Edgar Allan, 238
  Cottage (Bronx), 208, 255–56
  former residence of, 235
Poetry slams, 325
Police, 55, 83–84
Port Authority Terminal, 44, 81
Post offices, 84
Prospect Park (Brooklyn), 260
Provincetown Playhouse, 235
P. S. 1 Contemporary Art Center (Queens), 209, 261
Public Theater, 298, 308, 321

Queens, 62, 261–62
  attractions index, 180
Queens Museum of Art, 209, 262

Radio City Music Hall, 222, 311, 348
  Christmas Spectacular, 31, 222, 255, 311
Rangers (hockey team), 263
Red Cube, The (Noguchi), 199
Reservations
  accommodations, 15–16
    online, 343–44
  restaurants, 118–19
Restaurants, 5, 118–77. *See also* Restaurants Index
  best bets, 7–9
  by cuisine, 119–21
  delis, 8, 121, 130, 140
  money-saving tips, 18–19
  prix-fixe lunch deals, 9, 19, 128–29
  reservations, 118–19
  theme, 162–63
  Web sites, 347
Restaurant Week, 28, 128–29
Ricki Lake Show (TV show), 252
Rockefeller Center, 4–5, 71, 221–22
  Christmas Tree Lighting, 31
  ice skating, 30, 221
Rockettes, the, 31, 222, 255
Rock music, 311–16
Roller blading, 247
Roosevelt, Theodore, Birthplace, 207, 218
Roosevelt Island Tramway, 225
Rosie O'Donnell Show (TV show), 221, 252

Safety, 51, 81–83
St. John the Divine, Cathedral of, 30, 32, 207, 223
St. Mark's Place, 68, 269, 291, 314

St. Patrick's Cathedral, 72, 206, 225
St. Patrick's Day Parade, 26
St. Paul's Chapel, 200–201
St. Vincent Millay, Edna, 235, 237
  former residence of, 238
Saks Fifth Avenue, 31, 274
Sally Show (TV show), 252
Salmagundi Club, 240
Sample sales, 20, 60, 71, 265, 281
Sandy Hook (New Jersey), 227
San Remo, former site of, 234
Saturday Night Live (TV show), 5, 71, 221, 252–53
Schomburg Center for Research in Black Culture, 206, 218, 224
Sea-Air-Space Museum, *Intrepid,* 27, 212–13, 253
Seagram Building, 223
Seaport. *See* South Street Seaport
Seasons, 11, 24–25
Seinfeld (TV show), 161, 172, 228
Senior citizen travelers, 36, 301
Shakespeare Garden (Brooklyn), 258
Shakespeare Garden (Central Park), 246
Shakespeare in the Park, 21, 28, 183, 298, 308
Shea Stadium (Queens), 5, 228, 262–63
Shoe stores, 293–94
Shopping, 264–95
  money-saving tips, 20
  streets and neighborhoods, 265–72
Sidewalk vendors, 267
Sightseeing, 178–262. *See also* Tours
  cheap thrills, 182–83
  money-saving tips, 20
  by neighborhood, 179–80
Skating, 250
  ice, 30–31, 194, 221, 247, 250
  in-line, 247
Skyride, 220, 255
Skyscrapers, 4–5, 218–22, 255. *See also specific skyscrapers*
Smith, Abigail Adams, Museum & Gardens, 209
Smoking, 85, 119
Soccer, 263
SoHo, 67
  art galleries, 217
  attractions index, 180
  bars, 323
  restaurants, 132–35
  shopping, 266–67, 269, 275
Solomon R. Guggenheim Museum, 205–7
Sony Building, 223

Sony Wonder Technology Lab, 206, 209, 255
Sousa, John Philip, former residence of, 239
South Street Seaport, 64, 193–94, 254, 309, 348
 bars, 321
 boat cruises, 227
 ice skating, 31, 194
 restaurants, 122, 124–25
 shopping, 265, 275, 290
South Street Seaport Museum, 193, 254
Spanish & Portuguese Synagogue, 225
Special events, 25–32, 255
Spin City (TV show), 5, 253
Spirit Cruises, 228
Sporting goods, 294–95
Sports, 262–63. *See also specific sports*
 in Central Park, 247–48
Sports Complex, Chelsea Piers, 69, 250
Staten Island Ferry, 182, 184
Statue of Liberty, 3–4, 181, 348
Stock Exchange, New York, 64, 185, 193, 196, 198, 206
Stonewall Bar, 238, 337
Strawberry Fields, 5, 246
Striver's Row, 72
Student travelers, 37, 301
Studio Museum, 218
Styron, William, former residence of, 242
Subways, 14, 75–77, 349
 to/from airports, 40
 safety tips, 82
SummerStage, 28, 183, 303, 308
Surrogate's Court, 202
Swedish Cottage Marionette Theatre, 246
Swing music, 334
Symphony orchestras, 304–6, 309. *See also* Concerts, free

Taxes, 56, 85, 264
Taxis, 78–79
 to/from airports, 43
 for disabled travelers, 35
Telephone, 56–57, 85
Television & Radio, Museum of, 215, 254
Television shows. *See also specific shows*
 tapings, 5, 183, 251–53
Temperatures, average monthly, 25
Temple Emanu-El, 206, 225
Tenement Museum, 213–14, 254
Tennis, 29, 248, 263
Theater, 5, 297–302
 Broadway on Broadway, 29
 for children, 255
 current schedule, 60, 296–97

money-saving tips, 20–21
 pre-theater meal deals, 164
 ticket-buying tips, 300–302
 ticket prices, 298, 300
Theme restaurants, 162–63. *See also* Restaurant Index
Theodore Roosevelt Birthplace, 207, 218
34th Street Tour, 229
Tickets, 298, 300–302, 310, 312, 348–49
 money-saving tips, 301, 305
 TKTS booth, 5, 20–21, 301
Time Out New York, 22, 34, 37, 60, 216, 255, 265, 281, 296, 315, 332, 336, 346–47
Times Square, 70–71, 82
 accommodations, 98–104
 bars, 328–29
 guided walking tours, 229
 New Year's Eve, 32
 restaurants, 154–55, 158–65
 shopping, 270–71
 Visitors Center, 59–60, 84
Tipping, 58, 119
Tisch Children's Zoo, 246–47, 255
Titanic Memorial Lighthouse, 193
TKTS booth, 5, 20–21, 301
Today (TV show), 222, 251, 253
Top of the World, 4, 194, 200, 348
Tourist information, 21–22, 59–60
Tours, 225–31. *See also* Ferries
 by boat, 227–28
 by bus, 226
 Cathedral of St. John the Divine, 223
 Central Park, 244
 guided walking tours, 228–31
 NBC Studio, 222
 Radio City Music Hall, 222
 United Nations, 222
Town Hall, 311
Toy stores, 295
Trade Center. *See* World Trade Center
Train travel, 44, 53–54
 to New York City, 14
 to the suburbs, 81
Tramway, Roosevelt Island, 225
Transit Museum (Brooklyn), 207, 209, 254, 259
Transportation, 74–81, 349
 to/from airports, 14, 40, 42–44, 85
 for disabled travelers, 35–36, 76
 MetroCard, 14–15, 42, 75–77

money-saving tips, 14–15
 transit info, 40, 76, 85
Travelers Aid, 85
Traveling
 to New York City, 37–45
 money-saving tips, 11–14
 to/within the U.S., 51–54
Travel insurance, 32–33, 49
Travel Web sites, 12, 339–45
TriBeCa, 64, 66
 accommodations, 87–88
 attractions index, 180
 bars, 322
 restaurants, 125–27
Trinity Church, 198–99, 309
Twain, Mark, 257
 former residence of, 243
Tweed Courthouse, 202
Twin Towers. *See* World Trade Center

Union Square, 69–70
 bars, 327
 greenmarket, 70, 249, 285
 restaurants, 148–52
 shopping, 270
Union Square Park, 249
United Nations, 72, 222, 348
Upper East Side, 73
 accommodations, 116
 attractions index, 180
 bars, 330–31
 restaurants, 174–76
Upper West Side, 72–73, 82
 accommodations, 108–9, 112–16
 attractions index, 180
 bars, 330
 restaurants, 168–69, 172–73
 shopping, 271–72
Uptown, 62, 72–74. *See also* Harlem; Upper East Side; Upper West Side
 art galleries, 216–17
 shopping, 271–72
U. S. Customs House, 196, 216
U. S. Open Tennis Championships, 29, 263

View, The (TV show), 5, 253
Village, the. *See* Greenwich Village
Village Voice, 60, 296, 347
Vintage clothing, 20, 284–85
Visitor information, 21–22, 59–60

Walker, Jimmy, former residence of, 238
Walking, 15, 74, 178, 182
Walking tours, guided, 228–31
Wall Street, 64, 185, 193, 196, 198
Warner Bros. Studio Store, 290
Washington Heights, 74
Washington Mews, 239–40

Washington Place, 238–39
Washington Square, 27, 239
Washington Square Park, 69, 239, 249–50
Wave Hill (Bronx), 207, 257
Waverly Place, walking tour, 238–39
Weather, 24–25, 345
Web sites, 22, 265, 339–49
West Chelsea, art galleries, 69, 217
West Side, 63. *See also* Midtown West; Times Square; Upper West Side; West Village
West Village, 69. *See also* Greenwich Village
Wharton, Edith, former residence of, 239
Whitney Museum of American Art, 206–9
Wilson, Edmund, former residence of, 239
Winter Garden, 200, 309
Wolfe, Thomas, former residence of, 240
Wollman Rink, 30, 244, 247
Woolworth Building, 201
World Financial Center, 64, 200, 309
World Trade Center, 26, 64, 194, 199–200, 226, 255, 309
    food court, 19, 122, 124
    Greatest Bar on Earth, 200, 321, 331, 334
    shopping, 265, 272, 276–77
    Top of the World, 4, 194, 200, 348
Wright, Frank Lloyd, 204–7

Yankees (baseball team), 5, 262–63, 290, 348
Yankee Stadium (Bronx), 5, 228, 262–63
Yeshiva University Museum, 210
YMCAs, 18, 108, 114, 116, 249

Zoos, 246–47, 255–56, 260

ACCOMMODATIONS

Abingdon Guest House, 92
Americana Inn, 98
Amsterdam Inn, 108–9
Belvedere, 7
Belvedere Hotel, 98, 103
Best Western Manhattan, 107
Best Western President, 106
Best Western Seaport Inn, 106
Best Western Woodward, 106
Broadway Inn, 6, 98–99, 112
Carlton Arms, 7, 104
Chelsea Inn, 94
Chelsea Savoy Hotel, 95, 112
Colonial House Inn, 95
Comfort Inn Manhattan, 107
Comfort Inn Midtown, 99, 107
Cosmopolitan Hotel-Tribeca, 6, 87–88
Country Inn the City, 7, 115
Crowne Plaza at the United Nations, 91
De Hirsch Residence at the 92nd Street YM-YWHA, 116
East Village Bed & Coffee, 88
Gershwin Hotel, 7, 93
Gramercy Park Hotel, 94
Habitat Hotel, 7, 104–5
Herald Square Hotel, 99
Holiday Inn Broadway, 107
Holiday Inn Downtown, 107
Hostelling International-New York, 114–15
Hotel Beacon, 113, 115–16
Hotel Chelsea, 95–98
Hotel Edison, 6, 100, 112
Hotel Grand Union, 105
Hotel Metro, 7, 103–4
Hotel Newton, 6, 109
Hotel Riverside, 109
Hotel 17, 93–94
Hotel 31, 105
Hotel Wolcott, 100
Larchmont Hotel, 6, 92
Loews New York, 107
Lucerne, 7
The Lucerne, 116
Malibu Hotel, 112–13
Marriott Financial Center, 90
Marriott World Trade Center, 90
Milburn, 7
The Milburn, 113–14
Millenium Hilton, 7, 90
Millennium Broadway, 91
Murray Hill Inn, 105–7
Off SoHo Suites, 88
Park Savoy Hotel, 100–101
Pickwick Arms Hotel, 107–8
Portland Square Hotel, 101
Quality Hotel Eastside, 107–8
Quality Hotel & Suites Midtown, 101, 107, 113
Ramada Inn Milford Plaza, 101
Second Home on Second Avenue, 91
Travel Inn, 7, 102, 113
Urban Jem Guest House, 117
Vanderbilt YMCA, 108
Washington Jefferson Hotel, 102–3
Washington Square Hotel, 92–93
West Side YMCA, 114
Wyndham, 6
The Wyndham, 103

RESTAURANTS

Acme Bar & Grill, 135–36
Aggie's, 142
Alison on Dominick Street, 9, 135
Alley's End, 154
America, 148, 167
Amy's Bread, 154, 161
Angelica Kitchen, 136
Aquavit, 129
B. Frites, 161
Bar Pitti, 8, 142
B Bar & Grill, 136
Bendix Diner, 9, 135, 152–53
Bereket, 130
Big Nick's Burger Joint, 169
Boca Chica, 136
Bombay Dining, 137
Bop, 142
Bread & Butter, 8, 134–35
Bridge Cafe, 9, 124–25
The British Open, 165
Brooklyn Diner USA, 162
Burritoville, 124, 141, 147, 154, 173
Cafe Asean, 144
The Cafe at Aquavit, 161
Café Boulud, 129
Cafe de Bruxelles, 144
Cafe Gitane, 132
Cafe Habana, 8, 132
Cafe Spice, 148–49
Cafeteria, 153
Caffe Grazie, 175
California Pizza Oven, 151
Canova Market, 160–61
Carmine's, 162–63, 167
Carnegie Deli, 140
Chanpen, 160
Chanterelle, 129
Chat 'n' Chew, 149
Churrascaria Plataforma, 164
Clementine, 149
Coffee Shop, 9, 149–50
Comedy Nation, 162
Copperfield Magic Underground, 162
Corner Bistro, 144
Cucina di Pesce, 137
Delegates' Dining Room, 222
Devon & Blakely, 124
Dojo, 135, 144–45
Dosanko, 165
Drovers Tap Room, 148
Ecce Panis, 124
EJ's Luncheonette, 142, 167–68, 174
Ellen's Stardust Diner, 163
Emerald Planet, 141–42
Empire Diner, 153
ESPN Zone, 162
Ess-A-Bagel, 165
Eureka Joe, 151
Evergreen Shanghai, 127, 165–66
Fanelli's Cafe, 132–33
Fashion Cafe, 162
Fine & Shapiro, 122, 124
Florent, 9, 145
Franklin Station Cafe, 125
French Roast, 145
Frutti de Mare, 138
Gabriela's, 169
Gandhi, 137
Gemelli, 122

Gotham Bar & Grill, 129
Gramercy Tavern, 129
Grand Sichuan, 152
Grand Sichuan Chinese
  Restaurant, 127
Gray's Papaya, 147, 173
Hamburger Harry's, 154
Hangawi, 159
Hard Rock Cafe, 162
Harley-Davidson Cafe, 162
Haru, 173–74
Haveli, 137
Hi-Life Bar & Grill, 168
Hi-Life Restaurant &
  Lounge, 174
Home, 8, 147
Housing Works Used Books
  Cafe, 134
Hunan Park, 169
Il Bagatto, 138
Il Cortile, 130
Island Burgers & Shakes, 8,
  154–55
Iso, 138
Jean Georges, 129
Jekyll & Hyde Club, 163
Joe's Shanghai, 8, 127–28, 154
John's Pizzeria, 147, 155,
  167–68, 175–76
Josie's Restaurant & Juice Bar,
  169, 172
Katz's Delicatessen, 130, 140
Kelley & Ping, 133
Kitchenette, 125
La Bonne Soupe, 155
La Caridad 78, 172
La Paella, 138
La Taza de Oro, 153
Layla, 126
Le Gigot, 8–9
Lemon Tree Cafe, 155, 158
Les Sans Culottes, 158
Lombardi's, 8, 133
Los Dos Rancheros
  Mexicanos, 158
Mangia, 122, 161, 167
Manhattan Chili Co., 158, 167

Mars, 163
Medusa, 150
Menchenko-Tei, 122
Meskerem, 158–59
Michael Jordan's—The Steak
  House, 221
Mitali East, 137
Molyvos, 9, 164–65
Motown Cafe, 163
Moustache, 135, 145–46
New York Noodletown, 128
Nha Trang, 129
Nobu, 129
North Star Pub, 122
The Odeon, 126–27
Official All-Star Cafe, 163
Old Town Bar & Restaurant,
  8, 150
Oyster Bar, 8, 168
Pamir, 166
Papaya King, 175
Paradise & Lunch, 161
Passage to India, 137
Patsy Grimaldi's Pizzeria, 8,
  176–77
Payard Pâtisserie and Bistro, 9
Payard Patisserie & Bistro, 176
Petrossian, 129
Pintaile's Pizza, 151, 175
Pisces, 8, 138–39
Planet Hollywood, 163
Pó, 8, 146
Pongsri Thai Restaurant, 160
Popover Cafe, 172
Prime Burger, 166
The Pump, 168
Rainforest Cafe, 162
Raw Restaurant, 162
Republic, 150
Rice, 133–34
Rice 'n' Beans, 159
Riverrun Cafe, 126
Roettele A. G., 139
Rose of India, 137
Salaam Bombay, 125
Sammy's Noodle Shop, 146
Sam's Falafel, 124

San Domenico, 164
Sapporo, 135, 159
Sapporo East, 160
Sarabeth's Kitchen, 9, 173–74
Sbarro Pizza, 122
Second Avenue Deli, 8, 140
Serendipity 3, 167
Serendipity 3., 174–75
Shabu Tatsu, 9, 139, 174
Siam Inn Too, 160
Sofia Fabulous Pizza, 175
SoHo Kitchen & Bar, 122, 134
Soup Kitchen
  International, 161
Spring Street Natural
  Restaurant, 134
Stage Deli, 140
Steak Frites, 152
Sylvia's, 176
Taco & Tortilla King, 166
Tartine, 8, 146
Tavern on the Green, 129
Tavern Room at Gramercy
  Tavern, 9
The Tavern Room at Gramercy
  Tavern, 152
Tea & Sympathy, 147
Thailand Restaurant, 129–30
Time Cafe, 139–41
Time Cafe North, 168–69
Tom's Restaurant, 172–73
Totonno's Pizzeria
  Napolitano, 175
"21" Club, 129, 164
Two Boots to Go, 147–48
Union Pacific, 129
Veselka, 141
Village Yokocho, 141
Virgil's Real BBQ, 160, 167
Vong, 129
Walker's, 126
Wall Street Kitchen & Bar,
  122, 134
Won Jo, 159
Woo Chon, 159–60
Yura & Company, 175
Zen Palate, 151, 154, 169

FROMMER'S® COMPLETE TRAVEL GUIDES

Alaska
Amsterdam
Arizona
Atlanta
Australia
Austria
Bahamas
Barcelona, Madrid & Seville
Beijing
Belgium, Holland & Luxembourg
Bermuda
Boston
Budapest & the Best of Hungary
California
Canada
Cancún, Cozumel &
  the Yucatán
Cape Cod, Nantucket & Martha's Vineyard
Caribbean
Caribbean Cruises & Ports of Call
Caribbean Ports of Call
Carolinas & Georgia
Chicago
China
Colorado
Costa Rica
Denmark
Denver, Boulder & Colorado Springs
England
Europe
Florida
France
Germany
Greece
Greek Islands
Hawaii
Hong Kong
Honolulu, Waikiki & Oahu
Ireland
Israel
Italy
Jamaica & Barbados
Japan
Las Vegas
London
Los Angeles
Maryland & Delaware
Maui
Mexico
Miami & the Keys

Montana & Wyoming
Montréal & Québec City
Munich & the Bavarian Alps
Nashville & Memphis
Nepal
New England
New Mexico
New Orleans
New York City
Nova Scotia, New Brunswick &
  Prince Edward Island
Oregon
Paris
Philadelphia & the
  Amish Country
Portugal
Prague & the Best of the Czech Republic
Provence & the Riviera
Puerto Rico
Rome
San Antonio & Austin
San Diego
San Francisco
Santa Fe, Taos &
  Albuquerque
Scandinavia
Scotland
Seattle & Portland
Singapore & Malaysia
South Africa
Southeast Asia
South Pacific
Spain
Sweden
Switzerland
Thailand
Tokyo
Toronto
Tuscany & Umbria
USA
Utah
Vancouver & Victoria
Vermont, New Hampshire
  & Maine
Vienna & the Danube Valley
Virgin Islands
Virginia
Walt Disney World & Orlando
Washington, D.C.
Washington State

FROMMER'S® DOLLAR-A-DAY GUIDES

Australia from $50 a Day
California from $60 a Day
Caribbean from $70 a Day
England from $70 a Day
Europe from $60 a Day
Florida from $60 a Day

Hawaii from $70 a Day
Ireland from $50 a Day
Israel from $45 a Day
Italy from $70 a Day
London from $85 a Day
New York from $80 a Day

New Zealand from $50 a Day
Paris from $85 a Day
San Francisco from $60 a Day
Washington, D.C.,
  from $60 a Day

FROMMER'S® PORTABLE GUIDES

Acapulco, Ixtapa &
  Zihuatanejo
Alaska Cruises & Ports of Call
Bahamas
Baja & Los Cabos
Berlin
California Wine Country
Charleston & Savannah
Chicago

Dublin
Hawaii: The Big Island
Las Vegas
London
Maine Coast
Maui
New Orleans
New York City
Paris

Puerto Vallarta, Manzanillo
  & Guadalajara
San Diego
San Francisco
Sydney
Tampa & St. Petersburg
Venice
Washington, D.C.

FROMMER'S® NATIONAL PARK GUIDES

Family Vacations in the
  National Parks
Grand Canyon

National Parks of the
  American West
Rocky Mountain

Yellowstone & Grand Teton
Yosemite & Sequoia/
  Kings Canyon
Zion & Bryce Canyon

FROMMER'S® GREAT OUTDOOR GUIDES

New England
Northern California

Southern California & Baja
Washington & Oregon

FROMMER'S® MEMORABLE WALKS

Chicago
London

New York
Paris

San Francisco
Washington D.C.

FROMMER'S® IRREVERENT GUIDES

Amsterdam
Boston
Chicago
Las Vegas

London
Los Angeles
Manhattan

New Orleans
Paris
San Francisco

Seattle & Portland
Vancouver
Walt Disney World
Washington, D.C.

FROMMER'S® BEST-LOVED DRIVING TOURS

America
Britain
California

Florida
France
Germany

Ireland
Italy
New England

Scotland
Spain
Western Europe

THE UNOFFICIAL GUIDES®

Bed & Breakfast in New England
Bed & Breakfast in the Northwest
Beyond Disney
Branson, Missouri
California with Kids
Chicago
Cruises
Disneyland
Florida with Kids
The Great Smoky & Blue Ridge Mountains
Inside Disney
Las Vegas
London
Miami & the Keys
Mini Las Vegas
Mini-Mickey
New Orleans
New York City
Paris
San Francisco
Skiing in the West
Walt Disney World
Walt Disney World for Grown-ups
Walt Disney World for Kids
Washington, D.C.

SPECIAL-INTEREST TITLES

Born to Shop: France
Born to Shop: Hong Kong
Born to Shop: Italy
Born to Shop: New York
Born to Shop: Paris
Frommer's Britain's Best Bike Rides
The Civil War Trust's Official Guide to the Civil War Discovery Trail
Frommer's Caribbean Hideaways
Frommer's Europe's Greatest Driving Tours
Frommer's Food Lover's Companion to France
Frommer's Food Lover's Companion to Italy
Frommer's Gay & Lesbian Europe
Israel Past & Present
Monks' Guide to California

Monks' Guide to New York City
The Moon
New York City with Kids
Unforgettable Weekends
Outside Magazine's Guide to Family Vacations
Places Rated Almanac
Retirement Places Rated
Road Atlas Britain
Road Atlas Europe
Washington, D.C., with Kids
Wonderful Weekends from Boston
Wonderful Weekends from New York City
Wonderful Weekends from San Francisco
Wonderful Weekends from Los Angeles